Youth and Society

Youth and Society

The Long and Winding Road

Third Edition

Vappu Tyyskä

Canadian Scholars' Press Inc.
Toronto

Youth and Society: The Long and Winding Road, Third Edition
Vappu Tyyskä

First published in 2014 by
Canadian Scholars' Press Inc.
425 Adelaide Street West, Suite 200
Toronto, Ontario
M5V 3C1

www.cspi.org

Every reasonable effort has been made to identify copyright holders. CSPI would be pleased to have any errors or omissions brought to its attention.

Canadian Scholars' Press Inc. gratefully acknowledges financial support for our publishing activities from the Government of Canada through the Canada Book Fund (CBF).

Library and Archives Canada Cataloguing in Publication

Tyyskä, Vappu, 1956- [Long and winding road]
Youth and society : the long and winding road / Vappu Tyyskä. — Third edition.

Revision of author's Long and winding road. Includes bibliographical references and index. Issued in print and electronic formats.

ISBN 978-1-55130-543-1 (pbk.).—ISBN 978-1-55130-544-8 (pdf).—ISBN 978-1-55130-545-5 (epub)

1. Adolescence—Canada. 2. Adolescence—Canada—Social conditions. 3. Teenagers—Canada. 4. Teenagers—Canada—Social conditions. I. Title. II. Title: Long and winding road.

HQ799.C3T99 2013   305.2350971   C2013-905854-0   C2013-905855-9

Text design by Brad Horning
Cover design by Em Dash Design

Printed and bound in Canada by Webcom.

Canadä

MIX
Paper from
responsible sources
FSC **FSC® C004071**
www.fsc.org

Table of Contents

Acknowledgements

I am thrilled and honoured to have this book in its third, revised edition. I am extremely thankful to the managing and editorial team at Canadian Scholars' Press Inc. for their support toward the completion of this and previous editions, and I value their insistence that there is an ongoing niche for my work.

I have benefited from the help of a number of research assistants through the three editions (in chronological order): Jennifer Leung, Fiona Whittington-Walsh, Noula Mina, Jagjeet Kaur Gill, Mary Grace Betsayda, Ramon Meza Opazo, and Leslie Nichols. I thank you all for your contributions to the different editions of this book.

My love and thanks to my partner of over three decades, Allan Tyyskä, and our son Mikko, who are constantly supportive of everything I do. I dedicate this edition to our growing family that now includes my son's partner, Winnie.

Preface

This third edition of *Youth and Society: The Long and Winding Road* has undergone thorough updates and revisions. What has not changed is the comparative focus on Canada, the United Kingdom, and the United States. This comparative approach posed significant challenges for writing the second edition, as well as for making revisions to the third edition. I have made the following revisions:

First, statistics were updated where available. There are revised tables on most of the phenomena discussed in the second edition; only where no more recent comparative data were available were the existing tables left intact.

Second, in addition to the lists of discussion questions in the end of each chapter, each chapter now starts with a list of the key learning objectives, intended to guide readers.

Third, there are additional or revised boxes and narratives in most chapters, highlighting specific issues that have arisen more recently in young people's lives, including (in no particular order): the Occupy movement; the role of social media and new communication technologies; child sexual trafficking; cyberbullying; flash mobs; biracial socialization; unpaid internships; transgendered lives; sexuality and religion; social determinants of health; neoliberalism; changes in the juvenile justice system (including Bill C-10); eating disorders; use of tobacco products; Islamophobia; hate groups; and Black youth and sports.

Fourth, as in previous editions, I have updated the quotes from young people, making sure to continue to reflect their agency.

Fifth, the title of Chapter 8 was changed to "Crime and Moral Regulation," to better reflect the contents, and in keeping with prevailing realities.

Vappu Tyyskä
Toronto, Ontario
June 10, 2013

1 Concepts and Theories

In this chapter, you will learn that

- there are misleading and negative conceptions and myths about young people
- the category of youth is a social construction, subject to change over time and location
- young people's lives are subjected to conservative and critical theorizing
- this book will take a critical approach to youth, with a focus on diversity and inequalities in an era of globalization
- this book will deal with young people's lives in three Anglo-American countries: Canada, the United Kingdom, and the United States

---

Are today's young people troublesome or in trouble? Do they need controls and regulation or do regulations need to be changed? Are we granting youth too much freedom or too little? Do we need protection from or for young people? Should we show leniency and sympathy or should we show no mercy for their own good? What do young people want and need?

Every day, we are bombarded with the problems of youth. We get anecdotes about problematic adolescents from family members and acquaintances. Media feed us a daily dose of stories of young people in trouble. The range of issues includes concern over the economic futures of youth amidst youth unemployment. Matters related to education are constantly highlighted, with questions about school-to-work transitions and whether the education system is serving our youth adequately. There is also concern over the degree to which today's family pressures, including divorces, remarriages, and family violence, affect young people. At the same time, fear is expressed that different social pressures, combined with poor parental supervision, result in youth delinquency and crime. Youth subcultures, including music and peer-based social activities, are often perceived as threatening. Other areas identified include social problems associated with young people's withdrawal from communities, manifested in poor health, stress, suicides, drug use, poverty, life on the streets, teenage pregnancies, and sexually transmitted diseases.

While pointing to these and many other legitimate concerns about young people's lives, there is an unfortunate tendency in the media and among the general public either to vilify youth, or to blame them and/or their families for their plight. The voices of young people themselves are frequently missing. Where youthful views are presented, they are used to show the lack of concern by adolescents and people in their twenties with their communities, witness their passivity in politics, and their preoccupation with the trivial pursuits presented by the leisure industry. Where young people are associated with action, this tends to be negative. The media fuel this with negative and slanted coverage of youth crime, street youth, youth gangs, and other delinquent or criminal forms of activity, giving the impression of young people running amok in their homes, schools, on the streets, and in our communities. The actions of youth that get attention are portrayed as dangerous and destructive, exemplified in the ongoing reports about "raves," "rap," or "gangsta" music and youth cultural phenomena, or about the large youth-driven demonstrations against the power of global corporations and the international financial machinery. The views presented in media both shape and reflect generally accepted public opinions.

While some of the concerns outlined above have a real and factual basis, many of the popular notions about youth are based on a misreading of studies and statistics or a misdirection of attention. Many of these misconceptions will be presented, discussed, and criticized in the substantive chapters of this book. For now, we can note, for example, that the real problem of education is not with the individuals who drop out of the school system, but with the conditions in the education system itself that result in high school dropouts or stalled post-secondary education, including gender and race discrimination and a lack of resources. And the problems of youth employment have less to do with the lack of skills or unwillingness on the part of young people and more with the ways in which the labour market in general is becoming governed by jobs requiring low skill and offering poor wages and working conditions. And rather than living on the streets as a "lifestyle" choice, some young people's family lives are governed by abuse and neglect that leave them little choice but to get away. Lacking alternatives, they end up on the streets, and become targets of public fear and prejudice. While alone, they may garner some sympathy, but in groups they may become labelled as "gangs" with the expectation that they engage in deviant and criminal acts. This also goes for other youth who express a specific brand of youth culture, for example, raves, rap, or other musical forms. While actual youth gangs do exist, there is an unfortunate impression that all young people in groups have to be watched, especially if they happen to be members of racialized groups. All youth are painted with the same brush, that of a small minority of young people who come into contact with the police or the legal system. Even here, there are widespread misconceptions about increasing levels of youth crime and violence, or about the supposed lenience of the juvenile justice system.

Through the creation and perpetuation of misrepresentations and myths about youth, an atmosphere is created in which young people are likely to be viewed negatively, subjected to increasing controls, and given little or no positive feedback at a stage of their lives that is supposed to be full of hope and promise.

The Aim of This Book

The popular anecdotal, misleading, and negative views about young people need to be taken apart. We need to systematically analyze the root causes of the different ideologies and theories related to youth. The main argument of this book is this: We have to move away from dealing with youth as the problem to addressing the social, economic, and political circumstances that are problematic.

This book presents a comprehensive picture of the diverse youth population in the beginning of the new millennium. Taking a critical approach, this book deals with the overlapping power relationships of capitalism, racism, patriarchy, and heterosexism that shape the lives of all people but have special relevance to youth in societies in which age is yet another significant basis for power differences.

The different pathways in the history of adolescence and youth point to a fluidity and an ongoing social construction of youthful age categories that have emerged in a specific form out of the developing industrial capitalism. This book takes a look at three such Western countries, including Canada, the United States, and the United Kingdom. What unites young people in these countries is the link to a common historical Anglo-American heritage founded on colonialism, with its attendant historical similarities (see Box 1.1). From this shared past arise contemporary differences based on different pathways in state formation and the development of social institutions, including work, education, families, and the legal system. These will be the subject matter of this book from a critical sociological perspective. The aim is not to provide a rigidly comparative account of every aspect of young people's lives in the three countries, but rather to introduce some of the common and different themes related to young people's lives. This means that amidst a general summary of trends, in some instances specific aspects may be highlighted with regard to only one or two of the countries instead of all three.

In this chapter, I will begin with a discussion of the meanings of young age categories as we understand them today, and as they are used in this book. I will also outline the general theories and ideologies that drive both research and public views about young people. Some of these view young people as a problem to be dealt with. Others present a critical view that raises questions about the environment young people occupy, not youth themselves, as the problem.

Defining Youth

Worldwide, there is a distinct lack of consistency in defining the category "youth" (Galambos & Kolaric, 1994; Danesi, 1994, p. 6), both in everyday usage and government policy. This great variety signifies both the fluidity of age categories and the degree to which they are contested globally.

During the International Year of the Youth in 1985, the United Nations defined youth as those between 15 and 25 years of age (Brown, 1990, p. 62). Thus, youth overlaps with the category of "childhood," which is commonly defined as anyone under the age of 18

Box 1.1: The Anglo-American Connection

Stephen Gennaro (2005, p. 131) directs attention to some of the common and different elements in the experience of the three countries in question, with parallels drawn regarding Canada's "in-betweenness" and adolescent status:

> Much like adolescents, Canada has always struggled with its in-between identity: Not quite British dependent but not quite independent; not quite American yet not distinctly Canadian. Provincially, Quebec is not wholly French, but certainly not English. Globally, Canada is an "in-between" nation as well; not a powerful country in world politics, but still a First World country. Every year the United Nations ranks Canada as one of the best places to live in the world and yet Canadians flock at the opportunity to move south of the 49th parallel. Lastly, Canada was a good enough friend to house all of the displaced Americans and those travelling on flights to and from the United States on September 11, 2001, and the days that followed, but it was not a good enough friend to warrant any mention from President George W. Bush as he thanked America's allies for their support four months later in his State of the Union address. Being "in-between" in so many different ways, Canada itself appears to have a multiphrenic identity.

(De Waal, 2002, pp. 13–14). The distinctions between "childhood," "adolescence," and "youth" are ambiguous, based on historically and geographically specific usage (Gillis, 1981, pp. 1–2). Anticipating the more detailed discussion in Chapter 2, Table 1.1 illustrates shifts in idealized life stages based on European history (Gillis, 1981).

In fact, the term "adolescent" was used for a comparatively wide age category (15–24) in many Western countries in the 19th century. The term presently refers to anyone from age 10–18 (Arnett, 2001, p. 13), though it's also used interchangeably with the Anglo-American English language-based term "teen," or those aged 13–19. Meanwhile, the term "tweens" was introduced in the 1990s by marketers to refer to young people aged 11–14 (Media Watch, 2000, p. 2).

In its current Western usage, the category of "youth" is elastic and covers a range of distinct age groupings. While the lines between age categories are comparatively blurred, some have taken the extreme position that new information and communication technologies have bred the kind of extreme consumerism that defines everyone from childhood upwards in a state of "perpetual adolescence" (Gennaro, 2005), to be discussed in more detail in the chapter on youth culture. More commonly, though, researchers rely on different age categories, albeit with changing age parameters.

Table 1.1: Idealized Life Phases in European History

	Childhood	*Youth*		*Middle Years*	*Late Years*
Pre-industrial society	0–8	8–20		Parenthood 20–45	45+
1900 (Middle class)	0–10	Adolescence 10–20	Young adulthood 20–30	Parenthood 30–60	Death or retirement 60+
Post-industrial society	0–10	Adolescence 10–16	Postmodern youth 16–30	Parenthood 30–60	Retirement 60+

Source: Adapted from Gillis (1981, Figure 1, p. 2; Figure 3, p. 104; Figure 7, p. 208).

For example, Galambos and Kolaric (1994) distinguish between young adolescents (10–14), teens (15–19), and young adults (20–24). Arnett (2001, pp. 14–16) has a similar scheme, consisting of early adolescents (10–14), late adolescents (15–18), and emerging adults (18–25). "Emerging adulthood" characterizes industrialized societies in North America, Europe, Australia, New Zealand, and Japan. It is also called "post-modern youth" by Gillis (1981, pp. 207–208; see Table 1.1). While adolescents are still dependent on their parents and largely isolated from the adult world, emerging adults are experimenting with life chances in relationships, work, education, and world views, gradually moving toward full adulthood.

While outside of the much narrower scope of this book, it is worthy of note that the above categories lack relevance to most of the non-Western context (De Waal, 2002, pp. 13–15; Wyn & White, 1997, p. 10; Argenti, 2002, p. 125; Sharp, 2002, pp. 15–18; Allatt, 2001). Thus, while we may, in Europe and North America, understand the meanings of the narrow age categories within the groupings of "children," "adolescents," and "youth," the term "youth" is a wider and more ephemeral concept in non-Western societies, starting in some cases as early as age five and stretching till age 35, based on political and economic conditions (Allatt, 2001, p. 256).

It is therefore not surprising that increasing numbers of youth researchers try to avoid defining youth as strictly specific age categories (Allatt, 2001; Rahman, 2001; Wyn & White, 1997). There is a preference to define youth as "not a particular age range" but as "a social status" (Marquardt, 1998, p. 7), characterized by a period of life in which a person is either partly or fully dependent on others, usually adults and members of one's family, for material support. However, if we use dependence or semi-dependence as the sole criterion to define youth, we could just as easily fit other large segments of the population into this category, including stay-at-home mothers, and most wage-earners who are co-dependent. Therefore, we need to set some age limits for the categories of "adolescence" and" youth" as we understand them in today's society, as well as acknowledge the specific social conditions that separate the experiences of youth from other social categories. Noting the various official and everyday usages, and in general recognizing that the category of youth is socially constructed, the terms "youth" or "young people" are used in this book with sensitivity to historical variations. Overall, in relation to the contemporary situation, the age categories will generally stretch from the teen years (13–19) to the early twenties (20–24) and in some cases to the mid- to late twenties (25–29).

Overall, youth should be approached in relational terms, with reference to the "social processes whereby age is socially constructed, institutionalized and controlled in historically and culturally specific ways" (Wyn & White, 1997, pp. 10–11). The fluidity of age categories, influenced by changes in social and economic conditions, will be shown throughout this book. As will be demonstrated, there is presently a particular pressure to extend youth well into the twenties, if not beyond. This reflects a general sense that these are the years that are significant and formative, a period of transition to "full adulthood," a time of growing self-awareness and the pursuit of independence from one's family of origin, characterized by educational and vocational decisions, and the formation of new relationships and family units. This notion of youth as a transitional stage, in contrast with adulthood, is reflected in the common perceptions of youth in Europe and North America, as illustrated in Table 1.2.

I will further argue that the tasks and processes associated with youth are linked to the particular shape of capitalism and patriarchy, which limits young people's choices. Thus, the pressure to stretch "youth" in the industrialized West, based on their total or partial dependence on parents and/or the state, reflects social processes that presently include lengthened education and part-time or temporary employment. This process is gendered in that most young women's state of dependence continues while they are in their child-bearing years, an aspect that will be discussed below with regard to theories of youth.

Theories of Youth

According to dominant Western ideology, youth is the most wonderful, carefree stage of our lives, a time to gradually develop a distinct identity and place in society. This ideal acknowledges the relative wealth of the northern hemisphere. Some theorists focus on the positive aspects of this wealth, and on the role of social institutions in shaping young people. This approach is largely uncritical and conservative, and focuses on the biological and social development of human beings, most frequently expressed in sociobiology, and developmental and life stage theories. These views are popularized, among other things, in imagery of young people enslaved to their tumultuous biological states and requiring firm regulation, so that they will learn to modify their behaviours and act in accordance with mainstream rules and norms. In contrast, critical theories point out

Table 1.2: Perceptions of Youth and Adulthood

Youth	*Adulthood*
Not adult/adolescent	Adult/grown-up
Becoming	Arrived
Pre-social self that will emerge under right conditions	Identity is fixed
Powerless and vulnerable	Powerful and strong
Less responsible	Responsible
Dependent	Independent
Ignorant	Knowledgeable
Risky behaviours	Considered behaviour
Rebellious	Conformist
Reliant	Autonomous

Source: Wyn & White (1997, p. 12).

that despite the general abundance in industrialized countries, young people in general and women and non-dominant minority youth in particular do not benefit equally from societal resources, and their voices are largely unheard.

Conservative Theories: Conformity

Many contemporary conservative theories are rooted in social Darwinism, which flourished from the 19th century onward, premised on the evolutionary theories of Charles Darwin. His theory of biological adaptation and natural selection is extended to society by sociobiologists and structural-functionalists, with specific reference to changes that took place in age strata as industrial capitalism emerged. A new stage of youth presumably developed out of specific biological imperatives of maturation. This developmental stage involves biologically driven disruptive elements, often referred to as "hormonal hurricanes," as young people learn to adapt to their environment.

To elaborate, age strata, such as adolescence or youth, are seen to be a beneficial adaptation to new environmental conditions. As explained by Côté and Allahar (1994, pp. 16–19), functionalist theories of youth see it as a necessary stage of life, characterized by preparation to meet diverse societal needs. For example, industrialization is seen to have created a need for a longer stage of preparation for adulthood. With the onset of industrialism and gradual improvements in the standard of living of working people, the labour of young people was no longer required, and their stage of total or partial dependence on parents was prolonged. As the service economy expanded, youth became institutionalized as a stage for education and preparation for the demands of the new economy.

The functionalist theory mirrors a common everyday approach to adolescence and youth. It is generally accepted that prolonged education is necessary in order to prepare for adult life, including a full participation in the economy. It is equally accepted that this requires the postponement of other aspects of life, including having a decent income to live independently, and delaying marriage and family formation. This theory promotes the notion that youth is a stage for instilling conformity within the requirements of prevailing economic and social conditions. This conservative script calls for mechanisms of control on youth in order to ensure a smooth functioning of society. Conflict is seen to be detrimental to the system as a whole (e.g., Eisenstadt, in O'Donnell, 1985, pp. 5–8).

Not all structural-functionalists promote the doing away with potentially rebellious youth or age-based conflict through oppressive measures, but all structural-functionalists do promote the idea of common good over narrower group interests, which are seen to disrupt the orderly development of societies (O'Donnell, 1985, pp. 7–8). Little attention is paid either to the problems that youth may face through this stage of the suspension of their rights, or to any active role that young people may play in changing the ground rules or creating their own interpretations of a successful transition to adulthood.

The stamp of sociobiology and structural-functionalism is evident in a number of influential life stage or developmental theories of the 20th century. Most of these focus on the stresses of youth, and the need to bring their naturally destructive inner tendencies under control. The earliest and most significant contribution comes from the American youth theorist G. Stanley Hall, who is credited with "almost singlehandedly" creating the "concept of adolescence as an autonomous age group" (Springhall, 1986, p. 28). In 1904, Hall proposed that human development from birth to death mirrored the evolutionary path of the human race. Fuelled by Darwinism, Hall developed his recapitulation theory, proposing that adolescence was a stage of savagery, a period of *Sturm und Drang* (storm and stress) (Danesi, 1994, p. 7; Côté & Allahar, 1994, pp. 6–7; Jones & Wallace, 1992, pp. 7–8; Springhall, 1986, p. 28). The theory proposed that, as in human evolution, individual development and maturation was a gradual process in which each stage was crucial in laying the stepping stones for the next. In adolescence, as the physical, cognitive, and social development reached its peak, young people were also subject to biologically driven storm and stress. Because of this, their path toward adulthood and a higher stage of development is a stormy one as they learn to subject their instincts to their environment (Grinder, 1973, pp. 22–32).

Hall's contemporary, Sigmund Freud, developed his psychoanalytic theory, which was likewise rooted in Darwinism, and strongly supported the *Sturm und Drang* approach. Freud proposed that at each stage of human development, the narcissistic tendencies of the human being are gradually subjected to controls. However, the central drive toward maturity in Freud's theory, unlike in Hall's theory, is laden with psychosexual energies (libido), which become particularly important in adolescence. The onset of puberty drives the adolescent toward the conflicting forces of dependence and independence. The crisis is solved as new codes of societal conduct are internalized (Grinder, 1973, pp. 32–36).

In the mid- to late 20th century, the views of two other developmental stage theorists, Erik Erikson and Jean Piaget, emerged as dominant. Both theorists proposed a sequence of life stages in human development driven by biology and leading toward a fully developed, mature human being. The stage of adolescence is seen as particularly crucial for the development of a sense of self, or identity (Danesi, 1994, pp. 7–10; Grinder, 1973, pp. 4–6). For Erikson, successful identity formation in adolescence is a process through which a person gradually internalizes societal expectations. An unsuccessful integration of individual and society would lead to "prolonged identity confusion" (Grinder, 1973, p. 5; Howe & Bukowski, 1996, pp. 189–190). In other words, one common strand going through these stage theories is the view that unless a person learns to conform to the mainstream in adolescence, he or she is not likely to be a fully integrated, individuated being.

Alongside theories aimed at understanding the sociobiological drive toward maturity and self-awareness, attention has been paid to the role of physiological changes in adolescence. The psychosocial changes that take place in adolescence are linked to the biological and bodily changes accompanying puberty. These changes that signify a transition toward adulthood are seen to create a need to bond with others who are in the same stage of development, amidst a heightened awareness of the physiological and cognitive changes young people are going through (Danesi, 1994, pp. 11–12; Offer & Offer, 1972; Arnett, 2001, pp. 31–59).

Very few scholars and academics today would endorse a purely biologically based theory of human life stages. Most would see a combination of biological and environmental influences behind the transition toward adulthood by virtue of the power of cross-cultural and historical studies that show the diverse ways of signifying human life stages (Danesi, 1994, pp. 12–14; Arnett, 2001, pp. 56–58). Among others, Canadian youth researchers Côté and Allahar (1994, pp. 13–15) are critical of the "nature approaches" in that there is too much stress on the significance of biological factors in puberty. The theories show a profound misunderstanding of the correspondence between biological and social variables. There simply is no one-to-one correspondence between genetic, hormonal, or physiological developments and human social behaviour.

In contrast to the biological determinist strand of analysis, another type of determinism emerged in the early 20th century, that of cultural determinism. Spearheaded by Margaret Mead, whose *Coming of Age in Samoa* (published in 1928) was deliberately aimed at contradicting Hall's work, these theorists made a case that adolescence need not be stamped by the crisis and stress presumed by Hall and others but that it could be an orderly process of gradual maturation through which individuals move toward adult interests and activities (Springhall, 1986, pp. 31–33).

Debates between biological and cultural determinists waged on through the middle of the 20th century, with the work of the aforementioned Freud, Erikson, and Piaget lending further confirmation to the conventional view that the biological changes associated with puberty and growing up could place intolerable strains upon the adolescent (Springhall, 1986, p. 226). The prevailing legacy of this strand of theorizing is present in the persistence of the popular view of adolescence as "inherently pathological" and in need of intervention (Hill & Fortenberry, 1992, p. 73).

Springhall (1986, pp. 234–235), meanwhile, points to problems with both biological and cultural determinism:

> The shaping of adolescence by social and cultural forces does not mean there are no inherent biological and hormonal changes during puberty. For adolescent behaviour is determined by the interaction between cultural and biological forces in a particular society at a particular moment in history. The process of adaptation to these internal and external forces is spread over many years, so that stress on the adolescent is rarely concentrated at any one time. Adolescence, in other words, is not entirely a myth manufactured by social scientists and the media but it is, nonetheless, a highly debatable and charged term, not a given but an a priori concept which needs to be supported by actual historical and other forms of evidence. While it may be possible to abandon or at least to offer correctives to the traditional view of adolescence, it still needs to be not simply a biological fact associated with puberty, nor a period of emotional turbulence as a result, but a cultural definition of a certain stage in the life cycle with a long history that still remains to be unraveled.

From the 1980s onward, a different type of stage theory was developed, called the life-course perspective. These theorists examine the transitions to adulthood in different spheres of life, including employment and family. Though less focused on biology as the driving force of people's life stages, many life-course theories are nevertheless structural-functionalist in nature. Life-course theories see youth as a

> series of processes in transition to adult life, roughly parallel longitudinal processes which take place in different spheres, such as home and the labour market, but which must be understood together because they relate closely to one another. (Jones & Wallace, 1992, p. 13)

With significant changes in the economic structures and associated social behaviours in Western societies, the uniformity of youth transitions was being called into question. It was evident that the changing nature of the economy—including a shift toward a service economy and widespread unemployment, and significant changes in families such as women's labour force participation—lead toward lessening standardization in the lives of everyone, youth included (Jones & Wallace, 1992, pp. 10–13).

Related to this approach is the so-called "individualization thesis" developed by the German sociologist Ulrich Beck (Beck, 1986, in Jones & Wallace, 1992, p. 15; Bynner & Parsons, 2002, p. 290). This thesis argues that people's lives are an individual project for them to achieve in a competitive world. There are increased "risks" for people at all levels of society as people are dissociated from the old social structures and create their own pathways.

The idea of a "risk society" reflects the increasing uncertainty that young people will make good choices, amidst the supposed freeing and expansion of opportunity in society at large (Bynner & Parsons, 2002, p. 290; Miles, 2000, pp. 54–60). This view is exemplified by studies that examine the ways in which young people develop their own "trajectories" as they face a world that is different from that of their parents. Attention to trajectories and transition involves an examination of different aspects of young people's lives as they move from school to work, form intimate relationships and families, and take steps toward being full members of their communities and political entities (Jones & Wallace, 1992, pp. 17–18; Chisholm & Hurrelmann, 1995, pp. 129–158).

Alternately calling this in-between stage a career, stage, pathway, or transition, this brand of life-stage researchers can be criticized for focusing on youth as preparation toward something (adulthood) "and not a time important in itself" (Beauvais et al., 2001, p. 8). In other words, it is as if the stage of youth is interesting only to the degree that it can inform the more important stage: adulthood. Further, it is their focus on the atomization of individuals and the need for more social cohesion, while downplaying the analysis of power structures in societies, that puts many life-course/stage theorists within the structural-functionalist tradition.

If conformity to social norms is the hallmark of a successful transition to adulthood, these theories can be criticized for putting pressure on young people to adapt to society rather than changing societies to accommodate them. In fact, there has been extensive criticism of structural-functionalist theories, particularly from the 1960s onward, when youth in North America and Europe exhibited widespread discontent with their marginalized status—a clear indication that their ideas about transitions differ greatly from expected norms (Jones & Wallace, 1992, p. 10).

Finally, though the idea of "risk society" is potentially critical of social ills, it has been transformed by some conservative theorists into the notion of "youth at risk." Rather than correctly addressing the structural inequalities (risk society) that result in some youth being at risk, the notion is generalized to apply to all youth (at risk), who can then be targeted and blamed. As Males (1996, p. 26) points out, based on the American context, the idea of youth at risk

> illustrates the process by which frightening *general statistics* describing ghetto youth are blended with deplorable *individual anecdotes* about higher income youth to manufacture an image of *all youth* run wild. [emphases in the original]

With the structural-functionalist theories' conceptualization of youth as inherently troubled and troublesome, the main focus is on how to maintain social cohesion. In order for society not to suffer, youth need to be subjected to a number of control mechanisms. These controls are often presented as natural parts of preparation of adult life, through parenting and socialization in families, and through education.

As industrial societies require increased education levels to meet the demands of the developing economy, other aspects of life have to be delayed, including marriage and family formation. Functionalists promote the notion that youth is a stage for instilling conformity within the requirements of prevailing economic and social conditions. This conservative script calls for mechanisms of control on youth in order to ensure a smooth functioning of society (e.g., Eisenstadt, in O'Donnell, 1985, pp. 5–8; Côté & Allahar,

1994, pp. 16–19; Jones & Wallace, 1992, pp. 8–11). A central role in the functionalist scheme is played by family members, particularly mothers, who socialize and educate their children toward taking their proper roles in the economy and the family (Parsons, 1956, pp. 16, 19, in Jones & Wallace, 1992, p. 9).

In addition to primary socialization in families, secondary socialization is taking place through schools and peers (Parsons, 1961 and 1973, and Coleman, 1961, in Jones & Wallace, 1992, p. 9). In the 1960s and 1970s, scholarly attention in Britain and the United States turned to peer groups and youth subcultures as vessels for transmitting proper work values, social attitudes, and behaviours to young people (Jones & Wallace, 1992, p. 11). Brake (1985, pp. 24–27; see also O'Donnell, 1985) notes that this approach is exemplified by the works of Karl Mannheim, Talcott Parsons, and his student S.N. Eisenstadt.

In this functionalist variant of subculture theory related to youth, there is a tendency to dwell on the problematic aspects of delinquent youth subcultures, and the problem of how to control this element (Brake, 1985, p. 57; Blackman, 1995, pp. 2–4). The destructive actions of youth are seen to reflect "status frustration" arising from a mismatch between "cultural goals" and "institutional means." Thus, youth subcultures are seen as results of inadequate socialization of young people into their "proper" position in society (Blackman, 1995, pp. 2–4). In other words, if only young people were made to understand their place in society, they would not be so troublesome. Another variant of conservative subculture theories focuses on the biological and bodily changes accompanying puberty, mentioned above. The changes that signify a transition toward adulthood are seen to create a need to bond with others who are in the same stage of development amidst a heightened awareness of the physiological and cognitive changes young people are going through (Danesi, 1994, pp. 11–12; Offer & Offer, 1972).

To summarize, this group of structural-functionalist theories can be criticized for putting pressure on young people to adapt to society rather than changing societies to accommodate them. They essentially endorse the prevailing social order, unlike theories that pay attention to society from a more critical perspective that is sensitive to power differences.

Critical Theories: Age and Stratification

In contrast to conservative theories, critical theorists point to the institutionalized powerlessness of youth. Especially in the last two decades, studies and reports point to the many problems that young people face and are finding difficult to confront and change due to the rules and boundaries set by adult-led social institutions, including the family, the economy, and the state (Marquardt, 1998, pp. 4–6; Carrigan, 1998).

The Marxist or political economy approach, when applied to different social positions by age, is a type of age stratification theory. There are several varieties of age stratification theory (Dowd, 1981; O'Rand, 1990), but in the Marxist variant, economic inequalities are linked to age inequalities because of the specific features of the capitalist economy. In order to exploit the workforce to the fullest, different age categories of workers are recruited into different types of work, allowing for the exploitation of the young as a part of the weakest segment of the working population. At the same time, age categories provide useful divided groupings of workers whose interests differ. This mass of working people is prevented from the realization of their common interests by employers' divide-and-conquer methods. A further element of control is present in the ideological forces that are utilized by the capitalist class, including the education system and media. These provide a form of control and ongoing indoctrination of people into the expectations of the economic system (Côté & Allahar, 1994; Mattson, 2003; Strickland, 2002). Thus, whereas structural-functionalists see education and media as necessary for the creation of beneficial social cohesion, Marxists view them more negatively as systems of "brainwashing" with the aim to turn young people into willing participants in the machinery of capitalism. The underlying idea is that capitalism is exploitive and we need to resist the ideological machinery of the school system (and other systems, such as media) that try to make youth into adults willing to perpetuate the exploitation of themselves and others.

Thus, Marxist theorists argue that youth have been effectively disenfranchised. Employers and the state have created, over more than a century, a system in which youth are deprived of full access to economic and political rights. They are processed through an education system that creates credentials, while the jobs in the labour market do not require the kind of extensive education that young people are made to believe they need in order to succeed. Rather than having access to economic institutions, youth are exploited as an underpaid working mass, and form a convenient target market for goods that are sold to them as a part of a ready-made package of corporate-driven youth culture. This process of turning youth into secondary producers and primary consumers has escalated since the 1970s with neo-conservative and neo-liberal state policies in Western industrial countries (Côté & Allahar, 1994).

The pros and cons of employment of young workers are constantly debated. The loaded term "child labour" is characterized by extreme conceptual ambiguity, partly because of the definitional difficulties of youth and child categories outlined above.

Estimated numbers of child labourers (depending on the age parameters of the statistics) range from 73 million to 500 million worldwide. Whereas the prevalence of child labour has previously been established in the southern hemisphere, it is also noted increasingly that the phenomenon is an essential part of the industrialized nations of the northern hemisphere where ever-increasing numbers of children and youth combine education with part-time wage work (McKechnie & Hobbs, 2002, pp. 218–219).

Alongside the objectionable imagery the term "child labour" evokes, debates are ongoing in the industrialized North regarding the detrimental vs. beneficial effects of employment for young people. Among the negative effects is the potential for a delayed or stalled education due to both the pressures and financial allure of wage work. Among the positive outcomes are those related to personal autonomy, independence, and sense of self-worth (Tienda & Wilson, 2002b, p. 16; McKechnie & Hobbs, 2002). These positive terms in themselves are interesting as they individualize a widespread social phenomenon into a psychological benefit rather than something that requires attention as a collective phenomenon. At the same time, the terminology of self-fulfillment and personal growth convey the centrality of the idea of an independent and autonomous individual, which is the main pillar of the liberal ideology that is associated with capitalism.

Indeed, Marxist theorists point out that the economic disenfranchisement of youth is accompanied by their political disenfranchisement manifested in their lack of political decision-making power and political apathy, and their harsher treatment as they are policed and incarcerated at ever-younger ages, particularly in North America (Giroux, 2003; White, 2002; Jones & Wallace, 1992, pp. 146–156; Mattson, 2003). In other words, as youth are, by their partial and low-wage work status and through the institutions of public education, rendered into a state of dependency or semi-dependency on adults or the state, they are also stripped of political power and are increasingly seen as a problem to be controlled.

On the one hand, Marxist age stratification theory is compelling and powerful in explaining the emergence of and the present condition of youth (to be elaborated in later chapters). On the other hand, we are still left with only a partial picture of the many facets in the lives of young people. Adolescence and youth are age strata, but they are also age strata that are differentiated along other dimensions. Increasing numbers of critical youth theorists point to the necessity of taking into consideration the social divisions of gender, race, and ethnicity (Chisholm, 1990, in Wyn & White, 1997, p. 3; Tienda & Wilson, 2002a; Ghuman, 1999). It is emphasized that regardless of region, nation, or hemisphere, young women and members of numerical and status minorities fare far worse than the young men who are used as a point of comparison, and who themselves may not be faring that well overall (Tienda & Wilson, 2002a, pp. 11–17; Heitmeyer, 2002; Back, 1996; Rozie-Battle, 2002).

Adding to the discussion of youth diversity, Aapola et al. (2005, p. 149) point out that the notion of adolescence as a stage for developing identity and autonomy is inherently a heterosexual and male model. The notion of a gradual separation from parents and becoming independent applies to young men, but not to women for whom becoming an adult involves managing relationships with their (heterosexual) partners, children, and other family. Young women's transition is still seen to be gradual transference from father to husband, with the associated imagery of dependence rather than independence. This will be discussed more below in connection with the issue of citizenship. Of importance is also the fact that other groups of youth, such as those with disabilities, are not necessarily able to define their adult status through independence.

Gender, race, immigrant status, disability, and other bases of social inequality are increasingly addressed by critical variants of theories of peer groups and youth subcultures. Peer groups provide freedom from parents and other authority figures, and provide alternative norms and information about expected behaviours, and a setting for conforming to these expectations about "a given group's *own* norms, attitudes, speech patterns, and dress codes" (Kendal et al., 1997, p. 145, emphasis in the original; also see Côté & Allahar, 1994, p. 20; Elkin & Handel, 1989, in Kendal et al., 1997, p. 145). At the same time, peer groups are formed based on socio-demographic factors including "grade level, age, gender, religion, and ethnicity" (Akers et al., 1998, p. 1; also see Kelly, 1998, pp. 78–82; Brake, 1985; Holmes

& Silverman, 1992, p. 38; Danesi, 1994, pp. 59–60; Strickland, 2002, pp. 10–11). Many researchers have found that young males and females tend to engage in different peer group activities (Holmes & Silverman, 1992, p. 38; Brake, 1985, pp. 163–183). Some researchers also point to bonding among minority high school students, partly in reaction to racist attitudes and practices around them (Kelly, 1998, pp. 67–72; Ghuman, 1999, pp. 5–6).

Unlike conservative youth theories of peer groups, critical approaches to peers and subcultures reflect an understanding of youth subcultures both as manifestations of youth rebellion and as mirrors of the dominant power relations under capitalism, patriarchy, and racism (Blackman, 1995, pp. 4–6; Jones & Wallace, 1992, p. 10; Côté & Allahar, 1994, p. 20; Brake, 1985; Ghuman, 1999; Giroux, 2003). The neo-Marxist reinterpretation of youth subculture as a reaction to capitalist oppression by young working-class males was largely based on the work of scholars at the Centre for Contemporary Cultural Studies (CCCS) in Birmingham, UK (Blackman, 1995, pp. 4–5; Rattansi & Phoenix, 2005, p. 102; Raby, 2005b, p. 153). Their cultural studies approach dominated youth research in the 1970s and 1980s. Though criticized for their lack of attention to gender issues (Rattansi & Phoenix, 2005, p. 102), their work and the research of their followers allowed theorists to develop an understanding of youth subcultures in a richer way, acknowledging youth as active agents (see e.g., G. Tait, 2000; Raby, 2005a).

Subsequently, youth subcultures are alternately seen either as a reaction to oppression, as an expression of youthful creativity (Filmer, 1977, in Blackman, 1995, p. 5; Raby, 2005a), as emotionally satisfying activities, or as a means toward an identity and a sense of community (Doherty, 1988, in Danesi, 1994, p. 56; Brake, 1985, pp. 189–191; Kendal et al., 1997, p. 145). On the negative side, critical theorists also note that youth subcultures can be co-opted with targeting of youth as a consumer group (Strickland, 2002, pp. 4–5; Brake, 1985, pp. 184–189; Côté & Allahar, 1994, pp. 109–111).

Authors such as Furlong and Cartmel (1997, in Miles, 2000, pp. 59–60) also suggest that consumer societies produce stresses on youth, and may compel them toward increasingly risky behaviours. This is a more radical reading of the notion of "risk society" than is offered by the structural-functionalists described earlier as it points to the problems of the social environment rather than the individual. Miles (2000, p. 60) proposes that the stresses that are created around consumerism in a society characterized by "poverty, inequality, and discrimination" may be responsible for risky behaviours like youth's increased drug and alcohol consumption. At the same time, youth consumerism has been interpreted by some as potentially "subversive" in that pockets of resistance arise in reaction to the corporate marketing strategies (Strickland, 2002, p. 13). At issue in approaches to youth subcultures are the ways in which different theorists see youth either as active or passive, or as victims or actors/agents in their own destinies (Raby, 2005a; G. Tait, 2000).

Postmodern Youth: Agency, Subjectivity, and Fragmentation

Overall, a main strand underlying the debates of power and agency in the post-subcultural theory era is the question of what the nature of youthful resistance is and what it implies. Raby (2005b, p. 157) points out that depending on the theoretical outlook of each author, the same youthful activity can be "described as resistance, rebellion or even deviance," in other words, implying either protest or delinquency. Overall, actions can be interpreted as any one of these. In other words, not all youth action can be interpreted as having some radical significance, but neither can youth's acts be automatically dismissed as a natural part of growing up. In understanding power and youth resistance, Raby proposes that a synthesis of different post-structuralist and postmodern theories is helpful in illuminating how youth's actions may hold contradictory components. Here, Raby relies on Michel Foucault's (1978, in Raby, 2005b, pp. 161–163) concept of power as expressed in social relationships, which are constantly shifting and situationally dependent. Thus, people occupy different relationships with regard to one another, and engage in various relationships in which they either resist or comply or both. Other postmodern and feminist theorists build on Foucault's work by turning toward examinations of the role of language and communication and identity development in youth's acts of resistance. The question here is to what degree are youth's expressions in language, or their adoption of specific personae and identities, rebellious or delinquent? Raby's (2005b, pp. 166–168) conclusion is that depending on the social position and specific relationships (social class, gender, race, etc.) that youth occupy, there are moments ("fissures") that provide an opportunity for youth to resist, contest, or refuse to identify with the status quo.

Raby's (2005b) approach relies heavily on a postmodern notion of youth. As Bibby (2001, pp. 161–165) summarizes, this school of thought emerged in the 1960s and is characterized by extreme pluralism, arising from its four main characteristics: (1) rejection of the idea of science and progress as the driving forces of history; (2) rejection of grand theories in favour of ones focusing on multiple location-specific perspectives; (3) rejection of a totalitarian (all or nothing) concept of power; (4) embracing "deconstruction," a process of uncovering the context and multiple meanings of phenomena. This means that we cannot claim that any one perspective is any more accurate or "truthful" than any other; in other words, there is no one reality. This plurality of conditions, perspectives, and views, some argue, is the condition of today's youth. For example, Long (1997, in Bibby, 2001, pp. 164–165) suggests that whether young people acknowledge it or not, postmodernism defines their experiences and is present in their tendencies to "(1) reject reason; (2) emphasize the subjectivity of truth; (3) place primary importance on experience; and (4) question authority."

Thus, though the same range of issues, loosely wrapped around issues of education, work, and youth culture, emerges from youth research in the 20th and 21st centuries, they are interpreted quite differently by youth theorists. While conservative or structural-functionalist theorists emphasize the disruptive features of youth and a concern over how social cohesion is promoted best, critical theorists attempt to analyze the underlying inequalities resulting in youthful disruptions, and are concerned with how societies can best respond to or remedy any problems that arise. To add to this, conservative theories tend to want youth to be passive and pliable so that their presumed negative tendencies can be harnessed toward maintaining system stability. Critical theories, in contrast, tend to view youthful energy in positive terms and see young people needing encouragement so they can both live fulfilling lives and be an important source of social change toward a more just and equal society. Postmodernist theories' focus on agency and subjectivities adds to this by addressing the fragmentation of youthful categories and the need to take apart the multiple conditions and motives of young people.

Current Trends: Globalization and Citizenship

The main tendency in current sociological theories of youth is an apparent wane in mainstream theorizing and an increase in critical approaches (both structural and post-modern) that take to task the complex effects of globalization, capitalism, patriarchy, and racism as interrelated phenomena.

The continuing need for a critical structural analysis is premised on the stark economic aspects of globalization. With global economic restructuring associated with demographic shifts in the age structure of populations, governments all around the globe are faced with enormous challenges. In the southern hemisphere, the invasion of the capitalist economy puts pressure on the large child and youth populations. In the northern hemisphere, there is an associated pauperization of youth as their families' economic well-being deteriorates, and their needs are pitted against those of the increasing population of the elderly (Tienda & Wilson, 2002b, p. 4; Allatt, 2001, pp. 256–257; Rahman, 2001). The realities of an increasingly interconnected world with linked problems have resulted in global attention to the citizenship rights of children and young people (Giroux, 2003; Earls & Carlson, 2002; Helve & Wallace, 2001; Tyyskä, 1998; De Waal & Argenti, 2002; Jones & Wallace, 1992, pp. 18–23, 145–156).

Citizenship is seen to consist of full and equal access to the rights and responsibilities expected within one's living area, typically a nation-state. Importantly, in the Western context, full citizenship implies independence, defined as having a direct relationship with the state that is not mediated by anyone. Applied to youth, this means that you are considered to be a full citizen at the point that none of your relationships to the state are mediated by your legal guardians (usually parents) (Beauvais et al., 2001, pp. iii, 2–3).

There are four main aspects of life in which citizenship is played out: (1) preparation for (in schools) and participation in wage work; (2) participation in family/domestic relationships; (3) civic and political participation; and (4) participation in leisure, recreation, and consumption. Each of these comes with specific expectations that define when one becomes a "full citizen." However, there is a distinct hierarchy and a narrowness of definition: A "full citizen" is a person who is financially self-supporting and/or able to form and support a domestic relationship, and exercises voting and consumer rights. It can be argued that citizenship is being defined narrowly and in a manner that excludes youth. Full-time wage work and political participation (through voting) are considered the main criteria for citizenship while school work, part-time work, and youth-based, less formal community activities are not. Further, citizenship is defined through the ability to support a domestic unit through wages, while aspects such as performing domestic or caring work or other non-wage activities, such as school work, are not considered avenues toward citizenship. Finally, leisure and consumption are the right of adult wage earners. The end result of citizenship this narrowly defined (as pointed out by Smith et al., 2005, pp. 428–429; Hall & Williamson in Smith et al., 2005, p. 429; Beauvais et al., 2001, p. iii) is that it is possible to refer to young people as "citizens in the making," a notion that denies their citizenship status.

Primarily, independence translates to being able to have financial resources in order to maintain one's own living space (Beauvais et al., 2001, p. 10). Indeed, it is the employment-oriented conceptualization of citizenship that dominates the literature on youth and citizenship. Young people's secondary and marginalized labour force status (to be taken up more fully in the chapter on work) is most commonly highlighted as an example of how they are deprived of citizenship rights (Smith et al., 2005; Beauvais et al., 2001). On the other side of this argument is the notion that any wage earning produces social value that should be recognized rather than belittled. Thus, youth's part-time and occasional employment should entitle them to full citizenship.

Additionally, feminist and youth researchers alike have pointed out that the narrow notion of economic citizenship of full-time (and male) wage earners hides the fact that wage work is actually dependent on different kinds of non-waged activities. Examples of these not only include women's and children's domestic and caring work that supports families' economic viability, but also young people's school work and part-time work that all support the economy and the domestic unit both in the short and the long term. Thus, wage work as the hallmark of citizenship instantly renders into non-citizens the majority of women and all children and youth (Smith et al., 2005, pp. 428–429; Hall & Williamson in Smith et al., 2005, p. 429; Beauvais et al., 2001, p. iii; Thomson et al., 2004, p. 229), regardless of the actual social or economic value of their contributions.

As much as a gendered understanding of youth is required, so is a racialized one. Alexander, 1996 (pp. 157–160) points out that the citizenship and nationhood concepts that emerged in Europe and North America were built on colonialism (see Chapter 2). Non-Whites were denied citizenship rights in the emerging colonial nation-states. The colonized indigenous peoples and the Black slaves who were forcibly brought into the emerging capitalist nation-states faced a hierarchy based on both race and gender. Since colonialism was a White male project, the large numbers of racialized people posed threat. All Black people were denied the right to a family life through forced separation of men and women into different living quarters. Black males were further "emasculated" through the denial of the economic privileges accruing to White males, while Black women were vulnerable to the sexual exploitation of their White owners. bell hooks (1992, p. 89, in Alexander, 1996, p. 159) argues that as a legacy of this process, Black men have not been able to "fulfill the phallocentric masculine ideal" and are seen to turn their powerlessness against Black women. In the post-colonial northern hemisphere, Black men are seen to be down and out while Black women are considered somewhat economically and emotionally successful. This has resulted in contestation of power and control among Black men and women, a situation that is often depicted as misogyny by Black males. Thus, the legacy of colonial history is reflected in the ambiguity in the relationships between Black women and men, which are negotiated in their personal peer and romantic relationships in their younger years (Alexander, 1996, pp. 159–186). Neo-colonialism is present in the continued denial of Black people's citizenship rights directly in education, wage work, and family life, and indirectly through their marginalization in the areas of political participation and leisure/consumerism.

As a part of preparing young people toward financial independence, or making them into full citizens, educational institutions play a central role, but the role of schools is more than work preparation. Schools engage in significant political and citizenship education of youth, as well as in education about life skills, including community involvement, health issues, and sexual behaviour, to name a few (Beauvais et al., 2001, p. 14). As discussed above (and more fully in the chapter on education), schools have always been and continue to be the main and continuingly contested ground for citizenship education. Leaving this major institution outside the definition of citizenship renders young people's educational rights invisible and denies them participation in decisions related to their own education and school environments. Thus, it is possible to impose rules and regulations on students as is seen in the zero-tolerance and school uniform policies in increasing numbers of schools.

In addition to preparation for and engaging in wage work, the second pillar of formal citizenship is official political participation. The concerns with young people's lack of engagement with official political parties and their low voting percentages in many industrialized countries have led to a chorus of lament over youth's political disengagement (Burfoot, 2003; Vinken, 2005; Smith et al., 2005).

Meanwhile, Smith et al. (2005) point out that young people themselves may have a much wider definition of citizenship. While the young people in their study acknowledged the above features assigned to full citizens, they identified a wider range of socially constructive activities that are not customarily acknowledged as a part of political citizenship. These include informal political action (e.g., campaigns), activities with political implications (e.g., membership in ethnocultural groups), awareness-raising (e.g., challenging discriminatory views), altruistic acts (e.g., charitable donations), and general social participation (e.g., neighbourliness, volunteerism). All of these go beyond formally organized activities and underline the importance of taking into account youth's everyday lives and activities, which may be different from those of adults. Based on this argument, Smith et al. (2005, p. 441) as well as Vinken (2005) and Burfoot (2003) call for a more inclusive view of citizenship that gives value to the activities that are driven by young people. Though young people can be construed as non-citizens because of their lack of wage-work status and formal political rights, we also need to heed the demands for an alternative vision of citizenship that would also redefine youth and reassess their contributions.

In fact, this reconceptualization of citizenship as co-operation and interdependence goes counter to the standard model of citizenship, which emphasizes individualism and independence. The value of the individualistic emphasis is seriously questioned by research showing that it is connectedness to social institutions and communities that is required for best youth outcomes (Burfoot, 2003; Picard, 2005). Vinken's (2005, p. 147) more inclusive approach defines citizenship as the process in which (young) people develop trust in others and in society's institutions and produce competences to participate in social networks, institutions, and associations that to some degree serve a public cause.

The main question in the area of political citizenship, arising from Vinken (2005), is: To what extent are young people expected to conform and participate within the parameters of official political systems, and to what degree are their own efforts welcomed and heard as they try creating a different citizenship space?

This question is indicative of the benefits reaped from the critical and postmodern theorizing on youth and citizenship in increased attention to youthful subjectivities, i.e., the ways in which young people themselves define their experiences and their identities (Thomson et al., 2004; Rattansi & Phoenix, 2005; Alexander, 1996). With this emphasis, there is a renewed appreciation of the fluidity of youth and the infinite nature of identity formation. Identities are not simply "established" but

> they are seen as always in process, always in relative state of formation, and any "closure" around a particular identity—masculine or "young" or British, etc.—is seen as provisional and conditional in a literal sense, that is conditioned by and within specific social contexts, for example, particular peer groups in specific locales, whether the playground street, "neighbourhood," and so forth. (Rattansi & Phoenix, 2005, p. 105)

This reorientation of attention to youth's own varied interpretation is owed to postmodern influences in the era of globalization. Postmodernists remind us that globalization is not only an economic phenomenon but also a cultural one. In this regard, the two main issues are the encroachment of American popular culture into the world, on the one hand, and the impact of consumerism, on the other (Miles, 2000, p. 61), both of which will be discussed in the chapter on peers and youth culture.

The final frontier in understanding and defining citizenship of youth is in the area of recreation, leisure, and consumption. As explained above, in the Marxist analysis youth form target markets in the capitalist economy, and are pushed into using their increased purchasing power gained through part-time employment in the leisure and consumer industries (Côté & Allahar, 1994). Jones and Wallace (1992, pp. 117–140) pointedly state that "much of the consumption of young people is not related to their leisure or cultural styles at all, but concerns of their day-to-day living expenses: for food, clothing and shelter" (p. 118). Thus, the authors argue, the generalized consumerism of young people's lives is premised on a level of affluence that not all young people possess. There are not only social class differences at issue, but also young women's lower capacity for consumerism due to their lower wages, and the existence of a racialized underclass of youth who are excluded from the wide array of temptations in shopping malls as "cathedrals of capitalism."

Despite this reality check, however, young people are not merely victims; they have a capacity for resistance and active creation of their niches within leisure and consumerism. For example, Thomson et al. (2004, p. 228; see also Miles, 2000, pp. 63–66) point to the crucial role of consumption and leisure as forms of activity that provide a space of privilege and freedom from school work or part-time jobs while allowing young people to exercise their spending power. Consumption and leisure, the authors argue, is an arena for experiencing "responsibility, competence and recognition" that shapes youth's present and future lives. Vinken (2005) makes this point even more strongly, arguing that consumerism takes up a lot of young people's time and serves the purpose of creating new civic action through social linkages both in their local communities and worldwide. Though Vinken acknowledges the dangers of a global "McWorld-culture" (2005, p. 154), he argues that consumerism through the new media can also be harnessed toward the common good, exemplified in political consumerism (e.g., making purchases based on ecological considerations, boycotting goods on political grounds), which creates networks and social movements among youth. The context youth are creating for their civic participation is unlike the formal adult world, eschewing hierarchies and formal organizations outside of adult control, and making it more creative, fluid, and dynamic. Thus, though consumer goods are appealing to youth, the ways in which they construct their identities out of them are not fully predictable (Miles, 2000, pp. 64–65).

Thus, in the view of youth researchers, the concept of citizenship is in dire need of an overhaul, based on its poor applicability to the lives of youth. On the one hand, the debate on young people's lack of citizenship rights brings attention to important and significant inequalities in their lives. On the other hand, authors tend to fail to illuminate areas in which youth make unique and active contributions and create new definitions of their own citizenship. Unbridled optimism seems to prevail among large numbers of youth. For example, Bibby's (2001, pp. 159–205) analysis of the attitudes and views of the most recent teen cohorts in Canada finds that, compared to preceding teen generations, youth tend to manifest a similar range of world views and expectations, tend to work toward autonomy, tend to think that they are going to be able to challenge or ignore the odds in pursuing their lives, and tend to have buoyant expectations for their future.

Conclusions

The definitions and parameters of youth categories are admittedly in flux, and there is a wide array of theories attempting to interpret the lives of young people. The key challenge is to make sense of young people's lives amidst the chaos of competing theories while doing justice to the diversity and fluidity of youth populations. This task requires sensitivity to social change and historical factors as well as issues of diversity and inequality. It is this mediation between the specific and the general that makes sociological analysis of youth challenging and frustrating yet exciting.

In the chapters to follow, I will outline the main components in youth's lives in three Anglo-American countries: Canada, the United Kingdom, and the United States. We will begin with a brief historical orientation to youth in these three countries in the next chapter, and will continue with a more detailed look at youth's relationships with adults and peers, and the main social institutions: (1) family; (2) education; (3) work; and (4) the state and the legal system.

Critical Thinking Questions

1. Do you think young people today are overindulged and too demanding?
2. What do the "age of majority" requirements in different areas of young people's lives (e.g., drinking, driving, sexual consent) tell us about societies' views of youth?
3. How much choice and freedom do you think youth have in their lives?

2 A History of Childhood and Youth

In this chapter, you will learn that

- young people's histories and current conditions are diverse, based on social class, gender, race, and immigrant status
- young people's histories in the Western world bear a post-colonial legacy, rooted in the development of capitalism
- there is a prolongation of young people's dependence on adults and adult-led institutions, established through socio-economic developments

In order to better understand the meanings of contemporary youth categories, I will outline some of the history of young people in Canada, the US, and the UK, particularly as it relates to education and employment of young men and women.

Given the ambiguities and historically specific uses of the terms "childhood," "adolescence," and "youth," what follows is a historical account of the lives of young people from their years of semi-dependence on parents to the point of independence, which Gillis (1981, p. 2) suggests spans years from around the ages of seven or eight to the mid-twenties. The historical discussion will concentrate on the period from around the 17th century till the early to mid-20th century. The trends and legacies of past histories will be summarized at the end of this chapter as a preamble to more detailed discussion of youth's lives in the late 20th and early 21st centuries.

Before getting into the details, a note of explanation is in order regarding the different countries. While Canada and the United States are unitary nation-states based on a federalist model, the United Kingdom or Britain requires a brief explanation. The terms United Kingdom (UK) and Britain are the shortened forms for the full name of the political unit of the United Kingdom of Great Britain and Northern Ireland. The UK is a political union of England, Scotland, Wales, and Northern Ireland. The largest of these is England, with its 50 million people constituting 83 percent of the UK population. Because of the vast complexities and historical distinctions, the data pertaining to the discussion of British youth will focus mostly on youth in England unless otherwise specified.

Young people's history is diversified by the complexities of hundreds of years of migrations, colonialism, conquest, and slavery. Thus, we need to pay attention to the ways in which the lives of young people were shaped differently based on whether they belonged to the White European-based middle class or the working class, or if they were colonized indigenous peoples or slaves forcibly torn from their families.

Generally, the history of youth in the upper and middle classes is characterized by material privilege and gains from education, while nevertheless being subjected to the use of parental and patriarchal power in families. In the working classes, children and youth have a history of arduous and low-paid physical labour. Over the centuries, the lives of young Aboriginal peoples in North America, slaves, and immigrant labourers have been marred by hard labour, discrimination, and marginalization. Currently, ongoing and increasing immigration from the southern hemisphere to the northern hemisphere of the globe has resulted in a mixture of peoples unique to each of the three countries in question, with notable similarities in the experiences of racialized groups compared with White immigrant groups.

Race, Ethnicity, and Immigrant Status

One of the most striking features of the 20th century has been the ethnic and racial diversification of the populations in the three countries in question. This is the legacy of colonialism and ongoing population migrations in the past few centuries due to both voluntary and forcible dislocations of peoples from the non-industrialized South to the industrialized North.

Both the United States and Canada are immigrant-receiving nations. As of 2001, the former boasts a foreign-born population of 11.1 percent, while 18.4 percent of the Canadian population is foreign-born (Liu & Kerr, 2003). There has been a shift in the source countries of immigration over the last century. Whereas in the 19th century and most of the 20th century, British and other European immigrants were preferred, the last quarter of the 20th century has seen an influx of immigrants from non-European countries who now make up over three-quarters of all immigrants entering Canada (Momirov & Kilbride, 2005; Ambert & Krull, 2006).

In contrast to the White European immigrants of the past, recent immigrants to Canada tend to be from racialized minorities: over half are Asian, with three of the largest groups being Chinese, South Asians, and Blacks (Ambert & Krull, 2006). The change began with an influx of Caribbean, South American, and Asian immigrants from the 1960s onward. By the mid-1970s, immigration from Third World regions accounted for 40 percent of all immigrants (Thomson, 1979, p. 105). While immigration from Europe and the United States declined dramatically between 1961 and 1996, there have been several cohorts of immigration from Central and South America (peaking in 1981–1990), the Caribbean and Bermuda (peaking in 1971–1980), and West-Central Asia and the Middle East (growing since 1981). Immigration from Asia and Africa is steadily growing. The diversity of the immigrant population is also reflected in the presence of over 90 ethnic groups in Canada, each with 15,000 members or more (Albanese, 2005).

Given that most immigrants are in the younger age groups and of child-bearing age, this translates to increasing proportions of first- and second-generation immigrants in the population. For example, a growing number of Canadian children and youth were born outside the country. The number of immigrant children grew by 26 percent, and the number of immigrant youth (15–24 years of age) grew by 7 percent, between 1991 and 1996. In Toronto and Vancouver, over one-quarter of youth in this age group were born outside Canada (Canadian Council on Social Development, 1998). Of the estimated 200,000 immigrants who arrive in Canada annually, approximately one-third are under age 25 (Canadian Council on Social Development, 2000). Between 1991 and 2001, 1.8 million immigrants came to Canada, and over 17 percent of these (or 310,000) were children between the ages of 5 and 16, accounting for 17.2 percent of immigrants during this time period (Statistics Canada, 2008a).

Similarly, immigration to the United States is leading to a "new American majority" (Hernandez et al., 2007). In 2012, the US had a total of 1,031,631 immigrants (Monger & Yankay, 2013, p. 3). Hispanic Americans continue to be the fastest growing group (Small, 1994). Immigration from Asia and Latin America has resulted in a population of 14 million children—nearly 20 percent of the population—who have at least one foreign-born parent (US Department of Health and Human Services, 2003). As of 2011, 29.8 percent of the Hispanic population was under 15 years of age (US Census Bureau, 2011a). Within the US, Asian children account for 19.8 percent (US Census Bureau, 2011b) and Black (non-Hispanic) children for 23.7 percent of the population under 15 years of age; meanwhile, the White (non-Hispanic) population has maintained a steady percentage of 16.9 percent (US Census Bureau, 2011c).

Similar to North America, UK National Statistics (2003a; also see Small, 1994, p. 195) show that immigration and fertility patterns have resulted in a younger age structure among minority ethnic groups than in the White population. Those of "mixed" ethnic backgrounds had the highest proportion of young people aged 16 and under, followed by Bangladeshi, Pakistani, and Black (grouped into Black Caribbean, Black African, and other Black, of which the last has the highest proportion of young people aged 16 and under). Of the different ethnic groups in the post-World War II era, the earliest were Black Caribbeans who migrated to the UK immediately after the war and in the 1950s. The 1960s were characterized by immigration from India and Pakistan, and the 1970s saw more immigration from Africa, especially Uganda. Chinese and Bangladeshi people arrived during the 1980s, and more Black Africans during the 1980s and the 1990s. According to Small (1994, p. 195) Asians outnumber African Caribbeans in England and their numbers are also growing faster.

As of mid-2009, there were 10,554,600 youth under 15 in England and Wales. White youth (including British, Irish, and other White) accounted for 81.6 percent, or 8,607,400 individuals. Meanwhile, the number of mixed race youth are growing: as of mid-2009 they accounted for 4.7 percent, or 442,400 individuals. At the same time, the Asian population (including Indian, Pakistani, Bangladeshi, or other Asian)

accounted for 6.4 percent of the youth under 15 (or 677,300 individuals), with South
Asian youth forming the majority. The Black youth population grew to 3.6 percent (or
339,300 individuals) of the entire youth population in mid-2009, the majority being
Black African, followed by Black Caribbean. The smallest ethnic category of youth in
England and Wales are Chinese and Other Ethnic, accounting for 1.1 percent of the
entire youth population, or 117,100 individuals, with Chinese youth in the majority.
Therefore, as of mid-2009, 15.8 percent of youth under 15 were not from a White
ethnic group (National Statistics, 2011a).

Given this wide variety of racialized, ethnic, and immigrant groups, it is impossible to
deal exhaustively with all of them. Therefore, amidst general information about selected
groups throughout this book, I will pay particular attention to the experiences of Aboriginal youth in Canada and the US, and Black youth in all three countries. This reflects
differences in the colonial and post-colonial histories of the three countries. The United
Kingdom has a long colonial history, reaching widely into the world. Given the long-term
British colonization of India, I will address some aspects of the lives of South Asian youth
in Britain. In the nascent North America, colonialism had a devastating impact on indigenous populations and in all three countries there were long-term consequences for Black
slaves and their descendants. Twentieth-century population migrations have affected the
three countries slightly differently, but the post-colonial legacy related to racialized groups
remains. The historical account to follow will focus on the experiences of these youth, and
will also outline the experiences of mainstream youth, while paying attention to social class
and gender differences. The historical focus will be on young people's family lives, employment, education, and treatment in the justice system.

The historical account will help us to understand both the age parameters of contemporary youth categories in society at large, and the ways in which they are diversified
based on race and gender. Further, the social construction of youthful age categories
in history will set the stage for a more detailed discussion in the following chapters of
the different social, economic, and political aspects of young people's lives in contemporary society. In later chapters, specific aspects of the lives of minority youth will be
discussed, including their experiences of racism and discrimination in education and
employment, relationships with the police and the legal system, intergenerational relationships between immigrant parents and their native-born children, and the cultural
manifestations of youth culture. These will show that, both historically and presently,
the lives of young people are differentiated by social class, gender, race, ethnicity, and
immigrant status.

The Legacy of Colonialism

More so than in the northern hemisphere, approaches to childhood and youth in the
southern hemisphere explicitly acknowledge the legacy of colonialism. Margaret Mead's
work in Samoa (see Chapter 1) is echoed in other more current studies showing that
youth in some less complex and non-industrialized societies can make a smoother tran-

sition to adulthood than youth in industrialized societies (Evans-Pritchard, 1951, and Mead, 1943, in Jones & Wallace, 1992, p. 8; Sharp, 2002, pp. 13–21). For example, despite great diversity in traditional pre-colonial African societies (and also in large parts of Asia—see Manderson & Liamputtong, 2002, pp. 8–9), an orderly transition into adulthood was based on gradual gender-based pathways (Argenti, 2002, p. 125; Rhodes et al., 2002).

Though the economic and gender-based hierarchies of pre-colonial societies can be criticized, the relative orderliness of youthful transitions in many countries in the southern hemisphere was destroyed by colonialism, resulting in "disrupted age categories" (Argenti, 2002, p. 124). Multiple problems in young people's lives ensued, including high mortality and morbidity rates due to war, poor sanitation, lack of clean water and proper nutrition, and lower school enrolment, particularly for girls (Tienda & Wilson, 2002b, pp. 6–8; De Waal, 2002). Rather than being the results of mysterious "crises," the disrupted transitions are a result of colonialism itself (Argenti, 2002, p. 124). In the atomized and frequently impoverished post-colonial urban environment, these problems may multiply and result in youth anger, violence, and armed conflict (Rhodes et al., 2002, pp. 205–206; Rahwoni, 2002; Everatt, 2001; Argenti, 2002, pp. 127–130).

Colonialism and slavery are embedded in the history of Canada, the United States, and the United Kingdom. Though a full history of colonialism is outside the scope of this book, I will present a brief outline here of European colonial exploits that date back to the 15th century when the Portuguese and Spanish sent ships to Africa and the West Indies. Among other early entrants to colonial explorations were France and Denmark. The British and Dutch colonial exploits began in the 17th century. Among other later imperial nations were Germany, Italy, and Belgium (Africa Reparations Movement, 2007; Wilde, 2007; McElroy, 2004).

According to the chronology of colonialism by Wilde (2007), the process of colonial expansion by Europeans spanned from the 15th century to the 19th century. South America was conquered and divided through warfare and agreements between Spain and Portugal, and North America was divided between France and England. In the wars in North America, England retained Canada and though it won the war against the French and Dutch in the present United States, the latter fought a successful war for independence. At the same time, Europeans colonized most of Africa, India, Asia, and Australasia. England's presence was particularly notable in India, and many European countries participated in carving up Africa in the second phase of colonial imperialism in the 19th to the early 20th century. As World War I ended, many colonies fought for and won their independence in the third phase of colonialism.

Colonialism was inextricably linked with the slave trade. The Atlantic slave trade got its start in 1441 with the seizing of 10 Africans at Cape Brojador, and continued unofficially beyond the late 19th century when slavery was officially abolished in the New World (Africa Reparations Movement, 2007; Wilde, 2007; McElroy, 2004). The transatlantic slave trade was abolished in the British Empire and the United States in 1808, and slavery itself was abolished throughout Europe and the Americas during the 19th century, for example, in 1833 (although it actually went into effect in 1834) in

England, 1838 in the British Empire, and 1865 in the United States (Africa Reparations Movement, 2007). The year 2007 saw the 200th anniversary of the abolition of the slave trade in the British Empire. Gradual abolition of Black slaves in some states in the US began in the late 18th century, but it remained in practice in some southern states at least through the first two decades of the 19th century (Span, 2002, p. 113).

Estimates of the numbers of slaves brought from Africa to Europe and the Americas are difficult to establish due to lost or incomplete records. There is now agreement among most historians that an estimated 12 million slaves (some say as many as 50 million), mostly men, were forcibly transported from Africa, and that 10–20 percent of them perished on board ships (BBC World Service, 2007; National Archives, 2007).

Colonialism and the British Empire

The British Empire played a key role in the Atlantic slave trade. Slave traders originating in Bristol, Liverpool, and Glasgow sold their slaves in British ports in West Africa from where they were sent for the "middle passage" to the Americas (National Archives, 2007). It is estimated that in the late 18th century, 44,000 slaves were transported across the Atlantic annually (BBC World Service, 2007). Those who survived the horrible ocean voyage were sold in the southern US, the Caribbean, and South America to work in the sugar, cotton, and tobacco plantations. These goods sold in Britain enabled the rise of the fledgling merchant class to full industrial capitalism (National Archives, 2007; also see Pryce, 1986, pp. 2–5).

It was among these merchant classes and also among the aristocracy of the 17th century that the first slaves were brought into Britain directly from Africa. Later on, as the slave trade took full wind, more were brought in by White Britons returning from the British West Indies (Patterson, 1965, pp. 42–43). At the end of the 19th century there were small Black communities in the port towns of Liverpool, London, Cardiff, and Bristol (Solomos, 2003, p. 44).

It is difficult to imagine the cruel multiple losses suffered by the people who were stolen from Africa and taken off to forced labour in Europe, the Americas, and the Caribbean. They lost their families, languages, religions, and their original cultures. The biographies of West Indians in Bristol, who grew up in the Jamaican colonial regime under independence, recount the multiple layers of loss and cultural recreation. One woman (in Pryce, 1986, p. 4) said:

> I look and wonder what is my custom. Because if I was coming from Africa as an African, in my passport would be written a name like Shulu Afyung or something like that. Instead I found myself at birth with a name like McGilpin, that makes me know that the man who owned my forefathers as a slave was a Scot, a McGilpin. I said, so I lost my name there.
>
> And then I realize I am not speaking in an African language, but I am speaking English language and I realize that my food, instead of being fufu, is crushed potato....

I would have landed at the airport in a sari or other pretty tie-head, instead I'm wearing my same clothes, so that all that's left of me is the pigment, and I said this is what I dearly cling to, I wouldn't change it for anything.

The role of Britain in the colonization of India is of key importance in the history of youth. Through the British colonial period in India, and particularly between the two world wars, it was customary for sons of high-status families of India, as well as from the West Indies and West Africa, to be sent to Britain for their education. This system of receiving foreign students expanded in the postwar years, reaching nearly 36,000 entrants by 1960–1961, the majority of whom were from West Africa, followed by students from India and Pakistan and the British Caribbean (Patterson, 1965, pp. 43–44). Another part of the history of establishing an Indian presence in Britain dates back to the early 19th century when Indian as well as Caribbean and Chinese seamen settled in port towns despite attempts to get rid of them through repatriation legislation and racist violence by the public (Solomos, 2003, pp. 45–46).

Throughout the 20th century, the lives of racialized people in Britain were stamped with racism and discrimination to the degree that the multiplication of social problems led to serious social tensions between the White and Black populations. Low educational standards, lack of employment opportunities, political disengagement, and general marginalization led to pervasive race riots. In 1958, serious rioting took place in Notting Hill and Nottingham, mainly consisting of attacks on Blacks by Whites. The Black populations were by this time called the "Negro Problem" and were associated by the Whites with social problems, including poor housing and crime. Young "half-caste" children were particularly targeted as a problematic group. The 1958 riots in towns populated by Blacks helped to establish their image as "'undesirables' from the colonies" (Solomos, 2003, pp. 117–121).

More rioting and urban protests by racialized British youth and adults followed throughout the 1980s up till the early 2000s (Benyon, 1984, in Solomos, 2003, pp. 117–143, 167–169; see also Gilroy, 1987, pp. 32–33). Though the Black British unrest of the mid-20th century never reached the magnitude of the American civil rights movement (see below), there were significant organizations modelled after the American "Black Power" groups, which were scattered by the end of the 1960s (Cashmore & Troyna, 1982, p. 29). There are more recent examples of unrest among youth, including the riots in Manningham which were caused by segregation of ethnic groups (BBC News, 2001).

The riots and emerging awareness of the social problems among British Black populations led to a widespread concern with Black youth from the 1960s onward, leading to a depiction of this population as one "in crisis" (Cashmore & Troyna, 1982). Their problems were summarized by Solomos (2003, p. 121) as "high levels of unemployment, low levels of attainment in schools and homelessness," as well as police harassment, to be discussed in more detail in the chapters to follow.

It is gradually being recognized that the British Empire, as well as the rest of western and northern Europe and the United States, were built on the backs of slaves. While slavery has been condemned as a practice, past British Prime Minister Tony Blair refused to apologize for it and opposed reparations to slaves even though slave owners were compensated handsomely when slavery was abolished (Cooper, 2007, p. A15).

Slavery in the United States

As stated, the majority of the slaves were men, but women and children were also transported. The first group of American slaves was brought to Virginia in 1619 (Infoplease, 2000–2007). Of note is the mostly overlooked fact that the millions of African people uprooted through slavery were children and youth who were seen to be more controllable as slaves than the older age groups. American scholar Useni-Eugene Perkins (2005, pp. 6–19) has filled in a big gap in the literature on slavery by addressing specifically the conditions of slaves with acknowledgement that they were young people. One slave trader (in Perkins, 2005, p. 5) described his human cargo as follows:

> The cargo consisted of a hundred and thirty slaves of whom two-thirds were males and one-third females. The two sexes were kept separate by a partition or bulk-head, built from side to side, across the ship, allotting to the waist to the men and to the women, the quarter deck. A great majority of them were very young, being from ten to eighteen years of age.

An examination of old newspaper records confirms the young age of many of the slaves. For example, the *Vicksburg Daily Whig* (in *The Mirror*, 1844, p. 374) offers a 13-year-old "negro girl" for sale.

As Perkins (2005, pp. 6–19) says, these children and youth were ripped away from the security of their families, transported across the world, stripped of their African names, given English names, and put to work in conditions that were totally dehumanizing. Children born to slaves were kept with their mothers and typically separated from their fathers, who were kept in male quarters by the slave owners. Mothers had to work in the fields from morning till night and saw little of their children, who were kept in plantation nurseries. These young slaves grew into servitude and were brought up to accept their miserable condition. One former slave, Frederick Douglass (Perkins, 2005, p. 12), recalled his treatment at age 16 in the hands of Mr. Covey, a "Negro Breaker":

> I shall never be able to narrate half the mental experience through which it was my lot to pass, during my stay at Covey's. I was completely wrecked, changed, and bewildered, goaded almost to madness at one time, and at another reconciling myself to my wretched condition.

Young female slaves were subjected to sexual exploitation by their owners and essentially by any White male, their most important function being "that of breeding children" (Perkins, 2005, pp. 14–16). Linda Brent (in Perkins, 2005, p. 15), recalls reaching adolescence:

But now I entered on my fifteenth year—a sad epoch in the life of a slave girl. My master began to whisper foul words in my ear. Young as I was, I could not remain ignorant of their import.... He peopled my young mind with unclean images, such as only a vile monster could think of.... No pen can give an adequate description of all the pervading corruption produced by slavery. The slave girl is reared in an atmosphere of licentiousness and fear.

Slave owners deliberately kept the young slaves separated from the older ones so they wouldn't get ideas into their heads about running away or rebelling. Despite the threat of beatings or death, young slaves, male and female, resisted or ran away. Those who rebelled were quickly sold and replaced with more docile slaves. Runaways were also dealt with fast and harshly, as exemplified by this ad from the *Vicksburg Daily Whig* (in *The Mirror*, 1844, p. 374):

A reward of £5 is offered for the recovery of a "dark brown mare," and a "negro boy," captured on suspicion of being "a runaway," is advertised as being "committed to gaol," until the owner comes forward, pays charges, and takes him away; failing which the boy will be dealt with as the law directs.

As the abolitionists began their efforts to ban slavery in Europe and North America starting in the mid-1700s, they faced resistance justified by arguments ranging from the economic importance of slavery to fabrications about how well treated and contented the slaves were. The realities of slave life were in stark contrast to this white lie: six-day work weeks at 10–12 hours a day in the hot sun (National Archives, 2007). As part of their campaigns, in order to awaken the consciousness of White Europe and North America, anti-slavery reformers published heart-wrenching depictions like this one, published in *The Mirror* (1825, p. 100), in Virginia:

The sun was shining out very hot, and in turning an angle on the road, we encountered the following group:—first, a little cart, drawn by one horse, in which five or six half naked black children were tumbled, like pigs, together. The cart had no covering, and they seemed to have been actually broiled to sleep. Behind the cart marched three black women, with head, neck, and breasts uncovered, and without shoes or stockings; next came three men, bare headed, half naked and chained together with an ox chain. Last of all came a white man,—a white man! Frank,— on a horseback, carrying pistols in his belt, and who, as we passed him, had the impudence to look us in the face without blushing. I should have liked to have seen him hunted by bloodhounds. At a house a little further on we learned that he had bought these miserables in Maryland, and was marching them in this manner to some of the more Southern States.

After slavery was abolished, Black Americans faced a long period of struggles toward their full civil rights. Congress established a legal framework for equality: the Civil

Rights Act was passed in 1866; the 14th Amendment to the Constitution in 1858 provided Blacks with citizenship and legal equality; and the 15th Amendment in 1870 gave Black males the right to vote. Despite these measures, in the so-called Reconstruction Period (1865–1877), the southern states resisted ratification of the 14th Amendment (McElrath, 2007a). Instead, in 1865—the year when Abraham Lincoln was assassinated and the US Civil War ended—they created Black Codes to regulate the ex-slaves' marriages, property ownership, residence, and work lives. In the same year, the Ku Klux Klan was founded in Tennessee. The federal government moved to protect Black rights through the Freedmen's Bureau, and deemed the Black Codes unconstitutional in 1866 (McElrath, 2007a, 2007b; Brunner & Haney, 2000–2007).

The legislation by no means guaranteed any rights in reality, especially in the southern states, and the struggle that began in 1865 and lasted till the 1970s and beyond marked the civil rights era. Early challenges in the late 19th century included the struggle to counter the "separate but equal" facilities for Blacks and Whites. The National Association for the Advancement of Colored People (NAACP) was founded in 1910 to press for improvements in the lives of Black people, and to create a "Black consciousness." Between the two world wars, there was the great migration of Blacks from the South to the North to look for jobs, even as young Black men served in the armed forces, mostly in segregated units, during World War II (Wynn, 1993).

The deprivation of Black children and youth during and after slavery was reflected in their exclusion from education to the degree that many states put in place legislation to prevent the education of Black slaves, even if they paid school taxes. While Blacks put in place their own schools for educating their children, starting in the early 1800s, it wasn't till the end of that century that they gained some access to public schools within a segregated system and inadequate resources. And only just under 60 percent of Black youth attended public schools as of 1910 (Perkins, 2005, pp. 91–116).

There were gradual improvements in the lives and education of Black children and youth during a highly violent period of the civil rights movement starting in the 1950s. The peak years of the modern civil rights movement were 1954–1968. The movement involved many Black youth, exemplified by an NAACP member, Rosa Parks, who, in 1955, refused to give up her seat in the "coloured section" of the bus to a White passenger in Montgomery, Alabama. After she was arrested, the Black community launched a year-long bus boycott, which ended with the desegregation of Montgomery buses in 1956. The following decade was filled with other landmark struggles and events in the civil rights movement history, marred by violence, injuries, and the deaths of many Black people at the hands of police, the Ku Klux Klan, and other hate-filled civilians (Brunner & Haney, 2000–2007).

The modern civil rights era began in 1954, when the "separate but equal" doctrine was finally overturned by the Supreme Court, which declared separate schools inherently unequal. Three years later marked a watershed test of the school desegregation law in Little Rock, Arkansas, where desegregation of other facilities had already taken place after the Supreme Court decision. However, the desegregation of schools did not go smoothly (Rains, 2000). The NAACP filed a suit in 1956 because 33 Black students had been denied entry into four schools in Little Rock. Following a period of court action on the suit, the school board was ordered to proceed with the desegregation plan (Dortch-Tiger, 1957). Nevertheless, Arkansas governor Orval Faubus brought in the National Guard to prevent Black students from entering as the school year started in Little Rock Central High School. The National Guard was removed just over two weeks later, following a federal injunction. The school was surrounded by Little Rock policemen as students arrived on September 23 to start their school year, with approximately 1,000 White people waiting in front of the school. Nine Black students, often referred to as "The Little Rock Nine," were escorted in by police through a side door. With the White mob threatening to storm the school, the nine students were taken out before noon. In order to resolve the situation, President Eisenhower dispatched troops to Little Rock and took away the Arkansas National Guard from the governor. On September 25, "The Little Rock Nine" were escorted to school by 1,000 members of the army (Rains, 2000).

Throughout the school year, tensions were high, with the school and the community bitterly divided over desegregation and the Black students subjected to taunts, harassment, intimidation, and violence by the White students. One student, Melba Pattillo, got stabbed, had lighted sticks of dynamite thrown at her, and acid sprayed into her eyes. The Black male students got beaten up. One of the nine students, Minnijean Brown, was expelled in February 1957 for retaliating to the harassment by dumping her lunch tray onto two White boys and for calling a girl who was taunting her "white trash." Upon her expulsion, White students in the school made up cards saying "One down … eight to go!" The other eight stayed, and the year ended with the first Black student, Ernest Green, among the graduates of the high school (Cozzens, 1998).

In addition to the NAACP, the largely Black National Coalition of Advocates for Students (NCAS) led the ongoing struggles for educational equality for Blacks from the 1980s onward (Perkins, 2005, pp. 91–116). With their influence, the notions of racial socialization and education began to enter American schools to redress racially based inequities and to instill an appreciation of their racial and cultural heritage in Black children and youth, a topic that will be addressed in more detail in the chapter on education.

Overall, it should be noted that the modern civil rights movement by no means ended in 1968. The struggles are ongoing and each decade has brought new challenges and changes, including the 1971 Supreme Court decision to uphold busing of students as a legitimate means for integration, and legislation to prevent employment discrimination through the 1990s and early 2000s (Brunner & Haney, 2000–2007).

In the US, there are continuing instances of protest by racialized groups, including the Mount Pleasant Riot of 1991, in which Hispanics rioted due to injustices (*Washington Post*, 1991). Also in 1991, minority and religious groups rioted against each other in the Crown Height Riot (Gourevitch 1993, pp. 29). The 1992 Los Angeles riot following police brutality was one of the largest riots in American history, which illustrates the challenges of Hispanic population growth in the southern US (Newman, 1992).

Slavery in Canada

Canada was also a part of the Atlantic slave trade. For example, "at least 60 of the slave ships used in the British slave trade were built in Canada" (Cooper, 2007, p. A15). The first African slave to arrive in Canada landed at Quebec in 1628 (Walker, 1985, p. 8). He is reported to have been from Madagascar, and was named Olivier Le Jeune, after a Jesuit missionary who was his teacher. Although at this time slavery was officially illegal in colonial New France, it was upheld by both the French and the English until the early 1800s. Until the late 1700s, almost all Canadian Blacks were slaves, mostly in domestic service to White colonizers (Walker, 1985, p. 8; Thomson, 1979, pp. 17–18, 96). In 1760, there were approximately 4,000 Black and Indian slaves in Quebec (Thomson, 1979, p. 96).

As in the United States, Canadian slaves were generally subjected to harsh treatment, including public whippings and death, for misdemeanours or attempts to flee (Thomson, 1979, pp. 18–19). They were mostly illiterate (Winks, 1997, p. 364). Even as slavery was gradually abolished in the British Empire, the general image of servitude remained, and there were still cases of indentured service after this, including a 12-year-old girl by the name of Maria Walker, who was reported to be a slave in New Brunswick in the 1830s (Thomson, 1979, pp. 19, 98; Walker, 1985, pp. 80–90), and two 11-year-old slaves sold by public auction in Halifax in 1852 (Thomson, 1979, p. 18).

As the practice of slavery gradually disappeared, more Black people arrived in Canada, ostensibly free, but in reality running away from slavery in the United States. Several thousand Black people (the so-called "Black Loyalists") arrived in Canada in the century before Confederation (1867). They settled in Nova Scotia, New Brunswick, and Ontario, where they engaged in labour on farms and in industry, and constructed roads and cleared land (Walker, 1985, pp. 8–11; Thomson, 1979, p. 89). Another group of some 700 Black people arrived on Vancouver Island in 1858–1859 (Walker, 1985, pp. 11–12).

Canadians cannot claim much pride in their treatment of Black people despite such well-known phenomena as the "underground railroad," which secretly brought fugitive slaves to safety in Canada. Although conditions for Black people in Canada improved gradually, racism and colour barriers prevailed. White immigration to Canada was welcomed, while Blacks continued to be segregated into the lowest-paying jobs despite economic expansion. One such story is that of Harry Gairey, a well-known figure in the Toronto Black community, who emigrated from Cuba at age 16, just before World War I began (Hill, 1981, p. 7):

> There was a cigar factory on Front Street, between Yonge and Bay, by the name of Androse, I can remember well. They wanted a cigar maker, and I was one, I learned back home. I saw this sign in the window, "Help Wanted," and then I saw it in the paper. When I went into the factory, it didn't take me long to see that it was all white there. But I applied. They says, "No, we have no job for coloured people." Then I saw a job advertised for one of the boats. For help. I went down to the employment place, where the people phone in for help. They phoned up and then said, "No, they don't want you." That was in the early twenties. And when I got the

job on the road, I never turned anywhere else. Never bothered, because I knew I was blocked everywhere I went; it was no use to butt my head against a stone wall; I'd have a railroad job and I'd make the best of it.

The time period between Confederation and World War II was characterized by the return movement of large numbers of fugitive slaves to the slavery-free northern United States, or their movement to Sierra Leone or Trinidad, reflecting an unwelcoming Canadian public opinion (Walker, 1985, pp. 8–9; Thomson, 1979, p. 98). Racist ideologies promoting the natural biological superiority of White people fell on receptive ears and Black people's presumed inferiority gained public acceptance (Walker, 1985, pp. 12–14; Thomson, 1979, pp. 21–22).

This is evident in the open segregation that was practised in the emerging public school system, echoing the American experience. School segregation existed in law and in practice in Ontario and Nova Scotia (Thomson, 1979, pp. 20, 99–106; Winks, 1997, pp. 367–370). From the early 1800s onward, resistance of White parents to the presence of Black children in schools led to the creation of separate schools for Blacks, run by churches and by Black communities themselves even though the majority of Blacks paid public school taxes and wanted access to public schools (Winks, 1997, pp. 365–366). Growing anti-Black prejudice in the 1850s was manifested in the seating of Black children on separate benches in mostly White schools, and the withdrawal of White children by their parents from schools that admitted Black children. Meanwhile, the separate schools for Blacks had poor resources, poor teachers, most had no library, and attendance was irregular. Toward the end of 1800s, protests against segregation led to a gradual integration of Black students into public schools (Winks, 1997, pp. 371–380).

Racist practices prevailed in the 20th century with regard to the Black population. While Black people were blatantly being excluded from mainstream activity in the early 20th century, they continued to collectively resist the colour divide as they had with regard to the segregated school system. Segregation in all aspects of life persisted. During the war, young Black men, mainly from Nova Scotia and New Brunswick, were recruited into a separate battalion to provide auxiliary services for White troops (Walker, 1985, pp. 15–17), even as numerous Black organizations across Canada raised money toward the war effort (Thomson, 1979, p. 102).

In the school system, the official segregation of Black students was gradually abandoned. All but one separate school had closed in Ontario by 1900, and a single separate Black school existed in Alberta till the 1960s. In Nova Scotia, the last separate school is reported to have closed in 1917, but de facto segregation of Black students continued well into the 20th century through the exclusion of Black students at some schools, and by not operating school buses for Black communities. It took until the 1960s for Ontario and Nova Scotia to revise their legislation and practices related to separate schooling for Black children. By this time, there had been disastrous consequences for Black children's education as manifested in high rates of illiteracy (Winks, 1997, pp. 371–389; also see Kelly, 1998, pp. 33–47).

Racial discrimination in employment and in community life continued in the interwar years even though by 1921, nearly 75 percent of the Black population was Canadian-born (Thomson, 1979, p. 103). The hostility of the interwar climate toward Blacks was fuelled by the entry of the Ku Klux Klan into Canada in the 1920s and 1930s, mostly concentrated in the four western provinces and Ontario (Thomson, 1979, pp. 103–104).

After learning of the horrors of Nazi concentration camps (see Box 2.1) following World War II, Black communities became increasingly active as they challenged discriminatory legislation related to employment, accommodation, and public facilities. In the 1960s, human rights legislation federally and provincially began to emerge to ban limitations based on race, sex, or religion (Walker, 1985, pp. 16–18). This also reflects the gradual revitalization of the Black community through immigration. The first cohort of West Indian immigration to Canada began in 1960 (Thomson, 1979, p. 105), and the population grew from 12,000 in 1961 to 200,000 in 1981. An additional 50,000 Blacks had arrived from Africa in the same time period. Meanwhile, the indigenous Canadian Black community, the descendants of the arrivals from the previous centuries, numbered around 40,000 or 15 percent of all Black people in Canada (Walker, 1985, pp. 17–19).

As of 2006, there were approximately 783,000 Black people in Canada, or 2.5 percent of the total Canadian population, making them the third largest racialized group in Canada after people of South Asian and Chinese descent. About 11 percent are of Canadian origin, over half are from the Caribbean, and nearly 40 percent are from Africa (Statistics Canada, 2006a).

According to Cooper (2007, p. A15), the significance of the slave trade remains today:

> Institutionalized racist practices, anti-black racism, the colour line, colonialism, African underdevelopment and also that of former slave societies in the New World, duplicity of western governments, white supremacy, economic disadvantage, racialization of black peoples, and psychic distance between black and white have all been identified as legacies of the slave trade and slavery.

Aboriginal Youth and the Colonial Legacy in North America

The North America that colonizers arrived in had been populated by Aboriginal peoples since 30,000–40,000 years ago. It is estimated that at the time of the colonizers' arrival, the indigenous population of the western hemisphere was about the same as that of western Europe—around 40 million. An estimated 2–18 million of them were Native Americans living in the area that is now the United States (USInfo, 2007). Canadian estimates of the size of the Canadian indigenous populations at time of European contact range from 221,000 to over 2 million, with the most widely accepted conservative estimate around 500,000. Both the American and Canadian Aboriginal populations were decimated by the many European diseases that the colonizers brought with them. In Canada, the Aboriginal population had shrunk to 102,000 by the 1871 Census (Royal Commission on Aboriginal Peoples, 1991).

Box 2.1: Holocaust War Orphans

Before, during, and after World War II, large numbers of Jews attempted to flee from what was a great tragedy of the 20th century: the Holocaust, the systematic killing of millions of European Jews by the remorseless genocidal machinery of Adolf Hitler and the German Nazi regime. Child survivors of the Holocaust were sent to displaced persons' camps and orphanages across Europe. Robbie Waisman (Romek Wajsman), a Polish Jew, was liberated from the Buchenwald concentration camp at age 14 only to find out that his father, mother, and brother had been killed in the camps. His sister Leah survived, and he later found his paternal aunt. He ended up in an orphanage in France and was soon sent to get his high school education. He left Europe for Canada at age 17 and lived, educated himself, and worked in Calgary and later moved to Saskatoon and Vancouver. Mr. Waisman (2002) recalls this:

> I remember being told that no country in the world, with the exception of Palestine, wanted us…. The other two options open to us were Canada or Australia. Australia was attractive to many of us because of its distance from Europe…. Getting into Canada was tough. The process was a very lengthy one and you had to be absolutely healthy. Wearing glasses was enough to disqualify you. I had trouble getting approval because of my very low blood pressure. I had repeated blood tests and had all but given up hope when I finally got a letter accepting me into Canada…. I was seventeen when we landed in Halifax on 3 December 1948. I was disappointed to learn that I was not going to either Montreal or Toronto. As I spoke French and not English I was hoping to go to Montreal. My second choice had been Toronto because I had some contacts there. I wasn't told that I was going to Calgary until I was already on the train…. Calgary seemed so new and so friendly. I was astounded to learn that I did not need a passport or ID card on a day-to-day basis and that I could travel to other provinces without a visa…. The availability of food stuffs was amazing to me. Everything was a discovery. Although I appreciated the material things, the most important thing for me was just living and experiencing. I could not get enough of the life around me…. Later I brought my sister, her husband, and son over from Israel…. I would ask young people to keep an open mind when they see and meet newcomers to this country. Do not stop by looking at the surface of people. Experience the adventure of getting to know other kinds of people. Each one of us possesses unique, wonderful qualities, regardless of colour or religion.

The indigenous populations of North America are diverse and cover many language groups and cultures. Cook and Howe (2004, pp. 294–309) list 55 languages spoken in Canada, the largest Aboriginal language groups being Cree (80,000) and Ojibwe/Anishinaabemowin (45,000) in the Algonquian language family. American sources estimate that there were approximately 2,000 languages spoken in the western hemisphere whereas there are currently 175 indigenous languages spoken today in the United States, with 155 considered "moribund" (Crawford, 1995).

Despite the rich diversity of language and culture, official statistics collect information for much narrower sets of categories. According to the 2001 Canadian Census, the total Aboriginal population is 3.4 percent of the Canadian population, and numbers around 1,066,500. The Inuit are the smallest group, with around 60,000 people, and the Métis number around 300,000. The largest category is the approximately 700,000 First Nations people, formerly called North American Indians (Statistics Canada, 2005c). The Inuit are Aboriginal peoples who live in the North American Arctic—Arctic Canada, Alaska, and Greenland—and are related to groups in Russia. The Métis live largely in western Canada, and are the descendants of Canadian First Nations women and European colonizers.

In the United States, the 2000 Census counted American Indian and Alaska Native (including American Indians and Inuit) populations as 1.5 percent of the total population, at 4.3 million people who report multiple or combined American Indian or Alaska Native identities. Approximately 1.8 million report their only racial identity as American Indians and nearly 100,000 report being Alaska Native as their only grouping (US Census Bureau, 2006, pp. 1–2).

Despite the multiplicity of languages and tribes, these groups share similarities based on colonial history, and continue to bear the consequences of the colonial legacy in reduced and young populations that continue to live in economically dire conditions with associated multiple problems that amount to much lower quality of life than that of the general North American population. Because of the complexities involved in dealing with such diverse groups, the examples in this section refer only to Native Americans in the US and First Nations in Canada.

By early settler and missionary accounts, the lives of children and youth in pre-colonial Native American communities—largely a combination of foraging, hunting, fishing, horticulture, and agriculture—showed an orderliness marked by everyone's economic contribution as soon as they were able. Children and young people were gradually integrated into adult activities, which were generally divided by gender. Members of the community were responsible for the education of the young in their daily practices, aimed at ensuring material and cultural survival (Wotherspoon, 1998, p. 47). Further, as Bradbury (1996) has documented extensively, old Jesuit records of Huron life also show that children were treated with kindness, and harsh punishment was not generally used.

Arnett (2001, p. 179) summarizes the general history of colonialism and the decimation of Native American societies and cultures in the United States as follows:

In historical terms, during the 19th Century Native American cultures were decimated and finally overcome by the spread of European American settlement into the vast areas of the United States that Native Americans once dominated. The devastation of their cultures was deep and thorough, as they were betrayed repeatedly by the U.S. government, killed in large numbers, forced to leave their homelands, and ultimately herded into reservations in the most desolate parts of the country. This alone would be enough to explain substantial disruption to their cultural life in the present, with consequent effects on the socialization and development of their young people.

The serious disruption that was brought on by colonization also meant significant changes in the lives of young people. As Canada was colonized by the French and the English from the 17th century onward, First Nations communities were gradually pushed out of the way, and many died out as a result of disease, war, or deliberate extermination by the settlers. Most of the settlers and colonizers were men, and most of them were single. In many cases, men married girls (some as young as 12) or young women a great deal older than themselves. Solutions to their wifelessness were also found through marriages to First Nations women (Bradbury, 1996).

Among devastations to the Native American communities in the US was the practice of taking children away from their families to be "schooled" by non-Natives, which destroyed their links to their families, communities, and culture (Arnett, 2001, p. 179). This system was put in place in both Canada and the United States in the last two decades of the 19th century and continued past the mid-20th century (Crawford, 1995; Wotherspoon, 1998, p. 48; Battiste & Barman, 2003).

Young First Nations peoples were pulled into missionary schools or boarding schools aimed at assimilating them as they were viewed as less civilized, naive, or backwards. The residential school system became official government policy in Canada in the 1870s (Wotherspoon, 1998, p. 48; also see Marquardt, 1998, p. 23; Battiste & Barman, 2003), and was launched in a systematic way in 1908 as a part of the Canadian government's paternalistic and racist attempt to assimilate the Aboriginal population. Most of the schools closed in the 1960s. By the time the last of the schools closed in 1988, there had been losses of life due to poor conditions, malnourishment, and disease. There had also been denigration of culture, and destruction and torment imposed on countless First Nations families whose children were torn away from them and put into institutions where they were denied access to their families and culture under the thin disguise of "civilization" and "education." In fact, it has been estimated that there were no educational benefits to at least half of the children who went through the residential school system (Henry et al., 2000, pp. 125–127; also see Battiste & Barman, 2003). The so-called education consisted of harsh discipline for offences such as speaking their own language, and students saw their family members only a few times a year (Wotherspoon, 1998, p. 48; Battiste & Barman, 2003).

Lois Gus recalls his life in a Canadian residential school for First Nations children (Wotherspoon, 1998, p. 49):

Normally, in a Native family, a child is allowed to learn by trial and error, with love and support being freely given. My experiences in residential school were a sharp contrast to this. There, our natural curiosity was impeded by the outlook of nuns, who had no experience in life and no experience as a parent. Even the natural curiosity of the opposite sex was discouraged and one was made to feel ashamed for even having had such curiosities.

There were very few times you could enjoy life as it was so regimented. There was no freedom of thought or expression allowed. Everyone had to conform to a rigid set of standard rules: pray, learn, pray, obey, pray, eat, pray. Up at 6:30 a.m., Mass at 7:00 a.m., breakfast at 8:00 a.m., class at 9:00 a.m., lunch at 12:00 noon, class at 1:00 p.m., sewing and mending at 4:00 p.m., supper at 6:00 p.m., bed at 9:00 p.m. The next day it started again.

Even our bodily functions were regimented; there were certain times to go to the washroom, and castor oil was administered once a year. We had a bath once a week, and laundry duty every Saturday. We attended church once a day and twice on Sunday. On Sundays we had a few hours of free time but we were unaccustomed to such freedom, so we usually looked to an older student to organize our activities.

As the survivors of this repressive system gradually came forward and revealed the extensive abuse they suffered in these institutions, the Canadian government offered to compensate survivors at the offensively low rate of $24,000 each. The House of Commons issued an apology in April 2007, and in June 2008, a formal apology was issued by the Government of Canada. A Truth and Reconciliation Commission was struck, conducting hearings on the residential school experience. A report was published in 2012, entitled *They Came for the Children*, outlining 100 years of abuse and maltreatment of Aboriginal children, ostensibly for educational purposes.

The cultural isolation engendered by residential schools meant that generations of young people were lost to their families even though they resided in their original communities. Patterns of livelihood were disrupted as young boys and girls were taught the ways of the colonizers (Fiske & Johnny, 1996, pp. 230–232). The damage to First Nations cultures has been severe as most groups face the near disappearance of their languages. Most languages survive only as long as the elders are around. In the US, official estimates find that there are fewer than 100 home speakers in one-third of Native American and Alaska Native languages (Crawford, 1995). In Canada, Cook and Howe (2004) find that 43 of the 55 languages they list have fewer than 1,000 speakers, and of those, 17 have 100 speakers or fewer.

Meanwhile, as will be detailed in future chapters, social problems continue in North American Aboriginal communities, manifested in high rates of illiteracy, poverty, unemployment, poor health, substance abuse, and suicide, particularly among the youth. This amounts to a major catastrophe in societies in which the proportion of young people exceeds the national average.

Mainstream White Youth

The lives of youth in the White mainstream follow similar pathways in all three countries, with some variation in the timing of major life changes and definitions of childhood and youth. Generally speaking, all three countries' social class divisions resulted in different life paths and experiences; while all children and youth experienced child labour for several centuries, the children of middle and upper classes were freed from the yoke of wage work to undertake the task of education earlier in history from the 17th century onward. For the children of labouring urban and rural classes, physical labour was the order of the day until the reform movements of the late 19th century outlawed child labour and heralded public education systems.

The United Kingdom

In the White mainstream of 16th- and 17th-century England, social class divisions separated the lives of children and youth. The children of the small segment of the upper classes were sent to private schools at early ages to gain an education, and obtained a mature status through practices such as dressing in adult garb. However, their total independence would be gained only through marriage or inheritance, and they would be held in a state of dependence or semi-independence for extended periods of time. One example of the subordination of those in the wealthier classes was the use of corporal punishment in educational institutions such as Oxford University, reserved for those whose station in life was deemed to be lowly (Gillis, 1981, pp. 7–9). In wealthier families, males were favoured, as evidenced by inheritance practices leaving them either all or the bulk of parental property. The male siblings of the eldest male heir were destined for different trades and professions, while the females were expected to marry (Gillis, 1981, pp. 11–13).

In 16th- and 17th-century England, as well as elsewhere in western Europe, children of middle and lower classes under the age of puberty customarily left their homes to work as servants or apprentices. This was seen as a "rite of passage" and provided youth with an opportunity for independence and identity (Springhall, 1986, pp. 16–21). Children were seen as an investment for their parents' old age and/or disability, resulting in families with large numbers of children. In England, children formed between two-thirds and three-quarters of the population, compared to the between a quarter and half of the population today (Gillis, 1981, p. 11). With the system of primogeniture, sons of peasants had to wait till their late twenties to gain family farms, resulting in average ages of marriage of around 27 or 28 for males and 24 or 25 for females, who were often pregnant at the time of marriage. Children were used as farm labour as soon as they were able, from around age 6 or 7. As children got older, the pressure of having younger siblings would often force them out of their own households and into those of others (often relatives) as farm workers and servants, since small landholdings were not capable of sustaining all family members. Some estimate that two-thirds of males and three-quarters of females lived away from home from their early teens until the time they got married (Gillis, 1981, pp. 13–18). Thus, children and youth were mobile or "surplus children" from around age seven or eight until their mid- to late twenties, spending time in servitude, apprenticeship, or, for the financially fortunate, in schools (Gillis, 1981, p. 17).

Gillis (1981, pp. 21–26) points out that two institutional forms were required to maintain rule over such a large proportion of superfluous children and youth. One of them was the patriarchal rule of heads of household and masters of trades and schools, including strict rules and regulations that dictated everything from the manner of dress to the length of hair of the youth under their charge. The other rule enforcers were peer-based brotherhoods (and some sisterhoods) in schools and trades with their initiation rites and internal moral codes.

During the 18th and 19th centuries, rapid population growth ensued in all of Europe, accompanied by both agricultural revolution and industrial revolution. The enclosure movement drove peasants off land and into emerging industrial centres. The labour of youth was in demand, with intensification of the pace and scale of production of both agricultural and industrial goods, and with a breakdown of the apprentice system. With access to wage work, young people set up their own households and got married earlier (Gillis, 1981, pp. 39–45). It is estimated that in the late 1800s, some 80 percent of the migrants to cities were 15–25 years old, most of whom lived in or near poverty (Gillis, 1981, pp. 55–56). Family strategies of survival were reflective of the economic utility of child employment as it was now beneficial to pool resources of all family members rather than send children away to work or apprentice (Gillis, 1981, pp. 58–61). In the early 19th century, illiteracy was widespread and young working-class men and women worked in the mills and coal mines. After Queen Victoria ascended to the throne in 1837, an evangelical turn in British Christianity led to the emergence of a middle-class movement of morality focused on youth (Rogers, 1997, p. 9).

With industrialization and the emergence of a full-scale capitalist economy in the 18th and 19th centuries, compulsory mass education was established and provided the basis for "adolescence" (Springhall, 1986, pp. 16–21), with the aim to produce work-ers and citizens as well as help in the formation of identity and the transmission of knowledge and skills (Chisholm & Hurrelmann, 1995, p. 130). Throughout this time, childhood and adulthood became sharply distinct phases, with a gap widening between them through the emergence of adolescence, a process that was accelerated from the mid-19th century onward (Chisholm & Hurrelmann, 1995, pp. 129–130). Specifically, Gillis (1981, pp. 95–131) puts the time of "the discovery of adolescence" to 1870–1900, starting with the upper and middle classes and spreading to the working class with a change in family strategy toward lower fertility. With no real property to pass on to offspring, the middle classes had an interest in educating adolescent sons toward profes-sional careers in public schools and socializing daughters toward good marriages within the confines of their homes. The typical life cycle became established as childhood (until around age 10), adolescence (10–20), young adulthood (20–30), parenthood (30–60), and death or retirement (Gillis, 1981, p. 104).

Middle- and upper-class boys were subjected to strict school discipline. In the Victorian climate of repression, "puberty" emerged as an acknowledgement of juvenile sexuality toward the end of the 19th century. While boys were schooled for longer periods of time and their age at marriage was approaching 30, regulation of youthful sexuality was seen as a challenge. Though it is impossible to determine the full extent of homosexuality, it has been noted that sexual relations between boys were commonplace in the public schools. Robert Graves (in Gillis, 1981, p. 113) is reported to have said:

> In English preparatory and public schools romance is necessarily homosexual.... The opposite sex is despised and treated as something obscene.... For every one born homosexual, at least ten permanent pseudo-homosexuals were made by the public school system.

Attending and staying in school was rather difficult for working-class children. Although in 1880 children under the age of 11 (raised to 14 in 1918) were legally obligated to attend school, working-class children's obligation to contribute to the family economy made their schooling difficult and truancy rates were high. As these children left home to make their own way, they recreated the poverty of their parents (Gillis, 1981, pp. 123–131).

In this time period, class-divided youth cultures emerged, characterized by the urban neighbourhood gangs among working-class youth and by student movements and bohemianism among the middle and upper classes (Springhall, 1986, pp. 16–25; Gillis, 1981, pp. 129–130; Rex, 1982, p. 56). Associated with the idea of working-class youth "gangs," in the 1890s and 1900s, British educators and social scientists became concerned with the problem of "boy labour," or the recruitment of school leavers into short-term menial jobs, and the associated juvenile delinquency. Instead of seeing the problems of these youth as rooted in urban working-class poverty, adolescence became the culprit of the vagrancy and uprootedness of urban youth, who were seen to be in need of spiritual and moral guidance (Springhall, 1986, pp. 25–27; Gillis, 1981, pp. 61–66).

The boundaries between youth and adult worlds gradually became more evident, manifested in the setting up of juvenile courts for young offenders (Rogers, 1997, p. 10). Through the latter part of the 19th century and the early 20th century, concern over the perils of adolescence was manifested in fears of delinquency (Gillis, 1981, pp. 133–134; Shore, 1999). In fact, youth delinquency was the ground for the biggest debates about crime and punishment in Britain. Juvenile criminals were depicted as the "monster roots of vice" of professional criminals. They were treated and depicted as adults or as "'stunted little men' (or women)" (Shore, 1999, pp. 2–3). These youthful "offenders" were mostly not guilty of major crimes but had been captured for their vagrancy or misdemeanours, or had been found "unruly" by their parents or guardians, who brought them in front of the magistrate. They were mostly in custody without trials or juries. Those under 14 (raised to 16 in 1850) were summarily processed in petty sessions allowed by the Juvenile Offenders Act of 1847. In 1854–1857 they were put into alternative juvenile institutions under a series of reformatory and industrial school acts. These reform schools became places for "moral and social education" where youth were divided into "good" or "bad" offenders, i.e., those who were misguided and those who were seen to be hardened (also see Box 2.2 for the conditions resulting in juvenile delinquency) (Shore, 1999, pp. 3–9).

Criminality in youth was understood in clearly masculine terms. The prevailing typification was that boys were thieves and girls were prostitutes. Girls' offences were perceived in sexual ways; they were more likely to be prostitutes or "criminal molls" with a corrupting influence on boys and men. Even assertive and aggressive behaviours among girl offenders were interpreted based on sexualized images. The institutions aimed at female offenders, such as the work of Elizabeth Fry, were primarily depicted as "rescuing" female juvenile offenders from themselves and "rescuing" society from their influence (Shore, 1999, pp. 9–11).

According to Shore (1999, p. 151), a stark reality of urban poverty among the industrial working class lurked behind the growing numbers of children and youth who populated the reform school and juvenile facilities:

> For example, many working-class children experienced problems at home, exacerbated by poor housing, ill health, unemployment, the drudgery of menial and often erratic work, and limited educational opportunities. Fourteen-year-old James Edwards, who was found guilty of burglary at the Central Criminal Court in March 1835, lived and committed his crime around Kingland Road, Hackney. Here he lived with his mother, a clog-maker. His father had left, and since then James's mother had taken to drink. Her situation was no doubt worsened by worry over James (who had previously spent time in prison) and about his brother who was on board the *Euryalus* under sentence of transportation. James had two other siblings, a married sister and another brother still at home. He had had some limited education, attending a national school. However, he could neither read nor write. Clearly he felt thieving to be a remunerative occupation, considering between 8s. and 10s. a "middling day's work." The family were on the verge of destitution, making up a meagre income by a variety of methods. All the family went out begging, James sang and sold matches. His mother also made extra money by purchasing old leather from a bellows shop in Bethnal Green and after cleaning it, selling it on to a Shoreditch shoemaker for 9d. or 1s. This story of debilitation, of poverty, of the makeshift strategies of the poor is recognizable in a number of the sources.

The close of the 19th century saw protective legislation aimed at youth to increase state control over children despite their parents' interests. The targets of legislation were families living in impoverished neighbourhoods where it could be argued that they should be saved, through legislation, from child labour, family violence, and from the perils of tobacco and alcohol (Gillis, 1981, pp. 156–159).

With the 20th century came the wider democratization of education, aimed at the children and adolescents of all social classes. As adolescence emerged, so did a whole industry of social and psychological theories of youth (see Chapter 1) and specialized services, including extracurricular activities (exemplified by the Scout movement), and employment services (Gillis, 1981, p. 133).

However, adolescence still continued to be a class-divided notion (Gillis, 1981, pp. 134–148). Working-class adolescents were still absent from the education system to a large degree due to the economic depressions that lasted well into the 20th century. Poverty was accompanied by poor housing, illness, and high death rates among the young. As young men lacked real work opportunities, poverty persisted among the working class well into the years of World War II. These conditions were accompanied—by necessity, as Gillis argues—with excessive concern over delinquency. Thus, the pulling of working-class youth into education was a means to curb their poverty and "hardened" ways and to instill into them a middle-class sensibility of conformity. Alongside this effort was the reform movement toward saving children from 1900–1950, which was populated with volunteer men and women of the upper and middle classes (Gillis, 1981, pp. 166–167). Their efforts, accompanied with the early 20th-century theorists discussed in Chapter 1, contributed to the emergence of one "of the twentieth century's social stereotypes, namely the aggressive, anti-social image of the modern juvenile delinquent" (Gillis, 1981, p. 170). This was particularly aimed at youth from the lower socio-economic classes:

> The youth most likely to be brought before the regular courts were those young people who had no institutional affiliations aside from work. In other words, the more independent the youth, the more responsible he or she was for his or her own conduct, the more likely the stigmatization by society as a real or potential delinquent. Indeed, the very customs of the adult-centered working-class family contributed to his vulnerability, since, in the eyes of the middle classes, it deprived its children of proper care and protection by sending them into the world so early. Failing to understand, or even to tolerate, the way the working class brought up their young, the self-appointed care-takers of the younger generation viewed the "deprived" child as the potential delinquent. (Gillis, 1981, p. 181)

In the early to mid-20th century, World War I and World War II drew youth into military service and associated industries. The result was an emergence of generations of traumatized and shell-shocked male youth, and somewhat liberated young women who had tasted economic independence in wartime industries and war-support work. During and after World War II, English youth culture experienced an "Americanization" with the influx of American popular music and movies. The 1950s were dominated by American-led images of youth in films such as *Rebel without a Cause* (1955), starring James Dean. By the "swinging sixties," London had become the world's "style capital" for youth (Rogers, 1997, pp. 11–15).

However, amidst all the swinging in the 1960s, there also emerged a renewed wave of youthful protest and political activism, and a freeing of youthful sexuality, particularly among middle- and upper-class youth (Gillis, 1981, pp. 185–186). For them, many walls were breaking down and freedoms from parental and social watchfulness were removed in social activities as well as the education system. With an earlier onset of puberty, adolescent sexuality became more widely accepted and the age of marriage dropped with the introduction and widespread use of contraceptives (Gillis, 1981, pp. 186–191).

The increased affluence of the postwar period also had an impact on the working class in lower birth and mortality rates and a reduced likelihood of needing the labour of all family members for survival. There was some convergence of class attitudes toward adolescents in the area of freedom of movement. However, in comparison to middle-class parents, working-class parents still expected their children to get employed sooner, and education was valued "for the skills its offers and not ... as a source of social status or social control" (Gillis, 1981, p. 193).

For working-class youth themselves, the value of schools was in forming peer groups for support and recreation (Gillis, 1981, pp. 195–196), while middle-class youth were more likely to join formal youth organizations outside school, such as Boy Scouts (Gillis, 1981, pp. 197–199). Meanwhile, specific musical expressions, such as Beatlemania, were distinctly working class in origin (Gillis, 1981, p. 199).

The 1970s in the UK were stamped by cosmopolitan influences and diverse cultural flavours from a range of immigrant communities (Rogers, 1997, p. 15). In the 1970s and 1980s, youth began to be "much more at ease with their own sexuality, far less concerned with questions of masculinity and femininity, most of which they have already resolved in early teenage" years (Gillis, 1981, p. 207). Gillis argues for the "obsolescence of adolescence" (p. 207) as middle-class youth have a psychological stability unknown to people of their age before. They are ready to face social and political issues and responsibilities at an earlier age than ever before, and are thus more likely to engage in radicalism and bohemianism at an ever-younger age. This is likened to Kenneth Keniston's (in Gillis, 1981, pp. 207–208) notion of "post-modern youth," the children of the wealthy and educated privileged classes who, from ages 15 or 16 onward, are fully adult in the sexual, intellectual, and political, but, significantly, not in the economic sense. As Rogers (1997, p. 16) reminds us, the 1980s were a time for Margaret Thatcher as prime minister and the associated unemployment, inner-city problems, and widespread disillusionment among youth.

The United States

In the early colonial period, it was common for young people in their late teens and early twenties to live outside their parental homes with family members or friends who employed them for farm work, go into service in wealthier households, or work in apprentice training. As the population grew and the nation industrialized in the 18th and 19th centuries, young people flocked to the cities in search of employment. Demand for children's cheaper labour translated to approximately 750,000 children aged 10–13 working in industrial work settings as of 1900, labouring up to 12 hours a day for pennies (Arnett, 2001, p. 8).

Concerns over young people's work conditions and their independent lifestyle, including crime, sexuality, and alcohol use, met with increasing controls and legislation by adults, through adult religious and community organizations, in the last decades of the 19th century and the early 20th century. Legislation was put in place to limit child labour and to instill compulsory education. While only 5 percent of 14–17-year-olds had been in school in 1890, the figure stood at 30 percent as of 1920. This was a signifi-cant turning point in that the meaning of adolescence changed with its increased separa-tion from the adult working world. This so-called "age of adolescence" (1890–1920) also saw the emergence of adolescence as a scholarly field, specifically due to the influence of G. Stanley Hall (see Chapter 1) (Arnett, 2001, pp. 8–10).

Mandatory education was historically put in place as an "antidote to child labor" (Redmount, 2002, p. 136). However, at least one study (Redmount, 2002) found a link between local economic cycles and school attendance among the working class and immigrants in Massachusetts in 1881–1899. Middle-class children's attendance increased during economic upturns while affluent neighbourhoods were not affected by business cycles. However, school attendance among working-class and immigrant male children declined each time that opportunities for wage work increased. Girls' school attendance is less tied to local economic fluctuations, suggesting that in low-income families, girls were able to stay in school partly because boys obtained wage labour. This may have planted the seeds for developing a future sense of the value of education among working-class and immigrant families.

As in the UK and also in Canada (see below), juvenile delinquency was an issue in the 18th- and 19th-century US. Concern arose in major urban centres like New York City over adolescent gangs and vagrants. In New York City, street gang membership drew from Irish, Italian, Jewish, and Polish immigrant children, as well as from among Black youth. However, it was concern over the White ethnic youth, not African-American children, that led to the establishment of juvenile justice and reformatory systems (Span, 2002). Span (2002, p. 116) points to the well-established link between underclass status and juvenile crime. As this underclass shifted from White to Black and brown, so did the makeup of the population of juvenile delinquents and responses to those youthful criminals. While the White immigrant children were put into reformatory institutions for clearly criminal behaviour, Black youth were perceived as more of a threat and were incarcerated for vagrancy, not for crimes committed.

Canada

In Canada, among both English and French colonial families, young people's eco-nomic and social independence emerged amidst strict codes of filial obligation and parental (particularly paternal) power over children's lives. Fathers had absolute rights to their children, including the right to mete out harsh physical punishment. The major social institutions, including families, communities, churches, and schools, were based on the notion that young people needed a firm guiding hand. The transi-tion from childhood to adulthood was abrupt in that children were expected to be pre-pared to participate in adult activities as soon as they were physically able. This meant that children as young as six began training for different work through apprentice-ship or home-based vocational training (Mandell, 1988, pp. 53–54; Moogk, 1982). Apprentice programs were not as common as in continental Europe, but some youth, more commonly boys, entered into a period of semi-independence as they lived away from home while learning a trade (Bradbury, 1996; Mandell, 1988, pp. 53–59, 66; Moogk, 1982, pp. 52–54).

There were different pathways for boys and girls, marked by social class differences. Boys would follow the occupational and status positions of their fathers, specializing in trades or professions. There were fewer choices for girls, who were expected to learn domestic skills to prepare for their future as wives/mothers, or their future in domestic service for wealthy households (Mandell, 1988, pp. 53–56; Moogk, 1982). As the colonizers began to form permanent settlements, standard work patterns emerged within their families, with the labours of all family members, including children and youth, needed to make a living. Not yet enrolled in any formal education (see Box 2.2) working-class boys would generally leave home by age 15 to work in lumber camps, on fishing boats, or in town. Girls more commonly entered domestic service and learned wifely domestic duties, such as making clothes (Bradbury, 1996, p. 62; Baker, 1989, p. 35; Marquardt, 1998, pp. 15–20; Moogk, 1982). Industriousness in children was expected. Sometimes this resulted in racist perceptions, as exemplified by the views of British colonialists toward French settlers' children (see Box 2.2).

Farm work dominated the lives of children and youth, and their labours made a real contribution to their families, as illustrated in the following proverb: "children are the

---

Box 2.2: "Les Petits Sauvages"

Children of 18th-century New France were given the racist name *les petits sauvages* to describe their unruliness, likened to Aboriginal peoples. Moogk (1982, p. 36) explains:

> In French Canada today little children are sometimes called *les petits sauvages*. This characterization of Canadian children as little Indians or savages would have been accepted by the administrators of New France. In their correspondence French officials described the youth of the North American colony in the blackest [*sic*] terms. Young *Canadiens* were rarely mentioned and then only with adjectives that expressed censure and disapproval. The boys of the colony were reproached with being lawless and disobedient; the girls were portrayed as vain and lazy. Even Father Charlevoix, a Jesuit teacher who knew the *Canadiens* well and excused many of their faults, ventured his own criticism of their children. The healthful climate and fertility of New France ought to have retained the native Canadians, he wrote, "but inconstancy, aversion to assiduous and regular work, and the spirit of independence have always caused a large number of young people to leave the colony."

riches of the poor" (Moogk, 1982, p. 54). On farms, young people were expected to participate to their fullest capacity. Parr (1980, pp. 82–83, in Mandell, 1988, p. 64) describes typical farm work as follows:

> Young boys of 8 fetched wood and water, gathered eggs, fed and herded animals. As they grew older, boys chopped wood, hoed potatoes, dug turnips and helped with the haying. Fourteen-year-old boys worked like men, ploughing in the spring and fall, threshing and husking corn in the winter, cutting wood.... Girls from age 6 on participated in the household chores by babysitting, cleaning, cooking and sewing and they helped the men outdoors. Their responsibilities increased as they grew older. Hired girls between 14 and 18 did more heavy housework and helped in the cash-earning dairy and poultry enterprises on the farm.

Children of the upper classes had more time on their hands, and they were subjected to other types of control over their time and behaviour, including religious training and schooling. In Europe, there were schools for the children of the upper classes from the end of the 17th century onward. Although this was mainly meant for male children, some upper-class girls were also given general instruction in basic literacy. For this privileged group of children, there was thus a gradual lengthening of childhood through education. This was slowly introduced to the lower classes and girls (Mandell, 1988, p. 59). Education in Canadian families was not only academic education but also religious instruction and vocational training (Moogk, 1982, p. 49).

The great changes in economic organization that ushered in capitalism also marked the continuity of child labour for the vast majority of the population. Marquardt (1998, p. 20) notes that the employment of youth was not only important to the financial survival of their families but also to the "business strategies of early industrial capitalists." That there was need for child labour was demonstrated in the importation of British children between 1867 and 1919 when approximately 73,000 children immigrated to work as labourers and servants. Children under 9 years of age were adopted, but those 9 to 18 years of age became indentured labourers. Under contract, they got room and board, clothing, and literacy in exchange for performing household chores that freed adults for heavy farm tasks (Mandell, 1988, p. 66).

Social reformers worked hard to combat the negative effects that child labour had on the development or even survival of young people. For example, city children regularly worked 60-hour weeks (Mandell, 1988, p. 66). It was not until 1887 that child labour laws in Canada limited the labour of children under the age of six. From the 1880s onward, the legal age limits were gradually raised, first to 12 for boys and 14 for girls in 1886, and to 14 for both sexes in 1895 (Baker, 1989, p. 35; see also McIntosh, 2000). This was not only a result of actions by well-meaning child protectionists, but coincided with economic recessions that led to adult male protectionism in work areas where child labour was seen to threaten their employment (Mandell, 1988, p. 67).

Both women and children were regularly paid lower wages on the assumption that they were not as productive or that they were not required to support a family (Baker,

1989, p. 35). In fact, fewer girls than boys worked in industries, and the participation of young women tended to diminish proportionally as they got older, reflecting the practice of women stopping wage work as they got married or had children (Bloomfield & Bloomfield, 1991, p. 31). As Canada became industrialized, the gender divide gradually hardened as boys and young men had a range of jobs to choose from, and girls' and young women's choices were limited (Bradbury, 1996, p. 69).

It was expected that marriage was possible once you were economically self-supporting. Given the poor availability of work and the low wages offered by the industrializing economy, young people in the mid- and late 19th century stayed dependent on their families for a longer time. The age of marriage was delayed, and more young people continued living at home for longer periods. Men would typically marry in their late twenties and women in their early twenties. At that time, women would leave the paid labour market (Marquardt, 1998, p. 17). This prolonged stay in the parental home also meant that youth were increasingly under parental supervision (Mandell, 1988, p. 65). In southern and eastern Ontario, young people preferred factory work over farm work or personal service work because the former offered comparatively higher wages, shorter work days, and more personal autonomy (Baker, 1989, p. 35).

The entry of young working people into industrial centres was accompanied by concerns about vagabond and delinquent youngsters on city streets. For example, Katz (1975, in Marquardt, 1998, p. 16) reports that in mid-19th-century Hamilton, Ontario, there were large numbers of "idle" young people whose presence and possible tendencies toward negative pursuits on the streets caused social reformers a great deal of concern. At that time, almost half of young people aged 11–15, and approximately a quarter of 16- to 20-year-olds, were neither employed full-time nor attending school.

The entry of women into industrial centres, such as Toronto, was also accompanied by concerns about "urban perils" that may lead young women into "sin" and a neglect of their domestic responsibilities once they had tasted the freedom brought by wage earning. This preoccupation with the morality of young women reflected the trend, by the mid- to late 19th century, of a shift in women's employment from domestic service to industrial work. These new work opportunities, created by industrialization and paid labour, took young women away from the supposedly safe confines of their own family or the families of strangers that they worked for (Strange, 1997, pp. 8–9; see also Coulter, 2005).

Young working women lived either with their own families, in boarding houses, or in their employers' homes. The latter setting made them particularly vulnerable to sexual exploitation. For example, Bailey's (1991, p. 8) study of Upper Canada in the early to mid-1800s tells of servant girls' vulnerability to sexual abuse by their masters, who were immune from prosecution. In 1837, the Seduction Act was passed, which permitted a girl's parents (mostly the father) to sue a guilty master and get support for any illegitimate children.

The concern over morality in the new industrial centres had a double edge, portraying young women either as hapless victims of urban vice or as "brazen," sinful beings. Both images were based on the increased freedoms of young working women who wanted to participate in the amusements offered in a big city. Increased social controls on women, brought on by morality-minded reform, were evident in the increased presence of female police officers, women's courts, and longer terms for female morals offenders. In extreme cases, those young women who defied convention were also sent to psychiatric clinics and diagnosed as mentally unfit for wanting to do what they pleased (Strange, 1995, 1997, pp. 11–13).

That young women's freedoms were seen as a threat is not unusual during a time when their futures were defined in terms of motherhood. Exemplifying this, in Quebec from 1880–1940, girls were expected to act like *petites mères* or look after their younger siblings while participating in occasional work, with their wages going to their parents. There is little evidence of education other than for a small number of girls (Lemieux & Mercier, in Bradbury, 1993, p. 162). A similar trend toward domesticity is noted in English Canada by Strong-Boag (in Bradbury, 1993, p. 162) and Davies (1995), who report a differential schooling for boys and girls, with the latter being groomed for motherhood and homemaking through domestic science classes and moral education.

On to the 21st Century: The Prolongation of Adolescence and Youth

During the 19th century we see the first references to adolescence as a distinct life stage among White youth in the mainstream of the three countries marked by semi-independence while being educated or engaging in some form of wage labour. Adolescence emerged first among the middle and upper classes where mortality and fertility rates dropped earlier, and where apprenticeship programs gave way to formal public education. This pattern gradually spread to the working class, where adolescence was, for a longer time, characterized by wage-work participation.

The emergence of adolescence is a direct reflection of the prolongation of youth. Within the working class, adolescence is intricately connected to the decline of the working family as a unit of production. As industrial wage labour became the way of life for increasing masses, wage work was the main way toward a livelihood. Adolescence became a time of occupational choosing and preparation for work through prolonged education and the removal of children from the labour market, as seen in the histories of the US and the UK as described earlier. Côté and Allahar (1994, p. 17) call this process the "disenfranchisement of youth." During the advancement of industrialization, families began to rely less on the labour of the young. The youth population started to move from being economic assets to being economic liabilities. In urban areas, education formed the basis for adolescence among working-class youngsters, and the standard of living rose to the point where the wage work of all family members was no longer needed.

As in the UK and the US, educational reformers in Canada extended compulsory school to the age of 16, with a resulting "partial idleness" (Marquardt, 1998, p. 16) among youth and the rise of advocacy for vocational training. Gradually, from the mid- to late 1800s onward, public school systems emerged for all of the population to add to the private schools available to privileged and well-to-do families (Baker, 1989, p. 37; see also Bradbury, 1996, p. 67; Marquardt, 1998, pp. 21–23, 28; Janovicek, 2003).

The first public schools were aimed not only at creating a literate population, but at raising a patriotic citizenry and instilling into "idle youth" habits that were valuable in the workforce, such as obedience and punctuality (Marquardt, 1998, pp. 21–23; Côté & Allahar, 1994, pp. 40, 120–124; also see Mandell, 1988, p. 72), while reproducing the social order based on divisions of social class, race, and gender. For example, even in the early 20th century, working-class youth tended to leave school sooner to take up jobs, while their middle-class counterparts continued their education (Marquardt, 1998, pp. 27–31; Strong-Boag, in Bradbury, 1993, p. 162; Bradbury, 1996, p. 69). Indeed, the time period for education has gotten ever longer since the 1960s, when federal and provincial governments started investing in all levels of the educational system, including universities and community colleges (Marquardt, 1998, p. 42).

In general, Côté and Allahar (1994, p. 40; also see Bradbury, 1996, p. 69) argue that in the 20th century, mass education prolonged youth and made young people more vulnerable to capitalist exploitation, both as students working part-time and as graduates who cannot find work that actually corresponds to their level of education. The concern over the generally deteriorating quality of jobs available to youth (Marquardt, 1998, p. 43) continues in the era of the "McDonaldization" of the labour market (Ritzer, 1993) and the "McJob." Though youth labour markets will be discussed in more detail in the chapter on work, it is worthy of note that, since World War II, while engaging in education, youth were generally employed in such settings as

> 1) large secondary firms (for minimum wage): security businesses, grocery stores, cleaning services, and construction companies; 2) small businesses (low-paid casual work): bakers, news stands, restaurants, gas stations, or convenience stores; 3) under the table (one-off opportunities usually neighbourhood based): babysitting, shovelling snow, painting houses, repairing cars, or some construction. (Marquardt, 1998, pp. 39–40)

The period of prolonged youth has possibly lengthened in the early 21st century, with ongoing problems related to education, work, and family formation among young people. That these issues among youth persist means that they are not a high priority on the political agenda (see e.g., Di Done, 2002).

Conclusions

It is clear from this short history of youth that a full understanding of young people's lives is possible only against the complexities of a past marked by different layers of inequality and oppression. Colonialism and its by-product capitalism, along with the hierarchies based on gender and race, form a disturbing mixture in which the significance of age hierarchies is revealed. The history of young people's oppression and abuse is the history of people in the United States, the United Kingdom, and Canada.

Out of the historical developments in all three countries arises a picture of youth prolonged, or a "generation on hold" (Côté & Allahar, 1994). Adolescence and youth are ever-longer periods, stamped by a suspension of full social, economic, and political rights to this age group while youth are in educational institutions. Young people's dependency or semi-dependency on adult-led institutions provides a foundation for a multitude of situations of conflict based on age. Power is held by adults, who hold positions of economic and political importance, while young people's lives are held in an ever-lengthening period of suspension.

As will be seen in the chapters to follow, these historical patterns continue today. An examination of young people's lives in relation to different social institutions will reveal an age hierarchy in which today's youth are allowed to reach a full, independent adult status much later than in any previous period in history. Youth today are unable to gain full access to socially valued goods and services, which were taken for granted by their parents at the same age. For the luckiest among youth, this prolonged dependence causes continued economic hardship, extends education way beyond the actual skill requirements of the labour market, and delays relationship and family formation. Those youth who are less fortunate are cast adrift in society due to no fault of their own, and become casualties in the statistics of high-school dropouts, unemployment, homelessness, and crime. All young people have to constantly mediate between different adult-led institutions that offer them few options amidst a tide of negative media and popular imagery. This is all the more daunting for young people who are not part of the White and male mainstream.

Critical Thinking Questions

1. Do you think colonialism and slavery can be used to explain the current and ongoing problems among Black and indigenous peoples?
2. Do you think the descendants of Black slaves or the indigenous youth in residential schools deserve a formal apology from governments? Should they be given reparations?
3. Do you think that industriousness is still a central value expected of youth today?

3 Families and Socialization

In this chapter, you will learn that

- families are sites for the exercise of power and control, based on age and gender hierarchies
- there are a variety of families and parenting practices, each impacting young people in different ways
- young people are socialized in families where they also learn about their gendered and racialized selves
- many young people's lives are challenging, including adjusting to parental divorce, remarriage, and changing economic circumstances, such as poverty
- immigrant and racialized youth face a number of additional challenges, including transnational family lives and parenting practices that may differ from the mainstream
- the residence patterns of young people vary: some live with their parents off and on, and others end up homeless or without families
- the meaning of independence is changing for young people, as they face a prolonged period of education and low-paid wage work

When we think of families, we don't tend to see them in terms of power and control. Yet, families are the most common site for children and youth to be subject to expressions and effects of power relations, both indirectly and directly. First, families, as social institutions, are shaped by the power relations prevalent in society based on social class, gender, race, and ethnicity. Second, there are also direct manifestations of power and control in families based on differentials in gender and age.

This chapter will focus on young people's family lives and on their relationships with their parents. The topics to be explored include parenting and socialization, including gender socialization, and the manifestations of intergenerational power and the "generation gap." Another major area of interest is young people's patterns of leaving and returning to their parental homes.

There is a prevailing stereotype that the stage of adolescence is characterized by intensified and hormone-driven processes that necessarily lead to conflict with parents. Its corollary in immigrant families is heightened intergenerational conflict in which "Old

World" parents are pitted against their "New World" children. The accuracy of these views will be discussed drawing upon North American studies.

Families are commonly seen as places that protect and nurture children and youth. However, large segments of youth are subjected to abuse and neglect by their family members. This topic will be addressed in more detail in the chapter on health, but it needs to be emphasized here that as serious a health issue as family violence is, it reflects power relationships within families. A lot of young people put up with years of violence; some run away and become "castaways," living on often hostile streets, which will be addressed in this chapter. Though these youth have families, they are beyond reach, leaving them without a significant support network at a crucial time in their lives.

Thus, families can be positive sites where youth learn to become members of society and get templates for their future relationships with the world. Families can also provide a host of negative influences for young people that lead them toward alienation and personal challenges. In short, the family is a contested site filled with both promise and threats to young people's well-being and adjustment.

In this and subsequent chapters, a range of studies and statistics will be presented from Canada, the UK, and the US. It needs to be noted that full comparability of statistics is not possible at all times because each country in question collects statistics differently based on their nation-specific interests and social conditions. As seen in Chapter 1, the analyses and theoretical traditions that inform data collection are somewhat different in the three countries in question and consequently emphasize different aspects of youth's lives. This should be noted for all the remaining chapters as well. Where possible, international statistics and studies are used, but readers should expect neither fully comparable reporting nor analysis. Attention should be paid to the overall patterns of behaviour rather than the issue of exact comparability of data.

Family Structure

Research into adolescents' relationships with their parents is complicated by the wide variety of family contexts. We are increasingly hard-pressed to find a "typical" family setting. There are general changes in families across Western industrial countries in the last half a century that are linked to shifts in the status of women, including their increased labour force participation, resulting in dual-earner families. There has been a rise in divorce rates and a linked rise in single-parent, female-headed families and remarriage families. Cohabitation is more common, and age at first marriage has risen. Added to this are the effects of population migration, resulting in families that are more diverse in form than ever (Aapola et al., 2005, pp. 79–80; Kamerman et al., 2003, p. 20).

Thus, since the "golden age" of marriage in Western nations from the 1950s to the 1970s (Kiernan, 2003, p. 2), there has been a decline in the proportion of traditional two-parent heterosexual families in all three countries. In the 2001 Census, 44 percent of Canadian families consisted of married or common-law couples with cohabiting children under age 24, a decline from 55 percent in 1981 (Statistics Canada, 2002a).

Two-parent households continue to be on a decline: in 2006, legally married couples with children only made up 34.6 percent of families within Canada. Meanwhile, single parents made up 15.5 percent and common-law couples made up 15.6 percent of households within Canada (Human Resources and Skills Development Canada, 2013).

The numbers from the UK and the US tell a similar story. In 2004, there were 17 million families in the UK, with 12 million (70.6 percent) families consisting of legally married couples. Lone-mother families rose to 2.3 million (13.5 percent) and cohabiting increased to 2.2 million (12.9 percent) (National Statistics 2005c). In the United States, two-thirds of households are composed of married couples, while single parenthood amounts to 27 percent, significantly higher than in Canada and the UK. A further difference is that cohabiting families only account for 7 percent of households (Federal Interagency Forum on Child and Family Statistics, 2012).

Divorce rates in the three countries are similar. The divorce rate in Canada has maintained a range between 35 percent and 42 percent (Statistics Canada, 2011a). In 2010 in the UK, 30.5 percent of marriages were expected to end in divorce by their twentieth wedding anniversary (National Statistics, 2011b), and in the United States, 3.4 marriages per 1,000 population ended in divorce in 2009 (US Census Bureau, 2012a). Divorce rates amount to large numbers of children and youth living in single-parent families, while more children also live in stepfamilies.

In 2001, there were 503,100 stepfamilies in Canada, representing 12 percent of all Canadian couples (Statistics Canada, 2002b). In 1999, 6 percent of all British families with children lived in stepfamilies (Finch, 2003, pp. 2–11, 34–35). The trend is likely to continue, as in 2010, remarriages accounted for 15 percent of all marriages for both partners and 19 percent for marriages where one partner was previously married (National Statistics, 2010).

Some differences are present, based on racialized categories. American statistics show that marriage rates are the lowest among Black women (27.2 percent) and men (34.2 percent), and divorce rates are lower among Asians (3.3 percent of men and 13.7 percent of women) than among other groups, and higher among American Indians and Alaska Natives, whose rates are around 11–14 percent (US Census Bureau, 2003a). These trends have continued in more recent years (US Census Bureau, 2012b).

As indicated above, the high rates of divorce are reflected in single-parent families. In Canada, well over 80 percent of them are female-headed (Nelson & Robinson, 1999, p. 29). Similarly, 90 percent of British single parents are mothers (Finch, 2003, p. 31), and 74 percent of such American families are headed by women (US Census Bureau, 2003b).

Sole parenthood is more prevalent in some ethnoracial minority groups than others. Black children are more likely to live in lone-parent households. The 2001 Canadian Census noted that 46 percent of Black children lived with only one parent compared to 18 percent of other children (Milan & Tran, 2004, p. 5). Within Black Canadian communities, Canadian-born children had a 47 percent chance of living with one parent, while foreign-born Black children had a rate of 40 percent (Milan & Tran, 2004, p. 5). Lone parenthood in Canada makes up 10.2 percent of all living arrangements for visible minorities (Statistics Canada, 2006d).

The US Census Bureau (2012b) notes that marriage rates are the lowest among Black Americans, as 11 percent are divorced—leading to more lone-parent households. Racialized lone parents are also common within Great Britain. For instance, the largest groups are various Black ethnicities, including Mixed White and Black Caribbean, Mixed White and African, Black Caribbean, Black African, and Other Black (Platt, 2009, p. 22). All of the Black ethnicities make up 54.5 percent of all lone-parent families in Great Britain (Platt, 2009, p. 22). The percentage of Chinese or Asian lone parents is significantly smaller, at 2.7 percent and 30.6 percent, respectively (Platt, 2009, p. 22).

The consequences of living in a female-headed single-parent family are manifested in family instability, poverty, racism, and discrimination (Christensen & Weinfeld, 1993, p. 41; Calliste, 1996, pp. 252–259). Sole-parent families are more likely to live in poverty and be stigmatized—even more so if they are members of racialized groups.

Another increasingly common family type is same-sex families. When the 2001 Canadian Census provided—for the first time—information about same-sex partnerships, they found that 0.5 percent (34,200) of all couples fall into this category (Statistics Canada, 2002b). Between 2006 to 2011, same-sex families were up 42.4 percent, of which 43,560 were common-law same-sex couples and 21,015 were married same-sex couples (Statistics Canada, 2011c). This period includes the first five years that same-sex marriages were legal in Canada. In this same time frame, common-law same-sex couples increased by 15 percent compared to 13.8 percent for opposite sex common-law couples (Statistics Canada, 2011c). In the US, where same-sex marriages are recognized in 12 states, same-sex couples accounted for 11.6 percent of all families (0.8 percent of all households) (US Census Bureau, 2012d, p. 5). In the UK, where same-sex civil partnerships have been recognized since 2004, same-sex couples accounted for 0.09 percent of all households, increasing to 0.24 percent in 2012 (National Statistics 2012c, p. 4).

Family Poverty

Out of the US, the UK, and Canada, the US is the leading country with childhood poverty, according to the Organisation for Economic Co-operation and Development (OECD, 2009a). Macartney (2011, p. 9) notes that the US child poverty rate in 2010 was 21.6 percent, compared to 15 percent in Canada and 10 percent in the UK (OECD, 2009a, p. 93). Since the mid-1990s, the US child poverty rate has decreased by 1.7 percent, while Canada's has increased by 2.2 percent and the UK's has decreased by 3.7 percent (OECD, 2009a, p. 93). In 2010, more than one in five children in the US (or 15.75 million children) lived in poverty (Macartney, 2011, p.1).

Race and ethnicity matter. In the US during 2010, White and Asian children had the lowest child poverty rates, below the US average. Black Americans had a higher rate of 38.2 percent, Hispanic children suffered from poverty at 32.3 percent, and children of mixed races at a rate of 22.7 percent (Macartney, 2011, p. 1). In 2006, children with recent immigrants for parents had a higher chance of living in poverty in

Canada (39.3 percent), followed by First Nations children (33.7 percent), children in racialized families (34 percent) and children with disabilities (28 percent) (Statistics Canada, 2008b).

The most significant factor contributing to the poverty of children and youth is that their parents do not earn enough income to support them. Canadian studies show that most families living in poverty are intact families (Richardson, 1996, p. 238; see also Cameron, 2000), demonstrating the deterioration of overall family incomes over the last few decades. Most families who live in poverty have at least one family member employed outside the home. The myth of poverty being associated with not working for pay is exploded by statistics on the "working poor." For example, in 1993, 56 percent of Canadian couples with children were among the working poor, as were 51 percent of poor couples without children, and 50 percent of poor, unattached women (Cameron, 2000).

Nevertheless, there are some family types that are more likely to live in poverty. With the increased prevalence of divorce, sole-parent mother-headed families are facing poverty at staggering rates. The comparative poverty rates for children by family type in the mid-1990s show that around 52 percent of American, 43 percent of UK, and 46 percent of Canadian children living in single-mother families live in poverty (Di Done, 2002, p. 9). There have been some improvements in the poverty rates in Canada since the mid-2000s, after the worst rates in the mid-1990s. Still, one in four children currently living in poverty come from single-parent households (Statistics Canada, 2009a, p. 14), with over one-half of the heads of these households unemployed (Vanier Institute of the Family, 2010, p. 105). Similar results were obtained in the US, where, in 2011, 31.2 percent of children living in poverty were in a household headed by a lone female (DeNavas-Walt et al., 2012, p. 17).

The poverty of single-parent families has complex reasons. At least in the short term, both members of marriage are impacted by the divorce, due to the new maintenance of two households. Gadalla (2008, p. 232) found, in a study of low income after divorce from 1999 to 2004, that 7.6 percent of males compared to 19.8 percent of females lived below the low-income line in the year following divorce. As well, she found that one in 5 women and one in 13 men became poor after a marriage breakdown (Gadalla, 2008, pp. 232–233). This is in keeping with previous studies showing that the economic consequences of divorce are worse for women than men (Richardson, 1996, p. 238; Nelson & Robinson, 1999, p. 412).

Similar results are found in the UK, where studies confirm the greater risk of poverty for divorced women and children than that of divorced men. This is compounded by the fact that lone parenthood is linked to social class, as those in the lower classes are more likely to marry as teenagers. Because young age at marriage is linked to a higher incidence of marital breakdown, these people are at a higher risk of poverty (McAllister, 1999, pp. v–vi). Further, Odekirk and Lochhead (1992, in Nelson & Robinson, 1999, p. 407) point out that "lone-parent mothers are more likely to be younger, less well educated, have lower earnings and less income, and typically are responsible for younger-aged children than are lone-parent fathers."

The situation is even worse for racialized women and their families. For example, the 1991 Canadian Census shows that 85 percent of young Black female lone parents aged 15–24 in Canada, and 91 percent in Nova Scotia, earned less than $20,000 (Calliste, 1996, p. 257). The 2006 Census showed that 25.6 percent of lone parents in Canada were Black women (Chui & Maheux, 2011, p. 16). This is alarming amidst studies that continue to identify the factors that increase the occurrence of divorce, and demonstrate that Black women are more likely to become lone parents. As listed by McKay (2002, p. 16), these include:

> early marriage, pre-marital cohabitation, pre-marital birth, having children early in marriage, couples from poor economic backgrounds, couples with low educational achievement, couples from different social classes, experience of marital breakdown among close family, having been married previously, experience of living apart, access to alternative partners, access to an alternative home (e.g., parents' home), and ethnicity.

One significant reason for the poverty of mother-child families is "deadbeat dads," or fathers who don't pay child support regularly or at all. In Canada, as of March 31, 2012, 45 percent of payers of child support were in arrears of at least two monthly payments (Kelly, 2013). In the UK, support was often low and privately arranged, often leading to the non-custodial parent not providing financial support (Andreß et al., 2006, p. 537). This was remedied with a more restrictive and better enforced child support payment system, resulting in a compliance rate of 79.7 percent in December, 2012, when £112.4 million in arrears was collected of the total £1,214.9 million owed (National Statistics, 2012d, p. 13). In the US, compliance of child care support decreased from 46.8 percent in 2007 to 41.2 percent in 2009, while 29.6 percent received partial payments (US Census Bureau, 2011d, p. 9). Child support compliance varied with custodial arrangement: custodial parents who had joint child custody or visitation privileges had 83.2 percent compliance, while 60.5 percent of custodial parents who did not have joint custody or visitation arrangements received full or partial child support payments (US Census Bureau, 2011d, p.10). Interestingly, non-custodial mothers are more likely (61.7 percent) to pay child support than non-custodical fathers (54.6 percent) (US Census Bureau, 2011d, p. 6).

Societal factors compound the problem of poverty in sole-parent families: there is a lack of support mechanisms (such as affordable child care) to assist women in finding and keeping employment, and women generally work in lower-paying jobs as a result of the gendered division of labour. Di Done (2002, p. 20) stresses that child poverty is lowest in countries where a higher percentage of the GDP is devoted to public social expenditure. Thus, countries such as Germany, France, Norway, and Sweden have child poverty rates that are several times lower than those in the UK, the US, and Canada, where social expenditure is relatively low. Although other consequences of divorce on children and youth will be discussed below, it is important to note that the greatest negative effect on children of divorce is poverty (Ambert & Krull, 2006, p. 407).

Changing Families: A Detriment to Children and Youth?

There is a heightened awareness and even a sense of panic about the profound changes taking place in North American and European families. Coontz (1997, in Davis & Friel, 2001, p. 679) captures this as follows:

> The development of new family forms and the breakdown of the "traditional" intact two-parent family have been held responsible for everything from teenage pregnancy and juvenile delinquency to urban violence, unemployment, and federal budget deficits.

This prevailing crisis mentality problematizes the changes, and particularly women's choices related to employment and family. There are outcries over "abandoned" children as women spend more time outside of their families (Kamerman et al., 2003, p. 20). This trend toward woman-blaming or mother-blaming has been observed by others (Aapola et al., 2005, pp. 81–83; also see Finch, 2003; McAllister, 1999) who question this practice. Instead, they propose a shift toward the recognition of a wider responsibility for families: Societies need to accommodate women's employment and men need to share unpaid domestic work, including child care.

The sense of despair over families and their crucially important roles in creating the life conditions for youth is expressed in this reaction in an editorial (*Globe and Mail*, February 22, 2007, A16) to yet another report of bad news about children and youth:

> If everything works against children except attentive, stay-at-home, well-off, non-materialistic, non-permissive, religious parents who discourage individualism, aren't overworked, don't leave their children "with serial caretakers," don't have a "critical mass" of low-income neighbours and shield their children from the media that saturate their lives, modern society might as well just pull the covers over its head.

Two specific areas of concern in the literature on the "family crisis," to be briefly discussed below, are the impact on children and adolescents of divorce and remarriage, and living with gay or lesbian parents.

Impact of Divorce and Remarriage

Large numbers of children and youth live in non-traditional family arrangements. Thus, one of the areas of concern for adolescents and youth is how they cope with parental divorce and remarriage. First of all, it is worth noting that most young people, regardless of age, do eventually adjust to shifts in their family situation. Nevertheless, there are negative consequences over the short term, and the types of consequences vary by gender and the age of children upon divorce and/or remarriage.

Findings on the impact of divorce on children come in two varieties. Some find that there are negative consequences for children. Though not supported in all research

(Toomey & Nelson, 2001), much of the research shows that divorce has an impact on the offspring's beliefs about romantic relationships, their marital success, and their desire for children. Generally, children from divorced families have sexual intercourse earlier, have more sexual relationships, form lasting relationships later than offspring from intact families, and have more negative views about their relationships (Mahl, 2001, p. 91; Toomey & Nelson, 2001, pp. 54–56). Some research shows that young adults from divorced families tend to have issues with trusting their partners and more pessimism about their relationships (Mahl, 2001, pp. 92–93).

Research also shows that the gender of children is important. Boys tend to be more negatively affected by divorce than girls. This may have to do with the fact that in the vast majority of the cases, custody goes to the mother (Richardson, 1996, p. 233; Nelson & Robinson, 1999, p. 410). The boy may miss the same-sex parent, whereas girls have their mothers present.

Age of the child is similarly a factor: Teenagers tend to have more problems adapting to parental divorce and remarriage than younger children, possibly because they dislike having an additional authority figure around at a time when they seek autonomy (Ambert & Krull, 2006, p. 416). Teenagers have also lived for a longer time with their two biological parents, and tend to make negative comparisons between their biological and step-parents, and step-siblings and half-siblings may be seen as intruders. There are also additional problems for young people as they adjust to the presence of step-siblings and half-siblings. This has been shown to result in diminished marital satisfaction and increased instability in remarriage relationships, which may contribute to further conflict and dissatisfaction among all members of a remarriage family. As will be discussed in the chapter on health, some of the adjustments by teens may also be manifested in violence toward parents (Baker, 1996b, pp. 31–32; Richardson, 1996, pp. 244–245). Children of divorced families are also at risk of becoming overly dependent ("needy") on their relationships as they reach adolescence because they may see the divorce experience as a type of parental neglect (Toomey & Nelson, 2001, p. 65).

Another approach to the impact of divorce on offspring shows that these negative effects are explained not by divorce itself, but by the presence of parental conflict, lower socio-economic status, and inconsistent parenting (Mahl, 2001, p. 90). As indicated above, the prevalent poverty among single-parent families alone is an extremely negative factor. The stresses of divorce can also lead to emotional changes in parents that manifest in yelling, withdrawing from children, or being busy. Parental conflict in marriage and divorce will also result in stress and anxiety in children (Ambert & Krull, 2006, pp. 407–409).

However, some researchers suggest that rather than viewing parental divorce as completely negative, we should examine the varied effects it has on offspring, including the possibility that divorce actually "results in improved family relationships" (Mahl, 2001, p. 89). Indeed, research shows that there are positive and stabilizing effects for both children and their parents. Stepfamilies are found to be a better alternative than remaining in an intact but conflict-ridden family or one-parent and poverty-stricken household (Baker, 1996b, pp. 31–32). In terms of other outcomes for youth arising from non-traditional families, it has been found that parents in these types of situations are "less likely to gender stereotype their children than parents living in traditional families" (Nelson & Robinson, 1999, p. 129).

In sum, though children and youth undergo significant stresses during divorce and remarriage, many of these are short term and also depend on the age and gender of the offspring. The biggest effects come from the poverty imposed on many children raised in mother-led households without adequate financial support. Adjustments seem to be more difficult for teenagers who have a longer period to develop loyalty to their biological parents and who may have been exposed to more conflict in their families preceding their parents' splitting up and forming new partner relationships.

Impact of Gay and Lesbian Parenting

There is general agreement in the social science literature that homosexual parents don't differ from heterosexual parents in their parenting skills or in their psychological, moral, and physical health (Arnup, 2005, p. 196). North American research on lesbian and gay parents finds them essentially capable, caring, and committed despite the negative stereotypes that prevail in the public consciousness. In fact, gay fathers compare positively with heterosexual fathers in their caregiving capacity and sensitivity to their children's needs (Arnup, 2005, p. 196).

Given the lack of difference between heterosexual and homosexual parents, their children are found in both North American and European studies to be similarly happy and well adjusted, showing the unimportance of sexual orientation on parenting skills. Nor are children's sexual orientations affected by that of their parents; they are not any more or less likely to grow up homosexual when raised by same-sex parents (Arnup, 2005, pp. 197–201; also see Saffron, 1998, p. 35).

Children raised by homosexual parents manifest positive adjustment over a long term, as evidenced in British longitudinal studies of young adults raised by lesbians (Arnup, 2005, pp. 197–199; Saffron, 1998). This is noteworthy given the stress and harassment that children of gay parents experience in their peer relations. For example, the Nova Scotia Advisory Council on the Status of Women (1996, p. 2, in Arnup, 2005, p. 199) presents the following quote from a child (age unknown) of lesbian mothers:

> Having gay parents isn't always easy for me. I often hide the fact that I have two mothers instead of a "normal" mother and father or even a single parent. Kids at school or camp, even fairly close friends, say things like, "Oh, gross, she's a lesbian," or "He's gay," and the people around them laugh. I feel really awkward at times like this because if I laugh, it's like I'm laughing at my parents for being who they are, and if I don't laugh, the kids will make fun of me.

Despite stress, children of homosexual parents tend to view their family life positively. Arnup (2005, pp. 199–200) proposes that fears and anxieties may be more likely among children whose parents had "come out" relatively recently rather than among children who were born into planned gay or lesbian families. Arnup (2005, pp. 200–202) also summarizes research that finds that offspring raised by homosexual parents develop sensitivity and tolerance toward differences. Saffron's (1998, pp. 34–47) interviews with 17 British teenagers and adults with lesbian mothers supports the view that having a lesbian mother is beneficial for moral development in that these offspring were more accepting of diversity and homosexuality, more flexible toward gender relations in general, and more inclusive about their definition of family. For example, 17-year-old Katrina said:

> When I say family I use it as a broad term. A family includes anyone who's going to love and care for you unconditionally. That doesn't necessarily have to be your biological mother or father. (Saffron, 1998, p. 44)

Parenting and Socialization

Socialization is the process through which we develop a sense of who we are, and learn to function in our social group or society (Nelson & Robinson, 1999, p. 123). This learning process is lifelong and happens in the context of human interaction. It is commonplace to distinguish between *primary* and *secondary* socialization. Primary socialization takes place in the context of significant others, usually family members. Secondary socialization takes place in the wider society, in the context of socializing institutions, e.g., schools, workplaces, the media, and peers (Nelson & Robinson, 1999, pp. 122–127). Future chapters will explain how peers, schools, and workplaces socialize youth. In this chapter, we will focus on primary socialization in families, usually described in terms of parental functions (see Box 3.1).

The most prevalent theories in this area are learning theory and social learning theory. The former sees socialization as a process directed by socializing agents and individuals based on rewards for normatively acceptable behaviours and punishment for unacceptable behaviours. Through this process, a child learns and adopts normative limits. Social learning theory arose in response to the criticism of learning theory as too mechanical a representation of the complex learning process. This theory puts more emphasis on the way young people process information, and examines the many different ways in which this takes place, including imitation (Howe & Bukowski, 1996, pp. 183–184).

In practice, social learning theory is characterized by a near-obsessive attention to parenting practices. There is a wide range of socialization literature that is essentially parenting literature, i.e., it concentrates on examining the kinds of "effective" parenting strategies that produce good outcomes in terms of young people's socio-emotional competence and their capability for behaving in a mature and responsible manner (Noller & Fitzpatrick, 1993, p. 145). This includes research into parents' role in juvenile delinquency, school and career success, sexual behaviour, and general attitudes and values. One widely cited finding is that parents have an influence on their adolescents' decisions about educational, financial, and vocational choices, whereas peers are more influential in decisions about adolescents' social activities (Noller & Fitzpatrick, 1993, p. 145).

Box 3.1: Parental Functions

Acknowledging that parenting is something that requires minimal training or preparation, American family sociologist Marvin R. Koller (1974, pp. 265–270) offers an exposé of parental functions in United States, including eight tasks:

1. *Denaturalization:* The general teaching of a child to be "human," in that they learn to "socially restrict their biological natures."
2. *Disciplining:* Exerting controls on children, through a system of external measures that are gradually internalized, allowing children to be social beings.
3. *Protection:* Keeping children out of harm's way and to teach them to protect themselves.
4. *Interpretation:* The screening and transmitting of culture to children.
5. *Personality development:* Moulding your children, and instilling in them generally valued "virtues" in society.
6. *Freedom giving:* Teaching children to value their freedoms while acting responsibly.
7. *Enrichment of family life:* Provide socializing influences that make family life fulfilling and vitalized rather than routinized and boring.
8. *Problem solving:* Dealing with the many dilemmas of child rearing that occur daily as children deal with their families and the outside world.

Parenting outcomes are seen to be mediated by different types of parenting styles, a relatively popular topic in American research. Parenting styles are usually classified as authoritative, authoritarian, permissive/indulgent, and indifferent (e.g., Anderson & Sabatelli, 1999, pp. 212–214; Paulson & Sputa, 1996; Howe & Bukowski, 1996, p. 188). These parenting styles are generally seen to be based on two main dimensions: control and warmth. From the different combinations of these, four categories of parenting are created: authoritative (high control/high warmth); authoritarian (high control/low warmth); indulgent/permissive (low control/high warmth); and indifferent/neglecting (low control/low warmth) (Paulson & Sputa, 1996; Howe & Bukowski, 1996, p. 188). It is authoritative parenting that is linked to the most positive outcomes, measured through high levels of adolescent adjustment, psychosocial competence and maturity, high self-esteem, and academic success.

Further, in taking apart the dimensions of control and warmth, specific aspects of these dimensions are found to correlate positively with adolescent outcomes. In the control category, it is involvement, not strict controls on behaviour, that results in good outcomes. Involvement refers particularly to parental values, parental expectations aimed at school success, parental interest in the child's grades and helping with homework, and involvement in school functions. The authoritative parenting pattern can be linked to the notion of "sponsored independence," which is specific to adolescence and involves a gradual relinquishing of parental control over the child in a supportive and warm atmosphere that allows the adolescent to gain more control over his or her decisions and actions (Nett, 1993, p. 196).

There is a growing body of research linking good parenting to positive outcomes in terms of adolescent development, including preventing involvement in anti-social behaviour, and general benefits to psychosocial development. In contrast, poor parental support, whether lack of warmth or lack of adequate supervision, has been linked to adolescent difficulties, including deviant and criminal behaviours, poor academic performance, and increased alcohol and drug use (Claes et al., 2005, pp. 401–402).

In comparison, there is far less research on the perceptions of children or adolescents of parenting styles. In fact, an extensive search found no Canadian studies, and only one American study that asked young people's views on their parents' parenting styles (Paulson & Sputa, 1996). This study of mostly White and middle-class families in the American Midwest interviewed children and their parents while the children were in grade 9 and later in grade 12. Their study was aimed at distinguishing between the parenting styles of mothers and fathers, including adolescents' perceptions about parenting styles. The results are generally consistent with other research. First, the results showed that regardless of the age group, both adolescents and parents perceived mothers to be more demanding as well as more responsive than fathers. Further, both mothers and fathers perceived themselves to be more demanding and more responsive than adolescents perceived them to be. Overall, both adolescents and parents perceived mothers to be more involved in homework/schoolwork and school functions than fathers were. However, both parents were seen to be equal in their values toward achievement. Further, the study found that parents reported themselves to be more involved with their adolescents than the adolescents reported. This is consistent with the concept of generational stake (Koller, 1974, p. 224; Nett, 1993, pp. 199–201), which proposes that parents have a higher investment in their children than vice versa. Because of this, parents tend to report being closer to their children than children report being to their parents.

Some age-group-specific results arose, but have to be treated with caution due to the smaller size of the follow-up group. Nevertheless, the study found that both adolescents and parents reported that mothers and fathers were less responsive in grade 12 than in grade 9. Parents also reported that they were less demanding when their children were in grade 12. This reflects the increasing level of autonomy and independence of adolescents, and is linked to the process of "sponsored independence" whereby particularly middle-class parents tend to support the increased independence of their adolescents and gradually relinquish parental control. Consistent with this, both the older adolescents and their parents reported lower levels of parental involvement in school work, and of maternal involvement in school functions, but no changes in parental values toward achievement. The results are consistent with the generally perceived decrease in parents' involvement in adolescents' school work and activities as they get older. An important omission from this study is the fact that even though parental gender was a variable, the results were not reported based on the gender of the adolescents. This issue of gender and parenting will be taken up below.

Parenting styles and socialization practices seem to vary by social class. It has been found that working-class parents are more likely to use "power-assertive" (or authoritarian) techniques, including physical punishment, and demand more conformity from their offspring. In comparison, middle-class parents use less overtly punitive methods. Instead, they use reasoning and withdrawal of privileges, love, and affection to guide their children toward self-control while encouraging their curiosity and self-expression (Nelson & Robinson, 1999, pp. 130–131; also see Nett, 1993, p. 196).

Ironically, social learning theory—on which a lot of the parenting literature rests— seems to be at least as mechanical if not more so than learning theory. Social learning theory can be criticized for its lack of attention to the relationship involved in socializing. There is an emphasis on one-directional socializing in which the active participation of the socializers, or parents, is paramount, while the young people remain targets or objects of socialization rather than active participants in the socialization process (Ambert, 1992). In fact, socialization involves an active bi-directional relationship. While parents socialize their children, children also socialize their parents. In the interactive process, children are not likely to just go along for the ride, but push the limits and mediate them according to their own wishes. Becoming knowledgeable about societal limits, norms, and expectations does not necessarily translate into following them. The active role of adolescents in their socialization is evident in prevalent myths about how difficult it is for adolescents and their parents to find common ground, and the general view of adolescents as challenging their parents.

Parents of adolescents often have difficulty dealing with youngsters who are becoming aware of their own individuality and independence, and are looking to put their own mark on their environment. This is especially problematic for young people with disabilities whose parents tend to want to protect them, especially if they are female. Though the young people with disabilities participating in a study by Hussain et al. (2002) reported loving and caring families, they also commented on their parents' low expectations and overprotectiveness. One Asian female youth with disabilities said this:

> I'll get angry if they put me in cotton wool or something like that, if they watch me every minute.

Impact of Children on Parents

It is still quite rare to see studies that examine the way in which older children, i.e., adolescents, or young adults influence their parents, or the manner in which the intergenerational relationship evolves (Ambert, 1992, pp. 16–19). This notion is embedded in the criticism of traditional socialization theories, and carries the name "bidirectional socialization" (Nett, 1993, p. 203).

Where the impact of children or adolescents on parents is acknowledged, they are most commonly seen as a drain on or a problem for parents. Examples of the wide range of these are: limitations to parental residence and community involvement due to the educational and recreational needs of children; diminished social, intimate, and sexual lives of parents; increased domestic work; disruptions to parental and particularly maternal wage work patterns; and the general financial drain from children and particularly adolescents (Ambert, 1992, pp. 33–43), not to mention the worry that particularly adolescent children cause their parents by sex, drugs, and their choice of peers and leisure activities (Noller & Fitzpatrick, 1993, pp. 208–209; Ambert, 1997, pp. 102–103).

It is rare to see studies that entertain an idea that there are positive aspects to the presence of children and adolescents in their parents' lives. One such finding is in some studies that children provide companionship and support to their parents (e.g., Boulding, 1980, and deMause, 1974, as reported in Ambert, 1992, pp. 41–42). A select few studies found that divorced custodial parents are grateful for the structure and stability that having children provided at the time of divorce (Ambert, 1992, p. 165). Nett (1993, p. 203) also reports a study from the mid-1980s that showed that university-attending youth influence their parents in a variety of ways, ranging from sports to politics to personal care habits. The parents reported having become more tolerant and acknowledged that they had gained from the knowledge passed to their children from their university courses. The influence was more evident for fathers than mothers. Nett (1993, p. 203) suggests that the closing of the gap might be more evident for fathers who had a longer distance to make up with their children. Putting it in other terms, mothers may already have been primed to being accepting and learning from their children through their years as primary caregivers, while fathers may just be adjusting to this more recently.

Where parental attitudes are explored, it is usually in terms of the presence of children, not in terms of the interaction between parents or children, or with an acknowledgement of the active role of children. For example, a standard sociology of the family textbook approach is to address how parents adjust their parenting techniques to the child's age, temperament, or gender (e.g., Baker, 1996b, pp. 193–194). A typical example of the latter is from research by Ganong and Coleman (1987, reported in Ambert, 1992, pp. 46–47), who suggest that the presence of children of different sexes may lead parents to think in more sex-typed ways. The authors found that parents of sons were more sex-typed than parents of daughters. This is explained by the higher value societies put on sons than daughters, which would lead parents to invest more in raising their sons in sex-appropriate roles. The possibility is not raised that the interactions between adolescents and their parents would influence this in whatever manner. It is not surprising, therefore, that young people themselves are oblivious to the impact they have on their parents, or even when they are asked about their relationships with their parents, they are not likely to spontaneously report their impact on their parents, but focus on their parents' impact on them (Ambert, 1992, pp. 133, 147).

It is even rarer to see studies in which the parents are being socialized into parent-hood by their children, or where young people are shaping their family environment. There is a huge literature on the parental transmission of values to their children, but far less on the impact of children on their parents' values and attitudes (Ambert, 1992, pp. 42–46).

Family Democracy?

It has generally been observed that intergenerational relations between parents and their children have changed toward a more "modern" or "liberal" pattern of parents negotiating with their children rather than dictating their expectations to them (Aapola et al., 2005, pp. 84–85). According to yet another widely prevalent myth of contemporary family life, one of the biggest dangers of today's society is "permissive parenting." Bad parenting is equated with parenting practices that are seen to allow too much say to children and teens, with the negative consequences of youth being "out of control."

There is no question that parenting has become more "democratized" throughout the 20th century, with less social distance and more openness between parents and their children (Solomon et al., 2002, pp. 966–968). But is modern family life really demo-cratic? British researchers Solomon et al. (2002) take on "the democratic ideal in family life," premised on the notion of increased intimacy and personal disclosure between parents and their teens. Increased talk is seen to be the hallmark of parent-teen rela-tions, with more willingness by young people to talk about their personal thoughts and feelings. The authors interviewed 58 White families, including 56 mothers, 53 fathers, 43 daughters, and 40 sons, aged 11–16. While all of the parent and youth respondents valued openness and honesty with parents, there were also tensions in relation to this democratic ideal. Some young respondents emphasized that their relationships were still premised on parental power. This meant that the information they divulged to their parents was used by parents to reassert parental control. Indeed, some parents confirmed that this was, indeed, the fundamental intent of their information-gathering from their adolescents. Generally, children are also expected to divulge more personal information to their parents than vice versa.

Thus, behind the "intimate talk" of supposedly liberal parents is an undercurrent of teens wanting to move toward independence while their parents want to maintain their control over them. Some of this is cloaked in parental protectiveness of their children. Jamieson (1998, p. 163, in Solomon et al., 2002, p. 981) argues:

> The overwhelming majority of parents do not treat their children as if they were equal but protect their children from their own thoughts and feelings. Even child experts who advocate attentive, listening, responsive parenting, do not advocate a mutual disclosing intimacy between parents and children, because children are to be protected from adult worries and boundaries.

Gender Socialization

Feminist scholars have addressed the ways in which gender differences are socially created, affirmed, and changed instead of emerging naturally. The phrase "doing gender"
has been used to capture the notion that getting a sense of ourselves as gendered beings
is an everyday process, a "recurring accomplishment" based on minute details of daily
life (Mackie, 1987, p. 49). As an integral part of socialization, gender socialization is
the process by which individuals develop a gender identity and acquire the normative
behaviours associated with masculine and feminine in society (Nelson & Robinson,
1999, p. 128; see also Ambert & Krull, 2006, pp. 371–373). From our earliest years
onward we learn to understand the place and meaning of our gender in society, and we
learn shared ideas and meanings of femininity and masculinity that are culturally specific. These social behaviours, values, and attitudes are passed on to us in various ways
throughout our lives (Ambert & Krull, 2006, p. 371).

Thus, socialization of children and youth is a gendered process. It has been
observed that independence is encouraged more among adolescent boys than girls.
Girls are expected to be more passive and there are more controls on their behaviour. In this way, "sponsored independence" is more of a pattern associated with
the socialization of males than females (Nett, 1993, p. 196). It is more difficult for
girls than for boys to negotiate their growing need for independence and autonomy
as parents still tend to view their daughters as being closer to their families and
also expect more from them in terms of responsibilities in the household. Parents
typically grant more freedoms to sons than daughters, particularly in adolescence
(Ambert & Krull, 2006, p. 371). This is especially the case with some, though by
no means all, ethnocultural groups. For example, studies in the US on Mexican-
American families find that rather than gaining freedoms in adolescence like their
brothers did, daughters gained responsibilities that tied them more closely to their
families, including household work and babysitting of younger siblings (Williams et
al., 2002, in Aapola et al., 2005, pp. 86–87).

The issue of socialization into a gender-based division of domestic labour will be
taken up in more detail in Chapter 6 in the context of how these socialization patterns
continue from young people's families of origin to their relationships with their intimate
partners. Here, we need to note that even if they don't have household duties, parents
tend to put more controls over girls. This surveillance of girls is often done in the name
of "protection" and particularly applies to daughters with disabilities. While sons are
expected to develop independence, daughters are "protected," preventing them from
learning how to be independent (Aapola et al., 2005, pp. 87–93).

Traditionally, there are clusters of acting, thinking, and feeling associated with female
and male socialization (see Box 3.2). The dominant themes of female socialization are
"sociability, popularity, and attractiveness" (Udry, 1971, in Nelson & Robinson, 1999,
p. 128), "nurturance, sympathy and warmth," and submissiveness (Mackie, 1987, p.
49), while male socialization centres on "independence, emotional control and conquest" (Udry, 1971, in Nelson & Robinson, 1999, p. 128) and aggression (Mackie,

---

Box 3.2: Female Tendencies over Time

According to Bibby (2001, pp. 319–320), there is a remarkable consistency in the ways in which men and women "put life together," including

the greater inclination of females than males to:

- value relationships, including being more inclined to associate sex with love;
- value interpersonal traits, including honesty, politeness, forgiveness, concern for others, and generosity;
- exclude prominent professional sports from their major sources of enjoyment, particularly those that are violent;
- exhibit concern about almost any person-centred social issue, from violence in schools through child abuse, suicide, and crime, to poverty;
- hold opinions on social issues such as capital punishment, rights of homosexuals, mandatory retirement, and war that reflect such traits as compassion and the valuing of equality; and
- hold higher levels of beliefs in almost anything of a religious, supernatural, or spiritual nature.

At the same time, Bibby also contends that

women, whether they are young or older, tend to be:

- more concerned than men about their looks;
- have less confidence;
- exhibit more fear; and
- more quickly and in larger numbers, abandon the idea that hard work will lead to success.

1987, p. 48). The characteristics associated with masculinity include: "(1) the refusal of vulnerability and fear; (2) mastery over things, tasks and people; and (3) bodily prowess that might be expressed in sports, sex, or fighting" (Kaufman, 1994; Kimmel, 1994; Simpson, 1994, all in Schellenberg et al., 1999, p. 148).

Generally, there are gender-linked socialization practices in all social classes. However, social class differences in the socialization of boys and girls are exhibited in the degree to which gender-based differences are emphasized. Those in the upper socio-economic classes are most likely to promote relatively egalitarian gender relations. Those in the lower socio-economic groups are more traditional and less egalitarian in their gender expectations (Nelson & Robinson, 1999, p. 131).

The gender of the parent is also important in family dynamics. Despite hype about "new" and "more involved" fathers, mothers continue to provide most child care. Most men still have limited involvement with their children. The consequence is that by teenage years, young people are more likely to want to communicate with their peers, mothers, or other relatives than their fathers (Bibby & Posterski, 1992, in Nelson & Robinson, 1999, pp. 417–420). Other studies from the 1980s (summarized in Noller & Fitzpatrick, 1993, pp. 209–210) also show that there are gender differences in communication patterns between parents and their adolescents. Daughters communicate more with their parents than sons do, and mothers are seen as more communicative than fathers. This is supported by a recent Health Canada study (Fine, 1999) of 2,500 teenagers, which found that fathers have a big communication gap with both male and female children, but particularly with their daughters. In all age groups, representing students in grades 6, 8, and 10, both male and female children reported that they found their mothers much more approachable than their fathers. The trend got worse over time, with significantly fewer children in grade 10 than in grade 6 reporting that they could talk to their father about things that really bother them.

Racial Socialization

It is recognized (and will be discussed in more detail in the chapters on education and employment) that living in a racist, sexist, and capitalist society is a particular challenge for members of minority populations. For example, Calliste (1996, pp. 262–264) points to the problems of raising Black children to be physically and emotionally healthy in an anti-Black, racist society.

Racialized minority youth's identity development takes place amidst racism, discrimination, and stereotyping. Parents play a crucial role in mediating these influences through "racial socialization" that is focused on developing children's and youth's pride in themselves and their group. These positive messages translate into youth confidence, which protects them against the negativity of living in a racist society. Some researchers suggest that ethnic/racial identity develops in four stages, starting with ethnic/racial unawareness in early childhood. This is followed by ambivalence in adolescence, which is often characterized by preference for mainstream norms and a distancing from one's group. In late adolescence and early adulthood, individuals go through an emergence, i.e., they look for connections to their origins and groups. Finally, in adult years there is ethnic/racial incorporation in which any identity conflicts are resolved (Hébert, 2001, p. 160). Regardless of whether a rigid stage theory applies to the actual experiences of youth, the process of racialized identity development is bound to be punctuated by problems arising from the influences from within and outside a young person's family.

In American studies, Codjoe (2006) found that regardless of structural barriers, the success of racialized minority youth is linked to their general well-being arising from a sense of social connectedness and a strong sense of their cultural identity. This speaks to the fundamental importance of "racial socialization" by families. Similar results have been obtained from among many different minority youth (Codjoe, 2006, pp. 46–48). One of the Black students in Codjoe's study, Afua, who was born in South America, recounts the valuable knowledge she gained from her grandparents:

> [They will] sit me down and explain to me exactly [my] blackness; this is what it means to be black.... It gave me some kind of guideline. I came to realize, I am black, it's not going to rub off.... I don't think I would ever back down from anything.... Every once in a while I experience racism, [but] I have very high self-esteem [and it helps me cope with it].... I know where I came from, I know my heritage. A lot of the [black] children today don't know; they're not interested. They're interested in partying, having a good time, that's about it. They need to know this is it, don't turn a blind eye. They have to know where they came from; they need to know their heritage (Codjoe, 1997, p. 231, quoted in Codjoe, 2006, p. 45).

The issue of racial socialization becomes more complicated when addressing the socialization of bi-racial youth. In these instances, the racial socialization strategies of parents are complicated by their own racialized identities. American studies suggest that African American parents may emphasize racial awareness and prepare their children for discrimination, whereas White parents may focus on answering their children's questions and teaching equality (Katz & Kofkin, 1997, in Rollins & Hunter, 2013, p. 142). Rollins and Hunter (2013, p. 143) suggest that in addition to the equality education in multiracial families, there may be more emphasis on "self-development socialization messages" rather than developing an ethos of solidarity and group membership. They may also be more likely to be silent about racialized groups and steer away from the harsh reality of racism.

Intergenerational Power

Young people are at the bottom of the age hierarchy. Adults, and particularly those in their middle years, hold economic, political, and social power and also control access to information, knowledge, and research. Adults in their full wage-earning years have access to most of the resources and thus have power and control over their children's behaviour, goals, and values. At issue are the power and control of parents over their children (Nett, 1993, p. 204).

Developmental Stake and Generation Gap

As noted earlier, parents have a greater developmental stake in their children's lives than vice versa. This notion comes from the aging and life-course research of Bengtson and associates (in Koller, 1974, p. 224; also see Nett, 1993, pp. 199–201). It is suggested that parents have a greater investment in their children because they represent continuity. On the other hand, children need to distance themselves from their parents as they develop a separate identity. This distance is exhibited, e.g., in adolescents' attitudes, which are more negative than those of their parents about the communication in the family. Adolescents tend to report less openness and more problems than their parents (Noller & Fitzpatrick, 1993, p. 267).

Interestingly, it has been reported that parents tend to see more similarity in the values and ideas of themselves and their adolescent children, whereas adolescents tend to downplay those similarities and point to differences. This is a normal part of the developmental process, and relates to the notion of "generational stake," in that older people have more of an investment in the younger generation than vice versa. Parents want to minimize the differences between themselves and their adolescents because they are the ones experiencing the loss of the youngsters as they gradually move away from them. Meanwhile, adolescents are in the process of leaving their family of procreation and moving toward other relationships. In this process, they are more likely to emphasize differences in order to make the separation more palatable. As pointed out by Baker and Dryden (1993, p. 209), it is only later on that young people once again are able to realize that perhaps they and their parents have more in common than they previously thought.

This power imbalance between the generations is particularly exhibited in the line of thinking that flows from it. It is assumed that if parents engage in controlling behaviours, this will naturally cause conflict as young people strive toward independence and start to rebel. This expectation of a generation gap and resultant intergenerational conflict is reinforced by psychoanalytic and developmental stage theorists who see adolescence as a period of identity confusion that needs to be resolved by the adolescent becoming autonomous (Koller, 1974, esp. pp. 208–209; Seltzer, 1989, p. 227; Beaumont, 1996). This phenomenon is rooted in the 1960s and 1970s with the associated student and youth rebellions (e.g., Duncan, 2000). However, the concept has been less clearly demonstrated empirically in the post-1970s era (Nett, 1993, p. 175).

Generally, we do expect some type of intergenerational conflict to emerge between parents and adolescents. The 20–30 years separating young people from their parents' age group are likely to lead to a generation gap. There is so much social change taking place that it would be quite abnormal if there weren't any areas of disagreement about values and expectations between parents and adolescent children. Also, those parents who were adolescents in a different era often go through a developmental process themselves, and have a very selective memory about the kinds of things they did when they were adolescents. Not surprisingly, it was noted in a survey of young women in Canada (Holmes & Silverman, 1992, pp. 31–32) that young people's satisfaction with their family life decreases with age. Even though most adolescents, male and female, are satisfied with their family relationships, there is a decrease between ages 13 and 16 from 87 percent to 80 percent for girls, and from 92 percent to 85 percent for boys.

It seems that this sequence of parental control leading to rebellion is generally culturally accepted in North America. For example, in one rare study, Canadian sociologist Ambert (1992) explored the perceptions of 109 university students of their effect on their parents as teenagers. Notably, all but seven reported having had a negative or more negative effect on their parents as teenagers than in any other age group. They linked this factor to having been more "rebellious/difficult," or to their parents' parental styles, which they experienced as challenging (Ambert, 1992, pp. 131–149).

Interestingly, Ambert (1992, pp. 133–137, 148) also found that the students went on to explain that as their parents adjusted to their new behaviours and needs, life became much more harmonious, indicating that the children had a socializing effect on their parents. The general trend was that, with the exception of the rare few who engaged in truly delinquent acts, "not a single student ever questioned their *own* mentality or the need to change it." The sense was that parents need to adjust, and the peer culture supported this view (Ambert, 1992, pp. 133–137, 148).

Beaumont's (1996) study of 28 grade 11–12 girls and 28 grade 5–6 girls in southwestern Ontario found that girls perceive their conversations with their friends to be more positive than those with their mothers. It is suggested, based on other research, that as adolescents begin to engage in intimate communications with their friends, they learn that all relationships can be based on a more reciprocal model. This then can influence them to shift the basis of their interactions with their parents from a unilateral authority model toward a more adult model of interaction.

Some researchers now question the applicability of the control/rebellion model, or the generation gap, in present times (Nett, 1993, p. 201). For example, Seltzer (1989, pp. 228–229) suggests that this may be both a self-fulfilling prophecy and a matter of interpreting regularly occurring parent-child conflicts in a new light once the child enters adolescence. In the words of Koller (1974, p. 224), it seems that "generational dissension is far easier to contemplate than consensus."

Adolescent-Parent Relations in Immigrant Families

They were raised 40 or 50 years ago in Sri Lanka and I was raised ten years ago in Canada.... Some parts of them, they still hold on to some values they learned when they were a child. Things like what girls should do and what boys should do and what they should wear. But for us, everything is changed. It's not the same—what girls should do here is not the same as what girls should do there. So, I think ... the generation gap—how we are raised. (A female, age 18, in Tyyskä, 2006, p. 23)

A number of studies have documented changes in newcomer parents' roles and relationships with their children in North America (Ambert, 1992; Anisef et al., 2001; Dhruvarajan, 2003; Foner, 1997; Kilbride et al., 2001; Tyyskä, 2003a, 2005, 2006). Many immigrant parents feel that their parenting ability is under serious stress in a number of ways (Fuligni & Yoshikawa, 2003; Noivo, 1993; Tyyskä, 2005, 2006). Poverty alone creates situational and systemic obstacles that undermine attentive and nurturing parental behaviours (Beiser et al., 2000). As immigrant parents struggle with unemployment, underemployment, multiple jobs, and shifts in gender-based economic roles, their children may not get the attention they deserve, while parents also put added pressures on them in areas of education and future employment (Creese et al., 1999; Tyyskä, 2005, 2006). Because their families are likely to face economic hardship, youth poverty is a big issue (Beiser et al., 2000). For some immigrant groups, there is a danger in both Canada and the US (Hernandez et al., 2007) alike that the economic hardships experienced by parents will leave a legacy of intergenerational pauperization despite the promise of upward mobility through education.

Children often learn the official language faster than their parents due to the influence of schools and peers (Hernandez et al., 2007). This can lead to two types of intergenerational problems. First, language differences can create conflict in intergenerational communication and transmission of culture and identity (Anisef et al., 2001; Bernhard et al., 1996). Second, role reversals and shifts in parental authority may result as parents rely on their children as mediators of official language, social institutions (schools, hospitals, social services), and culture (Ali & Kilbride, 2004; Creese et al., 1999; Momirov & Kilbride, 2005; Tyyskä, 2005, 2006). However, while immigrant children may claim new roles and responsibilities in their families, parents often expect to retain the same degree of authority over the children (Creese et al., 1999).

Added factors in the realignment of parental authority are shifts in maternal and paternal work and family roles and authority patterns that change parents' relationships with one another and their children (Ali & Kilbride, 2004; Anisef et al., 2001; Creese et al., 1999; Grewal et al., 2005; Haddad & Lam, 1988; Jain & Belsky, 1997; Momirov & Kilbride, 2005; Shimoni et al., 2003; Tyyskä, 2005). The resulting tensions can also contribute to the onset or increase in severity of family violence against women and children (Creese et al., 1999, p. 8; MacLeod & Shin, 1993; Smith, 2004; Tyyskä, 2005; Wiebe, 1991).

Immigrant youth often feel torn between their desire to fit in with their peers and their desire to meet their parents' expectations (Tyyskä, 2003b, 2006). Much of the research into intergenerational relations in immigrant families tends to focus on intergenerational conflict (the generation gap) in terms of the conflicting expectations of "Old World" parents and their "New World" children (Tyyskä, 2005, 2006), including issues such as peer relations and social behaviour (Wong, 1999; Wade & Brannigan, 1998), dating and spouse selection patterns (Dhruvarajan, 2003; Mitchell, 2001; Morrison, Guruge & Snarr, 1999; Zaidi & Shuraydi, 2002), educational and career choices (Dhruvarajan, 2003; Fuligni, 1997; Li, 1988; Noivo, 1993), and retention of culture (James, 1999).

It is true that particularly stark differences emerge in some immigrant communities with regard to parental expectations of male and female children (Tyyskä, 2003b). Adolescent girls in some immigrant families have much less freedom of movement and decision-making power than their brothers (Anisef & Kilbride, 2000; Anisef et al., 2001; Dhruvarajan, 2003; Handa, 1997; Shahidian, 1999, p. 212; Tyyskä, 2006). The parental fears for daughters relate predominantly to dating, which is equated with premarital sexuality, while fears for sons centre on drugs and violence (Anisef et al., 2001; Shahidian, 1999; Tyyskä, 2006). It is most often presumed that immigrant families (especially Muslim and Asian) are more restrictive than Western cultures with regard to their children, particularly daughters. Indeed, American studies of Asian immigrant families indicate that daughters buy into the notion of American gender equality in contrast with their own families' patriarchy (Aapola et al., 2005, pp. 93–94).

Girls hold a special place as "cultural vessels" in many immigrant communities, and their conduct is seen to reflect the family and the whole community. Nevertheless, families with girls and young women may need interventions in order to prevent the escalation of family conflict and possible violence, and the alienation of girls from their families. North American studies (Handa, 1997; Tyyskä, 2006; also see Aapola et al., 2005, pp. 94–95) document the kinds of dual lives that some young immigrant women live in order to mediate the demands of their families and their own need to establish their identity that adopts some elements from the mainstream society. This includes practices such as carrying different clothes so that they could change into garb deemed acceptable either by their peers or their parents. One 18-year-old Tamil woman (Tyyskä, 2006, p. 26) reflects on her parents' dilemmas:

> Even though they're adapted to Canadian culture, they didn't completely lose the aspects of Tamil culture. They do have little enforcement. Some things … they don't bend on to—some things that girls can't do and it's fine with me too. Sometimes, they're little bit strict on some stuffs and I can understand that too.

Transnational Families

> I came from a culture where we had extended family that participated in raising children who gave the mother the help and relief that she needed. On the contrary here I find parents with less children going through so much stress—especially those working parents. (Somali mother, in Tyyskä & Colavecchia, 2001, p. 57)

As stressed from the beginning, the definition of families is not limited to the traditional nuclear family. At the same time, the distinction between nuclear and extended families does not adequately capture the richness of local, national, and international/transnational networks that immigrants rely on (Creese et al., 1999). The impact of globalization is evident in the multiple border crossings across the boundaries of nation-states. Transnational families (or "astronaut families") are often characterized by members living together for limited periods and separately for long periods with especially teenage children living on their own. They are the result of migrations related to the search for work for adults and education for children, and are characterized by separation and reunification of different members of the family unit over time (Ambert & Krull, 2006; Panagakos, 2004; Waters, 2002; Wong, 2007).

Though some families arrive as multi-generational units (Noivo, 1993), others experience fracturing due to a combination of restrictive definitions of "family" in immigration policies and the circumstances of their departure from their countries of origin. For example, some immigration policies don't allow unification of family members outside of the immediate nuclear family unit. Some families undergo continuous transnational shifts over generations (Gordon, 1999; Panagakos, 2004; Shahidian, 1999), creating intergenerational ruptures and complex family dynamics over distance. One major change in some immigrant communities is that the loss of extended family in helping to raise children may lead to new parenting arrangements and parenting support networks (Anisef et al., 2001; Tyyskä, 2002, 2003b, 2011).

Transnational family arrangements stress spousal and parent-child relationships. In some cases, spouses may remain separated for several years. These lengthy separations often result in extramarital affairs (Cohen, 2000; Shahidian, 1999); spouses growing apart; and a host of negative emotions, including jealousy, hostility, depression, and indifference (Cohen, 2000; Man, 2003). Parent-child relationships are particularly stress-ridden in these circumstances. Children may grow into their teen years with other family members or friends, to be reunited with their parents at a later age. One type of transnational family in Canada centres on women who are brought here under the Foreign Immigrant Domestic Program from developing countries such as the Philippines and the Caribbean nations (Arat-Koc, 1997; Bakan & Stasiulis, 1996). These women leave their children behind to come and work as low-wage domestics and nannies in order to escape the poverty created in their home countries by the legacy of colonialism and expanding global economic exploitation (Ambert & Krull, 2006; Arat-Koc, 1997; Bakan & Stasiulis, 1996).

Regardless of the circumstances of their immigration, mothers are commonly held responsible for their children, and face stigma and social disapproval if they leave them behind as they search for better opportunities abroad (Ambert & Krull, 2006, p. 112; Bernhard et al., 2005). Immigration policies don't make it easy for families to reunite as the process takes a long time. This means that by the time children are reunited with their parents, families face a lot of adjustment issues, including fear of abandonment, or anger toward and jealousy of siblings who accompanied the immigrating parent. Parental authority may be undermined as a number of children grow up separated from their parents and without anyone to step into the role of parents. At the same time, there is a double loss for children who first were separated from their parents, and now face another separation from a caregiver they have grown attached to (Ambert & Krull, 2006; Bernhard et al., 2005; Cohen, 2000; Wong, 2007). Newly reunited children can also become overly dependent on their mothers, preventing the latter from connecting with their communities (Creese et al., 1999).

Living Arrangements: The Empty Nest and the Crowded Nest

Leaving home is a normative expectation when people reach adulthood. The process of a young adult leaving the parental home and establishing independent living quarters is commonly seen to mark an important life-course transition, a passage to adulthood. There is ample evidence to show that there is a sense of normative timing for this to take place (Mitchell, 1998, pp. 22–24; Aapola et al., 2005, pp. 99–101).

Leaving home is usually associated with significant life-course events, such as higher education, employment, or marriage (Zhao et al., 1995, p. 32). However, young people leave home for a variety of reasons and at different ages, some voluntarily, and others compelled by difficult family situations, including family violence. Some stay away and may become castaway youth on the streets. Others return temporarily and leave once again more permanently. Notably, some youth are less able to live on their own, including those with disabilities, who may need a lot of assistance with their daily lives (Aapola et al., 2005, pp. 99–100).

The lives of youth in northern European countries, including the United Kingdom, are characterized by leaving home early, with multiple returns and departures through the span of marriage and parenthood. Young women generally tend to leave home earlier than men due to their comparatively lower age at marriage and childbirth. Though the size of this gap varies by country, it is present in all European countries (Iacovou, 2002, pp. 42–43). The average age in the UK during 2007 to leave home was 24.3 for men and 23.8 for female (Eurostats, 2009, p. 29).

In the UK, there is a growing trend toward young people leaving the parental home before forming partnerships to live alone or with their peers, while getting educated, or to start new jobs. The patterns are changing in that young people are getting married and forming families later. Between 1971 and 1990, the median age at first marriage rose from 21.4 years to 24.9 years for women and from 23.4 years to 26.8 years for men. The average age at first childbirth among married women rose from 24 to 28 years between the early 1970s and 1993. One of the problems with young people leaving home is that the housing market is aimed at families, and affordable single-person housing is difficult to find (Jones, 2000, pp. 185–190). Eurostats notes that for all Europeans, including the UK, the issue of affordable housing is a major factor in staying in the parental household longer, and that 44 percent of all youth between the ages of 15 to 30 consider this to be the greatest reason why the parental house is a better option (Eurostats, 2009, p. 30).

UK and American studies also show differences based on ethnic background (Jones, 2000; Iacovou, 2002, p. 42). For example, more 16 to 20-year-old African Caribbeans in the UK leave home than other ethnic groups, while Asian women are generally least likely to leave home earlier. Children of stepfamilies also leave earlier than those living with two biological parents or a lone parent. Early home-leaving usually manifests negative factors in the family life of youth (Jones, 2000, pp. 185–186; also see Finch, 2003, p. 41).

Iacovou (2002) reports that in the United States, the age by which 50 percent of people have left home is 22.0, 24.0, and 23.9 for White, Black, and Hispanic men, respectively, and 21.0, 21.7, and 22.4 for women in respective categories. Similarly, the ages at which 50 percent of people are living with a partner are 24.3, 28.9, and 24.4 for White, Black, and Hispanic men, and 21.9, 28.0, and 23.4 for White, Black, and Hispanic women. Finally, the ages at which 50 percent of people live with children are 30.3, 34.8, and 30.6 for White, Black, and Hispanic men, and 26.1, 20.7, and 23.5 for White, Black, and Hispanic women. White Americans are more likely to have left their parental homes than are Blacks or Hispanics. American women are particularly likely to have left the nest early, around 17 or younger. Hispanic Americans are most likely to live in an extended family. By the ages of 25–29, only 7 percent of White, 15.9 percent of Black, and 24.5 percent of Hispanic women live with their parents, while the corresponding figures for men are 15.7 percent, 29.7 percent, and 34.0 percent.

Many immigrant and racialized parents expect a closer relationship with their young adult children than is expected in the mainstream. The significant marker for them for a child leaving home seems to be getting married. For example, Asian parents tend to expect that as long as their children are unmarried, they should share a residence with their parents (Beishon et al., 1998). However, as youth grow up, some of their expectations may reflect those of other youth around them. Borgen and Rumbaut (2005) report that many college-aged offspring of mostly Asian and Mexican immigrants in San Diego, though not living with their parents, exist in an in-between stage, spending a lot of time in their parental home while not living there full-time. Similarly ambivalent feelings were reported by Beishon et al. (1998) regarding younger Pakistanis and Bangladeshis in the UK. Though they agreed with their parents about the benefits of extended family and multi-generational households, a few also preferred that their parents not share a household with them to ensure privacy and autonomy.

As in the US and UK, there has been a steady increase in the median age of home-leavers in Canada for cohorts born after the 1960s. There is general agreement that the prolongation of staying at home has to do with the worsening of the economy and multiple recessions (Zhao et al., 1995, pp. 32, 47; Boyd & Norris, 2000, p. 270). Further, as education has lengthened, the age of independence has risen (Nett, 1993, pp. 216–217). In 2011, 42.3 percent of young adults (20 to 29) lived with their parents, amounting to a total of 4,318,400 young adults, a significant increase from 27 percent in 1981 (Statistics Canada, 2002b; Statistics Canada, 2012a).

In Canada, women typically leave earlier than men, but for both women and men, marriage and living as a couple have declined as reasons for leaving home (Statistics Canada, 2012a). Instead, reasons for leaving home have more to do with a desire for independence and pursuing a post-secondary education. For men, employment was always a more important reason for leaving home, but the general importance of getting a job has declined (Ravanera et al., 1992, 1993, in Zhao et al., 1995, p. 32). As of 1996, 23 percent of young Canadian women aged 20–34 were living at home, an increase from 16 percent in 1981. Among young men, the increase was from 26 percent to 33 percent in the same time period. Thus, the notable trends are the increasing age of children living at home, and that the majority are men (Boyd & Norris, 2000). In 2011, young men with an average age of 29 were more likely to live with their parents than women of the same age: 46.7 percent compared to 37.9 percent (Statistics Canada, 2012b).

These gender differences in home-leaving patterns were noted earlier by Zhao et al. (1995, p. 47), who also cite four reasons (from Ravanera et al., 1992) to explain it: (1) earlier physiological and psychological maturation of girls than boys; (2) earlier age of marriage for women than men; (3) a longer period of preparation for males as breadwinners; and (4) more household tasks for girls than boys that may act as an incentive to leave.

It has been observed (Aapola et al., 2005, p. 101) that despite their lower wages compared to young men, young women are more eager to leave their parental homes and are more reluctant to return even if they face financial difficulties. This has been linked to more control over young women's lives by their parents as compared to young men, an aspect that will be discussed in more detail later in this chapter.

Zhao et al. (1995) examined the results of the 1990 General Social Survey on home-leaving in Canada. They found that there were important family and parental characteristics that explained the timing of leaving home. First, stepchildren and adopted children leave home earlier than other children. Second, except for widowed families, children in all different types of non-intact families (e.g., divorced, step, single-parent) leave earlier than children in intact families. Third, children in immigrant families, especially non-European families, leave home later, perhaps due to a greater emphasis on familial values that hold family members together for a longer period of time. Fourth, lone children tend to leave home later than children with siblings, except if the lone child is a girl who is more likely to be a target of parental protectionism. Further, female children whose parents have post-secondary education are more likely to leave later than females whose parents are less educated. This may be explained by more parental emphasis on their daughter getting an education and a career than getting married and leaving home.

Since the 1990s, the "empty-nest" stage has proven to be less permanent in Canada as more youth return to live with their parents as "boomerang kids" or "[V]elcro kids" (Kingsmill & Schlesinger, 1998, pp. 13–34) resulting in a "crowded" or "cluttered nest." This trend holds for youth in Great Britain; a study in Scotland found that between 1987 and 1991, there was a doubling in the return to their parental homes among 19-year-olds (Finch, 2003, p. 42).

This phenomenon of children moving in and out of their parental homes is common in the Western world, depending on what is happening with their relationships and economic lives. Living on your own is difficult when the labour market offers fewer good opportunities for youth and more education is expected (Aapola et al., 2005, pp. 100–101; also see Zhao et al., 1995; Matsudaira, 2006), as will be discussed in more detail in the chapters on education and employment.

In fact, Canadian statistics show a significant increase in the phenomenon of youth returning home compared with previous decades. As of 1991, for example, in the age group 20–24, 70.5 percent of unmarried men and 63.4 percent of unmarried women were living with their parents. These percentages reflect both extended residence by children who never left, and those who returned after having left (Mitchell, 1998, pp. 22–24). In 2011, of young adults between 20 and 24 years old, 63.3 percent of men and 55.2 percent of women were living at home. Out of those young adults living at home, 95.9 percent for all age groups were never married (Statistics Canada, 2012b).

As in the case of delayed departure from home, the return to the parental home is reflective of the economic conditions. Although intergenerational co-residence patterns and reasons behind it have shifted over the last century, Allahar and Côté (1998, p. 137) argue that "not until now … has it been a result of the inability of the young to support themselves." This argument will gain more support from the work chapter, which will present the poor financial situation of young people. Similarly, Boyd and Norris (2000, pp. 159–160) link extended co-residence with economic factors and the lengthening education of young people, both of which keep them dependent on others for a longer time. Matsudaira's (2006, p. 19) analysis of American census data related to youth's living arrangements leads him to propose that

> Young adults respond to changes in economic conditions by altering their living arrangements. In particular, declines in the job market and falling wages push 20-something men and women to share housing with their parents. The effects of the business cycle are more pronounced for adults in their early twenties rather than their late 20s, probably due to the higher cyclicality of their employment prospects, and appear more pronounced for men than for women.

This prolonged dependency of youth is manifested in shifts in public policy (discussed in more detail in Chapter 10). For example, in Britain since the 1980s, youth in the age group of 18–25 are increasingly seen as dependants of their parents. Social policies are more likely to be based on the assumption that parents will support their young adults. As their social benefits are cut, they will have to turn to their parents for support in order to survive. This contributes to a lengthened period of dependence, and puts the fates of young people in the hands of their parents, who may or may not be able to support them, and with whom they may not get along (Aapola et al., 2005, pp. 89–90).

Stigma of Parent-Youth Co-residence

There is a tendency in the Western world to depict adult child/parent co-residence in a negative light as typical of children who have "failed" at something, be it marriage or their careers, and are returning to further burden their parents (Kingsmill & Schlesinger, 1998, pp. 13–34; Allahar & Côté, 1998, pp. 136–138). Many depict the situation of co-residence as something that amounts to "the indulgence of an immature and spoiled generation" by their parents, who are "not only impeding their children's adult independence but also hampering their own post-parenting lives." A new buzzword, "B2B" (Back-to-Bedroom) has been developed by American pop trend goddess Faith Popcorn to describe those youth who are supposedly freeloading on their parents (Paul, 2003).

This negative depiction prevails despite the harsh realities of young people's lives in the 21st century, and in the face of large numbers of immigrant families that have closer intergenerational relations and mutual obligations between children and their parents as a natural part of family life. As noted above, in some cultures, children are expected to live with their families as long as possible. If fact, children leaving their parents while young is seen as problematic by many immigrant parents.

The normative expectation that adulthood equates to living in your own residence, separate from your parents, is something that many young people identify with strongly. Aside from education, living arrangements seem to give many youth a sense of whether their lives are going "forward" or "backward." One Minneapolis female in her late twenties (Settersten, 2006, p. 11) described her life in these terms:

It went in *cycles with me* [emphasis in the original]. I didn't really feel like an adult when I got married. I was just myself. [B]ut ... moving into our own place ... and probably 6 months into being married and really getting into that routine of what our life was, paying bills, paying rent, car payments ... that's when I really started to feel like an adult. I ... felt that way for a few years and then I ... went backwards a little when I moved home. [And] then [backwards] again, going back to being a student, [and then moving forward] to the full-time job.

That is not to say that parent-youth co-residence is always easy. No family is completely harmonious at all times, so this cannot be expected from adult children living with their parents. However, it can be expected to be more harmonious if there is a cultural agreement and understanding about mutual roles and responsibilities.

Reportedly, returning children in the Western mainstream society may find it difficult to readjust to togetherness, as appears in the following segment entitled "How Do Your Children Feel about Returning Home?" (Kingsmill & Schlesinger, 1998, p. 20):

Returning home is not easy. Many boomerang children feel they have failed, and envy their friends who have made it. It was exciting and stimulating living away from home, and it is often discouraging to move back. They have become used to living on their own and to doing things their own way; now, suddenly, they have to swallow their independence. They may be wondering if they will ever be able to leave home and make a life for themselves. They may be depressed and unsure of themselves.

Moving home can be a real blow to any adult's pride, self-esteem and self-confidence, and the worries of what the future holds can seem overwhelming. Most do not return home by choice, no matter what the precipitating event, and the return is usually temporary. Unfortunately, many people see young adults who return home as moochers and cop-outs scurrying home at the first sign of trouble. This is unfair: in any age group there are some deadbeats, but most boomerang children are home to regroup before leaving again.

Meanwhile, studies also report positive effects from generational co-residence, including sharing of household tasks and positive family interactions (Mitchell, 1998, pp. 22–24; also see Kingsmill & Schlesinger, 1998, pp. 13–34). For example, Mitchell's (1998) study of 420 families in the Greater Vancouver area found that co-residence can be both a positive and a negative experience for the parents. Most parents reported that the co-residence was working very well, and fewer than 10 percent reported that it was working out either somewhat well or poorly. This is contrary to the current negative views of co-residence as characterized by "intergenerational tension, conflict, and dissatisfaction" (Mitchell, 1998, p. 40). The most positive aspects were related to companionship and the child's helping at home. Further, if the child had a full-time job or if she or he had initially left to go to school, parental attitudes were more positive. Fathers were somewhat less positive than mothers, possibly because they are not likely to have as close a relationship with their children as mothers do. Single parents also reacted more negatively toward co-residence with their children because of possible privacy issues. Further, the return of sons was more welcome than daughters, possibly because of different expectations regarding marriage and participation in household tasks. Those who returned twice were welcomed more readily, probably because issues related to co-residence had been worked out previously.

Homelessness

To talk about homeless youth in a chapter on families is logical given that homelessness usually translates to reduced family support, if not a complete breakdown. Thus, homelessness can be understood as a form of "familylessness." In other words, homelessness is not only about not having a roof over your head, "it is the lack of a secure and satisfactory home" (Farrington & Robinson, 1999, in Rokach, 2005, p. 469).

Homelessness is a growing problem in Canada as well as in the United States in the 21st century. It is estimated that in 2007, 671,859 individuals in America were homeless (Sermons & Henry 2009, p. 6). Meanwhile, in Canada, the number of homeless people was estimated to be 157,000 in 2006 (Trypuc & Robinson 2009, p. 1) In America, 26 percent of homeless people suffered from serious mental illness, 13 percent were veterans, 15 percent suffered from domestic abuse, 19 percent were employed, 13 percent were psychically disabled, and 2 percent were HIV positive (United States Conference of Mayors, 2008, p. 18). The United States Conference of Mayors (2008, p. 19) notes:

> For persons in families, the three most commonly cited causes of homelessness were lack of affordable housing, cited by 72 percent of cities, poverty (52 percent), and unemployment (44 percent). In last year's survey, the three main causes of family homelessness were cited as lack of affordable housing, poverty and domestic violence. This year's top three causes of homelessness among singles were said to be substance abuse, cited by 68 percent of cities, lack of affordable housing (60 percent), and mental illness (48 percent).

Homeless youth are those young people (generally 12–24 years of age) who are homeless on their own rather than with their families. They are categorized as either runaways/runners or throwaways based on the circumstances under which they are homeless. Runaways leave home because they find the conditions unbearable, and throwaways are forced out of their home. There are further categorizations based on whether the getting away is permanent (runners) or temporary or impulsive (in and outers) (Duffy & Momirov, 1997; Webber, 1991; Fitzgerald, 1995). Runners typically have histories of physical and/or sexual abuse, an aspect that will be discussed more fully in the chapter on health. Significantly, in a British study, only one in 10 youth indicated they would be able to return home (Jones, 2000, pp. 191–192).

As of 2005, an estimated 100 million children around the world were homeless (Unicef, 2005). It is estimated that 65,000 youth were homeless or living in a shelter in Canada during 2004 (Raising the Roof, 2009, p. 13). In the UK during 2011, approximately 107,060 were homeless, which was an increase of 10 percent from the previous year (Crisis, 2012, p. 1). Outreach agencies throughout London note that 7 percent of homeless individuals sleeping on the street where under the age of 25 (Crisis, 2012, p.1). In the US there are approximately 1,682,900 youth who are homeless or runaways (National Coalition for the Homeless, 2008).

Van der Ploeg and Scholte (1997, p. 22) summarize some of the main trends in global youth homelessness. The age of homeless youth is dropping and the numbers are increasing among both solitary youth and families, particularly young single mothers with children (see Box 3.3). Though there tend to be more homeless young males than females (see, e.g., Miller et al., 2004, p. 736), van der Ploeg and Scholte (1997) report that there are an increasing number of girls on the streets. In the Western world, it is also noted with alarm that cultural minorities are disproportionately represented among homeless youth. For example, in the United States, 35 percent of the homeless youth are members of minorities, with even higher proportions depending on the location.

Box 3.3: Motherhood on the Streets?

Gaetz et al. (1999) found a large number of pregnant street youth. Indeed, the study found that young homeless women get pregnant at rates of two to three times that of their non-homeless peers. The chances of getting pregnant are greater among younger women and those who have lived on the streets for a longer time. Miscarriages are two to four times the rates among the general population due to lack of proper nutrition and higher rates of substance abuse and sexually transmitted diseases.

Studies from all three countries show that young homeless people are not youth in search of thrills; they are there because their family circumstances have become unbearable and leave them no alternative but to go away. They come from families characterized by persistent family conflict (not getting along with parents), family instability (e.g., living in dysfunctional stepfamilies), sustained sexual and/or physical abuse, parental substance-abuse problems (Baron, 1999, p. 3; Fitzgerald, 1995; Duffy & Momirov, 1997, pp. 89–91; Webber, 1991; Miller et al., 2004; Jones, 2000; van der Ploeg & Scholte, 1997), and lack of parental emotional and/or financial support (Miller et al., 2004, pp. 737–747).

A study in Toronto (Gaetz et al., 1999) of 360 Toronto youth in shelters reports a profile of homeless youth consistent with other studies. Additionally, a significant number of these youth are gay or lesbian (generally estimated between 20 percent and 40 percent of the street youth population), and left home due to conflict with parents or peers over their sexual orientation. They also found a higher proportion of females than males, and the young women left home at a younger age than the males. The youth are not clearly representative of any one type of background based on social class as measured by parental employment or education. On the other hand, the Gaetz et al. (1999) study found that a very high percentage (65 percent) came from families in which the parents do not live together, or where one or both parents are deceased (17 percent). These features of family structure indicate that street youth typify a situation where for one reason or another, their "attachment to a nurturing adult has broken down" (Gaetz et al., 1999, p. 9).

The Gaetz et al. (1999) study in Toronto found that life on the streets is harsh, and youth have to engage in a number of different ways to earn their living, an aspect that will be discussed in the chapter on work. Youth are at risk of engaging in criminal behaviours, including stealing and using and selling drugs. Young people are also subject to sexual predators, and particularly girls are likely to turn to prostitution to support themselves. These topics will be discussed in more detail in the chapters on health and crime.

Because youth are not on the streets by choice but because of their strained circumstances, they yearn for more stability in their lives. In a British study by Miller et al. (2004), the street youth expressed a lot of optimism about their futures and thought of their situation as temporary. Clearly, supports are needed for this to happen as it is shown that the situation can become permanent without them. Based on interviews with youth who were either homeless or at risk of becoming homeless, Miller et al. (2004, pp. 752–753) recommend that the following measures be used to strengthen the services:

> (1) build on the youths' optimism and determination through the development of peer networks; (2) mobilize and support interest in education and employment through contacts with employers; (3) support ties to family, including extended family or families of choice when available; and (4) use current living arrangements or create living arrangements which can facilitate education and employment.

Conclusions

Families are seen in popular culture as safe havens from the ills and temptations of the world. At a closer look, they both replicate the power relations of society and also have power relations of their own. When young people get exposed to the multiple direct and indirect effects of inequities, their lives can take a turn for a worse. Although large segments of youth live in perfectly well-functioning families, significant numbers end up as casualties of dysfunctional family life, subject to poverty, stress, discrimination, abuse of parental authority, neglect, and violence, with detrimental effects on their chances of optimum development and lower chances of making it in the world. Some abused teens and youth end up on the streets with no home or family to call their own except for other youth on the streets. For these youth, it would be a luxury to be a "boomerang" youth as the stigma associated with living with your parents is certainly outweighed by the stigma of living on the streets.

Families come in many varieties. Significantly, most children and youth tend to fare well regardless of the type of family they live in. Some of the problems are not accounted for by the type of family itself but by the circumstances of the family. Thus, it is not single-parenting or living in an immigrant family that is problematic but the conditions of poverty and/or stress in those families that make the lives of children and youth more difficult. In stressful conditions, however, families can ideally help their youth, as is the case with racialized youth, who can be empowered by the positive messages they receive from family members in dealing with racism and discrimination in their lives.

Families are primary sites for socialization of youth; parents pass on to their offspring messages about expected behaviours. Significant differences are uncovered in parents' treatment of daughters and sons, reflecting a continuation of traditional gender-specific patterns. Despite talk about family democracy or "permissive" parenting, it still tends to be more of a feature in middle-class families, especially in relation to the raising of male children, whereas daughters continue to be subjected to tighter controls. This may be particularly significant in specific, yet by no means all, immigrant families where intergenerational relations can be particularly tense, especially where expectations of youth and their parents clash.

By virtue of living in a world dominated by adults who earn the money and make the decisions, youth depend on their parents for increasingly longer time spans. This dependence is not fully appreciated in the mainstream sensibility. Western "malestream" capitalism instills into people the notion that they need to be independent, as explained in Chapter 1. Adulthood is measured in terms of financial and residential separation from one's parents. That is why there is such a stigma associated with young people living with their parents for "too long," for example. And patriarchal conditions make it impossible for young women to ever meet the measure of independence due to child-bearing and rearing and their lower positions in the workforce.

I am, therefore, arguing that people who expect today's youth to be independent before reaching the end of their twenties are out of touch with today's realities of extended education and lack of economic opportunities. They are also out of touch with the range of family forms and norms in an increasingly diverse society. Now more than ever, youth need the help, the support, and the solidarity of their parents and other adults, not their condemnation for living in an age they don't fully understand themselves but in which their youth have to live. These main features of young people's lives will be made clear in the next two chapters on education and work, respectively.

Critical Thinking Questions

1. Do you think you have more power in your family than your parents had when they were young?
2. What are the kinds of issues that emerge between immigrant parents and their teenage children? How do you think they affect these youth?
3. Under what circumstances do you think it's acceptable for young people to continue living with their parents well into their twenties or beyond?

4 Education

In this chapter, you will learn that

- education is the major occupation of young people
- educational institutions are powerful socializing forces
- although the majority of young people are literate, many of them drop out of secondary school and only between one-quarter and one-third complete post-secondary education
- there are inequalities in education based on social class, gender, and racialized and immigrant status
- financing post-secondary education is becoming increasingly difficult for young people, with growing numbers of them combining paid work with their schooling
- young women and members of racialized and sexual minority groups face harassment in schools and have to deal with a hidden curriculum manifesting dominant values

A long period of education is an expected part of being young. As much as adolescence is synonymous with finishing secondary school, it is seen as increasingly necessary for young people to devote their twenties to getting post-secondary education. This chapter will outline young people's experiences in relation to education, including secondary schools and post-secondary educational institutions.

Educational institutions are powerful sites of secondary socialization. They aim to provide the skill sets required for navigating one's life, including citizenship, education, and training for employment. As discussed in the chapter on history, public education emerged partly as a solution to the problem of "idle youth." While waiting for full entry into the labour market, young people are being prepared for the labour force, not only in terms of requisite skills, but the discipline and industrious attitude required by the work environment. We need to pay attention to what it is exactly that schools provide, and how young people manage in schools, including literacy levels, school/academic enrolment and completion rates, and access to higher education.

While education is valued for its own sake, and young people understand the importance of education, not all adolescents and young adults are equally equipped to get into educational institutions or to complete their education. Numerous youth fall between the cracks due to institutionalized constraints based on social class, gender, race, and ethnicity. The uneven results are manifested in high school dropout rates, debt loads, and the general school experience, which still favours those in the higher socio-economic groups who are male, White, and native-born.

Another socializing aspect of schools has to do with the informal and social elements, including interactions between educators and students, and between students. A part of this is the "hidden curriculum," which refers to implicit messages in education that emphasize mainstream values and social hierarchies based on social class, gender, and race. Also of interest in this area are students' peer interactions in schools, particularly recently raised concerns about bullying and school violence.

Literacy

There is more to literacy than reading and writing ability. According to Willms (1999, p. 9):

> [Literacy] refers to a person's ability to "us[e] printed and written information to function in society, to achieve one's goals, and to develop one's knowledge and potential."

Thus, literacy combines elements of "human capital" (skills and knowledge) with "cultural capital" (values, forms of communication, and organizational patterns) and "social capital" (use of language in social relations). This means that literacy is not a neutral concept as all of these aspects reflect economic and social inequalities based on social class, gender, race, and ethnicity (Willms, 1999, p. 9).

An OECD report, including results from the UK, the US, and Canada, estimates that large proportions of populations 16–65 are functionally illiterate, defined as "the inability to understand and use common channels of communication and information in every day context, from newspapers and books to pamphlets and instructions in medicine bottles." These rates are estimated to be 21.8 percent in the UK, and 20.7 percent in the US, rates that compare poorly to those in the Nordic countries where comparable rates are well below 10 percent (Di Done, 2002, p. 15). In Canada, in 2003, 15 percent of adults were deemed illiterate, compared to 17 percent in 1994 (Statistics Canada, 2005d).

Nevertheless, there is no question that youth in Canada, the US, and the UK are more educated than their parents' or grandparents' generations. For example, the median years of schooling for the Canadian population aged 25–44 increased from 7.7 in 1941 to 13.2 in 1991 (Nakamura & Wong, 1998, p. 9). The 1996 Census (Statistics Canada, 1998a) showed that the trend of attaining increasingly higher levels of education has been observed since the early 1950s. Canadians between the ages of 5 and 39 can expect to go through 17 years of education. Between 1999 to 2009, attainment of post-secondary education within Canada increased from 30 percent to 50 percent for the adult population between 25 to 64 years of age (Statistics Canada, 2012c, p. 4). As of 2006, 61 percent of adults aged 25 to 64 held a college diploma or university degree (Statistics Canada, 2006e).

Secondary Schools

There are differences among the three countries in the quality of education. A major international adult literacy survey was conducted in 1994, including Canada and the United States, along with a number of European countries. In comparisons of literacy scores with Europe, youth in Canada and the United States do not do well. For Canadian and American youth with secondary school–graduated parents, the skill deficit is about two years and three years below European youth, respectively (Willms, 1999). The Programme for International Student Assessment (PISA 2000, in Human Resources Development Canada, 2002, pp. 16–17) of reading and math literacy in 31 OECD countries ranked Canadian 15-year-olds second in reading, fifth in science, and sixth in mathematics. Canadian students continue to do well on literacy testing compared to most countries (Statistics Canada, 2010, p.15).

To a large degree, the US results are indicative of considerable differences in the quality of education among less advantaged youth (particularly African Americans and Hispanics), while in Europe, in general, the standard of education is more even among social categories. The significant variations between American states and Canadian provinces in literacy rates also reflect the extent of socio-economic divisions. Further, if parents' immigrant status is considered, the gap between Canadian and American youth stretches from one year of schooling to two years. Among notable gender differences is that American female youth had higher scores than male youth in all but the quantitative (math) tests. In Canada, females tended to do better than males in all tests only if their parents were highly educated. The reverse was the case for those with less than high school education where boys tend to outperform girls (Willms, 1999). The trends in education based on gender, social class, and race will be expanded upon below.

Secondary school attendance has become an expected part of young people's lives. Di Done (2002, p. 14) reports that 90 percent of American, and 94 percent of UK and Canadian youth of secondary school age were attending relevant educational institutions in 2002. The Census of 1996 (Statistics Canada, 1998a) found that only 35 percent of the population aged 15 and over had not completed high school, compared with 48 percent in 1981. OECD figures (Dearden et al., 2006, pp. 2–3) show that 87 percent of Americans aged 25–34 had completed high school in 2002. The corresponding figure for UK youth in this age group was 70 percent.

Dropping Out

I think nowadays teenagers just get fed up with school. They just can't take it anymore. The further you get into the year, the more kids have the urge to give up.

> Specifically in my school, I think many kids drop out because they want to work and just don't think that doing homework is going to get them anywhere. Many times the teachers don't help because kids can be easily annoyed so if they are bothered they are more tempted to give up. On one side of it, I would say start at a younger age to explain the importance of school, but at the same time, I think it's just more about the school and teachers and friends who may be there to support them. (Brittany S., Springfield High School, PA, in *Student Voices Pennsylvania*, 2006)

Not all young people make it through high school. There is worldwide concern with the school dropout problem (Dearden et al., 2006, p. 3). Di Done (2002, p. 14) reports a high school dropout rate of 15.1 percent in Canada in 1999 and 11 percent in the US in 2000, the latter amounting to 16 million dropouts aged 16–19. The dropout rate was somewhat more positive in Canada in 2006/2007, at 9.3 percent (Statistics Canada 2007c, p.58). American research (Nguyen et al., 2001, p. 2) indicates that approximately 13 percent of youth aged 18–24 have not completed high school, a rate that remained stable through the 1990s. The Canadian Youth Transition Survey found a comparable high school dropout rate of 12 percent in 2000, an improvement from the rate of 18 percent in 1991 (Human Resources Development Canada, 2001). In the UK, the dropout rate is particularly problematic, with 23 percent of those aged 15–19 not enrolled in an educational institution (OECD, 2004, p. 4).

Internationally, a link has been made between dropout rates and compulsory school age. The dropout rate is lower in countries where the legal school-leaving age is higher. That age is 16 in all Canadian provinces (Human Resources Development Canada, 1999c, p. 18) as well as in the UK, and it ranges from 16–18 in the United States, with the majority (30) of states legislating it at age 16 (Dearden et al., 2006, p. 3). Some experiments have been made in the UK and the United States regarding paying students an incentive fee to stay in school, presumably to offset the negative economic effects of extended education among those with low incomes. The Education Maintenance Allowance (EMA) was offered in the UK to low-income students nationwide starting in September 2004. Evidence shows that the EMA is effective in increasing the school stay rates among older (16–17-year-old) students from the lowest parental income categories (Dearden et al., 2006, p. 4).

Anisef (1998, in Anisef & Kilbride, 2000, p. 22) stresses that it is important to understand that dropping out is a process, not a single event. This means that there are multiple reasons for dropping out that have to do with the school, the family, the community, the labour market, and government policy. Among reasons for dropping out are school-related factors such as poor academic performance, lack of engagement with education, and lack of school peers and role models, as well as the use of alcohol and/or drugs. However, some young men also drop out for reasons of wanting to work and some young women leave school because of pregnancy and child-rearing. Also, a higher percentage of dropouts (32 percent) than high school graduates (16 percent) lived with a single parent, and were more likely (27 percent) than graduates (9 percent) to have parents who had not finished high school (Human Resources Development Canada, 2001).

Researchers have established a long-standing link with students' social class background as those in the lower socio-economic categories are more likely to drop out (Anisef et al., 1980; see also Davies, 1994, p. 345). Crysdale (1991) studied high school dropout rates among youth in the economically depressed downtown Toronto core. He found that there was a 60 percent school dropout rate among the youth in this geographic area, which is twice the national average. The dropout rate generally is higher among low-income families (23 percent) than among youth in other income groups. Further, those in the lower socio-economic groups are more likely to enrol in basic or general level programs. Based on Ontario data, Tanner (1990) reports that the dropout rates for general level programs are much higher compared with those for advanced level programs.

Some studies suggest that dropping out is related to combining work and schooling, which is increasingly common among young people. Dropping out is more likely if the student works over 10 hours a week, or when the minimum wage is higher. This has led to proposals for two levels of minimum wage: one for those aged over 17 or 18, and another for younger persons, to encourage them to stay in school longer (Human Resources Development Canada, 1999c, pp. 18–19; Taylor, 1997).

The dropout rates cover significant variation based on gender, class, and race. Studies in 1980s Ontario show that over 90 percent of all high school dropouts were White, Canadian-born youth, while the rates for immigrants and minorities were lower. There were two exceptions to this rule: (1) recent immigrants of visible minority background who had been in Canada less than four years; and (2) Aboriginal youth whose dropout rates were over twice the national average (Davies & Guppy, 1998, p. 135). Because of the link between low income and race and ethnicity, it is not clear which one is the more determining factor. Aboriginal youth dropout rates have been declining since 1998; however, they are still relatively high, particularly for Aboriginal males. Among Aboriginal youth, 13 percent drop out and do not return, while 26 percent drop out and then return to school around age 20 to 22, making them the largest group of second-chance high school graduates. While the dropout rates for immigrants are no higher than those of Canadian-born youth, 3 percent of visible minority immigrants drop out and never return to school, while 11 percent drop out and then later return. In comparison, 5 percent of visible minority Canadian-born youth drop out and never return to school, while 10 percent return to school. At the same time, the rates for White groups show a comparable pattern: 7 percent of European immigrant youth drop out and do not return, while 13 percent later return to school; and 8 percent of Euro-Canadians drop out of school without returning, while 9 percent of them return to school (Looker & Thiessen, 2008, p. 18).

In 2009, the dropout rate in America overall was 9.4 percent, but it was 9.1 percent among White non-Hispanic youth, 11.6 percent among Black non-Hispanic students, and 20.8 percent among Hispanic students (US Census Bureau, 2012f). In the United

States, Hispanics made up 19.5 percent of the youth population between 15 to 24 years old, while Blacks made up 15.5 percent (US Census Bureau, 2008). Significantly, Blacks and Hispanics account for a disproportionate number among those who drop out. In 2004, the dropout rate among Hispanics was around 30 percent, while the rate among Blacks was also higher at 21 percent. Though they make up 11 percent of the total population, foreign-born students also had higher (26 percent) dropout rates compared to US-born students (17 percent) (Child Trends Data Bank, 2006). Similar to Canadian indigenous peoples, the dropout rates are much higher among Native American and Alaska Natives, 23 percent of whom have not finished high school, and whose dropout rate of 15 percent is second only to that of Hispanic youth (National Centre for Education Statistics, 2003, Indicator 3.3. and Indicator 8.1).

Gender differences are also apparent. The dropout rate is traditionally somewhat higher for Canadian males than females (Côté & Allahar, 1994, pp. 41–42, 173, note 33; Tanner, 1990). From 2011 to 2012, 9.7 percent of Canadian male youth and 5.9 percent of Canadian female youth dropped out of high school (Statistics Canada, 2012d). In 2011, 7.7 percent of American male youth and 6.5 percent of female youth dropped out high school. While males make up about half the general population for this age group in 2011, they account for 55 percent of high school dropouts (Child Trends Data Bank, 2012, p. 4, 8).

Interestingly, earlier studies and surveys from the 1990s show that more young women than young men indicate liking school (Holmes & Silverman, 1992, pp. 42–45; Tanner 1990). These studies also found that many young people have antipathy toward school, including teachers and guidance counsellors. Additionally, Tanner's (1990) study suggests that dropping out may not be due to poor grades, but may be rooted in poor attendance or behavioural problems that leave youth few options but to drop out or be expelled. Tanner (1990) interprets this trend as indicative of adolescent antipathy toward the school environment, which the respondents reported to be authoritarian, denying them freedom and autonomy because they are young.

Another major concern for youth was fitting in and getting access to peer groups or disapproving of the peer culture. This argument has been extended by Davies (1994, p. 345), who found that school dropouts are more likely to form a subculture of students who "expend less effort than graduates, engage in more disruptive behaviour, experience greater difficulties with school, and have friends who are also dropouts," leading them to "disengage themselves from the culture of schooling, and learn to prefer the 'real world' of employment over 'irrelevant' schooling."

Tanner's (1990) study found that dropping out was an "ambiguous experience" for most young people. They reported a range of short-term positive consequences, such as freedom and making some money, but they were also aware of the long-term problems dropping out might create. Although most of the respondents (70 percent) were definitely in favour of getting more education, only 36 percent of the females and 27 percent of the males indicated they would like to return to finish their high school education. Education was seen as a central value by the majority of the high school dropouts in his study.

Post-secondary Education

One of the major developments of the 20th century was the growth in universities. Almost all OECD countries have had dramatic increases in their post-secondary education programs at the turn of the 21st century. In the early 21st century, university applications are up by an unprecedented amount, with more students vying for spots in higher education. For example, the UK experienced an increase of 20 percent from the mid-1990s to the mid-2000s. The 2006 attainment of post-secondary education in Britain was 30.5 percent of the entire population (OECD, 2009b). In Canada, the rate was 47 percent, and in the US it was 39.5 percent (OECD, 2009b).

There is continuing concern over vocational preparation for young people in Britain and the United States along the model of many European countries with strong systems of vocational preparation (Bynner & Parsons, 2002, p. 303). In Canada, community college enrolments have increased dramatically, corresponding with the decline in part-time university numbers. There seems to be something of a return to the mentality of the era before mass education, whereby young people entered apprenticeships in order to get a job (Statistics Canada, 1993–1997). This is supported by a report of the Council of Ministers of Education Canada (1999). While gaining knowledge and developing individual potentials are valued in their own right, education is primarily seen to serve the needs of the economy, and to help shape a cohesive society. Colleges are seen to be more rooted in their communities than universities are, and to be more responsive to the needs of business, industry, and the public sector. At the same time, they are seen to be stepping stones toward university.

Financing Education

Rising tuition fees are cause for significant concern among students. University tuition fees in Canada have risen at a pace faster than inflation between 1990–1991 and 2003–2004, averaging $4,214 per academic year as of 2005–2006. Fees for graduate studies have risen at over twice the rate for undergraduates (Statistics Canada, 2005a). The average tuition fee in 2012/2013 was $5,581 for an undergraduate student, but in 2008/2009 the average graduate studies fee in Canada was $5,695 (Statistics Canada, 2013a). Graduate fees, however, were significantly higher in Ontario, Nova Scotia, and British Columbia (Statistics Canada, 2011d, p. 7). Rates for different programs vary, with dentistry still ranked as the highest tuition in Canada, costing $16,910 for the 2012/2013 academic year (Statistics Canada, 2013a).

It is not surprising that students with higher-income-earning parents are more likely to attend university. According to a Statistics Canada study (2003a), about 83 percent of high school graduates with family incomes over $80,000 went on to higher learning in 2001, whereas the proportion fell to 55 percent when family incomes were less than $55,000. The average debt loads owed in 2000 by university graduates were $20,000 while college graduates owed nearly $13,000 (Statistics Canada, 2005a). As of 2005, college graduates owed an average of $13,600, while university graduates had borrowed $25,600 (Statistics Canada, 2009b, p. 30). Between 1993 and 2001, youth from high-income (over $100,000) families were twice as likely as those from low-income (less than $25,000) families to attend post-secondary institutions (Drolet, 2005, p. 12).

In American universities too, tuition costs are spiralling and financial aid is becoming out of reach for an increasing number of students (Giroux, 2003, pp. 154–155). Tuition fees went through significant increases in the 1990s (Males, 1996, pp. 13-15). In 2010, the average annual fee for an American four-year university degree was US$8,123. In 2008, the total annual costs, including living expenses, books, supplies, and tuition, amounted to US$10,128 (US Census Bureau, 2012g).

In the UK, the issue of fees is linked to the expansion of higher education "from an elite system to a mass participation system." While only 6 percent of high school graduates attended university in 1962, approximately 43 percent did so in 2002. The argument for increased fees in the UK was that it is unfair for the general and largely non-university-educated tax-paying population to cover the growing cost (estimated by the government to be £9 billion) of higher education that benefits only the graduates themselves (politics.co.uk, 2013).

In England and Northern Ireland, changes were made to university tuition fees in 2006. Fees had been at a flat rate of £1,175, but were raised to £3,000 (called "top-up" fees), with income-graded grants awarded to those in the income bracket of £17,501–£37,425, starting at £2,700 annually and reducing to nothing as a family's annual income reaches the maximum. The fee increase applies differently in the other UK countries, Wales and Scotland. In Wales, Welsh students will continue to pay the £1,200 while students from other parts of the UK will pay £3000. In Scotland, Parliament pays the top-up fees on the students' behalf, and claims about £2,000 from the students after they graduate. The fees are around £1,700 annually, with medical schools claiming a fee higher by around £1,000. English and Northern Irish students are allowed to accumulate their fees over their undergraduate study career, and these are repayable once they earn minimum of £15,000 (BBC News, 2007a; politics.co.uk, 2013; Policy Studies Institute, 2003).

The British coalition government, which was elected in 2010, noted its intentions to increase the top-up fee. The government set up plans to increase the top-up fee in 2012 from £6000 to £9000 in England. As a result, the maximum tuition fee that a university can charge is £9000, while the average university in 2012 has a set fee of £8,123 for full-time students. The base family income for a full Maintenance Grant was £25,000, while the grant itself only amounted to £3,250 (politics.co.uk, 2013).

Based on the exorbitant cost of higher education, many students in all three countries experience serious financial difficulties both during and after their schooling. Because of the rising cost of education, Canadian studies report that more young people accumulate enormous debts in order to finance their education. At the same time, more students are compelled to work part-time and seasonally to finance their education (Baker, 1989, p. 43). Statistics Canada data reveal that more students are working during the school year, during both high school and post-secondary education. In 2004/2005, students worked in significant numbers during the school year for the first time: 52 percent of female and 41 percent of male post-secondary students had a paid job. In 2009/2010, 45.4 percent of all students worked during the school year, amounting to 39.6 percent of men and 50 percent of women (Marshall, 2010, p. 9).

Many American students are likewise crippled by increased debt loads without adequate state or parental support. Only about one-quarter of American parents provide financial support for their university- or college-attending children (Males, 1996, pp. 13–15). In the United States, one-third of universities are privately funded. This means that university and college enrolments are much more dependent on household income than in Canada as there are fewer affordable state-supported universities available to students (Frenette, 2005).

The system is highly punitive to low-income students, who would be graduating with huge debts, having foregone paid employment while in university. As official student loans continue, students in the United Kingdom will potentially accumulate £3,415 annually if they live at home and £6,170 if they live away from home (BBC News, 2007a; politics.co.uk, 2013; Policy Studies Institute, 2003). Under recent changes to the system, the loan limits are increasing (Bolton, 2012, p. 9).

One major study of student fees and debts in Britain (Callender & Wilkinson, 2003, in Policy Studies Institute, 2003) points out that there has been an escalation in student debts to the extent that individuals carried, in 2003, two and a half times the debt load of students who graduated in 1998, the year that grants were replaced by loans. In fact, the move from grants to student loans benefits wealthier students more as they got 15 percent more money than those in the lowest income categories whose support fell 4 percent. Indeed, another study (Machin, 2003, in Bright, 2003) shows that there was a drop in the university attendance of students in the lowest social class category from 13 percent of that category in 1991–1992 to 7 percent after the introduction of tuition fees and the abolition of grants.

British students themselves estimate that they will graduate with a debt load of up to £30,000. The president of the National Union of Students was quoted saying:

> The student funding review was called in order to address the balance of contribution between the students and the state.... That balance has certainly been addressed today with students footing the bill. (BBC News, 2003)

Canadian graduates, whose debt loads have multiplied from the 1990s onward, face a similar fate. For example, Elton and Brearton (1997) and Bailey (1999) report that the average debt load for a graduate with first degrees in universities and colleges in 1996 was $17,000, up from around $8,000 in 1990. According to the Canadian Centre for Policy Alternatives (2004, p. 2),

> in real terms, student debt at graduation has increased by close to 100% for college, bachelor and masters graduates and almost tripled for doctorates (since the early 1990s).

This means that most Canadian graduates will have difficulty paying back their loans, since 85 percent of those aged 18–24 earn less than $21,000 per year. There were approximately 35,000 university and college graduates who declared bankruptcy between 1990 and 1997 before reaching age 30. Declaring bankruptcy on student loans is now possible only after a 10-year period. Moreover, the government turned over the management of student loans to the five big banks, which are less hesitant about using drastic measures to collect their monies from graduates (Elton & Brearton, 1997; Bailey, 1999). By the end of 1997, over $36.9 million was recovered through collection agencies (*Globe and Mail*, 1999). At the same time, government per capita funding of post-secondary institutions has fallen 30 percent (Galt, 1999b).

According to a report by Human Resources Development Canada (1999b, p. 12), the increase in debt level of those seeking to obtain post-secondary education does not seem to be discouraging youth from pursuing further education because they have come to recognize the importance of education in a knowledge-based economy. However, if the costs of education continue to increase, it will become financially impossible for some youth to obtain an education. Parental financial support is important even though most students rely on earnings from summer and part-time work earnings (Anisef et al., 1980). This is hardly surprising, considering that the average cost of one year of post-secondary education is barely covered by the money that would be earned in a minimum-wage full-time job. It is also not surprising that there are higher proportions of students who have to borrow money to finance their education. The conclusion from these trends is that social class will increasingly be linked to one's educational achievement "in the face of rising educational costs and reduced services and financial support for students" (Wotherspoon, 1998, pp. 184–185).

A recent Canadian study (Frenette, 2005) shows that while there is a clear link between university enrolment and socio-economic background, measures such as student aid can offset the ill effects. Following the steep tuition increases in the 1990s in Ontario, enrolments rose among students with parents who held graduate or professional degrees (and thus had higher earnings), while there was a decline in enrolment by students whose parents had less education. In provinces where tuition fees were frozen, no such patterns emerged. However, the most interesting result was that in Ontario, enrolment rose among students whose parents had no post-secondary education. This suggests that it may be the middle-income students, who don't qualify for student aid, who are the likeliest to suffer under tuition increases where aid programs are present. The implication is that student fees need to be controlled at acceptable and affordable levels and that student assistance needs to be widened to include middle-income families.

Students are quickly learning that market forces are at play in their education. One American example from 2001 is provided by two recent high school graduates, Chris and Luke, whose plan to finance their post-secondary education consisted of soliciting for corporate sponsorships. They offered themselves up as advertising billboards for companies willing to pay for their college tuition and other expenses (Giroux, 2003, pp. 154–155).

It is not only the students who are catching up to the trend toward corporate sponsorships of North American schools. It is now common practice to name new buildings after private corporations and donors, use private funding toward endowing chairs, and to select university presidents based on their links to the corporate world (Giroux, 2003, pp. 165–174).

Regardless of rising tuition fees, in all three countries youth understand that in order to get a foothold in the working world, educational credentials are required. Though the impact of the 2006 fee increases cannot be measured at this time, a UK study from 2005 (Ramsden & Brown, 2005, pp. 5–6) reports that universities are receiving increasing numbers of applications. Similarly, Canadian universities report a significant increase in applications. For example, between 2000 and 2008, applications to Ontario universities increased by 34.4 percent (Council of Ontario Universities, 2013). In the US, between 2007 and 2012, there was an increase of applications to university by 10.7 percent (Universities and Colleges Admission Systems, 2013).

Inequality in Education

The trends in universities, outlined above, speak of continuing problems with equity in education. Despite general perceptions that past inequalities in education have been remedied, numerous studies from the 1980s and beyond (e.g., summarized in Maxwell & Maxwell, 1994; also see Anisef et al., 1980; Livingstone, 1999, p. 57; Guttman & Alice, 1991; Baker, 1989; Anisef, 1994; Willms, 1997, 1999; Wotherspoon, 1998) have documented that social class, gender, and ethnicity have a significant effect on educational aspirations and attainment.

> Put simply, schooling has functioned as a mechanism of social reproduction, a sorting machine closely tied to, and serving to legitimate and perpetuate, the social hierarchy of power and privilege in American society. But is also a site where significant gains have been won as individuals and groups have struggled to make schools responsive to the needs of their children. (Farber et al., 1994, p. 7)

Thus, youth who live in poverty, or are women or members of racial or ethnic minority groups, are finding that their educational experience is qualitatively different from that of youth who come from dominant backgrounds (e.g., Anisef, 1994, pp. 10–11; Wotherspoon, 1998, pp. 182–185; African Heritage Educators' Network and Ontario Women's Directorate, 1996, p. 3).

Social Class

Though ability and other factors cannot be discounted completely, to a large degree, schools are shown to reproduce social class positions (Kingston et al., 2003). Studies comparing educational achievement in the United States and the United Kingdom have consistently found that despite different educational systems, the link persists between socio-economic status and educational attainment as well as later occupational status (Kerckhoff, 1990, pp. 7–14).

Generally, it has been found that academic attainment—and ultimately occupational attainment—are largely dependent on family origins and educational experiences. Children from privileged backgrounds have better access to quality education, are more likely to benefit from better finances, and have access to goods and services that enhance the general education experience. As previously intimated, they are also more likely to accumulate different forms of capital (cultural, social, and human) (Willms, 1999, p. 9; also see Wotherspoon, 1998, pp. 179–185). Children who live in poverty and whose parents have to battle with teacher discrimination and expectations of failure have low self-esteem and low motivation to excel (Anisef, 1994, pp. 10–11; Wotherspoon, 1998, pp. 182–185).

An analysis of the Statistics Canada 1991 and 1995 School Leavers Surveys found that parental education influenced post-secondary education both indirectly and directly. In fact, "each additional year of parental education increases the likelihood of university attendance by as much as five percentage points." Parental levels of education have a long-term effect through primary and secondary school grades, attitudes toward school, and parental views of the importance of education. These are also correlated highly with university attendance (Statistics Canada, 2005a).

It is true that a lot of negative stereotyping accompanies poverty. In some neighbourhoods, such as Toronto's Parkdale, students and teachers are fighting back against the ill effects of this negative imagery by encouraging community participation. Among the most recent contributions is a book produced by students at the Parkdale Collegiate Institute. Entitled *Not Poor in Spirit*, the book contains contributions from members of the community and school outlining the efforts they make to achieve their goals amidst difficult circumstances (Galt, 1999a).

Although these community-based efforts do a lot to remove some of the stigma, we cannot erase the real and observable consequences of living in low-income neighbourhoods. Canada-wide, youth from advantaged family backgrounds fare well in tests of literacy, whereas youth from disadvantaged backgrounds fare uniformly poorly (Willms, 1997, p. 25). Young people who live in poverty are faced with additional challenges that those with more advantages cannot even imagine, including the ill effects of hunger and sickness, housing conditions that make it difficult to do homework, limited access to educational materials such as books or computers, and lowered educational aspirations in the family environment (Anisef, 1994, pp. 10–11; Wotherspoon, 1998, pp. 182–185).

These disadvantages are likely to be perpetuated from parents to their children. Research from the 1990s has shown that educational inequality is reproduced across generations. A study by Clark (1991, in Wotherspoon, 1998, p. 180) showed that the educational backgrounds of parents of post-secondary graduates were much higher than those of trade/vocational graduates. Along these lines, Siedule (1992, in Wotherspoon,

1998, p. 180) has demonstrated that those with favourable backgrounds in terms of family income, family structure, province, and ethnicity had up to five years of educational advantage over those from less favourable conditions.

The link between parental education and children's education is clear. For example, 26.9 percent of high school dropouts in Canada had at least one parent who had not completed high school, 45.2 percent had at least one parent who graduated from high school, 16.9 percent had at least one parent who had some form of post-secondary education (like a diploma or certificate), and 11 percent had at least one parent who graduated from university (Bowlby & McMullen 2002, p. 30). For high school graduates in Canada, 8.7 percent had at least one parent who had not completed high school, 34.7 percent had at least one parent with a high school diploma, 26 percent had at least one parent who had some form of post-secondary education, and 30.6 percent had at least one parent who graduated from university (Bowlby & McMullen, 2002, p. 30).

Similarly, family structure is linked to educational outcomes. In 2001 in Canada, 81.4 percent of individuals from two-parent families completed high school, compared to about 15.9 percent of those from lone-parent families. Meanwhile, the dropout rate for youth from two-parent households was 63.6 percent, compared to 31.9 percent for lone-parent households (Bowlby & McMullen, 2002, p.29). Within two-parent households, 55.4 percent of dropouts were from biological or adoptive households, whereas 8.2 percent were from mixed households (e.g., one step-parent and one biological or adoptive parent). The graduation rate for two-parent biological or adoptive households was 75.8 percent, compared to 5.6 percent of mixed-parent households (Bowlby & McMullen, 2002, p. 29).

Thus, there are notable ill effects for children living in single-parent families, who are more likely to suffer from poverty, as discussed in the previous chapter. Studies also confirm the above patterns by showing both the material advantages of dual-income families and the disadvantages of marital breakups as they relate to children's education (Frederick & Boyd, 1998).

Britain arguably has an educational system that revolves around social class and status to an extremely high degree. Indeed, the system has been likened to that of "missionary" schools where teachers of poor, working-class students find "gifted" children whom they "save" from their lower-class status by recruiting them into academic careers at the big-name universities. Not only are these select children and youth exposed to a higher level of academic achievement, but they are also socialized into the elite language and recreational culture (Rex, 1982, pp. 55–56). The ongoing reproduction of the social class hierarchy has been confirmed in studies showing that there is little movement between social classes in terms of occupational placement following education. By and large, working-class children continue to place in working-class jobs, while middle-class youth go on to post-secondary education and obtain higher-status jobs (Charles, 2002, pp. 95–97). One contemporary manifestation of social class inequalities is that there are differences in use of and attitudes toward computers (see Box 4.1).

Box 4.1: Socio-economic Status and Computer Use

A survey of computer use by 855 children in southwest England and South Wales found that access to computers is patterned by socio-economic considerations. Families in low-income categories were less likely than high-income families to own a home computer, to have parents who were exposed to computers, or who endorsed the use of computers for education (Facer & Furlong, 2001, pp. 454–458).

Follow-up interviews revealed that interest in computers also reflected gender-based peer group cultures and identity. Among boys, attitudes toward computers seem to define masculine identity along either physical or technological social power. Thus, working-class boys equated computer use with a lack of physical prowess (Facer & Furlong, 2001, p. 461):

> When you think about computers you see nerds working on them—you imagine like people with glasses and shirts tucked right into their trousers pulled up and socks over their trousers. (Boy, aged 11)

The study also found that these schoolchildren were frustrated at adults' presumption that they can use computers comfortably. The authors found this "cyberkid" image to be problematic in that for young people, it "becomes a battleground in which they construct their definitions of being 'successfully young'" (Facer & Furlong, 2001, p. 463). They are highly critical of the "cyberkid" concept as it homogenizes a whole generation of young people and creates a sense of exclusion and of being outsiders on the part of those who aren't part of this dominant cultural practice, and prevents them from getting help with computers in schools. This "information inequality" needs to be combated in order to "develop a more inclusive and diverse construct of childhood in the digital age" (Facer & Furlong, 2001, p. 467).

Gender

Generally, it has been found that early socialization and sex-role stereotyping are responsible for the maintenance of traditional educational and career choice patterns (Guttman & Alice, 1991; OECD, 1986; Maxwell & Maxwell, 1994, p. 147). Young women continue to put a higher priority on marriage and family life than young men, and consistently choose traditional educational and career patterns (Guttman & Alice, 1991). This type of "gender tracking" (Mandell & Crysdale,

1993) prepares young men and women for different paths in relation to education, work, and family.

In 1994, seven countries, including Canada, collaborated on the first International Adult Literacy Survey. In reporting the survey's results related to the youth population aged 16–25, Willms (1997, pp. 24–25) notes that nationwide, males and females scored equally well. However, there were notable province-based variations. Whereas females substantially outperformed males in New Brunswick and British Columbia, the reverse was true for Ontario and Manitoba. This is explained by informal streaming mechanisms that prevail in some provinces but not others. For example, Ontario youth in this study would have come from "streamed schools," where presumably boys would be more likely than girls to enrol in science-based academic programs. On the other hand, New Brunswick has more girls enrolled in French-immersion programs than boys. On average, French-immersion students do better in reading and writing assessments.

There is no denying that women have entered educational institutions en masse. The main Canadian trend in the 1980s and 1990s was that men and women are equally likely to graduate from high school. Further, there has been a female majority among university entrants and those who receive Bachelor's degrees since the early 1980s. The present trend reflects a proportional representation of male and female students in the education system. In fact, females gain higher grades in high school, are more likely to graduate from high school, and are more likely to attend post-secondary institutions (Mandell & Crysdale, 1993, p. 21; Normand, 2000, pp. 73–77).

Similar trends have been observed in Britain. British secondary education offers the General Certificate of Secondary Education (GCSE) at ages 14–16. Though they are not mandatory, most students take the GSCE, which consists of a grouping of mandatory courses. An O-level certificate is granted as a general certificate while A-level exams results in a certificate that potentially qualifies students for post-secondary education. In Britain, by the end of the 1990s, the gender gap in secondary school graduation (called O levels) had reversed to contain more girls, and the gap in A levels has disappeared (Charles, 2002, pp. 90–91).

In Canada, women are a large presence not only in secondary schools but also in colleges and universities. The 1996 Census (Statistics Canada, 1998a) found that 51 percent of women in the age group 20–29 held a degree or a diploma compared with 42 percent of men. This shows a significant change from 1981 when 37 percent of both men and women held post-graduate degrees. These trends hold for universities as 21 percent of the women aged 20–29 and 16 percent of men aged 20–29 held a university degree compared with 11 percent and 12 percent in 1981, respectively. Significantly, in 2008, women formed 60 percent of all university graduates in Canada (Statistics Canada, 2011d).

Mass education has not served girls and young women as well as it could have. Canadian women are still underrepresented in graduate programs and among those with more advanced degrees, and overrepresented in part-time studies. Further, gender divisions persist in the choice of field of study. Women in secondary and post-secondary education continue to be overrepresented in traditionally female fields, e.g., education, nursing, social work, humanities, and social sciences. They remain underrepresented in areas such as engineering, math, physical sciences, and computer science, as well as dentistry, medicine, and law (OECD, 1986; Mandell & Crysdale, 1993; Normand, 2000; Bibby, 2001, pp. 26–27). Only 24.4 percent of all mathematics, computer, and information sciences enrolments were women in 2010/2011 (Statistics Canada, 2012e). According to King et al. (2008, p. 16), in Canada:

> Men made up the majority of graduates in engineering (86%), computer and information sciences and mathematics (82%), physical sciences (68%), and biological sciences (54%). Conversely, women were the majority in psychology (70%), education (62%), health sciences (60%), and social sciences (56%).

Similar patterns prevail based on level of university study. Women drop below 50 percent of enrolment at the doctoral level in almost every field. In the academic year of 2005/2006, women accounted for 44 percent of all doctoral graduates. At the same time, 62 percent of undergraduate graduates were women and 52 percent of master's level graduates were women (King et al., 2008, p. 15).

Similarly, career choices and employment outcomes in the UK "still reflect stereotypical patterns and girls often lose out in the employment market" (Department for Education and Employment, UK, 2000). Though British high school girls now have gender parity in mathematics examination passes, gender inequality continues in other hard sciences, including physics, computing, and technological fields, which continue to be male-dominated, while girls are still much more likely to take home economics (Charles, 2002, pp. 88–89).

Are Boys Being Left behind?

Though girls' and boys' careers still reflect traditional and stereotypical patterns, concerns with educational achievements of boys have been raised across the Western world. As an example here, the British debate is used, reflecting similar discussions in Canada and the United States.

Girls tend to outperform boys in English schools at all learning stages, leading to the advocating of additional attention to boys' school culture and educational experiences (Department for Education and Employment, UK, 2000). The gradually growing success of girls in education has led to widespread concerns over the "underachievement" of boys in all three countries. This is one of the latest shifts in the debate on schooling waged since the middle of the 20th century. According to Epstein et al. (1998) and Yates (1997) (reported in Charles, 2002, p. 108):

> While early post-war studies problematized the way the educational system reproduced the class structure, studies carried out in the 1970s shifted their attention to cultural reproduction and social interaction in the classroom. With the advent of feminist sociology attention was turned to gendered processes within schools, later encompassing ethnicity and sexuality as well as gender but moving away from the

attention to class. The 1990s were marked by the emergence of studies of masculinities in schools informed by concepts of discourses, subjectivities, and identities and reflecting popular concern with boys' alleged under-achievement. At the turn of the century some have blamed boys' "under-achievement" on the influence of feminism and equal opportunity policies in schools which have favoured girls at the expense of boys and which have, allegedly, contributed to a crisis of masculinity.

British educators argue that boys are in need of remedial teaching to keep up with girls, who are now privileged in the classroom. Ironically, remedial teaching has always been offered more to boys than girls. The general argument here is that attention to girls has gone too far, and studies are used to exaggerate the extent of the gender gap in girls' favour (Charles, 2002, pp. 106–107). In Britain, the phenomenon could more accurately be described as "overachievement" by girls, who have been gaining ground as the rates of education have improved for all children, male and female alike (Charles, 2002, pp. 90–91).

The debate about the supposed underachievement of boys is also a debate about its consequences for their later labour market performance. Girls should be outperforming boys in the labour market given their higher educational achievements. However, despite their levels of performance, boys and girls still fall within the traditional gender-typed work areas. This means that higher educational achievements still make women fit for female gender-typed jobs rather than posing a threat to men's traditional jobs. Additionally, British studies show that "at every level of the occupational hierarchy women had higher qualifications than men, suggesting that men can get further with fewer qualifications than women" (Charles, 2002, pp. 92–93).

In fact, Charles (2002, p. 107) argues that boys' underachievement has always existed, particularly with regard to the working class. Middle-class boys have always been and continue to be achievers. What is different, Charles argues, is that with the contraction of the manufacturing sector, working-class boys find it increasingly difficult to find employment while the girls' education makes them fit for the expanding feminized service economy.

The focus on boys' achievements or lack thereof is in keeping with the British research tradition, particularly emanating from the Birmingham school (see Chapter 1) of examining working-class behaviours based on boys' school subcultures but not those of girls (Charles, 2002, pp. 95–97).

Gender and Educational Aspirations and Expectations

Young women may not be aware of the challenges they are facing at all stages of schooling. Overall, young women do well, and realization of the consequences of the gender-based streaming processes in education may come much later. One Canadian survey of adolescent women (Holmes & Silverman, 1992, pp. 45–46) found that awareness of gender discrimination increases with age. For example, about 96 percent of 13-year-old boys and girls agreed that there are equal chances for success in schools for boys and girls. This decreased by 7 percent for women and 2 percent for men by the time they were 16 years of age.

Canadian studies have noted a persistent gap between the aspirations and expectations of young females (Nelson & Robinson, 1999, pp. 174–175; Wall et al., 1999).
Although a majority of young women as well as men aspire toward a good education
and prestigious, well-paid occupations, only young women show a gap between their
plans and what they actually expect to achieve. At a young age, females learn to antici-
pate that their career plans will not work out, and that they will be best off preparing
for marriage and motherhood. Meanwhile, young men are more certain that their
career aspirations and expectations will be the same. This gender difference is telling
of the persistence of traditional patterns whereby men will not expect that their marriage and parenthood will stop them from achieving their dreams. In contrast, young
women are prepared for the barriers that their family life will pose for the fulfillment
of their professional plans.

However, there are some signs that girls' educational and professional aspirations
rose through the 1990s compared with the previous decades. Some reports note that the
educational and life aspirations of young women and men are increasingly similar (e.g.,
Tanner, 1990, pp. 88–89; Bibby & Posterski, 1985, in Maxwell & Maxwell, 1994, p.
144). These studies are in dire need of updating, given the rising educational levels of
women in recent years.

It is a general finding (e.g., Wall et al., 1999; Mandell & Crysdale, 1993) that parental support is particularly important in adolescents' educational pathways. Wall, Covell,
and MacIntyre (1999) summarize research that shows that social supports are important
as they influence the level of aspirations and expectations of students. A supportive
school environment is particularly important for youth's aspirations and expectations
if familial support is missing. In their study of 260 students aged 15–18 in Atlantic
Canada, Wall, Covell, and MacIntyre (1999) found more social supports for girls than
for boys. For boys' perceived opportunities, family support was seen as crucial because
they did not perceive as many peer or school supports as girls did. This translates to girls'
higher perceived opportunities, as well as higher expectations of education and career,
and higher educational aspirations than their male peers. This study may indicate that
there is a shift in young women's perception of opportunities and aspirations, even as
gender divisions in education persist.

There is evidence that parents' attitudes and behaviours regarding gender roles and
gender equality play a role in young people's decisions about education and careers. Traditionally, parents have been more likely to encourage the education of their sons than
their daughters, and to promote gender-typed career and family-related choices for their
children (Nelson & Robinson, 1999, p. 132).

An example of this is Mandell and Crysdale's (1993) study of 324 Ontario youth
in their mid-twenties, which examined their experiences in the school-to-work transition. The study found that 18 percent were traditional in their expectations, while
15 percent were labelled egalitarian. The majority of the parents were found to hold
"quasi-egalitarian" views, i.e., supporting egalitarianism in some areas but not in others.
This means that there is support for some combination of wage and domestic labour
for both men and women, but this is characterized by "somewhat equal responsibil-

ity for children, a little sharing of housework, and equal educational and occupational aspirations for women and men, provided no financial problems or other hardships are involved" (Mandell & Crysdale, 1993, p. 26). In practice, this results in differential parental aspirations for sons than daughters, which in turn results in differential labour market outcomes.

On the other hand, social class differences intersect with gender in shaping educational and career outcomes. A Canadian study by Higginbotham and Weber (1992, in Nelson & Robinson, 1999, p. 132) on 200 career women from a working-class background indicated that parental support toward careers and postponement of marriage had been crucial in shaping their views and future success. Maxwell and Maxwell (1994) also lend support to the general finding that socio-economic status and education are linked. Both male and female students attending private schools have higher than average educational aspirations. The effect is more marked for girls who aspire to achieve a higher level of education than even their fathers do and a significantly higher level than their mothers do. They also plan to work even after getting married. Thus, private schools are an avenue through which a select group of women can gain entry into the national elite. This, however, will only perpetuate the existing class hierarchies and will do nothing for those students who are still battling against general structural barriers.

British studies also find that both social class and gender influence teens' educational choices. Social class differences exist in vocational choices as well, with working-class adolescent males aspiring to skilled manual trades and girls aspiring to the traditional fields of nursing, office work, child care, and hairdressing. Middle-class boys also still show a preference for engineering, while middle-class girls aspire to teaching. Subject choices in secondary schools are likewise differentiated, with middle-class boys and girls studying physics, middle-class girls studying biology, and working-class boys and girls studying general sciences. These choices are linked to their career aspirations in either high-status jobs (middle-class boys and some girls), middle-status jobs (middle-class girls and some boys), or lower-status jobs (working-class boys and girls). Thus, the traditional gender and social class patterns still hold, with middle-class boys tending toward the highest status choices and aspirations (Charles, 2002, pp. 89–90).

Social class and gender differences figure prominently in the educational achievements of British adolescents. Indeed, it has been noted that differences continue from the 1970s to the present:

> At each level of education the sex-gap is bigger for the working class than the middle class and the class-gap is bigger for girls than for boys. As the level of education rises the sex-gap widens for both classes, but widens more for the working class. The class-gap also widens for both sexes, but more for girls than for boys. (King, 1971, p. 171, in Charles, 2002, p. 92)

Studies of middle-class and working-class girls show that they are subjected to different types of regulation. Middle-class girls are expected to excel in school, both by parents and teachers. They have extensive social and cultural capital throughout their lives. One

British White, middle-class girl (Walkerdine et al., 2001, p. 179, in Aapola et al., 2005, p. 87) reflected on the pressure to perform well:

> I had musicianship classes, orchestra, I actually had more orchestra, choir, quartet, quintet, piano lessons, violin lessons … if you do something and you don't do it well … I didn't do it well, you didn't want people to think that I couldn't do something well. If I can't—if I couldn't do it well I wouldn't do it at all.

Working-class girls are subjected to different types of controls and much lower expectations and less support from educators and their families who are not as able to provide them with enrichment as the middle-class parents. If they succeed, they tend to feel like outsiders in the world they have reached through their education (Aapola et al., 2005, pp. 87–88).

Charles (2002, pp. 99–100) also concurs that British girls' behaviours in schools are in keeping with what they can realistically expect outside of schools. Since marriage and motherhood are still valued over education and paid employment in their lives, especially among working-class girls, they develop strategies that are in keeping with this, including downplaying their academic talents and spending time attracting boys. That this is the case is supported by at least one study from the 1990s (Darling & Glendinning, 1996, in Charles, 2002, p. 100), which showed that when job opportunities are more widely available, middle-class girls are more likely to choose traditional male subjects at school.

Racialized and Immigrant Youth

Nearly one in three immigrants who arrived in Canada in the 11 to 15 years prior to 2006 held a bachelor's degree. In 2006, 58 percent of recent male immigrants and 49 percent of recent female immigrants held a minimum of a bachelor's degree, surpassing the graduation rates of Canadians (Galarneau & Morissette, 2008, p.6).

Notably, trends among immigrants indicate levels of education that were not necessarily gained while in Canada, but are a result of Canada's immigration policies, which select for immigrants with higher levels of education. Therefore, it is important to look at the specifically Canadian educational experiences of racialized and ethnic minorities. One significant finding is that there is a high incidence of poverty among immigrant children, reported at 48 percent among recent arrivals (within the past five years) by Campaign 2000 (2012, p. 12), a coalition of anti-poverty groups. When counting all immigrants, it has been found that "30 percent of all immigrant children live in families whose total income falls below the official poverty line" (Beiser et al., 1999, in Anisef & Kilbride, 2000, p. 13). There is a strong link between the negative and marginalized employment experiences of parents and pressure on their children to drop out of school. Therefore, it is suggested that Band-Aid solutions are insufficient; it is not enough to offer language classes to newcomer youth; closer links are needed between the home and school, and the education system itself must accommodate the diverse needs better. Further, difficulties in school also stand in the way of successful employment of minority youth. Some studies suggest, for example, that the educational programs devised to aid the transition from school to employment may in fact unnecessarily label minority youth as "at risk," which reduces employers' willingness to engage them (Anisef & Kilbride, 2000, pp. 25–26). Starting school can be difficult for immigrant youth and many described it as "sink or swim"—a quick adjustment required by demands to learn the language and make friends. This allows youth to adjust to the host society much faster than their parents (Canadian Council on Social Development, 1999/2000, p. 14).

According to the Canadian Council on Social Development (1999/2000), immigrant youth in the age group 15–19 are as likely as Canadian-born youth to stay in school. Further, those in the age group 20–24 are more likely than Canadian-born youth to be in school. More recent immigrant youth in this age group are more likely than Canadian-born youth to be enrolled in educational institutions.

However, we have to note the range of ethnic groups and racial minorities embedded in the more general group of "immigrant youth." In his analysis of the 1996 Census in relation to Toronto, Ornstein (2000, p. 51) notes that groups with low chances of dropping out include Caribbeans and Indo-Asians, the Japanese, Koreans, West Asians, Europeans, Germans, Ukrainians, and Jews. In contrast, there are groups for whom high school non-completion is a particular problem. The Central Americans and Portuguese stand out, with nearly 30 percent of young people without high school diplomas or not in full-time school attendance.

The low educational rates of Portuguese-Canadian youth have long been a subject of concern. This lack of progress has been explained by the eagerness of Portuguese parents to have economic success, which was to be obtained by every family member's participation in wage work. Thus, children's schooling is sacrificed to their early entry into the labour force. Furthermore, parents have a problem communicating with the schools because of their lack of proficiency in English. However, these patterns were more prevalent in the 1970s, and have begun to change, at least in Vancouver, where Portuguese parents have shown high educational aspirations for their children (Arruda, 1993, pp. 16–18).

American studies find that immigrant status seems to increase parental aspirations for children's education (Kao, 2002). Asian-American students score consistently higher on standardized tests of mathematics ability, have higher grade point averages, and attend four-year colleges at higher rates than do students of other racialized minorities (Goyette & Xie, 1999). Goyette and Xie (1999) found that when treated as a homogeneous group, all Asian-American groups had higher educational expectations on average than Whites. However, when different ethnic heritages and histories are taken into account, differences emerge. Their study found that differences in educational expectations reflect socio-economic characteristics, measures of academic ability, and parental expectations. The higher income levels among Filipinos, Japanese, and South Asians explain a large part of their higher expectations compared to Whites. Standardized measures of academic ability are linked with high educational expectations of Chinese, Koreans, and Southeast Asians, but not of Filipinos or Japanese. The authors suggest that though there seem to be different pathways toward higher educational expectations, it may be that the generally higher expectations of Asians reflect a commonality and may be a "conscious strategy to overcome racial discrimination and achieve upward mobility" (Goyette & Xie, 1999, p. 33).

Other American studies (Kao, 2002) have also found variations in parental educational aspirations among race and ethnic minorities in the United States. Generally, minority parents are found to have high educational aspirations for their children. Measured as parental hopes that their 8th graders will graduate from college, Asians (80 percent) have the highest and Hispanics (50 percent) the lowest parental aspirations, while Black and White parents fall in between (60 percent). The high aspirations of Asian-American parents are combined with a higher level of savings than among other families with similar incomes. Kao (2002) also concludes that parental optimism about their children's education helps minority youth boost their own aspirations. Additionally, the saving patterns of Asian-American parents help explain the increases in Asian-American enrolment in higher education that go counter to the prevailing links between low socio-economic status and low educational achievements.

Kim (2002) found that Korean-American families have high expectations regarding their children's educational achievement, even in the face of limited financial ability. In fact, the lower the family income, the higher the expectations. Kim and Rohner (2002) also found that parental—and especially maternal—involvement was quite high, particularly among educated parents, with the children doing generally well in school.

It is unequivocally evident from studies in all three countries in question that racialized status matters in educational experiences and outcomes. Anisef (1994, pp. 8–9) reports that (with the exception of Asian students) Canadian racialized students perform generally more poorly in the school system. It has been found in Ontario that racialized students are more likely to be streamed into non-university tracks in high school, to be put in special education classes, or to be suspended. They are also more likely to drop out of school (Anisef & Kilbride, 2000; Sefa Dei, 1993).

Black Canadian students continue to face difficult educational circumstances. Sherwood (1993) reports that in the late 1980s, 76 percent of Asian students in grade 9 were in advanced programs in high school, whereas the comparative figure is 65 percent of White students and 45 percent for Black students. Meanwhile, 21 percent of the Black students, 9 percent of Whites, and 3 percent of Asians were enrolled in basic-level programs. Similar results were reported in the mid-1980s in the North York Board of Education in Toronto. While 55 percent of the White children were enrolled in advanced programs and only 15 percent in basic or vocational programs, the corresponding figures for Black students were 4 percent and 60 percent respectively (Christensen & Weinfeld, 1993, p. 31; also see Brand & Bhaggiyadatta, 1986, p. 282). In their analysis of the 1986 Census results, Christensen and Weinfeld (1993, p. 34) found that both male and female Blacks in the age group 15–24 have lower-than-average high school graduation, college entrance, and Bachelor's degree completion rates. The particularly difficult situation of young Black women students has been noted (African Heritage Educators' Network and the Ontario Women's Directorate, 1996, p. 3).

The legacy of colonialism and racism is also evident in the education gap of Aboriginal youths in Canada. They have made some modest gains from the mid-1980s to the mid-1990s; for example, more of them complete high school, and more attend and complete post-secondary education. However, gaps between Aboriginal and other Canadians are still grave. Based on 1996 Census data, Aboriginal peoples were 2.6 times more likely than the non-Aboriginal population to not complete high school. There was some slight improvement at the post-secondary level in 1996 compared with 1986. In 1996, Aboriginal peoples aged 20–29 were 50 percent less likely to complete their education than the same age group of average Canadians. The comparable figure was 60 percent less likely in 1986. At 21 percent, Aboriginal women have a slightly higher college completion rate than men, 19 percent of whom have completed a college degree. These rates were slightly more favourable among the Métis than among First Nations or the Inuit, who are more likely to live in remote or northern communities and thus have less access to post-secondary education. Generally, those in urban areas are more likely to have higher educational levels than those living in rural areas (H. Tait, 2000, pp. 258–259; see also Statistics Canada, 1998a; Van Wert, 1997).

The problems that Black and Aboriginal students face relate to poverty and lack of access to employment opportunities (Van Wert, 1997; African Heritage Educators' Network and the Ontario Women's Directorate, 1996, p. 3; Davies & Guppy, 1998, p. 135). Poverty is particularly prevalent in minority families in general. Black children are 2.5 to 3 times more likely than the Canadian average to be living in lone-parent family households, which are characterized by low incomes. This is even more pronounced among Canadian-born Blacks than foreign-born Blacks (Christensen & Weinfeld, 1993, p. 41).

The role of low socio-economic status in the educational fates of American Hispanic youth has, likewise, been noted. For example, low-income and Hispanic students' college enrolment lag behind those of their American White peers. Hispanic students also struggle with college costs more than other students. Banerji (2004, p. 10) states that "for every $1000 increase in annual tuition, 6 to 8 percent of the Hispanic population loses access to higher education."

Black students' academic underachievement is particularly well documented in American studies (Codjoe, 2006; Smith, Schneider & Ruck, 2005). The most common stereotype of Black students is that they are "loud, lazy, muscular, criminal, athletic, dumb, deprived, dangerous, deviant, and disturbed" (Niemann et al., 1998, p. 104, quoted in Codjoe, 2006, p. 34). They fall short on a number of school performance indicators, including test scores, grades, high school completion and dropout rates, and disciplinary action (Smith, Schneider & Ruck, 2005, p. 347). The most common explanation for these is the cultural-ecological explanation, which blames Black students' lack of success on their mentality of low achievement, which in turn is both an adaptive response to the barriers they face and perceive in their lives, and a way of maintaining their collective identity (Ogbu et al., 1978, 1987, 1993, in Smith, Schneider & Ruck, 2005, pp. 347–348). For example, Seyfried and Chung (2002) suggest that African-American parents' and their children's past school experiences stand in the way of sustaining high educational expectations. This approach presents Black students' academic achievement in terms that are incompatible with their Black identity. In contrast, more recent studies suggest quite the opposite, i.e., that not only are Black identity and academic achievement compatible, but that a strong and healthy identity is essential for academic success (Smith, Schneider & Ruck, 2005, p. 348).

As indicated above, parental encouragement and expectations are widely linked to student aspirations and achievement (Wang et al., 1996). Family influence, and specifically perceived parental support, is "the most consistent predictor of students' educational outcomes" in Canada, whereas American studies have found that peers and neighbourhoods are a stronger predictor. This does not mean that Canadian Blacks aren't subject to economic hardship, but they are less likely than American Blacks to be segregated in large, poverty-stricken neighbourhoods. The negative influence of peers on academic achievement of American Blacks was not found in Canada. Further, the extent of peer influence on American Blacks has been questioned of late through studies that focus on the school's role in the marginalization of Black children and youth (Smith, Schneider & Ruck, 2005, p. 356).

With regard to Britain, Rex (1982, pp. 58–71; also see Cross, 1982) points out that the educational system into which immigrant children enter is rife with social class differences. Through the overlap of social class and immigrant status, there is an education gap between immigrant children and those in the upper classes and in the working class. Significant differences in the histories of specific populations also spell traditionally different educational pathways for minority youth. Thus, for example, children of particularly well-to-do immigrants from India do well in schools as they are from large empires that have a history of long-term migration and command of the English language. They also have a culture centred on the role of the family, which serves as a support system. In contrast, West Indian children arrive from a different legacy of colonialism and slavery. They are more likely to be uniformly in the working class and have a history of forcible adjustment to their past masters' language and culture. Therefore, these children in the school system are worse off. Only a small number in the 1980s made it through the school system and, much to everyone's surprise, they did so with better grades than their White English counterparts. Nevertheless, large numbers of them ended up in remedial or disciplinary classes, left school earlier, and ended up in a racist and unwelcoming labour market.

Though there is a historic gap in the educational performance of Whites and ethnic minorities, a youth cohort study conducted in 1999 revealed that this gap is narrowing in England and Wales (Department for Education and Employment, UK, 1999). Asian youth (particularly Indian) and Black youth were more likely to be studying for higher education qualifications than White people and were more likely to be studying for qualification overall. The highest full-time education attendance of 16-year-olds was recorded for Asians (86 percent) while it was 82 percent for Blacks and 67 percent for Whites. Also, the grade-based performance of Indian and Chinese students was higher than that of Whites.

At the same time, education gaps seem to be quite high within some ethnic groups in Britain, with high proportions of highly educated but equally high rates of no educational credentials. For example, nearly a third of Pakistanis and almost half of Bangladeshis had no qualifications (National Statistics, 2002; see also Rex, 1982).

As is by now evident, immigrant status, race, and cultural origins intersect with gender and social class in complex ways. For example, in all ethnic groups in Britain, girls outperform boys (Charles, 2002, p. 92). One study found that, in 1999, girls outperformed boys in every ethnic group, with the highest performance by Indian girls and boys overall (National Statistics, 2002). Charles (2002, pp. 92–93) summarizes results from a survey from the late 1990s showing that educational performance is widely varied among different ethnic groups, that there is variation based on gender, and that the gender gap is different based on ethnic group. South Asians performed on par with Whites, while West Indians fell behind. Among South Asians, Pakistani and Bangladeshi youth do poorly, with the young Bangladeshi women doing the worst. In comparison, young Caribbean men do worse than White men and worse than Caribbean women, but fare better in comparison with the Pakistani and Bangladeshi males. These kinds of studies point to the importance of considering the complexities of gender and ethnicity, as well as social class, in educational outcomes.

In the United States as well, "women from all racial and ethnic groups are attaining higher levels of schooling than men" (Lopez, 2002, p. 67). A particularly notable trend in American racism related to education is stereotypes linked to Blackness and gender. While young Black males are viewed as criminally suspect and therefore not interested in education, Black women are stigmatized about their sexuality, which supposedly leads them away from education. In fact, at least one researcher found that the young second-generation Dominican, West Indian, and Haitian women in New York City responded to their stigmatized racialization by "affirming their commitment to furthering their education as a means of combating racism and sexism" (Lopez, 2002, p. 80). Furthermore, these women's responses reflected the important role their mothers had in their educational aspirations. Their mothers' hardships in bringing their children to the United States provided them with a contrast that encouraged educational achievement.

One recent Canadian study (Smith, Schneider & Ruck, 2005, pp. 355–356) confirms that in Canada, as well as in the United States, females do generally better in school, and that Black females in particular do better in school than Black males. This tends to be explained in the literature by several factors, including the lack of role models for Black males, particularly in the primary grades where teachers tend to be women; differences in teachers' perception and treatment of Black male and female youth; and the bigger negative impact of economic disadvantage on Black males than females. Smith, Schneider and Ruck (2005) found in their study of Black students that the more recent Caribbean immigrant population in Toronto was more optimistic about their education and their future than the long-term Halifax population that had faced racist barriers for centuries. This research is also in line with the generally more optimistic stance of recent immigrants, also confirmed in American studies.

The Hidden Curriculum

A major part of the reason for the continuation of unequal education patterns and experiences lies in the institutionalization of classism, racism, and sexism manifested in a pro-middle-class and Eurocentric male mentality that dominates the educational system. These biases are often captured under the general term "hidden curriculum" (Deem, 1980, in Mandell & Crysdale, 1993, p. 33). The term includes a range of dominant attitudes, values, norms, and practices by educators and administrators that create a cultural and social ethos within the academic institution that prevents the full and equal participation of subdominant groups (Henry & Tator, 1994). Among these are: course streaming (or "tracking"), invisibility of one's group in educational materials and among faculty and students, discriminatory practices by guidance counsellors, and lack of teachers' positive attention and encouragement, as well as generally discriminatory attitudes by educators, administrators, and peers (Côté & Allahar, 1994, p. 89; Mandell & Crysdale, 1993; Anisef, 1994, pp. 9–12; Henry & Tator, 1994; Anisef & Kilbride, 2000; Sefa Dei, 1993).

For example, studies have established the presence of Eurocentrism in educational content and materials, evident in the neglect of the history, geography, social science, science, literature, and culture of anyone who is not in the White mainstream. Mostly, however, the hidden curriculum is about pedagogy, including overt and covert biases toward specific student populations, manifested in expectations and evaluations of those students. It is noted, for example, that assessment and placement practices often stream non-White students into lower academic categories (Henry et al., 2000, pp. 233–244; Hébert, 2001, p. 161). According to Hébert (2001, p. 161), in schools, "a multitude of timeless voices, texts, events, practices, and gestures tell minority students that they are intellectually, emotionally, physically, and morally inferior."

The hidden curriculum includes the values, assumptions, and expectations of educators, and the social and physical environment of the educational institution. The physical and social environment includes a wide assortment of items ranging from the choice of which holidays to celebrate, the content of school-based cultural and club activities, and acceptable behaviours (e.g., whether racial harassment is tolerated or not) (Henry et al., 2000, pp. 236–244). A typical experience has to do with not being able to identify with school celebrations as narrated by Dayna (James, 2003, pp. 77–78), a Jewish student in a Christian-dominated school:

> Although there may have been diversity in my school, it was overpowered by the large Christian white population. We always had Christmas plays and decorations that celebrated the Christian holidays. I always felt left out and different from my friends. We would have door-to-door decorating contests at Christmas and the entire school would look like a Christmas pageant but the staff never seemed to celebrate other holidays. I remember in Grade 11 math, I had a test on a holiday that I couldn't be at school for. It really irked me that a teacher could not look past her calendar to see that her test was on a day that Jewish people viewed one of the holiest of the year. My cousin lived in a more predominantly Jewish area, and at their high school, the cafeteria served matzo bagels during Passover. It always bothered me that my school barely acknowledged other religions at all, especially mine.

In Canada, secondary school guidance counselling has been specifically identified as highly problematic in the way this process sustains and promotes traditional career choices based on gender (Russell, 1987; Cassie et al., 1981, in Guttman & Alice, 1991). It has been suggested that the counselling processes limit young women in several ways, by (1) not having female counsellors available for female students, (2) not having an appropriate range of career information available for women, (3) not having ready access to career programs designed for women, and (4) not providing support for non-traditional careers for women. New innovations in the career counselling programs have begun to address the problems in the last two decades (Cassie et al., 1981, in Guttman & Alice, 1991).

The general educational environment reproduces traditional gender divisions. Feminist scholars have shown that there is pressure from male peers and teachers that creates an unwelcoming classroom and school environment. This unwelcoming character of educational institutions in general and of traditionally male disciplines in particular is referred to as a "chilly climate" (Mandell & Crysdale, 1993, p. 21; Reynolds, 1998, p. 237). In the educational system, girls and young women get the message that they are not welcome, and that they do not matter as much as boys and young men do. It is typical that in classrooms, males get more attention and approval and help from teachers than females do (Larkin, 1994, pp. 49–53; Reynolds, 1998, p. 237). In universities particularly, women who venture into the traditional male bastions of physical sciences and engineering face a hostile environment that is antithetical to learning. Women tend to receive less attention and less feedback than male students from the predominantly male faculty. They are also more likely to face disparaging comments about their work or their commitment to studies, or comments that focus on their appearance rather than performance. Young women are likely to be counselled to pursue lower career goals than men. As graduates, they are less likely to get faculty support, such as co-publications. Furthermore, women who interrupt their studies or attend part-time while raising children are not taken seriously.

British studies confirm that schools are traditionally more receptive to boys than girls. Classrooms are places for reinforcing traditional gender-based behaviours. Thus, even similar behaviours by boys and girls are interpreted differently. Whereas boys are expected to be noisy and disruptive and challenge teachers, such behaviour in girls is discouraged because it's not in keeping with traditional femininity. Furthermore, boys get more attention than girls in the classroom. Teachers and boys, therefore, act as police to check that girls behave in acceptable ways. Thus, even though we need to consider social class and ethnic variations, schools teach children about gender hierarchies and power relations (Charles, 2002, pp. 97–100, 106).

Charles (2002, pp. 103–106) also points out that masculine identities are shaped through the school experience. British studies identify multiple types of masculinities and masculine subcultures in the school environment, ranging from "macho lads" to "academic achievers" and "new enterprisers," all of whom are working class, heterosexual, and from multiple ethnic backgrounds. Additionally, there is a group of "real Englishmen" who are White and middle-class, and share the macho lads' disdain for academics. By and large, all masculinities are wrapped up in being heterosexual and "cool," which stands in contrast with school achievement, which is seen as a threat to traditional masculinity and is likely to be perceived in heterosexist and homophobic terms.

As indicated, one area of criticism relates to school curricula and testing practices, particularly as it pertains to racialized groups. Generally, African-American students tend to underperform in standardized school tests compared to White students. In their criticism of such standardized tests, Edwards, Gonsalves, and Willie (2000) point to biases in their content against disadvantaged populations. The American educational system is punitive toward minorities, in denying diplomas and holding back grades from students whose performance in biased standardized tests is less than satisfactory. Schools are generally failing African-American students by a lack of attention to their different pedagogical needs and their need for material and human resources.

Perkins (2005, pp. 108–109) developed a typology of American teachers based on their approaches to Black students (see Box 4.2). Of the types of educators, Perkins argues, only the Social Advocate is appropriate to teach Black students, but is also the rarest type.

Interestingly, unlike gender discrimination, which goes largely undetected by young people, race and cultural discrimination are more clearly identified. In a Canadian Advisory Council on the Status of Women survey (Holmes & Silverman, 1992, p. 45), only a minority of young men and women identified gender discrimination as a problem, whereas discrimination based on race and ethnicity was recognized more readily.

Box 4.2: Teachers and Black Students

Perkins (2005, pp. 108–109) characterizes American teachers of Black students as belonging in one of eight categories, including:

1. Benevolent Misfit allows benevolent attitude toward Black students to compensate for an inability to teach them.
2. Frustrated Cynic is repulsed by having to teach Black students and constantly complains about the school system, but does nothing to improve it.
3. Confirmed Racist hates Black students.
4. Social Technician uses Black students as guinea pigs to reinforce deficit concepts.
5. Bureaucratic Freak is addicted to regulations and has no flexibility.
6. Social Advocate believes Black students can achieve and works diligently to provide them with a quality education.
7. Chronic Apologist makes excuses for everything that goes wrong in the classroom.
8. Accommodationist is willing to go along with any policy, regardless of its effect on Black students.

One issue that emerges in schools in relation to immigrant youth is the primacy put on the mainstream way of speaking English. Like other languages, English is spoken in a variety of ways, yet there is normative English that is acceptable and anything else is seen as an accent. In Canada, schools offer English as a Second Language (ESL) classes, which are a useful way for immigrant and non-English-speaking youth to develop their ability. However, many English-speaking children are also sent to ESL classes because of their accents even though they speak fluent yet accented English (Scott, 2003). One Caribbean female in Toronto said:

> I already knew English. But when I came here I could understand them, but they could not understand me. They wanted to put me into an ESL program, probably because I had an accent and spoke fast. (Scott, 2003, pp. 112–113)

Furthermore, Black students have reported (African Heritage Educators' Network and the Ontario Women's Directorate, 1996, p. 3) the following experiences:

- I told my teacher that I wanted to be a lawyer but she said that I should be a cook because the food I prepared for the school event was good.
- I was pushed into sports and my schoolwork suffered.
- I told my teacher that I was interested in law but she said I should be an actor.
- I was counseled to drop math without being told how it would affect my
- chances to go to university.
- My guidance counselor told me that I should be a hairdresser.

In the late 1990s, the Canadian Council on Social Development (2000) ran focus groups of a total of 50 immigrant youth aged 15–24 in Toronto, Montreal, and Vancouver. The study found that most of the participants, and almost all of those who were of visible minorities, had experienced bigotry and racism in Canada:

> The issue of racism was raised spontaneously in all of the focus groups. Often it arose as part of the discussions about negative aspects of Canada. Younger participants in particular felt that … teachers could be racists. Even participants who did not raise the issue themselves and those who had not faced racism from teachers agreed that certain teachers and school administrators seemed to single out certain students or groups of students for harsher treatment based on their ethnicity. "I have a teacher who hates the Hispanic kids." "Teachers don't like me because I'm Greek." "I had a teacher who deducted 20 points from an oral presentation I gave because of my accent. She said that she marked everyone on their diction and she was going to treat me just like the others because it was the only way I was ever going to learn." "If a white kid does something and I do the same thing, there is no question that I'm going to get into worse trouble. In fact, teachers don't even bother with me. I go to the principal's office for the slightest offence."

Interesting links appear between gender and race, reflecting the studies of school performance reported above. British studies find that Black Caribbean families strive to support their daughters' educational aspirations, and these young women grow up with higher occupational aspirations than their mothers (Mizra, 1992, in Charles, 2002, pp. 100–102; Aapola et al., 2005, pp. 88–89; Fuller, 1982, pp. 87–99). This trend in high educational aspirations and motivations is, in many ways, contradictory as these young women have to make their way through the racist and sexist school system. Girls who aspire to non-traditional areas or non-gendered occupations are discouraged with messages by educators that their aspirations are "unrealistic" (Mizra, 1992, in Charles, 2002, pp. 100–102).

Yet another aspect of the hidden curriculum is the lack of role models of students' backgrounds in schools. Fuller (1982, p. 91) reports that in the UK, some of the Black Caribbean girls find role models in woman teachers who had "made it." In the American context, Howard (2002) reports that Black students tend to generally respond positively to Black teachers who can establish connections with students based on an understanding of their family lives and communities.

Anti-racist Education

As seen in the multitude of literature on youth and education, there is a general tendency to overemphasize negative experiences, particularly in research on Black youth's education. In contrast, Codjoe (2006, p. 33) examined the success stories among Black American youth, showing that "pride in one's heritage and knowledge of one's culture contribute to academic success."

This type of anti-racist education strategy was first formulated in Great Britain and the United States, and appeared in Canada in the late 1980s. The aim of anti-racist educational reform is to eliminate discrimination in institutional and organizational policies and practices (Henry et al., 2000, pp. 250–251). Various strategies are used to accomplish this, such as teaching Black heritage and history, including personal stories of resistance; emphasizing the positive aspects of being Black; and stressing education (Calliste, 1996; Brand & Bhaggiyadatta, 1986; Perkins, 2005, pp. 93–116). Codjoe's (2006) research and call for action (see Box 4.3) are in contrast with the well-demonstrated racial inequalities and the neglect of Black cultural values in North American school curricula. Black students are failing because schools fail to engage in more inclusive cultural practices.

Some youth are also active in grassroots anti-racist organizations. In reaction to persistent racism in Nova Scotia, Black high school youth organized themselves into the Cultural Awareness Youth Group (CAYG) in 1979. Most of the participants are high school students aged 15–19, the majority are female, and most come from communities where segregation, accompanied by unemployment, lack of recreation, and isolation, are major problems. Since its foundation, the CAYG has organized a number of events for Black youth and the wider community in schools and other venues.

Box 4.3: Helping Black Students Succeed

The direct quote below comes from Codjoe (2006, p. 48), who calls for changes in schools' practices. These issues are most recently reflected in the controversial calls for Afrocentric schools.

> From the narratives of students, I provide this summary of a critical factor that is significant in contributing to the academic success of black students.
>
> A secured, clarified and developed self-identity and pride in African cultural/racial identity positively affects academic success of students by
>
> - serving as an important buffer against racism and devaluation of African peoples
> - providing students with requisite coping skills
> - affirming that black students do not need to "act White" in order to succeed academically
> - providing the appropriate cultural foundation for learning via an African-centered learning environment.
>
> [B]lack students affirm their culture, heritage and identity by
>
> - an awareness of and pride as African-Canadians
> - a demonstrated depth of knowledge about black and African history, politics, literature, arts and culture
> - seeking a culturally-based education
> - participating in black organizations and community activities.

Some of them are annual, and focus on Black history and culture, as well as contemporary issues faced by Black people (National Film Board, 1992). In the words of Shingai, a member of CAYG:

> There has been a black community in Nova Scotia for over three hundred years, but you wouldn't know it by the history books. You won't find our faces on the post cards, you won't find our statues in the parks. The only time white people seem to notice us is when they want to call us "nigger" and say we've got an attitude. Well, my name is Shingai, and my attitude is this: You don't have to be from Scotland to have a history. (National Film Board, 1992)

School Climate and Safety

There is a sense that particularly secondary and, increasingly, post-secondary schools have become a boot camp for school administrators and educators to instill law and order in the student population. As discussed in Chapter 2, schools are traditionally sites of citizenship education, a training ground for acceptable collective behaviour and common civic culture (Hébert, 2001, pp. 162–166). A part of these is the reliance on codes regarding appearance and conduct in educational institutions. For example, Raby (2005a, p. 5) argues that

> dress and discipline codes are sites through which subjectivities are created (e.g., the "respectable" student and the "responsible" citizen) and governance is individualized—creating students and future adults fitting for neo-liberal capitalism.

Raby's conclusion is based on her analysis of the Ontario government's Safe Schools Act, passed in 2000 and aimed at improving school safety and discipline, and mandating school boards to develop their codes of conduct, including dress codes and a zero-tolerance policy. This policy is aimed at controlling youth by instilling in them the idea of self-discipline, and promoting the creation of restrained and obedient workers for the capitalist economy.

The political climate in American schools has likewise become increasingly oppressive following the 9/11 attacks and a slate of well-publicized school shootings (e.g., Columbine). Giroux (2003, pp. 90–109) argues that in the 9/11 aftermath, schools have been turned more blatantly into "agencies of social and cultural reproduction." In the school reforms under George W. Bush's administration, "character" education was elevated over the ability to think and evaluate critically. The themes of "patriotism" and "moral education" were present in teaching, and following the rules was emphasized. The tone of Bush's school reform document, called *No Child Left Behind*, was one in which those values are presented against the fearful alternative of gun-toting children and youth intent on injuring themselves and others. New policing measures were put in place while nothing positive was done to school budgets, which were either cut or not increased. At the same time, the administration provided tax breaks to the tune of $1.6 trillion to corporations and the wealthier classes.

President Barack Obama's approach to education has been to focus on individuals' learning from "preschool to the day they start their careers" (Obama, 2013). In his plan, there is an increasing focus on standards of learning and teaching under the slogan "Race to the Top." This appears to be in keeping with the main values of America and the Western industrial world in general—individualism and competition—as discussed in previous chapters.

School Violence, Bullying, and Harassment

School violence and bullying are terms that are used in the media constantly. Extreme criminal and violent elements—in the form of well-publicized yet rare instances of school shootings—will be addressed in the later chapter on youth delinquency and violence. In this segment, the focus will be on bullying and harassment.

A 1998 national health survey in Canada (King, 1998; in Bibby, 2001, p. 83) found the self-reported rate of bullying (defined as physical, verbal, or psychological intimidation) to be just under 30 percent among grade 10 students, and males were disproportionately represented among the victims. Bullying was found to be cyclical; in other words, bullies are likely to have been bullied in their past.

Another survey done in Alberta in 1999 by the Canadian Research Institute for Law and the Family found that 40 percent of grade 9 students and 32 percent of grade 12 students said they had slapped, punched, or kicked someone in the past year. Over half of the students said they had been victimized at least once in school, and nearly the same number had been victimized outside of school. Approximately 16 percent said they had brought weapons to school, the most common ones being knives or replica weapons (plastic guns, bats, clubs), and least common being handguns and pellet guns (Bibby, 2001, p. 85). Bibby's (2001, pp. 78–79) survey of teens found that large numbers of them, and particularly girls (59 percent compared to 40 percent of boys), think that school violence is a "very serious" problem.

Bibby (2001, pp. 84–86) is critical of the way in which adults in recent years, as compared to youth themselves, have raised the bar on what defines school violence. It is reasonable to punish young people for serious violence and use of weapons, but the typical punitive reactions exert a measure of control (such as increased police presence) on youth in schools under a zero-tolerance approach that is unwarranted by the extent of actual serious violence.

A notable major flaw with the debate regarding bullying is that it makes it appear as if every child and youth is at risk in schools. When this wide definition of the victim population is combined with the widest possible definition of violence, it creates a false sense that (1) all youth are running dangerously amok and need to be watched and policed; (2) violence in schools is a more important issue than violence against young people in their homes; and (3) violence has no specific structural patterns, but has to do with the personal or psychological qualities of the individual bully and the victim.

The latter point is particularly important when we consider the lack of attention to gender-based and/or sexual harassment or racial harassment in schools. It is interesting, to say the least, that comparatively small-scale instances of bullying and school violence are gaining media attention while more prevalent and structurally based expressions of sexism, racism, and homophobia are barely acknowledged.

Racialized students work very hard to try to fit in. Desai and Subramanian's (2000, pp. 118–161) study of South Asian youth in Toronto found that those in schools with a higher proportion of South Asian students were better adapted and self-confident than those in White-dominated schools. According to the Canadian Council on Social Development (2000), immigrant students note that cliques developed in high school along racial lines. The majority of the youth reacted to racism by ignoring it and by developing closer relationships with members of their own ethnic group.

The "chilly climate" for minorities in schools is starting to be acknowledged, including increased attention to racial harassment and hate activity on university campuses

(Henry et al., 2000, pp. 245–248). In a study of immigrant youth by the Canadian Council on Social Development (2000, p. 13), immigrant youth reported that racism in high schools is a problem. New arrivals in particular faced taunts and slurs based on their appearance and their accents.

One currently recognized concern is over boys' sexual harassment of girls. Sexism and harassment have been recognized in Britain as detrimental to girls' educational engagement and outcomes (Charles, 2002, pp. 100–101). American studies of sexual harassment in schools indicate that around 80 percent of secondary school girls report having been verbally and/or physically harassed by boys, while 60 percent of boys report sexual harassment with more reported verbal abuse and more commonly by other boys. Harassment typically occurs between adolescents who know one another rather than between strangers. Alarmingly, harassment is accepted by young people as a normal part of their school day. Mostly, girls tried to ignore it. Despite anti-harassment policies and rules in schools, intervention is not inevitable, and girls mostly have to deal with harassment on their own, manoeuvring their way through the aggression of boys (Tolman et al., 2003).

In Canada, Larkin's (1994; also see Nelson & Robinson, 1999, pp. 171–172) study reports a range of male behaviours aimed at girls, including comments on their body or appearance, sexual innuendo, and unwelcome touching. These are part of a behaviour pattern aimed at putting girls "in their place," and have negative consequences for adolescent girls' self-esteem and their sense of power in an education setting. In Ontario, Larkin's study and others (reported in Orton, 1999, p. 132) have found that 80 percent of female secondary school students reported being subjected to sexual harassment at school, compared with 30 percent of males, who reported being afraid of harassment by other males. Reportedly, 27 percent of Ontario high school girls have been pressured into unwanted sexual behaviours, and 46 percent reported being recipients of "unwanted sexual comments or gestures in the last 3 months" (CAMH Centre for Prevention Science, 2008, in Girls Action Foundation, 2011, p. 13).

Although it is possible that young men are less likely to report or admit fear, the results also indicate that harassment is seen as a serious issue by more young women than men. While sexual harassment of males does occur, it is not as prevalent as harassment of females. Further, based on traditional gender-based expectations, sexual harassment of females in high school is more likely to be perceived as either "natural or as a threat," whereas female harassment of males is more likely to seen as an "invitation" (Larkin, 1994, p. 35). The issue of sexual harassment in schools has also gained attention in the United States, as reported in Box 4.4.

The report from the American Association of University Women (2011) in Box 4.4 also points to the newest form of harassment, cyberbullying, defined as "sending or posting harmful or cruel text or images using the Internet or other digital communication devices" (Willard, 2004, p. 1, in Li, 2006, p. 2). This type of harassment has gained notoriety of late, with highly publicized incidents of suicide among school-aged bullying victims.

According to Statistics Canada (Perreault, 2011), young or single people, those who are homosexual or bisexual, and those with activity limitations are more likely to face cyberbullying. This large-scale survey found that "young adults between 18 and 24 years

---

Box 4.4: Crossing the Line

A new national study, *Crossing the Line*, reveals some staggering statistics on school sexual harassment. The survey was conducted by the American Association of University Women (2011), a nonprofit research organization whose mission is to advance equity for women and girls through advocacy, education, philanthropy, and research. A group of nearly 2,000 students across the United States were surveyed in May and June of 2011.

The study reveals some striking results, including the following:

- Nearly 50% of 7th to 12th graders experience sexual harassment
- 44% of students said they were harassed in person—subjected to unwelcome comments or jokes, inappropriate touching, or sexual intimidation
- 30% of students reported online harassment—unwelcome comments, jokes, or pictures via text, email, Facebook, and other tools, or having sexual rumours, information, or pictures spread about them
- 87% of those who experience harassment reported negative effects such as absenteeism, poor sleep, and stomach aches
- Girls reported being harassed more than boys—56% compared with 40%
- Boys were more likely to be the harassers
- Children from lower-income families reported more severe effects

---

of age were about three times more likely than those aged 25 and over to report having been the victim of cyber-bullying, at 17% versus 5%" (Perreault, 2011, p. 1).

As indicated above, young people who are gay, lesbian, bisexual, or transgender (LGBT) are likely to be the targets of disparaging behaviour and taunts, through virtual and face-to-face means. The 2009 National School Climate Survey by the Gay, Lesbian and Straight Education Network (GLSEN) found that 9 in 10 LGBT students experience harassment in schools: "84.6% of LGBT students reported being verbally harassed, 40.1% reported being physically harassed and 18.8% reported being physically assaulted at school in the past year because of their sexual orientation" (GLSEN, 2009). In the UK, recent reports indicate that 8 out of 10 gay youth have experienced harassment in schools, with a similar distribution of types of harassment as reported in the US (Morgan, 2012). Canadian surveys from 2009 also find high levels of harassment among LGBT youth, including verbal harassment (59 percent), physical harassment (25 percent), cyberbullying (31 percent), and generally feeling unsafe at school (73 percent) (CBC News, 2010).

The harassment of sexual minority youth and its detrimental academic, physical, and emotional effects have been demonstrated (Frank, 1994; Bishop & Casida, 2011). British studies show that while young women may face taunts about their sexual orientation if they show an interest in traditionally masculine areas of study (such as physical education or mechanics), boys (particularly working-class boys) in school are likely to face terms of abuse ("poofter" or "girl") if they take their school work seriously (Charles, 2002, pp. 104–106).

Frank's (1994) study of 14 White young men, aged 16–20 in a Canadian high school in 1987–1988, is an early examination of heterosexual privilege. The young men in this study are clear about "what it takes to be a man": sports, building your body, acting tough, and getting girls. Among the least acceptable behaviours were "acting like a girl," homosexuality, not doing sports, and being friends with girls. Negative reactions were likely to originate from male peers if one "acted like a girl" or a homosexual. Actions were to follow, including verbal, physical, and psychological abuse. These experiences are repeated in the daily lives of many sexual minority youth, and the culprits are not only other students, but also teachers and staff. A study done in California by McQuire et al. (2010, pp. 1182–1183) found that young transgendered people

> expressed a belief that schools were a place of considerable harassment and vic-
> timization for gender nonconforming and transgender youth. Reports of physical
> violence were common with descriptions of gender nonconforming youth (both
> masculine females and feminine males) being "pushed around," "getting the crap
> beat out of them," and "getting their asses kicked," by other students. Verbal harass-
> ment and "teasing" were also common. Peer rejection was another major theme.
> One participant reported, "I had some nasty people who were like 'Eww, that's
> gross'." It is possible that harassment served the function of reigning in or polic-
> ing the gender nonconformity of youth. One youth described the motives of the
> harassers: "they would do anything they can to take them out, to make them think
> that you … shouldn't be doing that."

Sexual harassment takes on additional overtones based on one's social class or race. Huerta (2007, p. 5; also see Tonnesen, 2013) points to the racial stereotypes and myths behind harassment, whereby some racialized women are targeted in specific and deroga-tory ways. For example, black women are depicted as "loose" and "hypersexual," and Hispanic women as "hot-blooded." These stereotypes, with their emphasis on sexuality, can result in harassing behaviors. Sexually and racially laced epithets and slurs are a part of the high school environment, and can leave a serious mark on a person's self-esteem (Larkin, 1994, pp. 28–29).

The end result of sexual harassment is that girls and young women get discouraged. They tend to underestimate their academic abilities and experience a decline in their aca-demic aspirations (Côté & Allahar, 1994; Larkin, 1994, pp. 101–115). There is a large body of research documenting that girls' self-esteem takes a significant plunge during late childhood and early adolescence. Additionally, academic performance (particularly in traditional male subjects) tends to decline (Nelson & Robinson, 1999, pp. 170–171).

However, harassed youth do not always remain completely passive victims. Although young women facing harassment are silenced in their fear, they also develop tactics for coping with and retaliating against harassment, including confrontation and public humiliation of the perpetrators (Larkin, 1994). One form of resistance more commonly documented by the popular media is the prom, where some sexual minority youth are making a point by taking their partners out publicly. There are reportedly official "queer proms" organized by activists in several Canadian cities (White, 2010). Some youth are challenging school authorities by taking a date to formal school proms, as exemplified by this story in the southern United States:

> Morgan Frieden, a 15-year-old girl in Huntsville, Ala., developed a "huge crush" as a sixth-grader on an eighth-grade girl just out of the closet, sending the entire school "into an uproar." By the time Frieden got to high school, she was even gutsier. Only a few teachers and students knew she was a lesbian when she arrived, but in the fall of her ninth-grade year, she took her girlfriend to the homecoming dance. "It was a blast!" says Frieden, who is now a sophomore. "We got a few evil looks, a few 'Ooh, can I butt in?' looks, and many 'Way to go!' looks." (Kirby, 2009, p. 29)

In the end, schools are not safe havens for a lot of students, particularly those who are underprivileged, female, homosexual, or racialized. Bullying and harassment are definitely an issue, but not in the randomized, individualized, and sensationalized ways they are being depicted. There are patterns to hateful behaviours, rooted in the general and tacit acceptance of unequal social relations in schools and other social institutions. While the notions of increased policing, codes of conduct, and proper attire are being peddled as solutions to the "discipline problem" in schools, there is no critical attention being paid to widely prevalent and systemic patterns of destructive behaviour rooted in fundamental inequalities. In the end, researchers suggest that only "zero tolerance" policies are effective, requiring the coordination of the efforts of schools, teachers, parents, and students (Holt & Espelage, 2007; Bishop & Casida, 2011).

Conclusions

Education is synonymous with being young. Adolescents are seen to belong in high schools, and those in their twenties belong in colleges and universities. Specifically, as argued by Côté and Allahar (1994), the expansion of the post-secondary education system in the second half of the 20th century signifies the prolongation of youth as a stage of life. However, despite the popular imagery of happy and fulfilled youth roaming the hallowed halls of colleges and universities, social class, gender, race, and ethnicity continue to determine one's access to, experience of, and success in the educational system. Dropping out of secondary education, ending up in serious debt through post-secondary education, and being excluded from school curricula are common experiences for youth who are not male or not fortunate enough to have been born into well-to-do, White families. Not only are many youth subjected to a range of overt and covert discriminatory practices by adults as educators and administrators, but they also mirror inequalities in behaviours among themselves in their peer relationships. The social life of the powerless in educational institutions can be unpleasant. These institutionalized patterns of advantage and disadvantage are likely to be perpetuated as young people situate themselves in the labour market, which will be the subject of the next chapter.

Critical Thinking Questions

1. What are the barriers that youth face in secondary and post-secondary education? How can these be overcome?
2. Do you think the college or university program you are enrolled in is gender-typed? How do you explain this?
3. Do you think separate race-based schools are a good idea? What about faith-based schools?

5 Work

> **In this chapter, you will learn that**
>
> - although young people are better educated than ever, their credentials don't always lead to well-paid and secure work
> - economic recessions are particularly detrimental to youth employment
> - young women, members of racialized and immigrant groups, and people with disabilities are particularly disadvantaged in the labour market
> - young people are unjustly blamed for their lack of professional advancement
> - unionization of young people is particularly challenging, due to their precarious work status
> - more young people combine ongoing education with paid work
> - some youth fall through the cracks and end up living on streets, engaged in marginalized work

Paid employment is encouraged among young people to build character and future employment prospects. Hopes are high among young people as they embark on their prolonged educational path with a view to attaining career success and financial stability. In reality, whether combining education and employment or in transition from education to full-time employment, young people face a range of problems that have less to do with their qualifications and preparedness for the labour market, and more to do with the structure of the economy.

This chapter will outline the central features of the youth labour market. The patterns of inequality that emerge in secondary and post-secondary education (outlined in the previous chapter) are mirrored in young people's work experiences. The streaming based on social class, gender, race, and ethnicity continues in the labour force. These divisions and the transient nature of the youth labour market reduce young people's chances of resisting the further deterioration of their work experience.

Youth Labour Markets

Some authors propose an "epistemological fallacy" among youth, referring to a mismatch between the way they conceptualize their lives and the actual constraints they operate under (Furlong & Cartmel, 1997, p. 4, in Thiessen & Blasius, 2002, p. 74). For example, Thiessen and Blasius (2002) analyzed the views of 1,209 youth aged 17 regarding their views of and aspirations for their future occupations in three different urban locations across Canada. They found that across the board, these young people all want and expect to hold professional jobs, though realistically, not all of them will. The one exception to this lack of realism was working-class boys in rural Nova Scotia, who expected to end up in the manual work that characterizes the region. Generally, the young people in the study were oblivious to the constraints of their social class position while some acknowledged the influence of gender on their choices.

This general ethos of unfettered choices is fuelled by popular media. Judging by the popularity of the many TV shows in the UK, the US, and Canada that select "ordinary people" as their stars, achieving fame and, with it, fortune, is an ever more popular daydream for youth who are tired of projecting into their distant futures the kind of security that comes with gradual academic and professional advancement. Monbiot (2006) reports that, in Britain,

> declining mobility is accompanied by rising expectations. In January [of 2006] the Learning and Skills Council found that 16% of the teenagers interviewed believed they would become famous, probably by appearing on a show like Big Brother. Many of them saw this as a better prospect than obtaining qualifications; 11% of them, if found, were "sitting around 'waiting to be discovered'." The council claimed that the probability of being chosen by Big Brother and of becoming rich and famous as a result is 30 million to one. But the promise held out to us is that it can happen to anyone. The teenagers seemed to believe it can happen to everyone.

In reality, the labour markets of the three countries have little good news to offer young people. The 1980s and 1990s were particularly characterized by "global economic restructuring, new technologies, unemployment and underemployment, the growth of low-tier service industries, and an increase in temporary, part-time and other 'flexible' forms of work" (Lowe & Krahn, 1994–1995, p. 3; also see Blanchflower & Freeman, 1998; Tannock, 2001, p. 4). Consequently, youth are facing a worsening labour market with fewer opportunities for good jobs that match their education, often captured in the term "precarious labour" (Panitch & Swartz, 2006, p. 347). Degrees and diplomas do not translate to good positions in the youth labour market. Most of the jobs offered are in the service sector, which utilizes young people as a pool of poorly paid, temporary, part-time, and flexible workers.

Globally speaking, there is reason for extreme concern over young people's labour market fates (see Box 5.1). The International Labour Organization's (ILO) statistics and projections are grim. However, they also reflect a stark global imbalance in that of the over 1 billion young people in the world, 85 percent live in developing countries. Those who are part of the economically fortunate 15 percent of the world's youth population may have reason to be encouraged. Indeed, the gross domestic products of the three countries—the US, the UK, and Canada—ranked first, second, and third position, respectively, among the G8 countries in 2004. It is particularly good news for Canada because its population is the smallest among the G8 nations (Statistics Canada, 2005b).

Box 5.1: Global Concern over Youth Employment

The International Labour Organization's 93rd Session of the International Labour Conference (ILO, 2005, p. 1) outlined the "key issues" in global youth labour market trends:

- Globally, less than half of the youth available for work had jobs in 2004.
- Many young people are underemployed as involuntary part-time employees, temporary (short-term) workers or in work of inadequate productivity.
- The vast majority of the world's youth work in the informal economy.
- An estimated 59 million young people aged 15 to 18 years are in hazardous forms of work worldwide.
- The youth unemployment rate is persistently high throughout the world, most recently estimated at 88 million young people or 47 per cent of the global unemployed, with young women in many countries more likely to be unemployed than young men.
- Youth unemployment rates are much higher than overall unemployment rates in all regions of the world. In every country for which ILO data are available, youth unemployment rates significantly exceed adults' unemployment rates.
- Sustained unemployment can make youth more vulnerable to social exclusion.
- Global labour force participation rates for young people decreased by almost four percentage points between 1993 and 2003, mainly the result of increasing numbers of young people attending school, staying longer in education and training, and withdrawing [from] or never entering the labour force.
- Particular groups of people, such as young women and men with disabilities, youth affected by HIV/AIDS, indigenous youth, demobilized young soldiers, young migrant workers and other socially disadvantaged youth are more prone to unemployment and underemployment, with many opting out of the labour force in countries where the possibility of reliance on social security payments exists.
- Some 238 million young people are living on less than US$1 a day and some 462 million young people are living on less than US$2 a day. This means that almost one-quarter of young people in the world (22.5 per cent of the world's population of 1.1 billion 15–24-year-olds) are in extreme poverty. On the broader measure of US$2 a day, over 40 per cent of all young people can be categorized as living in poverty (43.5 per cent of the 1.1 billion 15–24-year-olds).
- In 2015, 660 million young people will either be working or looking for work—an increase of 7.5 per cent over the number of youth in the labour force in 2003.

Additionally, the International Labour Organization's (ILO, 2013, pp. 1–2) update on the status of decent work for youth worldwide noted that the youth employment crisis is exacerbated by a skills mismatch, and that long-term unemployment is an "unexpected tax" on the youth of today. The ILO also noted that the 90 percent of youth living in the global South are particularly hard hit, lacking good employment opportunities.

Youth in the more fortunate countries of the global North, however, have little reason to celebrate. Though their situations are significantly better than those of their Third World counterparts, similar age-related inequalities prevail as revealed in the ILO's global statistics. From 2008 to 2012, the unemployment rate among youth in developed economies grew by 25 percent, or more than 2 million (ILO, 2013, p. 4). Worldwide, the difference between youth and adult unemployment rates has not changed much; in fact, the ratio was only 2.7 during 2013. As a result, young workers have three times the unemployment rate of adult workers (ILO, 2013, p. 3). In the US, the youth unemployment rate was 16.4 percent in March 2012, while in April 2013 the adult unemployment rate was 7.5 percent (OECD, 2013a; Bureau of Labor Statistics, 2013). In Canada in April 2013, the youth unemployment rate was 13.9 percent, while the adult unemployment rate was 7.2 percent (OECD, 2013a; Statistics Canada, 2013b).

In January–March 2013, 36 percent of all youths in the UK were economically inactive (National Statistics, 2013b). During the same time, the youth unemployment rate was 21.9 percent, while the adult unemployment rate was 7.8 percent (OECD, 2013a; National Statistics, 2013a). There are differences between the unemployment rates of young men (20.1 percent) and women (16.9 percent) in the age group 16–17, as of 2000 (Charles, 2002). When accounting for a slightly older age group of 16–24, men's unemployment was still quite high at 14.8 percent in 2013 (National Statistics, 2013b).

Further, the unemployment rates among British ethnic minority men are higher than those of ethnic minority women or White men (Charles, 2002, p. 112). In 2012, the youth unemployment rate for White men in London was 20.9 percent, while it was 47.5 percent for Pakistani youth males, 51.3 percent for any other Asian background, and 46.6 percent for Black/African/Caribbean/Black British people. These averages were calculated for three months ending in March 2012, with White male youth having the lowest unemployment and any other Asian background having the highest rate of unemployment during the studied period (National Statistics, 2012e).

Moreover, youth employment is extremely vulnerable to economic fluctuations. Among youth under the age of 25, unemployment was more severe in the 1990s than in the 1980s. Youth make up 35 percent of the unemployed, and their ranks among part-time workers in so-called "McJobs" in the lower-tier service sector are increasing. This has resulted in increasing numbers (64 percent of those 16–24 years of age) of young people living with and depending on their parents. Among others, Miles (2000, p. 43) confirms that "the period of dependency of youth has been extended by an extension of training and education, the shrinkage in the youth labour market and a reduction in state support."

Reflecting these diminishing returns, the notion of "Status Zero" youth has emerged in Britain to describe mid-teens youth who aren't engaged in education, training, or employment, and are in a marginalized status. Instead of choosing official paths toward economic security, they opt out from a system they see as not responding to their needs, and engage in informal sector employment or illegal activity. It is estimated that 16–23 percent of the age group 16–17 can be described as "Status Zero." They share a background of family "fracture" and violence, but not all are necessarily opposed to education or lack career aspirations. These youth blame their parents, politicians, and professionals for letting them down (Miles, 2000, pp. 43–45).

Young Canadians are also less likely to be employed and more likely to be unemployed than people over 25 (Archambault & Grignon, 1999; Jennings, 1998). In 2011, the employment rate for youths in Canada was 55.4 percent (Statistics Canada, 2012f), and the unemployment rate of youth aged 15–24 was 14.2 percent (Human Resources Development Canada, 2011). Teenagers tend to have higher unemployment rates than those in their early twenties: as of 2003, the age cohort of 15–19 had an unemployment rate of 18 percent, which was much higher than among those aged 20–24 at 11 percent (Service Canada, 2005). Young women's labour force participation rates and unemployment rates have historically tended to be a few percentage points lower than those of young men (Statistics Canada, 1999b), but in the age group 15–24, there has been a gender equalization of labour force participation since 2006 (Canadian Council on Social Development, 2007).

Echoing the "Status Zero" youth of UK is the growing proportion of non-student Canadian youth who are dropping out of the labour force (Jennings, 1998). Associated with this are ever-longer periods of unemployment among youth since the 1970s. The proportion of youth unemployed for more than a year increased threefold between 1976 and 1995 (Kerr, 1997).

An equally alarming feature of youth employment is the fact that high proportions of employed youth live in poverty. In the United States, official statistics from 2004 show that 5.8 percent of full-time employed youth aged 18–24 and 3.7 percent of those aged 25–34 in this category lived below the poverty level (US Census Bureau, 2007, Table 691). Indeed, a study by Bell et al. (2006) of six industrialized countries, including Canada, the US, and the UK, concludes that economic self-sufficiency among 18–34-year-old men and women has generally declined between the mid-1980s and the year 2000. This general pattern holds despite a relative stability in the employment and earning levels of American males aged 26–34 and American females aged 26 or over. The results will also have to be interpreted against inequalities based on race and ethnicity (addressed below) as well as levels of disability (see Box 5.2) where significant differences emerge in young people's labour market fates.

There is general agreement that youth employment is more sensitive to aggregate economic conditions, i.e., when the economy is poor, youth are more likely to suffer disproportionately in comparison with older age groups (Blanchflower & Freeman, 1998; Kerr, 1999), and youth labour markets are less likely to recover from economic downswings. While the numbers of jobs for Canadian adults increased by 1 million between 1992 and 1997, youth were offered 100,000 fewer jobs (Elton & Brearton, 1997). The economic upswing of the late 1990s brought youth employment rates up,

Box 5.2: Youth with Disabilities

An estimated 7–10 percent of the world's population consists of people with disabilities. Subject to social isolation, discrimination, and prejudice, they are among the poorest of the population. Their access to and success rates in education, training, and employment continue to be blocked:

> Society tends to view disability in isolation, that is, without reference to other social issues. Stigma and prejudice are perpetuated by schools, employers, society as a whole, and even by the families of disabled people. Due to the many misperceptions about disability, disabled youth are often seen as incapable of contributing to society. Employers tend to assume that a person with a disability is unable to handle the competitive work environment, and that hiring disabled people will create problems or necessitate additional investments and, therefore, result in higher costs for the company. (Roggero et al., 2006, p. 647)

Consequently, the levels of employment are lower and rates of unemployment and poverty are much higher among people with disabilities than in the general population. This is confounded by the great variation in definitions of disability, generally referring to some degree of loss or limitation of community or work opportunities due to physical or social barriers (Russell, 1996–1997). Statistics from Canada, the UK, and the US show that there is a big gap in the employment of people with disabilities as compared to those who don't have disabilities, amounting to 20–30 percentage points in each country (Office of Disability Issues, 2013; National Statistics, 2011c; Galarneau & Radulescu, 2009, p. 7; US Department of Labor, 2013a).

The differences in the employment and unemployment rates among young people with disabilities are less severe but equally significant. For example, in 2001, UK youth with disabilities in the age group 16–19 had an employment rate of 53.4 percent compared with 54.7 percent for non-disabled people. The comparable percentages for those aged 20–24 were 71.3 percent and 73.2 percent, respectively. The unemployment rate of disabled youth aged 16–24 in 2001 was 19.1 percent and 28.2 percent among disabled youth aged 25–34 compared to 9.6 percent and 22.9 percent in the same non-disabled age categories (Smith & Twomey, 2002). Among Canadian youth with disabilities, 30.5 percent of those aged 15–34 were unemployed within the previous year, based on reports from 2001. A high percentage (19.8 percent) of this age group also worked in non-permanent jobs (Canadian Council on Social Development, 2005). In the United States, as of 1999, the general labour force participation rate for people 18–64 years old was nearly 83 percent, but was only about 52 percent for those with disabilities, including youth. Moreover, only about 38.6 percent of Blacks and Hispanic/Latinos with disabilities are employed (National Council on Disability, 2000). These statistics are reflected in the overall low income levels of youth with disabilities in all three countries.

with an added 145,000 jobs, and led to a reduction in the youth unemployment rate (Statistics Canada, 2000c).

Youth were impacted globally by slow economic recovery in 2012 and 2013. The ILO notes that the inability to access jobs has led to a youth job crisis, and the length of waiting for employment has led some to give up. As well, those who are able to access employment are less selective about the type of employment, a trend that pre-existed the economic crisis. Thus, there has been movement toward precarious employment, including part-time work and temporary jobs. Globally, the unemployment rate for youth in 2013 was 12.6 percent (ILO, 2013, p. 1).

Earnings: Are Youth Too Greedy?

One persistent public image is that young people are lazy. Not only that, they are too inflexible and demanding in their expectations of starting-level jobs. In other words, youth themselves, and particularly their "excessive" demands and expectations, are to blame for youth unemployment. This argument has no bearing on reality. In fact, in virtually all OECD countries, including Canada, the UK, and the US, workers in the younger age groups experienced declines in their earnings relative to older workers in the 1990s (Blanchflower & Freeman, 1998), a trend that has continued in the early 21st century with increased youth poverty rates (OECD, 2013b).

The Canadian Economic Observer (Corak, 1999, p. 3.2) reported that in 1994 young men (aged 17–24) were earning the same as their counterparts in 1969. When inflation is accounted for, there was a 19 percent decline in the earnings of full-time working males aged 17–24 between 1979 and 1992, while there was a similar drop of 10 percent in the age group 25–34 (Picot & Myles, 2000, p. 131). Meanwhile, those in the age group 45–54 earned over 30 percent more than their counterparts in 1969. It is said (Corak, 1999, Table 3.2; also see Beaujot, 2000, pp. 302–303) that

> these changes reflect a pervasive decline in the earnings capacity of the young regardless of industry, occupation, union status, and the prevailing macroeconomic climate. Even if unemployment had been the same, youths in the 1980s would have started their careers with earnings almost 20% lower than their counterparts ten years earlier.

The beneficial effect of education is demonstrated in Canadian earnings. In 1990, there was a difference of nearly $10,000 a year in income between those who have Bachelor's degrees and those without (Kerr, 1997). In 1990, high school graduates earned approximately $22,600 a year compared with $46,000 for doctoral graduates (Education Today, 1996, p. 5). Doctoral graduates in 2007 made a median income of $65,000 per year (Desjardins & King, 2011, p. 27). Nevertheless, a decline in earnings for youth workers has occurred "regardless of industry, occupations, education level, or union status" (Marquardt, 1998, p. 93).

The low earnings of young people are reflected in their living conditions. In 2005, 58.1 percent of unattached Canadian individuals in the age group 18–24 were found living in low-income situations, with significant convergence of the male and female low-income rates (Feng et al., 2007). This is hardly surprising, with increasing proportions of the youth population working in dead-end service jobs and minimum-wage conditions that do not provide them with a subsistence income. In 2013, Canadian minimum wages range from the low of $9.75/hour in Alberta to the high of $11/hour in Nunavut (Munroe, 2013). The US federal minimum wage stands at $7.35/hour, while the different states set their minimum wages from a low of $5.15/hour in Wyoming and Georgia, to the high of $9.19/hour in Washington (US Department of Labor, 2013b). In the UK, the minimum wage varies depending on one's age: those under 18 earn £3.68/hour, those 18–20 earn £4.98/hour, and those 21 and over earn £6.19/hour (gov.uk, 2013).

The image of young people as lazy slackers is put in a new light. If young people are lacking in faith in the benefits of hard work, it is because they see no evidence that their efforts are being rewarded. Whatever slacking may be taking place (and there is no real evidence for it) would be rooted in knowing that you will have to work twice as hard as your parents or even the cohorts of youth before you to obtain a smaller share of the wealth around you. It is surprising that so many young people can still bring themselves to keep on trying.

Where Are the Jobs?

American research on school-to-work transitions is primarily preoccupied with the phenomenon of youth "floundering" in the labour market, with reference to youth entering and leaving the workforce during a period that is seen to be transitional, along the way to full and steady employment. It is of particular concern that young people without post-secondary education will be stuck in the floundering stage. Interestingly, rather than being linked to the labour market itself, floundering tends to be depicted as a result of youth immaturity. The picture these proponents of the "floundering thesis" paint is this (Tannock, 2001, p. 28):

> Youths … are not responsible enough when they first finish high school to take career jobs. Recent high-school graduates are more concerned about their social

lives than work—they are interested only in jobs that won't demand too much, that can provide a quick supply of cash, and that they can pick up and drop as fancy strikes. Youths just out of high school ... don't really know what they want out of life and are certainly not ready to settle down. As a result, career employers, who make considerable investments in training their employees, are forced to wait until these workers have had time to "mature." Only employers such as restaurant and retail outlets, which depend on a cheap supply of unskilled and temporary labor, are willing and able to hire the young and give them a chance to develop as workers.

Tannock (2001, pp. 28–31) objects to this argument that blames youth for their "deficit," and points out that the evidence from school-to-work studies goes counter to this common depiction. Instead, it is shown that employers are unwilling to hire youth who are stereotypically labelled as "irresponsible, lazy, self-interested, and antisocial" (p. 29). Thus, youth take anything they are offered because the doors to good jobs are closed to them. Thus, the "job-hopping" they are seen to be doing arises out of young people's frustration with the economy that offers meagre returns. In the absence of real policy solutions that would help bridge the gap between school and jobs, young people will continue to work in low-wage, low-status jobs.

Indeed, North American research has generally debunked the myth that young people are immature and unreliable as employees, and thus not as desirable as employees as their older counterparts. In fact, some researchers puzzle over the finding that many young people enjoy their work in the lower-tier services sector and exhibit a lot of commitment to it. Youth are desirable as employees to the McJob sector precisely because they are reliable and offer a convenient pool of flexible labour. Tannock (2001, pp. 24–27) suggests that the best way to understand youth labour markets is to acknowledge that youth and adults are in competition in the labour market. This means that the poor youth employment outcomes result from the collusion of interests, on the one hand, by employers looking for cheap youth labour, and adult men, on the other hand, who take the good jobs at the expense of youth, women, and members of minorities.

There is a distinct pattern to the type of employment youth are able to get. In the past, major employers for graduates (regardless of level) were found in the public sector: health, education, and public service. In contrast, during the 1990s and beyond, youth employment is generally found in the service sector. Regardless of educational level, young people are substantially overrepresented in the traditional service industries, in clerical, sales, and service occupations, where wages and benefits are poor, promotions rare, and the workforce transient. In contrast, youth are underrepresented in the good non-service job sectors. There has been a trend toward higher concentration in "bad jobs" since the mid-1970s (Betcherman & Leckie, 1996, in Nakamura & Wong, 1998, p. 8; Marquardt, 1998, pp. 81–82; Côté & Allahar, 1994). Graduates are also competing for jobs in the private sector where the levels of stress and competition are high (Marquardt, 1998, pp. 81–82).

Another significant feature of the youth labour market is the persistent part-time employment of young people (Beaujot, 2000). This partly reflects the trend toward precarious employment among young people discussed above, and the general trend toward precarious employment, discussed in Chapter 4. Part-time employment of young people has gone hand in hand with the rising cost of education as young people's own financial contributions are needed in addition to parental contributions.

The kinds of jobs youth occupy in the McJob sector are low-skill, low-paid, and highly stressful. Tannock's (2001, pp. 40–58) study outlines the monotony, repetition, and demands for high volume as causes of stress. There is an increased push toward customer service strategies that place demands on youth to act according to specifically scripted instructions. One example of this is carefully worded greetings to customers, or standard wordings to customer inquiries or complaints. Additionally, companies spend a lot of time creating schemes to motivate workers and to make them feel a part of a "team" through company social gatherings (e.g., picnics, parties, games) and incentive programs accompanied with material rewards (e.g., cash, dinners, prizes) or by appealing to the intrinsic rewards of being the "best," whether it's for the most sales or for the cleanest work area. One standard feature of a lot of lower service sector work is the increased use of "just-in-time" methods, i.e., the increased efficiency of service delivery (productivity) based on detailed analyses of workflows and habits. This means that work can be scheduled to fit the peak times, with resulting shorter shifts for workers and the loss of hours of work. The team spirit created will keep workers committed and avoids the hassles of more direct control exerted by managers. Overall, the effectiveness of these schemes at least partly explains the puzzle of why young people keep on reporting some degree of satisfaction with their jobs. Working with other youth, in an atmosphere of being "treated" to games and awards, creates a semblance of youth subculture, which young people respond to more positively than may be realistically expected given their dismal work conditions and poor wages.

The stress that young people face at work is coupled with abuse from customers and managers. Tannock's (2001, pp. 40–46) study of young workers in the fast-food and retail industries in America uncovered a typical practice of customers' verbal abuse, frequently resulting in young workers having to explain and enforce company policy over which they have no control. Managers are also reported to "power trip" around workers; the younger the employee, the more likely she or he will be a target of verbal abuse. One practice is for managers to get rid of youth they don't like by targeting them for abuse until they quit.

Tannock (2001, pp. 46–51) also characterizes the fast-food and grocery industries—where large numbers of youth work—as places of employee surveillance. Young workers who are approached with suspicion of pilfering or giving unauthorized discounts to friends are subjected to hidden or visible security cameras and audio systems. Some companies require special tests for "personality" or "honesty" prior to employment. The level of surveillance and rules leaves no room for individual and independent decision making—everything has to be checked and authorized.

Starting in 2006, McDonald's in the UK has waged a battle with the *Oxford English Dictionary's* definition of "McJobs" as a "low-paying, low-status, and usually unstimulating job with few benefits and little possibility of advancement" (Grittani-Livingston, 2007). The term was coined in the 1980s and came to the public consciousness in Douglas Coupland's 1991 book, *Generation X* (BBC News, 2007b). The company launched wide publicity campaigns to persuade the public that their jobs really are not given justice in the dictionary definition. As mentioned earlier, many youth still feel that they are getting something out of their lower service sector work, as explained by Debbie Mansteed from Edinburgh (Winterman, 2006):

> I joined McDonald's at the age of 16 as a part-time crew member in order to save money to go to university. I am still with the company almost three years on and despite what people's perceptions are of the company, we work together as a team and have such a good time on shift. I was very shy when I joined but now people can hardly shut me up! It definately [*sic*] has a positive impact on your confidence and your self-esteem and the flexibility of work is excellent as I can fit it around my uni[versity] work....

One recent and disturbing trend is the exploitation of young people's lack of employment experience by hiring them for unpaid internships. A discussion of the ethics of this practice is emerging in Canada, as well as in the US and the UK, and is starting to be reported by the media. Estimated at 300,000 positions in Canada, these "jobs" represent huge profits for employers and huge losses for the young people who engage in them, and forego pay and benefits over long and short term. In the words of Andrew Lagille (2013):

> Students and young graduates are sold the idea of working for free with promises of experience, references, networking opportunities, acquiring new skills and the "potential" of an eventual, paying position. Most of the time internships do not act as a door to stable, secure employment as apprenticeships or entry-level jobs often do. For a lucky few, unpaid internships can lead to a well-paying job, but for the vast majority of youths, internships only lead to insecurity, precarity and alienation from the labour market.

Gender and Employment Experiences

Large-scale American surveys among young women confirm a general trend in the Western world: Young women are aspiring to fulfilling paid work over their lifetime, not only as a temporary phenomenon on their way to marriage and motherhood. At the same time, in both Europe and North America, young women's capabilities are being heralded and called for in the new economy (Aapola et al., 2005, pp. 64–69).

Despite hype about increasing gender equality in wage work, the labour force remains segregated by gender, both horizontally and vertically, premised on the traditional divisions outlined in Chapter 4 on education. Men and women occupy different work categories and different levels of hierarchy in the working world (Charles, 2002, pp. 22–26). According to Charles (2002, p. 31):

"[M]en's" jobs are heavy, dirty, dangerous, involving outdoor work, and are associated with qualities such as aggression, ambition, an ability to exercise authority and cope with stress, a natural affinity with machines, and superior intelligence. In addition, men's work tends to be more highly valued than women's…. "Women's" jobs, in contrast, are associated with low pay, are boring, low grade, low status, involve subservience, and are jobs that men would not want to do. They are associated with "feminine" qualities of caring, being good with people, and dexterity.

Not surprisingly, considering the gender-typing in education, the type of youth employment varies based on gender and levels of education. There has been only minimal entry of women into typically male-dominated fields. Female graduates continue to be overrepresented in education, fine arts and humanities, general social sciences, and nursing. Women are also more likely than men to work in part-time and temporary jobs (Human Resources Development Canada, 2001, pp. 14–15). Typically, Canadian studies find that most girls aspire to a narrow range of traditionally female occupations (Maxwell & Maxwell, 1994, p. 153). The patterns from the 1970s and 1980s indicated that young women find it very difficult to enter non-traditional work in a highly gender-segregated labour market. Their primary employment is in the clerical and service industries, and other female-dominated professions, such as teaching and nursing (Guttman & Alice, 1991; Anisef et al., 1980; Charles, 2002, pp. 23–26).

There is some evidence from Britain that while women are moving gradually toward some male-dominated work areas, men's work fields are more strictly male-based and they have not made similar excursions to traditionally female work areas. However, women's only inroads have been made in the professions. Nearly 70 percent of the professional jobs created from 1981–1996 went to women. The development is not taking place across the board. Women are particularly absent from the traditional male bastions of work in manufacturing. At the same time, British studies also find that women are still significantly underrepresented in management (Charles, 2002, p. 26).

Because of the significant drop in the incomes of young males, and the slight increase in young women's wages, Canadian researchers have concluded that "young men and women increasingly have more in common with their age-mates than with older persons of the same sex" (Beaujot, 2000, p. 304; Allahar & Côté, 1998; Conference Board of Canada, 2013). The common elements are: increasing job ghettoization, a general deterioration of wages, and being trapped in dead-end work areas with no chance of advancement (Allahar & Côté, 1998, p. 132).

Indeed, the general trend is that, with globalization, labour markets are becoming "feminized," with most growth in jobs taking place in areas that are traditionally women's work, including service, sales, and communications, while traditional male manufacturing jobs are declining. Feminization also refers to the female model of the preferred worker: well groomed, expressive, and mobile. The term "genderquake" (Wilkinson, 1994, in Aapola et al., 2005, p. 62) has been coined to describe this phenomenon in which women's increased education and workplace gender-equity programs and feminism are supposedly starting to put young men at a disadvantage. Interestingly, this debate can be linked to concerns raised regarding young men being left behind in terms of their education, as presented in the preceding chapter. This ideologically driven debate is not coincidental, and amounts to an anti-feminist backlash. The arguments are simply not supported by evidence.

Instead, studies show that young women in Europe and North America are faltering in the labour force. Not only are they exploited in the growing service sector, which relies on unskilled labour, but they are also forced into employment in the informal economy, exemplified by the garment industry, where the vast majority of workers are young women. While this is happening, the social safety nets are being eroded, leaving young women particularly economically vulnerable (Aapola et al., 2005, pp. 71–72).

According to Human Resources Development Canada's National Graduates Surveys, the starting salaries of women post-secondary graduates are moving closer to the starting salaries of men. However, men's earnings grew faster than women's earnings in the years following graduation: that is, the earnings gap widens in the years following graduation (Human Resources Development Canada, 2001, p. 8). In 2010, Canadian women aged 25 to 34 earned 78.3 cents for each dollar earned by men (Conference Board of Canada, 2013). This mirrors the wage gap in Britain between men and women, which amounts to women in full-time work earning 82 percent of what full-time working men earn (Charles, 2002, p. 29). Similarly, in the United States, the wage gap in median incomes of men and women as of 2003 stands at just under 60 percent. The gap in the wages of women and men aged 15–24 is around 75 percent, while the gap among those aged 25–34 is approximately 72 percent (US Census Bureau, 2007, Table 683).

Child-bearing and joint labour supply decisions within families explain some but not the entire earnings gap. For example, women are more likely to work part-time than men, largely due to family responsibilities. Even full-time women employees work on average two-and-a-half to four hours less than men (Human Resources Development Canada, 2001, p. 14).

Gender-based wages reflect the gender divisions in the youth labour market. Canadian male youths without a high school diploma are generally found in unskilled blue-collar jobs: delivery men, grocery clerks, kitchen helpers, or general labourers. By the age of 24 one-quarter will be in skilled trades as carpenters, welders, heavy-duty mechanics, and auto mechanics. A minority will be in supervisory sales or service positions. Meanwhile, two-thirds of female youth without a high school diploma will be in the consumer service industries as sales clerks, cashiers, and waitresses, while only 14 percent will have a blue-collar job like seamstresses or food processors. Even with a high school diploma, 70 percent of young women will be in clerical, sales, and service industries, with most in consumer services. Only 10 percent will be in blue-collar jobs in comparison with half of the males (Marquardt, 1998, pp. 77–78).

Of Canadian male graduates from community colleges or other non-university diploma graduates, over one-third work in skilled blue-collar jobs, while female graduates will find employment in "professional, managerial, and technical occupations, particularly nursing, teaching, and skilled administrative and business occupations" (Marquardt, 1998, p. 78). Almost half of the female post-secondary graduates and one-third of the males are still working in unskilled or semi-skilled jobs (Marquardt, 1998, pp. 78–79). Notably, the gendered wage gap persists regardless of industry or work area: for example, in 2010, it was 71 percent in managerial jobs, and 65 percent in processing, manufacturing, and utilities, all of which tend to be male-dominated. The corresponding gaps for the female-dominated areas of social sciences, education, and related jobs was 70 percent (Conference Board of Canada, 2013).

Holding a post-secondary degree is a key to workplace success relative to less-educated youth. Half of Canadian youth with a post-secondary degree will work in managerial occupations by the age of 24. Reflecting the gender patterns in the education system, women will more likely become elementary or secondary teachers, while men will be in "professional jobs in the natural and applied sciences, including engineering, as well as in business, finance, and administration" (Marquardt, 1998, p. 78). However, over a third of both male and female university graduates under 24 work in the typical student labour market, usually in the service sector or blue-collar labour market. The gender-based wage gap in the service sector in 2010 was 57 percent (Conference Board of Canada, 2013).

Studies document the effect of both socio-economic background and gender on education. Thiessen and Looker (1993) studied a sample of 567 young males and 639 young females, all 17 years of age, in Hamilton, Ontario, and Halifax, Nova Scotia. Their study suggests that working-class youth distance themselves from the manual work of their fathers, and middle-class young men and women expect a pattern of work after their fathers. This finding also supports a study by Weis (1990, in Thiessen & Looker, 1993) suggesting that there is a gender equalization in expectations, i.e., that young middle-class women take it for granted that their own work patterns would be those of middle-class males.

In the UK, young women's job market fortunes, likewise, continue to be dictated by their social class background. New opportunities are more readily open to young, White middle-class women, while other young women struggle. Young working-class women are handicapped by their lower educational credentials, and there is evidence that it is they, not the men, who suffer most from the deterioration of the traditional manufacturing work sector. They are likely to get trapped in the worst fringes of the economy, in poorly paid, insecure, and unsafe work with no prospects for advancement (Aapola et al., 2005, pp. 68–70). American studies also find that young African-American women's workplace success depends on the degree to which they can "act White." Particularly at a disadvantage are young women with disabilities whose post-school employment prospects are poor (Aapola et al., 2005, pp. 68–69).

Workplace Harassment

As in the case of education, work settings reflect general patriarchal power patterns. Women may be subjected to sexual harassment in the workplace (Nelson & Robinson, 1999, pp. 264–271, 345, 494). According to European Commission (1998, p. 1), "[f]orms of sexual harassment are usually divided into three different types: verbal (remarks about figure/look, sexual jokes, verbal sexual advances), non verbal ('staring and whistling') and physical (from unsolicited physical contact to assault/rape)." These behaviours are seen to be violations of a person's dignity. Further, sexual harassment in the workplace is typically divided into two varieties. The quid pro quo cases are the most obvious, involving threats to employment if the woman does not agree to sexual encounters. The other variety, called "poisoned work environment," is more difficult to recognize, and refers to subtle ways in which the work environment is intimidating, uncomfortable, or offensive to the worker (Nelson & Robinson, 1999, p. 268).

The Canadian Violence Against Women Survey found that 87 percent of Canadian women have experienced sexual harassment incidents of a "memorable" variety, and that nearly half of these were work-related. In these work-related incidents, co-workers were the most frequent perpetrator, followed by bosses or supervisors, and clients, customers, or patients (Johnson, 1996, p. 97). United Food and Commercial Workers (UFCW, 2010, p. 1) states: "It is estimated that approximately 90% of all female employees in Canada will face some form of sexual harassment while working on the job: with young women and unmarried women at greatest risk." This risk has been demonstrated in previous studies (Larkin, 1994, pp. 24–28; Johnson, 1996, pp. 103–104).

Charles (2002, p. 40) points out that aside from sexual harassment, which also prevails in the British workplace, women's work is "sexualized" in other ways. For example, in contrast to men, women's "attractiveness" is considered in many work areas where they have to deal with male customers and clients. This undermines their work skills and their status is diminished in relation to their male co-workers. Aapola et al. (2005, p. 71) also point out that the intersections of gender, race, and culture in many sexualized images make it difficult to disentangle gender and racial harassment.

Race, Ethnicity, Immigrant Status, and Employment Experiences

Immigrants to Canada have the promise of a good start, as the Canadian immigration system favours those with higher education (Shields, 2004). In fact, almost twice as many immigrants aged 25–54 hold university degrees (40 percent) relative to the Canadian-born population (Frenette & Morissette, 2005; Momirov & Kilbride, 2005), a trend that was more extensively discussed in the previous chapter.

The promise of a prosperous life in the new land is often unfulfilled as immigrants struggle to find employment. Both American and Canadian research has shown that immigrant newcomers experience economic difficulties for several years after immigration, in part due to discrimination (Ambert & Krull, 2006; Hernandez et al., 2007; Kaushal & Reimers, 2007; Li, 1988; Liu & Kerr, 2003; Momirov & Kilbride, 2005). Liu and Kerr (2003) summarize research showing that those of European ancestry are located in better jobs, while those from Africa, Asia, and Latin America are less successful, even if they are educated. They report a "substantial decline" in the "average levels of well-being" of immigrant families within the last 10 years. Low earnings among immigrants correlate with poverty, poor health, and poor housing conditions (Anisef & Kilbride, 2000; Beiser et al., 2002; Statistics Canada, 2004a, 2004b, 2004c, 2005a, 2005b; Shields, 2004).

The policy and program solutions in this area obviously have to do with increasing immigrants' access to gainful employment while reducing their welfare dependency. However, improvements in this area would require nearly a full reversal of the trends that began over two decades ago. Particularly since the 1990s, social and economic restructuring (see Chapter 10) has eroded the ability of the welfare state to provide for the needs of immigrant populations. The logic behind changing Canadian immigrant entry requirements in the early 1990s was to create a highly flexible, adaptable immigrant mass that had transferable skills (Arat-Koc, 1993; Shields, 2004). Instead, underemployment, unemployment (Arat-Koc, 1993), and poverty (Frenette & Morissette, 2005) have increased among immigrants. The problems are compounded by cuts in funding to social services and settlement services aimed at immigrants in Canada (Shields, 2004). Similarly, the 1996 welfare reforms in the US made non-citizens "ineligible for important public benefits and services" (Hernandez et al., 2007). All of this has created additional barriers for immigrants, who also have to combat racism and anti-immigrant attitudes in many aspects of their lives.

In the UK, one in three White, Caribbean, Indian, and African-Asian men are employed in manufacturing, while the proportions of Pakistani, Bangladeshi, and Chinese men are lower. Analyses find that these proportions are linked to the history of migration of each of these groups and reflect the recruitment and expansion strategies of different manufacturing sectors at the time. Generally, comparisons of White and "ethnic minority groups" in terms of employment show a higher pattern of concentration of both minority men and women in retail and service work (Charles, 2002, p. 28; also see Cross, 2003).

Minority youth in Britain have higher rates of unemployment than White youth. For example, the unemployment rate among Pakistani and Bangladeshi people aged 16–24 is around 30 percent compared to 12 percent among young White people. In response to this, the British government put in place the New Deal for Young People (NDYP) in 1998. The goal of NDYP is to improve both short- and long-term employability of youth, and it is mandatory for youth 18–24 who have been unemployed for six months or more. The program provides job search and personal support (called Gateway), followed by a six-month placement with either a public or private sector employer, in a voluntary organization, an environmental task force, or up to 12 months' education toward national vocational qualifications. Most participants prefer the employment placement, and the environmental task force placement is the least preferred. The dropout rate for the first two years of the program is about 12 percent, with ethnic minorities' dropout at 11 percent. Overall, around 31 percent of White participants and 41 percent of minority participants opt out of the Gateway, with the highest rate among Pakistanis at 45 percent (Fieldhouse, Kalra & Alam, 2002, pp. 500–509).

Statistics collected from the NDYP in the UK show that young people from ethnic minority groups are overrepresented in the program; they form 8 percent of the total population, but 14 percent among NDYP clients. This is a reflection of their higher levels of unemployment overall. There is also a gender imbalance in that one-third of the ethnic minority participants are women, while one-quarter of the White participants are women. Further, ethnic minority participants are more likely to go into training with the voluntary sector and are less likely to engage in employment afterward, which is the optimum outcome (Fieldhouse et al., 2002, pp. 500–501).

Disturbingly, and going counter to the "greedy youth" claims discussed above, young people are generally willing to work even for less money, as long as they don't see it as "overly" exploitive. One 23-year-old Pakistani male (in Fieldhouse et al., 2002, p. 508) who was looking for a placement under the New Deal for Young People, said this:

> Well, money matters, I don't want to work for £50 a week or anything, but then I don't mind working for a bit less if they are going to train me and give me a pay rise after a bit, but some places just take the piss. I went to this one guy who lives round our end and owns a factory, he said he had some packing stuff, it was 9 till 7 every day and Saturday half day and all he was paying was £60, but he said that I could sign on as well if I wanted to, but that's just using you, it's slave labour.

Generally, in the UK, men earn better pay than women in nearly all ethnic groups. The exceptions are Pakistani and Bangladeshi men, who earn lower wages than women, while women in these groups are also the worst off compared to other women (Charles, 2002, p. 29).

Racialized status in Canada typically translates to being underemployed in the labour market. Although members of racialized groups are likely to have more credentials, racist barriers continue to exist in job entry (Livingstone, 1999, p. 215). Young racialized people and immigrants aged 15–24 have lower rates of labour market participation and employment, and higher underemployment rates compared to the national average for this age group (National Council of Welfare, 2012, p. 10; Galabuzi, 2005). Based on the 2001 Census, the labour force participation of immigrant youth was 3.4 percent lower than the national average, and nearly 15 percent lower for racialized youth. At the same time, unemployment rates among these groups were 1.5 percent and 2.8 percent higher than the national average, respectively (Galabuzi, 2005, p. 14).

The higher education levels of Canadian racialized groups don't seem to result in higher pay. Taking into account the effect on higher earnings potential of education levels and fields of study, these groups had earnings *penalties* of 1–10 percent, based on a 1992 survey (Human Resources Development Canada, 2001, p. 19). Galabuzi's (2005, pp. 16-18) analysis of later trends confirms this, and points to an increase in the earnings gap between educated racialized people and the national average.

The fact that increasing numbers of racialized people are living in poverty is often referred to as the "racialization of poverty" (e.g., Galabuzi, 2005, p. 16). This term is particularly appropriate for Canadian Aboriginal populations, where unemployment is a particularly serious problem, and is a result of the poor educational histories discussed in the previous chapter and the long history of colonization discussed in Chapter 2 (also see

H. Tait, 2000, p. 260; Marquardt, 1998, p. 76). According to Statistics Canada (2011f), the employment rate for Aboriginal youth in 2009 was 45.1 percent, more than 10 percent lower than their non-Aboriginal counterparts. The same source records that Aboriginal youth were particularly hard hit by the 2008–09 recession, as employment rates plummeted by almost 7 percent. Overall, Aboriginal youth aged 15–24 are twice as likely to be unemployed as their non-Aboriginal counterparts (Centre for Social Justice, 2007–2013).

Another racialized population that is facing serious problems with employability is Black youth. James (1990, p. 93) reports that Black-Canadian youth believe that "as visible minority individuals they would be labelled, stereotyped and discriminated against, and that their race would impact on their occupational experiences and opportunities." These fears are well founded. Ornstein's (2000, p. 59) analysis of the 1996 Census in relation to Toronto found that there are three groups with "frighteningly high" youth unemployment rates: Africans and Blacks, Jamaicans, and Trinidadians and Tobagonians. What is significant in relation to these groups is that their high youth unemployment is not due to settlement difficulties. For example, "70 percent of the African and Black group are born in Canada and another 10 percent arrived before 1976." Galabuzi (2005, p. 14) reports that the 2001 Census found a 33.2 percent youth (aged 15–24) labour force participation rate and 21.4 percent unemployment rate among Black Canadian-born youth, the worst rates compared among non-Aboriginal groups.

In the United States, the legacy of slavery and the ongoing marginalization of the Black population are, likewise, reflected in unemployment statistics. The unemployment rate among White youth aged 16–19 was 14.2 percent in 2005, while the corresponding figure for Black youth of this age was 33.3 percent. This means that Black youth have an unemployment rate that is nearly two-and-a-half times the White youth's unemployment rate and almost twice the unemployment rate of Hispanic youth of same age (18.4 percent). Similar patterns prevail among those aged 20–24, with the unemployment rates of 7.2 percent among Whites, 18.3 percent among Blacks, and 8.6 percent among Hispanics (US Census Bureau, 2007, Table 608; also see Cohen et al., 2007). It is not surprising that one national study of American youth found that 61 percent of Black youth agreed with the statement "It is hard for young Black people to get ahead because they face so much discrimination," and that only 11 percent believe that "it is *very* likely that racism will be eliminated in their lifetime," while 42 percent believe "racism will *not* be eliminated during their lifetime" (Cohen et al., 2007, pp. 18–19, emphases in the original).

Immigrant youth are at a particular disadvantage in searching for employment. They lack contacts and networks, may have language difficulties, and may deal with different sets of familial expectations regarding combining responsibilities to one's family, school, or workplaces (Canadian Council on Social Development, 1998). This is reflected in the lower rates at which immigrant youth combine work and education. The Canadian Council on Social Development (2000, p. 5) reports that while about half of Canadian-born youth aged 15–19 combine school and employment, only one-quarter of immigrant youth in this age group who have been in Canada less than 10 years are holding a job while in school. In the age group 20–24, 79 percent of Canadian-born students work, while under half of the immigrant youth who have been in Canada for less than 10 years work. However, the study also found that 80 percent of immigrant students of this age group who have resided in Canada for longer than 10 years did work.

Workplace Dangers

Lately, more attention has been paid to the dangerous working conditions that young people face in their workplaces. Despite the popular perception of youth as a healthy workforce, they are prone to workplace injuries, accidents, and attacks (Tannock, 2001, pp. 53–54). For example, in 2006, workplaces claimed 97 workers aged 15-29 (Government of Canada, 2013). It is also reported that about 48,000 young people are injured annually seriously enough to require time off work (Canadian Centre for Occupational Health and Safety, 2013). Among the fatality cases that made the news were David Ellis, who died at age 18; Jared Dietrich, aged 19; and 16-year-old Ivan Golyashov, all of whom died of separate workplace injuries suffered while dealing with a dough-making machine (Freeze, 1999; Hargrove, 2000). Another youth, 20-year-old Steve MacDonald, died after being entangled in a metal lathe (Hargrove, 2000). James MacMillan was crushed at age 24, pinned to his truck while a 10-tonne agricultural sprayer lurched from its trailer (Philp, 2000).

In 2006, a Europe-wide campaign was launched to address the high risk of injury of young workers. In the UK, the second-highest workplace non-fatal injury rates are among young men aged 20–24, while women of this age had the fifth-highest rates (Hazards, 2006). In American workplaces, nearly 70 teenaged workers die annually, with males at a higher risk. Further, an estimated 64,000 teens receive emergency care annually due to workplace injuries, with 15–45 percent resulting in "work restrictions or permanent disabilities" (Runyan & Zakocz, 2000, p. 247). A study by Dunn et al. (1998) of 562 adolescents aged 14–17 in North Carolina, US, found that over half of them had been injured at least once at their workplace. The most common injuries were cuts and burns. Injuries of young males were also linked to working around loud noises or using workplace equipment such as ladders, scaffolding, forklifts, tractors, and ride-on mowers. Young women suffered from assaults because they were more likely to hold jobs that required handling money.

In the American industries studied by Tannock (2001, pp. 54–55), the most common injuries in the fast-food sector were related to hot shortening—burns are considered a part of the job. Additionally, youth suffered physical injuries from slipping and falling, and injured their backs while lifting heavy loads. In the grocery store, respiratory problems and skin conditions arise as a reaction to foodstuffs they handle or the chemicals used to clean the store. Problems with back, hips, or knees and feet result from prolonged standing and walking on concrete floors. Additionally, some customers don't limit their abuse to verbal slurs, but either threaten or physically attack the workers. Workers who handle cash are also at risk of being robbed. This is a double whammy in a low-trust work environment as they can be penalized for not following company rules about how to behave during robberies (not resisting) or for having had too much money in the till without having dropped off the extra cash at the bank.

In the United States, the National Consumers League listed five particularly hazardous job areas for teens, including agriculture, which is the most hazardous of them all, with the risk of fatality for workers aged 15–17 at four times the rate of young workers in other workplaces. The second place on the list is claimed by retail work, which involves working alone or late at night, when robberies are a particular danger. The third most dangerous jobs involve construction and work in high places. The fourth place on the list belongs to operating workplace vehicles (tractors, forklifts). And the fifth most hazardous is work involving door-to-door sales where young people often operate without adult supervision (Career World, 2004).

Some of the blame for workplace accidents is put on young people themselves, who are described as seeing "themselves as invincible." However, most of the blame must fall on employers who do not provide health and safety training to their young employees (Philp, 2000; Tannock, 2001, pp. 53–57), workplaces that are small enough to be left outside the workplace safety training legislation, or those who give only lip service to informing young workers about factors regarding their health (Hargrove, 2000).

Tannock (2001, pp. 55–57) describes one common problem with workplace safety training: the inapplicability of the educational material to the specific circumstances of the workplace. One young produce clerk (in Tannock, 2001, p. 56), who suffers from back pain, explains:

> I saw the video [on safe lifting procedures]. Of course, it was all perfect on the video; everything was easy to get to. But, for example, the other day, I didn't trim celery because I would have had to reach over another case or two, grab it from the side, and pull it out and twist and lift up and over, with my arms over here—a fifty-five pound case of celery. I was just, like: Too bad, no celery; should have broken the load better. I didn't do it. Stuff like that happens all the time. A fifty-pound bag of onions—you gotta lift it straight up with one arm over something.

Regardless of the mismatch between the ideal world of safety training and the less-than-ideal world of actual workplaces, injuries of youth tend to be blamed on their carelessness. One young fast-food cook (in Tannock, 2001, pp. 56–57) explains his experiences after suffering a burn at work, and the ways in which the "just-in-time" workplace systems undermine safety:

> I was burned in the back of my leg, here…. It was pretty gruesome…. My boss tried to blame it on me—well, not blame it on me, but get mad on me for it, because I'm not wearing the extra type of apron [required by Fry House safety guidelines when workers carry hot shortening]. But I showed that with the exact burn location, it doesn't cover the apron, so I told him even if I was wearing it that it wouldn't have done nothing…. The Fry House safety guidelines are so much safety, it pretty much

takes three times as much time to [follow them] than to actually do the thing ... if you wear all that stuff, it just gets in the way, makes it [take] more time ... if it's really crazy, they say, "OK. Do it the way you do it. Get it done. We need your help."

The working conditions in youth-dominated jobs are often poorer than those in adult workplaces, and the rates of work-related injury are higher among young workers. They may be even higher than officially reported because many young people are not aware of their rights or are afraid to report them (Waldie, 1993). Meanwhile, job growth has "concentrated in the largely non-union private-service sector, where work is likely to be part time and precarious" (Eaton, 1997, p. E1). The shift from full-time union jobs in manufacturing and resources has had a disastrous effect both on incomes (Eaton, 1997) and on work conditions.

Combining Education and Work

One of the big debates in North America is over the impact of the increased work engagement of youth still in secondary or post-secondary education, either as summer employment or part-time employment through the academic year. In fact, this type of dual activity, outlined previously, is seen to be beneficial, as engaging in work is seen as useful for youth, building character and learning "real life" skills and work habits. This argument has been turned upside down with criticism that the kinds of work experiences available to youth neither offer real work training nor enhance their studies. Indeed, menial and boring jobs with longer than 20-hour work weeks repress educational performance, while more interesting jobs and fewer hours result in positive outcomes (Tannock, 2001, pp. 31–33). The Youth in Transition Survey (2002, in Human Resources Development Canada, 2002, pp. 18–19) found that those 15-year-olds in all Canadian provinces who did not participate in wage work during the school year performed much better in reading than those who had a job, and had a less significant difference in the areas of math and science. However, performance in all three categories worsens as the number of work hours per week increases.

Combining school with work is also highly stressful. The Canadian Council on Social Development (2000, p. 5) found that at least 50 percent of Canadian-born youth aged 15–19 combine school and full- or part-time employment. Statistics Canada (1999f) also reports that in 1998, 35 percent of full-time students had a job, an increase of 3 percent from the year before. This means that while the usual adult work week is on average 37 hours, the average working teenager's combined weekly time at school and work amount to 50–60 hours (Waldie, 1993). This doubling of hours spent at work and in activities preparing one for work is stressful without a doubt regardless of presumably higher levels of youthful energy.

Students' part-time work is often also seen as a good way for them to make pocket money while being primarily supported by their parents. This argument is severely criticized by Tannock (2001, p. 35), who points out that large numbers of students need the money for their education and upkeep, and calls "deeply suspect" the view that parents should subsidize the profits made by the large employers that hire their children at low wages.

There are general arguments that engaging in wage work is beneficial because young people learn valuable work skills, and the routines and time management skills required for participation in employment. The strongest arguments speak of the benefits of gaining a work ethic and discipline required for employment. Tannock (2001, pp. 183–210) is critical of this view, which represents as beneficial the fact that scheduling is not up to the youth but to the employers, who easily overlook required break regulations, expect workers to start before and finish after designated hours, and routinely ignore employees' time needs, "that is, their personal, family, work, and (in the case of working students) school time" (p. 184). That employers are not accommodating school time is a common complaint, as recounted by a young bakery clerk who was attending community college (Tannock, 2001, p. 188). She quit her job because of the lack of time accommodation:

> I was like, you know what, I can see that they are not going to give me any help with dealing with homework and school and stuff.... The week before last, they gave me a shift from 2 to 9 on a school day. Well, my last class lets out at 1. OK, I would have to skip my class in order to get to work on time.... They knew that and they didn't care. I missed [came in late to] work that day. I'm sorry, I do not.... If you give in once and skip class and go to work, they'll do it again, and they'll do it again, and they'll do it again. You cannot give in to that.

An additional concern is that combining education and employment seems to further suppress labour force performance. The National Graduates Survey (A. Clark, 1999) reports that those youth who had jobs before they graduated, to finance their education, were more likely to work in clerical, sales, and service occupations, and were more likely to stay in the same job. Those who started work after graduating were more likely to work in professional or technical jobs, and were more likely to have changed jobs.

Finding Employment after Graduation

Kerckhoff's (1990) comparative research on the transitional patterns of youth in Great Britain and the United States shows that young men and women left school and entered the labour force much earlier in Great Britain than in the US. British men and women left the parental home and married later than Americans did. Women in the two countries had their first child at about the same age. As a result of the timing of these individual events, the five events (leaving school, entering the labour force, leaving the parental home, marrying, and becoming a parent) were spread out over a wider range of ages, on average, in Great Britain than in the US. If we view the "normal" order of events in both countries to be school leaving, labour force entry, leaving home, and marriage, that order was much more common in Great Britain, and there were many more reversals of the expected order in the United States. The order of these five events has been shown to affect outcomes, and the effects also differ depending on the gender of the individual. For example, women who marry before entering the labour force obtain lower-status jobs, but men who do so obtain higher-status jobs.

Using longitudinal data from the 1970 British Birth Cohort Study (BCS70), Bynner and Parsons (2002) found that if young people are not engaged in education, training, or employment in their later teens, there will be long-term negative consequences. Both young men and women are more likely to face a long-term continuation of this status, and will reduce their chances of full and successful engagement in the labour market. Additionally, women are likely to marry or cohabit at a younger age, and will feel dissatisfied and lack a sense of control, and experience problems in life (pp. 300–310).

A high proportion of Canadian graduates from all the graduating classes find jobs. Two years after graduation, 82 percent of 1995 graduates found jobs, about the same percentage as 1990 graduates. Trade/vocational graduates had a somewhat lower percentage employed (79 percent) than other graduates, whereas PhDs had the highest percentage employed (87 percent) (Human Resources Development Canada, 2001, pp. 11–13).

According to many Canadian reports, including one by Human Resources Development Canada (1999b, p. 12), staying in school longer pays off as education increases one's chances of employment. In 2009, 82 percent of Canadian adults aged 25 to 64 who were university graduates were employed, while the corresponding rate was 55 percent for those with less than a high school diploma (Statistics Canada, 2012c).

Those with more education are more likely to be employed in the long term. According to OECD comparisons of young people aged 16–29 based on education levels, the employment rates in the US were 57 percent for less than high school, 74 percent for high school, and 88 percent for post-secondary education; in Great Britain, 55 percent, 75 percent, and 90 percent, respectively; and in Canada, 56 percent, 75 percent, and 88 percent (Scarpetta et al., 2010, p. 17). These trends also seem to hold over time. Allen et al. (2003, p. 5) compared Canadian high school, college, and university graduating classes of 1986, 1990, and 1995, and found:

> In all three graduating classes, young college and bachelor graduates were more likely to have a job than youth with only a high school diploma. College graduates made the transition to the labour market more quickly, but for the classes of 1986 and 1990, bachelor graduates caught up after five years. This was not the case for the class of 1995. The difference in employment rates diminished by 2000, but young college graduates were still more likely to have a job. Bachelor graduates were more likely than college graduates to hold a job requiring their level of education. For example, among 1995 young university graduates who were working in 2000, 23% held a job requiring less than their level of education, versus 38% of college graduates.

Educational Inflation, Credentialism, and Precarious Work

The terms "educational inflation" and "credentialism" have entered our vocabulary. As more people are getting educated, the value of education is inflated as credentials such as degrees and diplomas are required for even entry-level jobs, which previously required no such credentials (Côté & Allahar, 1994, pp. 36–37, 124–125; Naiman, 2000, pp. 176–177; Baker, 1989, pp. 41–43; Blanchflower & Freeman, 1998). For example, Vedder (2010) says that in the US "approximately 60 percent of the increase in the number of college graduates from 1992 to 2008 worked in jobs ... [that are considered] ... relatively low skilled—occupations where many participants have only high school diplomas and often even less." This story captures the increasingly commonplace experiences of post-secondary graduates:

> William Klein's story may sound familiar to his fellow graduates. After earning his bachelor's in history from the College at Brockport, he found himself living in his parents' Buffalo home, working the same $7.25-an-hour waiter job he had in high school. It wasn't that there weren't other jobs out there. It's that they all seemed to want more education. Even tutoring at a for-profit learning center or leading tours at a historic site required a master's. "It's pretty apparent that with the degree I have right now, there are not too many jobs I would want to commit to," Mr. Klein says. (Pappano, 2011)

Despite holding a degree, many Canadian youth find themselves underemployed in unskilled jobs offering the lowest wages and benefits. According to the 1994 General Social Survey, large numbers of well-educated Canadians feel overqualified for their jobs. Of those with college or university education, 22 percent felt overqualified for their job, with women more likely than men to feel this way. Those college and university graduates in the age group 20–29 were the most likely (37 percent) to feel overqualified, reflecting the fact that they are most likely (30 percent) to be employed in clerical, sales, service, or blue-collar positions (Kelly et al., 2000, pp. 182–183).

Another term that has entered our vocabulary when speaking of youth employment trends is "precarious work," referring to the instability of employment that is temporary or short-term. This trend is evident, regardless of levels of education, and young educated workers are much worse off than older educated workers in terms of unemployment and precarious employment (Foster, 2012, p. 4). According to the Canadian Centre for Policy Alternatives (CCPA) (Foster, 2012, p. 3):

> The proportion of young employees working non-permanent jobs has nearly doubled, from 6.9% in 1997 to 11.6% in 2011, while the proportion of older employees in these types of jobs has only grown from 4.0% to 5.7% during the same time period. This is important because permanent jobs are more likely to provide benefits, tend to be better paid, and offer a sense of psychological security: employees can rest assured that so long as they fulfill their end of their employment contract,

they will continue to be employed in the future. Notably, these numbers do not even include casual employment or employment secured through temp agencies.

The increase in precarious work among young people has given rise to the acronym NEETs, referring to youth who are "not in employment, education or training" (OECD, 2013c), an increasingly common fate for those aged 15-29. Of the total youth population, the OECD averages between 1997 and 2011 put the percentage of NEETs between approximately 14 and 16 percent for any given year. The long-term "scarring" of precarious employment marked with periods of unemployment is captured in an OECD report (Scarpetta et al., 2010, p. 14) in Box 5.3.

Employment Policies

In response to the economic crises in the late 2000s, the OECD (2010a, p. 4) paid particular attention to measures that would assist youth in the labour market. Their main recommendations encouraged the collaboration of all sectors, including governments, employers, unions, and NGOs, to: (1) develop and enhance youth job search assistance programs; (2) put in place temporary social safety net measures; (3) develop and enhance apprenticeship and other vocational education and training (VET) programs; and (4) develop special programs for the most disadvantaged youth, focusing on technical and computer skills as well as providing adult mentoring and work skills exposure.

An example of the second recommendation is the 2009 Recovery Act in the United States, which expanded unemployment benefit eligibility for youth and other workers with short work histories (OECD, 2010a, p. 4). The Canadian government's summary response to this call for action was equally feeble, despite claims of being "well ahead of most other OECD countries in responding to the education and labour market challenges faced by youth" (OECD, 2008a, p. 3). In response to the third OECD recommendation, it was noted that the 2006 budget offered grants and a tax credit to encourage young people's entry into trades. Canada's report states that three of the provinces, Alberta, Newfoundland, and Ontario, took initiative to address the high dropout rate in secondary education. Aside from this, the other measures consist of general approaches to the labour market and nothing to address the youth employment crisis. The "Advantage Canada" Strategy of 2006 aims to develop "the best educated, most skilled and most flexible workforce in the world," with no specific focus on young people (Department of Finance Canada, 2006, p. 6). A similarly general approach was present in the Aboriginal Skills and Employment Partnership (ASEP), which received new funding in 2007 (OECD, 2008a).

Efforts to respond to the youth crisis are more extensive in the UK, starting with measures to encourage young people to complete their secondary education. This includes a national Education Maintenance Allowance established in 2004, providing financial support to students under 16 years of age and extended to 17-year-olds in 2008. In keeping with the idea of partnerships and the second OECD recommenda-

Box 5.3: The Scarring Effects of Unemployment on Youth

"Scarring" means that the mere experience of unemployment will increase future unemployment risks and/or reduce future earnings, mainly through effects associated with human capital (i.e., deterioration of skills and foregone work experience) or signalling (i.e., periods of unemployment convey a signal of low productivity to potential employers). The longer the unemployment period lasts the more individual productivity will be affected, and the lower the level of initial qualification the longer the scarring effects are likely to last.

Most studies find that, on average, early youth unemployment has serious negative effects on incomes, but less of an effect on the risk of future unemployment (Mroz & Savage, 2006, using the US National Longitudinal Survey of Youth; Gregg & Tominey, 2004, and Arulampalam, 2001, using the UK National Child Development Study). While the reduced employment effects are estimated to be short-lived by Mroz and Savage (2006) in the United States, Gregg and Tominey (2004) suggests that youth unemployment does impose a long-lasting unemployment scar in the United Kingdom: an extra three months of unemployment before the age of 23 led to an extra two months out of work (inactive or unemployed) between ages 28 and 33. But most studies agree that the greatest impact of lost work experience is on wages. Mroz and Savage (2006) found that a six-month spell of unemployment at age 22 would result in an 8 percent lower wage at 23, and even at ages 30 and 31 wages were 2–3 percent lower than they would have been otherwise. Gregg and Tominey (2004), controlling for education, region, family wealth, and personal characteristics, found that one year of unemployment at the age of 22 impacted wages by 13–21 percent twenty years later in the United Kingdom. In particular, unemployment immediately upon graduation from college is associated with substantial and permanent future earnings losses (Oreopoulos et al., 2006). How long the effects of unemployment among youth last also depends on the overall labour market conditions at the time.

More generally, Bell and Blanchflower (2009) find evidence that periods of unemployment while young often create permanent scars through its harmful effects on a number of outcomes—happiness, job satisfaction, wages, and health—many years later. Moreover, spells of unemployment tend to be particularly harmful to the individual—and to society—when the most disadvantaged youth become unemployed. This involves significant social as well as economic costs. (Scarpetta et al., 2010, p. 14, Box 1).

tion, flexibilities were built into the New Deal program for youth suffering from long-term unemployment, in co-operation with employers, in 2009. In line with the third recommendation, the UK also launched the "14–19 strategy" in 2005, enhancing young people's choices for vocational training. Connexions Services were introduced in 2003, to provide "advice and guidance" to those aged 13–19, which follows the fourth OECD recommendation. Finally, since 2006, support is given to employers through the Train to Gain program, which gives referrals and other advice for training employees (OECD, 2008b).

As a general trend, the policies of all three countries, outlined above, reflect less of a concern with responding to the youth employment crisis and more of a concern with protecting and enhancing business interests through financial and other government incentives. It has been noted in Canada that the programs aimed to create good jobs and ease work-to-school transitions are complemented by policies that support the "expansion of low-wage employment to reduce the jobless rate" (Marquardt, 1998, pp. 109–119). This includes measures such as lowering or eliminating the minimum wage, and lowering employers' other labour costs, such as unemployment insurance premiums and pension plan contributions. It is expected that as labour costs fall, the number of jobs will increase. On the other side of the coin are measures to create incentives for workers to accept low-paying jobs, such as lowering unemployment insurance benefits and social assistance (Marquardt, 1998, pp. 109–110). Part of this strategy includes wage subsidies for employers who hire young workers. The ironies are multiplied in that, as this trend is taking place, youth wages are deteriorating, with a significant drop in the last two decades.

Aside from these general problems that apply to all youth, not enough has been done to assist either female or visible minority youth in their educational or employment experiences. For example, Aboriginal youth need a range of different support programs to help them make their way on their own (Gabor et al., 1996; Wood & Griffiths, 1996). Young women also need a range of programs, not only employment equity or anti-harassment policies, to help them along the way (Varpalotai, 1996). One of the major policy challenges is to help young people establish a healthy connection between wage work and family life in a way that does not unduly penalize women (Looker, 1996, p. 160).

Canadian Youth Employment Programs (YEP) provide work opportunities for people 15–30 years of age through community-based organizations. Many programs target youth "at risk," i.e., those youth who live in impoverished neighbourhoods or who are homeless. In criticism of YEPs, Tam (2005) points out that these programs ghettoize young women into stereotypically feminine work areas such as clerical work or personal service work. They give the appearance of offering choices while funnelling young women into gender stereotypes and cheap labour. Programs are also run as if they don't have to account for young women's child-care responsibilities. They also do a disservice to youth "at risk" through their individualistic approach, which doesn't take into account the systemic poverty, racism, sexism, and discrimination that need to be addressed on a collective level rather than by targeting specific segments of the population. This approach individualizes the problem and does nothing to alleviate the conditions of these youth who can now be blamed for their own situation.

A main element of American youth employment programs is that they target at-risk or underprivileged youth, many of whom are from racialized backgrounds. The US Department of Labor (2008) offers "a wide variety of programs to ensure that all youth have the skills and training they need to successfully make the transition to adulthood and careers," including Job Corps, Youth Discretionary Grants, Youth Formula-Funded Grant Programs, and Apprenticeships. All three are targeted at marginalized or at-risk youth. Heckman (1994, p. 112) concludes that the Job Corps alone has been shown to have a positive effect on earnings of disadvantaged youth. This program offers on-site job training and placements to young people in private companies, state and federal agencies, and unions.

A key area of interest for American policy makers since the 1990s has been school-to-work transition programs, including President Bill Clinton's added investment in the Summer Training and Education Program (STEP). A new program initiated by President Clinton starting in 1991 was the youth apprenticeship program, with a view to easing the transition of youth from school to work in a labour market that offers diminishing opportunities for young people (Heckman, 1994, pp. 102–103).

Both programs have faced criticism based on poor outcomes. The STEP program was deemed a particular disappointment, having failed to increase the employment skills of the marginalized youth participants. Heckman (1994, p. 101) concludes that even intensive summer youth programs are not a reasonable investment into youth employment. Though "they may protect the peace, prevent riots, and lower the summer crime rate," they simply do not provide returns for the participants.

Similarly to the North American pattern, increasing attention was paid in Britain to continuous job training, particularly since the conservative Thatcher years of the 1980s and continuing in the 1990s (Miles, 2000; O'Higgins, 1997). There have been a series of work training and experience programs, including

> the Work Experience Program (WEP, 1975–78); the Youth Opportunities Programme (YOP, 1978–83); the Youth Training Scheme (YTS, 1983–88); and, most recently, Youth Training (YT, 1988–) and the Modern Apprenticeship (1995). (O'Higgins, 1997, p. 54)

O'Higgins (1997, pp. 54–55) argues that though the form and content of these programs have varied over the years, they have enhanced the human capital (skill levels) of youth and lowered their wage expectations. The reasoning arose out of an analysis—akin to the reasoning behind similar Canadian programs—that corporations needed incentives to train young people who would move ahead to another firm, leaving the training site without returns for its investment.

The irony is that such schemes still fail to produce what their expressed goal is—jobs. O'Higgins (1997, p. 55) concludes that the programs have only "a small positive influence" on youth employability. Meanwhile, youth spend their time as virtual slave labour in poorly paid research training schemes. Overall, the schemes provide youth with "skill-attainment rather than knowledge-attainment," resulting in their vulnerability to economic fluctuations (Miles, 2000, pp. 39–40).

O'Higgins (1997, p. 56) also points to uneven effects of the programs among young women and ethnic minorities in the UK. Lowe and Krahn (1994–1995) raise similar concerns related to the Canadian context about increasing labour market polarization as most of the job training programs favour young, well-educated male workers as their programs are more likely to take place in larger work organizations and among full-time workers. Other research (Côté & Allahar, 1994, pp. 124–125; Naiman, 2000, pp. 176–177; Baker, 1989, pp. 41–43; Blanchflower & Freeman, 1998) supports the conclusion that the current system favours those who have the means to pursue education, i.e., it discriminates against those who are from lower-income groups, women, or members of ethnoracial minorities.

Echoing this conclusion, Aapola et al. (2005, pp. 72–76; see also O'Higgins, 1997, pp. 56–57) are critical of the fallacy of credentialism and lifelong learning as it pertains to young women living in Western democracies. The realities of a trained workforce do not match the demands of a largely deskilled youth labour market that offers increasingly few real career opportunities. It has been pointed out that despite their higher qualifications, young women's chances are especially circumscribed, particularly since they are concentrated in female-dominated work areas where there is great competition over few opportunities.

O'Higgins's (1997, pp. 59–60) analysis of the reasons for the lack of impact of the work training programs finds that they fail fundamentally because they lay blame on young people (lack of skills, high expectations) for their poor employment records instead of where it belongs—namely, labour market conditions. Additionally, there is great variability in the quality of the programs, including poor monitoring of the schemes; lack of certification of skills obtained; being out of step with the educational system; and lack of partnerships between employers and unions. With reference to the above information about American programs, the success of the Job Corps program may be at least in part attributed to the fact that unions were involved in youth work training and placement.

Youth and Unions

The difficulties of collective organization in the part-time and transitional lower-tier service sector translate to low unionization rates among youth. The lack of success of unions is mirrored in the apathy and lack of awareness among youth about the benefits of unionization. Bryson et al. (2001, p. i) note that "what is particularly striking in Anglo-Saxon economies"—namely, Britain, Canada, and the United States—is that "all display youth unionization rates that are two and a half times lower than those of adult workers." For example, as of 2011, the unionization rate of young people 30 years of age and under with post-secondary education was 15.1 percent, while the corresponding percentage was 29.9 for those over 30 with post-secondary education; in these age groups, those without post-secondary education had unionization rates of 28.2 percent and 38.0 percent, respectively (Foster, 2012, p. 5).

As young people of both sexes have entered the ghettoized youth labour force, unions are changing in composition. Nearly half of all union members in Canada are now women, compared with only one-sixth 30 years ago. Women are unionizing at a more rapid rate than men, reflecting both their increased numbers in the labour force, and the increasing attempts at unionization in the female-dominated, part-time labour force (*The Kitchener-Waterloo Record*, 1998). There are similar patterns of union representation among American (US Census Bureau, 2007, Table 646) and British (Grainger, 2006) women and men.

Tannock (2001, p. 131) describes young American employees as having a "deep sense of alienation from their union." The nature of youth employment and other factors are significant barriers to young people's unionization, as indicated in Box 5.4.

Box 5.4: The Unionization of Young Workers

According to Fontes and Margolies (2010, p. 3):

> There are many challenges to organizing and involving young workers including the following:
>
> - Young workers often do not view their current jobs as a career so when faced with objectionable working conditions they are more likely to find a new job than organize.
> - Young workers tend to work in industries and jobs with high turn-over rate making organizing more difficult.
> - Some unions using older organizers and traditional methods of communication are not able to effectively connect with younger workers.
> - Younger union members are more likely to experience union give-backs and two tier systems at the same time as older union members unsuccessfully try to get their younger peers to appreciate the union struggles of the past.
> - Union cultures reflect the tastes and experiences of older members and these often don't appeal to younger members.

Conclusions

Education is seen as an important pathway toward gainful employment. However, the kinds of jobs and wages young people are getting do not match their extensive and expensive education. The dramatic economic shifts of the 1980s and 1990s, continuing in the 21st century, have hit the youth population particularly hard, leaving some segments especially vulnerable. The patterns of youth employment mirror their educational experiences: those from lower classes, women, and members of race and ethnic minorities are at a disadvantage as reflected in the gendered and racially divided labour market with associated wage gaps.

The depiction of young workers as lazy and greedy is counter to studies showing that young people are willing to work at wages so low that a large proportion of them live in poverty. The image of the shiftless youth worker puts blame on young people themselves for conditions that are created by the capitalist marketplace. In the relentless search for cheap labour, youth become large-scale casualties of the drive for profits. At the same time, increasing workplace controls, combined with enticing "team building," employee gifts, and outings, create a working environment in which large segments of the youthful workforce seem to get some measure of enjoyment out of their exploited condition. While some youth resist and fight back through unionization, their transient work conditions make it nearly impossible to create and sustain a long-term battle against corporations that hold money and power. The challenge of unionizing this shifting labour force remains one of the key struggles of the 21st century.

While increasing numbers of young people combine their education with part-time wage work, the longer weeks they spend in these "constructive" pursuits work to their detriment. Combining part-time work with education is not shown to be beneficial in terms of future employment. Lifelong learning programs and youth work training initiatives are largely ineffective and discriminate against youth who are women or members of racialized and immigrant minorities. Targeted programs, focusing on the most marginalized youth, do not show the returns they promise. In the end, government priorities are in supporting employers in their strategy to offer youth low-paying and menial work that in no way reflects the years of effort and investment they spend in their education. Educational inflation and credentialism are rampant with the tacit approval of governments. These issues are intensifying with the serious economic crises that have hit Europe and North America in the 2000s and 2010s, and require serious attention, not only lip service, by governments.

There is a sidebar to this story of youth and employment: the work-related fates of those youth who fall outside of the radar of their families and immediate communities. As shown in the chapter on families, many youth end up as casualties on the street, having escaped violence and conflict at home. The chapter on crime will show that at least some of these marginalized youth attempt to gain a livelihood in an informal economy that provides them with more dignity than begging or engaging in illegal activities. Their efforts prove to be in vain as they are subjected to draconian legislation, excessive policing, and social ostracism. Their fates reflect the depth of the double-think around youth employment: The more marginalized young people are, the less opportunity they are given to climb out of the pit created by uncaring adults who seem to be more willing to condemn and incarcerate than to make room for youth in their privileged world.

Critical Thinking Questions

1. Do you think the kinds of jobs you have held provide good training for your future employment?
2. What are your work-related goals? What do you think are your chances for attaining them? Why?
3. Have you combined your education with holding a job? How accommodating is or was your employer of your situation?

6 Sexuality and Intimacy

In this chapter, you will learn that

- there is a range in the sexual and intimate relationship patterns among young people, including practices of dating and courtship
- sexist, racist, and heterosexist double standards still prevail in sexual practices
- there are both alarmist and critical views regarding teenage pregnancy and motherhood, particularly related to the experiences of young racialized women and those who live on limited income
- there is an increased diversity in couple formation among young people, including common-law and marital situations for heterosexual and sexual minority youth
- young women continue to perform the largest share of domestic work in heterosexual couples

---

Forming sexual and intimate relationships is a large part of the adolescent and young adult experience. This chapter will explore young people's sexuality, sexual orientation, and relationship formation, including dating, marriage, and common-law relationships.

Relationship formation reflects the society around us, and is subject to the same kinds of power issues that characterize other social relationships, particularly patriarchal power, including heterosexism. These are manifested in the variety of both subtle and overt pressures put on single young people to form lasting intimate and sexual relationships as they get into their twenties. Youth receive these signals from their parents and other adults, their peers, and a wide range of media influences, including popular magazines and television. They also learn gradually that societal preferences are toward heterosexual relations. Thus, young people who are gay, lesbian, or bisexual are frequently shunned or rejected by their families and friends.

In all intimate partner relationships, there are issues of power and control; old double standards still tend to prevail in dating practices and young people's intimate relationships, including the way they negotiate division of domestic work. As young people form cohabiting and marital relationships, they are faced with multiple pressures as they combine work and career pressures with forming relationships and having children. Some young women end up dealing with single motherhood, making it doubly difficult for them to navigate their lives through education and careers. At issue are the kinds of social and financial supports they can access, amidst stigmatization and vilification.

It is worth noting here that reproductive health is an integral part of the dynamics and power relations in intimate partner relationships. There are some specific issues in the area of sexuality and intimacy that will be discussed separately in the chapter on health, including the use of contraceptives and the troublesome prevalence of relationship violence.

The Single Life

Young people may be seen as preoccupied with relationships, but not everyone forms lasting partnerships, nor does everyone live with other people. The term "single" refers to people who were never married. In Chapter 3, it was noted that most single young people tend to live in their parental homes for an extended period of time, meaning that fewer live on their own. Although directly comparable data are not available, some of the trends are quite similar in all three countries, with only one in ten young people in their twenties living alone in the 21st century. About 11.4 percent of people aged 20–34 in the UK were single and living alone as of 2001 (OECD, 2010b). In Canada, based on the 2011 Census, 9.2 percent were single people living on their own (Statistics Canada, 2012b). In the US, 10.6 percent of young people aged 25–34 lived alone as of 2004 (Kreider, 2007, pp. 15-16).

About 10 percent of all Canadians are likely to remain single throughout their lives, an increasing trend since the 1970s. Rising numbers of single people have similarly been observed in the UK, where Finch (2003, p. 14) found that while 7 percent of women born in 1946–1950 were not married by age 32, 28 percent of women born in 1961–1965 had not married by that age. The high percentage among those in the 1961–1965 cohort likely reflects the acceptability of a later age of marriage, meaning that some of these women may still marry.

Iacovou (2002, pp. 57–58) reports that living alone forms a gradually growing proportion as young people in the UK and the US move through the youth age categories from 15–34. In the UK, the percentage for 15–19-year-old women living alone is 1.3, while it gradually increases to 3.6 percent (ages 20–24), 6.0 percent (ages 25–29), and 6.4 percent (ages 30–34). There are variations based on race, ethnicity, and gender. The corresponding numbers for White American women are higher for the first three age categories (1.7 percent, 9.9 percent, and 9.6 percent, respectively), and lower for the oldest age category, at 4.1 percent. Among Black American women, the numbers are lower for most age groups, at 0.8 percent, 5.2 percent, 5.6 percent, and 4.9 percent, respectively, and significantly lower among Hispanic American women, at 0.6 percent, 2.2 percent, 2.3 percent, and 1.3 percent, respectively. The percentages are higher for men in all age groups, particularly in the case of Black American men, one-fifth of whom live alone at ages 30–34. According to Iacovou (2002, p. 68), living alone and cohabitation without legal marriage are "transitional" because they are more common during one's twenties than in one's thirties.

Traditionally, there used to be a strong stigma attached to being a "bachelor" or a "spinster," particularly for women, whose unmarried status carried a host of negative associations. Men's singleness was more readily accepted as a chosen stage of "sowing your wild oats," while single women were pitied because "nobody asked them yet." Today singleness as a choice is more socially accepted, but the pressure toward relationships is still there, and single people are still faced with having to explain why they haven't found "the right one" yet. Well-meaning friends and relatives will go to any length to try to set up single people with potential partners. The general acceptability of singleness has to do with the lengthening of education and the increased acceptance of casual relationships due to contraception and the women's movement (Nett, 1993, p. 223; Baker & Dryden, 1993, pp. 64–67). Singleness for women does not hold the same stigma as it did before, but some research still finds that parents may try to interfere with their single daughters' lives because they have difficulty perceiving them as independent individuals (Gordon, 1994, in Aapola et al., 2005, p. 149).

Interestingly, never-married people are less happy than married people, but single people are happier than those who are divorced, separated, or widowed. The circumstance that singles are less happy than married people is attributed to a lack of a readily available sexual partner, costs incurred from living on one's own rather than sharing a household, more effort needed to find company, and the general pressure toward a "couples' culture" (Nett, 1993, p. 224).

Interesting gender differences appear in satisfaction with one's marital status. Never-married women at all ages are healthier and better satisfied with their singleness than never-married men. This is quite the opposite of the stereotype. The exception is women in their thirties due to increased pressures from family and friends, and the wish to have children, generally expressed as hearing the "biological clock" ticking. Generally, for women, being single is associated with higher educational levels, higher median income, and higher occupational status. Women who delay marriage and live independently, compared with those who continue to live with their parents, are more likely to plan for employment, lower their expected family size, be more accepting of employment of mothers, and be non-traditional in their sex-role expectations. Women who never marry also retain stronger family ties to their family of procreation and extended kin (Nett, 1993, p. 224).

Nevertheless, it is a fact of life that only a small portion of people remain single throughout their lives. Most young people select mates and form long-lasting—even if not lifelong—relationships and family units at some point in their lives.

Courtship and Dating

Mate selection is traditionally associated with courtship, defined formally as "the institutional way that men and women become acquainted before marriage" (McCormick & Jesser, 1991). This was historically prevalent and still continues today in some societies where young women and men are kept apart as much as possible during puberty and early adult years. In these kinds of societies and cultures, courtship is a way of introducing young men and women to their prospective mates. Traditional courting behaviour includes formal visits between the young woman and man, traditionally with the presence of an adult (chaperone). There are strict limitations on the way in which the time together is spent. Sexual self-control is valued, but there is generally a double standard whereby the sexual indiscretions of young men are tolerated more readily than those of young women (Hobart, 1996, p. 144).

Fundamentally, courtship and arranged marriages are about the use of parental power. Parents play a big role in mate selection, with some degree of input by the young people themselves, and courtship usually does end in marriage (Hobart, 1996, p. 144). The practice is still somewhat prevalent in southern Europe, especially in countries where Catholicism is the dominant religion, and it is also normative in large parts of Asia and the Middle East, as well as southern Africa. With population mobility and the increased presence of immigrants and their descendants, more conservative mate selection practices are increasingly common in other European and North American countries.

In general, the prevalence of courtship and arranged marriages declined in Europe and North America from the middle of the 18th century onward, and romantic love became the basis for marriage. With this transition, in modern industrial societies, the free choice of mate became the standard, and dating gained in popularity (Hobart, 1996, pp. 144–145; Nett, 1993, pp. 205–207).

Dating refers to an institutionalized pattern of association among adolescents and young unmarried adults that provides a series of companions for purposes of recreation and socialization (modified from Nett, 1993, p. 206). It is more casual than courtship, based on mutual fun, is on a short-term basis, and is without any immediate expectations about the future of the relationship. This practice in Western countries dates back to the 1920s and the 1930s, and especially to the 1950s, when this form of freer social association of young women and men was formalized, particularly in North America. With the 1960s, the dating setting changed, and formal dates began to be described in more casual terms, as "going out," "seeing," or "getting together with" someone (Albas et al., 1994).

The meanings of dating are shifting and can be a source of confusion, especially among younger age categories. For example, Darling et al. (1999, pp. 475–476) found that students in grades 6 and 7 are uncertain about the meanings of relationships, i.e., whether they are romantic in nature, imply time spent together, or refer to formal dating. There are also gender differences in perceptions about dating, with younger boys reporting a higher incidence of dating than young girls. This may reflect different definitions of dating or an overreporting by boys.

It is customary to view young people's dating relationships and first relationships as "puppy love" or "infatuation" in contrast with adults' presumably deeper and more committed relationships. However, at least one study (Connolly et al., 1999) involving 1,755 Canadian adolescents aged 11–14 found that their views of romantic relationships and friendships "show parallels" with those of adults. Specifically, they found that adolescents, just like adults, identify passion and commitment as the distinguishing features of romantic relationships, while strong affection was seen to be a hallmark of friendship. Further, passion was linked with infatuation and sexual contact, while intimacy was seen to be a part of both romantic relationships and friendships. Among the differences between parents' and adolescents' views was that adults put more emphasis on emotional intimacy in both relationships, and had a stronger sense of commitment in terms of romantic relationships. The authors found that generally the views of older adolescents got closer to those of adults. Further, the study found no significant differences between boys and girls. The authors suggest that age may change this as gender patterns in behaviour become more established.

It has been argued by some researchers (Orton, 1999; Darling et al., 1999) that not only are young people ill-prepared for relationships, but that there are gender differences. Of particular note is the argument that boys have more problems. Orton (1999, p. 133) claims that adolescent socialization gives poor preparation to young men to be responsible and nurturing in relationships, or to young women to maintain their independence in relationships. It is difficult for youth to strive toward a balance of nurturing and independence in their relationships, but, as these authors argue, it is particularly difficult for boys.

Darling et al. (1999) contrast two hypotheses related to the shift from solely single-sex to mixed-sex social networks that takes place in adolescence. One is the "stress hypothesis," which notes the decline in especially girls' self-esteem in the transition to romantic relationships. Many propose that this is due to the increased significance of physical appearance in girls' lives, which makes them vulnerable in mixed-sex settings if they are deemed to be unattractive. The other one, the "leisure hypothesis," proposes that high self-esteem results from the positive correlates of time spent together, such as "positive feedback, shared goals, [and] spontaneous activity." In this model, boys are more vulnerable because they have fewer interpersonal skills than girls (Darling et al., 1999, pp. 462–463). More specifically, the authors' study of students in grades 6–8 in a primarily White, semi-rural, mid-Atlantic community in the United States found that both boys and girls tend to experience the transition into the dating scene positively, in line with the "leisure hypothesis." However, positive self-perceptions among girls are linked to their comfort with boys, and positive self-perceptions among boys seem to correlate with having spent more time with girls. Boys who felt pressured into dating, even though they didn't feel ready for it, had lower self-esteem than other boys. Further, boys' self-esteem was linked to the degree of their actual exposure to girls, whether in peer groups or as girlfriends. For girls, their self-esteem was predicted by their level of comfort with boys, in keeping with girls' tendency to express friendship and intimacy by reflecting on and talking about their feelings. Though this model may overestimate and privilege feminine ways of dealing with relationships and intimacy, it also illustrates the difficulties of relationship formation amidst social pressures toward dating at young ages.

Because all three countries considered in this book have large numbers of immigrants, traditional courtship practices still prevail among some ethnic and racialized groups. However, through the processes of urbanization and the global migration of populations, children are more likely to be exposed to alternative relationship patterns, creating ground for potential clashes between generations.

For example, Canadian studies find that some parents from India and Pakistan arrange marriages for their children, even if they are university graduates (Hobart, 1996, p. 144). However, even where marriages may be arranged, there is more intergenerational consultation involved than may be the case traditionally. Also, Dhruvarajan's (2003) study of Hindu Indo-Canadian families in Winnipeg indicates that parents first screen potential matches based on considerations of caste, class, and linguistic background. After that, the young people have the final say about their choice for a partner. Further, it is becoming more acceptable for young people to date and seek their own partners.

Netting's (2001, pp. 15–20; see also Netting, 2006) study of 27 Indo-Canadian youth in their twenties addresses the ongoing pressures toward arranged marriages in this community. The standard practice in North America is to engage in a system of "introductions" upon the completion of a girl's formal education or a son's achievement of a steady income. "Introductions" consist of the parents "putting the word out" through friends, relatives, newspapers, or Web sites that they are searching for a suitable match for their child. The search is customarily limited by religion, caste, and mother tongue. Parents and youth go over photos and biographies together and make a selection, based on thorough background checks. A formal meeting is arranged with the young people and their parents. Young people have a say in the outcome of the meeting, and it's usually acceptable to terminate the negotiations if there are no romantic feelings between the two. However, parents need to feel that the families are a good match as well, as marriage is about not only the young couple, but also the union of the families. After an agreement is reached, the young couple has a few months to get acquainted and finalize their agreement or disagreement. If all is agreed, a marriage ceremony takes place.

The young people in Netting's (2001) study put high importance on love in choosing a partner, and the majority were not accepting of the introduction system. Only four of the 14 women—whom Netting calls "traditionalists"—and none of the 13 men accepted the introduction system. Five of the youths were "rebels," rejecting the system completely. The largest group—"negotiators"—consisted of two-thirds of the respondents. These youth tried to bend the rules of introductions as much as they felt they could. Their strategies involved not telling their parents about romantic relationships they were engaged in, and selecting only culturally acceptable dating partners. About half of this group indicated willingness to accept an introduced marriage if they were not successful in finding a partner themselves. Many also engaged in free dating temporarily with the intent to eventually bow to the introduction system. Netting's study also found a high degree of mutual negotiation between youth and their parents of boundaries and acceptable partners. She concludes that the "Indo-Canadian marriage system is gradually converging with standard North American practice" (p. 29), a conclusion that gains support from her later study (Netting, 2006).

Studies from the UK and the US confirm that many immigrant parents frown upon the Western practice of dating. The young Vietnamese-American women studied by Zhou and Bakston (1998, in Aapola et al., 2005, pp. 97–98) spoke of their parents' negative attitude toward dating. Similarly, Ghuman (1999, pp. 112, 118–119) reports that Asian girls in the UK are subjected to strict controls in their education and career choices while their families will choose an acceptable marital partner for them. One 22-year-old Indian woman said this about her strategy to resist her parents' wishes:

> My father would not let me go away from home to a university in London. Then I suggested that I could stay with my uncle and travel daily to the university. He agreed ... then my parents were concerned that I was getting too old ... and they should arrange a match for me. I said, "Definitely not from India." To which they agreed. Then I said, "Let me finish my diploma course." After that I turned down several boys and chose the one I really liked; it was a sort of compromise.... There was never any question of dating or going out with boys. (Ghuman, 1997, p. 5, quoted in Ghuman, 1999, p. 119)

Heterosexual Sex

Sexuality is definitely an expected part of adolescent and young adult life, and it is clearly linked to the shift from formal courtship to dating practices. Studies from the three countries are indicative of normalization of sexual activity among young people. This less restrictive social ethos is captured by Greenwood, Fernández-Villaverde and Guner (2010, p. 2):

> The last one hundred years have witnessed a revolution in sexual behaviour. In 1900, only 6% of US women would have engaged in premarital sex by the age of 19, compared to 75% today. ... Public acceptance of premarital sex has reacted with a lag; in 1968 only 15% of women had a permissive attitude towards the act, despite the fact that about 40% of 19 year-old females had had premarital sex. The number with a permissive attitude had jumped to 45% by 1983, a time when 73% of 19 year olds were sexually experienced.

Indeed, the large-scale National American Survey of Family Growth (1982–2002) shows that premarital sex seems to have become normative over time; by age 20, three-quarters of the respondents had premarital sex, and by age 44, all but a small percentage had premarital sex. Further, among "women turning 15 between 1964 and 1993, at least 91 percent had had premarital sex by age 30" (Finer, 2007, p. 73).

Among American youth, being a teen is synonymous with being sexual; nearly 80 percent of males and 66 percent of females engage in sexual intercourse in their teen years (Button & Rienzo, 2002, p. 4). It is found that though American males tend to have a lower age for first sexual experiences than females, this gender gap was closing toward the late 1990s. In their study, Davis and Friel (2001, pp. 672, 675) found the average age of sexual initiation to be 14.3 years for boys and 14.9 years for girls. Ramirez-Valles et al. (2002, pp. 418–419) report that while 54 percent of high school students were sexually active in 1990, the rate in 1997 was 48 percent, reflecting a general downward trend in reported adolescent sexual activity compared to the previous two decades of increases.

Following the 1960s sexual revolution, sexual encounters in dating patterns became more common for both young men and women. According to Hobart's research, there was, between 1968 and 1988, a general increase in the proportions of all young Canadian men and women who thought that premarital sexual intercourse was acceptable if you loved someone, or if you had sex "for fun" (Hobart, 1996, pp. 148–149; see also Belyea & Dubinsky, 1994, p. 20).

The relaxed sexual norms of today are due to wider availability of contraceptives (an issue that will be further discussed in Chapter 9), and the general relaxation of sexual standards among adults, including the portrayal of sex in the media. There is less morality associated with sex, and Hobart (1990, in Hobart, 1996, p. 151) found that only 8 percent of young Canadian people believe that premarital sex is morally wrong.

In Britain, likewise, sex outside of marriage is definitely not a taboo; in a 1994 national survey it was only disapproved of (considered "wrong") by 8.2 percent of men and 10.8 percent of women. There has been a drop in the age for first intercourse in the postwar years. Thus, the median age in 1994 was 17 for both women and men, and men are only somewhat more likely to have had sexual intercourse before age 16 than women. Though this pattern holds for Whites, there is also race and ethnic variation, with Asian women the least likely to report sexual intercourse before age 16, and Black men the most likely (Charles, 2002, p. 130).

Similar patterns of intergroup differences are found in the United States. Ramirez-Valles et al. (2002, pp. 418–419) report that rates of sexual activity vary by gender, race, and social class. In 1997, the rates of sexual activity of high school students were 72 percent for African Americans, 43 percent for Whites, and 52 percent for Hispanics. The rates are the highest among African-American males. These general patterns have been confirmed in later research (Manning et al., 2005).

Some differences between ethnic groups are also reported in Canada. Earlier studies from the 1960s to the 1980s indicated that premarital sex was traditionally less prevalent among French-Canadian than English-Canadian youth, but this distinction diminished due to the declining influence of the Roman Catholic Church in Quebec following the Quiet Revolution (Hobart, 1996, pp. 148–149). As discussed in Chapter 3, recent studies of children of Asian immigrants in Canada suggest that there is considerable tension between first-generation parents and second-generation children over issues of dating and intimacy (Giguère et al., 2010, pp. 20-22). Though there are no large-scale studies, the reported intergenerational conflict would suggest that even if the rates of premarital sex are lower among second-generation youth than in the general youth population, their acceptance of premarital sex might be higher than that of their parents.

Sexual activity outside marriage is by far the norm among university-age youth. While in the late 1960s, only approximately one-third of Canadian university-aged males and one-fifth of females had sexual intercourse, by the 1970s and the 1980s, the majority of males (60–70 percent) and females (50–60 percent) had sexual experience (Hobart, 1996, pp. 149–151). By 1988, the gap reduced to 77 percent and 73 percent of Canadian college and university male and female students, respectively (Netting, 1992; Hobart, 1996, pp. 149–151), reflecting the normalization of sexual activity among young people observed above.

Nevertheless, not all university or college youth fall within the same sexual culture. Netting's study from 1990 (reported in 1992) of a sample of college students at the Okanagan University College suggests that there are distinct types of sexual culture among Canadian youth. About one-third of both men and women were celibate, i.e., they reported that they practise celibacy or sexual abstinence. About one-third of men and almost half of the women reported being monogamous, i.e., having had only one lover in the past year, whereas 30 percent of men and 20 percent of women had more than one partner. Most men (60 percent) and women (53 percent) had had more than one partner since they began dating. The third group consist of free experimenters; that is, more men (33 percent) than women (14 percent) reported at least one one-night stand, and more men (28 percent) than women (6 percent) reported that they currently have multiple sexual partners.

Netting's (2001) updated study, incorporating data from 1996–1998 and 2000, looked for any changes in students' sexual decisions and behaviours from the earlier surveys. The later survey found that the "proportion of committed partners rose as proportion of strangers fell," i.e., by 2000 14 percent of men and 8 percent of women reported having had one-night stands, while 35 percent of men and 48 percent of women reported having had sex with a steady partner. Additionally, 51 percent of men and 44 percent of women reported having had sex with a friend or an acquaintance. This means a trend toward more serious relationships for both sexes, though men still have more casual partners than women (Netting, 2001, p. 8, Table 4). Of the three types of approaches to sexuality, those who were celibate showed most stability, with approximately one-third of the students (23 percent of men and 35 percent of women). Monogamous relationships were by far the most common, with 59 percent of men and 58 percent of women, while 18 percent of men and 7 percent of women indicated being free experimenters (pp. 13–15). Overall, the three subcultures have remained relatively stable over the years (p. 20).

Whereas having sex seems to be natural among young people in their late teens and early twenties, it has also now become a natural part of being a younger teenager. A national Canadian study of high school students in 1992 found that the vast majority (90 percent) of both males and females approved of premarital sex if a couple was in love. The percentage declined to 51 percent for women and 77 percent for men in cases where the couple liked each other (Hobart, 1996, p. 151). These approval ratings are reflected in actual sexual activity. Canadian health studies have found that approximately 16 percent of male and 12 percent of females have had sexual intercourse before age 15. By the time they are 17 years of age, 47 percent of males and 45 percent of females have had sex, and 36 percent of the males and 17 percent of females have had more than one sexual partner. These rates are much higher among high school dropouts aged 16–19, i.e., 89 percent and 84 percent, respectively; and were 95 percent and 93 percent among street youth aged 15–19. Among college and university students aged 18–21, 70 percent of males and 66 percent of females had experienced sex (Orton, 1999, pp. 131–132).

More recently, in 2005, the Canadian Community Health Survey and the National Population Health Survey showed similar patterns to the 1990s: of young people aged 15–19, 43 percent had had sexual intercourse. The percentages were higher for older age groups, with about one-third of those aged 15–17 and two-thirds of those aged 18–19 having had intercourse at least once. Sexual intercourse was less common among those below age 15, at 8 percent (Rotermann, 2008, p. 1). At the same time, the available data indicate that there was a slight decline in sexual intercourse among Canadian teens from the 1990s to 2010 (Sex Information and Education Council of Canada, 2012). Likewise, a national study indicates that 38 percent of males and 51 percent of females reported being virgins at age 18 (Ambert & Krull, 2006, pp. 226–227). These declines are possibly due to the HIV/AIDS epidemic and the impact of sex education. A similar decline has been noted in the United States since the 1990s. Compared to 1991 (67 percent), fewer American grade 12 students reported having had sex in 2001 (61 percent) (US Department of Health and Human Services, 2012).

The percentages above, as well as other large national studies, indicate a steadily higher rate of sexual experience for young men than young women in all age groups (Rotermann, 2008, p. 1). The decline in young women's sexual activity may be linked to an increased attempt, in the United States at least, to curb young people's sexuality, exemplified in the rise of abstinence education in the 1990s. Some argue that this campaigning has resulted in increasing fearfulness toward sex among young girls. Some argue that this may, in fact, lead to more sexual victimization, as these girls become more adept at hiding their sexual activity from their parents rather than discussing it with them (Aapola et al., 2005, p. 97).

What Predicts Adolescent Sexual Activity?

Peers are often cited as influential in a range of young people's behaviours. That sexuality is a part of youth culture is borne out by the fact that most Canadian adolescents find out about sexual matters from their peers, not their parents; and about birth control at school, not at home (Nett, 1993, p. 210). Maticka-Tyndale, Herold, and Mewhinney (1998, pp. 155–157) studied the spring-break sexual behaviours of Canadian university students. The self-reported rates of casual sex (having sex with someone they met) were 21 percent of men and 17 percent of women, similar to rates among British beach vacationers (22 percent and 20 percent). Peers had an influence on the youth's actions, as the spring-break atmosphere is one of a big party with drinking and picking up sexual partners. However, gender differences were noted. For both men and women, peers influenced their decisions about having casual sex, commonly through pacts with the intent to have casual sex. However, male peers' actions did not directly affect the males' actions, while their female peers' actions did have an influence on the women's casual sex behaviour. It seems that while young women are influenced by their peers, young men are more influenced by general environmental cues.

Aside from peer influence, which seems to be at least situationally relevant, multiple studies have uncovered factors behind young people's sexual initiation and the level of their sexual activity. Factors behind the initiation to and the frequency of sexual intercourse include social class, level of education, religiosity, and parental—particularly maternal—norms, values, and supervision. Generally, studies indicate that later sexual initiation is associated with parents' higher social class position, living in a two-parent family, higher school achievement, and religiosity (Ambert & Krull, 2006, p. 227; Charles, 2002).

Studies also suggest that the acceptability of premarital sex is tied to religion: those who adhere to religious beliefs tend to be less permissive (Das et al., 2011). For example, a recent study by Adamczyk and Hayes (2012) found that Muslims and Hindus are less likely to report premarital sex than Christians and Jews. Given that religious affiliation and observance are a part of the socialization pattern of young people, and that populations are becoming more varied with the influx of immigrants, future studies will likely further illuminate the links between religion and the acceptability and practice of premarital sex among young people.

American studies on adolescent sexuality and family structure have found that young people from intact two-parent families are less sexually experienced and begin sexual relations at a later age than those from divorced families. Thus, girls from single-parent families or cohabiting families are more sexually active and experienced. These links are generally explained by these parents' more permissive attitudes about sexuality, and weaker parental authority and control over their adolescents (Davis & Friel, 2001, pp. 670–671; Wu & Thomson, 2001). It is easier for two parents to control their teens' sexual behaviours. Greater parental supervision in general has a dampening effect on teens' sexuality (Wu & Thomson, 2001, p. 684).

Linked to this is the debate on the impact of divorced and remarried families on youth sexual activity. The "turbulence" argument holds that parental divorce provides for an unsettled context in which teens are more likely to enter into earlier sexual relationships. Stepfamilies have generally more complex internal dynamics and some research supports the notion that their supervision of adolescents is similar to single-parent families (Wu & Thomson, 2001, pp. 684–685). Interestingly, Davis and Friel (2001, p. 676) found that living in a lesbian family does not make a difference for the sexual timing or number of sexual partners of adolescents.

Parental values and norms, through family culture, have generally been established to have an effect on adolescents' sexuality. In other words, parental approval or disapproval of sexual activity seems to be reflected in the adolescents' behaviours (Davis & Friel, 2001, p. 679). Most of the studies of parental influence focus on mothers, which is in keeping with their role as primary caregivers (Wu & Thomson, 2001, p. 683). Davis and Friel (2001, pp. 679–680) demonstrate that what seems to have an impact on both teenage males' and females' sexual initiation is "the mother-child relationship, the level of interaction, and the mother's attitudes toward and discussion of sex." However, they found that once a teenager has begun to have sex, family context or structure have very little effect on their sexual partnering. Other studies support the notion that the closer and more supportive the parent-child relationship, the later the sexual initiation (Wu &

Thomson, 2001, p. 684). Further, in their nationally representative sample of American adolescents in grades 7–11, Dittus and Jaccard (2000) found that perceived maternal disapproval of adolescent sexual activity and mother-adolescent closeness were likely to delay onset of sexual activity and deter teenage pregnancy. Additionally, the more satisfied teens were with their relationship with their mother, the more likely they were to use birth control.

The general factors behind young racialized people's decisions about sexuality confirm the complex influences of social class, gender, family type, religiosity, and parental supervision and closeness. For example, Wu and Thomson (2001, p. 694) found that family turbulence had an impact on the sexual activities of White American women, but not Black women living in single-parent or father-absent families. In comparison, what seemed to be more influential for Black women's sexuality was their living in single-parent families where their mothers were sexually active, suggesting that maternal norms and values play a role.

Further, in their three-year longitudinal study of sexual behaviour among 558 African-American high school students, Ramirez-Valles et al. (2002) found different predictors for males and females of timing of first intercourse. Young African-American women were more likely to delay first intercourse if they participated in church activities, spent time with their mothers, or had mothers with less than high school education. The explanation for these effects is that church activities and time spent with their mothers reinforce more conservative outlooks, particularly if the maternal education levels are indicative of more time spent at home and thus a chance to monitor their daughters' behaviours. For the males, timing of first intercourse was delayed if they were motivated to complete school, lived in two-parent families with time spent with their father, participated in family decision making, and lived in more affluent neighbourhoods. This translates to a situation in which the combination of parental control and raising sons' expectations about their future is reinforced by living in a neighbourhood that is not financially deprived. Indeed, other research has found a strong link between neighbourhood poverty and African-American youths' early sexuality (Ramirez-Valles et al., 2002, p. 435).

The Double Standard

Up until the 1950s, premarital sexual abstinence and virginity in heterosexual relationships were normative for women, while the double standard allowed men to engage in premarital sex. This meant that women would be of two types: potential wives or "easy" sexual partners (Hobart, 1996, p. 148). Though not quite as blatantly expressed anymore, the double standard in sexuality prevails in the present day. In fact, adults tend to view adolescent sexuality, and particularly that of their daughters, with a great deal of alarm, convinced that young people are obsessed with sex (Belyea & Dubinsky, 1994, pp. 22–23).

Meanwhile, a survey of Canadian adolescents by the Canadian Advisory Council on the Status of Women (CACSW) (Holmes & Silverman, 1992, pp. 37–39) found that girls are much more concerned with their families and friends than with boyfriends. The CACSW survey also found that sex is not as high on the list of priorities for young high school–aged girls as are friends and getting good grades. This stands in contrast with the image of young girls as "boy crazy." This reflects the general sense that "it is still not considered appropriate for young women to take control over their sexual lives." Thus, young women's sexuality is along the lines of social expectations, i.e., they remain passive (Holmes & Silverman, 1992, pp. 39–40).

Indeed, gender differences persist in British youth's reasons for sexual intercourse, with love and intimacy rating higher in women's reasons and peer group pressures and ridding themselves of their virgin status more prevalent among young men. Women are also less likely than men to report multiple sexual partners and more likely to prefer monogamy. Other aspects of the double standard are still alive and well, with women and more so men thinking that sex at a young age is more acceptable for men than for women (Charles, 2002, pp. 130–131). Young men are also reportedly less interested in developing intimacy than having a sexual conquest, which can be narrated to male peers (Charles, 2002, pp. 144–145). This conclusion of women's greater emphasis on emotional aspects of the relationship and men's emphasis on the sex act is supported in Canadian research (Hobart, 1996, p. 151).

Many point to the reduction of the male-female sexual experience gap as evidence of liberalization of sexuality for both young men and women (Hobart, 1996, pp. 150–151; Otis et al., 1997, p. 17). However, the double standard still prevails, witness the continuation of assumptions of "availability" of single women who date many men (Baker, 1996a, p. 304). In keeping with the discussions on bullying in Chapter 4, studies continue to show that girls can lose their reputation if they engage in sexual activities such as being flirtatious or having more than one boyfriend (Belyea & Dubinsky, 1994, pp. 32–34). Young women still get the reputation of being "slags," "sluts," or "hos" if they are seen to be too solicitous of male interest. Suzy, a young British woman (Hey, 1997, p. 117, in Aapola et al., 2005, p. 140), said this:

> I think a slag is someone who's ... just ... there's a lot of them around this school. They walk around sort of clicking their heels, sort of their bums swaying from side to side and they're caked in makeup. And it's so obvious that they are out to "get the boys" really. That's it! That's what I'd say a slag is.

These patterns are manifestations of patriarchy. Male power in sexual relations is exhibited in three major indicators: (1) the ability to choose the place and time and progression of sexual activity; (2) the ability to communicate one's sexual demands explicitly; (3) sexual pressure or strategies used to obtain sexual favours (Otis et al., 1997). There is an asymmetry based on the privileging of male sexual needs over women's, and the association of male sexuality with aggression and pleasure, and female sexuality with passivity in the context of wanting love and romance. Thus, women who express their sexuality more aggressively and freely are more likely to be labelled as deviant or promiscuous (Otis et al., 1997, p. 18).

Further, despite the numerical equalization between men and women in sexual expression, the quality of the first sexual experience differs for young women and men. In Britain, based on large national surveys in the 1940s and the 1990s, women continue to be consistently dissatisfied with the quality of their emotional and sexual experiences with men (Charles, 2002, p. 132). Meanwhile, young men's first sexual intercourse is usually enjoyable and they think their female partner is also enjoying it, while young women's accounts are more negative and indicate limited satisfaction. This is rooted in the idea that sexual encounters are geared toward men's needs; men are the actors and women are passive recipients who are expected to get fulfillment from meeting the male's needs. Additionally, young women are fearful of unwanted pregnancy, sexually transmitted diseases, or a loss of their reputation, and the focus on this makes it more difficult to experience desire and pleasure. It can be argued that "first intercourse turns boys into men whereas girls do not experience it as turning them into women; this is much more likely to be associated with menstruation" (Charles, 2002, pp. 144–145).

Similarly in North America, young men tend to describe their first sexual experience as "exciting and satisfying." In contrast, young women are more likely to have an experience in which they lack control and report negative emotions like "fear, anxiety, embarrassment, and even guilt." One young woman (in Ambert & Krull, 2006, p. 227) said this:

> I did not enjoy my first sexual experience at all because I was not ready for it and that's why I mention it here because it became something I regretted for a long time after and made me feel dirty. It took me three years after that, until with my boyfriend, to consider it again and the experience was so different because I felt loved.

At the same time, the differential valuing of sexual performance by young women and men is challenged by some young women. Mariah, a 17-year-old American (Gray & Phillips, 1998, in Aapola et al., 2005, pp. 143–144), says:

> I tend to think I'm an exception to the female role in terms of sexuality. I view sex as a notch in my belt and don't have a problem picking up a guy. Sex is an experience for me, and I don't have to be in love. The TV and the media never show women as that outgoing, unless they're evil characters. I find that when I initiate sex, it can scare guys. But if the guy's not ready, then I can take on the role of "Hey, that's cool" and pick up whatever we were doing and not go any further.

Even though young women are not expected to take charge in sexual matters, they are still by and large held responsible for their encounters. While young men have freedoms and are seen to be subject to their inherent sexual desires, young women are expected to "act responsibly" for both their sexuality and for contraception (Aapola et al., 2005, pp. 150–151). This issue will be taken up in more detail in the chapter on health with regard to reproductive health issues, birth control, and sexually transmitted infections. What has to be noted here, though, is that despite this expectation of responsibility and maturity, girls are subject to more parental control regarding their sexuality. Their vulnerability to sexual exploitation is raised as the reason for their surveillance, even as many of them continue to be abused in their homes, harassed in schools, and accosted by male friends, acquaintances, and strangers. The irony is that even today, there is a sense that if a girl is subjected to unwanted and uninvited attention, she is still somehow to blame for her own victimization (Aapola et al., 2005, pp. 153–156).

Aside from the double standard associated with sexuality, the prevailing image of sex also presumes perfect bodies. An added complication for young women is the emphasis on having attractive bodies. While young women strive to attain this ideal, they may also have difficulties with accepting their bodies even as they are engaging in sex (Belyea & Dubinsky, 1994, pp. 29–30; Otis et al., 1997). The idealized bodies associated with sex also exclude youth with disabilities, who are often considered asexual and whose sexuality is denied (Box 6.1).

Box 6.1: Sexuality Denied

Harilyn Rousso (1988, p. 2, in Aapola et al., 2005, p. 144), a disability rights activist, recounts the prevailing social attitudes about disability and sexuality prior to her realization that it was not written in stone:

> One of the myths in our society about disabled women is that we are asexual, incapable of leading socially and sexually fulfilling lives. When I was growing up, my parents and I accepted this myth without question. We simply assumed that because I had a disability, I could not date, find a partner, or have children. As a teenager and young adult, I put aside any hope of a social life and concentrated on my studies. It never occurred to me that I had any alternative, that I could have both a career and a romantic life.

The Sexualization of Blacks

The issue of the double standard also has racialized components. There are suggestions of different dating and sexual patterns and expectations based on racialized group membership. British youth researcher Alexander (1996) studied the lives of three groups of Black British male youth aged 18–24 in London. She points to the ambiguities in Black males' attitudes toward women. As indicated earlier in Chapter 2, the history of Black people in Europe and North America is one of denial of masculine privilege and of the sexual oppression of Black women. This was manifested in the group studied by Alexander through the young men's engagement in frequent sexual relationships even though they had steady girlfriends whom they referred to as "wives." The women in casual flings were called "bitches," a term often extended to all women. The contrast between "wives" and "bitches" mirrors the ideas about the good girls you have at home as opposed to the not-so-nice women who are designated for casual sex. One of the young men, Shane (Alexander, 1996, p. 163), explained it this way:

> I treat the one I'm serious about like a flower, like a butterfly; I treat the other one like a dog.… And that's it—either you like it or leave it.

The "bitches" were mainly White women whom these men saw as being good for casual sex, but not for committed relationships. The young men depicted Black girls as harder to get and White girls as "easy," illustrated by a young man by the name of Darnell (Alexander, 1996, p. 174):

> It must be true because I'm finding it hard at the moment.… Yeah, a lot of them are harder to get. Like with a white girl, you can go and whisper two things in their ears and within a week you're regular every night, right? With a black girl, you have to say "Praise Allah and everything," and then they *might* give it up. [emphasis in original]

Meanwhile, the very men who engaged in sexual dalliances had a strict possessiveness about their "wives." Many of Alexander's informants said they could never have a wife who had been with some other man because she would have "belonged" to some other man. This possessiveness and the sexual liberties taken by these young men resulted in conflict with their wives, but wives who became too demanding were left behind. Shane (Alexander, 1996, p. 165) had done this to his past girlfriend, Marion:

> I was really in love and she abused it, so I dropped her.… I felt that she was in control and I wasn't, so I decided to drop her.

An important subtext to the complex relationships is provided by the ideologies regarding Black sexuality. In Alexander's (1996) study, the young Black males reported both White and Black community hostility toward interracial relationships. As these males objectified White women, they were also objectified themselves. They spoke of the stereotype and myth of Black male sexuality, including the stories of penis size, some of which they were proud of as much as they rejected it. For example, Shane (Alexander, 1996, p. 180) said:

> We're well-toned, we're physical, we're funny, we're rhythmic.… We have nice bodies, we look good. Just look at a white man—look at a 25-year-old white man to a 25-year-old black man.

The sexualization of Black women and men is a well-documented phenomenon in both Britain and the US. Small (1994, pp. 98–100) situates this legacy in the era of slavery when

Black women were established as breeders of more slaves, and their public image has remained sexually charged to this day. The images of Black women as sexual threats and breeders are repeated in the current depictions of the "welfare mothers" and the "ho." Meanwhile, Black males are portrayed as sexual brutes. These depictions are present in complex ways in the lyrics of rap and hip-hop music, as will be discussed further in Chapter 7.

Gay, Lesbian, and Bisexual Intimacy and Relationships

National surveys report levels of non-heterosexual orientation in the range of a few percentage points of the total population. For example, in Canada, just under 2 percent of the population identified with being gay, lesbian, or bisexual in the 2003 and 2005 Canadian Community Health Surveys, the largest group being gay men, followed by bisexual women, lesbians, and bisexual men (Statistics Canada, 2008d). A 1994 British national survey reported homosexuality among 6.1 percent of men and 3.4 percent of women; the percentages were higher among those who had been in boarding schools (Charles, 2002, pp. 131–132). According to nationally representative survey results from 1994, 1.4 percent of American women and 2.8 percent of men identified themselves as gay, lesbian, or bisexual. The numbers are higher depending on the wording of the question. When asked whether they had ever thought of having sex with someone of their own gender, 5.5 percent of women and 6 percent of men responded affirmatively. The numbers rose even higher when asked if they had at least one event of same-sex desire to 7.5 percent for women and 7.7 percent for men. Studies generally estimate the rate of adolescent homosexuality or bisexuality to be 1–3 percent. However, this is likely higher as "coming out" to oneself and to others is a gradual process in the face of negative social attitudes and a resistance to being labelled. Additionally, whether heterosexual or non-heterosexual, not all youth engage in sexual behaviour at a young age (Savin-Williams, 2001, pp. 9–11).

Heterosexuality is still the norm throughout the globe, and though attitudes are changing gradually in the Western world, homophobia and heterosexism continue to prevail, expressed in negative behaviours toward homosexuals, including verbal and physical harassment and violence. Attitudes differ by age, gender, and level of education, with acceptance levels generally higher among women, and rising with age and level of education (Schellenberg et al., 1999, pp. 139–141; Charles, 2002, pp. 131–132; King et al., 1988, in McKay & Holowaty, 1997, p. 34). There has been increased acceptance of homosexuality over time as a result of the battles of gay rights activists (Baker & Dryden, 1993, pp. 66–67).

Bibby (2001, pp. 90–91) found that approval of homosexuality is still not universal among Canadian youth: 66 percent of teenage girls and 41 percent of teen males indicate approval for homosexual relations, and 87 percent vs. 62 percent think that homosexuals are entitled to the same rights as other Canadians. Reflecting the gender gap in views in this area, one grade 11 male from Alberta said:

> One thing I would like to stress is that homosexuality is wrong. If they really want to be gay, they should do it in secret and not adopt kids.

Generally, and despite some relaxation of norms over the past few decades, the hegemony of heterosexuality (Aapola et al., 2005, p. 149) or "compulsory heterosexuality" prevails and is taken for granted (Rich, 1980, in Charles, 2002, pp. 134–137). We still live in a heterosexist, homophobic, lesbo-phobic, and bi-phobic society. Homosexuality is by and large seen to be socially undesirable. It is still illegal in many countries, or is socially constructed as a mental illness. In most countries, despite some relaxation of laws and attitudes, homosexuals continue to be subjected to ill treatment, harassment, discrimination, and hate (Aapola et al., 2005, pp. 155–156). In her book on postwar Canadian youth and the "making of heterosexuality," Adams (1997) maps out the ways in which teen sexuality was geared toward heterosexuality in the 1950s through the demonizing of homosexuality and its association with abnormality and delinquency (see also Maynard, 1997).

There is a debate over whether gays or lesbians are more reviled. In their study of Canadian university students' (101 male, 98 female) attitudes toward homosexuality, Schellenberg, Hirt, and Sears (1999) found that lesbians were viewed more positively than gay men, that woman students were more positive than men, and that students in arts or social science were more positive compared to science or business students. Male students' attitudes toward gay men seemed to become more positive with increased years of education. The levels of acceptance of lesbians also improved regardless of the study respondents' gender or field of study. The authors conclude that "college education may promote a reduction in anti-homosexual prejudice among young people, particularly among young men" (p. 139).

Some argue that gay men are more negatively viewed than lesbians due to narrow definitions of masculinity (Schellenberg et al., 1999, pp. 139–141). Canadian researcher Frank (1994, p. 57) argues that the hegemony of heterosexual masculinity is very difficult to work against because it permeates every aspect of social life. Meanwhile, Aapola et al. (2005, pp. 148–149) point out that lesbianism is still stigmatized. Societal views hold heterosexual penetration as the hallmark of having sex. Thus, young women are seen to be initiated into "normal" sexuality through heterosexual crushes and boyfriends. Despite contemporary hype around sexual liberation, lesbianism is still out of bounds as a serious transgression of the unwritten sexual code. For example, in Britain, lesbianism was never criminalized while male homosexuality was decriminalized in the 1970s (Charles, 2002, p. 132). If these views are taken together, the masculine privilege is revealed to be behind both types of stigmatization and it may be futile to engage in debates over who is more oppressed when both gays and lesbians are victims of the same hierarchy.

Same-sex dating and mate selection have not been studied extensively so far. Not only is the population comparatively small, but many youth also tend to stay in the closet and date heterosexually. If "coming out" is more likely to take place later in adulthood, same-sex dating during one's teens or early twenties is not an issue (Ambert & Krull, 2006, pp. 207–210). The stigma of "sickness" is still associated with homosexuality, and it was not too long ago that young people were encouraged to be "cured" of their same-sex sexual attraction by forming heterosexual relationships, including getting married (Lenskyj, 1990) or having children (O'Brien & Weir, 1995, p. 119).

What little is known about partner selection among gay and lesbian people seems to indicate that homogamy—the selection of mates based on similarities in the potential partners' characteristics—is not as important as it is for heterosexuals. It is speculated that their nonconformist sexual orientation may be associated with other non-traditional behaviours. There is also more difficulty matching criteria due to the small numbers of gays or lesbians from the same kind of background, including race, ethnicity, social class, etc. Additional findings seem to suggest that gays may be more concerned than lesbians with the physical appearance of their partners (Ambert & Krull, 2006, pp. 207–210).

With a still slow increase in the acceptance of homosexuality and bisexuality, some teens come out to their families amidst benign responses, as exemplified in the experience of Angie, a 17-year-old American girl (Gray & Phillips, 1998, in Aapola et al., 2005, pp. 95–96):

> I came out to my mom by leaving a poem on the kitchen table about a girl I liked. My mom said, "I guess you are bisexual or something." I said, "Yeah, I don't think about it too much," which wasn't totally true. "Don't you think it would be easier if you picked gay or straight?" I told her, "Mom, I can't change the way I am."

More generally, though, coming out is a trying process for young people who are gay, lesbian, or bisexual (Aapola et al., 2005, pp. 155–156). It has been said that rather than being supportive, "families are a hazard for gay and lesbian youth" (O'Brien & Weir, 1995, p. 121). The experiences of coming out to families tend to be mostly negative, ranging from conflict to parents disowning their child, to the youth feeling that they have to hide their true identity and aspects of their life from their family (Crago, 1996; Lenskyj, 1990; Aapola et al., 2005, pp. 98–99). Typical family reactions to coming out include lack of support, anger, harassment, and parental attempts to restrict the young people's activities. Parents may also be misinformed about sexual minorities, engage in denial, or think that the child is too young to decide. Parental and sibling abuse as an outcome of coming out is well documented (O'Brien & Weir, 1995, pp. 119–120).

In a rare study of 72 gay, lesbian, and bisexual youth (aged 16–27) about their process of maturing and separating from their parents, Floyd et al. (1999) found results similar to heterosexual youth. The sexual-minority youth faced similar developmental challenges that were made more difficult if the parents had a negative view of their children's sexual orientation. Additionally, sexual-minority youth face their identity development alone as their parents are unable to socialize their children in this regard, lacking similar experiences. However, parental acceptance seems to help in their development. Similar to other studies, this one shows that mothers are generally more approving than fathers, and that maternal positive attitudes have an impact on these youth's sense of well-being. The study also shows that adjustment problems found among sexual-minority youth arise not from their identities but from stressors in their families.

Discovering that you are gay or lesbian or bisexual can be a frightening experience. Homophobia and hostility are exhibited in schools, workplaces, and families. As indicated in the previous chapter, gay and lesbian youth in schools are subject to ill treatment, including physical and psychological abuse by students and teachers. Some young people feel that they are particularly rejected by the older generation, who represent power and authority in these social institutions. This is combined with the general ideology in heterosexual and queer communities alike that being young means that you cannot possibly know what your sexual orientation is. Seventeen-year-old Anna-Louise Crago (1996, p. 15) has this to say:

> When I began coming out, somewhere between 14 and 15, I started playing around with the word bi. No one believed me. They swore I'd change when I matured. (I'm 17 and still here). I worked tirelessly on gay and lesbian issues hoping I might gain credibility. I didn't, nor did I gain shelter from the queer-bashing in high school as the only one out. Biphobia fed into ageism and vice versa. Established lesbian and gay groups were there for people in their thirties. They did/do not have the resources or necessarily the understanding of the gamble of being out *in* and *dependent on* one's home. [emphasis in the original]

Stages of "Coming Out" or Flexible Sexuality?

Because of the fear of rejection, taunts, and hostility, sexual-minority youth may be forced "into the closet" for longer than they would like, covering up their true sexual identities. Because of their economic dependence on their parents, and because of fear of loss of family affection and rejection, they are likely to delay the coming-out process (O'Brien & Weir, 1995, pp. 118–119).

Typical developmental stage theories of sexual identity formation propose a progression, starting with a gradual awareness of one's sexuality and moving through different stages of self-acceptance and disclosure ("coming out"). These theories presume a fixed, inborn sexual identity that is gradually revealed to a person through time. Typical models propose a move through stages that reflect an attempt to achieve congruence between sexual orientation, sexual behaviour, and sexual identity. The stages of identity formation move from budding awareness of one's sexual orientation, to starting to question whether you may be non-heterosexual, to exploring the emerging identity, to involvement in social and sexual activities of non-heterosexuals. Through the stages, individuals "come out" to themselves and their family, friends, and society, and establish a comfort level and positive attitudes toward their sexuality (Rosario et al., 2006, pp. 46–47) (see Box 6.2).

Though the idea of one's sexual identity as fixed and uncontrollable is popular and is also reflected in the personal narratives of many gay, lesbian, bisexual, and transsexual youth, some authors question the fixed pathway model. Instead, they propose that sexual identity and expression are more fluid and context-dependent than proposed in the stage model, and that in fact our sexual identities continue to change over time rather than follow a fixed path with a final end point (Horowitz & Newcomb, 2001; Rosario et al., 2006).

Longitudinal studies have found that the majority of young people sustain their sexual self-identification over time. For example, American studies have found that around

---

Box 6.2: The Pathway of "Coming Out"

Chandler (1995, pp. 124–133) maps out a typical pathway based on the most prevalent models of "coming out" in the social science literature. According to this now-contested model, an individual goes through six phases along the way to the ultimate acceptance of his or her homosexual identity and orientation. It is to be noted that the notion of bisexuality is not acknowledged as a possibility in this early model:

1. *Sensitization-Insight:* The earliest (typically around age 9 to 11) feelings of "being different" that are not labelled but are based on same-sex attraction.
2. *Identity Confusion-Isolation:* Beginnings of the realization, in adolescence, that one might be homosexual. This is associated with stigma, fear, and avoidance.
3. *Identity Tolerance-Disclosure:* Acknowledgement and toleration of one's homosexuality, which is shared with trusted people because of the risk of disclosure. Initial sexual experimentation and exploration of gay and lesbian culture takes place.
4. *Identity Acceptance-Socialization:* Though still somewhat conflicted, teens accept and seek to validate their sexuality by developing same-sex love relationships and get more involved with the queer community.
5. *Identity Pride-Commitment:* In the face of prejudice, teens become more solidly committed to their sexual orientation and the queer community, and make their homosexuality public. Some may become active in queer politics.
6. *Identity Synthesis:* Homosexuality becomes just one aspect of the many in the teens' self-definition, and there is less threat perceived from the heterosexual world.

50–70 percent of youth maintain their sexual identity, while a lesser proportion (around 15 percent) experiences shifts over time. Though the results in this regard are mixed, some studies also suggest that women are more flexible in their sexual identity than men, with more young women than young men reporting bisexuality (Rosario et al., 2006, pp. 47–48).

Aside from the issue of flexibility in people's sexual identity over time, another problem with developmental stage theories is the homogenizing of the experiences of people in the sexual-minority category. Often conclusions from one category (e.g., gay males) are extended to others (e.g., lesbians). Thus, the coming-out models for gay men are not applicable to lesbians, who have been shown to deal with the stages (awareness, labelling, disclosure, and acting on their feelings) within a shorter period of time, and with different pathways and earlier experiences than gay men (Savin-Williams, 2001, p. 8). Lesbians tend to come out later than gays, and lesbians' same-sex attractions tend to be in conjunction with close bonds of affection (Floyd et al., 1999, p. 724).

Further complications arise for transgender and transsexual individuals as they come to terms with their needs and external pressures (Push Projects, 2013):

> I finally came out about being Transgender when I was 23 to my counsellor after watching the previous weeks Sharon Osborne Show, when she had a female to male transgender person (F2M) as her final guest, who was talking about how he went through the process of first deciding he was a lesbian before finally coming out as Transgender. This was only after he had tried to overdose on prescription pills and painkillers. Luckily his Mum found him. I was sitting there watching and listening, and just thinking that was me because although I hadn't tried to kill myself, I was identifying with everything else that he said. For the next week I was nervous because this was huge to leave myself open like this to ridicule or to be dismissed as just being silly, the effects of which would have been crushing for the one person who I trusted above all others to be able to talk about anything with, but thankfully she didn't do that, she was brilliant, and she helped me by going on the internet with me and finding out about the whole process. It was funny because pretty much every keyword she typed in like 'female to male Transsexual' or 'Transgender' came up with results pages pretty much full of links to Transgender porn sites, but eventually we got there and she printed out loads of information for me to take home and read. She even sent a letter to my doctor on my behalf explaining the situation because I was so worried about sitting there and talking to the doctor about it. That night I sat at home and chose my new name which was quite fun. I was originally going to choose the name my Mum would have given me if I had been born a boy, which was Scott, but I decided I didn't like that. After some more thought I chose Ben because when I was a kid we had a dog called Benny, and he was like my big brother.

Young men and women from racialized backgrounds have an even worse time with gay and lesbian identities as they see themselves being "the only ones" in the world, and are alienated from their own cultural communities as well as the mainstream gays and lesbians (Charles, 2002, p. 147). There are differences in the sexual and romantic experiences of Latino, Asian-American, and African-American gay men. For example, Dubé and Savin-Williams (reported in Savin-Williams, 2001, p. 8) found that there was variation in the number of sexual and romantic relationships, with Asian Americans having the fewest. Further, these men were most likely to have a gay or bisexual identity before their first same-sex experience while African Americans' gay or bisexual identity followed their first same-sex experience. Both Latinos and Asian Americans had lower levels of internalized homophobia.

Age is also a factor in the behaviours of sexual-minority young men. In Savin-Williams's (2001, pp. 8–9) study, young men in their teens rather than in their twenties or thirties were likely to label their gay or bisexual attractions before engaging in same-sex behaviour. The younger cohorts (16–25) also had fewer sexual partners relative to romantic relationships.

How Are GLBT Youth Coping?

As a consequence of family and peer rejection, the risk of substance abuse and suicide among gay and lesbian youth is significantly high. They also often become isolated from family, friends, and schools. Further, it is estimated that the homeless street youth population has extremely high proportions of gay, lesbian, and bisexual youth (O'Brien & Weir, 1995, pp. 120–121).

In his criticism of the scholarly community's approach to sexual-minority youths, Savin-Williams (2001, p. 5) criticizes their preoccupation with "problematic concerns" rather than the actual experiences of these youth:

> A plethora of data document the suicide attempts, drug usage and HIV infection rates of youths who define themselves as gay, lesbian or bisexual; largely ignored are the data that document the daily lives of most youths with same-sex attractions.... Because researchers may want to better the lives of sexual-minority youths, they call attention to the *difficulties* these youths face—their victimization and early death— rather than their *strength* and *resiliency*. [emphases in the original]

Savin-Williams (2001, pp. 6–7) argues that it is a false contrast to compare sexual-minority youth with heterosexuals as populations that are distinct. This approach has contributed to the stereotyping of sexual-minority youth as hypersexualized based on presumed biological differences from heterosexual youth. Another stereotype is the presentation of sexual-minority youth as pathological, based on studies of mental health and self-destructive behaviours. These behaviours can reasonably be explained as responses to the ostracism that sexual-minority youth face from society at large.

Though studies of adolescent suicide indicate that 30–50 percent of sexual-minority youth have attempted suicide in the past year and often multiple times, this is likely to be a vast overestimation based on the use of populations at risk or attending services for youth at risk. Additionally, the categorizations used for determining sexual-minority status are so wide as to be meaningless (Savin-Williams, 2001, pp. 9–10).

According to Savin-Williams (2001, pp. 7–8), it is necessary to get away from the "gay versus straight" research and move toward an examination of within-group differences, i.e., the diversity among sexual-minority youth. For example, rather than just showing the higher risk of suicide by sexual-minority youth, research should identify which youth are at risk, why they are at risk, and determine if the risk factors are the same for heterosexuals and sexual-minority youth.

Teenage Pregnancies

Generally, the age at which young women experience their first pregnancy and childbirth has risen across the Western world due to prolonged education and young women's increased focus on their careers along with family formation. Nevertheless, some young women still get pregnant and give birth in their teens (Aapola et al., 2005, p. 101).

Physiologically, many 11–13-year-olds are ready for intercourse and young girls can potentially bear children as young as age 11. One of the significant phenomena of the 20th century in Canada has been the reported rise in babies born outside of marriage. While in 1921, only 2 percent of babies were reported born outside of marriage, this rose to 27 percent by 1991. The lower rates for the earlier decades of the 20th century no doubt reflect the unacceptability of births outside of wedlock, and there may have been many more births than we know. The most rapid increase in non-marital birth rates took place in the 1980s. The increase reflects the increased acceptability of sex before marriage, and the increased prevalence of common-law relationships, a trend particularly significant in Quebec (Belle & McQuillan, 2000, p. 115; see also Baker, 1996a, p. 29; Nett, 1993, pp. 214–215).

The Canadian Contraceptive Study found that 4 percent of women in the age group 15–17, 31 percent of 18–24-year-olds, and 16 percent of 25–29-year-olds had an unplanned pregnancy. While a minority of the women in the age groups 18–24 and 25–29 miscarried, among the youngest age group, all pregnancies were terminated. Also, those in the 18–24 age group were equally likely to either terminate the pregnancy or carry the baby to term and keep it. Among the age group 25–29, 52 percent chose termination of pregnancy while 44 percent kept the baby and 6 percent opted for having their baby adopted (Fisher & Boroditsky, 2001, pp. 85–86). Overall, pregnant teens increasingly choose abortions and consequently give fewer births over time since 1974 (Ambert & Krull, 2006, p. 246).

The rate of babies born to unwed mothers is higher in Quebec, where more couples live common-law. Still, only 20 percent of these births are to women under 20 years of age, while 60 percent are to women aged 20–30. In fact, and contrary to popular imagery, there has been a significant decline in teenage birth rates since the 1950s, partly due to better contraception and legal abortions (Baker, 1996a, p. 29; Nett, 1993, pp. 214–215). Teen pregnancy rates continue to decline in Canada (Fisher & Boroditsky, 2000, p. 86).

The majority of teen pregnancies are unplanned (Orton, 1999, p. 125). Also, the majority (81 percent) of the teenagers who gave birth in 1994 were single compared to only 25 percent in 1974. This reflects the increased social acceptability of single motherhood as opposed to the compulsion to marry when pregnant. The pregnancy rates of older teenagers (aged 18–19) were twice that of the younger group (15–17). The total of those aged 18–19 who gave birth in 1994 was around 16,000. Nearly 8,000 women in the younger teen age group gave birth in 1994, and approximately 700 of them for at least the second time (Wadhera & Millar, 1997, pp. 12–14).

In 1994, there were close to 24,700 babies born to mothers aged 15–19, while another 21,000 pregnancies in this age range were terminated, and there were 2,000 stillbirths or miscarriages (Wadhera & Millar, 1997, p. 9). However, the age of unmarried mothers is rising, and today, most of the mothers are 25 years of age and over (Belle & McQuillan, 2000, p. 116).

Overall, what is significant about teen pregnancy is not the decrease in the actual rate, but the greater numbers of young women who want to keep their babies rather than have an abortion or give them up for adoption. Indeed, Canadian statistics indicate a drop in the birth rate to teens to under half the rate between 1960s and the 1980s

(Wong & Checkland, 1999, p. xv). By 1989, only 3.6 percent of unwed mothers under 25 gave up their child for adoption (Orton, 1999, p. 125).

Table 6.1 presents a comparison of teen pregnancy and abortion rates in Canada, the UK, and the US. The notion of "teen pregnancy" as a negative phenomenon is historically specific. Only 10 percent of all teens giving birth in Canada were single in 1974, while currently about 80 percent are. The prevalent hype in North America about a crisis of teen pregnancies is based on American experiences; the US teen pregnancy rate—at nearly 50 percent in 2001—is over twice that in Canada, which is 20 percent of the teenage population. This distinction has resulted in moralistic debates in the United States but less so in Canada (Ambert & Krull, 2006, p. 246; also see Aapola et al., 2005, p. 101).

Table 6.1: Teen Pregnancy and Abortions in Canada, the UK, and the US

Country	Age	Pregnancies per 1,000 Females (actual numbers)	Rate of Abortions per 1,000 Females (actual numbers)
Canada (2003)[1]	Under 15	(411)	1.5 (302)
	15–17	(10,285)	9.5 (5,785)
	18–19	(22,857)	28.1 (11,871)
England and Wales (2005)	15–17	41.3 (42,187)[3]	
	Up to age 19		(39,099)[2]
Northern Ireland (2006)	15–19	26.7 (3,040)[4]	
	Up to age 19		(74)[5]
Scotland (2003–2004)	13–19	39.8 (8,741)[5]	
	Up to age 19		(206)[5]
United States	10–19 (2005)[6]	(421,124)	
	Up to age 19 (2002)[7]		12.0 (121,178)

Sources:
1. Statistics Canada (2003c).
2. East Midlands Public Health Observatory (2005).
3. Department of Health, UK (2006).
4. O'Keeffe et al. (2006).
5. Department of Health, UK (2006b).
6. Hamilton et al. (2006).
7. Strauss et al. (2005).

Indeed, statistics in the US and the UK show a similar pattern of a higher rate of teen births among all young women, and particularly among young racialized women, who are also more likely to be single mothers. The latter are more likely than young White mothers to be employed full-time because they have their partners' support (Aapola et al., 2005, pp. 102–103). In the United States, "1 million teenage females become pregnant each year" and approximately 40 percent get pregnant at least once before they turn 20, and 4 of each 10 pregnancies are terminated by abortion. Nearly half a million babies are born to teen mothers (Button & Rienzo, 2002, p. 4). The US birth rate to teens (aged 15–19) has been stable since the mid-1970s, at about 12–18 percent of all births, or 27–29 births per 1,000 (Aapola et al., 2005, pp. 100–101).

The teenage pregnancy rate in the UK is the highest in western Europe (Department of Health, UK, 1999). In the mid-1990s, 35 percent of all births were outside marriage, an increase from 5 percent over the mid-1960s. Lone-parent families increased from 570,000 in the mid-1960s to 1.5 million in the mid-1990s (Charles, 2002, p. 46). Finch (2003, pp. 16–29) reports a steady increase since the 1990s in births outside marriage in England and Wales, approaching 40 percent of all births by 2002, mostly by cohabiting couples. At the same time, there has been a decline from 25.5 percent in 1991 to 18.4 percent in 2001 in the proportion of births in this category to young, never-married women who don't have a partner. In 2001, 90 percent of all births to mothers under the age 20 were outside marriage. Overall, the teenage conception rate in England and Wales is the highest in the European Union, with 47 per 1,000 women under age 18 getting pregnant in 1998. Of those conceptions, 34–52 percent are terminated, with more terminations in the northeast of Britain compared to London.

Is There Reason for Alarm?

Teenage pregnancies and births to teenage mothers tend to be viewed in a way that can be described as alarmist. Having a baby as a teenager is associated with medical risks for both the baby and the mother, including a greater chance of premature births and identifiable congenital abnormalities, or having a low birth-weight infant (Wadhera & Millar, 1997, p. 9). Having a child also causes multiple economic and social problems for teenage mothers, especially if they remain single and without support from either a husband or their own parents. A recent analysis of the Canadian National Longitudinal Study of Children and Youth (Dahinten & Willms, 2002, pp. 255–257) identified three key factors in the outcomes for children of adolescent mothers: (1) children's academic and behavioural outcomes improve as maternal age at child-bearing increases; (2) the outcomes for teen mothers are bleak, including low education and income associated with poor mental health; and (3) children born to adolescent mothers are delayed in their vocabulary development and have behaviour disorders, particularly in preschool years.

The kinds of items that cause concern are high school dropout rates, which lead to lower-level wage work involvement or dropping out of the system to be reliant on social assistance. This means that these young women can create and perpetuate a cycle of poverty for their children. Generally, single-parent, mother-headed households are at a high risk of poverty as are young families in general due to their lower earning power. Concerns are also raised about the emotional maturity of young parents, whether on their own or with a partner, to raise their children (Baker, 1996a, pp. 29–30; see also Wong & Checkland, 1999; Orton, 1999, p. 127).

A typical story is that of Debbie from Newfoundland (National Film Board, 1990), who got pregnant after having been with her boyfriend for one month because they did not use birth control. The boyfriend became abusive toward her while she was pregnant. She reported it to the police, and he got a jail sentence. She tells of the "struggle to get by" on a welfare cheque of $823, $550 of which goes toward rent. She gets most of her stuff from garbage, is constantly hungry, and has no money. She sometimes eats in restaurants and slips out without paying, just to have a meal. She did not finish her education, nor is she gainfully employed.

In contrast to the alarmist approach to teenage motherhood, there are critical voices pointing to the general shifts in societal attitudes over time. Wong and Checkland (1999, p. xv) point out that "the age at which it is 'normal' to begin raising children has varied across cultures and times." They further ask why it is now that the issue is raised, and how it is framed. Among other things, Wong and Checkland (1999, p. xviii) conclude:

> The issue of teen parenting ... should bring to the forefront the needs and status of adolescents and "youths," a group towards which political, ethical, and social theory have generally been ambivalent. Adolescents are poised between the legally full autonomy of adulthood and the dependent, non-autonomous status of childhood. Psychologically, adolescents—perhaps especially female adolescents, given the changing conceptions of women's rights and roles—are also in a "no-man's land" that has been neglected in public discussion. Developmental paradigms and common sense ... locate the adolescent as capable of much that "adults" are capable of, but at the same time suspect as a decision maker because of attributed immaturity. Clarifying the appropriate weight to give to developmental considerations unavoidably complicates issues of responsibility, blame, opportunity, entitlement, rationality, and choice.

These critical voices do not question the real and largely negative consequences of teenage parenthood on mothers and children. However, many researchers (e.g., Orton, 1999, pp. 127–128; Perkins, 2005, pp. 126–127) question the stigmatization (as illiterate, dependent, immature) of teenaged women who choose to keep and raise their children. Orton (1999) raises important issues rooted in the prevailing social inequalities, including unequal or inadequate access to pregnancy prevention. Teenage pregnancy is far more prevalent among the lower socio-economic classes. For example, the Ontario Health Survey found in 1990 that 18 percent of teenage women in households with incomes below $30,000 reported a pregnancy in the past five years compared with only 4 percent in households with incomes over $30,000. Meanwhile, pregnancy-prevention and educational programs are concentrated in more affluent areas.

Teenage pregnancy has social class, gender, and racial components. Perkins (2005, pp. 119–136) outlines the crisis of pregnancies to Black teens in America, among whom 83 percent of births occur outside of marriage. This is accompanied by high infant mortality, high school dropout rates for the mothers and the fathers, higher chances of child abuse and neglect, and more chance of substance abuse and crime by parents. Perkins argues that in addition to being a by-product of higher poverty among Blacks, unwed Black teenage pregnancy is a legacy of slavery in that it mirrors the image of Black females as bearers of children. They are also denigrated by White and Black men alike, who "have been indoctrinated with the image of the oversexed, promiscuous, exotic woman" (p. 126), as discussed above in relation to Black sexuality.

Males (1996, pp. 10–12) is emphatic that high poverty rates are to blame for the high teenage pregnancy rate. There is the strongest possible link between race, age, and poverty in the United States, which translates into high rates of unplanned pregnancy among Black and Hispanic youth. In fact, the link between poverty and teenage childbearing is strong enough that the teen birth rate from 1960–1993 could be calculated with 90 percent accuracy by relying on the previous decade's child poverty rates. In fact, the reasons for the lower pregnancy rates among European compared with American teens are directly linked to levels of affluence. In other words, racialized groups that have lower levels of poverty also have lower levels of teenage pregnancy. For example, Finch (2003, p. 30) reports that there are ethnic differences in teenage birth rates in Britain, with higher rates in 2001 among Bangladeshi and Caribbean women compared to Whites, while Indian and Pakistani women's rates are lower. The teenage birth rates among Bangladeshi women, though high, have decreased significantly since the 1980s.

Kaufman (1999, p. 30; also see Aapola et al., 2005, p. 103) also points to the vilification of teenage mothers while the role of the young fathers who sired those children is taken less to task. Indeed, less is known about teenage fathers than about mothers. Males (1996, p. 16) points out that the majority (93 percent) of American unwed births are to couples either one or both of whom are 20 years of age or older. Further, the main reason for the mothers to be on welfare is that they were recently divorced and/or laid off employment, and the father of the child is not paying child support. Significantly, the problem is, according to Males (1996, p. 17), that the fathers of the children of teen mothers tend to be adult males: half of the fathers of children born to mothers 15 years or younger are post-high school–aged males who are, on average, five to six years older than these teen mothers. Another outrage is the high proportion of raped and sexually abused females among the mothers. For example, a study in Washington, DC, found that two-thirds of the teen mothers had been either sexually abused or raped, and the victims averaged 10 years of age at the time of abuse. The abusers were mostly adult family members, on average, 27 years old. Indeed, a 1995 survey by a University of Chicago sociologist found that "childhood sexual abuse was the single best predictor of teenage pregnancy over the past 40 years" (Males, 1996, p. 17).

A study by Redmond (1985) examined the attitudes of 74 White adolescent males in Kitchener-Waterloo, Ontario, regarding adolescent pregnancy and fatherhood. Approximately one-third of them had been involved in a teenage pregnancy. The study found that most young men want to be included in the decision-making process about the pregnancy and are supportive during this time. The majority (80 percent) were of the opinion that mothers should keep their children, while 67 percent endorsed either abortion or adoption. The majority (85–90 percent) were also willing to discuss options with their girlfriends. Overall, two-thirds agreed with the teen mom's decision about the pregnancy, and were willing to go along with the decision even if they disagreed with it. The young men also found that their inclusion in the decision making about the pregnancy was a positive experience. The young men's ability to earn an income was a major factor in whether they supported keeping the baby and providing assistance. Overall, the preferred desired outcome of pregnancy for males who were in a serious dating relationship was to have the baby and get married (40 percent) or to provide assistance (32 percent), while those who were in a casual dating relationship with the pregnant girl preferred either adoption (38 percent) or abortion (32 percent). Only a minority of either group of young men suggested that the mother have the baby and bring it up herself. Redmond (1985, p. 342) suggests that there is reason to include young fathers in the solution to the problem and not only as the problem.

Echoing this conclusion is American research by Perkins (2005) on young Black parents. The popular image of young Black men is that they are unwilling to take the responsibility and support their children after they have gotten their sexual gratification. In contrast, Perkins (2005, pp. 130–136) outlines some of the problems that prevent Black teen fathers from fulfilling their paternal obligations, including school interruptions and lack of finances to support their children because they lack marketable skills. Recognizing the multiple problems facing unwed teen parents, many Black American communities have developed programs that offer multiple forms of assistance, including "pre-natal and post-natal care, parenting education, family counseling" (Perkins, 2005, p. 133).

While the real needs and responsibilities of the teen fathers go by and large unnoticed, the young women get the negative attention as unsavoury "unwed mothers," to be contrasted with "good girls" whose life path involves an orderly and planned sequence in which sex and children follow marriage (Addelson, 1999, pp. 85–87). This attitude reflects the general allocation of responsibility for sexuality to young women rather than young men (Aapola et al., 2005, pp. 104–105), as indicated above.

To be sure, social class differences prevail in attitudes about teenage pregnancy. Research in Britain finds middle-class parents less accepting than working-class parents, many of whom provide material, emotional, and practical support to their daughters (Aapola et al., 2005, pp. 104–105). The issue is also racialized as teen pregnancy among Blacks is seen as a sign of "widespread social dysfunction," whereas White girls are subjected to an interpretation of psychopathology, while their offspring are at least seen to contribute to good-quality stock (Caragata, 1999, pp. 103–104). Further, because of the correlation with poverty, teen mothers are more likely to be seen as evidence of "those poor who breed like rabbits." In fact, Susan Clark (1999) questions whether the poverty of teenage mothers is an effect of early parenting or whether it was the poverty that led the young woman to make a rational choice given her circumstances. In fact, motherhood may be a pathway toward independence and maturity, and a way out of a bad family situation (Davies et al., 1999, pp. 46–47).

Indeed, Ladner (in Perkins, 2005, pp. 127–130) points to the contrast between the White American middle class and lower-income Black people's attitudes toward teen pregnancy. She argues that premarital sex and teen pregnancy are perceived as normal as opposed to alarming. Many Black girls part with mainstream values in their acceptance of unwed teen pregnancy, and are willing to take on the responsibility for their children despite economic or emotional strains, or see them as the responsibility of the women in their extended family rather than the state. They object to the stigma on these children and their mothers, except for mothers who have more than one child out of wedlock.

Thus, a critical approach to teenage pregnancy does not see births by young women as unproblematic, but it frames them in a different way, with attention to the power relations involved and the interpretations of the young people going through the experience. Particularly important consideration is given to the way in which young single mothers are seen to be a drain on the public purse (Caragata, 1999, p. 106; Kelly, 1999; Ambert & Krull, 2006, pp. 246–248). The vilification of teen mothers is unrelenting in the US media, with accusations that they are a burden on the public, are shamed for their immoral behaviour, and are the targets of baseless accusations that they are responsible for "breeding 90 percent of all violent criminals" (Males, 1996, pp. 27–28).

In fact, North American studies show that neither do welfare payments entice young women to become pregnant, nor are teen mothers any more likely than older mothers to be welfare recipients (Kelly, 1999, pp. 56–59). The conclusion from this is that the negative attitudes toward teenage pregnancy have more to do with (1) ageism grounded on the generally upheld view that young people are incapable of looking after themselves or their children, (2) the conservative discourse on dependency, and (3) moralistic middle-class values about "proper" families than with the actual circumstances among teenage mothers.

There is a direct link between the weak youth job market and the dependency of teen mothers on welfare. As more jobs are becoming part-time, short-term, and temporary, wages are declining. As teen mothers try to support themselves and their children, they often have tough choices to make between welfare and a poorly paid job that would not allow them to cover the cost of child care and other expenses. Davies et al. (1999, p. 48) interviewed 16 teen mothers who were forced onto welfare, and had to make difficult choices between going on welfare or spending large proportions of their wages toward new costs that come from living with a child. Pam, who had supported herself as a factory worker and cashier, observed:

> The way I see it, I could go to work right now, but I wouldn't really make it, because I would be making about $600 a month and that's not even enough—already with the money that you get from welfare, you don't get enough for the month. And imagine, if I go to work, I'm going to have to pay the babysitter, the bus pass, this and that, so it wouldn't really work…. Some people might imagine that it's fun for us to get pregnant because we get out of working, and we get out of going to school or whatever, but it's not. It's pretty hard, you know.

Intimate Partnership Formation

Some family patterns were discussed in Chapter 3, particularly with regard to the families from which young people originate. In this segment, the focus will be on the intimate partnership formation of young people themselves.

We tend to view modern intimate partnership formation as the freedom to date or marry anyone, but there are several factors that contribute to the selection of dating partners. There are a number of features of this "assortative mating" (OECD, 2011, p. 26). First, prospective dating partners' proximity to each other's neighbourhood, community, school, workplace, or school tends to predict couple formation. Second, there is homogamy: people tend to select mates who are similar to themselves in terms of social class, education, religion, and race or ethnic group. Third, hypergamy is also prevalent for men, meaning that they tend to marry "down" in terms of education, income, social class, or even height (Hobart, 1996, p. 145; see also OECD, 2011).

Overall, the partnership patterns of young people aged 20–34 are changing in almost all OECD countries, with cohabitation more common than among the previous generation of the same age. This increase has been linked to young people's concern about getting into a potentially financially precarious situation, related to the poor working conditions and chances reported in Chapter 5.

Cohabitation rates are high in anglophone countries (OECD, 2011, p. 24). However, marriage is still the most common type of intimate partnership. For example, whereas 92 percent of Canadian families were married couples in 1961, it declined to 67 percent in 2011. There was a corresponding quadrupling in common-law couples (Eichler & Pedersen, 2012), which had already doubled their proportions from 6 percent in 1980 to 13.5 percent in 1996 (Baker, 1996a, p. 16; Vanier Institute of the Family, 2000, p. 36). Today, cohabitation is more common as a first union, reflecting greater social acceptance (Eichler & Pedersen, 2012). The increase in cohabiting rates has been particularly notable in Quebec, reflecting the secularization of the population with the waning influence of the Roman Catholic Church. By 1995, 25 percent of Quebec couples lived as common-law, compared with 11 percent in other provinces (Turcotte & Belanger, 2000, p. 107). That cohabiting is a common premarital living arrangement, or a "trial marriage," was demonstrated in 1990 when over one-third of Canadians in their twenties followed their cohabitation by getting married (Baker, 1996b, p. 305).

Similar trends took place in the UK. While in the mid-1960s only 5 percent of all couples in the UK were cohabiting, this had increased to 70 percent by the mid-1990s (Charles, 2002, p. 46). Iacovou (2002, p. 55) reports that, of women aged 20–24 in the UK, 25.3 percent are cohabiting while 18.9 percent are married. In the age group 25–29, 18.8 percent are cohabiting while 50.3 percent are married.

There has also been a general trend toward increased age at first marriage for both women and men in all three countries (Charles, 2002, p. 46; Statistics Canada, 1999c; OECD, 2011). In Canada, average ages at marriage have increased from 27 for women and 29 for men in 1992 (Nett, 1993) to 30.9 years for women and 33.5 years for men in 1997 (Statistics Canada, 1999c). In the UK in the mid-1990s, the average age at first marriage was 26 (Charles, 2002, p. 46), rising to around 30 in 2005 (Office for National Statistics, UK, 2005). Current marriage ages in the three countries are depicted in Table 6.2.

Table 6.2: Average Age at Marriage, Canada, England and Wales, and the US

Country	Year/s	Average Age at Marriage	
		Male	Female
Canada	2003[1]	30.6	28.5
	2008[2]	31.1	29.1
England and Wales	2005[3]	31.7	29.5
	2010[4]	36.2	33.6
US	2000–2003[5]	26.7	25.1
	2010[6]	28.2	26.1

Sources:

1. Statistics Canada (2007b). Data exclude Ontario.
2. Human Resources and Skills Development Canada (2011).
3. National Statistics (Online) (2005a).
4. Office for National Statistics, UK (2010).
5. US Census Bureau (2002–2003).
6. Infoplease (2010).

The rising age of marriage should be generally good news because the younger the age at marriage, the more likely a couple is to get divorced. The divorce rates for those who marry between the ages of 15 and 19 are significantly higher than for people who marry at an older age (Oderkirk, 2000, p. 97).

There are some differences based on racialized group membership. In keeping with similar results (above) regarding premarital sex, Iacovou (2002, p. 55) reports that, in the United States in the age group 20–24, 12.2 percent of White women, 9.1 percent of Black women, and 7.8 percent of Hispanic women were cohabiting, while the figures for married status are 36.2 percent, 16.2 percent, and 32.6 percent, respectively. In the age group 25–29, the percentages for cohabiting were 10.8 for White women, 12.1 for Black women, and 8.9 for Hispanic women, while the figures for marriage are 68.4 percent, 38.6 percent, and 57.3 percent, respectively. There is also similar ethnic variation in cohabiting rates in the UK: it's less common among South Asians, and especially among Pakistanis and Bangladeshis, while it's more prevalent among Caribbeans.

For example, Pakistanis and Bangladeshis in the age group 20–24 are seven times more likely to be married than Caribbeans in the same age group (Charles, 2002, pp. 46–47).

Living common-law is correlated with age, in that young people are more likely than older people to live common-law. For example, in 1996 in Canada, 77 percent of those aged 15–19 and 56 percent of those in the 20–24 age group were living common-law. In the older age groups, the percentages were 32 percent for 25–29 year olds, 20 percent for 30–34 year olds, 15 percent for 35–39 year olds, and 12 percent for 40–44 year olds (Vanier Institute of the Family, 2000, p. 38).

Common-law unions differ from legal marriages in that they tend to last for a shorter time and tend to produce fewer children. Further, if marriage follows, it is more likely to end in divorce, possibly because cohabiting people hold less traditional views and see divorce as a legitimate way out of an unhappy marriage. However, as cohabiting becomes more prevalent, these distinctions seem to be diminishing (Baker, 1996a, pp. 17–18; Hobart, 1996, pp. 155–156; see also Milan, 2000). One of the important factors in the equalization of marriage and cohabiting couples are the legal changes that have given equal status to these relationships (Hobart, 1996, p. 156).

As indicated in Chapter 3, one of the biggest hurdles to cross in terms of equalizing relationships is the question of the rights of gay and lesbian couples to marry, a debate that is currently taking place in Canada, the UK, and the US. Same-sex unions were legalized in Canada in 2005 (see Box 6.3).

Young People and Division of Domestic Work

As discussed in Chapter 5, young men and women are almost equally likely to be found in the wage labour force. This raises important questions regarding possible changes in the gender division of labour in the family/household. We would like to think that younger generations are more likely to share all tasks. One the other hand, we know that gender divisions are pervasive, leaving women in charge of most domestic chores, including child care, and men responsible for "helping" and doing more of the outdoor chores and household repairs.

As noted in Chapter 3, studies of intergenerational relationships are strongly influenced by social learning and gender-role learning theories. Male and female patterns are learned in the context of family. Thus, household work becomes an arena for "doing gender." Male and female children are rewarded and compensated differently for their participation in domestic activities. Studies consistently find that girls' time spent in domestic work outweighs that of boy. Girls also tend to do routine tasks, including cleaning and child care, while boys engage in tasks such as garbage clearing and lawn maintenance (Robson & Anderson, 2006, pp. 2–4).

Parental behaviours predict teens' household work participation. For example, sons with mothers who work long hours do more, while sons in single-parent families do less than sons in dual-parent families. Where fathers participate in domestic work, children are more likely to think that men should do this (Robson & Anderson, 2006, p. 4).

Box 6.3: Bill C-38: The Civil Marriage Act (Canada)

Hurley (2005) summarizes some of the main elements in the history of legalizing gay unions in Canada:

> Bill C-38, an Act respecting certain aspects of legal capacity for marriage for civil purposes, or the Civil Marriage Act, received first reading in the House of Commons on 1 February 2005. The bill codifies a definition of marriage for the first time in Canadian law, expanding on the traditional common-law understanding of civil marriage as an exclusively heterosexual institution. Bill C-38 defines civil marriage as "the lawful union of two persons to the exclusion of all others," thus extending civil marriage to conjugal couples of the same sex.
>
> [...] *The Civil Marriage Act came into effect with Royal Assent on 20 July as Chapter 33 of the Statutes of Canada for 2005. With its enactment, Canada became the fourth country to legislate same-sex marriage, the others being the Netherlands (2001), Belgium (2003) and Spain (2005).* [emphasis in the original]
>
> [...] As anticipated, reaction to Bill C-38 throughout the legislative process was mixed, both within and outside Parliament.
>
> Bill C-38 critics focused on perceived threats to the institution of heterosexual marriage itself as a stabilizing force in society, to the family unit, and to the religious and expressive freedom of those opposed to same-sex marriage. It was argued that the legislation fails to adequately protect clergy and other public officials, such as civil marriage commissioners, who do not wish to recognize or officiate at same-sex marriages. Opponents pointed to provincial jurisdiction over solemnization of marriage, as confirmed in the Supreme Court of Canada Reference decision, as evidence that federal guarantees in this area lack substance. Fears of harm to children raised by same-sex parents were also expressed. Advocacy groups for gay and lesbian rights and human rights organizations, on the other hand, welcomed the bill as landmark equality rights legislation that would end exclusion of and discrimination against gay and lesbian conjugal couples. In this view, Bill C-38 represents final endorsement of long-standing claims to equal access to the institution of civil marriage in a manner that does not undermine religious freedom guaranteed by the Charter.

A rare study of adolescent males' household work participation in Great Britain is a welcome piece of research in an area sorely lacking in literature. Robson and Anderson

(2006) analyzed the results from the 1970 British Cohort Study, of people born April 5–11, 1970, in England, Scotland, Wales, and Northern Ireland. The authors focused on the characteristics of males aged 16–19 who kept a time diary of their leisure and household activities (including housework) over a four-day period. They compared these diaries with the activities of the males at age 29–32, 13 years later (a total of 1,594 married and mostly White males). The authors found partial support for their hypothesis that early participation in domestic tasks does have some influence on adult males' tendency to share household work. However, the authors also conclude that experiences over the life course influence men's housework participation.

There is some evidence in the UK that attitudes are changing among younger couples regarding domestic division of work toward increasing gender equality (Charles, 2002, p. 65). This raises the question whether young couples forming cohabiting or marital relationships are entering increasingly into egalitarian domestic relationships. Some studies, in fact, suggest that cohabitation increases the likelihood of more egalitarian relationships (Baker, 1996b, pp. 304–305). South and Spitze (1994, reported in Robson & Anderson, 2006, p. 6) found that compared to married couples, cohabiting couples are more likely to divide housework equally.

At the same time, Canadian and British studies suggest that women's participation in household work tends to increase upon marriage, while men's time input decreases. Further, the presence of children tends to result in an unequal division of domestic labour, with women doing more (Robson & Anderson, 2006, p. 6; Charles, 2002, pp. 61–62). Child care is still overwhelmingly work for women, while men's role is seen predominantly as providing for their children and families. British studies suggest that fathers want more involvement with their children, but that their paid labour is seen as a hindrance. American studies, meanwhile, show that when women are co-providers for children and when workplaces encourage more involvement by fathers, there is a general increase in fathers' involvement in both child care and housework (Charles, 2002, p. 84).

Mostly, this has to do with the realities of the gendered labour market, which has to be negotiated with family responsibilities. It is logical for young couples to choose to rely on the higher incomes of males while going through the child-bearing and rearing stage. Thus, particularly when couples have children, most of the domestic work falls on women, who now largely depend on the male wage for the domestic economy. Thus, women's wage work participation is not posing a challenge to the domestic division of labour as motherhood interferes with women's wage-earning capacity but not men's. The prevailing ideology still is that wage work excuses men's lack of domestic work participation but not women's (Charles, 2002, pp. 61–62). Nevertheless, Canadian studies have found that younger husbands who are married to full-time working wives are most likely to share child care and housework (Marshall, 1993, in Baker, 1996b, pp. 307–308). Studies in the UK confirm that men's participation in domestic work is higher in couples where the woman is in full-time employment rather than part-time work (Charles, 2002, p. 59).

Although there is an increasing pressure on men to share household labour, it is still the case that the shift is more ideological than actual. Studies from the early and mid-1990s indicate that although young couples say they favour equality in marriage, traditional roles and task divisions prevail in most households (Baker, 1996b, p. 308; Charles, 2002, pp. 58–60). Robson and Anderson (2006, p. 10; see also Charles, 2002, p. 59) suggest that there is a "cultural lag" as societal attitudes about housework are changing, but actual behaviour is not changing along with it, and that there is definitely resistance by both men and women based on the ways in which gender identities are constructed in the family context, and the consequent emotional investment that men and women put into it. These mostly unspoken and taken-for-granted sentiments are reflected in the words of a young British male and a young newlywed woman (Mansfield & Collard, 1988, p. 127, in Charles, 2002, p. 62). The man said:

> I think it gets back to my image. I follow my dad—it was always the wife who cooked the meals and did the ironing and did the vacuum cleaning and washed the kitchen floor and I do all the decorating because they're the more masculine jobs.

And the woman said:

> I knew before I married what I would have to do. I knew that by seeing other people being married—my sister has been married a long time before me.

Conclusions

Moving from being single to forming intimate and sexual relationships can be a mine-field of challenges. Today's young people face age-old problems with a new twist. As dating has replaced traditional courtship, many young people are faced with expecta-tions of sexual involvement as a regular part of a relationship, while others—particularly youth in immigrant families—struggle to reconcile their peers' dating norms with those of their parents.

Sexual activity is inextricably linked to dating and youthful intimacy at increasingly young ages. While some may question adolescents' preparedness for intimacy and sex-uality, the fact is that it is taking place within gendered, heterosexist, and racialized boundaries. Relationships are negotiated in a complex net of power relationships, with the most negative consequences for young women, non-heterosexual youth, and racial-ized youth who may either buy into or resist the scripts they are dealing with. More studies of patterns of young people's sexuality are required, accounting for population diversity in terms of immigrant status and religious observance. Studies to date suggest that these are significant factors, and future studies will undoubtedly shed light on the degree of difference they make.

Intimate and sexual relationships are gradually shedding the heterosexual bias, though patriarchal behaviours and attitudes prevail in the continuation of the double standard. Nevertheless, gay and lesbian youth still face concerns with their physical and emotional safety in a heterosexist environment. In heterosexual relationships, concerns continue over male power and control over women, manifested in the perpetuation of the double standard in sexual and dating relationships, and the tenacity of a gender-based domestic division of labour.

Many young people's relationship decisions are made without adequate supports. There is little room for change as societies set up and run by adults make life difficult for young people by not creating opportunities for them to be self-supporting through real gainful employment. This is particularly evident in the area of teenage pregnancies. Lacking an economic foothold or social supports, often including that from the father of their babies, young mothers find themselves stigmatized and forced to choose between different kinds of hardship. In the end, this issue also demonstrates the prevalence of an ideology that sees young people as individually incapable of looking after themselves. That they are doing remarkably well considering the obstacles they face in their daily lives is overshadowed by the real consequences of deprivation for themselves and their children.

Critical Thinking Questions

1. What is love? How do you know you are "in love"?
2. Do you think that norms about sexuality and sexual orientation are changing? What do you think explains it?
3. Do you think it's possible to have equality in heterosexual cohabiting or marital relationships? What about gay or lesbian relationships?

7 Peers, Identity, Politics, and Youth Culture

In this chapter, you will learn that

- young people actively participate in politics in multiple informal and formal ways that differ from those of middle-aged and older adults
- young people's political participation is influenced by their parents, peers, the media, and popular culture
- there is a wide range of youth cultures and subcultures among young people, based on immigrant status, racialization, and gender
- there is a large and steadily growing prevalence of communication technologies and social media in young people's lives
- marketing and consumerism are powerful forces in young people's lives and are reflected in music and popular cultural expressions

Although the influence of families in the development of youth identity cannot be overestimated, adolescence is generally seen as a time of forming friendships and getting more involved with one's own peers than one's family. For young people, youth groups and the culture that evolves around them form a basis for creating their own culture (Delgado, 2002), which establishes and validates their own identity in contrast to the adult-dominated world with its own norms, rules, and regulations. Friends and peer groups provide a comfortable setting for testing one's individual limits and expanding one's horizons. This includes both positive and negative aspects. Among the negative ones is the link between peers and substance abuse, which will be discussed in the chapter on health.

Youth's lives are organized in many ways and forms and by many sources. There are formal and informal youth organizations and groups, both large and small. Formal organizations are those that have an official structure, including formal hierarchies and written functions. These are mostly bureaucratic organizations, such as political parties and large-scale organizations, that are typically created for youth and not led by youth themselves. Among youth, there are also informal organizations and groupings, such as cliques and gangs. These are put together by youth themselves, in an informal context, for purposes defined by group members. Though some may have a structure and hierar-chy, including leadership positions, these tend to arise quite organically from within the group. Youth participate in both formally organized community (adult-led) activities and informal youth-led organizations. There are youth organizations and groups that are either acceptable/desirable or unacceptable/undesirable in relation to the mainstream. Youth gangs, as one such socially unacceptable organizational form, will be discussed in the chapter on youth crime. The focus in this chapter is on normative activities that fall within acceptable, socially desirable youth activities. Some of these activities may be barely tolerated, though they may be seen as undesirable and suspect by some adults, including some youth subcultures or music that do not match adult tastes, but that are not necessarily seen as criminal or deviant.

Miles (2000, pp. 1–34) is critical of the applicability of the term "subculture" to youth's ways of spending their lives at the beginning of the 21st century. Instead, he proposes that the term "lifestyle" is more appropriate. According to Miles, the term "subculture" evokes a sense of youth's deviancy or delinquency. The term "lifestyle" is not as laden with implications of youth in relation to the dominant order, but points to elements of conformity and creativity (or structure and agency) in young people's lives. The notion of lifestyle both captures the wider availability of options to young people today, and opens the door for consideration of gender and ethnoracial concerns and also the impact of consumer culture.

Van Roosmalen and Krahn (1996) divide normative youth culture into five distinct areas, including home-based youth culture, social youth culture, the culture of work, participatory youth culture, and street youth culture. Work-based youth culture was extensively discussed in Chapter 5 where part-time and casual labour was established as a major aspect of young people's lives. This includes the ways in which workplaces serve as a space for finding meaning through working relations with peers. Some aspects of social youth culture relating to dating and sexuality were discussed in Chapter 6. Social culture was also raised in Chapter 4 on education in the context of youth social interac-tions in the school setting. Some aspects of home-based youth culture were raised in the chapter on families, particularly with regard to immigrant youth.

This chapter will delve into youth culture in more depth, including patterns based on race, ethnicity, and gender. The chapter follows the division between mainstream, adult-led social outlets versus youth-driven social activities. In the latter category, home-based and street-based youth cultures will be examined. The culture of consumerism is brought to these areas by business and media through a range of consumer goods and services aimed at capturing young people's minds and pocketbooks. However, youth may integrate these mass-produced items in ways that are unique to them, while also engaging in activi-ties that can be interpreted as protest or resistance, such as political involvement and social movements as a part of participatory youth culture. In each of the sections to follow, it is shown that there is a delicate balance between accommodation and resistance in young people's engagement with their peers and the social outlets that society offers. Fundamen-tally, as outlined in Chapter 1, young people's social and political involvement evokes questions about the nature of civic responsibility and citizenship.

Youth in Adult-Led Institutions

Given the heightened media attention to young people's presumed political apathy, this chapter will begin with consideration of the meanings and realities of youthful political engagement. What emerges is a pattern of disillusionment with official party politics among youth, accompanied by a corresponding increase of interest in alternative politics among those who are politically minded, and an increase in commercially fuelled youth subculture among those who are younger and/or less interested in politics. And, indeed, as some youth researchers have argued (see Chapter 1), it is at least open for debate that some of the seemingly leisure-based subcultural forms could be, to some degree, a form of political statement among select categories of youth.

Another major aspect of young people's adult-defined social lives centres on their school-based activities. Here, sports are taken as an example of the many clubs and activities offered to youth in educational institutions and in society at large. Participation in athletic activities is an agreed-upon way of positively channelling youthful energies. Sports are also gendered and racialized to an extreme degree, with associated stereotypes and expectations.

Youth and Political Participation

Political and socially aware groups and organizations are a part of young people's lives. In Chapter 2, we addressed the historical mobilization of Black youth, and Chapter 4 gave examples of some ways in which some Black high school youth have organized to inform themselves and others about their own history and living conditions. In Chapter 5 we discussed the issue of youth unionization. These are just a few examples of the wide range of general political activities in which young people participate.

Despite these types of evidence of young people's political participation, there is widespread concern throughout the Western world regarding one specific aspect of their political lives: the presumed apathy of youth in relation to official politics compared to older adults (Charles, 2002; Gillis, 1981; Flanagan, 2006, p. 2). Based on interviews at Laval University in Quebec, Hudon et al. (1991, pp. 8–14) show that, indeed, youth's interest in official politics is low, particularly among young men.

Official statistics lend support to the concern over youth's political apathy. As indicated in Table 7.1, youth voting percentages are low in all three countries in question. Indeed, voting percentages rise with age, and the rates among the youngest eligible voters are particularly low compared to older adults. For example, the US Census Bureau (2007, Table 405; also see Kirby & Marcelo, 2006) reports that only 15.1 percent of youth aged 18–20 and 18.7 percent of those in the 21–24 age group voted in the 2002 congressional elections, while the voting percentage among those aged 44–64 was 53.1 percent.

As discussed in Chapter 1, young people's definition of what constitutes effective political citizenship is much wider than formal political participation through membership in political parties and using one's vote. In keeping with this notion of the wide

Table 7.1: Selected Youth Voting Percentages

Country	Age	Voting Percentage
Canada (Federal elections)		
2000[1]	18–20	22
	21–24	27.5
	25–29	38
2004[2]	18–21½	39
2008[3]	18–24	37.4
Great Britain (National elections)		
2005[4]	18–24	45
2010[5]	18–24	44
United States (Federal elections)		
2006[6]	18–29	58
2008[7]	18–24	49

Sources:
1. Service Canada (2005).
2. Canadian Council on Social Development (2006).
3. Library of Parliament Research Publications (2010).
4. National Statistics (2005b).
5. Ipsos-MORI (2010).
6. Kirby & Marcelo (2006).
7. US Census Bureau (2009). Youth voter turnout is generally higher in presidential elections than midterm elections.

scope of youth politics, Canadian studies indicate that though young people's organizational participation is generally relatively high, their interest in political organizations is comparatively low. Youth tend to be more interested (in order of importance) in sports or cultural (theatre, music, dance) organizations, or organizations with social objectives (cadets, Scouts, religious movements), than in organizations with political objectives or political organizations per se (Hudon et al., 1991, pp. 28–29).

Further, Gauthier (2003) and Martinez (2002) note the trend among Canadian youth of increased political activation, albeit in support of numerous ideologies instead of one single agenda. Youth take on local, regional, and global issues (Gauthier, 2003; Flanagan, 2006), and exhibit an emerging opposition to corporate power (Martinez, 2002).

Notably, many youth seem to be searching for a "new politics" involving militancy and participation on their terms. They approach traditional politics with suspicion and form their own associations (Hudon et al., 1991, pp. 3–8). This image is perpetuated with media reports of "disaffected" youth, who "see no point in casting ballot," which was part of a headline of a major national newspaper (MacKinnon, 2000a) during a Canadian federal election campaign. The article goes on to quote the views of six people in their "late teens and early 20s," exemplified by one 21-year-old woman's views (MacKinnon, 2000a):

> There is a certain sense of hopelessness.... You feel like a million young people could vote for the same party and they'd still never get in.

Young people's lack of interest seems to reflect their view that traditional politics has little of substance to offer, and that it may be based on deceit and trickery. A large segment of these students saw politics as necessary, but disagreed with current practices (Hudon et al., 1991, pp. 8–14). There is a very real sense of disillusionment among youth. However, a part of the problem in interpreting young people's behaviours is that studies tend to deal with a very large age segment, which may distort the differences between the younger and older age groups and also present a false picture of "averages" (Hudon et al., 1991, pp. 3–7).

As in other areas, there are differences in political participation based on gender, race, and social class. One Canadian study found that levels of interest in politics and confidence in political parties are somewhat higher among boys than girls. There are also significant social class differences: private school girls, but not boys, seem to be more interested in politics than public school girls. Levels of interest in politics are higher among those whose fathers were from upper-middle-class backgrounds (Hudon et al., 1991, pp. 14–17). These patterns of generational and social class differences are echoed in British research. Gillis (1981) cautions that the generation gap in political activities has to be interpreted with sensitivity to the significant divisions, including those based on social class, among the population:

> Nowhere in Europe or America is there very much evidence of a severe "generation gap," despite the student and worker upheaval of the 1960s and 1970s. Studies of "young rebels" indicate that, while there is a certain degree of child-parent tension, the major thrust of youthful discontent is directed not at family but outward, at social, political, and academic institutions that are only indirectly identified with the older generation. Young people and their parents are more likely to be united than divided on basic political and social issues, tensions arising over means rather than end, a reflection of the normal pace of historical change rather than any intra-familial disruption or severe hostility between groups on the basis of age alone. In

many contemporary situations, the confrontation between the young and the old is actually conflict between persons of differing class position—students versus police, young workers versus employers. Therefore, we must be careful not to mistake these events as evidence of deep generational divisions. (Gillis, 1981, p. 205)

Likewise, Hudon et al. (1991, p. 17) conclude that "the phenomenon of indifference to politics is not confined to young people." International studies show that the general level of interest between the young and older age groups tends to be similar. Further, questions about political interests tend to be ambiguous at best, subject to multiple interpretations by respondents. Therefore, it is important to use carefully phrased questions. The authors went on to ask more specifically in their high school surveys whether "they felt personally concerned about the decisions made by government." There was a correlation between concern in this regard and being fairly or very interested in politics. However, more notably, more students reported having personal concerns than actually indicated an interest in politics. This result is interpreted as a sign that students distinguish between an image of the word "politics" compared with "political actions" or decisions. This is supported by other studies showing a general level of cynicism and lack of trust in politicians, political parties, and institutions.

The lack of trust also speaks to the lack of identification with the faces presented in the political parties. Some of the poor voting patterns among young voters, and particularly women and members of racialized minorities, reflect their poor presence as members of major political parties or governments. For example, over three-quarters of British women have no involvement in any type of political party activity, and the levels of non-involvement are particularly high among those who are young, Black, and female (Charles, 2002, p. 155). Ethnic minority representation in Britain is 1.8 percent in the House of Commons and 0.4 percent in the House of Lords. Local councils in England and Wales have 2.5 percent membership from ethnic minorities (House of Commons Library, 2004).

In the United States, Black youth have a great degree of faith in being able to make a difference, but they don't necessarily think that they are being heard. In one national study, young people were asked if they think that government leaders care very little about them, and there were significant race-based differences. While 44 percent of White youth agreed with the statement, 52 percent of Hispanic and 56 percent of Black youth agreed (Cohen et al., 2007, p. 9). Given the degree of distrust and poor representation, it is no surprise that political party affiliation and voting percentages among youth are low.

As noted, political parties are only one aspect of the wide spectrum of political interests and involvements. Hudon et al. (1991, pp. 24–27) also examined some of these other aspects. For example, a large majority of the Canadian high school students he surveyed would sign a petition if they believed in a cause. Another third would write to newspapers or politicians or belong to a group or association. A further quarter would stand for election. Overall, if those who would "perhaps" engage in these activities are included, at least half of these young people would engage in these activities. There were also fewer gender differences in willingness to get involved through these means.

Overall, only approximately one-third in the Hudon et al. (1991, p. 26) study indicated that they were never willing to take some form of political action. At least one-third of those who indicated little or no interest in politics were willing to lobby for an idea they believed in. This general willingness may not result in actual participation. In comparison with the much higher levels of willingness found by Hudon et al., the Canadian Youth Foundation survey (in Hudon et al., 1991, p. 26) found:

> Forty percent of those surveyed have signed a petition while only 18 percent have participated in a demonstration, 13 percent have written to an "official" and 8 percent have boycotted products in stores.

Thus, political action is being taken by young people, but they seem to prefer alternatives to joining established political parties. Studies charting youthful action in the three countries in question are starting to document that the apathy of the young is largely a myth and that there is a lot more than meets the eye once we pay attention to alternatives to official politics (Braungart & Braungart, 1990; Matthews & Limb, 2003; Gauthier, 2003; Schiff, 2000; Green, 2007; Kingsnorth, 2001; Ferman, 2005; Gingwright & Cammarota, 2006; Akom, 2006; Sherrod, 2006; Noguera & Cannella, 2006).

Presently, large environmental, anti-globalization, and anti-war demonstrations continue around the globe, showing a large youth presence and activism (Lojowsky, 2001). The numbers of young activists within these demographically diverse movements are difficult to estimate, but youth are among them. For example, Verhulst and Walgrave (2007, pp. 128–129) interviewed anti-war demonstrators, who organized coordinated demonstrations in several countries on February 15, 2003, against the American invasion of Iraq. They found that 11 percent of the American demonstrators and 16 percent of the British demonstrators were under 24 years of age.

A Canadian example of a youth-driven social movement is the Environmental Youth Alliance (EYA) of British Columbia, with membership consisting of young people aged 14–24. Its membership went up to 20,000 in the first few months since its founding in early 1990. Another youth environmental group is the Canadian Student Environment Network, also founded early in 1990, and aimed at college students nationwide (Lowe, 1990). Van der Veen (1994) interviewed a group of 30 young people aged 15–25 in British Columbia. The grassroots young environmentalists felt that "adults do not respect them or accord them equal status," and they see themselves as a marginalized population group. They do not have much respect for decision makers, and question traditional institutions.

However, this does not mean that all youth are alike. Young environmentalists may have different values and motives for participating. Van der Veen (1994) found seven different categories of participants. First, there are the "peaceful revolutionaries" who want to overthrow the whole system through non-violent means. Environmental activism is only one aspect of their general humanist stance to life. Second, those who are "socially responsible" feel personally responsible for the environment.

It is their duty to help others, and hold on to Christian ethics or beliefs. Third, those who are "pursuers of a simple life" want to live in harmony with the environment, while pursuing creative activities. Fourth, the "spiritualists" have devoted themselves to protect the environment in all aspects of their lives. They see the Earth as a spiritual mother, interconnected with everything around. Fifth, the "self-seeking operators" don't have the environment as the primary focus of their lives, and are more concerned with possible benefits to themselves first, and then to the environment. The sixth category is the "sacrificialists" who value non-humans over humans, willing to discard humans if other species can be protected. Lastly, there are the "conscientious explorers" who want to learn about everything possible, whether it is the environment or anything else. They want to make their "own small contribution" toward a specifically defined environmental cause.

Another large-scale example of young people's political activity is the anti-globalization movement that spans multiple continents. Primarily, globalization refers to the economic system of transnational corporations (TNCs) that dominates the world and helped remove trade barriers and undermined of the role of nation-states. Contemporary information technologies and communication systems make it possible to coordinate production and to open up a global consumer market. As such, they promote a homogenization of global cultures while creating a backlash in the form of emerging local heterogeneities. Thus, there is an increased fragmentation and emergence of local movements for autonomy. The consequences have been many, including relocation of manufacturing from the industrialized world to the lower-cost and low-paid Third World. Overall, workers are expected to be more "flexible" as work becomes fragmented and less standardized (Charles, 2002, pp. 186–187).

One of the biggest examples of the actions of the anti-globalization movement was the string of global demonstrations starting with a day of riots and demonstrations by an estimated 60,000 people shutting down the World Trade Organization (WTO) Ministerial Conference in Seattle in November 1999. This was followed in other parts of the world through 2000 and 2001 (Hatcher, 2003; also see Báez, 2003). This "globalization of activism" (Hatcher, 2003, p. 112) is also part of young people's political scope throughout the 1990s and 2000s.

The recent global Occupy Movement is an example of young people's activism. In a startling and unexpected development, a crowd largely consisting of young people occupied Wall Street, in New York, in September 2011. The focus of the discontent was with how the wealthy (Wall Street, banks, and corporations, with the help of governments) claim 1 percent of the world's wealth, leaving 99 percent of the population in an increasingly deprived condition. This "waking up" was a reaction to recurring news about how the distribution of wealth is increasingly polarized, not only in the global South but also in the wealthier industrial North. Within a few weeks, the Occupy Movement's global reach was an estimated 1,500 cities (Van Gelder, 2011, pp. 1–2). Occupy locations included London, UK, and Toronto, Canada. Box 7.1 outlines some of the hopes and pitfalls of this newest form of youth political activism, dispelling the myth of their presumed apathy.

Box 7.1: Youth and the Occupy Movement

This shortened version of Paola Loriggio's (2011) article for the Global Network captures the different ways in which young people engage in activism in the Occupy Movement, including the widespread use of social media, discussed later in this chapter.

TORONTO—Long chided for their lack of political and civic engagement, Canadian youth showed signs of mobilizing this year, raising hopes and questions about the role they will take in shaping the country's future.

While the majority stayed out of the fray, clusters of young Canadians rose up in outbursts of support or outrage, hints of a simmering discontent that some say could emerge as full-blown movement.

"One thing we're beginning to see ... is a space for a lot of young people to start to ask more systematic questions of our society," says Jamie Biggar, co-founder of LeadNow, a youth-led group that advocates civic engagement....

Occupy Canada may have gone underground following the dismantling of camps across the country, but some experts say it capped off a year-long string of events that could trigger a more united and influential youth movement.

It may take time for a broader effort to take shape, they say, and whatever emerges might not fit the familiar mould.

Studies show young Canadians have long shunned conventional forms of political participation: they're less likely to vote or join political parties, less interested and less informed about politics than other population groups....

Meanwhile, observers continue to sound the alarm over an aging leadership unable and seemingly unwilling to recruit much-needed new blood.

For now, at least, young adults favour petitions, boycotts and ethical spending, demonstrations and volunteering.

Yet today's fragmented and fickle Internet generation is ill-suited to the persistent campaigns of the 1960s and '70s, preferring a pop-up style of protest, says Henry Milner, a political scientist at McGill University in Montreal.

The way this generation communicates is "very short-term" and more likely to spur sporadic participation in specific events or causes, says Milner, the author of "The Internet Generation: Engaged Citizens or Political Dropouts."

Social media, live-streaming and other technological tools played a key role in mobilizing Occupy protesters and summoning backup in the face of eviction.

The key for the next wave of activists will be to harness their powerful but shifting networks and turn them into something sustainable, says Biggar.

"(Young people) are really good at information-sharing and co-ordination," allowing them to muster large crowds on short notice while keeping everyone on equal footing, he says.

"Now we're working on building organizational models that take the best of that but also allow us to take collective action together for the long term," he says.

It's impossible to predict when that will happen, but "the process of finding those answers is accelerating, partially as people try to figure out what to do with the Occupy movement," Biggar says.

"And I think that may be actually one of the most interesting and powerful things our generation does."...

The challenge is in articulating specific demands without losing sight of the bigger picture...

Still, some issues—the environment, the erosion of democratic rights and a growing economic insecurity—are taking centre stage....

...Occupy itself is working to broaden and solidify its social networks across the country to form a more unified front, Batty says.

But there are still significant barriers keeping Canadian youth from traditional politics, a central mechanism for social and economic change.

An Elections Canada survey found that lack of political interest and the sense that issues important to youth aren't being addressed deter young people from voting as much as difficulties accessing the polls.

The agency has called for a long-term approach "supporting civic education to increase youth knowledge about politics and democracy in Canada" in the hopes it will boost turnout among young voters.

At the same time, the country's major political parties and institutions must make space for the younger generation if they want to foster the next wave of leaders, says Biggar.

There is no question that the numbers of youth in the so-called new social movements are not insignificant, and their endorsement of the central ideals of environmentalism and protection of the globe from war and rampant exploitation is a focus of much of their energies. The central messages of this latest wave of activism among youth are captured by Lojowsky (2001, p. 11):

The demands of the new movement are clear and straightforward. In fact, the movement has only one demand: equal rights for all. This means the freedom to earn a livable wage; the freedom to speak out; the freedom to decent education; the freedom to accessible health care, home and food; the freedom to preserve and celebrate our many cultures; and the freedom to live upon a healthy and sustainable planet, regardless of nationality, race, gender, sexual orientation, age, ability, or religious belief. There is nothing confusing about it; there are no hidden agendas. It is our basic and inalienable right as citizens of the Earth to demand nothing less.

What Influences Young People's Political Activity?

It is generally held that parents influence young people's political attitudes because they provide the setting for primary socialization, our earliest highly personal and continuous experiences, which have more credibility for the child. The pivotal influence of parents and families on young people was generally discussed in Chapter 3, including the importance of their social and economic background, reiterated above by Hudon et al. (1991) and Gillis (1981). Further, school, peer groups, and television have also been found to play a role in forming young people's political attitudes (Mintz, 1993).

Young people also seem to be influenced by the increasing numbers of celebrities speaking for different political causes. American research has found that first-time voters are at least moderately swayed by celebrity endorsements (Jackson & Darrow, 2005, p. 81). Following McCracken's "meaning transfer theory," Jackson and Darrow (2005) propose that politics can be sold through celebrity endorsements just as readily as consumer goods can, especially if the celebrities are popular rock or pop musicians who are able to offer new meanings of adolescence to their audience, including having political and social beliefs. They conclude that in order to be effective, there has to be a good match between the celebrity, the product, and the audience. Thus, they found, for example, that Alanis Morissette had no influence on the views of the 456 Canadian anglophone university-aged youth because she appeals to a slightly older audience. In comparison, Wayne Gretzky, as a well-known Canadian hockey hero, influenced the youth's views. Strong effect was also found for two young performers who were closer to the age of the respondents: popular music star Avril Lavigne, and pop/punk band leader Deryck Whibley.

Not surprisingly, fashions follow the footsteps of celebrities in creating political messages or capturing popular political trends. Designers such as FCUK and DKNY have capitalized on these by creating slogans encouraging youth to vote with slogans like "FCUK You, I'm Voting!" and "You have the power." Though these marketing attempts are called "activism light," they nevertheless both create and reflect prevailing political ideologies among young people (Thompson, 2004).

Peers, Schools, and Sports

Peer groups emerge based on connections made in one's communities and schools. In an American study, Stewart (1998, p. 26) calls high schools and their environments "mini cities," and teenagers are likened to citizens with their own language and value system. In the contemporary urban society, young people potentially spend a long time without adult supervision after school. However, most children and young people, and particularly girls in the upper and middle classes, have their time increasingly structured and preoccupied with organized activities, including clubs and sports (Aapola et al., 2005, p. 115).

Hudon et al. (1991, pp. 27–33) found in their survey of 1,003 Canadian grade 11 and grade 12 students that participation in sports groups is highest among all organized activities: 41.6 percent of the young men and 22.8 percent of women indicated participation in sports organizations. That sports is more popular as a pastime among young males than young women is confirmed by Bibby's (2001, pp. 22–24) finding that 77 percent of males aged 15–19 and 57 percent of females in the same age group list sports as a major source of enjoyment.

According to the 1992 General Social Survey (Corbeil, 2000, pp. 214–215), 77 percent of young Canadian people aged 15–18 participated regularly in sports compared with 53 percent of those in the age group 25–34 and 25 percent of those aged 55 and over. The favourite sports of youth are basketball, volleyball, hockey, baseball/softball, and some downhill skiing. There is a gender gap in that sports tend to be mostly male; 89 percent of males and 64 percent of females aged 15–18 were active in sports. Men tend to dominate numerically in sports like hockey, rugby, football, soccer, squash, racquetball, baseball/softball, golf, and weightlifting. Women's presence exceeds that of men in figure skating, equestrianism, swimming, bowling, and cross-country skiing.

Likewise, Van Roosmalen and Krahn (1996) found gender-based differences in the types of sports that youth engage in. They also found that most youth participated in sports (73 percent) or clubs (61 percent), with higher participation among boys than girls, who were more likely to engage in either arts or outdoors-oriented clubs. Interestingly, outside team sports, in areas such as working out or running, girls had a higher level of participation. Whereas 82 percent of girls participated in unorganized or individual-type sports, about 59 percent of the boys participated in these areas and another 41 percent participated in team sports. Males also engaged in a wider variety of individual and team sports. These results confirm the gender divide in that young women's culture is generally found to be geared toward neatness and looking good, whereas young males' culture is more competitive. It also signifies fewer opportunities and supports for sports for younger women.

Aapola et al. (2005, pp. 160–164) point out that there has been an increase among girls of physical activities that are seen to be masculine. Working out in the gym is more popular, including bodybuilding and fitness training. While bodybuilders tend to be males, fitness trainers tend to be females who don't want to build muscle but want to develop a shapelier body. Studies find that males and females use the same machines, but may use them differently to get the desired results. The issue of bodies and body image will be taken up in more detail in the chapter on health.

Sports can also offer a basis for a hierarchy of popularity. Eder et al. (1995, in Aapola et al., 2005, pp. 121–122) report on a US middle school where students who belonged to school sports teams gained status, whereas those who did not were lower status and avoided the "snobbish" high-status students. The divide was social class–based as only the better-off students could afford the social activities associated with high-status and popular students, and those from rural areas and from the working class were excluded.

Popularity among girls and young women can also be tied to sports events through specifically gendered elements. In the United States, the tradition of cheerleading has been associated with team sports for over 100 years. It provides a venue for highly skilled athleticism for young women, while it also feeds into traditionally feminine stereotypes (see Box 7.2).

Box 7.2: Go Team! The Cheers of American Girls

A cheerleader by the name of "Bri" (Niemiere, 2008) captures the spirit and spunk in the American tradition of cheerleading:

> Let's get physical
> Get down, get hard, get mean
> Let's get physical
> And beat that other team!

Cheerleading holds captive an estimated 3 million young people, of whom half a million are enrolled in cheer camps that provide both athletic and aesthetic training. This now well-established tradition was started by Princeton University in the 1880s and has blossomed into an impressive network of 72 regional or national competitions involving students from high schools and colleges. Full or partial scholarships for cheerleaders are offered by 225 colleges and junior colleges. It is not unusual for cheerleaders to practice several hours during the school week and more before competitions. Though the vast majority (95%) of cheerleaders are young women, young males are needed for stunts and catching in the highly acrobatic events (Brady, 2002).

In addition to being gendered, sports are an arena for racialization (James, 2005; Stahura & Parks, 2005). This is an area in which Black students can be subjected to stereotyping. Some of this is not necessarily negative, but no less unfair than the blatantly negative ones because of the persistence of an either/or approach. Thus, while the stereotype of Black youth as academically poor prevails, the stereotype of Black male youth excelling in sports completes the picture. In the words of one teacher in a school in Alberta, "They get positives for being athletic but not for being good students" (Kelly, 1998, p. 71).

Many researchers using critical race theory confirm the long roots and the prevalence of the image of Black youth as natural athletes in the US (Small, 1994; Hodge et al.,

2008; Simiyu, 2009) and Britain (Small, 1994). Attitudes and myths prevail about the presumed superior speed and physical prowess of Black athletes contrasted with the quick thinking and mental agility of White athletes. Thus, schools and amateur and professional sport coaches both endorse and promote the idea that Blacks and Whites are suited for different sports, based on these differences in supposed innate ability. Explaining the racially divided sports world also requires an understanding of the attitudes and actions of sports organizations that most certainly perpetuate it, along with media endorsements (Small, 1994, pp. 100–106; Simiyu, 2009; Hodge et al., 2008).

Simiyu (2009; also see Hodge et al., 2008) summarizes the three major factors that compel Black youth toward athletics, namely, the persistence of the myth of the physical prowess of Blacks; the media message that sports are a route toward financial success for Blacks; and the narrow range of sports where Black youth have role models. In his view, these result in a "triple tragedy among Black youth: (1) their obsessive pursuit of success through sports which only a few will attain; (2) the resultant underdevelopment of other aspects of their lives; and (3) the deprivation of the Black community of other kinds of vital talents that these young people could pursue."

Youth among Themselves: Peer Groups, Diversity, and Identity

Peers are an important pathway toward identity formation of young people. Close friendships and the idea of a "best" friend "provide support and feedback during identity formation" (Akers et al., 1998, p. 1). Peer groups and friendships provide freedom from parents and other authority figures, and provide alternative norms and information about expected behaviours, and a setting for conforming to these expectations about "a given group's own norms, attitudes, speech patterns, and dress codes" (Kendal et al., 1997, p. 145; also see Matsueda & Heimer, 1997). At the same time, youth are a part of something that is emotionally satisfying and a means toward an identity and a sense of community (Doherty, 1988, in Danesi, 1994, p. 56). On the other hand, Côté and Allahar (1994, p. 20) suggest that insofar as youth culture is created from within, it is also a reaction to an exclusion from adult culture and a way of creating something of their own aside from the roles that are granted by adults. In the words of Elkin and Handel (1989, in Kendal et al., 1997, p. 145), the "peer group is both a product of culture and one of its major transmitters."

Young people tend to value their relationships with both their families and friends. While relationships with family members are still important in adolescence, peer relations and friendships become particularly central (Sippola, 1999). Moreover, youth tend to be more satisfied with their friendships than with their family relationships (Holmes & Silverman, 1992, p. 38). Reflecting this peer orientation, Bibby (2001, pp. 20–24, 32–33) found that for the majority (94 percent) of Canadian 15–19-year-olds in a national study, peers were the number-one ranked source of enjoyment, and that youth are more likely to turn to their friends than to their parents when they have a serious problem.

Peer groups do not arise randomly. Similarities among friends are great in terms of socio-demographic factors, including "grade level, age, gender, religion, and ethnicity" (Akers et al., 1998, p. 1). Age is a particularly important criterion, and friendships usually arise within a narrow age range (Aapola et al., 2005, pp. 120–121).

This is manifested in clique formation. Danesi (1994, pp. 59–60) writes:

> When a clique is formed it normally consists of young teens. Moreover, at its inception it tends to be mainly unisexual and isolated from other cliques. A little later on the cliques typically start to interact with other cliques. During subsequent stages, the clique opens itself up more and more to members of the opposite sex. Finally, heterosexual bonding occurs within the clique signaling its disintegration.

Membership in particular cliques involves acquiring certain specific behavioural characteristics similar to other members. For example, Danesi (1994, p. 59) points out:

> A teeny-bopper who sees himself or herself as a hard rocker, for instance, will eventually develop a "hard" personality. The hard rocker will typically manifest aggressive behaviour, utter obscenities regularly, wear ripped jeans, boots, and long hair, and listen to heavy metal music.

In the 21st century, some negativity has been associated with cliques, which are sometimes equated with school bullying, discussed in Chapter 4. This negative association is rooted in the main feature of cliques: homogeneity in terms of social class, gender, and race. Some peer groups may develop negative behaviours, based on the "othering" process that is implied by shared demographic and behavioural characteristics.

Subcultures of Immigrant and Racialized Youth

As indicated in Chapter 1, youth is seen to be a crucial stage for the development of identity. "The development of a stable sense of identity is one of the central processes of adolescence" (Hébert, 2001, p. 156). This is made more difficult in diverse societies as individuals are depicted as being "caught between two cultures."

Immigrant youth have to negotiate their identities amidst often conflicting factors. A study of immigrant youth by the Canadian Council on Social Development (2000, pp. 11–12) found that though a majority of young immigrants felt comfortable being in Canada, they did not "feel Canadian." They were not certain about what "being Canadian" means. Nearly all felt that maintaining their culture, language, and heritage was very important. This is easier for larger immigrant groups from China and India, but more difficult for the smaller groups.

The shifting frames of reference for immigrant families have resulted in an increasing attention by sociologists to issues of identity and belonging (Driedger, 2001; Kalbach & Kalbach, 1999). Fuelled by postmodernist theory, an increasing number of studies focus on the different interpretations of national and ethnic identity among immigrants, stamped by gender and age differences (Handa, 1997; Karakayali, 2005; Tyyskä, 2003b). These analyses move the debate beyond the traditional "acculturation thesis," which measures degrees to which immigrants adapt to the host society. According to this thesis, acculturation is seen as a natural progression in which each successive immigrant generation adopts more of the "behaviours, rules, values, and norms of the host society" (Boyd, 2000, p. 3; see also Berry, 2007).

Instead, the focus in more recent sociological literature is on multiple and "hybrid" identities (Gordon, 1999; Berry, 2007; Karakayali, 2005; Tyyskä, 2003b; Dallaire & Denis, 2005; Alexander, 1996, pp. 38–69; Hébert, 2001, pp. 156–159; Kalbach & Kalbach, 1999). In other words, the premise of recent studies is that identities are flexible, subject to multiple influences and interpretations of equal validity.

In a Canadian study of the narratives among second-generation youth in their early twenties whose families originate from India, Pakistan, and Bangladesh, Tirone and Pedlar (2005) found a profound appreciation of their heritage and origins even as they participated in dominant peer culture. This is echoed in Karakayali's (2005, pp. 325–343) research on 30 immigrant autobiographies in 20th-century North America (Canada and the United States). The author challenges the widely prevalent view that children of immigrants are a "problem group" living in "two worlds," caught between their culture and the mainstream. The "two worlds" discourse is widespread in the literature from the 1950s onward, either explicitly or implicitly. Karakayali's analysis reveals a wide range of relationships and patterns in immigrant families. Similarly, the lives of immigrant children reflect multiple relationships, experiences, dreams, and desires, well beyond "two worlds." The reported experience of two worlds seems to be, in fact, something that is imposed on the children by the outside world, which identifies them based on their culture. Thus, this constructed reality is imposed on immigrant children and does not necessarily reflect the complexity of their relationships in their communities.

Similar results are revealed in Alexander's (1996) study of Black youth in London with regard to some of the dilemmas of living in a society delineated by a colour divide. These youth, many of whom were born in Britain but had either visited or moved back and forth between Britain and their parents' home countries, told of varying degrees of identification with Britain, the West Indies, and Africa. One example is Angelina (Alexander, 1996, p. 49), who spoke of the multiple identities:

> All the history they're learning here is *their* history basically, whereas in respect, it should be *my* history as well. But I've also got the fact that I've got another history—I've got the history of the Caribbean, history of slavery and the mother country, Africa, where our roots come from ... so I've got another history. Maybe that's why we are special—we've got two histories, not just one; or three in my case. [emphases in the original]

In this sense, being part of an entity, such as the Black community, is very much a process of being in an "imagined community," one that is constantly changing; it is a set of shared experiences rather than a fixed place (Alexander, 1996, pp. 69–70).

Consequently, more attention has been paid to the transnational identities of young people, reflecting the major changes and challenges arising from population mobility. The reference point of identity is definitely malleable in an increasingly connected world. Visits and communications with relatives and friends in a young person's family of origin, for example, can result in manifestations of different mixes of cultures. One young woman in Somerville's (2008, p. 29) Canadian study said: "I have a cousin who is the same age as me and when I go [to India] I'd take clothes to wear and we'd compare and sometimes I'd borrow some things or go with her to buy them." These kinds of everyday behaviours reflect a multiple and complex adoption of behaviours, in keeping with the quote from Angelina in Britain, above.

As was discussed in earlier chapters, the educational and work context for youth differs by race and ethnic background. As well, educational institutions are a context in which youth culture diversifies along race and ethnic lines. Anyone who has either attended or observed the cafeteria and recess groupings in schools can attest to the power of race and ethnicity in the formation of peer groups.

Following up on the theme of cliques and friendship formation along racialized lines, Kelly's (1998, p. 82) study of high school youths in Alberta indicated that where friendships develop between Black and non-Black youth, they were generally based on the students' common experiences and support for each other through difficult times. One respondent explains:

> Little kids hanging out together, having snowball fights, doing little kids things, being there for me when I was getting busted for doing this and that. I was there for him. We went skateboarding together. We just did things as little kids and as you grow up you begin to have respect for those things. It's easier to be friends with somebody at that age than it is now. At our age everything is about money and it's a different aspect.

More commonly, the Black high school youths "chose their close friends mainly, though not exclusively, from the Black student population." This, Kelly (1998, p. 78) argues, is because for many of these students, "high school offered the first opportunity to mix with Blacks who were not members of their church or from their immediate neighbourhood." She quotes a student:

> There was not that many Black people in my elementary school so I had to get along with other people. In junior high there was still a little bit more [Black students] but not that many. But it was in high school in grade 10 that you associate more [with Blacks].

Some of the bonding among Black students was due to stereotypes (also discussed in Chapter 3 and above, in relation to sports). The students in Kelly's (1998, pp. 67–72) study were aware of the ways in which their identities and group formation were influenced by how others viewed them.

Further, one of the dominant Black cultural forms in the United States and elsewhere is hip-hop culture, including "rap music, graffiti, break dancing, and djing" (Cohen et al., 2007, p. 13). Because hip-hop is a major musical force, it will be discussed in more detail in that context below.

In the US and the UK, the racial divide is stark. As discussed in Chapter 2, American Black-White race relations were forged out of colonialism, slavery, and the civil rights movement. According to Cohen et al. (2007, p. 1), on a scale unlike any other groups, "Black youth reflect the challenges of inclusion and empowerment in the post-civil rights period." This is reflected in the depressing statistics presented in previous chapters on education and employment, and will be further proven in the chapter on youth crime.

In the UK of the 1980s, the conservative political climate was dominated by the notion of "Englishness" as an exclusively White category. An influential book by Paul Gilroy (1987, in Back, 1996, pp. 9–11), entitled *There Ain't No Black in the Union Jack*, began to challenge this racist notion.

In the UK, Rastafarianism is perhaps the most influential Black religious, political, and cultural expression. Rastafarianism is "an international mass movement of resistance against white supremacy and neocolonialism" (Pryce, 1986, p. xiv), hailing back to November 1930, when Prince Ras Tafari was crowned emperor in Ethiopia and given his official title, Haile Selassie I, King of Kings, Lord of Lords, The All-Conquering Lion of the Tribe of Judah. When the news got to Jamaica, it galvanized the followers of Marcus Garvey, the founder of the Negro Improvement Association in the early 20th century. Garvey had prophesied that there would be a Black king arising from Africa, heralding the dawn of a new era for Black people, and their return to their roots in Africa. His followers linked the prophecy to Haile Selassie, who was expected to bring an end to "Babylon," or White domination. Though Garvey never endorsed the notion and also disparaged Selassie publicly for his politics, the myth and vision gained strength. It spread among Black youth in Britain and by the 1970s it became a central political and cultural force among them (Cashmore & Troyna, 1982, pp. 72–86; Pryce, 1986, pp. 18–19). The main observers and followers of Rasta are males aged 18–45 and older (Pryce, 1986, p. 144).

As much as Rastafarianism is a political movement, it is inextricably linked with new Black cultural forms, including religion, dress, and music. Jah Haile Selassie was seen as the true God, so Rastafarians rejected conventional Christianity as a mockery created by White people to dominate Black people (Cashmore & Troyna, 1982, pp. 73–74). Marijuana (*ganja*) plays a role in religious observance; it is a sacred "weed" as described in the book of Genesis, and is seen as a means toward spiritual unification and as a "wisdom weed" (Pryce, 1986, p. 148).

Followers of Rastafarianism adopt Ethiopian national colours (red, green, black) and grow their hair into dreadlocks as symbols of their rejection of White society. They also choose to speak a Jamaican patois and avoid association with anything that expresses the domination of Babylon. The main musical form is reggae (Cashmore & Troyna, 1982, pp. 73–74; Pryce, 1986, pp. 147–151), which will be discussed in more detail below.

According to Cashmore and Troyna (1982, pp. 74–86; also see Pryce, 1986, pp. 143–166), the "Journey" of becoming a Rastafarian (Rastaman)—also known as "the road to Jah"—among the British Black youth in the 1970s took place in four phases: (1) the apprehension; (2) the loss; (3) the drift; and (4) the acceptance. The final stage of the journey consisted of accepting Haile Selassie as the God who will destroy Babylon and return Black people to Africa. That journey began with the apprehension phase, whereby youth in the education system who were looking for employment realized their racial disadvantage in the British context. Having been born in Britain or lived there most of their lives, these Black youth rejected the idea that you can go "home" to the West Indies. Instead, they learned to value their own Black youth groups ("gangs") as sources of power and transformation in the British society. The second phase consisted of loosening ties to their parents' values whom the youth regarded as having been brainwashed by Babylon. This process of loss was aided by the gang structure of mutual support. The third, or drift phase, consisted of extensive debates among the different gangs on all possible topics that would be interpreted through the filter of the inspirational messages that were embedded in the reggae music (see below) of the biggest Rastaman of them all, Bob Marley, and others.

Another offshoot of Rastafarianism in Britain is the so-called "rude-boys," which is a Jamaican expression for lower-class delinquent Black youth. Unlike the pacifist Rastas, rude-boys were secular and promoted a violent solution, including redistribution of wealth, especially to the historically wronged Black population. Another group, called "rudies," is similar to them. Also called teenyboppers, this group of Black youth has influences ranging from the Rastas to the rude-boys and the American Black Power movements as well as pan-Africanism arising from freedom struggles (Pryce, 1986, pp. 143–166).

The British literature of Black youth culture has been accused of pathologizing Blacks through the excessive reliance on their association with "cultures of deprivation" and decaying inner cities (Alexander, 1996, p. 10). I would argue that the information collected by the various authors' work summarized here can also be given a different interpretation, one that emphasizes the richness and variety of Black youth cultures while making room for an understanding of their varied meanings to the youth themselves. As expressed by Gilroy (1987, 1993, in Alexander, 1996, pp. 16–17), though many Black youth experience subordination, they also engage in ongoing struggles to create positive cultural experiences.

Those positive experiences are difficult to create by immigrant and racialized youth who have to come to terms with discrimination based on their cultural practices. A good example is the intensification of public hostility toward the most visible symbols of Islam in the post-9/11 era, accompanied by controversies regarding Islamic clothing and symbols worn by children and youth in schools (Franz, 2007; Maira, 2004). Among the symbols of Islam, the *hijāb* (traditional Muslim women's headdress) has become hotly debated and contested in the context of school and sports clothing regulations. One of many such incidents took place in Canada, with the ban of an 11-year-old Muslim girl from a soccer game in Quebec for wearing a *hijāb*. Upon appeal, Asmahan Mansour's ban was upheld by the officials of the International Football Association Board, located in Manchester, England. Though the *hijāb* is by no means unanimously endorsed in the Muslim population, many questioned the ban, made on grounds of a "safety risk," because *hijābs*, turbans, and yarmulkes are habitually worn by players in Canada and across the world (Blatchford, 2007).

The discovery that even a few "homegrown" Muslims, born in the industrialized West, harbour resentments toward their hosts generated new studies showing the lack of socio-economic success of that population. In the UK, a 2004 government report, leaked to the public, listed high unemployment rates, high rates of school dropout, and high incidence of poverty among the Muslim population. This low status is combined with media vilification, depicting "Muslims as backward, uneducated religious fanatics who marry their daughters off like other people sell cars" (Franz, 2007, p. 98). It is particularly the high proportion of Muslim youth that is viewed with alarm; whereas among the general population one in five people are under age 15, one-third of Muslims are in that age category. And despite polls showing a high degree of Muslim support for their nations of residence, the fears of the general public are fuelled by a few incidents in recent European history (Franz, 2007).

The situation is particularly inflamed in the US, where a significant backlash has taken place against Muslims (also discussed in Chapter 8). Maira (2004, p. 220) describes many Muslim communities in America as feeling "under siege." Children and youth are not exempt from this negativity as exemplified in incidents from one high school in Cambridge, Massachusetts, where particularly South Asian Muslim immigrant youth were targeted with accusations of "You're a terrorist" or were being called "bin Laden" or "Muslim niggers." The White House's initial embrace and later neglect of American Muslims following 9/11 is not lost on young people. Khan, a young South Asian Muslim male (in Maira, 2004, p. 225), said this:

> Initially leaders, including Bush, has spoken up [against racial profiling], but afterwards, when it wasn't as critical, outreach to Muslim Americans has stopped completely. Now, it's bashing time.

Gender and Youth Subcultures

As is evident from the above discussion and from materials in previous chapters, gender divisions are stamped across the range of young people's experiences. Not surprisingly, gender patterns emerge in studies of young people's cultural expressions, including the value put on friendships and relationships. Holmes and Silverman (1992, p. 38) found that young Canadian women are more concerned than young men about their relationships with families, friends, and the opposite sex. Additionally, more young women express satisfaction with their friendships than with their family relationships, and twice as many young women are more dissatisfied with their family relationships than with their friendships. Young women consider friendships very important, despite possible conflicts. They also worry about peer pressure, but younger teens (aged 13) seem to worry more than older teens (aged 16). There is also research that suggests that young women are not generally as willing to engage in anti-social activities due to peer pressure as are young men. Holmes and Silverman (1992) conclude that as young women get older, they seem to be less concerned with conformity, and are more secure in what they do.

Girls' friendships are traditionally seen to be about training for their future as wives and mothers and require close affective bonding. This view is gradually changing as the multiple purposes and aspects of girls' peer relations are explored, including their bonding for the purpose of support in the male-dominated milieu. Female peer groups and friends provide young women with an arena to venture toward independence and develop their self-identity, characterized by an "autonomy/connection" tension. Because it is expected that women are emotionally responsible and connected, creating a sense of independence can be problematic, something that is alleviated by the presence of same-sex friends (Aapola et al., 2005, pp. 109–113).

These same-sex, activity-based peer groups result in some differentiation between the activities of young males and females. Overall, however, female youth culture tends to be studied less than male youth culture. Where attention to both exists, male culture tends to be identified with the public sphere (streets and public spaces) and the female culture with the private sphere (home and family). However, Canadian researchers Van Roosmalen and Krahn (1996) question this distinction because it trivializes the youth culture of females and tends to associate young males' culture with deviance and delinquency found on the streets and public spaces. Instead, they suggest that though youth culture is gendered, it is not completely dichotomous.

There is some evidence that the traditional gender distinctions in young women's and men's home-based culture is gradually breaking down. In Bibby's (2001, p. 24) survey of Canadian 15–19-year-olds, though more females (82 percent) than males (67 percent) ranked spending time in their "own room" as enjoyment, it was still third in overall combined rankings. Van Roosmalen and Krahn (1996) found that there were no gender differences in the degree to which Canadian youth spend time "just hanging around." Only one-third reported spending most of their time this way, and it was also usually combined with other activities, such as doing homework and chores.

Girls and Reading

There is one area in which gender differences are evident. Baker's (1989) study of Canadian adolescents found that girls were more likely than boys to read magazines (Currie, 1999, p. 43). This is not surprising considering that reading in general is more popular among young women than men. According to a survey by the Canadian Advisory Council on the Status of Women (Holmes & Silverman, 1992, p. 43; see also Bibby, 2001, p. 29), reading for pleasure and personal interest is more common among adolescent women than men. While 70 percent of the females reported reading three or more hours per week, only 43 percent of the men did. The percentage of men who do not read at all is also higher at 14 percent compared to 6 percent of young women.

Magazines aimed at the young female audience send a specific range of messages to their readers. For example, Currie (1999, p. 247) found in her research of female youth and magazines that despite being discriminating readers who want magazines that focus on the realities of their lives, girls are overwhelmed by the difficulties in pursuing the "cultural mandate to 'look good.'" Currie (1999, pp. 247–248) states:

> Because physical attractiveness is based on the assumption of others, comments from peers can be both reassuring and devastating when self-esteem is linked to physical appearance. As a consequence, learning how to look good is important for girls growing up in a patriarchal culture.

Further, Durham (1999, p. 193; see also Aapola et al., 2005) writes:

> Much attention has been paid over the last decade to the role of the mass media in this cultural socialization of girls: clearly, the media are crucial: data paint a disturbing portrait of adolescent girls as well as of the mass media: on the whole, girls appear to be vulnerable targets of detrimental media images of femininity.

Graydon (1997, p. 2, Appendix A) identifies some of the most pervasive trends in media, particularly in advertising, that have a negative effect on young women. Young women are presented as objects; their bodies are subjected to unnecessary sexualization (see also Zurbriggen et al., 2007); they are presented as infants who need guidance or rescuing, or are defined in terms of their domestic relationships with men or children, or are portrayed as natural victims of male brutality. Media messages portray the ideal young woman as White, slim, and beautiful by mainstream standards, to the exclusion of anyone—arguably the majority of the female population—who do not fit this unrealistic and unattainable image (Aapola et al., 2005, pp. 134–135). Currie (1999, p. 52) concurs:

> If we look at the content of women's magazines, the evidence seems incontrovertible: the representation of women within women's magazines associates femininity with the sphere of domesticity and heterosexual romance; it emphasizes youth and the physical beauty of whiteness; and it under-represents the diverse identities and concerns of women as a social category.

The pressures are great to conform to the images offered for sale, witness the large sums of money spent on the beauty industry, including cosmetics, surgical procedures, dieting, and exercise, by young women (Aapola et al., 2005, pp. 137–141). The body-image issues and eating disorders that arise from this obsession will be discussed in Chapter 9 on health.

Nevertheless, Aapola et al. (2005, p. 135; also see Schilt, 2003) point out that even as young women are voracious consumers of magazines, they are also critical of the images. Nevertheless, those who rebel are quickly silenced. Monbiot (2006) observes the following about a popular British girls' magazine, *Sugar*:

> A couple of readers seek to rebel against these impossible dreams, but they are slapped down. "After reading 'How to be sexy by Christina Aquilera [*sic*],'" one girl

writes, "I realized: how can a girl say she's individual but look plastic?" The letters editor replies: "She has an individual approach to fashion, image and attitude—which is why we think she's fab." Another letter asks: "Why is a celebrity always on the cover of *Sugar*? People who aren't celebrities are people, too, and readers would respond better to seeing their mate's older sister than a star who they wish they were!" She's told: "We've done our research and most of you'd prefer to see a celeb on the cover."

Some girls actively participate in creating girl-friendly content. In addition to traditional magazines, there are "girl-zines," defined as "do-it-yourself publications made primarily by and for girls and women" (Green & Taormino, 1997, p. xi, quoted in Schilt 2003, p. 73). Though they may seem to cater to traditional or revamped ideas about girlhood and femininity, some girl-zines also take on the tough topics related to living and growing up female, including sexuality, sexual abuse, sexual harassment, psychological problems, and reproductive issues. In doing that, they provide a space for young women to develop agency, and to challenge the treatment they are subjected to. One editor of a girl-zine put it like this:

> And see, right now there is an 11-year-old girl … she is telling her story. She too was sexually molested. She is crying. I am crying too. I just want to hold her and tell her I am proud of her. And that she is brave. And I wanna tell her that maybe everything isn't alright right now, but we can make it alright. I wish for every one of us to come out, that could change things. We can come out, come on strong. Yell and kick until the world finally listens and takes action. (Carlip, 1995, p. 5, in Schilt, 2003, p. 88)

Girlfriend! BFF!

Studies of girls' friendships find a set of social rules, including "reliability, reciprocity, commitment, confidentiality, trust and sharing" (Hey, 1997, p. 65, in Aapola et al., 2005, p. 117). At the same time, there are tensions as young women balance the ethics of friendships with both vying for social position and responding to the male gaze. Girls' friendships tend toward cliques, and it is often difficult to include new friends in the tightly knit groupings (Aapola et al., 2005, p. 117). Further, according to studies summarized in Aapola et al. (2005, p. 123), girls with a shared level of development or shared experiences also tend to bond together. Thus, girls who have begun to menstruate, girls who share ideas of physical beauty and attractiveness, and girls with disabilities may form friendship groups.

The ethical rules and foci of girls' cliques vary depending on social class and culture. "Niceness" or getting along with everyone is something that is associated with middle-class femininity, whereas among working-class girls this may be construed as "kissing up" to authority, or being a "snob." Working-class girls are also found in American and British studies to present a tougher image and to manage their conflicts more openly than middle-class girls (Aapola et al., 2005, p. 118). An American study of girls also found that girls tend to think of their group as the norm, labelling the others as lacking, whether it is in regard to their clothing, school performance, or their overall conduct (Finders, 1997, in Aapola et al., 2005, p. 124).

A "problem" approach to girls' friendships has emerged, emphasizing the negative aspects of the "indirect forms of aggression" among girls, especially when they are younger, including social exclusion, talking behind someone's back, sulking, or making other friends as a form of revenge. It has been suggested that these types of behaviours are a reaction to young girls' realization of their powerlessness and that as time goes by, they come to terms with it and aggression declines. At the same time, indirect aggression is socially more appropriate for girls, as any aggression in women tends to be unacceptable. Thus, middle-class girls who are intent on being "nice" hide their group conflicts, whereas working-class girls more openly "bitch" about other girls (Aapola et al., 2005, p. 119).

Indeed, Aapola et al. (2005, p. 129) argue that the attention to the negative aspects of girls' friendships and "tough girls" (see a further discussion of the "nasty girls" phe-nomenon in Chapter 13 on crime) reflects the notion that aggressive girls in a public space are a threat to the traditional gender order. Traditional views see girls involved in an invisible "bedroom culture," which does not pose a challenge, whereas girls in public spaces do, especially if they seem like "girls running wild."

Girls' friendships tend to be not only stamped by social class–based groupings but also racially based groupings. Hey (1997, in Aapola et al., 2005, p. 121) found that the White British working-class girls in her study distanced themselves from Pakistani girls, labelling them negatively as "slags" in the process. At the same time, one British researcher (Wulff, 1995, in Aapola et al., 2005, p. 124) found that the girls in her study transgressed ethnic boundaries in their friendship groups.

The Media Invasion

Aside from print media, which are more closely identified with young women, there are multiple visual and auditory media, which provide content for young people as they hang out. Television and film viewing and listening to music are major activi-ties, while other activities include computers (including Internet and computer games), video games, and spending time on the cell phone, Facebook, Twitter, and other new communication technologies and social media. All of these media absorb a large chunk of youth's time and expose them to rampant consumerism.

The Old Foe: TV

Television is traditionally identified as one of the major influences in the lives of young people. Conrad Kottak (1995, in Wilson, 1998, p. 16) coined the term "teleodition-ing" to capture the significant impact of TV on young people, namely that they "dupli-cate, albeit inappropriately, in other areas of their lives, behavior styles developed while watching the tube." A common complaint, included among Kottak's examples, is that students don't seem to read unless there is background noise, to come and go in class as they please, to bring food, or even kiss or ask the instructor to wish Happy Birthday to a fellow student. One major complaint among professors is that students seem to want to be entertained while being educated, something that is disparagingly called "edutainment."

Television viewing takes up a lot of time among young people (see Table 7.2). In Canada, young people aged 12–17 spend, on average, 20 hours a week watching television. Indeed, a Canadian government study from 1996 showed that by age 12, an average child spent twice the time watching television (12,000 hours) than going to school (Gennaro, 2005, p. 129). According to Bibby (2001, p. 24), television viewing is a major source of enjoyment for 60 percent of Canada's youth. One notable phenomenon that is not yet captured in research is the increasing viewing of programs and movies on computers, tablets, smartphones, and other personal communication devices (Stald, 2008).

Although there seems to be a levelling off recently, young men have tended to watch more TV, a trend confirmed by Bibby (2001, p. 24) and Van Roosmalen and Krahn (1996). Instead of watching TV, young women are more likely to do chores. The males

Table 7.2: Television Viewing among Youth

Country	Age	Hours per Week
Canada		
2004[1]	12–17	12.9
	18–24 (males)	12.3
	18–24 (females)	14.9
2011[2]	12–17	19.9
United Kingdom		
2006[3]	16–24	15.9
2011[4]	10–15	16.5
United States		
2005[5]	15–18	23.8 (based on 3.40 per day)
2011[2]	12–17	22.9

Sources:
1. Statistics Canada (2006b).
2. Television Bureau of Canada (2013).
3. BBC Commissioning (2006).
4. Broadcasters Audience Research Board (2012).
5. Henry J. Kaiser Family Foundation (2005).

tend to also report the content of viewing (e.g., cartoons and sports), whereas the females tend to report the context for viewing (e.g., with family, with friends). In fact, more females than males spend time with friends, through visits, on the phone, or in the mall, reflecting a traditional focus by women on relationships (Van Roosmalen & Krahn, 1996).

These results are echoed by McKinley (1996, p. 118) who found that the conversation young women engaged in during and after TV shows was important because it "established a community among the viewers, a community with shared experience and expectations—a shared expertise, if you will, in terms of how females look." She suggests that this is indicative of an ongoing process of identity formation linked to everyday interaction. These gender distinctions also have to be seen in the context of the content of television, which tends to marginalize women. For example, Gerbner (1995, p. 3) found that women's presence is smallest in the news and children's programs (where they tend to be minor characters) but tends to increase in daytime serials.

Black youth likewise have difficulty finding non-stereotypical positive images in films, television, and music. Kelly (1998, p. 61) found that a part of Black youth's positive sense of identity came from films and shows that depicted Black people in a positive way. Still, with the American domination of the air waves, Gerbner (1995, p. 5) found that African Americans are largely invisible in program content, while their numbers are larger at peak viewing times. Kelly (1998, p. 60) also found that even though films can provide a powerful sense of identity and togetherness, Black youth are also aware that films present Blacks in a particular way. Eldridge, one informant, said:

> The [films] always show that the Black man is always saved by White people. We can never save ourselves, I can't understand that. We do stuff for ourselves, but they always show the White man trying to save the Black person.

American entertainment media, including TV and film, are generally found to underrepresent Blacks and perpetuate stereotypes about Black youth. According to Perkins (2005, pp. 171–193), the colonial depiction of Blacks as criminals continues in the media today. In her analysis of pre- and post-1960s images of Blacks in film (see Table 7.3), images prevail that "will never motivate our youth to achieve their true potential or make a notable contribution to the improvement of black people" (p. 182). The post-1960s "blaxploitation" films are filled with sex and violence and characters that seem to be heroic but feed into the worst stereotypes of ghettoized behaviour. They continue to distort the image of Black youth as dangerous criminals. Perkins (2005, pp. 191–192) coins the term "mediacide" to depict this practice:

> It is the systemic process of creating, distorting and depicting images of a people that are dehumanizing, stereotypic, hostile and dangerous; thereby targeting them as being worthless and expendable.

Table 7.3: Historical and Contemporary Images of Blacks in Film

Pre-1960	*Blaxploitation Period*
Contented Slave	Stupid Militant
Tragic Mulatto	
Brute Negro	Brute Negro
Wretched Freedman	Suicidal Militant
Sensuous Female	Sensuous Female
Black Stud	Black Stud
Happy Coon	Celebrated Hustler
Timid Nigger	Super Nigger
Noble Slave	Cool Pimp
Bad Nigger	Bad Nigger

Source: Perkins (2005).

The New Foes: Communication Technologies

For many youth, TV and films are becoming boring because they are not interactive or amusing enough (Ferguson, 2000, p. 3). A recent survey among youth found that "85% of Canada's teenagers were wired [to the Internet], three-quarters of them at home." The study also found that boys are online for up to 10 hours a week and girls for 8 (Ferguson, 2000, p. 1). Although the technology connects one via chat rooms and email, it is basically an individualistic activity and also provides a method of youthful resistance. For example, two Montreal boys, in separate incidents, were arrested and charged with cyber-vandalism. One of them, a 17-year-old, was charged with interfering with data systems at NASA, Harvard, and the Massachusetts Institute of Technology (Ferguson, 2000, p. 1).

If television has been blamed for an increasing number of ills among youth, we can now add to this the explosion in telecommunication technologies, including laptops, cell phones, personal music and video game devices, multimedia gadgets including cameras, and other multiple forms of communication and entertainment that are easily transportable. There are many new communication and entertainment technologies that go well beyond the notion of "cyberspace" (Delgado, 2002). Young people who grew up in a world rich in media and communication, using electronic devices and occupying digital spaces for multiple aspects of their lives, have been referred to as the "Net-generation," the "millennium generation," and "digital natives" (Mesch, 2009).

One of these media is Facebook, which is used primarily by youth to develop friend-ship networks for the purpose of sharing updates, pictures, comments, and event infor-mation. It reports over 1 billion active monthly users worldwide. Twitter, a social net-working medium relying on short messages known as tweets, was reportedly used by 23 percent of American teens in 2013, an increase from 16 percent in 2011 (McDiarmid, 2013). Additionally, the same report found that in 2013 "twenty per cent of teens … posted their cellphone number online, compared to just 2 per cent who did in 2006. More than 90 per cent have posted a photo of themselves, up from 79 per cent six years ago" (McDiarmid, 2013).

Instant messaging (IM) is used in lieu of email by large numbers of high school stu-dents to hook up with others (AdweekMedia, 2007). American research shows that an average teenager texts 60 times a day as of 2011, compared to 50 texts a day in 2009. The increase is being led by older teens, males, and Black youth. It is the dominant way of communicating among teens (Lenhart, 2012). Similar trends are reported in the UK, where texting and social networking are used more than phone calls or person-to-person communications among people aged 16-24 (Ofcom, 2012).

Texting is used by some youth as a way of breaking up dating relationships. One example is that of Katie Barnard, an 18-year-old from near Lethbridge, Alberta, who got a five-word text message of cancellation from her prom date, an hour before her limo was scheduled to pick her up. In shock, she shared the news with her younger sister, who tracked down a new date for her using her cell phone, in time for Katie to make it to her prom with her new date dressed in a borrowed tuxedo and a corsage his mother helped find for Katie (Anderssen, 2007, p. A8). Cell phones have become standard equipment among young people, for whom they are a regular form of communication. Text messaging shares a spot with Face-book, Twitter, YouTube, and IM for keeping in touch with friends, dates, and lovers.

Youth created a large proportion of the 4.6 million text messages sent in 2006. With the widespread use of these communication technologies, the lives of young people are becoming increasingly public as news about their private lives is flashed in text, photos, and video clips to anyone who has access to the same technology. The invasion of pri-vacy is too much for some youth, but most continue using these sites for socialization (Anderssen, 2007, p. A8; also see AdweekMedia, 2007).

Though TV viewing still outranks new communication and entertainment technolo-gies, Internet use is going up in all three countries (see Table 7.4). Among the activities of Canadian youth, 47 percent of teens report computers, 42 percent report the Inter-net, and 33 percent report email as sources of enjoyment. Indeed, while the Internet was touted to eventually replace television as a source and medium of youthful entertain-ment, it seems the two are complementary (Bibby, 2001, pp. 24–26).

Computer games are very popular. In the UK, 82 percent of youth aged 16–24 report playing them (BBC Commissioning, 2006). American youth aged 15–18 clock an aver-age of 33 minutes per day playing video games (Henry J. Kaiser Family Foundation, 2005). Though some girls also play, video games tend to be associated with young males; in Canada, 69 percent of young males (15–19) indicate playing computer/video games daily to weekly, while only 26 percent of young women do so (Bibby, 2001, pp. 28–29).

Table 7.4: Youth Internet Use

Country	Age	Percentage of Youth
Canada		
2000[1]	15–19	90
	25–29	70
2007[2]	16–24	96
United Kingdom		
2006[3]	16–24	83
2011[4]	16–24	98.8
United States		
2003[5]	15–17 (at home)	91.5
	18–24 (at work)	70.6
2007[6]	12–17	93

Sources:
1. Dryburgh (2001).
2. Statistics Canada (2008c).
3. BBC Commissioning (2006).
4. European Travel Commission (2012).
5. US Census Bureau (2003c).
6. Lenhart et al. (2010).

The extensive use of computers and computer games (see Table 7.5) worries many adults. Games are particularly seen as "addictive" to the so-called "Nintendo genera-tion" of 12–17-year-olds starting in the 1990s. It is especially young males who are being socialized in this fashion as there are gender inequalities embedded in the use of this technology. Whereas young women's culture has always been ignored, this pattern continues and, ironically, in a setting that has been traditionally described in feminine terms. It has been found that access to and control over domestic space is gender-based; young men command a lot more space and access to computers and computer games than their sisters do (McNamee, 1998, in Miles, 2000, pp. 78–79).

Communication technologies also allow for the creation of a completely new space for youthful connections that cuts across the private and the public. There are those who see the computer and the Internet as signs of youth's adaptability and creativity. They allow youth to share information in a new way and in a forum that allows them to help themselves and one another through advice to peers and help for youth in trouble, e.g.,

Table 7.5: Youth Videogame Playing in Canada, 2005

Age	Percentage	Time Used per Day (in minutes)
15–17	31.7	1–10
	14.6	10–60
	12.3	65–120
	22.8	125+
18–19	32.7	1–10
	7.3	10–60
	7.1	65–120
	12.0	125+
20–24	0	1–10
	8.0	10–60
	14.0	65–120
	15.8	125+

Source: Statistics Canada (2007a).

those victimized by bullies. Thus, they call for more understanding and acceptance by adults and parents, rather than condemnation and policing of young people's computer use (Wilson & Jette, 2005, pp. 81–82).

Through their extensive use and enjoyment of new communication technologies, young people are literally creating new languages, such as leet speak (see Box 7.3). They also allow for the creation of both global and localized peer links and new freedoms that are also increasingly contested by parents and other authorities (Aapola et al., 2005, p. 116). In 2007, the use of cell phones was banned in Toronto public school classes and hallways, ostensibly because "the technology is a disruption in class and can be used to cheat on tests" (Alphonso, 2007, p. A13). The ban was lifted in 2011 (Hammer, 2012). A complete ban of cell phones applies in New York schools, and schools in Milwaukee are banning them following "an incident in which students used them to call in reinforcements in brawls (Alphonso, 2007, p. A13).

One major concern among the users of extensive networking technology, raised in Chapter 4, is cyberbullying. A related concern is predatory adults and strangers who may do harm to children and youth. The American report on social media, cited above, noted that among teens, one is six had experienced this kind of unwanted contact, with twice as many girls than boys (McDiarmid, 2013). Though there are serious incidents involving proposed contact and actual harmful consequences, critically oriented social

Box 7.3: Leet Speak

This original piece to this book, written by Jennifer Brayton (2007), introduces leet speak, commonly used by youth in text messaging.

Leet speak is basically Internet-based slang that is used as shorthand when communicating with other people. It's short for "elite." In leet speak, "leet" itself is written as "l33t" or "1337."

While many people today assume leet speak is new and used only by youth, it originated in the early 1980s when people with technical skills and knowledge were using early online bulletin boards to share information and files. Leet speak originated because, for one, it was faster to type using abbreviations than full words and sentences, and, secondly, because some of the topics under discussion were controversial or forbidden. Using slang or abbreviations hid the topic from possible censorship or removal from the bulletin boards. Using leet speak also indicated to other people that a person had more advanced technical knowledge or higher status in the bulletin board community and thus more access to content than others. As video gaming became more of a mainstream media industry in the early 1990s, leet speak became a significant part of video game communication. With the public acceptance of the Internet in the mid-1990s and its success as a new communications and information medium, leet speak gradually became part of contemporary mainstream culture.

Leet speak is often grammatically incorrect, using all lower case (upper case is usually used for emphasis), mixes letters with symbols and numbers, and includes the intentional misspelling of words. Leet speak now appears in most forms of interactive computer-mediated communications (CMC), such as online massive multi-player games, instant messaging, text messaging, on social networking sites, cell phone communications, and in many more Web-based or virtual spaces.

While this may be appropriate for use in certain social situations, it is not appropriate for all communications with other people. Using leet speak when emailing a supervisor or a teacher will not be accepted in the same way as using leet speak while playing an online video game.

Some commonly used and known phrases and words in leet speak:

- LOL: One of the earliest acronyms, shorthand for "laughing out loud."
- pwned: To own—seen especially in video gaming, where to pwn is to spectacularly defeat one's opponent and to have advanced player skill.
- noob: Someone who is new and inexperienced, who does not yet know and understand the conventions of the community. May also be used sarcastically to refer to someone who is being annoying or arrogant.

- w00t: A cheer or positive exclamation.
- warez: Short for software, and usually refers to illegal or pirated software. (The z at the end of words indicates it is plural, not singular.)

These can be combined together to create shorthand sentences. For example, "i <3 u" is short for "I love you."

researchers have concluded that there is a "moral panic" (further discussed in Chapter 8 on youth crime) related to this issue. Labelled "technopanic" by some (Marwick, 2008; see also Potter & Potter, 2001), these "media–fueled moral panics that concern uses of technology deemed harmful to children" are seen to "rely on the idea of harm to children as the justification for Internet content restriction."

Music: We Will Rock You!

Music has historically been associated with youth. Beginning in the 1950s, with the American rock 'n' roll influences in North America and Europe, by the 1960s this musical trend was linked inextricably with youth on both sides of the Atlantic. Analyses of the 1950s' and 1960s' music trends reveal that the audiences for this music were by and large middle-class or educationally successful working-class youth. It was also noted that the rock 'n' roll trend was primarily male in nature while the "teenybop" trend was aimed at young women. Notably, the bulk of European youth music trends originated either in the United States or the Caribbean (Roe, 1999).

In its multiple expressions, music is a major part of the leisure activities of youth (Van Roosmalen & Krahn, 1996; Kelly, 1998, p. 62). Indeed, a large-scale national study in Canada found that music ranks as a major source of enjoyment for both female and male youth, second only to spending time with their friends. Among the music-related activities of young people, male and female alike, are jamming/working on music, and attending concerts and raves (Bibby, 2001, p. 20, 29).

As summarized by Roe (1999), analyses of youth and music reveal different dimensions to youth's relationship to music, in relation to "family, peers, achievement/success, gender," or "ethnicity." Choice of music signifies youth's distancing themselves from their parents while they form closer bonds with their peers. Rock music is generally associated with youth who reject their parents' culture and expectations. Music has also been found to reflect school achievement. Specifically, youth who have knowledge of a wide variety of music, or listen to classical music, jazz, or blues, tend to be high achievers, while those who like heavy metal rock tend to be discontented low achievers. Interestingly, however, many high achievers are heavy metal fans, but generally because they hate the regimentation of school, although they are committed to their education. Studies also find links between social mobility and music preferences. Youth who have a strong preference for disco music have been found upwardly mobile in terms of occupation; a strong preference for heavy metal rock is linked to downward educational mobility; and classical music lovers tend toward upward educational mobility. A preference for mainstream pop seems to be linked to young people not anticipating or projecting significant downward or upward social shifts.

While the 1960s' and 1970s' musical trends were perceived in terms of youth as a homogeneous generation, more recent analyses note the multiple gendered, culturally based, and racialized aspects of youth's musical engagement, and the role of music in expressing and creating group identities (Roe, 1999).

Roe (1999) summarizes some gender patterns in young people's relationship to music. Girls tend to have a higher interest in music than boys up till age 19–20, and their interest peaks at ages 9–12 and 15–16, with the overall peak year around age 15. Boys' interest in music tends to surpass that of girls as they reach age 20, and their interest begins somewhat later than for girls, at around age 12–13, peaking at around age 24, or much later than for girls. Pop music with its romantic themes is particularly appealing to young women (Roe, 1999).

Along with the arguments presented previously in this chapter, researchers tend to characterize boys' and girls' musical cultures based on the public/private split, or boys as "performers" and girls as "private consumers" (Frith, 1983, in Roe, 1999). Many describe girls' culture as "bedroom culture," in which girls' leisure is spent at home while boys are more in the public realm. Nevertheless, dancing is a very public act and is associated more with femaleness than maleness. Some researchers argue that girls express themselves and come to terms with their bodies through dance, while young males use dance as a venue for meeting women. Additionally, different musical subcultures imply different roles and expressions for young women and men. For example, in the American punk slam dances, the space is dominated by aggressive male dancers, while women have to negotiate their space in order to stay out of the way while still participating (Roman, 1988, in Aapola et al., 2005, pp. 162–163).

Hear Me Roar: Grrrl Power!

Starting in the early 1990s, influenced by popular music and media, a phenomenon of "girl power" emerged in Europe and North America. Aapola and colleagues (2005, pp. 19–39) point to the different roots of the phenomenon in the UK and the US. The term is attributed to the early 1990s when a group of young, White, middle-class, and mainly queer women called themselves "Riot Grrrls," the latter word designating both aggression and autonomous pride in being a young woman. This punk music-driven message with its criticism of women's oppression soon spread to the UK, Europe, and Australasia. They largely spread their objections to the abuse and harassment of girls through zines (photocopied self-made publications) and cyberspace via the Internet and e-zines. With the spread of "girl power," it also became more diffuse as some aspects were co-opted by the mass media and the consumer market. Perhaps the most famous face of the girl-power trend is that of Buffy, a young vampire-slayer popularized in the American TV series. The most famous all-girl pop band that emerged with the movement was the enormously popular Spice Girls from Britain, whose first CD sold over 50 million copies in its first year. Indeed, Aapola et al. (2005, p. 28) point out that British girls aged 12–17 represent £1.3 billion and American girls aged 8–18 represent US$67 billion in spending power. While the message may be empowering to young women in other ways, its effects can be certainly measured in the lightening of young women's purses and bank accounts.

Aapola et al. (2005, p. 37) question the actual effectiveness of the girl-power movement in the lives of working-class girls. In the 1990s, it was announced in Britain that young women were outperforming their male peers (see Chapter 4). Working-class girls were forming school groups (e.g., "spice girls" or "girlies") based on the girl-power message, their defiance manifested in behaviours such as rating the boys for physical attractiveness. Their acts may have given them a sense of power in their girlhood, but they faced negative reactions and overt hostility from their teachers who moved to limit their freedoms. These initiatives by girls, circumscribed as they are by traditional notions of femininity (in heterosexual attention to boys), continue to be viewed negatively, witness the general panics over "mean" or aggressive girls, to be further discussed in the chapter on crime.

Meanwhile, as Aapola et al. (2005, pp. 32–35) stress, the origins of the term "girl power" have been contested as the term coincides with the emergence of hip-hop music in the 1980s and the popular phrase of encouragement "You go, girl." According to one young African-American woman:

> I remember growing up to the flavor and stylings of teenage female rappers like Salt 'N Pepa, McLyte and Queen Latifah and seeing "girl power" served up constantly as a spicy dish of independence, pride and assertiveness throughout hip hop music. For me girl power is in no way a particularly nineties thing, and it certainly does not have a White girl's face. (Hues, 1998, p. 8, in Aapola et al., 2005, p. 33)

Indeed, the original Riot Grrrls had an anti-racist message that arose from the context of the previous decade's popularization of hip-hop music. At least one author (Jacques, 2001, in Aapola et al., 2005, p. 34) argues that the "whitening" of the face in media attention to the girl-power movement indicates a preference for young women over angry Black men.

Music of Black Youth in North America

Since rock 'n' roll took hold in the 1950s, music has been marketed for the adolescent audience. Elvis Presley, the Beatles, punk, rap, and hip-hop all have been empowered by the youth movements of the day. Up until the 1990s, rock 'n' roll has been a part of White youth culture, while Black youth have their own music, which has "acted as a catalyst for their social lives. It provided meanings and themes with which the students could identify, and indicated adherence to their raced origins" (Kelly, 1998, p. 62). In the 1990s, with the rise of rap and hip-hop, White youth are relishing Black culture through its music. Rock 'n' roll has freely borrowed from Black music since its beginnings.

Rap music emerged in 1976, and is attributed to Black dance clubs in New York where disc jockeys started to switch music between two turntables without stopping, with their own spoken commentary added to the mix. Though performance of rap music continues to be nearly completely (with Eminem as its best-known exception) a Black phenomenon, the majority of the albums are sold to White males (Bibby, 2001, p. 110).

Rap and hip-hop surged in the 1980s as an urban Black phenomenon in the US, and it soon spread elsewhere. One form that also spread to the UK was the "human beat box," which involved amplifying the voice to produce rhythms and beats. Significant elements in the development of rap are an emphasis on boasting or "lying" and "inversion" in which words are used in their opposite meaning, e.g., "bad" means "good" (Back, 1996, p. 203).

The majority (58 percent) of Black youth in the American study by Cohen et al. (2007, pp. 14–15) said they listen to rap music daily, while only 3 percent reported never listening to it. It's also popular among Hispanic youth, 45 percent of whom reported listening to rap every day. It's somewhat less popular among White youth, but 23 percent of them reported daily rap listening.

However important it is for Black youth culture, rap is criticized for its violence, hate, and negative portrayals of women (Kelly, 1998; Cohen et al., 2007). Cohen et al. (2007, p. 14) report that the majority of young Black American men (59 percent) and women (70 percent) find the content too violent, while 57 percent of the males and 66 percent of the females agreed strongly with the statement: "Rap music videos portray Black women in bad and offensive ways." Interestingly, 56 percent of the young Black males also agreed with a similar statement about Black men. One Black high school student in Kelly's (1998, pp. 64–65) study said:

> Snoop [Dogg] is disrespectful to women by calling them bitches. I don't think they should be disrespectful to their own people when your people are being brought down by outside forces [mainstream White society].

Another 17-year-old male in the American study by Cohen et al. (2007, p. 13) adds this comment about the demeaning content of the music and music videos:

> In the videos … I dislike the way they objectify women.… I think … if you were just to watch music videos and never have met a Black person in your life, you probably would think ill of Black people altogether.… White people probably think that Black people don't care about anything but sex and selling drugs and partying all the time. I mean, that's the images you get from rap music videos, pretty much.

A study of 522 Black girls aged 14–18 living in non-urban, lower socio-economic neighbourhoods in Birmingham, Alabama, found that those who watched gangsta videos at least 14 hours per week were far more likely to hit a teacher, get arrested, have multiple sexual partners, get sexually transmitted infections, and use drugs or alcohol (DiClemente, in Kirchheimer, 2003). The study did not control for the presence of violence in the family or the subjection of these girls to other violence.

However, Back (1996, pp. 203–210) points out that the sexualized bravado in rap is contradictory. Although some of it reflects misogyny, there is also an element of parody and social criticism in the music of many of the artists and groups. This is exemplified in the presence of female rap and hip-hop artists who are developing their own kinds of music and agendas. One example is the adoption of Black male masculinity and bravado in lyrics, or forming groups with men or other women, or developing new messages that don't take on issues of gender and sexuality. Meanwhile, American media have jumped on the bandwagon of condemning the misogyny and homophobia in West Coast gangsta rap, represented by artists such as Dr. Dre. Though they make a point about the messages of hatred in some rap, these condemnations also have the tendency to demonize Black youth culture. Not all rap is about oppressing women; the main messages have to do with coming to terms with the dominant society and developing an identity that has elements of self-determination and power.

Music of Black Youth in the UK

As stated previously, Afro-Caribbean migration to the UK increased in the postwar period. With this, Jones (1988, pp. 33–57, also see Roe, 1999) explains, there was a burgeoning of music and leisure activities in many urban centres. The majority of the immigrants (about 60 percent of all Afro-Caribbeans) are Jamaican, so their influence dominates in the UK's cultural scene.

It should also be noted that there have been powerful musical trends emerging among Indo-Pakistani youth in the last three decades. Since the 1980s, new South Asian musical forms emerged among youth. The biggest influence has been the Punjabi-based bhangra music, which has been reinvented in the UK, and cuts across the nationalities of India, Pakistan, and Bangladesh, and across religions, including Sikh, Muslim, and Hindu, and across caste or class. The bhangra evolved into more complex fusions through the 1990s, including mixes of reggae and bhangra, called bhangramuffin, exemplified in the music of Apache Indian, from Indo-Punjabi origins, and Maxi Priest, a Black reggae singer whose "Fe Real" tour and music captured the imaginations of both Black and South Asian youth (Back, 1996, pp. 211–229). Back (1996, p. 227) argues that this kind of music defies classification or specific identity: It is "reggae plus bhangra plus England plus Indian plus Kingston plus Birmingham." It signifies, according to Back (1996, p. 228), the common yet distinctive themes of youth in diaspora, or "the particularities of local cultures while being alert to the global matrices of diaspora cultures."

Though Afro-Caribbean musical traditions have a longer history, two prominent trends have emerged since the second half of the 20th century. The first one, from the 1960s and 1970s onward, was the predominance of Rasta and African themes. This coincided with the general politicization in the Black community, reflecting the poor education and employment prospects of Black youth, accompanied by excessive and oppressive White policing tactics in Black residential areas. Black cultural expressions, parties, and dances were targeted for suppression. Rastafarian influences, dress, and music became more prevalent. Since the mid-1970s another trend has been centred on reggae, which built on Rastafari but was also influenced by Wailers music. At this time, the key element was dissociation with Jamaican roots and the development of British-based music content. In the words of Keith Drummond, lead singer of Black Slate:

> You don't know what they're going through in Jamaica. You can only read about it secondhand. So sing about the sufferation you're going through here.... They say you can't make reggae unless you're a sufferer. Well, it's not just the Jamaicans who suffer. We suffer too, and now we're singing about our own condition. (in Black Music, July 1977, p. 18, quoted in Jones, 1988, p. 50)

The positive and self-affirming messages of reggae music to Black youth are illustrated in the lyrics from the tune "Young, Gifted and Black," which calls for young people to dream big instead of feeling low and fearful (Pryce, 1986, p. 164). The stable interactions in Rasta gangs formed the basis for the creation and internalization of positive messages about being Black, and closing the ranks to non-Rastas. Reggae music was central to the youth's development of their personal understanding of Rastafarian themes:

> First time was reading through Rastaman Vibrations [a Bob Marley LP]; I always thought he was chatting rubbish then I read the words—played back his other records and found that it wasn't rubbish he was chatting. It was about the Rastas. (Cashmore & Troyna, 1982, p. 79)

The rejuvenation of Black Caribbean music continued in the 1980s with not only British but also US Black influences. Significantly, Jones (1988, pp. 232–240) argues that the power of Black culture and Rasta and reggae traditions, along with their political messages of anti-oppression and rebellion, have influenced White and Asian youth as well. Jones (1988, p. 232) argues that Afro-Caribbean culture "has become the dominant culture among all youth, regardless of race."

Since then, other research emerged to address the ways in which Black cultural forms are influencing White youth. Examples of this are skinhead styles that adopt Jamaican music, including ska and bluebeat, while proclaiming White pride. Other studies have examined reggae as a site for Black/White exchanges (Back, 1996, pp. 12–13). Likewise, bhangra, described above, is an example of music that transcends boundaries of race. The meanings of this blending and boundary shifting remain to be analyzed.

Marketing and Consumerism

Wilson and Jette (2005, pp. 73–78) question the notion of passive youth who unquestioningly consume everything that is thrown at them. Rooted in the Frankfurt School of Social Research, there is a group of theorists in whose view youth are being duped into uncritical conformity through consumer culture. Indeed, many others have contradicted this finding, pointing to many expressions of resistance and countercultural forms that arise in reaction to consumerism among youth. The researchers at the Centre for Contemporary Cultural Studies (CCCS, see Chapter 1) are particularly influential in addressing youth's resistance to the hegemony of corporations and upper classes. Examples of this are down-loading music from the Internet or purchasing used clothing. Some youth subcultures, such as punk, have also been interpreted as being intentionally anti-establishment and expressing this in their style. Though the point about active youth resistance is well taken, this approach has been criticized for its overemphasis on youth's capacity to resist. Thus, depending on their particular social location (gender, race, social class, etc.) and their environment, youth can be more accurately described as either/or and both compliant or rebellious with regard to their consumerism.

In a national American study focusing on Black youth, Cohen et al. (2007, p. 10) found that one way young White, Black, and Hispanic people express their political views is through "buycotting." Almost 23 percent of the young people had either shunned products or services they disliked or bought products or services because they liked the political or social values of the company in question. This echoes the results, presented above, of the different forms of youth's political expression compared to the adult mainstream.

Despite some selective consumer practices among youth, many researchers make the case for youth run over and swept away by the lure of stuff to purchase. There is an overload of consumerism embedded in North American and British television aimed at youth (Miles, 2000, pp. 81–82).

Millions of music albums have been sold by individual artists alone in North America. For example, in March–May 2000, the albums of N'Sync (2.4 million), Eminem (1.7 million), and Britney Spears (1.3 million) broke records in their first week of sales (Bibby, 2001, p. 21). The emergence of music television has transformed music into a "comprehensive source of youth culture" and some argue that it is no longer authentic (Hampson, 1996, p. 77), or that it has led to a simplification of ideas, expressed as "cool attitudes" (Danesi, 1994, p. 85). More recently, in 2011, Canadian pop star Justin Bieber became the first musician to achieve 2 billion views on his YouTube channel (Fowler, 2011), showing the influence of social media among youth over that of TV.

There is no denying that marketing to youth is a major business. It is clear that youth groups from 9–19 are the major advertising demographic. In Canada, this age group spent $13.5 billion in 1998 (Clark & Deziel, 1999, in Wilson & Jette, 2005, p. 69). American teens were estimated to have spent $208.7 billion in 2012 (Statistic Brain, 2012). It is especially among the "Millennials" (those born between 1980 and 2000) that the buying of luxury items, such as most recent electronic gadgets, has increased a third (MSN Money Partner, 2012). The generally high level of comfort among young people in relation to new communications technologies and the Internet is providing ever more means for businesses and advertisers to reach youth (Ferguson, 2000, pp. 1–2).

It was American mass production from the second half of the 19th century onward that made it possible to package and sell a wide range of consumer goods. The basis of this successful sales pitch is brand-name products and brand recognition. One of the earliest and biggest success stories of branding and marketing was the packaging and commodification of Elvis, including radio and television appearances, record sales, movies, and brand-name products, such as clothing and makeup, soft drinks, etc. Between the start of his career in

July 1954 and the end of 1957, there were 78 different Elvis products out for purchase for fans, with the gross value of about $55 million (Gennaro, 2005, pp. 126–130). Since then, by the year 2000, there are five multinational mega-media corporations that dominate the culture industries: Disney, News Corp, Viacom, Vivendi Universal, and AOL-Time Warner. As Gennaro (2005, p. 129) says, "One does not have to be a conspiracy theorist to see the magnitude of the convergence that controls the media."

Media sources gear their aid campaigns to teens, and ages 14–18 are the most valuable target group (Stewart, 1998, p. 26). By the year 2004, there will be an estimated 4.4 million Canadian teens between the ages of 10 and 19, and in 1998 that age group spent $13.5 billion in Canada alone (A. Clark, 1999, p. 42). Whether referred to as "GenY," "echo generation," or "screenagers," teens are a force with a lot of spending to do.

Following Côte and Allahar's (1994) argument, as young people have been excluded from a full participation in the economy and the political process, they are also targets to be exploited. They are both producers and major consumers. Marketers encourage a self-image of youth as major consumers. Anton Allahar says: "We are taking more from them than we are giving to them" (National Film Board, 1997).

According to Gennaro (2005, p. 119), the message conveyed by culture industries to young people through media, is simple: "(1) to be young is to be happy; (2) youth is 'hip'; and (3) the way to be young is to buy products that give you a youthful feeling."

This message is clear in the Coca-Cola advertising campaigns of the 1990s, presenting a utopian view of the world, in which everyone is happy and gets the "feeling" of sharing in that utopia. British studies of young people's reactions to the American ads confirm the appeal of the carefree American teens laughing in the sun and enjoying their ideal lives (Miles, 2000, pp. 82–83).

Indeed, Gennaro (2005, p. 120, also see Miles, 2000, pp. 8–9 for a summary of similar arguments) makes the point that the media have created an "imagined community of youth," the lines of which are blurred to the degree that adults of any age can continue to live in "perpetual adolescence." This ongoing state starts with the purchase of the first commodity and it never ends, as illustrated by 13-year-old girls wearing thongs, 20-something young males playing video games, and 50-year-old men buying Harleys. In this process of linking childhood to the rest of one's life, Americans dominate the North American (and arguably all Western and some non-Western) culture through their preponderance in the information and communication technologies.

Thus, media and advertising feed into the establishment of a range of goods associated with specific trends. It is easy to make the argument that there is a process of indoctrination of youth in the ideology of individualism and self-fulfillment, through media and advertising, leading to a primary identification with consumerism with its leisure and identity industries. These become a major basis for identity formation of youth (Côte & Allahar, 1994, pp. 109–111). In the words of Gerbner (1998, p. 75):

> Most of what we know or think we know, we have never personally experienced. We know the world, and in a way, we know ourselves, by the stories we're told by others; the stories that we can see, read and write. We live in a world that is directed

by these stories, and a major change in the way in which they are told is represented by the shift from the time stories came from parents, schools, churches, communities and even nations, to our time when stories are being told not by anyone who really has anything to tell, but essentially by big major global conglomerates that have something to sell.

Teenagers have disposable incomes and this is seen in a wide range of goods and brands and clothing and labels in stores. "It's all about pop culture," says Grainger, an grade 11 student from Toronto, "and pop culture is all about buying" (A. Clark, 1999, p. 42).

Gordon Tait (2000) argues that youth subcultures are not examples of "resistance to a dominant culture." Instead, they are a reflection of the ways in which governments and power politics have defined youth. There is no defiance by youth in subcultures, but they reflect the conventions and customs within youth culture and teen consumerism. Youth has been managed and turned into self-regulating entities in school and the family. This is expressed in youth subcultures that express particular and diverse types of consumerism.

Similar to the American pattern of luxury spending described above, British male and female teens alike spend most of their money on "clothes, records, stereo equipment, entertainment and travel," and shopping has become their favourite social activity and a part of their lifestyle (Miles, 2000, pp. 115–116). Miles (2000, p. 131) offers the following example from his interviews with British youth regarding how important it is to buy something on a shopping trip:

> *Jack:* Yeah, you walk around Leeds and you don't really see wot you like and you come home and you're thinking, that was a real waste of time. If you buy something, you're thinking, yeah, this has been really worthwhile, this. It's been a good day. It's like incentive really.

And further:

> *Jill:* You get a good feeling if you walk back with something. If you go out willing to buy something and you come back without anything, then you're thinking, oh my God!

Whole subcultures can be bought. The subculture theorists in the UK have paid attention to the defining characteristics of Goths, including dress and appearance (black clothes, jewellery, makeup, Doc Marten shoes or boots), activities and behaviour (loners, anti-church, criticize others, hold seances), and relationships with adults (dislike, rebel) (Denholm et al., 1992, p. 23, quoted in G. Tait, 2000, p. 207). Goths are most frequently depicted as young people struggling against the establishment, though others interpret them as merely creating a specific look through fashion choices. Indeed, the fashion industry has catered to the creation of the Goth look through well-managed marketing strategies (G. Tait, 2000, pp. 207–214).

In the end, Miles (2000, pp. 145–146) concludes that teenage consumers are wrapped up in a lifestyle that is limited only by the resources at their disposal. Their purchases give them a sense of security and belonging in a world filled with constant change and demands. That is its lure, and escaping from it is all the more difficult.

While it is a dream come true for those with something to sell, Dupont (2000, p. 2) argues that the teen market is a difficult one to stereotype, and that youth today have grown up with advertising and have become smart and able to evaluate advertising better. One teenager, Brendan (National Film Board, 1997), has this to say as he went to a mall to spend $200 in birthday money:

> Music is a huge part of youth culture. So naturally the first place I wanna go is the record store.… There are so many bands out there and they're all trying to sell me the goods. Everyone likes to have what's cool, and it's important to keep up with the trends. But it's not like I'd buy everything they're trying to sell me, even if I could. I'm not as gullible as people seem to think I am.

However, the fact that youth make the choice to buy "stuff" to begin with is telling. Andrew Clark (1999, p. 42) states:

> Annie Grainger, 16, says she is wary of commercials and marketing, yet spends $50 a pop for body piercing. Eighteen-year-old Mike Landon proudly wears hip-hop clothes with the Phat Farm label and says: "Show me a commercial that says 50-percent off—that's a good commercial to me."

The multibillion-dollar video game industry is a good example of the success of marketing over youth, particularly males in their late twenties. Gennaro (2005, p. 123) reports that over 80 percent of video games are bought by those over age 18, nearly 70 percent of them male, with the average age of a player at 29.

Numerous research studies in North America have demonstrated the effectiveness of celebrity endorsements in increasing sales of consumer items. Matching market goods to celebrities is a highly evolved business. McCracken (1989, in Jackson & Darrow, 2005, p. 83) suggests that there has to be "meaning transfer" for the endorsement to create marketability. This notion refers to the match between the product and the meanings the celebrity brings, including "social status, class, gender, age, personality, and lifestyle type" (p. 83). These meanings are first transferred from the celebrity to the consumer good and then passed on to the consumer. Thus, particularly young consumers would be affected as they are in the process of moving from one age category to another and are looking to "invent and reinvent themselves."

Street-Based Youth Culture: Partying

> Young people are hedonists. They are more concerned about enjoying themselves from one minute to the next than they are worried about what the future may or

may not hold for them.... The state of the environment, social inequality, access to Higher Education, all these issues pale into insignificance compared to the God-given right to party. (Miles, 2000, p. 87)

In saying this, Miles (2000) is being pointedly sarcastic, and is in fact questioning this widely prevalent attitude about youth.

Danesi (1994, p. 66) writes about the signs and meanings of adolescent youth:

There are many ways in which teens can socialize with their peers. But the desire to be involved in a party scene stands out in all surveys of teen social activities.... The main reason the party scene has become such a common locus for socialization is that it involves the enactment of three affective states—sexuality, peer bonding, and identity construction in the peer context....

An article published in *Maclean's* (2000, p. 43) magazine outlines the forms of marginalized party activity that captivated kids—and, in most cases, scandalized parents—over the past 80 years:

Flappers, 1920s:
Music: Dixieland
Look: Short, bobbed hair and slim-cut dresses for women; fedoras for men
Drug of choice: Alcohol and roll-your-own cigarettes
Ritual: Dance-hall parties and the Charleston

Swing Kids, 1940s:
Look: Sleekly coiffed hairdos, fitted blouses and skirts for women; pleated trousers, sports jackets, or the clean-cut GI Joe look for men
Drug of choice: Alcohol and cigarettes
Ritual: Music-hall parties and cutting a rug with the jive and the jitterbug

Rock 'n' Rollers, 1950s:
Music: Elvis Presley and other early rockers, Paul Anka
Look: Bouffant hairdos and bobby socks for women; greasy ducktails and white T-shirts for men
Drug of choice: Alcohol and cigarettes
Ritual: Parties in darkened rec rooms, group excursions to drive-ins and pool halls, high school dances

Hippies, 1960s:
Music: Folk and acid rock, the Beatles
Look: Tie-dyed garments, ethnic wear, jeans, bell-bottoms, miniskirts
Drug of choice: Just about every legal and illegal mind-altering drug, especially cannabis, LSD, and alcohol
Ritual: Love-ins, happenings, rock concerts, and festivals

Disco Diehards, 1970s:
Music: Mindless dance music
Look: Platform shoes, loud shirts, big collars, halter tops, and hot pants
Drug of choice: Cannabis, cocaine, heroin, alcohol
Ritual: Dancing till you dropped at discotheques

Punkers, Late 1970s to Mid-1980s:
Music: The Sex Pistols and other punk rock
Look: Safety pins, Mohawks, studded leather
Drug of choice: Cannabis, heroin, speed, alcohol
Ritual: Concerts and mosh pits

Hip-Hop Kids, 1980s to the Present:
Music: Rap music
Look: Extremely baggy sportswear, sometimes worn backwards
Drug of choice: Cannabis, crack
Ritual: Parties, concerts

Raves

Raves emerged as a new youth party phenomenon in the late 20th century. A rave is a large party where the primarily youth population dance to electronic music created by DJs orchestrating synthesizers and turntables (Oh, 2000). Raves began in Britain in the 1980s, and are based on illegal parties, drug use (particularly ecstasy), and a challenge to police authority (Miles, 2000, p. 88; Hier, 2002). Though raves are not totally uniform in make-up, the majority of ravers tend to be White middle-class youth who are either employed or attend school (Hier, 2002, p. 53).

Raves have been described as resembling the rock festivals of the 1960s and 1970s. And like those "celebrations of youthful exuberance, gatherings of the idealistic tribe" have caused outrage and concern from greater society, even though ravers often "frown on alcohol" (Oh, 2000, p. 39). Many in and out of the rave scene see raves as a positive celebration, and a way of finding a family (Oh, 2000).

The rave scene was originally a drug-free environment where youth would go to dance and have a good time (Silcott, 2000b; Oh, 2000). However, owners distributing and encouraging the use of the drug ecstasy, and gang infiltration and control over the drugs, changed the rave scene (Silcott, 2000b; Oh, 2000), with the majority of attendees using illegal drugs (Oh, 2000, p. 40). Highly publicized drug fatalities (Kingstone, 2000, p. 1; Bethune, 2000, p. 1) resulted in a moral panic (Hier, 2002), subsequent bans, and legislation increasing surveillance by police, in cities such as Toronto (*Toronto Star*, 2000b).

The multiple meanings of raves for youth who participate in them have been studied by Wilson (2002; 1999, in Wilson & Jette, 2005, pp. 78–81; see also Miles, 2000), whose list of motives among youth include being part of a counterculture, someplace to go after bars close, a safe space to use drugs, a place to listen to music and dance, or where one might pick up a one-night stand. Thus, the rave scene is characterized by both active social critics and passive conformists and cannot be reduced to one set of elements. Nevertheless, the movement to lift the ban on raves mobilized a group of youth who were not closely connected before (Stanleigh, 2000, p. 2), providing an example of the spontaneous political mobilization discussed in the first part of this chapter. Hier (2002) points out that the rave organizers in Toronto used media to organize a movement that offered counterpoints to the moralizing tone of their opponents depicting raves as a risk.

But as with other forms of youth celebrations spanning the past few decades, acceptance by greater society leads to an exploitation of the cultural form. Marketers have capitalized on this cultural celebration through movies, music, and merchandise sales (D. Gordon, 2000), as well as expensive ticket prices netting as much as $40,000 per event (Oh, 2000, p. 3; Miles, 2000, p. 93-95). In the words of Miles (2000, p. 101), "Rave is potentially subversive, but can ultimately only be subversive in a submissive form."

Following the decline of raves, flash mobs emerged as a collective expression of a "street party" variety, starting in 2003 when the first one was organized through social media by Bill Wasik of *Harper's Magazine*. He professes starting this to test the susceptibility of "hipsters" (under 35s) to marketing ploys, as "an authority experiment" (Wasik, 2006, p. 9). According to Wasik (2006, p. 1), the end result was an addition to the 2004 *Oxford English Dictionary*: flash mob was defined as "a public gathering of complete strangers, organized via the Internet or mobile phone, who perform a pointless act and then disperse again." Since these early days, flash mobs have appeared in various forms, and with varied messages or lack thereof, in different locations. Although it's difficult to estimate how prevalent this phenomenon is among young people, the initial critical intent of its founding father, Bill Wasik, seems to have been lost in a sea of consumerism (see Box 7.4).

Box 7.4: Using a Flash Mob to Create Brand Awareness

This excerpt from magnifydigital.com (2013) illustrates the ease with which any collective expression can be turned into a business venture:

> Since its emergence in New York in 2003, the flash mob has been used as a successful visual marketing tool for many companies. Here are two companies whose flash mob video productions have become among the most viewed on YouTube.
>
> The title for the most viewed flash mob video on YouTube goes to an Ontario-based company called Alphabet Photography. This company shows that you don't need a large budget for your flash mob production, just talented performers, clever planning and lots of surprised onlookers. Their flash mob video, "Christmas Food Court Flash Mob, Hallelujah Chorus—Must See!" went viral soon after it was posted on YouTube and has received over 38 million views. After its release,

the video was featured across world media and the company has since received royal approval from Prince Charles himself! The end board of the video lists information about Alphabet Photography's website and a season greeting, which serve to heighten awareness of the company.

Mobile Phone Company T-Mobile has two flash mob videos appearing in the "Top Ten Flash Mob Videos on YouTube." Their UK-based "Life's for Sharing" campaign features flash mobs taking place in the busiest transport hubs in the UK. Collectively, their big budget, all-singing, all-dancing flash mobs have received over 46 million YouTube views. T-Mobile also creates individual campaigns around each video with a behind the scenes look at the flash mob organization, and reaction from the public after the flash mob has taken place. Before you check out the flash mob videos...be warned that "The T-Mobile Welcome Back" is quite a tearjerker!

So what lessons can we take from the examples shown above?

Conclusions

Youth culture is diverse in membership and content. The one unified theme of youth culture is that it offers an alternative to the adult-dominated world. Young people band together in order to create something for themselves, a space and an identity that is uniquely theirs. Youth culture takes place in the mainstream and against it, whether it involves adult-led or youth-led activities. Despite concerns about youth apathy, many young people are engaged in politics and social movements, but they want to do it on their own terms and are inventing new political venues. Here, as in other aspects of youth culture, these activities may not necessarily involve forms that are expected by the adult-dominated world but that break new ground and pose new questions and challenges about the nature of collectivity and citizenship.

Youth have developed different subcultures or lifestyles, expressed in new ways of communicating, dressing, partying, and enjoying music. All of these form ground for distinctive lifestyles and identities, differentiated by social class, gender, and immigrant and racialized status. Many of the new subcultures fall below the radar of the adult world unless they directly violate any of the rules and tastes of mainstream adult culture. When this happens, outcries of concern among the most authoritarian public usually result in curtailment of any suspect activity.

A large portion of youth activities is dominated by the adult world. Social institutions, such as education, politics, and business, are adult-led and exert their influence in areas where young people are creating something of their own. These institutions also take an active role in organizing cultural endeavours to direct youthful energies and wills. Some of this provides a welcome outlet for youth, such as sports and other recreational activities in schools. Other elements are more exploitive, as even genuinely youth-originated activities, such as raves, which originally began as youth's own expressions, can be usurped by commercialization.

There is a mainstreaming of youth culture, including music, television, computers, clothing, communication technologies, and other material aspects. Each fad is accompanied by relentless marketing and advertising campaigns. Young people—one of the major groups of cheap labourers—are also one of the major consumers targeted by businesses. As will be discussed in the chapter on health, these businesses include more sinister elements in the form of drug pushers, and tobacco and alcohol producers and sellers. A significant segment of youth are vulnerable to these, particularly those who are already marginalized. The same media that carry advertisements for tobacco and alcohol tend to emphasize these negative aspects of youth culture over its many positive elements, and create unnecessary concern over the "state of the youth."

Critical Thinking Questions

1. Can youth have genuine impact on society if they opt out of official politics?
2. Is there a way of creating a unified youth culture for all young people regardless of gender or race?
3. Are there positive messages for youth in contemporary music such as rap?

8 Crime and Moral Regulation

In this chapter, you will learn that

- young people's activities are subject to moral panics, a form of moral regulation
- the majority of youth crimes are property- and drug-related, and a large proportion of perpetrators are repeat offenders
- despite media hype, violent crimes by youth are not on the rise, and their victims tend to be other youth, not adults
- gun violence is a particular issue for American youth, due to the constitutional right to bear arms
- racialized youth are disproportionately represented in the criminal justice system, accounted for by conditions of marginalization and racial profiling
- youth crime and gang formation are largely explained by economic deprivation
- the criminal justice system vacillates between the ideas of rehabilitation and punishment of youth
- despite the myth of young women run amok, they form a small proportion of perpetrators of youth crime

In the next chapter on health, I will discuss the many ways in which young people are victimized in their families, by acquaintances and strangers, and by the authorities and agencies that have been created to protect them. This chapter will focus on the role of youth as perpetrators of deviant and criminal acts, and their treatment by the legal system. The main problem areas addressed are youth violence and youth gangs, including hate groups. The gendered and racialized aspects of youth delinquency will be dealt with using a critical focus on the "moral panics" that create a system in which marginalized youth are particularly victimized.

There is a disturbingly persistent image among the public: that young people pose a danger to the public by engaging in delinquent and violent behaviour. This seems to be both a historical (see Chapter 1) and contemporary phenomenon. As outlined earlier, the prolongation of youth, and youth's tenuous connections to the labour market, raise fears that "idle hands are a devil's workshop." Youth who occupy public spaces in increasing numbers are seen as a potential threat. The imagery by Brearton (1999) from *Toronto Life* magazine (see Box 8.1) shows that the late 1900s seem eerily like the late 1800s.

Box 8.1: What's Wrong with Them?

Brearton (1999, pp. 2–3) captures some of the main sentiments prevailing about youth in Toronto during different time periods:

> What's with kids today? Take the squeegee punks. We've beaten them up, had them arrested, tried to legislate them out of existence and even shot at them, and they still won't go away. But these sponge-wielding street urchins aren't the first ne'er-do-wells to raise the ire of local citizenry. Here, a brief history of our wayward youth.

> **1891** Police move to regulate the 500 or so newsboys—you know, the little chaps in tweeds and knickers yelling "Extra! Extra!"—who work the city's street corners. Authorities cite the need "on the one hand ... to protect and encourage boys in an honest and industrious course, and on the other, to prevent dishonest boys from making newspaper selling a cloak for idleness and thieving." As a result of the crackdown, children aged seven and younger are prohibited from selling papers.

> **1945** An increase in crime prompts a city social agency to study the rising problem of "unattached groups" of urban youths. Their subsequent report describes in lurid, first-person detail the street kids' affinity for loitering, playing craps, "relative open immorality (both heterosexual and homosexual)." The report concludes that "it is a serious matter that at a time when human resources are so greatly needed many persons cannot or will not restrain their anti-social tendencies and play a manful part in the present world crisis."

> **1949** In a *Saturday Night* article, parents complain that the influx of violent American crime comic books is "poisoning the minds" of our children. The House of Commons introduces a bill aimed at banning the comics and prosecuting their publishers. Legislators assure the nation that they are not targeting legitimate "funnies," and subsequently amend the Criminal Code to outlaw the printing, selling or distributing of crime comics unless the "public good was served" by their publication. The law is still on the books.

> **1977** Following the legalization of pinball machines by the federal government in 1976—they were previously banned as "games of chance"—Metro officials move to regulate pinball establishments, limiting their hours and banning kids under the age of fourteen. Critics claim that the evil amusements lead to truancy, drunken-

ness and begging, but the Metro Licensing Commission rules that the city has no grounds to restrict access to the machines. A lawyer representing the owner of a pinball machine-operating lunch counter near Central Tech high school argues: "I'd be better having them play pinball machines than off in a car someplace smoking a marijuana cigarette."

1987 The city at large becomes alarmed over reports of "swarming"—gangs of teens swooping down on their victims, usually other teens, demanding money or, in some cases, the victim's shoes. In one incident reported in the *Star*, twenty-four youths storm a Fran's restaurant and make off with "$20 to $25 worth of pastries." Metro councillor Norm Gardner expresses concern that this gang activity will sully the imminent Shriner's Convention, the biggest convention in the city's history. Police form a special undercover unit to deal with the crisis, then announce a month later that the problem has been defused.

1998 Squeegee kids—who are initially lauded in a *Globe and Mail* editorial as "traffic-dodging impresarios" with a plucky adherence to the tenets of capitalism—are now regarded as a serious threat to public safety. In mid-July, one squeegee kid is threatened with a gun by a motorist while another's dog is shot in the head by police. The *Globe*, lamenting its earlier charity, suggests licensing the kids as a way of controlling their activities and collecting taxes on their no-doubt sizeable earnings.

Similar listings and comparisons have been compiled by others. In the United States, Males (1996) points out that the kinds of concerns that are being raised by today's adults and senior citizens about the immorality and unbecoming behaviour of youth were directed at the very same senior citizens in the 1930s. At the time, there was alarm over school problems (fewer than half of teens were in high school), teen violence, and drugs as exemplified by horror over "Reefer Madness" and "Cocaine Fiends." A "drug crisis" was looming in the mid-1930s as media and other alarmists sounded warnings about "armed" kids roaming the land, "out for what they can get, while it lasts" (Leighton & Hellman, 1935, in Males, 1996, pp. 259–266).

Most recently, these negative media-driven depictions have taken on racialized and gender-based overtones. Groups of youth, and particularly young (and Black) males are perceived as "gangs." In recent years, young women have been targeted for the same kind of treatment, with media hype about "girl gangs."

Moral Panics

According to Cohen (1972, in Welch et al., 2002, p. 4), "moral panic" occurs when

> a condition, episode, person or a group of persons emerges to become defined as a
> threat to societal values and interests; its nature is presented in a stylized and ste-
> reotypical fashion by the mass media; the moral barricades are manned by editors,
> bishops, politicians, and other right-thinking people.

Cohen's earliest uses of the term are linked to societal reactions to British youth in the 1960s, the so-called Mods and Rockers whom media depicted as threatening public safety. With this ideological ammunition, increased police powers were justified. A simi-lar reaction ensued in New York City in 1989 after five youth were convicted of raping a young woman in Central Park. Similarly to the British case, tougher police and legal measures followed. Moral panics also customarily have racial overtones as it is urban racialized youth who are frequently stereotyped (Welch et al., 2002, p. 4; see also Bar-ron, 2000, pp. 21–22; Charles, 2002, p. 114).

According to Welch, Price, and Yankey (2002), moral panics have a predictable path of development, starting with (1) concern over the behaviour in question and its effect on society; followed by (2) some degree of consensus among the public that the problem is real and requires action by politicians and the legal system; (3) hostility toward and vilification and negative stereotyping of the group identified as the culprits (folk devils), who are distinct from ordinary people (folk heroes); (4) disproportionality of the danger or the potential harm the phenomenon threatens; and (5) volatility, that is, a sudden eruption followed by the panic's disappearance. The latter two aspects are reflected in the avalanche of reporting on the topic immediately after it happens, and its quick disap-pearance from the headlines soon after.

However, Welch, Price, and Yankey (2002, pp. 18–22) also point out that the long-term effects of moral panics linger; there are changes in legislation and policing practices, as well as continued stereotyping of the vilified population, and particularly of the racialized minority criminal. Moral panics are also arguably laden with social class implications as a contrast is made between the "yuppie" victims and the lower-class and racialized perpetrators who live in marginal conditions. In the United States, the negative public image is associated with young Black and Latino males. Thus, in their Marxist or political economy analysis, Welch and colleagues argue that the real impact of moral panics is to maintain the political and economic order by redirecting the attention of the increasingly exploited population from the real source of their problems—the capitalist class and their political puppets—to the sup-posed and vastly exaggerated danger of the American disaffected underclass.

Moral panics also misdirect the attention of the public. Males (1996, pp. 280–281) makes the point that the idea that children and youth need more restraints and punish-ment diverts attention from adult behaviours and particularly that of adult men. Adult males are most of the offenders in all areas of crime, yet it is adolescents and particularly adolescent males who are targeted for negative attention and restrictions.

In the United States, after the terrorist attacks of September 11, 2001, a climate of fear gripped the government and the population so tightly that Giroux (2003, p. xvi) argued that "the United States is at war with young people," who are being targeted for all its "class and racial anxieties." Even prior to the fateful events of 9/11, and despite evidence to the contrary, most people in North America seemed to "know" that there was a lot of youth crime, particularly of the violent kind, and that we needed to do something about it because the current laws were "too lenient." In fact, Canadian and American studies show that the public's understanding of youth crime and justice systems is inaccurate, and that most people's opinions are based on misinformation and sensationalism bred by media. Thus, public views tend to correlate youth crime with violent crime, contrary to what crime statistics actually tell us (Sprott, 1996; Jaffe & Baker, 1999, pp. 22–23; USA Today, 2001). For example, Sprott (1996, p. 271) found that while "most (94%) of the stories about youth crime appearing in a sample of Toronto newspapers involved cases of violence," youth court statistics indicated "that fewer than a quarter of youth cases in Ontario involved violence." Similarly, a Berkeley media studies report on youth, race, and crime in the news found that from 1990–1998, American network news coverage of homicide rose 473 percent, while the actual homicide rate decreased 32.9 percent. And while youth homicides declined by 68 percent between 1993 and 1999, 62 percent of the public thought that youth crime was increasing (USA Today, 2001). These widely prevalent "moral panics" over youth crime create an image of youth as "out of control" and create negative stereotypes of "bad youth" (Schlissel, 1997, in Bell, 1999, p. 31).

In fact, and as will be shown in this chapter, where youth engage in delinquent or criminal behaviour, most of it is non-violent in nature. The media's creation and perpetuation of the image of violent youth reflects yet another way in which young people are oppressed. What is often neglected, and is partly addressed in the chapter on health, is that young people are more likely to be victims than perpetrators of violence.

Youth as Perpetrators of Violence and Crime

The concern over youth crime, particularly violent crime, is shared among the three countries. Indeed, young people do commit crimes disproportionate to their presence in the population, as will be presented below. However, their criminal offences do not amount to the kind of violent rampage portrayed in the media and by the public. In looking over the statistics, one must keep in mind that they reflect various types of reporting. For example, in Canada, there are self-reports, official records of convictions, charges, and victimization surveys, all of which provide slightly different results. This is all the more important to keep in mind with international comparisons.

When addressing youth crime statistics in England and Wales, we must first note that the low minimum responsibility age of 10 in Wales is contrary to the commonly held minimum age of around 14 worldwide (Natale & Williams, 2012). According to official statistics from England and Wales in 2011/12, "10–17 year olds accounted for

15.5 percent of all arrests but were 10.7 percent of the population of England and Wales of offending age" (Youth Justice Board, 2013, p. 7). Reflecting the issue of proportionality expressed above, in England and Wales, as of 2010/11, 23 percent of all crimes were committed by young offenders, defined as those aged 10 to 17 in England and Wales, amounting to about one million crimes in total. While 15 percent of youth offences were violent crimes, the adult violent crime percentage was higher at 22 (Cooper & Roe, 2012, pp. i-1). According to official statements: "There is no evidence that the number of violent crimes committed by young people is increasing. The rise in cautions and convictions represents better enforcement and an improved criminal justice response to violent crime" (Leapman, 2008).

In the United States, reflecting a trend of decreasing youth crime rates, the youth (10–17) arrest rates declined by 47 percent between 1994 and 2009 (Office of Justice Programs, 2013). In 2010, there were over 1.6 million reported arrests of young offenders under 18 years of age, and 76,000 of these were classified as violent crimes, based on the FBI index (John Jay College of Criminal Justice, 2012). In 2010, 8 percent of all homicides were committed by youth (Office of Justice Programs, 2013). The violent crime rate for young men aged 10–24 was halved between 1995 and 2011, from 850.8 per 100,000 population, and declined significantly for young women of the same age, from 139.6 to 99.7 per 100,000 population (Centers for Disease Control and Prevention, 2013).

Canadian crime rates are higher among those aged 12 to 18, and the peak age is 18. There is then a gradual decline through the twenties, a levelling off in the thirties, and a steady decline until age 55. The crimes committed by youth in 2010 amounted to 13.1 percent of all crime, and youth crime rates have declined gradually over the last decade, including violent offences (Public Safety Canada, 2012). Long-term trends from Statistics Canada show that there was a 7 percent decline in the number of cases completed in youth court in 2010/11, following fairly steady declines by around 25,000 cases over the previous decade. Of the total number of 52,904 cases in 2010/11, 38 percent were violent crimes, whereas the majority, or 62 percent, were property crimes (Brennan, 2013).

Victimization by youth tends to be against other young people rather than adults older than them. According to the Office of Juvenile Justice and Delinquency Prevention (2004), data from 1997–1998 show that 62 percent of victims of juvenile violent crime were aged 18 or under. Similarly, in 2003, 54 percent of Canadian victims of youth homicides were other youth (*National Post*, 2006). As indicated in Chapters 4 and 5 in relation to issues of harassment and bullying in schools and workplaces, there are gendered and racialized patterns. For example, young men tend to be the highest risk group for sexual offending, particularly against other youth (Moore et al., 2008, p. 5). This issue will be taken up in more detail in Chapter 9 on health.

Notably, recidivism, or the chance of reoffending, is a significant feature of youth crime. The statistics of all three countries indicate that rather than more youth being responsible for the crimes committed, a significant portion of youth crime is committed by repeat offenders. Although there is great variation in this based on location, in 2002 the rate of juvenile reoffending was an appalling 76 percent in New York City (Calvin, 2004, p. 57). Similarly, in England and Wales, 75 percent of the 18 to 20-year-old men released from prison in 2004 reoffended within two years (Natale & Williams, 2012, p. 12). A summary of Canadian studies from the 2000s indicates that the chances of recidivism increase with the number of times a young person is incarcerated (Caputo & Vallée, 2010). This phenomenon calls into question the effectiveness of incarceration as a response to youth crime. According to Natale and Williams (2012, p. 14): "Locking up young offenders also makes them more likely to commit further crimes and be unemployed later in life." Similarly, a Canadian meta-analysis of relevant research studies by Public Safety Canada (2002) indicated that harsher punishment had the opposite of its intended effect, increasing the chance of reoffending by 3 percent. This topic will be taken up below, in the section on the police and juvenile law.

Guns and Violence

Children and youth in the United States are particularly at risk of being shot. The Second Amendment to the United States Constitution grants the right to people "to keep and bear arms" (Reich et al., 2002, pp. 5–6). A rare individual would argue for the right of children to bear arms, and US federal law restricts the sale of handguns to those 21 years or over, and the sale of rifles and shotguns to those 18 years or older. However, it is easily demonstrated that the wide availability of firearms is exacting a toll within the youth population. This is particularly likely as studies estimate that only 30–39 percent of gun-owning parents in the United States store their guns unloaded behind lock and key. The carrying of guns among youth has risen since the 1980s, with a corresponding increase in the homicides committed by young people. According to a 1999 survey, 833,000 American youth aged 12–17 had carried a handgun at least once in the preceding year. Many youth also lend their guns to others. In the same year, approximately 9 percent of the illegal guns seized by authorities belonged to juveniles and another 24 percent were seized from 18–24-year-olds. Gun violence is exacerbated by the rise in the use of drugs, particularly crack cocaine, and a rise in child poverty and gang activity (Reich et al., 2002, pp. 7, 13–14, 17; see also Doob & Cesaroni, 2004, pp. 103–108).

In the United States, use of firearms is not only responsible for youth victimization rates but also contributes to perpetration rates. Generally, the firearm-related homicide rate among children under 15 years of age is nearly 16 times higher than the combined rate in 25 other industrialized nations. In 1998, youth under age 25 were responsible for 54 percent of gun homicides, and youth under 18 accounted for 12 percent. The perpetrators are more likely to be African American than White or Hispanic. Thus, Black youth are overrepresented among victims as well as perpetrators (Reich et al., 2002, p. 8, also see Fingerhut & Christoffel, 2002). In fact, Black males aged 15–19 are five times more likely to die from gunshots than Whites or Asian/Pacific Islanders and twice as likely as Hispanic and American Indian males (Fingerhut & Christoffel, 2002, p. 29). The risk of death from guns increases with age for all males and females, but the rates are multiple for males compared to females. For example, the death rates per 100,000 population are around 5 among females aged 18–19, while the rates are nearly 45 among the comparable male population. The states in the West and South have the highest firearm death rates for the 15–19 age group, compared with the Northeast and Upper Midwest, with Louisiana's rate alarmingly at nearly 20 percent higher than any other state (Fingerhut & Christoffel, 2002, p. 31).

In comparison to the extremely high rates in the United States, the death rates of teens aged 15–19 from gunshots are low elsewhere in the industrialized West. Whereas in the 1990s, there were 20 deaths per 100,000 youth in this age group in the United States, the rates were approximately 4 in 100,000 in Canada and less than 1 in 100,000 in England and Wales (Fingerhut & Christoffel, 2002, p. 28). In the United States, *The Future of Children* (2002, p. 1) reports that the annual death toll from firearms among young people aged 20 and under is around 20,000, and that the risk of gun homicide is particularly high among African American and Hispanic young males.

Cook and Ludwig (2002) estimate that the nationwide cost to the United States of gun violence is approximately $100 billion annually, with $15 billion or more due to gun violence against youth. The costs cover not only the tangible ones of medical expenses, personal injury suits, and loss of productivity, but the costs of minimizing fear through measures toward general community safety, including safer neighbourhoods and schools.

School Shootings

The issue of violence in schools is illustrated in the tragic killing of 32 people, mostly students, at Virginia Technological Institute in Blacksburg, Virginia, in a shooting spree by a young "dark and demented student" (Leeder et al., 2007, p. A1). The previous high-profile school shooting spree took place in 1999 in Columbine High School, where 14 students and a teacher were killed and 23 others were wounded (Muzzatti, 2004, pp. 144–146). That same year, on April 20, two students were shot, and one of them died, in a school in Taber, Alberta (Bibby, 2001, p. 79). Most recently, in March 2013, a 20-year-old male's shooting spree cost the lives of 20 children and 6 adults in a Connecticut elementary school (Reuters, 2013).

Fingerhut and Christoffel (2002, p. 32) point out that

> despite the high-profile shootings at schools like Columbine High School in Littleton, Colorado, school shootings account for a very small percentage of all youth firearm deaths. In each year from 1993 to 1998, fewer than 1% of all firearm deaths among young people ages 5 to 19 occurred in schools.... The number of deaths was higher in 1992–1993 than any later academic year.

Indeed, some point out that twice as many American youths are struck by lightning than are killed in school shootings (Doob & Cesaroni, 2004, p. 104).

Arguably, the Columbine episode gained notoriety not because there had been no violence in high schools before, or because of the unusually high numbers of dead and wounded, but because it happened in a school in an affluent White suburban community. Also, as is further argued by Muzzatti (2004, pp. 144–146; also see Tanner, 2001, pp. 122–128), the issue that the shootings evoked was not gun control but scapegoating.

In this instance, the targets of the public debate that ensued were "teen super-predators, poor parenting, violent video games and the moral bankruptcy of Hollywood and the music industry," and particularly Marilyn Manson and Goth youth culture. Following the shooting, local police rounded up, detained, and went through the personal computers of 22 young people whose image matched the "Goth" image that was broadcast over news channels. These "Goth" youth were subjected to public ostracism and at least half a dozen of them dropped out of school due to harassment by other students. Public fear resulted in further tightening of zero-tolerance policies already in effect in most US schools. The policies were widened to include not only suspected weapons or violent misbehaviours, but also anything that was seen to threaten teachers' authority. Muzzatti (2004, pp. 148–149) reports that, according to the Centre on Juvenile and Criminal Justice in 2001, over 60 percent of student suspensions were meted out on grounds of non-violent disciplinary infractions. The irony of the situation is not lost on Muzzatti (2004, p. 150), who points out that all these surveillance techniques are taking place at a time when educational funding is being cut and child poverty is high. Interesting parallels can be drawn with the general crackdown on students in uniform and conduct codes, as discussed in the chapter on education.

According to Sternheimer (2007), these new "folk devils" also include video games, which are often touted by moral crusaders to have created the problem of violent youth. The fact that school shootings are extremely rare is lost on the panic-stricken public. Meanwhile, the video game connection to youth violence was omnipresent in the American media in the years following the Columbine shooting. The main problem with the reporting is that video games are depicted without their social context, devoid of any understanding of the structural factors that accompany them, including "poverty, neighborhood instability, unemployment, and even family violence." Also, notably, youth are depicted as passive victims of media messages (Sternheimer, 2007, p. 16).

Race, Ethnicity, and Youth Crime

Some race and ethnic minorities have distinct patterns of criminal and delinquent behaviour. For example, North American youth of Chinese descent tend to have lower than average rates of delinquency. Among this ethnic group, acculturation was found to be strongly correlated with increasing delinquency, while adherence to Chinese culture was found to lower delinquency (Wong, 1999). Similarly, Jang's (2002) study of nationally representative longitudinal data from the United States indicates that Asian-American adolescents commit fewer acts of deviance (measured as school misbehaviour) than do White, Black, Hispanic, or Native American adolescents, explained by the higher socio-economic status of Asian Americans, combined with their higher chances of living in two-parent families, factors that encourage school attachment and success. Additionally, their low assimilation into mainstream culture may serve as a protection against negative peer influences.

Cultural explanations for youth crime or delinquency are gradually being proven faulty. These explanations claim either that violence or criminal behaviour is somehow inherent in some cultures as opposed to others. Instead, what is being shown is that a host of negative factors in the immigration or minority experiences result in higher as opposed to lower youth offending and delinquency rates. One historically based argument comes from Waters (1999), who analyzed several American immigrant groups in terms of youth criminality. He concluded that in those communities where youth delinquency rates were higher, the numbers of teenage males were high overall, and were combined with a lack of social cohesion in a particular community, and a lack of legitimate alternatives for youth. Low socio-economic status alone does not explain youthful criminality, but it has to be combined with a rupture in the intergenerational relations between parents and their teen sons in the community in question in order to result in higher levels of youth crime and delinquency. In other words, the immigrant communities that experience a high rate of juvenile offending are those in which the parents have experienced a loss of economic status through immigration, combined with the disaffection of their sons, who turn to crime because they lack legitimate opportunities. For example, Waters shows that historically, potential youth criminality has been staunched by the opportunity to enter military service, which provided a legitimate means toward alternative institutions away from gangs and crime.

On the other hand, some racialized minorities have more than their share of brushes with the police and the legal system. For example, the Canadian Centre for Justice Statistics (1997–1998) confirms a widely reported phenomenon of Aboriginal youth being disproportionately represented at all levels of the criminal justice system. The marginalization of Aboriginal populations puts them in a position of living in high-risk communities where poverty, substance abuse, and violence are common.

In Britain, compared to Whites, crime rates are higher among Afro-Caribbean youth and lower for Asians (Charles, 2002, p. 111). In the United States, similar patterns have been reported for African-American and Hispanic youth, their situations being linked with higher incidence of poverty, school problems, and substance abuse, accompanied by higher rates of juvenile crime and delinquency (Cervantes et al., 2000). This pattern also reflects the information, above, regarding the higher risk of these racialized groups of death from gun violence.

In fact, research shows convincingly that when levels of income are controlled for, racially based differences in the incidence of violent youth crime disappear. Similarly, when poverty rates are held constant, age-based differences disappear, with the highest rates appearing among adults in their twenties and thirties. Thus, teen violent crime can be largely explained by conditions of stress created by poverty (Males, 1996, p. 21). The strong links between poverty and youth violence were affirmed in the Government of Ontario's *The Roots of Youth Violence Report* (2008, p. 7) which stated that "poverty without hope, poverty with isolation, poverty with hunger and poor living conditions, poverty with racism and poverty with numerous daily reminders of social exclusion can lead to the immediate risk factors for violence." This will be discussed more fully below, in the section on why young people engage in criminal behaviour.

Racial Profiling and Police Harassment of Youth
In the criminological literature, racial profiling is said to exist when the members of certain racial or ethnic groups are subject to greater levels of criminal justice surveillance

than others. Racial profiling, therefore, is typically defined as a racial disparity in police stop and search practices, racial differences in Customs searches at airports and border crossings, increased police patrols in racial minority neighbourhoods, and undercover or sting operations that selectively target particular ethnic groups (Wortley & Tanner, 2003, pp. 369–370, in Wortley & Tanner, 2005, p. 583; also see Amnesty International, US, 2004, p. v).

Britain has a particularly long history of racial profiling of Black West Indian youth dating back to the race riots of 1958 through which a link between Blackness and crime was established in the public mind. The 1960s and 1970s were marked by attempts to study and establish the veracity of accounts and accusations by Black male youth of extensive police harassment, racist labelling, and brutality (Solomos, 2003, pp. 117–141; see also Cashmore & Troyna, 1982, pp. 1–9).

During 1980 and 1981 there were three major outbreaks of unrest. First, in April 1980 violent confrontations took place in the St. Paul's district of Bristol between groups of predominantly Black residents and the police. Second, during April 1981 violent confrontations between the police and crowds of mostly Black youth occurred in Brixton and London. Finally, in July 1981 there were widespread outbreaks of unrest in the Toxteth area of Liverpool, the Southall area of London, and various other localities in London, including Brixton. Other, smaller-scale disturbances took place and attracted attention in the media and within government (Benyon, 1984, in Solomos, 2003, p. 143).

More rioting followed in September and October 1985 in four locations, and some smaller altercations took place in 1986 and 1987. After the earlier race riots, the issue led to police initiatives to improve race relations by recruiting more Black and Asian police in the more racially diverse cities. These measures proved ineffective as the later riots of the 1980s took place in areas considered to be models of good community policing (Solomos, 2003, pp. 117–141; see also Gilroy, 1987, pp. 32–33). Thus, the 1980s was a period of widespread unrest among Black youth, not only in reaction to policing but to their general marginalization. Additional but smaller-scale outbreaks of unrest took place in 1992 by Asian youth and in 1995 by Black youth following the death of a young Black male, Wayne Douglas, who was in police custody. Further rioting took place in 2001 in a number of economically depressed locations largely by South Asian youth (Solomos, 2003, pp. 167–169), showing that relations between the police and racialized youth continue to be inflamed. This was clearly demonstrated in 2011, when there was widespread rioting and demonstrations by young people in London and other cities in reaction to the police shooting of a young black male, Mark Duggan.

Recently, the media have tended to downplay the race issue in their reporting of these incidents, possibly equating a lack of racial identification to "sensitivity," or perhaps attempting to not inflame the situation further. It is difficult not to read the media silence about the role of race in community unrest as complicity with the state. In these instances, there is a difference between racial profiling and having the issues identified clearly by linking youth unrest to the continuing marginalization of racialized communities. One social commentator wrote this:

What colour is Mark Duggan? Mark Duggan is the man who was shot dead by the police on Thursday in Tottenham. The Tottenham riots last night were sparked when people protested his death. This morning, I first heard of the riots on the radio, then on the television. I read articles on the internet. But oddly, no one would say what colour Mark Duggan was. No one would say the unsayable, that the rioters were, I suspect on the whole, black. Then, finally, Toby Young's *Telegraph* blog post on the riots was published. Is Toby Young the only journalist out there who will dare say that these riots are about race? Still, one paper did carry a photo of Mr Duggan. When I saw the photo, it confirmed what I knew instinctively: black youths once again have set London alight. (Birbalsingh, 2013)

Brownfield, Sorenson, and Thompson's (2001) analysis of the Seattle Youth Study data (Hindelang et al., 1981, in Brownfield et al., 2001), and their analysis of North American studies, showed a link between arrests and youth's "master status" based on social class and race. In other words, if youth are Black or lower class, they have a higher risk of being arrested. The conclusion is that there is profiling going on based on race and social class. Specifically, in this study, Blacks had 1.75 times the likelihood of being arrested compared to Whites. Further, having a father with the minimum of college education reduced the odds of being arrested. Profiling is based on a variety of different possibilities. One of these is that Blacks and lower-class youth have higher visibility in the community, based on where they live. The second possibility is that the police are more likely to use their discretionary powers where these social categories are concerned. A third possibility is that there may be a link between gang involvement and arrests. However, Brownfield and Sorenson's study rejects this interpretation as they found that gang status was not linked to arrests. They suggest, however, that this may play a larger role since gangs have been identified as an urban menace starting in the 1980s.

In Canada, Aboriginal and Black youth have been subjected to racial profiling. For example, the Canadian Centre for Justice Statistics (1997–1998) reports that Aboriginal communities are more visible and subject to more police presence, and this is reflected in higher arrest rates. Similarly, Black youth are particular targets for excessive negative police attention (Wortley & Tanner, 2005, p. 597; Commission des droits de la personne et des droits de la jeunesse, 2011). James (1998) has outlined the negative effects of racial profiling on the relationships between police and Black youth and their communities. These are some of the comments from the Black youth themselves:

They drive by. They don't glimpse your clothes, they glimpse your colour. That's the first thing they look at. If they judge the clothes so much why don't they go and stop those white boys that are wearing those same things like us?

There is a stereotype of Blacks—baggy pants, flashy jewellery, baseball caps, flashy colours, and so on. All Black people [who] dress like this are [seen] as pimps or drug dealers. White people dress like this too, [but are] not seen as pimps, etc. (James, 1998, p. 166)

James also found that social class and gender differences overlap with considerations of race. The perception that Black people are poor means that if they are wearing good clothes or walking in a wealthier neighbourhood, they are more likely to be questioned or harassed. Further, although both young Black males and females seem to fall under suspicion, the girls tend to be treated less harshly by the police. However, there was a perception that both males and females get the same kind of harassment in malls and schools (James, 1998, pp. 166–167, 169–171). These results were confirmed by Wortley and Tanner (2005) whose 2000 survey of 3,393 Toronto high school students shows that Black youth report much higher rates of being stopped and searched by police than youth from other racialized groups.

Notably, studies of racial profiling in Canada are still few as Canadian police do not collect data on the racial background of those stopped and searched. However, studies done in Great Britain and the United States (where police must record the racial background of people they stop and search) are consistent with racial profiling. The point worthy of note here is that racial profiling results in skewed crime statistics as the groups that are subjected to more surveillance are also more likely to show a higher preponderance of specific types of criminality regardless of whether it is factual or a result of the excessive surveillance itself. Thus, racial profiling is perpetuated based on faulty data (Wortley & Tanner, 2005, pp. 598–600).

Though racial profiling has existed as a practice for a long time, the practice was kicked up several notches in the early 21st century. Following the September 11, 2001, terrorist attacks against Americans in New York City and the Pentagon, the United States led the way in establishing counterterrorism measures that effectively established a portrait of Muslims and brown people as potential terrorists and criminals (Centre for Human Rights and Global Justice, 2006; Bahdi, 2003). The London bombings in July 2005 heightened the fear and public hysteria over the presumed potential for every Muslim in the world to be labelled as suspect, as expressed by Paul Sperry, of the Hoover Institution at Stanford University, in the *New York Times* (reported in Harcourt, 2006, p. 2):

> Young Muslim men bombed the London tube, and young Muslim men attacked New York with planes in 2001. From everything we know about the terrorists who may be taking aim at our transportation system, they are most likely to be young Muslim men.

New York City police commissioner Raymond Kelly (in Harcourt, 2006, p. 3) countered this claim by saying:

> If you look at the London bombings, you have three British citizens of Pakistani descent. You have Germaine Lindsay [the fourth London suicide bomber], who is Jamaican. You have a Chechen woman in Moscow in early 2004 who blows herself up in the subway station. So whom do you profile? Look at New York City. Forty percent of New Yorkers are born outside the country. Look at the diversity here. Who am I supposed to profile?

Amnesty International (2004, pp. vi–viii) asks a similar question, noting how widespread racial profiling is in the United States: approximately 32 million Americans report having been victims of racial profiling, and 87 million are at risk of racial profiling during their lifetime. The long list of "usual suspects" is so long that it makes one wonder who is left. Among the affected populations are:

> Native Americans, Asian Americans, Hispanic Americans, Arab Americans, Persian Americans, American Muslims, many immigrants and visitors, and, under certain circumstances, white Americans. (Amnesty International, US, 2004, p. vi)

Examples on the Amnesty International list of police harassment in America include police interference with targeted groups when driving, walking, travelling through airports, shopping, at home, and travelling to and from places of worship, while there is no clear or justifiable cause to do so. In fact, we all have heard the expressions "DWB" or "driving while Black" or "TWA" or "travelling while Arab," which, according to David Tanovich (interviewed by McKenzie, 2006), originated in the community in reaction to unnecessary and unwarranted police and authority interference.

As listed in the Amnesty quote above, and illustrating the pitfalls of profiling, the culprit in the previous case of American terrorism was a White American, Timothy McVeigh, who killed 169 people, including children, by blowing up the Murrah Federal building in Oklahoma City in 1995. There was no discourse about racially profiling Whites after this incident because it was seen to be individually based (Bahdi, 2003, p. 312). It is easier to see racial representation in non-Whites. It is observed in the US, the UK, and Canada that incidents of racial profiling against Muslim and brown youth have become firmly established after 9/11 (Harcourt, 2006; Bahdi, 2003; Jimenez, 2006; Frankel & Jones, 2005; Amnesty International, US, 2004; Maira, 2004). The ensuing US-led war against terrorism has resulted in significant measures that curtail immigration and civil rights of Muslims and Arabs in all three countries in question, and has led to the reinforcement of their image in the Western world as "violent, fanatical, irrational, immoral, untrustworthy, and incorrigible barbarians bent on destroying peace" (Bahdi, 2003, p. 304). This kind of extreme stereotyping has resulted in "false positives"; while everyone is tainted with the same brush, large numbers of innocent individuals are harmed (Bahdi, 2003, p. 309).

Indeed, the association of clothing and specific behaviours with being suspicious, as reported by the Black youth above, reached its pinnacle during the post-9/11 era. It was revealed in 2005 that both American and British policing authorities had in place a number of "shoot-to-kill" policies regarding suspected suicide bombers. These policies are endorsed in guidelines by the International Association of Chiefs of Police (IACP), a body facilitating police training and co-operation in the US and worldwide. In their discussion of these practices, the Center for Human Rights and Global Justice (2006, p. 7) reveal the checklist for a "suicide bomber profile":

These indicators include:

- wearing loose or bulky clothing in the summer
- pacing back and forth
- fidgeting with something beneath one's clothing
- failing to make eye contact
- being in a drug-induced state
- having strange hair colouring
- wearing too much cologne
- wearing talcum powder
- being overly protective of one's baggage

Even without the confirmation of Fekete (2006), any critical reader could see that several of these descriptions apply to many American, Canadian, and British youth whose regular attire is "bulky clothing," or whose tastes may run to different hair colours, and that many of the behaviours listed can also be signs of physical or mental illnesses. Additionally, the list stigmatizes behaviours that fall within a normal range of conduct in normal daily circumstances.

This profile has, nevertheless, had deadly results, with a number of innocent people killed for their "clothing and behaviour," including a Brazilian national, Jean Charles de Menezes, who was shot to death by the London police two weeks after the July 7, 2005, bombings (Centre for Human Rights and Global Justice, 2006, pp. 7–8; Fekete, 2006). Similarly, on a flight from Miami to Orlando, a Costa Rican–American, Rigoberto Alpizar, was shot dead by two air marshals. Alpizar fit the profile because he was agitated. In fact, he had not taken his medications for bipolar disorder. He was shot as he tried to reach for his bag.

Even aside from the rare fatalities, American and Canadian studies find that racial profiling has a dramatic impact on the targeted individuals and populations. There are a host of negative feelings ranging from fear to anger and frustration, and may include stress reactions, including post-traumatic stress disorder, as well as a profound distrust in social institutions (Wortley & Tanner, 2005, p. 601). The psychological harm caused is described as "fear and humiliation," and children are particularly vulnerable when their families and communities are perceived as potential enemies (Bahdi, 2003, p. 310). Behaviour changes may follow that impinge on people's quality of life through restrictions of their movements in public and avoidance of specific neighbourhoods. Racial profiling also results in heightened perceptions of racial discrimination and injustice (Wortley & Tanner, 2005, p. 601).

Wortley and Tanner (2005) also raise the possibility of racial profiling as a self-fulfilling prophecy, a conclusion that is supported by research by Manzo and Bailey (2005), who found that Black Canadian young offenders' views and actions are influenced by racial stereotypes, particularly the "gangsta" and "nigga" images. In doing so, they distance themselves from the rest of society. Ricky, one of the young males in the study (Manzo & Bailey, 2005, p. 293), said:

Gotta act hard ... acting like a gangsta, a thug or something ... just talk like it, walk like it—with a limp, you know. All that stuff like they don't care ... like if someone ticks them off they'll go beat them up or whatever, you know. That's how acting hard is like, like you don't care man.

Why Do Youth Engage in Criminal Behaviour?

If you were interested in creating a criminal you would have a pretty good chance if you took a young person from a seriously troubled home, put them into a series of foster and group homes, changed their primary worker on a regular basis, let them run away from "home" at an early age, allowed them to drop out of school and enabled them to develop a drug and/or alcohol addiction. Your chances would improve if, somewhere in their lonely and painful existence, they had been sexually, physically or emotionally abused. If in those few instances that they sought for help you would ensure that there were no accessible services, that the workers they encountered were rushed and overwhelmed by heavy caseloads, and that they would be seen first and foremost as trouble rather than troubled, is it surprising then that these young people would become perpetrators or victims of crime? (Youth voice, National Crime Prevention Council, 1997, p. 1)

Above, poverty is identified as a significant factor behind youth violence. There is a long list of other reasons for criminal behaviour in North America, and for youth offending in particular, ranging from psychopathology to personality traits to factors related to social class, family life, educational and occupational achievements, and interpersonal problems (Carrigan, 1998, pp. 280–281; National Crime Prevention Council of Canada, 1996; also see Stevenson et al., 2000, p. 225; Shields, 1995; Cervantes et al., 2000; Corrado et al., 2000).

Hill-Smith et al. (2002) indicate similar results in the UK. The authors found that compared to non-violent youth offenders, violent youth criminals are more likely to come from lower socio-economic backgrounds, had families where parenting (and especially mothering) was harsh, and had a history of problems with schools. Charles (2002, p. 112) points out that unemployment alone does not seem to result in higher crime rates. Additional factors in youth criminal involvement are "failure at school and low parental supervision."

Research in the UK has linked youth delinquency to "low family income, large family size, convicted parents, low non-verbal intelligence, [and] poor parental child-rearing behaviour" (including punitive parenting, poor parental supervision, explosive parenting) as well as generally anti-social behaviours, poor housing, and being tall. Studies also link delinquency to anti-social peers and educational problems. Other research points to personality factors, including hyperactivity and impulsivity (Hill-Smith et al., 2002, pp. 221–222).

Studies in the UK and the US on adolescents who have committed murder show clear links not only to neuropsychological abnormalities (which are extraordinarily difficult to measure) but also to social factors such as disruptive families, parental violence and sexual abuse, and alcohol abuse by the young person. Additionally, American studies have found that gang membership and educational problems are contributing factors (Hill-Smith et al., 2002, p. 222).

It is true that there are some teens and youth who have, for social or psychological reasons, embraced the view of young people as violent, and get satisfaction out of violent behaviour. For those who don't have the capacity to pursue other goals, violence can be a way of temporarily reclaiming the strength they feel that is rightfully theirs.

However, aside from the small proportion of violent individuals who are diagnosed with a psychopathology such as sociopathic personality, most violent behaviour can be explained by one's negative social, economic, and political circumstances. Thus, parental physical and/or sexual abuse are major factors contributing to youth involvement in criminal activities (National Crime Prevention Council, 2000, p. 4). A typical juvenile offender's background is that of having been a "repeat victim" as a child (National Crime Prevention Council of Canada, 1996). Childhood abuse or witnessing abuse can result in the kind of traumatization that can lead to violent and criminal behaviours (Jaffe & Baker, 1999, pp. 24–25; Stevenson et al., 2000, p. 225). This is one of the predictable outcomes of family violence as indicated in the chapter on health. Child abuse is a major risk factor for juvenile delinquency and particularly for violent crime (Herrera & McCloskey, 2001).

A youth's involvement in a dysfunctional family setting involving poor parenting and substance use or abuse is also a major factor (National Crime Prevention Council, 2000, p. 4; National Crime Prevention Council of Canada, 1996; also see Stevenson et al., 2000, p. 225; Claes et al., 2005; Cervantes et al., 2000; Bartollas & Miller, 2001, pp. 331–353). For example, a study by Correctional Service Canada (1999b) found that adult criminal activity was linked to teenage substance abuse in three ways. First, teenage drug use led to higher conviction rates for property crimes than for non-drug users. Second, regular teenage alcohol use was linked to higher rates of conviction for all types of crimes than for irregular or non-users of alcohol. Third, there was a wider variety of crime convictions for those convicts who have high levels of both drug and alcohol use as teenagers.

As stated, youth crime is significantly related to poverty and inadequate living conditions (*Law Now*, 1996; also see Stevenson et al., 2000, p. 225), but it must be noted that poverty itself does not cause delinquency. However, poverty may be associated with factors that can put youth at risk for delinquency, including family violence. Studies indicate that as income levels decrease, the rates of family dysfunction and parental depression increase. In addition, children's school readiness decreases, which can then lead to low achievement, school dropouts, and delinquency (Jaffe & Baker, 1999, pp. 24–25; Stevenson et al., 2000, p. 225; LeBlanc et al., 1993). So, as child poverty increases, so does the chance of juvenile delinquency (Jaffe & Baker, 1999, pp. 24–25; Stevenson et al., 2000, p. 225). Because of the link with poverty, youth in single-parent families are more likely to become delinquent (Stevenson et al., 2000, p. 226).

Bartollas and Miller (2001, p. 357) point out that chronic or repeat offenders are typically from lower income or impoverished urban backgrounds characterized by poor links to social institutions such as schools and workplaces. Poor education and unemployment can result in higher chances of engaging in ongoing criminal activity. American studies suggest a strong link between gang membership and low social class position. In Canada, Wortley and Tanner's (2006) results strongly support this conclusion.

A 1997 report by the Canadian Centre for Justice Studies found that one of the key indicators for youth involvement in criminal activity is the lack of legitimate means of earning money (Stevenson & Besserer, 1997, p. 21). With an unemployment rate of 22 percent added to the other societal pressures such as growing up in a lone-parent family, lacking adequate social bonds, belonging to a gang, dropping out of school, physical and sexual abuse, television violence, and poor parenting (Stevenson et al., 2000), many youth end up participating in criminal activity. The strong link between economic factors and youth delinquent behaviour gains support from studies that found that street youth who have a legitimate means of earning money (such as engaging in "squeegee-ing"—see below for a detailed discussion) are less likely than other youth to engage in criminal behaviours, including drug use and theft.

More generally, an attachment or "social bond" to different institutions, including school, work, and peers, can help reduce criminal behaviour. If youth fall outside the institutional support mechanisms, they are more likely to be attracted by alternative norms and values that support a delinquent lifestyle. Thus, dropping out of school is linked to youth crime as these youth are more likely to be unemployed, marginalized, and thus more likely to engage in anti-social activities (Stevenson et al., 2000, pp. 225–226; also see Shields, 1995). With the worsening of the youth job market and increased youth unemployment, there are concerns that this marginalization will lead to more young people becoming alienated from society (Hartnagel, 1998, p. 436).

Among social bonds, those with parents are highly significant. Claes et al. (2005, pp. 402–409) summarize North American research that shows that family conflict and dysfunction are major reasons for youth's susceptibility to deviant peers and behaviours. The research strongly supports the notion that parental bonding and supervision are important for all adolescent development, but it is not clear whether or not the effects are similar or different for boys and girls. The authors propose that particularly for boys, parental monitoring is important in determining whether they get involved with deviant peers. It is also suggested that parental bonding is important for protecting girls from deviant behaviours.

American research (Herrera & McCloskey, 2001) suggests that though family violence is a factor in both boys' and girls' criminal behaviour, it takes more severe abuse for girls to turn to criminality. Notably, the form of violent offending is almost exclusively domestic violence (against parents or siblings), a finding that supports the theory of an intergenerational cycle of violence for girls, but not for boys, who were more likely to act violently toward friends or strangers. They also found that witnessing marital violence predicted overall offending for both boys and girls, and that extreme poverty is also a factor. It has been suggested that a history of sexual abuse is a unique risk factor for girls' delinquency (Herrera & McCloskey, 2001, p. 1049).

Peers, Gangs, and Delinquent Subcultures

As seen in the previous chapter, peers provide youth with validation and social bonds if the adult world is seen to be of no help. North American studies demonstrate that peers are one of the strongest predictors of deviance and delinquency among youth (e.g., Wong, 1999; Brownfield & Thompson, 1991; Brotherton, 1999). For example, Brownfield and Thompson (1991) report results consistent with social learning theory in that peer involvement in delinquency was strongly and positively associated with self-reported delinquency. Further, Wong (1999) reports that association with delinquent peers was positively related to delinquency among Chinese-Canadian youth.

Given the role of peer influence, it is not surprising that there would be youth groups that bond together and engage in similar activities, including entities that can be called gangs. Confusion prevails, however, over the definition of gangs: When is a group a gang? The problem is that more restrictive definitions may underestimate the phenomenon, and wider definitions may create unnecessary fear and panic with their overestimation of gang activity in various communities. The main features associated with gang activity range from engagement in illegal or criminal group activity, to the presence of leadership and hierarchy (leaders vs. followers), identifiable colours or clothing, and initiation rituals (Wortley & Tanner, 2006, p. 20).

Doob and Cesaroni (2004, pp. 96–101) define a gang as a "relatively stable, somewhat organized, group with clear or formal leadership." According to this definition, not all youth in groups form a gang, and most of the groups committing offences are not gangs but more fleeting groupings. Such fluidity is observed in Canadian and American studies, suggesting a continuum of different groups ranging from transient and disorganized to more stable and organized. This makes it very difficult to estimate the actual extent of the youth gang problem across North America, but it seems to, at most, have increased only slightly over time. Indeed, Doob and Cesaroni argue further that the increased focus on gangs reflects an increase not in actual gang incidents but a skyrocketing number of media stories about gangs. At the same time, police have used the threat of gangs as a tactic to increase their budgets and to legitimate their use of force when criticized for police brutality. However, the consequence of increased media and police attention is that the idea that there is a rapidly growing gang problem is firmly planted in the public consciousness. Adults' attention to "youth gang" activity tends to be cyclical, and one of those cycles of increased interest began in the 1990s (Smandych, 2001, pp. 281–283).

Ultimately, at least some of the fear regarding youth gangs has to do with the way the term "gang" has been inflated to include any suspicious youth activity in groups. If the term is applied more selectively, actual gangs, as more permanent groupings with a criminal intent, are relatively rare (Brotherton, 1999; Smandych, 2001). Real gangs are toxic environments to their members, including increased involvement in violence and victimization (Bartollas & Miller, 2001, p. 323).

Large-scale American studies (summarized in Bartollas & Miller, 2001, pp. 321–322) propose a seven-stage path for the development of emergent gangs, from less serious to more serious crime activity, starting with small-scale sale of drugs (stage 1) which expands and becomes more organized (stage 2). There is a gradual emergence of a more distinct organization (stage 3), including formal membership symbols (e.g., clothing, signs) and initiation rituals as rival gangs distinguish themselves from one another. The competition between gangs (stage 4) can be manifested in open conflict in schools and other public places, with gang symbols openly displayed. Drugs are being sold more openly in schools and public spaces (stage 5) with a rise in adult leadership and victimization of teachers and students in schools. Eventually, gangs gain control (stage 6) in schools and communities, and commit more crimes that police are unable to control, resulting in public fear. The most common crimes tend to be larceny/theft, aggravated assault, and robbery. Finally (stage 7), the community environment deteriorates to the degree that there is migration away from the city and the population keeps children home from school and avoids public spaces (Bartollas & Miller, 2001, pp. 321–323).

In the United States, a nationally representative school crime study from 1991 indicated that 15 percent of the students surveyed reported that they had gangs in their schools. The reported rates were higher by Black students (20 percent) and Hispanics (32 percent) (Cervantes et al., 2000, p. 48). There were dramatic increases in the estimates of youth gang involvement in the 1990s. All but 10 percent of the largest cities in America reported youth gang problems, compared with half that in the early 1980s. Police estimate that there are 4,881 gangs nationwide with nearly 250,000 members (Laidler & Hunt, 2001, p. 656; also see Bartollas & Miller, 2001, p. 321). In 2001, the Justice Department reported over 400,000 gang-related crimes, a significant increase from the just over 16,000 in 1991 (Florian-Lacy et al., 2002, p. 4). Based on a national survey of law enforcement officials in 2010, "there were 29,000 gangs and 756,000 gang members throughout 3,500 jurisdictions in the United States," with some fluctuations over the previous 15 years (Egley & Howell, 2012, p. 1).

Urban gangs have been present in American cities since the 1920s, with such famous examples as the Chicago supergangs of the 1950s. One of the most famous ones was Conservative Vice Lords, started by a small group of youth under the leadership of a 15-year-old reformatory schoolboy. This gang flourished from the late 1950s to the late 1960s. Other famous Chicago gangs of the era were Cobras, Disciples, El Rukns, Latin Kings; Los Angeles had Bloods and Crips, and there were other notorious gangs in Miami and elsewhere (Bartollas & Miller, 2001, pp. 313–325).

Wortley and Tanner (2006, p. 19) point out that a lot of what is thought about Canadian youth gangs is, in fact, derived from American studies, in the face of lack of research into the Canadian gang situation. Overall, rates of violent crime are lower in Canada than in the United States. Along these lines, some studies suggest that Canadian youth gang members are less likely to engage in violent crimes than American youth gang members (Gatti et al., 2005, p. 1187).

Wortley and Tanner (2006) approached the subject matter without a fixed definition of gangs, but instead asked a large sample (3,393) of Toronto high school students and a sample of 396 street youth about their self-identified gang activity. The results were that

11 percent of high school youth and 27 percent of street youth reported belonging to a gang at some point in their lives. When asked about their present gang membership, 6 percent of the school youth and 16 percent of the street youth indicated in the affirmative. Interestingly, the activities identified with gang membership were social rather than criminal in nature. Indeed, the gangs that either high school or street youth belonged to were either "criminal" gangs or "social" gangs, based on the types of activities they identified. Though social time and partying were identified by both high school and street youth as most common activities, street youth reported higher rates of criminal activity, including selling drugs and committing property crimes. Members of both types of gangs reported having engaged in street/gang fights, but with much higher rates of fighting among criminal gang than social gang members.

Immigrant and Ethnic Youth Gangs

In the 1970s, the less restrictive immigration laws from the 1960s onward were blamed for an increase in Hong Kong–based youth gang activity "in the Chinatowns of San Francisco, Vancouver, New York, Los Angeles, and other cities" (Joe & Robinson, 1980, p. 337), and for a general rise in "Chinese" gang activity (Mark, 2000, p. 31).

Several Canadian studies from the 1990s point to a demographic pattern among gang members. Most are male and the average age of membership is 19, with the majority of members being in their mid-twenties or younger. The race and ethnic composition of gang membership depends on the geographic area one is looking at. For example, Gordon (1993, in R. Gordon, 2000, pp. 39–60) reports that gangs in British Columbia tend to have mostly Caucasian membership, with the Asians being the next largest group. Very few members are East Indian, Hispanic, Aboriginal, or Black. It has been noted that, although they tend to be small in numbers, street gangs in specific locations are "composed disproportionately of individuals from particular ethnic minorities" (R. Gordon, 2000, p. 50) and from among immigrant groups. For instance, in the Greater Vancouver Area Gang Study, visible minority members formed three-quarters of all gang membership, and the Vietnamese were the largest single group. In comparison, young Aboriginal males form the bulk of gang members in Winnipeg, and in Toronto there is a disproportionate representation of Caribbean, Hispanic, and Portuguese populations in gangs (R. Gordon, 2000, pp. 39–60).

Historically, North American gang membership draws from among disadvantaged Europeans, including Irish, Italians, and Jews. More recently, American gang membership is concentrated among African and Hispanic Americans. According to Wortley and Tanner's (2006, p. 31) survey, gang membership is more common among Black (8 percent), Hispanic (6 percent), and Aboriginal (6 percent) youth than among White (4 percent), South Asian (3 percent) and Asian (2 percent) students. The majority of criminal gang members are White (36 percent) while 26 percent are Black, 11 percent are Aboriginal, 10 percent are South Asian or Asian, and 7 percent are Hispanic. Wortley and Tanner's study shows a link between lower-class backgrounds and residence in community housing among Black, Aboriginal, and Hispanic students, as well as higher levels of reported alienation from mainstream Canadian institutions. The authors conclude that the key to alleviating gang activity is to "reduce racial discrimination and existing racial inequalities," including improvements in their relative social positions (p. 31).

Wortley and Tanner (2006, p. 29) found that among large samples of Toronto high school youth and street youth, gang membership was more common among Canadian-born youth than immigrant youth born outside of Canada. In other words, there is no cause for a public panic over "immigrant youth gangs."

Nevertheless, there are currently some notorious African-American gangs, including the Chicago supergangs and the Bloods and Crips in Los Angeles. Other racially based gangs are present across the United States, including Hispanic street gangs in the Southwest and Southeast, and Asian gangs that originated in California and are now spreading to other cities. White gangs also began on the West Coast and are increasingly becoming involved in satanic cults (Bartollas & Miller, 2001, p. 320).

These results clarify the links between ethnicity, immigration status, and socio-economic status in the formation of street gangs. These can combine with

> limited language competency and a lack of marketable skills to produce a variety of economic vulnerabilities; poverty, family disintegration, a lack of supportive community networks, and the lack of rewarding employment. (R. Gordon, 2000, p. 51)

The end result is the formation of street gangs that seek illegal ways for dealing with these problems (R. Gordon, 2000; Mark, 2000).

In addition to poverty and stresses caused by immigration and settlement, American studies suggest that—similar to general reasons behind juvenile delinquency discussed above—multiple factors are behind youth gang formation, including "poor family relations, low self-esteem, and the presence of learning disabilities" (Florian-Lacy et al., 2002, p. 12). Florian-Lacy et al. (2002, p. 14) found that gang members tend to be alienated from their families; feel academically inferior; join gangs to deny those feelings; and enjoy the sense of "family" associated with gang membership.

In multiple American studies, gang membership is linked to a higher incidence of criminal behaviour, and especially serious and violent crime and drug use. Generally, studies find that the link between gang membership and delinquency is attributed to three different processes: (1) the selection model (gangs attract youth already engaged in criminal behaviour); (2) the facilitation model (association with gangs encourages criminality in non-criminal youth); and (3) the enhancement model (joining a gang enhances criminality in youth who have some history of criminal behaviour). Each of these models has some support from different American studies. In a Canadian study of 1,161 French-speaking boys in disadvantaged areas of Montreal, support was found for the facilitation model for shorter-term gang members, and the enhancement model for long-term gang members. In other words, youth who had no history of criminality acted criminally in gangs, but their involvement was more transient. In comparison, longer-term gang membership is likely to escalate criminality in those youth who are already engaged in criminal activities. The long-term gang members showed much higher levels of criminality, violence, drug use, and drug selling in comparison with non-members and with transient gang members. However, drug use or sales are not necessarily enhanced by gang membership as these behaviours were present in gang members prior to their gang involvement and remained high after leaving the gang. Overall, the authors conclude that gang influence is specific and that gangs do exert an influence on their members' behaviours over and above the influence of the "social deficiencies" of their members (Gatti et al., 2005, pp. 1178–1179). Wortley and Tanner's (2006, p. 27) study of Toronto youth gang members lends support to the notion that both selection and socialization effects are in place, the latter supported by the drop in crime activity among former compared to current gang members.

Skinheads and Hate Groups

One youth delinquent subgroup that has been subjected to much study is the skinheads, particularly by journalists, special-interest groups, and law enforcement agencies. Their accounts depict skinheads variously as neo-Nazis, who are likened to terrorists, and misunderstood youth, who are alienated from a society that has rejected them. Some of these reports point to the wide variety of skinhead groups and their diverse politics, and the variety of backgrounds these youth come from (Khanna, 1999; Baron, 1997), ranging from stable middle-class homes to dysfunctional and abusive family environments. In recent academic studies, a similar trend prevails. Added to this, there is a more recent trend to examine skinheads as disaffected working-class youth. This approach is criticized for its lack of attention to the negative features of skinhead culture, including crime and violence (Baron, 1997).

The skinhead subculture originated in Britain in the mid-1960s, and was a movement by working-class youth intent on expressing their objection to capitalism. While British subcultural theorists from the Birmingham tradition noted this aspect of the youth's disaffection, they did not address their racism. As the skinheads spread into North America and became more overtly associated with neo-Nazism and racial hate, more attention has been paid to this aspect of their motives and behaviours (Tanner, 2001, p. 143).

What the British, American, and Canadian skinheads seem to have in common is that economic declines tend to produce deviant subcultures such as the skinheads (Tanner, 2001, pp. 149–150). American skinheads are intent on protecting their "American way of life" or their "Aryan heritage" (Bartollas & Miller, 2001, p. 312). Earlier American studies, such as Mark Hamm's (1993, in Tanner, 2001, p. 143–144) noted that American skinheads are distinctive as they revolve around racism, meaning that they are White, and their hatred and violence are pointed at non-Whites (including Jews) and homosexuals. According to Tanner (2001, p. 147), they are also "male traditionalists" as they allow only a small number of women in their midst, who hold a secondary status and a sexualized role. Second, Hamm (1993, in Tanner, 2001, pp. 143–144) points out that skinheads are distinctively violent compared to other youth subcultures. Like their British counterparts, American skinheads tend to be blue-collar working high school dropouts, whose disaffection was fed by the years of Reaganomics that expanded the American urban underclass.

The following Bush Sr. years brought recessions and unemployment that continued to feed the appeal of the skinhead subculture.

It has been estimated that by the mid-1990s there were 3,500–4,000 skinheads in the United States, along with approximately 25,000 hard-core activists in an estimated 300 different White supremacist organizations (Bartollas & Miller, 2001, p. 312). There are an estimated 1,000 skinheads in Canada (Khanna, 1999, p. 18). In a rare Canadian ethnographic study, Baron (1997) interviewed a group of 14 homeless Edmonton male skinheads, aged 15–22. They came from mixed social class backgrounds, but only three were from intact families. This supports findings of other studies suggesting that the conflict and tensions leading to a parental breakup are linked to some youths becoming "vulnerable to the influence of delinquent peers." The youths in this study had been subject to physical or sexual victimization in their families, particularly by their male guardians. These experiences left them filled with hatred and desire for revenge on their parents. The school environment, with its authority structure and requirements for order, was equally oppressive, and the youth got into serious problems due to their nonconformist and violent behaviour. The average education level was grade 9, and only one member of the group interviewed had his high school diploma. Consequently, their connection to the labour market was tenuous, and all were unemployed at the time of the study. Without means to support themselves, they ended up on the streets, where their anger and aggression are evident in a large number of one-on-one fights, resulting in serious injuries. The violence became a subculture, with a code of retributive justice, i.e., you are expected to "settle the score" if harmed by another, or come to the aid of a buddy in a fight, to show your loyalty to your group. Robbery and drugs are also part of the life of skinheads. Most of the male youth interviewed were involved in drug trafficking, and all were heavy users of drugs and alcohol.

One of the major questions for skinhead groups has to do with their neo-Nazi political views. In this particular study, the youth were not involved in, nor did they display "a great deal of racially motivated behaviour." Most of the youth reported no political views or agenda, but there were six extreme racists among them, who were willing to use violence to achieve political change. Although there is a small core group of those who seem compelled toward the neo-Nazi skinhead image, Baron (1997; also see Curry, 1997 in Tanner, 2001, pp. 146–147) does not think that this group is cohesive enough to be attracted to right-wing extremist organizations. Instead, they are "street crime" skinheads, more interested in crime and violence than organized political activity.

Tanner (2001, p. 147) points out that Canadian skinheads' activities and concerns are "not far removed from those held by ordinary Canadian adults." That racism is systemic and not only a feature of select fringe groups is also shown by American studies reporting a high incidence of hate crimes in schools, particularly in some of the most diverse cities like Los Angeles (Cervantes et al., 2000, p. 48). The typical offender is under the age of 20 (Bartollas & Miller, 2001, p. 312).

Hate activity is also present on Canadian campuses, manifested in Holocaust deniers and other racist groups who are using electronic and print media on campus to promote their messages (Henry et al., 2000, pp. 247–248). According to Khanna (1999, pp.

ii–6), the little research that has been done so far indicates that organized hate groups recruit youth in schools and universities, and through the Internet. There are at least 32 Web sites that directly target children and youth. The perpetrators of hateful acts against minorities come from diverse and varied backgrounds, but the majority are male and in their twenties. Khanna (1999, p. ii) notes that the prime target group for these recruiters are "lonely, marginalized youth seeking a sense of identity, or angry young people who are seeking a solution to the problems they are facing."

Interestingly, in this case as well as in other cases of crime, youth tend to be viewed more likely as perpetrators than as victims of hate crime. We discussed earlier (in the chapters on education and sexuality) that lesbian and gay youth tend to be subjected to harassment and violence in schools and in communities. However, hate crimes tend to be among the most underreported, and youth are particularly unlikely to turn to the police in these cases. The common reasons given for this reflect the powerless position of youth. For example, youth tend not to report hate crimes to the police because they are uncertain about the degree of seriousness that warrants reporting, and they resist getting involved in the justice system. In schools, youth feel that they have little support, and that they get blamed even before the perpetrator does. Students don't feel that adults take the incidents seriously enough. Instead, adults tend to minimize the acts and their consequences as nuisances or "childish pranks" that do not warrant serious punishment. Students also report that their peer group, and the fear of potential retaliation, also led them to deal with the incidents themselves rather than report them to adult authorities. Meanwhile, they suffer amidst serious consequences to their "self-esteem, school performance and sense of safety and security" (Khanna, 1999, pp. 21–27).

Recently, in the years following the economic recession, there has been at least an anecdotal increase in neo-Nazi activity, shown in instances of attacks on immigrants and members of racialized minorities. The perpetrators are not confined to youth, and the activities of hate groups are difficult to study, for obvious reasons. In general, racially motivated hate crimes form about half of all cases of hate crimes in Canada, which numbered 1,410 in 2010. However, this number is based on police reports, and it is known from victim surveys that only about one-third of hate crime incidents get reported (Dowden & Brennan, 2010). Similar percentages prevail in US statistics (FBI, 2012). In particular, anti-Islamic incidents have increased since 9/11, and tend to escalate immediately following new incidents (Dado, 2103). For example, there was a reported surge in attacks against Muslims in the UK following the public daytime killing of an ex-army officer by a Muslim male in the spring of 2013: within 48 hours, over 140 instances of Islamophobic hate crimes were committed (Press TV, 2013).

The Police and Juvenile Law

The three "post-industrial" countries in question have a shared "social, cultural, and legal background"; their contemporary legal and statutory systems developed from the legacy of English common law (Bartollas & Miller, 2001, pp. 388–390). Therefore, their patterns of criminal justice also fall into step, with a trend toward harsh punishment for the most serious and violent offences, and with alternative measures (e.g., restorative justice) for less serious offences. The debate over which is more effective is ongoing, with resistance toward increasingly punitive measures from those working with and providing services to young people (Caputo & Vallée, 2010).

According to Bartollas and Miller (2001, pp. 112, 391–397), the Canadian juvenile justice system is traditionally a welfare model as its intent is to rehabilitate and to help youth and address youth's needs outside of the criminal justice system, with the exception of violent and repeat offenders whose treatment is more in line with the crime-control model aimed at punishment. In comparison, the British and American models are somewhat more punitive in nature, but England and Wales moved increasingly toward a welfare model in the 20th century, while the US toughened its line. In the last three decades of the 20th century, both American and UK societies are grappling with the issue of well-publicized murders committed by youth, and the debate between the proponents of the crime-control and welfare models continues.

Youth law reform has been on the national agendas of all three countries since the 1990s. Debates continue between conservative hard-liners recommending juvenile punishment in adult courts, and more liberal child and youth advocates recommending leniency and acknowledgement of the young age of offending (see e.g., Sternheimer, 2007, p. 16). Meanwhile, starting in the 1990s, the juvenile justice systems of the three Anglo-American countries seem to be undergoing a liberalization. However, some aspects of the systems are indicative of attention to ever-younger offenders, or those "at risk," with increased surveillance of not only the young offenders but also their families.

The measures in the UK are indicative of the latter trend. There have been a number of measures put in place since the late 1990s. The youth crime reform includes early intervention measures combined with punishment and rehabilitation. A scheme including final warnings, reparation orders, action plan orders, child safety orders, and parenting orders (see Box 8.2) was put in place in 2000 as a part of the 1998 Crime and Disorder Act "to help communities live without fear of crime and to make sure that young offenders are diverted from their offending behaviour at an early stage." The focus is on prevention, and with fewer warnings to juvenile offenders than before. As a part of the overhaul of the system, sentencing times were reduced. For youth in court less than two years previously, there is an end to conditional discharges. As well, courts can "remand 12–14 year olds direct[ly] into secure accommodation" (Home Office, 2000).

A UK Home Office release (2000) recounts "success stories" based on the pilot studies done prior to the nationwide implementation of the new measures. One of them was John (no age indicated), who was subjected to a second and final warning for shoplifting in 1998, put through a community program including a reparation (letter of apology to the shop owner), subjected to monitoring for his school attendance, and is working with a team to make sure his wider needs are attended to. Another example is Steven,

---

Box 8.2: Criminal and Disorderly Conduct

The following measures are listed in the official directives used to explain the UK Crime and Disorder Act, 1998 (Home Office, 2000):

Final Warning Scheme: Repeat cautioning is replaced by a statutory final warning scheme. A final warning is followed by an intervention programme to address the causes of the offending behaviour. Once an offender has received a final warning, any further offence leads to criminal charges.

Reparation Orders: To make offenders face up to their crimes and the consequences of their actions. It can involve writing a letter of apology, apologising in person, cleaning graffiti, or repairing criminal damage. The Order can be imposed for any offence (for which the sentence is not fixed).

Action Plan Orders: A short intensive program of community-based intervention combining punishment, rehabilitation, and reparation. It lasts three months and is designed to address the specific causes of offending.

Child Safety Orders: To protect children under 10 who are at risk of becoming involved in crime. It can require a child to be at home at certain times or to stay away from certain people and places. The Order is made for between three and twelve months and will be available in the family proceedings court on the application of the local authority.

Parenting Orders: To help and support parents to control the behaviour of their children. It requires parents to attend counselling and guidance sessions and can require them to make sure their children go to school each day. The Order is made for up to 12 months. The pilots [pilot studies] found that parents generally welcomed the assistance they received, often for the first time, in dealing with their children.

---

who at 13 was given a reparation order (verbal apology) for two subsequent petty thefts. His single-parent mother and distant and alcoholic father were subjected to a parenting order, which was not held up by the father. Steven and his mother attend sessions with family services, and his problem behaviours at school seem to have been remedied.

Neither John nor Steven has reoffended "so far." The social cost may be that while societies are "protected from harm," ever-younger people and their families are subjected to increased government surveillance.

Indeed, the UK media feeds into this trend by publicizing stories about the notorious criminal lives of a few young people, against whom the nation needs to be protected. Examples of these individuals include young "bail bandits" whom the new legislation can now remand in custody. They name the "Boomerang Boy," who at 15 had committed over 1,000 crimes because he was continually bailed and allowed to continue terrorizing the community. Similarly, new measures allow magistrates to "name and shame" repeat young offenders, such as the "Terror Triplets"—three 13-year-olds sisters—who engaged in unspecified anti-social behaviour (BBC News, 2002).

The United States stands as a prime example of a nation where young offenders receive extremely harsh punishment. In 1989, the United States Supreme Court legislated the execution of 16–17-year-olds for crimes (Bartollas & Miller, 2001, p. 150). It was only in 2005 that the US Supreme Court banned executions of juveniles. A study released in 2007 puts the number at an estimated 200,000 of youth under age 18 who are punished under the adult justice system. This amounts to an increase of over 200 percent since the 1990s. The daily number of youth in adult jails is 7,000, either serving their sentences or awaiting trial. Connecticut, North Carolina, and New York automatically send 16–17-year-olds into the adult system. The offences are not only for violent or repeat offenders; more first-time offenders for non-violent crimes are subjected to adult courts. For example, in 2002, only 15 percent of the nearly 14,000 17-year-olds charged with crime in adult courts were arrested for violent crimes (Harper, 2007, p. A11; also see Bartollas & Miller, 2001, pp. 134–155). Finally, the US is the only country in the world that sentences children to life without parole for committing murder. In 26 states, this sentence is mandatory. In 1990, 2.9 percent of the children convicted of murder were sentenced to life without parole (Amnesty International, UK, 2005).

Generally, the prevailing myth of youth getting lenient sentences couldn't be farther from the truth. For example, a 1993 study from California shows that juveniles have 60 percent longer detentions, by nearly a year, than adults for the same crimes; and that there are wider sentencing disparities among youth for murder and other crimes. For example, youth got on average 60 months in prison while adults got 41 months for murder (Males, 1996, p. 36).

There was a move in the US during the 1970s and 1980s toward community-based corrections programs, which are generally found to be at least as successful as incarceration, and some studies have found them more effective in deterring youth crime. The caution here is with regard to the type of juvenile offender that will benefit from reintegration; the debate is ongoing about whether community-based programs should be offered to all but hardened juvenile criminals, or whether the programs should be offered only to a smaller segment of offenders who are deemed most likely to benefit (Bartollas & Miller, 2001, pp. 182–207).

The punitive nature of the US youth justice system also has racial overtones. For example, in 2005, not only were 58 percent of the youth crimes tried in adult courts non-violent, but 7 of 10 defendants were non-White (Harper, 2007, p. A11). In the United States, the overrepresentation of racialized youth in juvenile institutions is a formidable challenge. In 1997, Black youth were around five times more likely to be incarcerated than White youth, and the rates among Hispanic youth were double the rate of non-Hispanic youth (Engen et al., 2002, p. 194; also see US Justice Fund, 2007). Similarly, Black and Hispanic youth are overrepresented among those who were sentenced to life without parole (Amnesty International, UK, 2005).

The analysis by Engen et al. (2002) of a large number of studies on race and punishment shows that if anything, studies may underestimate the role that race plays in the youth justice system. Overall, these studies suggest that race plays a particularly important role in the early stages of youth criminal careers (arrest and detention), but that it diminishes in the process of petitioning and adjudication. This suggests that racialized youth are more likely to be seen as threats to the community as they are processed initially, whereas the nature of the offence is more of a determinant at later stages of the process. Etherington (1997, p. 83) confirms that that Canadian and American racialized minority youth are overrepresented in the court system.

Critics of the harsh approach to punishment point to evidence that rather than serving as a deterrent against further offending, harsher early punishments are more likely to produce hardened criminals. This realization has led to calls for reform of the youth justice system in several states, including North Carolina—in reaction to high reoffending rates among youth—and Connecticut, where a bill to disallow adult charges for those 18 years of age or younger is being considered (Harper, 2007, p. A11).

Adult prisons are harsh places, and they are often described as training grounds for hardened criminals. Juvenile offenders in American prisons are likely to get sexually and physically violated and they are less likely to get age-appropriate services for their physical and mental health issues or their education (Bartollas & Miller, 2001, pp. 147–148).

All jail systems, whether adult or juvenile, also develop problems related to informal hierarchies and power differences between inmates. Power relationships within prisons and institutions are manifested in victimization and degradation of those who are deemed to be weak. Bartollas and Miller (2001, pp. 265–266) provide the following example of a youth who became the scapegoat for the stronger inmates:

> In a revealing incident, a resident was making fun of a scapegoat one day when the scapegoat, much to the surprise of everyone, attacked the supposedly more aggressive youth. In the fight that ensued, the scapegoat clearly got the better of the other youth. Staff locked both youths in their rooms until a disciplinary meeting could be held. The youth who had had a higher position in the cottage until the fight tried to commit suicide by setting his room on fire; he clearly preferred to die rather than take on the role of the scapegoat. This youth did become the cottage scapegoat and later confessed to a staff member that he was committing oral sodomy on half of the 24 youths in the cottage.

American institutions for juvenile offenders (including jails and detention centres) came under severe criticism in the 1970s due to high levels of harsh treatment of youth by staff, including brutality. The sexual victimization and suicide rates of young offenders were alarmingly high. From the 1970s onward, shelter care facilities, ranches, and forestry camps became more common for minor offenders, as did the use of boot camps for youth who have a history of minor offences and need a deterrent. Training schools for serious offenders are also used, with the intent of gradually rehabilitating the youth and increasing their autonomy as their behaviour improves. The schools come in minimum-, medium-, and maximum-security varieties, depending on the nature of the offences, and they offer education and vocational training to the inmates (Bartollas & Miller, 2001, pp. 239–262).

There is also an increase in mental health placements among juvenile offenders, which is highly controversial because youth can be "voluntarily" admitted by their parents who deem them "unmanageable." The youth may not have committed any crime but are "acting out" in ways that are unacceptable to their parents. These institutions are blamed for medicalizing deviance as the residents tend to be troubled or troublesome youth whose conditions are deemed mental issues, with the consequent use of psychotropic drugs and psychiatric treatments. Some describe mental health placements as the last refuge for the "problems faced by the children of haves" (Bartollas & Miller, 2001, pp. 263–264).

An important feature of the Canadian youth crime scene is that while the youth crime rate itself has remained relatively stable, there has been a dramatic increase in the youth incarceration rate, which is significantly higher than for adults (Jaffe & Baker, 1999, p. 23). Further, in comparison with adults, average youth custody sentences are 22 percent longer, and youth, unlike adults, are not eligible for parole after one-third of their sentence (*Law Now*, 1996, p. 12).

The trends in sentencing seem to be contradictory to the spirit of the Young Offenders Act. To put it briefly:

> The Young Offenders Act is based on the premise that youths should be held responsible for their illegal actions, but that young people have special needs as they develop and mature. Therefore, the Act creates a youth justice system *separate* from the adult system. (Cuddington, 1995, emphasis in original)

Since being enacted in 1982, and in response to a public perception that it was "too lenient," the federal Young Offenders Act (YOA) was amended three times, in 1986, 1992, and 1995. The 1992 amendment lengthened the maximum sentence for murder from three to five years, and eased the transfer from juvenile to adult court. The 1995 amendment extended the sentence for first-degree murder to 10 years, and made it the defence attorney's responsibility to argue grounds for keeping 16- and 17-year-old offenders in the juvenile justice system rather than have them transferred to adult court. The toughening of the YOA means that incarceration is increasingly seen as the best solution to youth crime (Jaffe & Baker, 1999, p. 23).

The criticism of the "tough line" or "boot camp" approach to young offenders is simply that this approach focuses on individual-level solutions rather than linking juvenile offending to the significant structural problems outlined above. The overall criticism is summarized as follows (Jaffe & Baker, 1999, p. 23):

> The focus of legislative solutions has been misguided and has placed the emphasis on increasing the severity of consequences to crime rather than solutions aimed at preventing the development of criminal behaviour and changing persistent offending patterns.

This line of thinking is in keeping with the general findings in research showing that social supports, and particularly family supports, significantly reduce the chances of youth offending and reoffending. This is logical, given that family dysfunction is associated with both delinquency and adult criminality (Latimer, 2001; Currie & Covell, 1998).

The Liberal government put in place Bill C-68, which repealed the YOA and replaced it with the Youth Criminal Justice Act, aimed at both steering youth away from the juvenile justice system and providing more serious punishments for youth convicted of serious crimes, and for repeat offenders (Pate, 1999, p. 42).

In fact, all of this was already provided under the YOA. There were increased arrests and charges of youth as a result of Criminal Code changes that resulted in the hardening of the approach of police and courts toward young offenders (Bell, 1999, pp. 28–29). While the rates of police charging of youth increased by 21 percent after the introduction of the Young Offenders Act (YOA) in 1984, the numbers of crimes committed remained the same (*Law Now*, 1996).

According to Carrington (1999), there was a 7 percent increase in police-reported youth crime from the 1980s to the 1990s. At the same time, there was a 27 percent jump in the rate of young people charged by police, reflecting a "drop in the use of police discretion." In other words, the YOA seems to have led to changes in police practices in four provinces and one territory because while there was no jump in the proportions of youth apprehended, there was a jump in the proportions charged. Carrington (1999, p. 25) concludes that "there is no basis in fact for public concern about increased levels of youth crime or the supposed failure of the YOA to control youth crime."

Nevertheless, the new Youth Criminal Justice Act (YCJA) was put in place in 2003, offering a softer approach to youth crime despite some pressure toward taking a tougher line. The YCJA retained the minimum age of criminal responsibility at 12 instead of lowering it to 10, and the minimum age of youth being sent to adult courts was retained at 18 instead of lowering it to 16. There was no increase to maximum lengths of sentencing, and the YCJA rejected the proposal that an automatic adult sentence be meted out in some cases. The new measures introduced in the YCJA include more focus on rehabilitation and reintegration rather than punishment and incarceration; it sets out options for measures outside courts, including informal warnings, police and Crown cautions, referrals to community agencies and programs, and extrajudicial sanctions for non-violent offences that allow youth to accept responsibility for their offences and to comply with terms and conditions. A new concept of conferences was introduced to allow members of the police, judiciary, and the community to make plans toward restitution or rehabilitation of the youthful offender. The YCJA also allows for the involvement of child welfare authorities to assist youth in improving their situation. Overall, the YCJA also aims to set out sentencing principles that are proportionate to the offence and must promote rehabilitation (Barnhorst, 2004).

Since the Youth Criminal Justice Act was put in place in 2003, the number of juvenile offenders in jail has dropped significantly. As of 2005, there were approximately 13,100 juveniles under detention or on probation, which is a 12 percent decline compared with 2003–2004 (Harper, 2007, p. A11). The federal Conservative partly was determined to change the law, which they considered too lenient. A part of their platform was to charge anyone over 14 years of age in adult courts for "serious, violent or repeat offences" (Harper, 2007, p. A11). Indeed, significant changes to the Youth Criminal Justice Act were embedded in the 2011 Omnibus Bill C-10 (Safe Streets and Communities Act) which was enacted in March 2012, and were seen to lead to increased incarceration of young people, with longer sentences, and a rise in adult sentences (Justice for Children and Youth, 2011; Canadian Coalition for the Rights of Children, n.d). These harsher measures are inexplicable on any but ideological grounds, against the inarguable declines in youth crime outlined above.

Indeed, the reactions from other Anglo-American countries, including the UK, the US, and Australia, were of bewilderment, with all other countries favouring alternative measures to juvenile incarceration, which is proven to be both ineffective and costly (Paperny, 2012). In these times of neo-liberal cost-cutting, it is noted that youth incarceration is a costly alternative. For example, it costs £32 million a year, the equivalent of $49 million, to incarcerate 405 British youths for a year (Paperny, 2012). Earlier cost estimates from the province of Ontario put the cost of secure custody of a young offender at $167 per day while community supervision costs about one-sixth of this (*Law Now*, 1996, p. 12).

Community supervision falls under the "alternative measures" in the Young Offenders Act (1985), for offenders 12–17 years of age who would otherwise proceed to court. Instead, they are dealt with through "non-judicial community-based alternatives." There were 33,000 of these cases in 1997–1998 across Canada, excluding British Columbia. Participation rates are highest in the Prairies and lowest in Ontario. Most participants (70 percent) have been charged with property-related offences, with the majority of these being theft under $5,000. Only 8 percent were charged with violent offences. Cases of common assault, mischief, other property offences (e.g., arson, possession of stolen goods), and "other" Criminal Code offences (e.g., disturbing the peace) accounted for 7 percent each of the crimes. Community service is the most likely (22 percent) alternative measure, e.g., helping out in a non-profit community agency for a specified number of hours. Other measures include apologizing to the victim either personally or in writing (18 percent). Another category of measures (13 percent) involves financial compensation to the victim, educational sessions, and essays or presentations related to the offence. The least frequently used measures were personal service (2 percent) and counselling (1 percent) (Canadian Centre for Justice Statistics, 1997–1998).

The most likely offenders in these programs are males aged 15 years or older. While only 20 percent of youth charged and brought to court are female, they accounted for 36 percent of youth in alternative measures. Females tend to be younger on average than the males. Aboriginal youth, who form 4 percent of the youth population, are likewise overrepresented in the programs at 13 percent of all participants. The percentages are even higher in provinces such as Saskatchewan where Aboriginal youth account for 36 percent of the alternative measures cases, while they represent 15 percent of the province's youth population (Canadian Centre for Justice Statistics, 1997–1998).

Critics of Bill C-10 point out that it is particularly punitive toward marginalized populations. Nationwide in Canada, Aboriginal youth are incarcerated at eight times the rate of non-Aboriginal youth, with the rate as high as 30 times in the province of Saskatchewan. This has generally been recognized as a reflection of their historically marginalized status, combined with substance abuse and victimization. In their analysis of youth court data from five major cities across Canada, Latimer and Foss (2005, p. 481) show that Aboriginal youth tend to receive longer custodial sentences than non-Aboriginal youth "regardless of standard aggravating factors such as criminal history and offence severity." The authors conclude that discrimination is a factor.

These alternative measures make a lot of sense particularly because there is no evidence that long sentences deter youth crime. *Law Now* (1996, p. 12) points out that

> there is no evidence that longer sentences deter young offenders from future crime. There is growing evidence, however, that the type of social environment a young offender returns to will influence the likelihood of his or her returning to crime. Placing a young offender in an inappropriate (i.e., adult) corrections environment will likely reduce his or her likelihood of developing a normal life.

The consequences of the general pressure toward incarceration rather than rehabilitation are serious for young people. Totten (2009) summarizes research showing the particularly disastrous consequences for young Aboriginal people. North American research demonstrates convincingly that the chances of reoffending and staying in gangs are enhanced by incarceration. The irony of these conclusions should not be lost: what is the logic in using measures that increase rather than decrease the anti-social behaviour of marginalized young people?

Echoing the influential arguments of Schissel (1997) regarding moral panics over youth crime, Pate (1999, p. 40) notes:

> Rather than adopt a "zero violence" approach, "zero tolerance" policies are resulting in ever-increasing numbers of disenfranchised youth being jettisoned out of schools and communities, and usually through, rather than into, a thinning social safety net. Rather than nurturing our youth, we are increasingly scapegoating and disposing of them as though they were expendable human refuse.

The Criminalization of Marginalized Youth: Toronto's "Squeegee Kids"

The lives of street youth and their state of "familylessness" were addressed in part in Chapter 3. Additionally, Gaetz et al.'s (1999) study of street youth list a number of criminal behaviours used to make a living, such as breaking and entering or selling drugs (19 percent); social assistance (18 percent); or sex work, e.g., prostitution, escort services, stripping, or phone sex (10 percent). A surprisingly high percentage (21 percent) reported being employed at the time of the study, with 17 percent employed in the past three months. Similarly, although 10 percent reported the sex trade as their main economic activity, a much higher 31 percent of both men and women reported that they had engaged in one form of these activities at least once. In terms of criminal activity, 76 percent of the males and 52 percent of the females reported that they had been arrested at least on one occasion in the past, and another 63 percent and 36 percent, respectively, have served time in jail or a detention facility. Thus, there is a distinct connection between the duration of life on the streets and the likelihood of violent behaviours (Miller et al., 2004, p. 737).

A small but significant number of young people end up making their lives on the streets. Here, the subject of the informal "squeegee" work performed by these young people is taken up. Squeegee youth are young homeless people who earn their livelihood by offering to clean car windows at busy intersections in large urban centres, such as Edmonton, Calgary, Saskatoon, Montreal, Hamilton, and Toronto. Squeegee youth are the most marginalized of the youth population. They tend to be alienated not only from their families but also from the rest of society and the services geared to helping individuals who are homeless. This phenomenon is not just a product of the 21st century. As explained in Chapter 1, early stages of industrialization and urbanization led to the detachment of large numbers of youth. This process was then, as it is now, associated with fears of youth vagrancy and criminal activity.

As in the 20th century, street youth in the 21st century are also blamed for their precarious situations. Society on the whole has condemned squeegee-cleaning activity and culture. O'Grady et al. (1998, p. 315) argue that the public perception of Toronto's squeegee youth is that they are "tarnishing the image of the city, or more seriously, that these youths are responsible for elevating levels of violence in the urban core."

In response to that claim, many street youth advocates claim just the opposite. They argue that due to the visibility of squeegee youth, they themselves have become targets of police harassment. During the summer of 1998, a "war" was declared on squeegee youth. The attack was led by the mayor of Toronto, Mel Lastman, who was quoted as saying, "We're getting rid of the thugs.... The city is becoming safer and I like a safe city. And those who don't like it, it's too damn bad" (Spears, 1999).

The mayor created a law-and-order program that targets specific downtown areas with extra police whose purpose is to remove "squeegee kids, panhandlers and street criminals" (Nguyen, 1999, p. A18; Spears, 1999). The media overlooked the irony of his attacking homeless youth at the same time that the well-publicized interim report of the mayor's homelessness Action Task Force was released.

Following the mayor's initiative, the premier of Ontario, Mike Harris, joined the anti-squeegee bandwagon during the provincial election in the spring of 1999. In a bid to have "A Safer Ontario" (Progressive Conservative Party of Ontario, 1999, p. 27), the government of Mike Harris pledged to "stop aggressive panhandling by making threatening and harassing behaviour, such as blocking people on sidewalks, a provincial offence. We'll also give police the power to crack down on 'squeegee kids'" (Progressive Conservative Party of Ontario, 1999, p. 31). Local bylaws against squeegeeing are in place in Hamilton, Saskatoon, Edmonton, and Calgary. Ontario is the only government to pass a provincial law against this form of informal labour.

Bill 8, the Safe Streets Act, amends the Highway Traffic Act. It was passed by the Ontario Legislature on December 9, 1999, and was implemented on January 31, 2000. Under the new legislation, fines ranged from $500 for the first offence to $1,000 and/or six months in jail for repeat offenders. The Act made it illegal to engage in "aggressive panhandling" as well as stopping or approaching a "motor vehicle with the intent to offer, sell or provide any product or service." Andrew Bolter (1999), a London lawyer and poverty advocate, argues that "Harris's answer to the problem of poverty is to try to ban its visible manifestation; out of sight, out of mind." A Toronto lawyer, Edward Sapiano, and 30 of his colleagues offered to represent charged squeegee youth and challenge the Conservative government constitutionally all the way to the Supreme Court. Sapiano argued that "the challenge will turn on whether individuals are allowed to perform this type of job and whether the Constitution protects an individual's choice of employment" (*Cambridge Reporter*, 2000). On June 14, 2000, the lawyers were in court for the first time launching their constitutional challenge. Defence lawyer Peter Rosenthal argued that "the wording is so general it makes the simple act of asking a friend for money illegal" (*Toronto Star*, 2000a). The challenge failed, and the law was upheld in Ontario (CBC News, 2001).

Many poverty advocates, members of the Opposition, as well as squeegee youth are concerned that this law will force those affected by it into a life of crime. Liberal justice critic Michael Bryant argues that exactly that has occurred in Montreal, where "squeegee kids turned to prostitution, the drug trade and other crimes.… It's going to throw them into the revolving door of criminal justice" (*Cambridge Reporter*, 2000).

In fact, it has been shown that rather than being lazy and criminal, most street youth want to be gainfully employed. When involved in squeegeeing, this was the next best thing, "the most viable means of generating income that they are currently able to engage in" (Gaetz et al., 1999, pp. 19, 21). Further, O'Grady, Bright, and Cohen (1998, p. 319) found that rather than this activity leading people into crime and ruin, squeegee-cleaning street youth reported fewer criminal acts than non-squeegee street youth. These acts included: selling marijuana or other drugs (44 percent vs. 66 percent); breaking into a car or building (34 percent vs. 61 percent); taking something worth $50 or less (24 percent vs. 75 percent); damage to or destruction of property (30 percent vs. 60 percent); use of physical force to get money (39 percent vs. 59 percent); and getting into a fight "just for fun" (24 percent vs. 51 percent).

Thus, while left to conduct their squeegee work freely, these street youth compare positively with their non-working counterparts. There is a twisted logic in punitive acts that push marginalized youth further into the abyss.

"Nasty Girls": Gender and Youth Crime

Despite statistics to the contrary, there is a persistent myth prevalent about dramatically increasing crime, violence, and "gang activity" among young women (Pate, 1999). Over time, males have accounted for approximately 80 percent of all Canadian violent crime and they dominate at all age levels and are more likely to be repeat offenders (Jaffe & Baker, 1999, p. 23; Stevenson et al., 2000, p. 223). Girls accounted for 28 percent of youth crime charges as of 2009 (Mahony, 2011, p. 19). In the United States in 2011, women's arrests were 25.9 percent of all arrests, with 13.7 percent in the juvenile category of under 18 (National Criminal Justice Reference Services, 2012). Similar trends prevail in the UK, where 19 percent of offenders were women in 2002 (Youth Justice Board, 2009, p. 7).

There has been a lot of media attention over a seemingly dramatic increase in the number of violent crimes committed by women and girls. The increase in young women's crime rate in Canada was 128 percent from 1986 until 1994 (Kuryllowicz, 1996, pp. 20–23), while the violent crime rate of young males increased by 65 percent. Similarly, British statistics show a jump between 1992 and 2002 of 173 percent for women in custody, while men in custody increased by 50 percent (Youth Justice Board, 2009). In line with Canada and UK, young women formed 11 percent of juvenile arrests in the US in 1980, rising to 18 percent by 2000 and 30 percent in 2004 (Crime in America, 2010).

However, what is often neglected in the hype about increasing crime rates of girls is that the violent crime rate of female youth is still only a fraction of that of male youth, at about a third of the rate in Canada (Barron & Lacombe, 2005, p. 55). Canadian statistics show that not only are most crimes (around 80 percent) committed by men, but male youth tend to commit more serious violence, such as robbery and major assault (Paetch & Bertrand, 1999; Hung & Lipinski, 1995), while most female youth commit common assault. Female offenders tend to be younger than male youths, with peak years at 14–15, while young males peak at around 16–17 (Savoie, 1999; Stevenson et al., 2000, p. 223; Jaffe & Baker, 1999, p. 23). This pattern of higher young male crime rates is similar in the United States as well (Herrera & McCloskey, 2001).

Rates of crime among UK female youth are also lower than those of male youth. For example, the incidence of murder is considerably lower: In 1996 young males aged 19 or under were convicted for 22 murders, while only one young woman was convicted (Hill-Smith et al., 2002, p. 222). Similarly, though there has been a slight increase in reconviction rates of young women, they are still significantly lower than among young men (Jennings, 2002, pp. 2–3). Overall, though the gender gap in crime has narrowed since the 1950s, British juvenile delinquency is still overwhelmingly male. For example, males form about three-quarters of the 40 percent of crime committed by youth under 21 years of age, the highest crime rate being attributed to males 18–20. Women also have a lower peak age for offending (15) than men (18) and are likely to give up criminal behaviour earlier (Charles, 2002, pp. 110–111).

Canadian studies show that the types of crimes that young males and females commit are similar, with theft under $5,000 being the most common offence for both. The next most common charges for boys in 2000 were breaking and entering and common assault, while common assault and failure to appear in court were the next most common for girls (Stevenson et al., 2000, pp. 223–224). In general, there are isolated incidents of violence by young women, but the majority of the offences are non-violent (Corrado et al., 2000). Only 11 percent of all Canadian youth who kill are females. When women kill, the victims are more likely to be male and more likely to be a family member (Meloff & Silverman, 1992). Further, in 1995–1996, only 2 of the 44 cases of homicide were committed by girls (Doob & Cesaroni, 2004, pp. 132–137).

Most of the situations in which young women have been charged for violent crimes involve either defences against attackers or offences that have been reclassified as serious offences because of a zero-tolerance approach (Pate, 1999, p. 41). Thus, what is significant about the rising charges and convictions of young women is that the phenomenon is largely a reflection of changes in youth justice policy and charging practices. Despite the media and public image of girls run amok, there is little evidence to suggest that there is a criminal crisis among Canadian girls (Barron & Lacombe, 2005, pp. 51–52). In the UK, despite alarm over an increase in young female criminal offending and gang membership, the base rate is so low that the numbers remain relatively insignificant. Like Canadian researchers, Charles (2002, p. 111) points out that it is difficult to determine in the UK whether the changes are actual or represent a change in the treatment of female offenders.

Similar to British studies above, Wortley and Tanner (2006, pp. 31–32) found in their large study of Toronto youth gangs that females (6 percent) report much lower lifetime gang activity than males (17 percent), and that under 2 percent of females are currently gang members compared with 7 percent of males. Overall, criminal gangs are 80 percent male. The percentages are higher among street youth, with lifetime gang membership at 22 percent among females and 29 percent among males, and current gang membership at 11 percent among females and 16 percent among males. American studies indicate that girl gang membership is increasing, accounting for 10–30 percent of all gang members (Laidler & Hunt, 2001, p. 656; Bartollas & Miller, 2001, pp. 320–321). Girls join gangs for a number of reasons, including the need for social support in the absence of a financially and emotionally stable family or other social support mechanisms (Aapola et al., 2005, pp. 128–129). Female gang members are typically sexually exploited by the male gang members (Bartollas & Miller, 2001, p. 323).

Laidler and Hunt's (2001) longitudinal study involving interviews with over 600 girl gang members in the San Francisco Bay area found that in contrast to the "bad ass" image of girl gang members, the young women constructed a femininity that was based on the notion of respectability. A good reputation is something that they were willing to defend to the point of violence (aside from acting violently in other instances as well). They resort to "looking bad" instead of "being bad" in order to cope with their immediate environment as a protection against the patriarchy in their immediate lives with their families and their homeboys and their lovers. There are class and race differences in this as the members of largely White, middle-class girl gangs (who are benignly known as cliques or friendship groups in contrast to the working-class and racialized girl groups' more menacing label as gangs) have access to more resources and are able to defend their reputations through non-violent means such as social isolation of their critics.

British studies suggest that the lower involvement of girls in crime may be explained by their orientation toward marriage and motherhood. Young men, in contrast, associate masculinity with access to a wage. The pressures of the consumer society are thus greater on males, who may see themselves as failures unless they bring in money. Young men are, therefore, more likely to engage in crime as a reaffirmation of their masculinity in an environment in which legitimate means to gain money are unavailable (Charles, 2002, pp. 112–113).

In the United States, Schiff and McKay (2003) found that girls became more prone to aggression and delinquency by exposure to community violence, an effect that was moderated by maternal monitoring. The authors suggest that girls, compared to boys, need more connectedness and will turn to peers, even delinquent ones, when the connection to mothers is lacking.

Barron and Lacombe (2005) discuss the "Nasty Girl" phenomenon in the context of moral panics, the concepts of risk and risk management, and the backlash against feminism. The term "Nasty Girl" was coined by a CBC documentary in 1997 that examined high school girls' delinquent behaviour (see Box 8.3).

Barron and Lacombe's (2005; also see an American study by Laidler & Hunt, 2001, p. 657) analysis of the popular imagery of Nasty Girls as "folk devils" outlines how this false depiction of young women typifies "moral panics" through the distorted and sensationalized media depiction of rare and isolated acts of girl violence. This moral panic is rooted in a long history of depicting women criminal offenders as aberrations in conflict with the ideal of maternal and caring womanhood. Female aggression is equated with their claim for gender equality and its darker aspects: the masculinization of female crime patterns. Barron and Lacombe contend that this panic has had a "significant impact on legal, educational and social policy in Canada" (p. 59). For example, amidst one sensational case of girl violence, The Youth Criminal Justice Act (YCJA) came into effect in 2003 in Canada with measures for harsher treatment of violent youth.

Additionally, as discussed in Chapter 4 on education, there has been increased attention to school bullying. There is pressure to expand the definition to "teasing, gossiping, and quarrelling," behaviours typically associated with girls. School authorities and parents encourage "informal control of girls," reflecting the moral panic over girls "at risk" of becoming a threat to society (Barron & Lacombe, 2005, p. 61). Alongside this, hotlines have emerged that encourage a self-policing and surveillance by youth themselves, a measure that the authors claim encourages fear of youth and a victim mentality among young people. The authors conclude that the emergence of the moral panic over Nasty Girls coincides with the general anti-feminist backlash of the 1990s. As young women are increasingly becoming aware and acting on their autonomy through slogans such

---

Box 8.3: Nasty Girls

This excerpt from Barron and Lacombe's (2005, pp. 52–53) study outlines some of the roots of the "nasty girl" discourse:

> The expression, Nasty Girl, is not often used in journalistic or academic discourse on young female violence. It was, however, the title of a 1997 CBC documentary ("Nasty Girls," 5 March 1997) that examined high-school girls' experience of violence and incarceration (Barron, 2000: 81–85).... The documentary begins with old black-and-white film footage of two charming little girls playing with dolls.... The reassuring 1950s view of girls as essentially maternal and domestic is, however, shattered.... In the following scenes, we learn just how bad things have become.... The documentary proceeds to show how this metamorphosis from sweet to Nasty Girl is activated by a liking for gangsta rap music, rock videos, and teen magazines filled with scantily dressed fashion models. The disastrous effects of popular culture are illustrated by a succession of scenes of high-school girls pushing, kicking and fighting each other, followed by scenes of incarcerated girls being searched by guards or walking behind jail fences. This imagery is interspersed with shocking newspaper headlines announcing the increase in girl violence.... By disrupting social norms, popular culture has displaced the ideal role model of little girls—the mother/housewife—and thus produced a new species, the Nasty Girl, whose threat to the stability of our present and future society is only becoming apparent. The Nasty Girl, therefore, has become a folk devil in the 1990s.

---

as "girl power," their claims are mutated into "folk devils" that threaten the supposedly natural gender order.

This argument is supported by Aapola et al. (2005, pp. 48–53; see also pp. 128–130) whose discussion of the "mean girl" discourse in Europe and North America points to the emergence of school and community programs aimed at helping young women with their "aggression problems." While they provide some space for girls to "celebrate their girlhood," these programs also reinforce the view of girls as victims, as passive, and in need of rescue through the help of others or through individual self-improvement (e.g., anger management) rather than solutions addressing the sources of their legitimate collective anger over discrimination and sexism.

The real origins of the real phenomenon—the small minority of violent acts by young women—are not analyzed. These include the acknowledgement of the effects of economic and gender inequality and family violence in the lives of young female offenders, as well as the role of institutional racism (Artz, 1998, in Barron & Lacombe, 2005, pp. 57–58). And, as has been claimed by Faith and Jiwani (2002, in Barron & Lacombe, 2005, p. 58), it has passed by the media completely that racism may have been a factor in one of the most sensational cases involving girl violence: the brutal murder of Reena Virk, a teenager of Indo-Canadian origin, by a group of young male and female teens. These structural reasons for any violence require attention from both media and scholars.

Conclusions

There are distinct patterns in relation to youth and criminal or violent behaviour. First, youth are generally more likely to be victims than perpetrators of violence, a matter that will be discussed in more detail in Chapter 9 on health. Second, youth crime is generally decreasing and, third, it is less likely to be of a violent nature than adult crime. Fourth, young women continue to account for a fraction of violent crime despite media hype. Fifth, as exemplified in the case of Aboriginal and Black youth, there is widespread age-specific racism in the legal system, including police and the courts. And finally, only a small minority of youth engage in criminal or violent gang behaviours. Although there is a need to take these instances seriously, we also need to pay attention to youth as victims and not only as perpetrators of hate crime.

We also need to pay more attention to the structural conditions that marginalize youth, in order to find proper solutions that do not rely solely on a boot camp mentality toward young offenders. The widely prevalent "moral panics" over youth crime and violence manifest the generally negative experiences of youth in the new millennium. The fears are well founded in that the more poverty and discrimination people tolerate, the more likely it is that increasing numbers of youth will become victims of family violence, school estrangement, poor job prospects, and general community disintegration.

Critical Thinking Questions

1. Is collection of crime data based on racialized and ethnic status a good idea?
2. Should young offenders be treated the same as adults?
3. Should young female offenders be treated the same as young male offenders?

9 Health

In this chapter, you will learn that

- there are social determinants of physical and mental health for young people, based on their specific life conditions, including their social class, gender, and racialized status
- for young women, body image issues can lead to eating disorders
- the use of legal (alcohol, tobacco) and illegal (drugs) substances is normalized among youth
- the prevalence of sexually transmitted infections (STIs), including HIV/AIDS, continues among young people, linked to an information gap about use of condoms, transmission of STIs, and risky sexual practices, especially among the youngest sexually active youth
- young women continue to experience relationship violence, including date rape
- violence in families is a serious issue for young people
- marginalized youth face multiple health problems, including risk of sexual exploitation

The issue of health has emerged in many chapters of this book. As discussed, the education and work environments create health and safety concerns, including harassment and accidents. Likewise, while family life has many positive aspects, there are also health issues arising from that context, including family conflict and violence, with consequences for young people's mental, physical, and sexual health. Peer and intimate relations also hold the potential for violence, sexually transmitted infections (STIs), and substance use and abuse.

While some health issues were dealt with in the substantive chapters and in their specific institutional context, this chapter will give some more details about select areas of young people's health and well-being against the backdrop of different sets of power relations. Starting with the general state of young people's mental and physical health, this chapter will present information about a number of current health issues among youth, including body image, sexuality (condom use and STIs), violence in families and intimate relationships, and substance (tobacco, alcohol, and drugs) use. Finally, the multiplication of these concerns will be illustrated through a discussion of the health of marginalized and transient youth who occupy public urban spaces.

The State of Youth's Health

Health status is generally correlated with risks of morbidity and mortality, and is strongly predicted by social and economic inequality. The framework of Social Determinants of Health (SDH) (see Box 9.1; Mikkonen & Raphael, 2010; Raphael, 2009) has become nearly universally accepted for explaining health outcomes.

Box 9.1: Social Determinants of Health

Among the various models of the social determinants of health that exist, the one developed at a York University Conference held in Toronto in 2002 has proven especially useful for understanding why some Canadians are healthier than others. The 12 social determinants of health in this model are (Raphael, 2009, p. 7, Box 1.1):

Aboriginal status	health care services
early life	housing
education	income and its distribution
employment and working conditions	social exclusion
food security	social safety net
gender	unemployment and employment security

Each of these social determinants of health has been shown to have strong effects upon the health of Canadians. Their effects are actually much stronger than the ones associated with behaviours such as diet, physical activity, and even tobacco and excessive alcohol use.

Accordingly, researchers have shown that among young people, SDH explain more about health outcomes than mere attention to young people's risk behaviours, which are commonly identified without attention to the social conditions that lead toward those very behaviours (Woodgate & Leach, 2010). For example, North American research shows that, compared to low-income youth, high-income youth fare better in terms of health-related behaviours as well as self-reported health, growth, and obesity (Canadian Institute for Health Information, 2005). Youth from lower socio-economic categories suffer from a wide range of risk factors, including "substance abuse, sexual activity, delinquency, depression, and school problems" (Button & Rienzo, 2002, p. 3; see also National Center for Health Statistics, 2007). There are also well-documented gender differences in health status (see, e.g., Canadian Institute for Health Information, 2005), which will be discussed in more detail in the segments to follow.

Given the link between socio-economic status and health, a note is in order regarding access to health care. Canada and the UK have publicly funded health care systems while the United States does not. This means that in the US disparities prevail in access to health care and health insurance based on social class, race, and ethnicity. Meanwhile, the lives of racialized minorities (African American, Hispanic, and indigenous populations) manifest lower life expectancy, higher rates of risk factors, higher rates of chronic diseases, and higher levels of stress compared with White and well-to-do Americans. Youth are similarly underprivileged. In 2005, 16.4 percent of Americans under age 65 were uninsured, while a staggering 29 percent of youth aged 18–24 and 19 percent of children under age 18 were uninsured (National Center for Health Statistics, 2007). According to Button and Rienzo (2002, p. 3):

> About 12 million American youth are medically uninsured and millions of others have inadequate insurance that fails, for example, to cover even basic immunization necessary for school attendance. Studies also show that schools with poorer students report higher rates of unsafe school environments, another significant health risk for these children. Finally, according to a 1997 Institute of Medicine report (Eng and Butler, 1997), even adolescents with access to care rarely get help for problems of greatest importance, because most physicians are untrained and feel inadequate to address those issues. Those with mental health problems, which comprise a significant number of youth, go largely untreated (Allensworth et al., 1997).

However, publicly funded health care systems don't necessarily offer even levels of care across social categories. Health needs of specific populations are not always adequately addressed through the public health care system. For example, the Canadian Institute for Health Information (2005) reports language barriers to services among immigrant children and youth. There are also cultural differences in health behaviours among youth. Adolescent immigrants experience psychosocial adjustment issues based on the stresses of immigration and settlement, including discrimination, isolation, and intergenerational conflict (see also Chapter 3). Aboriginal youth, meanwhile, have suicide rates five to six times those among non-Aboriginal youth. American studies (Kaufman et al., 2004, p. 302) summarize the prevailing evidence of the poor state of health among Native American youth. Their lives are described as problem-filled through alcohol and drug use, suicide, and depression.

Thus, health outcomes among youth depend on their degree of closeness to or distance from mainstream institutions and lifestyles. Overall, we can conclude that good health outcomes for youth are likely if they belong in higher income categories, if they are male, and if they are White and non-immigrants. For example, in Canadian studies, good health status among youth is linked to good relations with and support from parents and engagement in school (Canadian Institute for Health Information, 2005), all of which tend to be characteristics of more advantaged populations.

Mental Health

Unacceptably large numbers of young people experience mental health problems, including depression and suicide. The many pressures of young people's lives, including school and work, sometimes create a situation in which a young person will find it difficult to function within the normal parameters of life. If, in addition, youth have problems with their parents, they are left without support from the family as the main social institution that is expected to be looking after them.

A British Medical Association (BMA) report (Monbiot, 2006) points to a steady deterioration in the mental health of children aged 5 to 16. Among the startling findings is that nearly one in ten (9.6 percent) of them suffer from persistent and severe psychological problems that affect their daily functioning, with more disorders among children living in poverty. Acts of self-harm are growing, with 11.2 percent of girls having committed acts like pulling out their hair, swallowing poison, or cutting or burning themselves. The BMA suggests that approximately 1.1 million British children under 18 years of age need counselling.

In the US, the Substance Abuse and Mental Health Services Administration (2006, pp. 7–8) reports that "serious psychological distress" was, in 2005, highest among those in the 18–25 age group. Also, about 13.7 percent (3.4 million) of youth 12–17 years of age had at least one "major depressive episode" in their lifetime, and 8.8 percent (2.2 million) of them had an episode in the past year. The report also notes the higher prevalence of psychological distress reported by girls (13.3 percent) in this age group than among boys (4.5 percent).

Results from Statistics Canada (1995, reported by the McCreary Centre Society, 1998) echo the gender-based findings: Depression among young women is nearly double (around 10 percent among those in their teens) that among young men, and the rates of depression and emotional distress rise from the earlier grades toward the end of high school (McCreary Centre Society, 1998; also see Sears & Armstrong, 1998). Bibby's (2001, pp. 36–38) survey of Canadian teens found that girls reported more negative mental health indicators than boys, including "feeling not as good as others" (43 percent vs. 27 percent), loneliness (33 percent vs. 25 percent), and depression (33 percent vs. 25 percent). A later survey from 2002 found that approximately one-quarter of boys and over one-third of girls in grade 10 reported feeling low at least once a week in the past six months (Canadian Institute for Health Information, 2005, pp. 30–32).

Studies also show that there are gender differences in the causes of depression. Girls' depression, for example, is often linked to anxiety whereas boys' depression is more frequently associated with substance abuse and anti-social behaviours (Sears & Armstrong, 1998). Similarly, the generally more positive rankings among young males of their state of emotional and psychological well-being can also be read as being part of the male code of behaviour in which expressions of weakness are frowned upon. This means that boys may be less likely to get help for their mental health issues as they mask their feelings (Pollack, 1998, in Bibby, 2001, p. 41).

The "stiff upper lip" among males may also explain why their suicide rates are higher than those among young women, who are more likely to seek help when they are feeling anxious or depressed. A mental health report from the World Health Organization (2001; see also Bridge et al., 2006; Haw & Hawton, 2007) shows that males in all OECD countries are more likely to commit suicide than females. The youth suicide rate is comparatively lower in the UK, with the suicide rate among males aged 15–24 at 8 percent and for young females at 2 percent. The Canadian and American rates are higher, particularly among young males. The rates for males aged 15–24 are around 16 percent in the US and around 17 percent in Canada while comparable rates among young females are around 4 percent in the US and 5 percent in Canada (Di Done, 2002). It is important to note that official statistics underestimate the actual rates because accidents (a leading cause of death among youth) and undetermined cases are not included. Some studies suggest that the rate may double or even triple if sources outside the official reports are used (Madge & Harvey, 1999; also see Links, 1998).

The Canadian adolescent suicide rate has increased fourfold since the 1960s, and is now one of the highest in the industrial world (Links, 1998). Similar to Canada, concern has emerged over the dramatic increases in rates of suicide among American adolescents. Suicide now ranks between second and third position in the list of causes of death among youth aged 13–19 (Watt & Sharp, 2002, pp. 232–236). Overall, the suicide rate of children in the US is twice the combined rate of children in 25 other industrialized countries (Reich et al., 2002, pp. 8–9). Comparisons of suicide rates in the three countries by age and sex are presented in Table 9.1.

Table 9.1: Youth Suicide Rates (per 100,000) by Age and Sex

Country	Year	5–14 Years			15–24 Years		
		M	F	All	M	F	All
Canada	2000[1]	1.4	0.9	1.1	20.2	5.5	13.0
	2004[2]	0.8	0.6	0.7	17.0	4.8	11.0
United Kingdom	1999[1]	0.1	0.0	0.1	10.6	2.5	6.7
	2009[2]	0.1	0.1	0.1	7.9	2.1	5.1
United States	2000[1]	1.2	0.3	0.7	17.0	3.0	10.2
	2005[2]	1.0	0.3	0.7	16.1	3.5	10.0

Sources:
1. Bridge et al. (2006).
2. World Health Organization (2012).

There are social conditions that facilitate different means of committing suicide. One of them is the degree to which guns are a prevalent part of the culture. As discussed in the preceding chapter on crime, guns are a bigger part of American lives than is the case in Canada or the United Kingdom. Gun violence in general exacts a cost in terms of the general mental health of children and youth. The trauma from gun violence, and particularly from directly experienced gun violence, is manifested in a range of psychological effects, including "sleep disturbance, anger, withdrawal, posttraumatic stress, poor school performance, lower career aspirations, increased delinquency, risky sexual behaviors, substance abuse, and desensitization to violence" (Reich et al., 2002, p. 11).

International comparisons of firearm suicides are revealing. While there are significant declines in firearm suicides in Canada, England, Wales, and Scotland, the rate of firearm suicides is several times those rates in the United States, where close to 60 percent of suicides involve the use of firearms (Adjacic-Gross et al., 2006). It is notable that in the United States in 1998, suicides by firearms accounted for 33 percent of all gun-related deaths among youth. Guns are used more frequently by youth than adults in committing suicide. The gun suicide rates are higher among White male adolescents and rural youth. Generally, the gun-related suicide rate among children 5 to 14 years of age is nearly 11 times higher than in any other industrialized country (Reich et al., 2002, pp. 8–9). Notably, the countries where firearm suicides are either stable or in decline are those with restrictive legislation related to the registration, licensing, and storage of guns (Adjacic-Gross et al., 2006).

It is notable that gun suicides among adolescent African-American males have risen sharply and are approaching the rates of White males (Reich et al., 2002, pp. 8–9). Males (1996, p. 34) reports generally higher suicide rates among Black adults and teens than among Whites. This represents a switch in a past trend. It has been a long-term paradox among African Americans that though they experience more social strain, their suicide rates have been lower than the rates for White Americans. The tide seems to have turned toward the beginning of this millennium.

Watt and Sharp (2002) suggest that the factors leading to suicide vary for different racial groups. In a large nationally representative sample in the United States, they show that 2–6 percent of the adolescents surveyed reported attempted suicides, the highest rates being for White females and the lowest for Black males. The study confirms the general finding that both Black and White females are more likely to attempt suicide than males. The authors conclude that the low rates of attempts among Black adolescent males show that status strain is not a risk factor for them, while it is a risk for White males and females. The measures that linked to Black males' suicide attempts were poor grades and relational strains, specifically feeling that their fathers or other adults don't care about them. For White males, wanting to leave home was linked to suicide attempts, while for White females the significant factors were poor or falling academic performance, the perception that they weren't socially accepted, and feeling that their parents don't care for them. For Black females, the significant predictive factors were feeling that it was their mothers who don't care for them and wanting to leave home. Feeling misunderstood by family is a predictor for both Black and White females.

Surprisingly, White females who lacked friends had fewer suicide attempts, suggesting that modelling suicide attempts in a peer group explains some young people's own attempts. Generally, the authors lend some support to the idea that "family and adult supports have been eroding in the Black community," resulting in increased suicides among Black adolescents. The study did not support the findings in the literature that religious attendance would suppress suicide attempts. This may be true for adults, but not for adolescents. The overall conclusion is that there are process differences between Black and White adolescents' suicide attempts.

As pointed out previously, suicides are a significant problem among North American indigenous peoples. Although there is wide variation based on geographic location, the suicide rates of Native Canadian youth on reserves are many times the national average (Chandler & Lalonde, 2008). The blame for these is put squarely on the legacy of colonialism, which has left these communities to struggle with no resources, no spirit, and at the mercy of financial mismanagement by misguided and unscrupulous leaders (Cheney, 1999; Barber, 1999). Young people commit suicide because they are left without any hope for improvements in the future, are often caught in a cycle of family violence, and engage in a range of self-destructive behaviours, including abuse of drugs, particularly sniffing of gasoline and solvents (Cox, 2000).

Based on all the patterns presented above, it is clear that there is a cluster of factors that explain suicides among youth, in keeping with the SDH approach that draws links between risk behaviours and the social conditions that generate them. There is a now well-established link between suicide and a number of situational "risk behaviours," i.e., those that challenge familial and social standards and pose some risk to their own or others' well-being. These include alcohol and drug use (to be further discussed below), school misconduct, and anti-social acts. Depression in youth rarely occurs on its own. It is usually experienced at the same time as anxiety, conduct disorder, substance abuse, and eating disorders. The majority of those who are depressed also suffer from other afflictions (Sears & Armstrong, 1998; Blum & Harmon, 1992; Watt & Sharp, 2002, pp. 232–236; Bridge et al., 2006). Several predictors of suicide have been identified, amounting to negative mental health correlates: depression, low self-esteem, economic and family strains, school difficulties, and isolation from peers. Significantly, a past history of attempted suicides is the best predictor of future attempts and completed suicides (Watt & Sharp, 2002, pp. 232–236).

The instability of family life and absence of support, combined with economic and social isolation, can lead to increased vulnerability of youth to mental illness. A general lack of social networks is detrimental (Picard, 2005; Canadian Institute for Health Information, 2005). As mentioned in Chapter 6, youth who are gay, lesbian, or bisexual have been found to have unusually high levels of suicide. This has been linked to a number of risk factors, including substance abuse, family rejection, and general victimization (Bridge et al., 2006).

Further, in keeping with the SDH framework, institutionally rooted discrimination based on race, sex, religion, or other characteristics is a contributing factor, as are cultural or political patterns that are not supportive of family life (Cochrane,

1988; King et al., 1988, p. S46). If this is the case, youth may not be any worse off than adults in similar situations. Indeed, Males (1996, pp. 29–30) argues that the so-called suicide epidemic among teens is mostly due to improved recording. Instead, Males suggests that the rates may have declined, as have other poor mental health indices among youth.

The difference is that young people are less equipped than adults to identify mental health problems and to pursue the help they need. They rely on adults to pay attention and to follow up with supports. According to Di Done (2002, p. 16):

> Suicide is frequently related to alcohol and substance abuse, which often stem from alienation, social exclusion and the breakdown of the family, and the inadequacy of state prevention and protective measures.... Support programs are either inadequate or insufficient to address the particular needs and behavioral changes ... during the high-risk period of adolescence. Again [this reflects] the low status of youths within our societies and their low priority on the political agenda.

Girls in Crisis: The Ophelia Discourse
In 1994, Mary Pipher's book, *Reviving Ophelia: Saving the Selves of Adolescent Girls*, launched a discussion on the crisis of girlhood in America, characterized by a pressure for them "to be someone they are not." They take a hit in adolescence, manifested in low self-esteem, a drop in IQ and mathematics scores, and a general loss in mental and physical alertness and energy. The road to Pipher's work was paved by previous work by Carol Gilligan (1982, in Aapola et al., 2005, p. 43) in which she outlined the "crisis in self-esteem" among adolescent girls. This work, compounded by that of Pipher, created a discourse that focused on the vulnerability of girls, particularly those in the White middle class (Aapola et al., 2005, pp. 41–45).

Aapola et al. (2005, pp. 45–55) laud the work that has increased attention to girls' mental health problems, including low self-esteem, eating disorders, depression, and risky behaviours. At the same time, they are also critical of a discourse that focuses on middle-class White girls who are seen to be deserving of our sympathy and whose problems can be individually addressed through therapy and different support programs. What is neglected are the issues facing girls who are marginalized based on social class and race, and the social structural conditions of inequality that are at the root of their problems. It was only much later that subsequent work focused on and found racial differences with regard to girls' self-esteem, with, for example, African-American girls more likely to retain their self-esteem than White or Latina girls.

Body Image
Western culture is obsessed with the body, and young people are bombarded with messages about the right kind of body (Aapola et al., 2005, pp. 157–159). Media messages about femininity were discussed in the chapter on peers and youth culture. Here, body image will be taken up as an important health issue, together with general preoccupation with appearance (beauty) as a central self-esteem issue among girls.

One of the central elements in this discussion is the glamourization and sexualization of youth culture, and particularly the ways in which youthful female bodies are displayed in media, advertising, pornography, and popular culture (Belyea & Dubinsky, 1994, pp. 29–30; Zurbriggen et al., 2007; Aapola et al., 2005, pp. 141–144; Hill, 2006). Music videos are particularly influential in creating an image that young women cannot possibly measure up to. Two British studies (reported by Bell et al., 2007, p. 143) measuring the impact of music videos show that

> adolescent girls exposed to thin models in music videos show a significantly larger increase in body dissatisfaction from pre- to post-exposure in comparison to girls who have listened to the songs without visual input.

This objectification of a specific type of "ideal" female body can lead young women to feel inadequate. For example, a survey conducted in 2000 by the teenage magazine *Bliss* found that only 8 percent of British teenage girls were happy with their bodies (Barton, 2005, in Hill, 2006, p. 376).

Most recently, there has been increasing concern with the health effects of obesity among young people (Wills et al., 2006), with their sedentary lifestyles in front of the screen to blame. For example, between 1981 and 1996, obesity rates more than doubled among Canadian girls (from 5 percent to 12 percent) and tripled for boys (from 5 percent to nearly 15 percent) (Tremblay & Willms, 1996, in Bibby, 2001, pp. 38–39). Though there are reasonable health concerns associated with being overweight, when linked with feminine concerns and pressures, the issue becomes less about health and more about the politics of appearance.

Preoccupation with appearance is common among young women, and weight preoccupation is one of the most common issues (Rossiter, 2000; Marchessault, 2000; Lafrance et al., 2000). The social ideal is a thin body, as seen in the high levels of dieting among young women. It is also reflected in the increased incidence of eating disorders such as anorexia.

Bibby's (2001, pp. 36–37) study found that Canadian teen girls are more concerned than boys both about their looks (51 percent vs. 38 percent) and weight (45 percent vs. 21 percent). Bibby (2001, p. 39) also found that nearly one-quarter of Canadian teen girls and approximately 7 percent of boys indicated they were "currently dieting." Similarly, an American survey of high school girls found that 34 percent of girls and 22 percent of boys saw themselves as overweight, and close to two-thirds of schoolgirls were trying to lose weight. Some racial differences appeared as White and Hispanic girls' body image was less positive than among African-American girls (Vobejda & Perlstein, 1998).

Eating disorders are more prevalent in North America than ever before, particularly among young women in their teen and young adult years (Belyea & Dubinsky, 1994, pp. 29–30; Zurbriggen et al., 2007; Aapola et al., 2005, pp. 141–144; Hill, 2006). In North America, 17 is the average age of onset for anorexia. It is estimated that there are approximately 5 million American (90 percent of them women) who suffer from anorexia and bulimia. The health toll is enormous; approximately 5 percent are expected to die and only half will make full recovery. About one-third of the bulimics will have recurrences during their lifetime (Lafrance et al., 2000, p. 227). There are complex socially created factors behind women's poor body image and associated eating disorders, further discussed in Box 9.2.

As Bibby (2001, pp. 37–38) points out, the problem is the continuation of the double standard that values women for their looks and men for their accomplishments. This cultural value, rooted in structural gender inequality, is to blame for the higher degree of eating disorders, including anorexia and bulimia, among girls and women. Kate Rossiter (2000, pp. 194–202) recounts her personal story of weight obsession:

> Once I had joined Weight Watchers, weekly weigh-ins and pep talks (for a stiff fee) marked my supposed progression towards happiness. But as I grew closer and closer to my ideal weight, a strange thing happened: the thinner I became, the more unhappy I felt with myself. What once may have been my "dream" body now looked to me as lumpy and fat as my "old" body. I still wasn't quite perfect. Despite my weight loss I still had not learned to accept myself. In fact, the constant body/ mind competition set out by Weight Watchers led me to further criticize my shape and size. In truth, it didn't matter what size my body was: I was stuck in an obsessionally [*sic*] self-hating mind frame which was supported by the world around me. After losing 30 pounds (13.6 kilograms), it seemed only reasonable to set my goal weight another 10 pounds (4.5. kilograms) lower. As a result, I was aware of everything I put in my mouth.

This is likely to strike a familiar chord with a lot of young women and some young men. If it does, it is time to seek counselling and support. Unlike so many others, Kate was fortunate enough to recover from her weight obsession, fat phobia, and self-loathing, albeit only after she became bulimic, which shocked her into seeking help. She also became angry at the societal pressures for young women to be thin, began to speak publicly, and founded a body-image support and awareness group at her university (Rossiter, 2000).

In the most extreme, the preoccupation with appearance and body-image significantly affects the numerous young people whose bodies and/or features are seen not to be "normal" or normative: people with disabilities and socially constructed deformities. Whittington-Walsh (2006) recounts the story of Ani, a young Canadian woman with a port-stain mark on her face. Ani has struggled all her life with outsiders' reactions to her facial difference. Since childhood, she has been subjected to attempts at changing her appearance, first through medical interventions that were based on labelling her as abnormal and hence in need of correcting, and then through the use of cosmetics to camouflage her face. Whittington-Walsh situates the violence squarely in both the ideal of White beauty and the consumerism of Western patriarchal capitalist societies. She paints a portrait of attempts in Western history to correct perceived flaws in the human face, in order to attain a mythological, racialized standard of beauty. She also addresses

Box 9.2: About Eating Disorders

This segment from a US government site (womenshealth.gov, 2013) illustrates the causes and perils of body image issues and eating disorders.

"Mirror, Mirror on the wall…who's the thinnest one of all?" According to the National Eating Disorders Association, the average American woman is 5 feet 4 inches tall and weighs 140 pounds. The average American model is 5 feet 11 inches tall and weighs 117 pounds. All too often, society associates being "thin," with "hard-working, beautiful, strong, and self-disciplined." On the other hand, being "fat" is associated with being "lazy, ugly, weak, and lacking will-power." Because of these harsh critiques, rarely are women completely satisfied with their image. As a result, they often feel great anxiety and pressure to achieve and/or maintain an imaginary appearance.

Eating disorders are serious medical problems. Anorexia nervosa, bulimia nervosa, and binge-eating disorder are all types of eating disorders. Eating disorders frequently develop during adolescence or early adulthood, but can occur during childhood or later in adulthood. Females are more likely than males to develop an eating disorder.

Eating disorders are more than just a problem with food. Food is used to feel in control of other feelings that may seem overwhelming. For example, starving is a way for people with anorexia to feel more in control of their lives and to ease tension, anger, and anxiety. Purging and other behaviors to prevent weight gain are ways for people with bulimia to feel more in control of their lives and to ease stress and anxiety.

Although there is no single known cause of eating disorders, several things may contribute to the development of these disorders:

- *Culture.* In the United States extreme thinness is a social and cultural ideal, and women partially define themselves by how physically attractive they are.
- *Personal characteristics.* Feelings of helplessness, worthlessness, and poor self-image often accompany eating disorders.
- *Other emotional disorders.* Other mental health problems, like depression or anxiety, occur along with eating disorders.
- *Stressful events or life changes.* Things like starting a new school or job or being teased and traumatic events like rape can lead to the onset of eating disorders.

> - *Biology.* Studies are being done to look at genes, hormones, and chemicals in the brain that may have an effect on the development of, and recovery from eating disorders.
> - *Families.* Parents' attitudes about appearance and diet can affect their kids' attitudes. Also, if your mother or sister has bulimia, you are more likely to have it.

the attitudinal violence that Ani has been subjected to all her life, ranging from jeering and name-calling to being subjected to the public "gaze." In Ani's own words (Whittington-Walsh, 2006, p. 18):

> I don't like being stared at on the subway.... On the subway it is another interest other than me ... they are just staring at the physical me. It makes me uncomfortable and uneasy because they can't know who I really am. I feel that people are looking right at the surface and at the same time looking right through me because to them I don't exist—I am just a "thing" to look at.

Whittington-Walsh likens the physical and emotional components of the medical gaze and public gaze to fascism, which significantly moulded Ani's self-image and resulted in a combination of reactions ranging from shame, fear, and sadness, to anger and resistance. Ani began to fight back: She refused to cover up her port-stain mark and began to challenge those who objected to her appearance.

That young people and particularly young women can express their resistance in their bodies is something that is noted by Aapola et al. (2005, p. 159), who point to tattooing, scarification, and piercing as common practices that are both beautification and political statements. Permanent tattoos and body piercings are becoming more common; according to Bibby (2001, pp. 71–73), 19 percent of Canadian teen girls and 6 percent of boys have piercings other than their ears, and 10 percent of girls and 7 percent of boys have tattoos. There is also a great deal of overlap in the two categories.

Aapola et al. (2005, p. 77) draw a link between issues of body image, appearance, and well-being and the lack of actual opportunities in society. The authors, citing work of many other scholars, note that since the returns for education and finding fulfilling work opportunities are diminished for young women, they focus on their appearance. In other words, self-improvement programs are a logical response to diminished returns; at least weight or beautification projects are aspects of life that young women feel they can control.

The Use of Legal and Illegal Drugs

The concern around substance use by youth is that it has become normalized, i.e., that previously stigmatized behaviours are becoming a part of everyday life and become "increasingly accommodated and perhaps eventually valued" (Parker, 2005, p. 205). There is ample evidence to show that this may be the case, particularly where social activities with peers are concerned. As is seen in the example of raves (Chapter 7), smoking, drinking, and doing drugs are associated with youth and particularly with spending time with peers. Here, the use of legal drugs (alcohol and tobacco) and illicit (street) drugs will be given a closer look.

General patterns of substance use and abuse vary by social class, gender, race, and ethnicity. Males tend to be more likely users of drugs and alcohol, particularly in younger age groups (Single et al., 1994; Van Roosmalen & Krahn, 1996; Jayakody et al., 2006). Men are also more likely to be smokers than women, except in age groups under 20, where young women are more likely to smoke than young men (Statistics Canada, 1996–1997). There is some evidence for a different pathway toward substance addiction among girls and boys. A report in an American newspaper (Barrett, 2003) proposes a gender-based trend in substance addiction:

> Girls and young women get hooked on cigarettes, alcohol and drugs more quickly and for different reasons than boys and should receive specialized treatment that reflects that, according to a study.… Teen girls often begin smoking and drinking to relieve stress or alleviate depression, while boys do it for thrills or heightened social status, according to the National Center on Addiction and Substance Abuse at Columbia University. [Girls] get hooked faster, they get hooked using lesser amounts of alcohol and drugs and cocaine, and they suffer the consequences faster and more severely, said Joseph Califano Jr., center chairman. Califano said prevention and treatment centers need to deal with the risk factors leading to female substance abuse. The study, based on a nationwide survey of more than 1,200 females aged 8 to 22, found little difference in the percentage of boys and girls who smoke, drink and use drugs. Approximately 45 percent of high school girls drink alcohol, compared with 49 percent of boys, and girls outpace boys in the use of prescription drugs, the study found.

Substance use patterns also show a link with race and ethnicity. While the specific issues related to this will be discussed below in relation to different drug types, the marginalized populations have been identified throughout this book. Thus, among Canadian minority populations, concerns have been raised over tobacco use of French Canadian youth (Government of Canada, 1998), and the abuse of drugs, tobacco, and alcohol among Aboriginal youth (Single et al., 1994; Government of Canada, 1998). British and American studies also indicate that immigrant youth are less likely to use illicit and traditional drugs than are longer-term residents, indicating that acculturation is a factor (Jayakody et al., 2006, p. 337).

The pattern that arises from the studies and statistics, presented in more detail below, is that although youth indulge in various drugs as a part of peer culture, the proportions of heavy users are low. Furthermore, heavy substance use tends to be specifically linked to lower socio-economic status, accompanied by adverse family circumstances, including abuse. Among marginalized groups, use of drugs is higher than average overall, not only among young people (Vertinsky, 1989; Single et al., 1994). Unemployed people and street youth are particularly vulnerable (Single et al., 1994), and their multiple health problems will be discussed separately.

Illegal Drugs

Notably, while among adults, abuse of prescription drugs (tranquilizers, sleeping pills, codeine, anti-depressants, and the like) is relatively common, it is much rarer among youth (Single et al., 1994). It is difficult to get reliable data on illegal drug use for obvious reasons.

Illegal drug use among Canadian youth is generally low and declining (Health and Welfare Canada, 1992; Stewart, 2002). Notably, the majority of youth, 63 percent of males and 69 percent of females, do not use any drugs. In the age group 15–16, 87 percent of males and 84 percent of females indicate no use. The figures are 71 percent and 73 percent for males and females in the age group 17–19, and 50 percent and 63 percent in the age group 19–24 (Hewitt et al., 1995).

In 2005, 9.8 percent of American youth aged 12–17 used illicit drugs (Substance Abuse and Mental Health Services Administration, 2006, p. 2). Similarly to the Canadian pattern, after a decade of rising rates, illegal substance use among American adolescents has stabilized and perhaps declined (Stewart, 2002, p. 99). Notably, in keeping with the higher prevalence of drug use among adults than youth, American studies show that the adult death rate from drugs is nearly 10 times that of adolescents, and only 1.1 percent of drug overdoses, suicides, and drug-related accidents in 1993 involved children and teens (Males, 1996, p. 24).

In the UK, illicit drug use among youth increased in the 1990s to the degree that they became known as "the most drug involved in Europe" with rates in the range of 30 percent for mid-adolescents. Nationwide, boys in the age group 15–16 are more likely to take drugs than girls in the same age group, at 40 percent and 33 percent, respectively. After the period of increase, drug use seems to have levelled off (Eddington & Parker, 2002, p. 98).

Eddington and Parker (2002) studied substance use patterns among British youth in the northern regions. They report that, in 1999, nearly half of the youth in the age group 16–17 had never taken drugs, just under 16 percent had experimented, around 22 percent reported being light users, and around 13 percent reported to be either moderate or regular users, with nearly even distribution between the two. The authors also report that only around 3 percent of youth have significant drug involvement in early adolescence (12–13 years of age), compared to 13 percent among older adolescents. This may increase to around 20 percent by age 17.

When drugs are used by youth, the most common one is marijuana, which is used by 19 percent of Canadian males and 12 percent of females in the age group 15–24 (Hewitt et al., 1995). In 2001–2002, nearly one in every three 12–17-year-olds said that they had tried marijuana while 13 percent had tried other drugs, such as cocaine or crack (Canadian Institute for Health Information, 2005, p. 32). Use of more serious street drugs (e.g., crack, speed) by young people aged 15-24 declined between 2004 and 2011, from 11.7 percent to 4.8 percent (Health Canada, 2011). Drug use is more common among younger age groups and generally declines with age (McCreary Centre Society, 1998; Health and Welfare Canada, 1992; Health Canada, 2011).

There was a reported decline in marijuana use among Americans aged 12–17 from 7.6 percent in 2004 to 6.8 percent in 2005 (Substance Abuse and Mental Health Services Administration, 2006, p. 2). The use of the so-called "dance drugs" (amphetamines, ecstasy, and cocaine) is less common among UK youth as well, at 10 percent among 16–17 year olds, while the drug of choice is cannabis (Eddington & Parker, 2002, p. 112; see also Jayakody et al., 2006), in keeping with the drug use patterns of North American youth.

As in the case of alcohol use (see below), drug use is more common among marginalized groups, such as street youth and runaways, and school dropouts (Health and Welfare Canada, 1992; Canadian Centre on Substance Abuse, 1999; Brands et al., 2005). For example, one study found that while approximately 30 percent of Canadian university students used cannabis, 92 percent of street youth did. Likewise, the corresponding percentages for cocaine use among university students and street youth were, respectively, 4.5 percent and 64 percent; for crack, under 0.5 percent and 39 percent; and for LSD, 2.6 percent and 70 percent (Single et al., 1994).

Among African-American adolescents, marijuana has recently increased in prevalence (Stewart, 2002, p. 100). Also parallel to the pattern with alcohol, drug use is more common among First Nations, with solvents (paint thinners, glue, and gasoline) among the major substances used (Single et al., 1994). In the United States, Whitesell et al. (2007) report that marijuana use among Native American youth may be highest among all American ethnic groups.

Aside from the most marginalized racialized groups, such as indigenous peoples, British and American studies find that drug use varies significantly among racialized and immigrant groups. In Britain, for example, the use of illicit drugs is low among Bangladeshi, Pakistani, and Indian youth. Young South Asians tend to be at a lower risk of using cannabis or amphetamines, while Bangladeshi youth have higher than average levels of glue/gas/solvent use. The drug use levels of Black Caribbean youth are higher than those among White British youth or Black British youth, while the drug use rates of Black African youth are comparable to those of Bangladeshi youth. Further, youth who immigrated within the previous five years had a lower drug use rate, suggesting that longer-term residents are at a heightened risk of drug use (Jayakody et al., 2006, p. 336).

There are treatment programs available for youth who are addicted to hard drugs such as heroin. However, Brands et al. (2005) report high attrition rates in North American drug use treatment programs for youth, particularly for homeless youth, who are at significant risk for associated mental and physical illnesses. Many youth are willing to enter a drug treatment program, but those have to be better designed to reach young people. There also seems to be a gender difference in the help-seeking behaviours of youth as young women are more willing to discuss their multiple problems and are more likely to seek help from others.

In addition to factors related to poverty and marginalization, American studies have linked substance abuse to negative factors in the family environment; overly harsh or lax parenting styles tend to contribute to a range of problems, including drug abuse. Positive parenting and parental monitoring are protective factors. Further, family structure—whether families have two parents or one—is not as important as the quality of the adolescent-parent relationship. Additionally, role modelling seems to have an effect; youth are more likely to abuse substances if their significant family members do so (Stewart, 2002, pp. 99–100).

Alcohol

Drinking alcohol is common among youth. For example, in 2011, 70.8 percent of Canadians aged 15 to 24—the same rate as among all people over age 15—reported having consumed alcohol in the past year, a decline from 82.9 percent in 2004 (Health Canada, 2011).

American adolescents demonstrate that this age group is where it commonly starts: approximately 50 percent of boys and girls have had at least one drink of alcohol by age 15, while 90 percent have done so by age 21 (US Department of Health and Human Services, 2007, p. 3). There is reason for alarm regarding teen drinking patterns. According to Vertinsky (1989, p. 9), 12 percent of Canadian youth begin drinking regularly at age 15. In 2002, 31 percent of Canadian youth in grade 9 and 44 percent of those in grade 10 reported having alcohol and getting drunk at least twice (Canadian Institute for Health Information, 2005, p. 32). There are American studies showing that 10 percent of children as young as 9 or 10 have started drinking (US Department of Health and Human Services, 2007, pp. 4–6).

Alcohol use is more prevalent than before also among British youth 11–15 years of age, having doubled in 14 years (Monbiot, 2006). British children in the age group 11–15 reported having drunk alcohol in the last week. In the UK, regular heavy drinking of a wider range of alcohol types by adolescents increased in the 1990s. Drinking tends to increase between the early and late teen years. In 1999, around 67 percent of 16–17-year-olds were weekly drinkers (Eddington & Parker, 2002, pp. 104–105).

North American males are more likely in all age groups to drink than females, and single young males are particularly likely to engage in high-volume drinking (Single et al., 1994, pp. 17–18; US Department of Health and Human Services, 2007, p. 8). The bigger volume of alcohol consumed by boys than girls is supported by British statistics, with 34 percent of boys and 25 percent of girls reporting weekly drinking (Association of Public Health Observatories, 2006, p. 57).

Earlier studies suggest that problem drinking is infrequent among young Canadians, and tends to be of the high volume (binge) variety (Hewitt et al., 1995). A similar pattern of binge drinking is found in the UK, where, in 2003, a significant portion (over 55 percent) of 15–16-year-olds reported having at least one binge-drinking episode in the past 30 days (US Department of Health and Human Services, 2007, 7; Eddington & Parker, 2002).

Also, more frequent and heavier drinking is more common among those in their early twenties rather than among teenagers. This may be partly explained by the higher numbers of people in their twenties who attend university and live away from parental controls on their behaviour (Hewitt et al., 1995). This proposal gains support from American data indicating that binge drinking rates peak around age 18–21, or when large numbers of young people are enrolled in college (Eddington & Parker, 2002; US Department of Health and Human Services, 2007, pp. 4–7). Just over 12 percent of 18–20-year-olds in the United States are described as having "alcohol dependence" (US Department of Health and Human Services, 2007, pp. 4–6).

Single et al. (1994) report that youth give many reasons for drinking alcohol. A study of New Brunswick youth found that the most often cited reason is curiosity ("to see what it is like"), followed by peer influence ("because friends drink"), for fun, to escape worries, because there was nothing else to do, and to feel good. Studies in Newfoundland and Labrador found that the most common reason was "to be sociable," followed by "to relax," "to feel good," "to forget worries," "to feel less shy," and "to add to the enjoyment of meals." These studies indicate a strong peer influence, also confirmed in other studies (e.g., Vertinsky, 1989; Hewitt et al., 1995; Coleman & Cater, 2005).

Coleman and Cater's (2005, pp. 129–130) interviews of 14–17-year-old binge-drinkers in the UK reveal similar motivations behind binging, including increasing one's comfort level in social situations, liking the "buzz," and peer pressure. For example:

> Sometimes I can be quite shy around new people.... When I'm drunk, I'm not like really over-friendly or anything but I can, I'll be like, Hi I'm Kate, who are you, blah, blah, blah. And you can talk to different people.... Yeah, it kind of opens doors. (Kate, 15)

> Peer pressure, 'cos I was hanging around the older kids and I thought, well, everyone else is doing it, why not. And it is a case of everyone else doing it, you feel, I better do this one, or I'm not going to be in with the crowd ... it was a case of having to 'cos everyone else was doing it and you didn't want to be out the group, you didn't want to be out the circle. (Maisie, 16)

> Probably just because everyone else did it and I wanted to be a part of them. It's not that I follow everyone else ... it's probably just because it's something that everyone does, innit, really? (Pete, 14)

In keeping with studies on illegal drug use (above), there are differences among youth based on ethnicity, race, and immigrant status. Both alcohol and tobacco use rates are lower among immigrant youth than among Canadian-born, but rates increase with longer residence. Partly this is a reflection of peer influence. As newcomers, youth may not have as many peers as those who have been in Canada longer (Canadian Council on Social Development, 2000, p. 7). Youth, including immigrants and longer-term residents, may also be influenced by religion. For example, Islam does not allow the drinking of alcohol; studies in this area are scarce, but one American study found that the rate of alcohol use among Muslim students is about half that of non-Muslim students (Abu-Ras et al., 2010).

American studies show a great deal of variety in drinking patterns between different racialized and ethnic groups. As of 2006, official statistics show that though all youth have high alcohol use patterns, African Americans and Asians tend to drink the least, while the rates of alcohol abuse are the highest among Whites, followed by indigenous populations (Native Americans, Alaska Natives, Native Hawaiian, other Pacific Islanders) and Hispanic or Latino youth. Stewart (2002, p. 100) reports that studies from the late 1990s indicate that although Black adolescents may generally drink less than their White counterparts, they may actually be more likely to engage in heavy drinking (Stewart, 2002, p. 100).

There are a number of adverse health consequences from alcohol consumption by youth, including motor vehicle accidents and other injuries, assaults, risky sexual behaviours, abnormal brain development, internal organ problems, and increased chances for abusing other substances such as tobacco and illicit drugs. All of these consequences carry heavy costs. For example, American studies show that approximately 1,700 college students die annually from alcohol-related injuries, including car crashes; about 600,000 are injured while under the influence, an added 700,000 are assaulted by other students while drinking, and about 100,000 are subject to sexual assault or date rape (US Department of Health and Human Services, 2007, pp. 10–13; see also Donnelly, 2007).

The youth in the Coleman and Cater (2005, pp. 131–132) qualitative study of alcohol use among UK teens reported a number of adverse health outcomes, expressed in the following statements by youth:

> I tripped over a wall, dislocated my kneecap went from the right round to the back, I cut my chin open and think [I] fractured my elbow or something, and I had to get rushed to the hospital.... I have done everything, and drinking is really bad. (Jane, 17)

> Some guy down [name of town] punched one of my mates in the face. And I went after him and he just pulled a knife out. And if I hadn't been drunk I probably wouldn't have gone after him. So that was pretty awful. But, there is something about being drunk that does trigger you off, because I hate violence. I can't stand it. But if I do see someone I don't particularly like at all, and I'm very drunk ... (Scott, 15)

Tobacco

One of the major areas of concern related to drug use among youth is tobacco. There are a wide variety of tobacco products available, including smokable varieties (cigarettes, cigars, pipes, bidis, kreteks, hookah/sheeshah), as well as non-smoking varieties (chewing tobacco, snuff). In this section, the focus will be on cigarette smoking, with a note that some of the statistics may include all tobacco products.

Smoking is prevalent among youth in the UK, with 1 percent of 11-year-olds and 21 percent of 15-year-olds identifying themselves as regular smokers (Association of Public

Health Observatories, 2006, p. 53). Approximately one-fifth of the Canadian population under age 20 are regular smokers (Hewitt et al., 1995). However, there are reports of some decline in smoking in the early 21st century, particularly among teens; as of 2003, 18 percent of Canadian teens smoked, down from 22 percent in 2002 (Canadian Institute for Health Information, 2005, p. 32). More recent findings show a decline in smoking by young people in grades 6–9 (aged 11–14) to 2 percent, from 3 percent in 2004, and a similar decrease among those in grades 10–12 (aged 15–17), from 13 percent to 10 percent (Health Canada, 2012).

Smoking is also common among American youth. Close to 47 percent of them have tried smoking by grade 12, with 22 percent of youth in grade 12 reporting that they are regular smokers. About a quarter of those in grade 8 have tried cigarettes and 9 percent are smokers (Johnston et al., 2006, p. 9). Similarly to Canada, smoking among 12–17-year-old Americans decreased from the 1970s onward (Males, 1996, p. 24), with further declines in this century, from 13 percent in 2002 to 10.8 percent in 2005 (Males, 1996, p. 24; Substance Abuse and Mental Health Services Administration, 2006, p. 4).

The gender gap has closed as more young women take up smoking. In the UK, more girls (10 percent) than boys (7 percent) in the 14–15 age category report being regular smokers (Association of Public Health Observatories, 2006, p. 53). Among Canadian teens, the gender gap in smoking is also relatively small. In 2008–2009, 4 percent of boys and 3 percent of 11–14-year-olds indicated being smokers, while the percentages were 13.1 and 11.3 among 15–17-year old boys and girls, respectively (Reid et al., 2012, p. 2). In the US, based on reports from the Centers for Disease Control and Prevention, 30 percent of boys and 18 percent of girls in the high school age groups use tobacco, and in middle school in 2011, the reports showed 8 percent and 5 percent for boys and girls, respectively (Sifferlin, 2012).

The use of tobacco products is higher among Canadian Aboriginal youth. For example, by the time they are 19 years old, 71 percent of Inuit and 63 percent of Dene and Métis in the Northwest Territories are smokers, with higher rates for females than males. The highest rate for smokers is among Inuit females aged 15–19, 77 percent of whom smoke (Single et al., 1994). These patterns confirm once again that smoking is more common among marginalized populations (Health Canada, 1995).

Alarmingly, about as many North American youth are exposed to their parents' second-hand smoke as take up smoking (Males, 1996; Canadian Institute for Health Information, 2005, p. 32). For example, nearly one in four youth aged 12–19 are exposed to second-hand smoke at home (Canadian Institute for Health Information, 2005, p. 32). A recent American report (National Center for Health Statistics, 2007, p. 9) identified high levels of blood nicotine in children living in low-income families, indicating exposure to second-hand smoke. This is mirrored in a UK report by the Association of Public Health Observatories (2006, pp. 53–54) showing that high saliva nicotine levels are associated with low-income households, and that child smokers are more likely in the poorest households. The irony is that although it's acknowledged in well-publicized studies that children's smoking patterns follow those of their parents, and that children are victims of parental smoking, it is children who are berated for taking up the habit and targeted for anti-smoking campaigns (Males, 1996, pp. 25–26).

There is a demonstrated link between youthful smoking, peer pressure, and parental smoking habits (Health and Welfare Canada, 1992; Males, 1996, pp. 25–26). In fact, a cigarette-smoking friend is the best predictor of smoking, while children of smokers are twice as likely to smoke as children of non-smokers (Health and Welfare Canada, 1992). As in the case of alcohol and drugs, peer pressure is identified as a major reason for smoking (Government of Canada, 1998). The combination of these pressures resulted in more smoking among Canadians in general and among youth in particular in the late 1990s after a decline that was reported in the early 1990s (Health Canada, 2000).

There are numerous public education campaigns that alert young people to the hazards of smoking. However, there is considerable public policy hypocrisy involved in dealing with tobacco in the United States. For example, while the Clinton administration in the United States launched a campaign to protect children from the ills of smoking by increasing the sale price of cigarettes, they also continued the federal subsidy to tobacco farmers (Males, 1996, pp. 25–26).

In recent years, there has been increased attention to the ruthlessness of tobacco companies in targeting youth as a market for cigarettes and tobacco products. The marketing strategies of Canadian tobacco companies were found by Health Canada to have "aimed marketing campaigns at children as young as 12" (MacKinnon, 2000b, p. A7). Secret documents from Canadian tobacco manufacturers were made public by the Canadian government in 2000. According to a marketing plan (marked "confidential") from 1971, for the Matinée brand (MacKinnon, 2000c, A1):

> Young smokers represent the major opportunity group for the cigarette industry, we should therefore determine their attitudes to smoking and health and how this might change over time.

Aggressive marketing is combined with a poor regulation of cigarette sales to minors. According to a recent Health Canada study (McIlroy, 1999), about 40 percent of retailers are illegally selling cigarettes to young people.

The rising cost of tobacco products may account for some of the decline in their reported (above) use among American youth. In addition to the appreciable rise in cigarette prices and the adverse publicity against the tobacco industry since the late 1990s, Johnston et al. (2006, p. 9) attribute the decline to the reduction in advertising of tobacco products and the increase in anti-smoking ads directed at children.

Meanwhile, with globalization, new types of tobacco products are being introduced and aggressively marketed to adults and young people alike in the northern hemisphere. One trend that is anecdotally noted, and needs further research, is the prevalence of hookah/sheesha, particularly among young people in their late teens and early twenties (see Box 9.3).

Box 9.3: The Unhappy Hookah

This segment, by Dr. Merlyn A. Griffiths (2013), assistant professor of business and economics at the University of North Carolina in Greensboro, illustrates the increasing presence of hookah on the post-secondary student scene:

Visit any American college campus today and you are likely to encounter an arresting sight: students gathered at a table, placidly taking turns inhaling smoke from a skinny hose connected to a glass container partially filled with water that bubbles with every smoker's drag.

At first the scene appears to be a sign of how relaxed the marijuana laws in the U.S. have become. But on closer inspection, these college kids are not smoking bongs in public. They're socializing at a hookah lounge.

Yes, many American campus-towns have begun to take on a Middle Eastern flair. As unlikely as that may seem, the appeal of the hookah lounge is easy to see. The exotic practice of smoking flavored tobacco holds great appeal for students too young for the bar scene, who see hookah lounges and their colorful, communal water pipes as a great place to gather with friends.

Unfortunately, the students also are often under the mistaken impression that using a hookah is somehow a healthy form of smoking. They're wrong.

The first myth is that the water in the pipe filters out harmful contaminants, making hookah smoking less risky than cigarettes. As a part of a university study, I interviewed more than two dozen students and young adults who enjoy hookah smoking who often cited this filtering quality in defense of the pastime. The respondents represented a cross-section typical of any college—male and female, student athletes, members of sororities, fraternities and other clubs. Each reported being drawn to hookah smoking as a way to socialize with friends. None of those interviewed was aware of any health risks. They shared a common belief that the water used in hookah pipes filters out harmful contaminants and "purifies" the smoke before it is inhaled.

"It's just common sense," one of the young men said. "You put the water in, you watch the smoke go through it, so you know for certain it's really filtering stuff out."

That's nonsense. The smoke from hookahs has been found to contain high concentrations of aerosols, carbon monoxide, nicotine, tar and heavy metals, which are ingested at greater rates than when smoking a cigarette. The charcoals used to heat the tobacco for smoking add to the toxic mix. None of these harmful substances are water soluble, and they are not "filtered out" by the hookah pipe.

During a typical hour-long session, according to a 2005 World Health Organization study, hookah smokers inhale 100 to 200 times the volume of smoke typically inhaled when smoking a single cigarette. The U.S. Centers for Disease Control says the practice raises the risk of oral cancer, lung cancer, stomach cancer and esophageal cancer, along with reduced lung function and decreased fertility. Include the risk of spreading herpes, hepatitis and tuberculosis through shared mouth-pieces and you have a recipe for a costly public-health problem.

Hookah smokers are also under the impression that their form of smoking is less addictive than cigarettes. This is a second myth. Tobacco consumed in any form is addictive, and hookah tobacco is no exception. Though it may be sweetened, flavored and mixed with herbs and other substances, the tobacco remains nicotine-filled. The greater volumes of smoke involved translate into greater levels of nicotine exposure.

Unfortunately there is little in the way of public discourse or public policy to counter the myths. Instead, the curious will find websites offering hookah "starter packs" and advice for first-time smokers. They also sell fruit-flavored smoking products—from bubble gum to ginger-bread—and infusions based on popular colas.

The websites invite smokers to post photos of their hookah friends and to blog about hookah smoking. One site even offers a "school-house student discount" to customers with an "edu" email domain. Coupons are available to fraternities, sororities and resident assistants in college dorms.

Since hookah lounges are typically based around college campuses, they seem not to have drawn attention from parents or lawmakers who might worry about the trend. Even in states with strong public policies governing when and where cigarette smoking is allowed, such as California and New York, hookah lounges appear to be flourishing. The phenomenon is so new that no reliable statistics are available about how many hookah lounges are in operation.

It is time for hookah smoking to be considered what it is: another form of tobacco use, and one that is, if anything, more dangerous than cigarette smoking. Public-education campaigns would help get the word out. Policy makers should take steps similar to those in 2009 when the Food and Drug Administration banned cigarettes flavored with clove, fruit or candy that might appeal to young people. Hookah smoking may look exotic, but its impact on public health is going to be all too familiar.

Health Issues in Intimate Relations

As discussed in Chapter 6, youth develop intimate relationships at ever-younger ages through the culture of dating, including sexual relations, which is increasingly regarded as normative. As indicated, this sometimes results in unanticipated consequences, such as teenage pregnancy. While pregnancy is not an illness, it does pose some health risks for young mothers, as discussed. The topics of sexuality and couple relationships, however, raise other health issues. One of them is sexual and reproductive health.

Here, the issue is not only how to prevent births but also how to prevent contagion and possible deaths from sexually transmitted infections (STIs), the most serious of which is HIV/AIDS. The second major health issue has to do with the most toxic aspect of relationships, namely relationship violence, including date rape. These issues are taken up below.

Sexually Transmitted Infections (STIs)

With regard to general contraceptive use to prevent unwanted and unplanned pregnancies, there is a range of options available to youth. The most commonly used contraceptives by teens in the developed world are oral contraceptives and different barrier methods (condoms, diaphragms). For example, the most common contraceptives used by Canadian youth are the condom, followed by oral contraceptives ("the pill"), while a sizable portion (particularly among the youngest age group at 22 percent) used withdrawal. A small minority use the rhythm method, injectable contraceptives, or the morning-after pill, while even fewer used foam, jelly, sponge, or a diaphragm (Fisher & Boroditsky, 2000, pp. 82–85).

Condoms are important not only in preventing pregnancies, but also in preventing STIs. They are, however, not generally properly used and younger teens in particular lack motivation to use them. Levels of condom use are low among teens in the UK (Olubusola & Appiah, 2006; Stone et al., 2006). Similar results come from Canadian studies. Though the use of contraceptives at first and most recent intercourse with a current partner is high (80 percent overall among women aged 15–29), they are not used at all times. Of the 15 to 17-year-olds, 60 percent indicated using contraceptives "always" in the past six months, while they were used by 68 percent of 18 to 24-year-olds and 82 percent of 25 to 29-year-olds. Overall, almost 28 percent of the young women across all of these age groups had unprotected sex at least once (Fisher & Boroditsky, 2000, pp. 82–85; also see Statistics Canada, 1998b).

Given the inconsistent use of condoms, it's not surprising that youth suffer from STIs. The most common STI in the Canadian Contraceptive Study was chlamydia, with 5 percent of the young women infected. About one in five sexually active Canadian women in the age groups 18–24 (17 percent) and 25–29 (22 percent) had been diagnosed with an STI (Fisher & Boroditsky, 2000 pp. 82–86). Over 36,000 cases are reported annually, with young people in the age group 15–29 accounting for approximately 85 percent of the reported cases. Infection rates vary by province; the highest infection rate was among youth aged 15–19 living outside of Whitehorse in more remote areas of the Yukon (Wack-ett, 1998; Burrows & Olsen, 1998).

Generally speaking, American youth tend to wait on average a year after starting intercourse before they get contraceptives. Condom use is rare and sporadic and their vulnerability to STIs is high. Of the over 15 million annual cases of STIs in the United States, at least one in four happens to a teenager, with associated complications of HIV infection, infertility, cervical cancer, spontaneous abortions, and low-birth-weight babies (Button & Rienzo, 2002, p. 4).

Despite claims of increased condom use by British teens, the statistics on gonorrhea and chlamydia tell a different story. In fact, similar to the North American pattern, rates have seen dramatic increases recently. The trend is alarming against the backdrop of the serial monogamous practices that are common among teens (Olubusola & Appiah, 2006; Stone et al., 2006; Fontes & Roach, 2007). Notably, between 1995 and 2003, rates of new cases of gonorrhea among males aged 16–19 increased by 197 percent, while the comparable rate for women aged 16–19 increased by 174 percent. The rates for chlamydia rose by 409 percent among the men and by 252 percent among women in the same age group (Stone et al., 2006). Rotermann's (2005, p. 41) analysis of the 2003 Canadian Community Health Survey found that 4 percent of the youth aged 15–24 who had experienced intercourse at least once reported that they had been diagnosed with an STI, an underestimation due to ignorance of symptoms or awareness.

Condom use is a significant issue given the danger of HIV/AIDS as a virulent and fatal STI. The period in which HIV/AIDS became a widespread concern saw an increase in condom use among teenaged males in the United States, from 56 percent in 1988 to 69 percent in 1995 (Murphy & Bogess, 1998, in Netting & Burnett, 2001, p. 3). Condom use among Canadian youth has similarly increased since the 1990s. Netting and Burnett's (2001, pp. 3–9, Table 5) study of condom use among Canadian university students confirms this, with 64 percent of men and 52 percent of women reporting using condoms always or usually in 1998, compared to 39 percent and 30 percent, respectively, in 1990. Age is a significant factor. Rotermann (2005) reports that in 2003, only 21.5 percent of the sexually active youngest age group (15–17) of Canadians reported having used condoms, while the percentages were higher for the older age groups: 32.5 percent among 18–19-year-olds and 43.6 percent for 20–24-year-olds. The still low rate of condom use among the oldest age group is explained by their lesser concern with condom use because they are in long-term relationships.

Though at least youth in the older age categories are increasing their condom use, sexually active teens seem to take unnecessary risks. The patterns are not only reflected in the general STI rates, but also in the prevalence of HIV/AIDS.

American researchers Wu and Thomson (2001, p. 682) report that as of 2000, 753,907 people in the United States were infected with HIV, translating to a rate of 265.4 per 100,000 population. Recent reports show a slow decline in HIV infections since 1998 (National Center for Health Statistics, 2007, p. 8). In Canada as of 2000, there were 17,165 people infected with HIV, amounting to 54.2 per 100,000 population. As in the US, the number of new cases is currently declining (Netting & Burnett,

2001, p. 2; also see Statistics Canada, 1999e; Frank, 2000). Alarmingly, the median age for people with HIV declined from 32 to 23 between 1982 and 1990 (Frank, 2000, pp. 61, 64). Most of the cases (84 percent in 1997) were among males (Statistics Canada, 1999e). In the UK, an estimated 63,500 adults aged 15–29 lived with HIV at the end of 2005 (Health Protection Agency, UK, 2006a). Youth aged 15–24 account for 11 percent of the diagnoses (Health Protection Agency, UK, 2006b).

The prevention of sexually transmitted infections, and specifically HIV/AIDS, raises questions about attitudes toward safe sex among youth. There is general concern over the failure of young people to practise safe sex (Nett, 1993, pp. 212–213; Belyea & Dubinsky, 1994). Many youth believe condoms interfere with their sexual pleasure (Belyea & Dubinsky, 1994, p. 31). Measor's (2006) qualitative study among British youth revealed a "culture of resistance" around condom use because not only are they seen to reduce erotic sensations during penetrative sex, but also because they are considered expensive, messy, and smelly. Additionally, some young men have a fear of erection difficulties during intercourse if condoms are used. This is a selection of some of the young men's attitudes, as reported by their female sexual partners (Measor, 2006, pp. 393–395):

He said, "Condoms—it's just such a turn off" and wouldn't use one. (Jan)

He was like, "Quick, quick, put it in." We were kissing or whatever and then he said "Let's have sex" so I'd try to put the condom on and you know he'd lost it so in the end I was just like "Stuff it in quick," and then we were doing it. (Amy)

It was like "enough girl with the condom thing! They make my skin crawl, and what you and I have—it's too intimate for condoms between us." And "Using one means it's fucking not making love!" and all that crap! (Lauren)

It is known that the presence of one sexual partner whose history you know is the best protection against AIDS (Netting, 1992). In 2000, Netting and Burnett (2001, p. 9, Figures 3 and 4) found that the most common reasons for not using a condom were being married or cohabiting, being monogamous, and being in love. This finding is supported by the Canadian Contraceptive Study, which concluded that lack of condom use corresponds with young women's belief that having a steady partner whom one trusts makes condoms unnecessary, and that a partner's real or perceived opposition also deterred condom use (Fisher & Boroditsky, 2000, pp. 87–88). Netting (1992) also found that in relation to STIs, most of the sample of university students believed their partners could not possibly be infected because they were too clean or too caring. This is completely counter to the results, which show that a large proportion of the students had multiple partners and past sexual histories.

As discussed in Chapter 6, there are at least three different types of sexual cultures among university students. Consequently, the HIV/AIDS scare is likely to have led to different reactions among these groups. Indeed, Netting and Burnett (2001, p. 20; also see Netting & Burnett, 2004) found that the students in each of the three subcultures have different approaches in the post-AIDS era, reflecting differences in values. The group of celibates is finding that the fear of AIDS reinforces their choice of celibacy. Monogamists rely on their trust in love and honesty. Experimentalists have increased their condom use to deal with multiple sexual partners. However, Netting and Burnett (2001, p. 11, Table 6) found that condom use was by no means constant among the small number of students (18 percent of males and 9 percent of females) reporting three or more partners in the past year. The infection risk posed by these young people is not insignificant.

That this failure to take STI infections seriously is not only an attitude from the past is shown in more recent studies done among youth suggesting a high level of ignorance about the transmission of STIs (Stone et al., 2006). Given the types of sexual cultures among youth, it is likely that a significant portion of young people are still either not fully informed of or wilfully ignore the risk of HIV/AIDS contagion. Another element in this information gap is the labelling of HIV/AIDS as a "gay disease" (Netting, 1992), giving heterosexual youth a false image and an associated false sense of security.

An added element in the information gap and ignorance regarding safe sexual practices is that some populations engage in risky behaviours due to their marginalization. For example, American research by Kaufman et al. (2004) proposes that young Native Americans are subjected to a great degree of stress and trauma through sexual abuse, experiencing and witnessing assaults, and other social stresses, including substance abuse. In these conditions, youth engage in unsafe sexual practices, including multiple partners and low condom use. In their study, the authors found that 55 percent of the Northern Plains youth aged 17–25 never used condoms, and another 22 percent used them some of the time. Only 14 percent used condoms every time. It is a reasonable interpretation that marginalized and traumatized populations don't have the same access to information and counselling that prevails in the mainstream. This is a parallel to the social class inequities that prevail in access to medical services, as discussed in the first part of this chapter.

Among Native Americans, the combined factors of higher-than-average rates of sexual intercourse and low levels of condom use put these youth at high risk for unintended pregnancies and STIs. In national surveys from the early 2000s, 59 percent of Native American adolescents, compared with 46 percent of all adolescents, report having had sexual intercourse. Corresponding rates of STIs among them are also higher, at nearly three times the incidence rate of the national average for adolescents (Oman et al., 2006).

An often neglected aspect of HIV and other STIs among youth is that the infections may not be linked to consensual sex between young people, but to rapes by adults. Males (1996, p. 18) reports that sexually transmitted HIV among American adolescents is partly attributed to relations with adult men. In other words, teens are being victimized by this population with deadly results. Thus, HIV infection among teens is not necessarily due to "risk-taking behaviour" by this population but due to forced sex by adults in their lives. Other aspects of victimization and disadvantage are layered upon this as Black and Latino teen females are dramatically much more likely than White teen females to contract HIV/AIDS.

What is becoming clear is the futility of the debates raging around sex education of the young (see Chapter 6). It is truly wrongheaded thinking to rely on youth's abstinence as a way of combatting STIs. We know that large portions of youth are sexually active, and they need the information that will help them make good sexual choices, and protect them from sexually predatory adults. Significantly, condom use is linked to the extent to which sexual topics are discussed at home. However, most young people find out about sexuality from sources other than their families or parents (Nett, 1993, pp. 209–210), which results in false information being circulated among young people. This shows that sex education is a social responsibility that should be shared by parents, schools, and health institutions.

Relationship Violence

As discussed in Chapter 6, young people form intimate relationships starting at increasingly earlier ages. The majority of youth live in a culture of dating and preoccupation with forming relationships. Though most of these relationships are characterized by the usual patterns of falling in love with the associated insecurities, lovers' quarrels, and emotional highs and lows, a portion of them are toxic, manifested in serious relationship conflicts and abuse.

One of the trends noted in Chapter 6 is the increased prevalence of cohabitation. This is not good news from the point of view of violence statistics. Canadian studies indicate that male violence against women is more common in cohabiting than married or dating relationships (Hobart, 1996, p. 152; Nelson & Robinson, 1999, p. 360). Marital violence is also much more likely if there has been violence during courtship (Nelson & Robinson, 1999, p. 360), another bit of bad news since a large proportion of cohabitations turn into marriages.

Violence in intimate relationships can be either ongoing between a dating couple or so-called "date rape" or "acquaintance rape" by a casual date. A Canadian study by Rhynard and Krebs (1997) shows that the age group most likely to experience acquaintance or date rape is women between 16 and 24. About 50 percent of all rapes are perpetrated by someone known by the victim. Sadly, knowing the perpetrator tends to suppress reporting rapes to the authorities.

North American research generally shows that the prevalence of late adolescence relationship violence is similar to that of wife assault. Depending on the study and methodology used, between one-third and one-half of high school–age and college-age young women had been abused by a dating partner. Significantly, prevalence does not depend on social class, ethnicity, or race (Hird, 2000, p. 69; Tolman et al., 2003, p. 159; Foshee et al., 2001, p. 128). The exception to this may be Aboriginal youth. Canadian studies report that dating violence is more common among Aboriginal youth, a legacy of the generally higher levels of violence and dysfunction among the colonized Aboriginal populations (Schissel, 2000, p. 969).

One large-scale, population-based study of 5,414 public high school students in South Carolina (Coker et al., 2000) found that nearly 12 percent of adolescents reported having been subjected to or having perpetrated severe dating violence, either physical beatings or forced intercourse. The rates were higher for females (14.4 percent) than males (9.1 percent). Forced-sex victimization was associated with thoughts and attempts of suicide. Both victimization and perpetration were associated with poor mental and physical health for both genders. The study was consistent with others reporting that adolescent female victims and male perpetrators suffer adverse health outcomes. However, severe dating violence is perceived as such only by a small fraction of female victims.

Prior to the study by Hird (2000), only one study of adolescence dating violence was conducted in the UK by Archer and Ray (1989). In a study of secondary school students in the south Midlands of England, Hird (2000) found that almost half of the young males and over half the females experienced psychological, physical, and/or sexual violence in dating relationships in the past 12 months. Forty-nine percent of the males and 54 percent of the females reported psychological aggression. The percentages for physical aggression were 15 percent for the males and 14 percent for the females, while just under 18 percent of the females but no males reported sexual aggression. Hird (2000) found no significant links with social class, religion, household composition, age, or the use of alcohol.

Depending on the type of sexual coercion, from kissing to coitus, studies estimate that anywhere between 20 percent and 80 percent of young Canadian women have been sexually coerced, with an increase in the last 30 years (Johnson, 1996, p. 115; Otis et al., 1997, p. 18; Price, 1989, pp. 22–24; Hum, 1993, in Hobart, 1996, p. 152; Nelson & Robinson, 1999, p. 360; DeKeseredy, 1992, in Lynn & O'Neill, 1995, p. 277). The prevalence varies depending on the category of violence. For example, DeKeseredy (1992, in Lynn & O'Neill, 1995, p. 277) reports that of women in colleges and universities, 79 percent report psychological abuse, 22 percent report physical abuse, and 29 percent report sexual abuse by the men they date. Further, in different studies, between 13 percent and 43 percent of young men admit to having coerced or inflicted some form of physical force on a young woman during a date (Mercer, 1988, in Price, 1989, pp. 22–24; Hum, 1993, in Hobart, 1996). Most violence in high schools tends to be verbal abuse (swearing, name-calling), followed by throwing an object, pushing or shoving, hitting or kicking. Overall, the results suggest a pervasive presence of verbal violence, with a small but significant proportion of male youth engaging in physical violence (Schissel, 2000, pp. 965–966).

In the UK, Hird (2000) also found that psychological aggression was most frequently manifested in name-calling and it was experienced more by girls, originating from both boys and girls. Typical taunts included references to sexuality, either perceived "promiscuity" or "frigidity." Boys were name-called less, usually by other boys, and for reasons of perceived homosexuality. Physical aggression was seen to be a part of "normal" dating relationships. While few boys talked about girls' physical aggression, most girls reported physical restraints, being hit, slapped, kicked, or punched. Most girls also talked about sexual aggression by males they knew, most commonly involving unwanted touching, but also coerced sex.

It was really, really dark and he took my top off and he said that if I didn't have sex with him he would finish with me. And I thought "what do I do, what do I do? I don't want to finish with him but I really, really don't want to have sex." And he started having sex with me and I started feeling sick and scared. And there had been loads of times when we had just spent the whole night getting off and kissing and he had always stopped and said "I had better go because you are really turning me on and I know you don't want to." ... Just because that was the one thing I really did not want to do. I was totally out of control. And he started shouting at me and he was angry it was like he had flipped ... and he just sort of got on top of me and it was over before I knew it. I was so scared. (Krista, 15, in Hird, 2000, p. 74)

One of the findings of Tolman et al. (2003, pp. 164–168) was that American secondary school teens believe that most boys are sexual predators by nature. The girls indicated being prepared for it and developed strategies for protecting themselves. Meanwhile, boys feel the pressure to behave in aggressive and sexually explicit ways toward girls in order to prove their heterosexual masculinity.

The majority of students in a study of Canadian high school students indicated they did not agree with the use of force, but young men were more likely to "excuse" violence than women (Head, 1988, in Holmes & Silverman, 1992, p. 48). Other studies confirm this tendency among both young girls and boys to tolerate abusive behaviour and to attribute it to "misguided love" (Belyea & Dubinsky, 1994, pp. 37–38). Abuse by boyfriends tends not to be reported (Belyea & Dubinsky, 1994, p. 38; Mercer, 1988 in Price, 1989). Since women are still held responsible for regulating their intimate relations, they are not likely to report date rapes, resulting in significant underreporting (Nelson & Robinson, 1999, p. 362).

A lot of researchers are engaged in attempts to explain why men behave violently toward women. There are some situational factors that surround violent acts. For example, the use of drugs and alcohol is common in violent incidents (Hobart, 1996, p. 153; Hird, 2000, p. 69; Tolman et al., 2003, p. 159; Foshee et al., 2001, p. 128; Schissel, 2000, p. 969). Rhynard and Krebs (1997) report that 26 percent of the rapists in their study were intoxicated at the time. Some studies find that alcohol use by the victim is also associated with rape. This is a point of contention because, in the past, alcohol consumption has been used by men as a defence to claim that they misread the woman's signals because of intoxication. Meanwhile, if a woman is using alcohol, she is less able to defend herself, and is more likely to be subjected to claims that she gave conflicting signals.

In the early 1990s, the Canadian Violence against Women Survey (CVAWS) found that although abuse is not confined to specific categories of males, young men under the age of 25 are the most likely abusers. In fact, over 10 percent of men in the age group 18–24 were reported to be violent toward their partners in the previous year, while only one in 100 males over the age of 45 had assaulted their female partners. This pattern is often explained by the difficulties for youth in modern society, and the lack of "resources or experience to make appropriate decisions." In fact, the CVAWS found that typically, abusers were in common-law relationships, with low levels of family income and education, or they were unemployed. Further, the association of low socio-economic status with some race and ethnic categories is used to explain the high levels of abuse in Aboriginal communities (Duffy & Momirov, 1997, pp. 37–39).

Other researchers point to the reported insecurities of young males that lead them to violate a young female (Larkin, 1994, pp. 96–98). Some researchers propose that violence is a way for young men to act out their relative powerlessness in society (Schissel, 2000, p. 970). Schissel's (2000, p. 970) study of teen dating violence provides the following picture of the violent male:

> Abusive young men seem to have relatively high alcohol and drug use, they were damaged as children by their parents' unpremeditated violence toward them, they are involved in a criminal lifestyle, they express themselves as being in loving relationships with their victims, and they are psychically disposed to depression and powerlessness.

Among male theorists, Horowitz and Kaufman (1987) argue that behind men's aggressive behaviour are fragile emotions and a need for reassurance. In a society that is based on male power, a woman's vulnerability ensures that she is there to stay, and will not abandon him. Any sign from a woman that she is not dependent anymore, or that she will not cater to the male needs, is seen as a threat. This threat is countered by the use of violence to ensure that she will not leave him.

The reasoning behind theories of male powerlessness and insecurities relies heavily on relatively tenuous psychological links, and comes very close to excusing violence. As Larkin (1994, p. 97) notes, using a sociological analysis, we can be sympathetic to the kinds of trying times that adolescence imposes on both females and males, while at the same time questioning "why young women are considered to be the legitimate recipient of the belligerence caused by males' frustrations."

Schissel (2000) links male violence to specific practices in communities where young abusive men's negative attitudes about women are formulated. He argues that male sports are an example of a community based on violence and misogyny that fosters violence against women. Schools contribute to this by segregating boys' and girls' physical activities, and by privileging and rewarding boys who participate in sports. Another community context for violence is the rural community where violence against women is more easily hidden behind closely knit community networks, combined with an economy that is male-based and excludes women. What unites both sports and agricultural communities is that they are linked with profit-making and male ownership. The stresses and trauma of having to live up to the expectation of economic success is expressed in violence against women. Schissel (2000) argues that there are examples of different types of communities that are successful in creating safer spaces for women, both in the school and the community.

Feminist theorists (e.g., Larkin, 1994; Duffy & Momirov, 1997; Lynn & O'Neill, 1995; Johnson, 1996, pp. 121–131) have advanced our understanding of violence against women. Generally, they argue that male violence is a part of patriarchal power structures based on male power over women. When social institutions are based on the practice and ideology of male superiority, male violence is to be expected, and women are put in a position where they are subject to the most extreme internalization of this message. Media perpetuate images of romantic relationships and traditional dating, which put women in situations where they are controlled by men, including the mode of transportation, choice of location, etc.

One of the ongoing debates is over the relative degrees of violence of males and females in dating or couple relationships. Some studies have found that males and females are similar in their frequency of reporting of violence toward their partners. These findings are criticized for neglecting the context of violence, noting that women tend to behave violently in self-defence and that women also tend to report and accept responsibility over violence more than men (Sharpe & Taylor, 1999, pp. 165–175; Duffy & Momirov, 1997, pp. 35–37; Johnson, 1996, pp. 116–118).

Girls are generally more likely to report even moderate physical aggression they inflict on others, while boys are more likely to report being victims of aggression as well as to be accepting of aggression and overtly sexual attitudes. This difference is said to reflect girls' greater willingness to accept the responsibility for problems in their relationships and possibly blame themselves for initiating aggression. Males, in comparison, tend to avoid such responsibility and are more likely to deny relationship problems (Feiring et al., 2002; Coker et al., 2000, p. 226).

It is known that both men and women engage in violent behaviour in dating relationships. However, more men than women are repeat offenders and abuse many different partners. Women are also more likely to have hit just one partner a single time (Hobart, 1996, p. 152). It is also known that women are more likely to use violence in self-defence rather than be the instigators of violence (DeKeseredy, 1996, p. 257; Sev'er, 2002). Hird's (2000, pp. 75–76) study of UK youth concludes that if the intent of physical aggression is taken into account, much of the girls' reported acts were self-defence against an act of aggression by a boyfriend.

> Someone I know got pushed against this wall by this bloke at a party and he was like pushing himself against her kind of thing and she hit him and I think that's exactly what she should have done … even if it hadn't gone any further he was still doing something that she didn't want and she made it clear that she didn't want it. And he didn't take any notice so she hit him. And I think that's what I would have done really. I hope I would have done that. (Gillian, in Hird, 2000, p. 76)

Standard tests of the frequency of dating violence are criticized for missing the impact and meaning of violence or its direction. The degrees of terror and serious injury are quite different for females and males (Coker et al., 2000, p. 226). Research suggests that women and girls are more likely to suffer physical injuries from relationship violence than men are (Sharpe & Taylor, 1999, pp. 165–175; Duffy & Momirov, 1997, pp. 35–37; Johnson, 1996, pp. 116–118).

Girls and women are also more likely to report self-defence as the reason for perpetrating violence, though self-defence alone is not an explanation for female physical violence (Feiring et al., 2002). Along the lines discussed in the previous chapter, many researchers call for more research into girls' aggression in order to fully understand it rather than "explain it away" (Feiring et al., 2002, p. 381).

Because young women and men occupy different cultural space with associated differences in norms, they have different expectations from and interpretations of social situations, including those involving sexuality and dating. There seem to be different motives and reasons behind the violence of young men and women. For example, Foshee et al. (2001) found that peer influence is a significant factor in both American boys' and girls' perpetrating dating violence. The use of alcohol was also a factor predicting girls' dating aggression. Socio-economic status has not been found to correlate with dating violence among adolescents, but girls' dating violence is linked to being a member of a non-White minority. Boys' dating violence can be linked to holding attitudes that are accepting of dating violence.

Hird's (2000, pp. 74–75) research in the UK suggests that young women and men are likely to interpret the process of negotiation in sexuality differently. While girls thought that "saying no" should be sufficient to deter men's sexual intentions, most boys in her study expected them to persist in physical resistance as well, not wanting to take the girl's word for it. For both, this is part of the pattern of gender relations in a patriarchal society in which "men initiate sexual activity which women are then supposed to regulate" (p. 74). If women don't resist "sufficiently," it's seen to be an invitation to press on. Larkin's (1994, pp. 95–96) study of high school girls in Toronto offers this account by a teenage female:

> During the March Break, my ex-boyfriend gave me a call and wanted to talk to me about "things" in our relationship.... When I arrived everything went smooth, but then there came a point when he was being aggressive. At that point, I was struggling for him to let go of me. When this occurred, he lifted me up and carried me up and carried me to the basement and I guess you can say he sexually harassed me.... When I told my best friend she said it was a date rape.... I said "no" to him and he still forced his way inside of me.

The issue is more complex as we consider the ever-younger ages at which adolescents start dating. Feiring et al. (2002, p. 381) found that younger high school students, especially girls, report a higher rate of physical aggression than is reported among older high school students. This may be explained by their lack of maturity in dealing with intense romantic feelings, and by younger girls being more likely to date older boys who have a physical and emotional advantage over them. This may reflect a growing similarity in gendered behaviours in that boys traditionally express interest in girls through physical acts like shoving and pushing. Feiring et al. (2002, p. 381) suggest that adolescent males and females may have "relatively equal power" compared to older age groups, and thus their aggression is more likely to be mutual "couple aggression" than "patriarchal terrorism."

As concluded in Chapter 6, the prevailing climate surrounding youth's intimacy is one of denial of their sexual and emotional needs and trivialization of the quality of their relationships. At the same time, the same double standard that governs the adult world is also present in the young people's world. This combination has negative consequences for young people's ability to deal with relationship violence. Thus, young women are easily victimized and young men are equally easily vilified, with neither getting help toward developing healthy relationships free from abuse. It is well documented that adults are having difficulty doing this, and it is rational to expect that young people deserve attention in this area to stop the cycle of violence.

Victimization of Youth

The preceding section shows that violence is present in young people's peer relationships. The previous chapter on youth and crime noted that some youth engage in criminal victimization of one another. These patterns cannot be overlooked, but it needs to be understood that they are rooted in youth's circumstances in which inequalities, challenges, and tensions may lead some of them to act aggressively. Large numbers of children and youth are subjected to violence by adults, whether strangers, acquaintances, or family members, adding to their burdens of navigating daily life.

Child and Adolescent Abuse in Families

Contrary to the popular image, strangers don't pose the biggest risk to youth. In Canada, most violence against children and youth that is reported to the police is by friends or acquaintances (51 percent). An additional 18 percent are violated by strangers (Brzozowski, 2004). In general, with the exception of sexual victimization, male youth are victimized at higher rates than females (Paetch & Bertrand, 1999).

Thus, not all families are safe havens for a secure transition from childhood into adulthood. Some young people's lives are marked by abuse and violence by other family members. We have quite a lot of information about the different types of child abuse, including physical, emotional, and sexual abuse, and neglect. Data are usually collected for children and youth under the age of 18. Youth are a neglected segment in the research on family violence. They are most often submerged in the category of children (Purkay-astha, 2000; Rees & Stein, 1999). According to Meyerson et al. (2002), there are nearly 3 million cases of reported child (including adolescent) abuse and neglect annually in the United States. Overall, the adolescent population tends to be submerged into the statistics, and they are a neglected population in studies of the effects of abuse.

The lack of attention to the abuse of adolescents and youth has been explained (Duffy & Momirov, 1997, p. 86) by the general stigmatization of adolescents. This time is seen to be generally confusing as young people are between childhood and adulthood and subject to more stresses. Because of this, there is the expectation of heightened family conflict, on the one hand, while, on the other hand, there is a perception that anything that teens and youth get may somehow be deserved because they are "difficult," "rebel-lious," or "obnoxious." There is also a perception that youth are better able to defend themselves as they are larger and more capable of handling themselves.

An international comparison of types of family child maltreatment investigations by police from the late 1990s shows that by far the most common reason for investiga-tion was neglect, standing at 58 percent of all cases in the US, 42 percent in the UK, and 40 percent in Canada. This was followed by physical abuse: 21 percent in the US, 31 percent in the UK and Canada; and emotional maltreatment at 11 percent in the US, 16 percent in the UK, and 19 percent in Canada. Sexual abuse was the reason for investigation in 19 percent of the cases in the UK and 10 percent in Canada, while in the US statistics the numbers are less clear (36 percent) because sexual abuse is included in a wider "other" category (Di Done, 2002, p. 17).

In 1998–1999, a nationally representative study (May-Chahal & Cawson, 2005) of British youth aged 18–24 found that 16 percent had experienced some form of maltreatment by family or non-family members. Of the sample, 25 percent had been subjected to some form of physical abuse while aged 16 or under (27 percent boys, 23 percent girls). The most common form of physical abuse was being shaken, followed by having been hit, kicked, thrown, or knocked down. The rate of serious emotional maltreatment was 6 percent (4 percent boys, 8 percent girls). The most common form of emotional abuse was being terrorized (33 percent boys, 34 percent girls), fol-lowed by psychological control and domination (22 percent boys, 26 percent girls) and humiliation (16 percent boys, 20 percent girls). Sexual abuse was reported by a smaller proportion of the respondents, with exposure or touching of someone's sexual organs or private parts at the top of the list (3 percent boys, 10 percent girls), followed by someone touching or fondling the child's sexual organs or private parts (2 percent boys, 8 percent girls). These rates are described by the authors as "unacceptably high" (May-Chahal & Cawson, 2005, p. 982).

Girls are more commonly than boys to be the targets of child sexual abuse. Another study from the UK among female university students shows that, consistent with other studies, 13.1 percent of them had experienced at least one incident of sexual abuse in childhood. In total, 3 percent of them were subjected to sexual abuse by a family mem-ber. Most sexual abuse incidents took place just once, but many went on for several years. Typically, the onset would happen during the victims' pre-adolescent years, and also consistent with other studies. All of the abusers were male, fitting with the pattern that most sexual abusers are men (Oaksford & Frude, 2001).

In Canada, children under age 18 are dramatically overrepresented among sexual assault victims. Physical assaults, however, are more common in general, and children and youth form one-fifth of all victims of physical assaults. Studies show that high school–aged males are generally more likely than females to be victims of physical violence by all categories of perpetrators, while females are more likely to be sexually assaulted (Ryan et al., 1993; in Paetch & Bertrand, 1999, p. 352).

Canadian girls (52 percent) are more likely than boys (48 percent) to be physically assaulted, but boys are more likely to be injured. Girls represent the majority of sexual assault victims at 81 percent of all cases, and their rate of sexual victimization by family members is four times that for boys. Girls' risk of being sexually assaulted peaks during their teenage years. In general, the rates of family-related assaults against children and youth are rising (Brzozowski, 2004, pp. 17–18). Whereas the sexual abuse of boys tends to end as they reach adolescence, the sexual abuse of girls tends to continue as they reach adolescence. This finding is consistent with other patterns of female victimization and abuse in families (Duffy & Momirov, 1997, pp. 67–72). These trends show the particular victimization of young people, and the continuing and escalating violation of adolescent girls by family members.

Parents are the most likely family members to engage in violent behaviour toward the young, whether it is physical or sexual assault. Significantly, fathers are more likely than mothers to be abusive regardless of the type of violence. Fathers were implicated in 98 percent of sexual assault cases and 71 percent of physical assault incidents (Statistics Canada, 2000b, pp. 31–38).

However, this is just the tip of the iceberg. There tends to be underreporting of incidents of abuse by children and young people in general, and of sexual abuse in particular (especially of male children—see, e.g., Mathews, 1996) and emotional abuse. The underreporting is due to several factors: children may not understand what is being done to them; children fear or depend on their abusers; and there is a lack of training of professionals to recognize signs of abuse (Statistics Canada, 2000b, p. 31).

Generally, American studies (Myerson et al., 2002) find that physically abused adolescents manifest a number of psychological and interpersonal difficulties, including poor social competence, language development, and school performance, as well as depression, anxiety, and conduct disorders. Sexually abused children tend to manifest these as well, but also additionally suffer from low self-esteem, aggression, and substance abuse problems. The Myerson et al. (2002) study of the impact of physical and sexual abuse on adolescents aged 16–18 found psychological stress and depression as common effects, with abused girls perceiving their families as less cohesive and more conflict-ridden. The results were more mixed for the abused males, with the physically abused males reporting their family environments as conflict-ridden, but not necessarily less cohesive, and with no perceived differences among sexually abused males.

One of the ongoing debates is whether corporal punishment—most commonly expressed as "spanking" of children—amounts to child abuse (see Box 9.4). Corporal punishment is arguably used by parents to control and exert power over children. It is an imposition on the child that, were it directed at anyone in the adult categories, would be a criminally punishable offence. If similar force was applied by one adult against another, she or he could be charged with assault.

Sibling Abuse

Abuse of young people by adult family members is at least an acknowledged aspect of family relations. On the other hand, sibling violence is mostly ignored. This kind of behaviour tends to be dismissed as "sibling rivalry," and parents tend to downplay its

Box 9.4: Corporal Punishment: Is It Child Abuse?

In Canada, the discussion of child and adolescent abuse is complicated by the Criminal Code, which allows the corporal punishment of children by their parents. According to Section 43 of the Code,

> every schoolteacher, parent, or person standing in the place of the parent is justified in using force by way of correction toward a pupil or child, as the case may be, who is under his care, if the force does not exceed what is reasonable under the circumstances. (Brzozowski, 2004, p. 19)

Those who have fought to strike down this section argue that

> corporal punishment is part of a continuum with spanking at one end and physical abuse and homicide at the other. It can sometimes be very difficult to assess when a parent or caregiver has crossed the line. (Mathews, 1996, p. 22)

Section 43 was upheld in 2004 after being challenged by the Canadian Foundation for Children, Youth, and the Law. The Supreme Court of Canada found it reflected a reasonable balance of interests and specified that only "minor corrective force of a transitory and trifling nature" is to be used, not involving objects or implements or to be directed at a child's head. The Supreme Court also limited corporal punishment to apply to children between 2 and 12 years of age (Brzozowski, 2004, p. 19).

severity and long-term consequences. A study by DeKeseredy (1996; also see Baker, 1996a; Duffy & Momirov, 1997, p. 84; Ambert & Krull, 2006, pp. 442–443) found that 47.8 percent of Canadian 215 undergraduate students reported having experienced harm inflicted on them by their siblings.

Brzozowski (2004, p. 17) reports that 29 percent of sexual and 18 percent of physical family-related assaults against children and youth are perpetrated by siblings. Some North American studies estimate that the actual rates of sibling abuse make it more common than child abuse by parents, and that sibling incest/sexual abuse is more common than parent-child incest/sexual abuse (Ambert & Krull, 2006, pp. 442–443).

Parents tend to normalize sibling violence, dismissing it as something that is irritating but harmless. Typically, because of parental tolerance for sibling violence, it tends not to be reported by its victims whose concerns are likely to be dismissed. This is particularly difficult for girls who are victims of sexual abuse by their brothers as it is the predominant type of sibling incest. The families in which sibling sexual abuse takes place tend to be ridden with other problems, making it all the less likely that the victims will ever divulge their experiences (Ambert & Krull, 2006, pp. 443–444).

Parent Abuse by Children and Youth

Family conflict can also be exhibited in the violence of young people against their parents. Even though parents have the power in the family, including control over resources, some of them become victimized by their own children. There are few Canadian studies in this area that involve children or adolescents (DeKeseredy, 1996; Pagani et al., 2003); most studies focus on the abuse of elderly parents by their adult and mostly middle-aged children.

American estimates of abuse of parents by their younger children put the incidence somewhere between 5 percent and 13 percent. Only a small minority, around 3 percent, involve severe instances, for example, the use of a weapon or severe kicking or beating (Duffy & Momirov, 1997, pp. 91–95). Based on a review of 11 American studies, Ulman and Straus (2003, pp. 42–43) estimate the incidence of child-to-parent violence anywhere between 7 percent and 96 percent. The highest figure captures very small kindergarten children whose actions can be excused on the grounds of their limited understanding. Generally, older children tend to have lower violence rates in this area, possibly reflecting their increased maturity and self-control. If sources dealing with institutionalized youth (police, mental health facilities) are excluded, the rates of youth violence against parents from the 1980s to the 1990s tend to be 7–18 percent. The rates are much higher among delinquent youth, as high as 56 percent in police reports from 1988 (Evans & Warren-Sohlberg, 1988, in Ulman & Straus, 2003, p. 43).

Ulman and Straus (2003, pp. 43–47) also report that studies generally find that boys are more likely than girls to hit their parents, and that mothers are the more likely victims compared to fathers. Studies also lend strong support to a link between child-to-parent violence and corporal punishment (see above) and the witnessing of violence between parents. Additionally, the rare cases of parent homicide by children "found that almost all have been victims of severe violence by the murdered parent" (Ulman & Straus, 2003, pp. 46–47).

In their analysis of a sub-sample of the 1975 National Family Violence Survey, Ulman and Straus (2003) found that 14 percent of the fathers and 20 percent of the mothers were hit by a child (either boy or a girl) aged 3 to 17 in the preceding year, the incidence declining with the age of the child to around 10 percent for children aged 10–17. The falling rates may be explained both by the increased self-control of maturing children and by the finding that parents use corporal punishment less as children get older. However, other results show that if subjected to severe violence by their parents, boys are likely to increase their violent acts toward them as they get older. The reasons for mothers being the more likely targets of their children's violence are complex. One general factor is women's lower levels of power and status, which make them more likely targets. Additionally, women's roles as primary caregivers also put them in more contact with their children, and also have them acting as disciplinarians more frequently than men do. Since 90 percent of American mothers and fathers spank young children, mothers are also more likely to be the targets of children's resentment of this practice. The study confirmed the general pattern that witnessing violence between parents increases the chances of violence by children. A disturbing and puzzling finding of the study was that all types of interparental violence—and particularly maternal violence toward fathers—resulted in heightened violence by children toward their mother, but not their father. In general, the authors conclude with the recommendation not only to avoid family violence but to specifically avoid corporal punishment of children as a way to prevent future violence by these children (Ulman & Straus, 2003, p. 57).

Pagani et al. (2003) studied the verbal and physical abuse of parents by a large sample of the general population of 15-year-olds in Quebec. Thirteen percent of the mothers reported that their adolescent children had directed physical violence at them (pushing, shoving, punching, kicking, or throwing objects) and 51 percent had experienced verbal violence from their teens, including yelling, swearing, or verbal insults. Their study linked the abusive behaviours to teacher-reported disruptiveness by these children at earlier ages. They also found that abuse was linked to stress brought on by parental divorce—associated with multiple parental and child adjustments—exacerbated by financial hardship and decreased social support. The study also lends support to the theory that abusive children may use "tyrannical strategies." In other words, they resist their divorced mothers' attempts to seek social support outside the family because they feel rejected, humiliated, or neglected, and those feelings are expressed in abuse of the mother.

This lends support to the view that abuse of parents is a way for young people to assert some order and control in a chaotic family setting. Abusive adolescents are most commonly detached from the school environment, and have experienced trouble with the law, have dealt with social services, or have been abused in their homes. They are more likely to have developed delinquent values and peer groups, and substance abuse is more prevalent than among other adolescents (Duffy & Momirov, 1997, pp. 91–95).

The central role of social learning theory is evident in studies of the impact of divorce on offspring's strategies for dealing with interpersonal conflict. Social learning theory, as applied to this situation, proposes that there are two stages. At the first stage, acquisition, a child learns from the parental behaviour pattern that aggression is acceptable in conflict resolution. In the second state, internalization, the pattern is learned and replicated in future relationships (Bandura, 1989, as reported in Toomey & Nelson, 2001, pp. 52–53).

Family Violence in Immigrant and Racialized Families

Family violence is found in all income groups and social categories. However, some minority groups have been found to be particularly vulnerable. The 500-year colonial legacy of large-scale pauperization and alienation experienced by Aboriginal communities is shown in the prevalence of family violence, which is estimated to be several times higher than in the general Canadian population. In the 1960s and 1970s, this resulted in the removal of large numbers of First Nations children from their families to be cared for in White foster homes. The outcome was the "removal of almost an entire generation of children" and a disruption of intergenerational continuity. The system was gradually changed, and Aboriginal communities have gained more control over what to do with their children and youth. However, this does not solve the larger problems of unemployment and poverty, which are at the root of the problem (Duffy & Momirov, 1997, p. 73, 184–185) and that are also manifested in the alarmingly high suicide rates and substance problems discussed above.

As also discussed in the previous chapter, there are country-specific factors behind violence. American youth homicide rates are particularly telling of a gun-based culture. Cervantes et al. (2000, pp. 43–44) report that homicide is the second leading cause of death among American youth 15–24 years of age, and the leading cause of death among African Americans 15–34 years of age. Other studies report that accidental shootings are the third leading cause of death among 10–29-year-olds. The common availability of firearms is linked to large numbers of child and youth victims not only among African-American but also Hispanic populations (Reich et al., 2002, pp. 7–9; Schiff & McKay, 2003, pp. 517–519).

Purkayastha (2000) studied violence against South Asian youth (mostly Hindu Indian-American) in the United States, from age 12 to their twenties, and who are still financially dependent on their parents. She concludes that instances of psychological and physical parental violence, and sibling violence and particularly brother-sister incest, as well as dating and relationship violence, are manifestations of the "position of vulnerability" or "liminality" of immigrant youth, torn between the norms and gender regimes of their families and the values in the United States, including heightened notions of masculinity and femininity. The cultural and structural elements work in conjunction, resulting in expressions of domestic violence. The very same issues are manifested in Canada, as expressed by this young Tamil girl:

> I think in life you need a peaceful life, no yelling or screaming. You need happiness.
> (Tamil female, aged 13, in Tyyskä, 2006, p. 30)

The multiple stresses of changing family circumstances among North American immigrants often lead to physical and mental health problems, and are an obstacle to the overall healthy functioning of the whole family unit (Ali & Kilbride, 2004). Health issues have been highlighted with increased attention to a range of social determinants of health in immigrant families (Beiser et al., 2002; Grewal et al., 2005; Beiser et al., 2000), as discussed at the beginning of this chapter.

Increasingly, family violence is recognized as an important health issue. There is an arguable link between loss of status and an elevation in the level of male/father aggression in some immigrant families (Tyyskä, 2005, pp. 127–128). Multiple reports suggest that some families experience an increase in violence following immigration (Ighodaro, 1997). As indicated above, some of this may be explained by women's newly found independence, which can come at the cost of escalating male violence (Creese et al., 1999, p. 8).

Though it is widely acknowledged that no population category is completely devoid of family violence, immigrant communities (and particularly racialized minorities) tend to be portrayed as inherently more violence-ridden than White Canadian–born families due to the former's presumed oppressive intergenerational and patriarchal cultural practices (Menjivar & Salcido, 2002; MacLeod & Shin, 1993; Maiter et al., 2003). This "cultural model" can be contrasted to the "situational/structural model," i.e., the proposal that violence in immigrant families may be, at least in part, a reaction to the multiple challenges of immigration and settlement, including language barriers, unemployment, poverty, lack of housing, isolation, and racism (Preston, 2001; Wiebe, 1991; Bui & Morash, 1999; Menjivar & Salcido, 2002; Martin & Mosher, 1995; MacLeod & Shin, 1993).

Though a number of these stressors are experienced individually by family members, the family unit also mediates external stresses. Families may undergo significant shifts in their internal roles and power relationships upon immigration. For example, the comparatively easier employability of women and teens over men in some immigrant communities may cause shifts in gender and age hierarchies that result in family conflict and violence (Smith, 2004; Jiwani, 2001; MacLeod & Shin, 1993; Wiebe, 1991).

Alternately, in some communities family violence has been present all along, and may be sustained or possibly escalate upon immigration (Martin & Mosher, 1995; MacLeod & Shin, 1993; Tyyskä, 2005; Pratt, 1995). Family violence may also become more pervasive but hidden as members of extended family may have been left behind and aren't there to act as social control, to provide support to end violence, or to protect specific family members from violence (Morrison et al., 1999).

Family violence is difficult to approach through policy measures. Many immigrant communities react defensively at the suggestion of family violence, afraid of public stigmatization. Solutions in this area require sensitivity and a full involvement of the communities in question, which can offer the best ways of alleviating the problem among people they know (Bui & Morash, 1999; Maiter et al., 2003; Martin & Mosher, 1995; Menjivar & Salcido, 2002; Pratt, 1995; Preston, 2001; Wiebe, 1991).

Marginalized Youth: Multiple Health Problems

It is clear that young people's health is inextricably linked to the degree to which they are linked to the important social institutions of family, schools, communities, and the state. As discussed in Chapter 3, many young people are compelled to leave their families. And as seen in the previous chapter, their lives on the streets can be made more difficult by lawmakers.

Canadian and British research shows that homeless youth have specific background factors, including parental substance addiction and child abuse, which are linked to youth's substance abuse, particularly alcohol abuse and use of soft drugs, such as marijuana (Baron, 1999; Mental Health Foundation, 2006). Brands et al. (2005, pp. 477–478) summarize research showing that Canadian street youth use at least 10 times the heroin compared to high school students, and that multiple drug use is normative. In the United States, four national surveys found that street youth (13.6 percent) and shelter youth (4.4 percent) use heroin at much higher proportions than youth living at home (0.5 percent) (Greene et al., 1997, in Brands et al., 2005, p. 478). Consequently, HIV infection levels are much higher among street youth both in Canada and the United States. Because of the high prevalence of mental health and psychological problems, heroin-use interventions are more difficult to put in place among this population (Brands et al., 2005, pp. 478–479).

Street life itself contributes to the drug and alcohol problem. Life on the streets is hard and the longer the duration of homelessness, the more likely youth are to turn to drugs for solace. Many turn to crime to finance their addictions, and the presence of like-minded peers encourages the cycle of drugs and crime. Life on the streets or in shelters is precarious, marked by unemployment or underemployment, poverty, hunger, poor health, and conditions of extreme deprivation (Baron, 1999; Mental Health Foundation, 2006).

Raychaba (1993) documented the lives of abuse that drives some young Canadian people to the streets, giving a rare glimpse of the youth's perspectives on both their families and the child welfare system. By the time some of them reach adolescence, they have been repeatedly physically abused by their parents or other adults whom they trusted. Others report sexual abuse and emotional violence. This is one such story (Raychaba, 1993, p. 19):

> I was more sexually abused and emotionally abused than physically abused.... To this day I remember certain things, as clear as if they happened yesterday. If you would ask my father the first time he sexually abused me, he'd lie to you and tell you that it was two years after it actually happened.... He used to make me sit and read stories out of *Playboy* magazines. These were stories with explicit swear words and explicit sexual things going on and he'd make me read them out loud to him and all that type of stuff which I thought was being weird. If I didn't do it, you know, it was "Do it, or else?" Yes. He'd do things like that or he'd do things like wake me up in the middle of the night when some porno movie was on and tell me to come and watch with him, that type of stuff. I mean, he did any and everything basically, you know. And it was just like, "if you tell anybody, I'll kill you." I mean, I've been threatened, I've been threatened with everything from being stabbed to being strangled and all that type of stuff.... I think my stepmother knew. I think she knew. I think she's a real bitch because she didn't do anything about it.... (Raychaba, 1993, p. 19)

The impact of violence on young people is serious. They are traumatized to the extent that their behaviours become both destructive and self-destructive, and they have difficulties trusting anyone, or forming lasting relationships. One common reaction is suicide:

> You know like with me, I've just about always slit my wrists. When I slit my wrists I used to always do it in an active way. It was fun. It was a way of taking things out

on myself. In one foster home I always took everything out on myself. It's scared me because I was very abusive toward myself, like my wrists and everything. In the foster home that I was at, where I'm at now, they felt "Well, if you believe in God then he should take your problems away." It's like, that was bullshit! How can you take away problems that have been there for ten years. And then they turn around and yell at you, "Well, you don't have problems. Your past is past. Just leave it. Go on." But you can't do that, man. (Raychaba, 1993, p. 25)

In British studies, an estimated 30–50 percent of young homeless people have been found to have mental health problems compared to 10–25 percent in the general population. One such study in London, England, found that two-thirds of young homeless people met the psychiatric diagnostic criteria for a mental disorder. It is possible that mental health issues were partly to blame for their homelessness, but it has also been demonstrated that transient living and its stresses exacerbate mental illness (Mental Health Foundation, 2006, pp. 4–5; Craig & Hodson, 2000). Physical health of youth is likely to suffer as a consequence of sleeping out in the streets, poor diet, and drug use (Wincup et al., 2003).

One of the big problems has to do with the lack of facilities and programs to deal with young people in need of help. It is difficult for any young person to find help with mental health and other issues, let alone for young people who are adrift on the street (Mental Health Foundation, 2006). It is estimated that 5–10 percent of all Canadians under the age of 16 suffer from "some significant social adjustment problem," but only one in 10 of these youth receive any form of treatment. Not only is there a problem with adults not believing or not wanting to hear what young people are telling them, but the existing child welfare services are so stretched that young people often experience this as an unwillingness or inability to help. Young people often also feel that they have no control and that they are being pushed around, coerced, and harassed by child welfare professionals (Raychaba, 1993, pp. 27–42).

In the most extreme cases, the family violence and dysfunction that young people are removed from gets replicated in the child welfare system itself. Young people in state care (foster families or child welfare authorities) face additional problems. British studies show that up to one-fifth of youth who leave state care experience homelessness in the two years after leaving care (Mental Health Foundation, 2006, p. 3): They have generally poor social supports and they are more likely than other youth to end up involved in crime, prostitution, and early parenthood (Mendes & Moslehuddin, 2004).

Large numbers of children and youth end up in state (foster) care. In 2004, they numbered 61,000 in England (Mental Health Foundation, 2006, p. 3), and over half a million in the United States (Administration for Children and Families, 2007). In Canada, there are an estimated 45,000 children and youth who live in state-sponsored alternative care settings, including approximately 30,000 in foster care homes, 10,000 in residential care settings, and 5,000 in institutions such as psychiatric wards, treatment facilities, and young offender centres. They are put in these facilities due to neglect, sexual, emotional, or physical abuse, or living in a setting where they are exposed to spousal abuse. In some studies, youth's behaviour problems, e.g., in the school setting, ongoing conflict and running away from families, or delinquent behaviour, are identified as the reasons for alternative care arrangements. However, these instances frequently cover up the true causes of youth's disruptive acts, i.e., violence and neglect by their families and by other social institutions (Raychaba, 1993, p. 4).

Sadly, the presence of many youth on the streets is explained by the difficulties they have in the foster care setting. The emotional and behavioural problems among traumatized children and youth pose a serious challenge to care providers, and risk a breakdown of the fostering relationship (Sellick, 2006). Not all foster families are the safe havens of healing and support they are supposed to be. It is estimated that up to 5–7 percent of Canadian substitute care providers abuse their wards (Raychaba, 1993, pp. 68–69). The problems of traumatized youth are extensive and the foster parents are not given adequate training to deal with the demands they pose. The stresses of caregiving by poorly trained foster parents in an inadequately funded and supported system make the situation ripe for abuse (Raychaba, 1993, pp. 68–96). In the words of one young ward of the state:

> I was being constantly told that I was worthless and a piece of shit and everything and stuff, being told how stupid I was. We had a foster parent who would physically beat all of us. He'd physically beat all of us kids, saying "You guys deserve it! You're all shits!" and saying that all of us deserved to die and everything else. I mean to me that was verbal attacking and stuff on me. I think he was crazy. I mean it wouldn't take anything really. He'd come home. He'd be upset. Somebody would do something or could drop something, could trip or whatever, and he would just fly. She [foster mother] was like that too. To cope I stayed in my room a lot, started bashing my head against the wall a lot, and then I finally just took off. It's really important to check more into the people who are being foster parents. The second most important thing is that somebody working in the system, whether it's a social worker or a children's advocate or whatever, has to be letting these young people know that if any of this stuff happens they can phone and that they're there for them. (Raychaba, 1993, pp. 69–70)

While on the streets, youth attempt many different ways of managing their lives, including staying safe and getting the food and clothes they need to survive.

One of these ways is cleaning car windows—being a squeegee youth—an activity discussed in previous chapters. In keeping with other positive effects discussed in that chapter, squeegeeing tends to have comparatively beneficial effects on young people's health. A study done in Toronto found that only 12 percent of squeegee-cleaning youth, compared with 33 percent of non-squeegee-cleaning youth, reported depression and/ or suicidal thoughts. O'Grady et al. (1998, p. 322) conclude that the non-traditional labour of squeegee cleaning provides not only financial and social support through closely linked groups but it also reduces depression and criminal activity and provides an indication that these youth are on their way off the streets.

Young homeless people are shunned by society and suffer profound depression, anxiety, and loneliness. Because of their personal histories of rejection, abuse, and lack of family supports, these youth are significantly more afflicted than other youth who are undergoing standard adolescent stresses (Rokach, 2005). Without significant intervention, including proper housing, education, and employment opportunities, and the mobilization of the support of family and friends, these youth are unlikely to gain a foothold on a normal life (Miller et al., 2004, pp. 752–754; Mental Health Foundation, 2006).

Sexual Exploitation: Child and Youth Prostitution

Sexual exploitation of children and youth is a worldwide phenomenon, manifested in sexual slavery, offering sex as a trade-off for basic survival, and in sex offered for sale to the presumably respectable world. One aspect of this is child sexual trafficking, but sexual exploitation of children is not limited to the transportation of children—it can take place within neighbourhoods as well as on a larger scale. Because of definitional difficulties and its illicit nature, it is difficult to estimate the actual numbers of victims; the range worldwide is estimated to be anywhere between 1–10 million (Gorkoff & Runner, 2003, pp. 15–16). American estimates of child prostitution range from tens of thousands to as many as 2.4 million (Bartollas & Miller, 2001, p. 349). Estimates from Europe and North America indicate that anywhere between one in ten and one-third of street youth have engaged in prostitution at some point. British studies estimate that around one in ten prostitutes is under the age of 18 (Cusick, 2002, pp. 232–233).

Usual estimates of prostitution come from police statistics in major cities. One Toronto police constable estimates that there are "hundreds of girls out there," with the youngest he had seen being 11 years of age (Gandhi, 2007, p. A7). In Winnipeg, police estimate that there are around 400 young people, mostly girls and in the age group 12–17, who may be victims of sexual exploitation, with other community agencies putting the number in the thousands (Friesen, 2007, pp. A1, A7).

Generally, the majority of adult prostitutes started when they were under the age of consent, a large proportion starting at the age of 12–15, a result also supported in British studies (Cusick, 2002, p. 233). Research across Canada gives an average age of a teen prostitute between 14 and 18 years, depending on the city, with some as young as 12. Girls enter prostitution at slightly younger age than boys, and though boy prostitution seems to be growing, girls form the majority, an estimated 75–90 percent (Gorkoff & Runner, 2003, pp. 16–17).

Aside from differences in age of initiation into the trade, other gender differences prevail, including: more girls than boys work with pimps; males work a more regular schedule with more clients; girls trade off sex for survival more; and males work more on the streets as opposed to rooms set up for the purpose of sex. Additionally, females tend to be victims of violence whereas males tend to both receive and use violence. Finally, female prostitutes are more likely to get arrested than males (Gorkoff & Runner, 2003, p. 17).

In 1999, the province of Alberta put in place the Protection of Children Involved in Prostitution Act (PChIP). By 2007, there were 1,038 children under age 18 apprehended, of whom 744 have been detained either voluntarily or involuntarily. The law grants powers to child welfare workers or police to confine these children for up to five days in a safe house to assess and help them leave street life. As of 2007, 347 agreements had been made to provide children with counselling and other services (Walton, 2007, p. A7).

Many studies blame child prostitution on abusive families and the failure of the child welfare system. Thus, prostitution is reasonably considered an offshoot of the same social forces that drive children and youth on to the streets. Their vulnerable status on the streets makes them targets of exploitation. Having to find ways to earn money for survival, they turn to prostitution (Gorkoff & Runner, 2003, pp. 19–20; Cusick, 2002).

There is a shared history for the vast majority of lack of parental support and prevailing abuse, and the fear that follows them to the streets. The majority of female prostitutes in the US, and in fact the majority of all female offenders, have been sexually abused as juveniles. It needs to be emphasized that juvenile prostitutes don't typically come from poverty-stricken families but from middle-class families that are described as having "high levels of violence and abuse." As a survival strategy, these juvenile girls run away from home and resort to selling sex in order to make a living (Bartollas & Miller, 2001, pp. 349–350).

It should be clear by now that young girls are prostituting not because of a lifestyle choice but because there is compulsion through economic need or by individuals who are enticing and pushing them into prostitution by normalizing it. This group is not necessarily always men; studies find that a large role is played by adult women, sometimes relatives and often friends already involved in the sex trade. In the study by Gorkoff and Runner (2003, pp. 31–33), about one-quarter of the girls were groomed by male pimps or boyfriends, while twice as many were initiated by other girls their age. Others followed the example of their female family members, and some were coerced.

One young Canadian woman (in Downe & "Ashley-Mika," 2003, pp. 46–68; also see Gorkoff & Runner, 2003) said:

> I knew I would end up on the street. As soon as that night when I was there and I was drugged up, the next night, I was on the street. I knew there was no turning back, I knew I would be out there.... I was scared. I was fourteen years old. You're not going to say no to some guy who is twice your age.

Interviews with young female prostitutes (Downe & "Ashley-Mika," 2003, pp. 46–68; also see Gorkoff & Runner, 2003; Bartollas & Miller, 2001, p. 350; Cusick, 2002) uncover a complex world in which the idealized image of "glitz, glamour, and easy money" is combined with the stark reality: fear of the streets, violence, pimps, and the police; drug use; and networks consisting of street families, including pimps and partners. Drug use, in the end, becomes an added reason for earning money through prostitution, as explained by one prostitute:

> I was fourteen [when I started]. I've worked for about eight years and it was completely for drugs. I didn't start heroin until five years ago, but before that it

[prostituting] wasn't every night, it was every second night or whenever I needed the money. When I was on junk, I'd get so sick without it that I'd have to be working. I'd have to have money for drugs to be OK. (Downe & "Ashley-Mika," 2003, pp. 46–68)

African-American street prostitutes typically drift into the trade through street networks; they are recruited by older and criminally involved African-American males who entice them with a romantic view of the lifestyle and the chance to make more money than they could in legitimate jobs (Bartollas & Miller, 2001, pp. 349–350).

The kinds of discrimination and marginalization that characterize social relations in the mainstream also apply to young female prostitutes. These young women are aware of differences in their status based on race. In Winnipeg, the majority of child prostitutes are First Nations. While Internet child exploitation is getting a lot of attention as a middle-class phenomenon, there is no similar outcry about these young women (Friesen, 2007, pp. A1, A7). This is confirmed for the general population by Gorkoff and Runner (2003, pp. 17–18), who point to the "history of colonization and cultural genocide" as causes of the exploitation of Aboriginal women. One young woman recognized the benefits of being White:

I was White in a highly Native population on the street. I had blond hair at the time.... I was blond. I was White. I was sixteen. I was ... Prime. (Downe & "Ashley-Mika," 2003, p. 63)

The issue of sexual trafficking has been noted in relation to North American Aboriginal women. Most of the victims of sexual trafficking in Canada are Aboriginal women and girls. Diane Redsky, member of the *National Task Force on Human Trafficking of Women and Girls in Canada*, has painted a detailed picture of the identity and fate of the victims and the profit that is being made from them:

The majority are marginalized women and girls who were sexually exploited at a young age, some as young as 10 years old, homeless youth, kids in the child welfare system, with a demand for young and younger girls.... For one young woman or girl, a trafficker will have a financial gain of $300,000 a year.... Many traffickers will have multiple girls, two to five young women. The younger the girls are, the more financial gain.... What do you think of when you hear the words juvenile prostitution? Someone older who chooses the lifestyle? Now how about when I say child abuse? Someone younger, and someone is hurting them. We should never call it juvenile prostitution. Those two words should have never been put together.... With younger girls, there is a bigger financial gain.... Sometimes they are as young as 10, with the average age being 13. Eighteen to 19 years old is less valuable, and those in their early twenties are almost of no value to the traffickers. The demand for them is not the same. That's who you will often see in the survival sex industry. (Wawatay News, 2013).

Given the horrors of life of prostitution, it is a given that young people attempt to get out. Some go through several attempts, only to return for lack of services or because they can't earn as much from legitimate jobs as from prostitution. Quite commonly, young women leave the streets for good after a significant event in their lives such as getting arrested, having been violated by their customer, or becoming pregnant. One thing is clear: They cannot leave if they cannot access agencies and programs and people who help them (Gorkoff & Runner, 2003; Cusick, 2002).

Conclusions

Though most youth seem to be in a good state of health and well-being, many of them struggle with health issues ranging from mental health problems, substance abuse, sexually transmitted infections, violence in their intimate and family relationships, and sexual exploitation by acquaintances and strangers. To the issues discussed in this chapter, we can add the discussions from previous chapters on workplace injuries and accidents, and school and workplace bullying and harassment, which exact a toll on youth.

Based on the studies presented, a most conservative calculation indicates that at least one in every five young people in their teens and early twenties experience at least one, if not multiple, health problems that require serious attention. These health issues are far from random; they manifest Social Determinants of Health: the layers of inequalities based on social class, gender, race, ethnicity, and immigrant status. Youth at the very bottom of these hierarchies—young people who are homeless on the streets, without institutional supports—are the worst off, subject to relentless exploitation, neglect, and punitive approaches, with the resulting disastrous consequences for their health. There is a tendency to pull youth down by blaming them for their problems rather than trying to bring them up through a real investment in social supports they need in order to regain their health and future. Health is the ultimate barometer of the degree of social inclusion of a population, and many youth seem to be frozen out.

Critical Thinking Questions

1. How do you reconcile the public view of youth as pampered and overindulged with the fact that many young people have extensive health problems?
2. What kinds of measures should be taken to address the health issues among youth? Who should be responsible for implementing them?
3. Are risky behaviours a natural feature of youth, along with their negative consequences?

10 Conclusions

In this chapter, you will learn that

- young people are not problems, but many of their life circumstances are problematic
- youth policies typically fail to address the real causes of young people's issues
- the neo-liberal political climate since the 1990s has worsened young people's life conditions
- policy solutions to youth problems require an integrated life-course approach

> We need a revolution in the way we think about youth and coming of age.
>
> Côté & Allahar, 1994, p. 160

So You Say We Need a Revolution?

This chapter will summarize the main areas of concern arising from the preceding chapters, and will raise general policy issues relevant to youth from a critical perspective.

In Western history, the second half of the 20th century was a period in which adolescents and youth were subjected to particular attention by the public, academics, politicians, and policy makers alike. Having emerged from the ferment of the first few decades of that century, adolescents and youth were identified as a population in crisis. In 1968, the first comprehensive worldwide report on youth was presented at the Unesco General Conference. Its concerns related to the political mobilization of youth in North America and western Europe. This large-scale collective fermentation of the baby-boom cohort (those born 1946–1966) of youth in Western society was relatively short-lived. Soon enough, it was replaced by the anxiety-ridden 1970s and 1980s, with a focus on young people's prospects for survival in school, work, and community (Unesco, 1981, pp. 13–20). These issues continue to preoccupy studies of subsequent cohorts of youth, identified under labels of "Generation X" (or the "echo" generation, those born 1960–1966), the "baby bust" (those born 1967–1979), and, most recently, "Generation Y" (or "echo boomers," those born 1980–1995) (Bourette, 1999). Sometimes, the echo and bust generations are collapsed into Generation X to cover the years 1961–1981 (Wilson, 1998, p. 9).

Of most recent interest in North America is the Millennial Generation, which spans from 1982 to the present. According to Bibby:

> This cohort is seen as living during a time of unprecedented peace and prosperity. They have been exposed to dramatic technological innovation relating to sight, sound, and, of course, the Internet. All this change, according to youth and culture expert Dawson McAllister [1999, p. 7] is something with which they are comfortable: "For Boomers, change was a mandate. They were out to change the world. Change was threatening to Xers, who felt unsafe and unstable in the world the Boomers created for them. Millennials, however, thrive on change. It is the air they breathe, and the more of it, the better." (Bibby, 2001, pp. 166–167)

Many European countries, the UK included, "have national youth policies and nationally funded youth councils and ministries" (Côté, 2005). More effort is put into directing youth policies, most recently targeted at 16–18-year-olds, in areas of education and employment (Bell & Jones, 2002). Nevertheless, policies are still approached in a piecemeal fashion, with poor coordination and general planning. Critics point to several areas in need of improvement (see Box 10.1; Bell & Jones, 2000).

These problems are even more serious in the United States and Canada where no coherent national youth policy exists (Côté, 2005; Kidder & Rogers, 2004). Repeated calls for a cohesive national youth agenda in the United States urge a move away from a problem-oriented paradigm of youth and toward a "holistic and positive" approach with a focus on youth development (American Youth Policy Forum, 1995; Yankelovich, 1998). Although issues related to youth have been highlighted in Canada through the 20th century (e.g., Ambrose, 1991), there has been a particularly active period of government attention from the 1980s onwards (e.g., Special Senate Committee on Youth, 1986; Marquardt, 1998, p. 4; Human Resources Development Canada, 1999a). Most recently, the National Longitudinal Survey on Children and Youth is attempting to address the issues and problems in the lives of the youngest of the population. A similar increase in attention to the condition of young people has been observed among academics. For example, Gfellner and Hundleby (1990, p. 133) found that there was, in a sample of 12 relevant journals from 1980–1987, "a 50% increase in publications on adolescents by Canadian authors."

This recent attention is well deserved considering the multiple problem areas outlined in this book, which indicate that the state of crisis among youth continues, and has possibly worsened. Some of the major areas under scrutiny and selected policy options have been identified in the preceding chapters. In this final chapter, I will summarize the issues and policies arising from the preceding pages, and put them in the general context of social forces.

Box 10.1: Problems with UK Youth Policy

Bell and Jones (2000) list the following problems arising from research of UK youth policy:

- Particularly over the last two decades, a range of policies affecting different areas of young people's lives has effectively extended the period during which they are economically dependent on their parents or carers.
- Different policies define youth in different ways.
- Social security policies use age as the main indicator of vulnerability and dependence. In practice, however, the transitions young people make to adulthood are not wholly based on age. Some other policy emphasis, such as health, use other measures based on notions of maturity and competence.
- The current policy emphasis on social citizenship, empowerment, participation, and consumer rights is not matched by policies that allow young people full economic independence.
- Responsibility for young people has shifted from the state to the family, as state support has been eroded. Parents or carers are now expected to exercise some parental responsibility for the first 25 years of their children's lives and to provide economic support where necessary.
- Policies in one area of legislation sometimes conflict with those in another, so that young people and their parents can receive confused messages about what is expected of them. Even within policy areas, young people can be treated as dependent children and independent adults at the same time.
- Policies that imply young people are dependent in some way are not balanced by policies that define the parental responsibility for that dependency. This puts many young people at risk.

Youth's Problems, Not Problem Youth

The main conclusion to be drawn from the range of problems that face youth today is that most of the problems have deep-seated roots in the general inequities prevailing in society, based on social class, gender, race, and ethnicity. Notably, young age itself is a basis of inequality that is linked with these other forms, and specifically has to do with the main features of living under capitalism. Youth is a liability in societies in which one's livelihood depends on the amount of wages earned. Youth are made to feel their state of dependency on others. The fates of adolescents and youth, more so than those of most adults in the working-age groups, are tied to the level of success of those with whom they live. Thus, families are the primary setting that can either provide youth with opportunities or seriously hinder their chances. At the same time, the prolonged education they are subjected to prevents them from participating in the labour force fully. However, there is a high likelihood that young people will work in jobs in which this education is not utilized. Notably, because of the links between social class, gender, race, and ethnicity, the problems of youth multiply as the number of relatively powerless (as opposed to powerful) categories they belong to are increased. Thus, whether through their families or while on their own and among their peers, young people's lives are governed by social institutions in which their position is that of powerlessness and marginalization.

Family Life

Most adolescents and youth live in families where their emotional and material needs are met. However, there is a significant proportion whose chances of making it in the world are seriously hampered by a multitude of problems. Some of these problems are a reflection of the wider social forces affecting families. Social class differences are manifested most starkly in the high proportions of families who live in poverty. The economic conditions of families are also indicative of the overlapping of social class with gender, and ethnic and racial inequality, as it is more likely to find female-headed and minority families among those who are living in economically stressed circumstances. These inequities have dire consequences for the children and youth in these families, who get a precarious start to their lives in a society in which those with material and cultural capital fare better in competition. At particular risk are Aboriginal populations where centuries of colonialism have created a crisis. Further, the phenomenon of young people leaving home later, or returning home to reside with their parents as young adults, is both a sign of the generally worsening economic conditions for youth, and a wake-up call for policy makers to take steps to help youth who face particular risks in getting established.

Inside families, young people are faced with the misuse of parental power. This power is rooted in the economic superiority of adults over youth, and in the presumed superiority of knowledge and experience based on age. Although most people would acknowledge that youth are in need of guidance, in some families the power that parents hold over their children is exhibited in aggressive and destructive ways. Youth are subjected to a range of abusive acts and neglect in their families. Consequently, their mental health suffers, and they risk becoming marginalized in society as castaway or throwaway kids on the streets, involved in a precarious life that offers little hope.

As discussed in Chapter 9, what makes the plight of young people at risk even worse is that those young people who are in the care of the state sometimes find a replication of the problems and abuse that they experienced in their families. Youth who are in state care also find it difficult to make a transition to normal life. This shows one of the fundamental flaws of programs that target specific populations. When a segment of population is subjected to a program, it is assumed that it is this population (in this case, traumatized youth) that is in need of treatment, while the causes (systemic inequalities that create the problems in the first place) are ignored. A more systematic approach is required, one that focuses on creating better opportunities for all families, so that all family members can flourish. This includes wide-ranging policies, including income equalization through taxation and social policies that help all segments of population achieve a standard of living that is acceptable in an advanced and affluent industrial society.

Education and Employment

The education system likewise reflects systemic barriers to those who occupy minority positions. There is ongoing concern over high dropout rates. Research tells us that the best predictors of dropping out are being from a lower socio-economic status, usually accompanied by visible minority status or being female. Rising tuition fees and debt loads are making it increasingly difficult for youth to obtain post-secondary education. Students without means address this problem by holding a job to finance their education, or by dropping to part-time studies. It is left up to the individual students to amass debt while the lack of funding for post-secondary education leads to staggering increases in tuition, which force students into serious amounts of debt even before they get a start in their working careers.

Youth in general have lower employment rates and higher unemployment rates than adults. Although these trends are sometimes blamed on the sizes of the different cohorts of youth in competition over jobs, most of the blame lies in the greater sensitivity of youth labour markets to economic fluctuations. Youth tend to work in the service sector, where they continue to provide a flexible pool of casual labourers who can be pulled in and pushed out of work, depending on the vagaries of the market. The high incidence of casual, and particularly part-time, work among youth is a sign of their expendability and precarious position.

These trends in the youth labour market are actively encouraged by the governments of the three countries discussed in this book. Official policies are founded on a twofold approach. On the one hand, governments aim to create good jobs with corresponding quality-control mechanisms in education. Transitions to work are facilitated by programs that combine schooling with workplace experience. The problem is that, overall, the opportunities given to students come at a cost of low wages, while the short-term employment opportunities do not necessarily result in good permanent jobs. On the other hand, there is also an aim to expand the low-wage work sector. Meanwhile, the problem with this element of employment policy is that the enticements offered to employers (in taxes and support payments) deteriorate the wages and the social safety net of the workforce, as there is pressure to lower the minimum wage and cut employers' unemployment premiums and pension plan contributions.

Aside from these general problems, the fates of youth also depend on their social category. Inside the education system itself, there is an institutionalization of inequalities, reflected in the "hidden curriculum," which provides selected minority groups—particularly Black, Aboriginal, and immigrant youth, and women—with a qualitatively different experience from the mainstream. Youth from disadvantaged backgrounds continue to fall between the cracks, and are caught in an intergenerational cycle of higher chances of dropping out of education and consequent low-wage employment or unemployment and attendant poverty. Of particular concern are youth from single-parent families, who are much more likely to live in poverty than their counterparts in two-income, intact families.

The gender segregation in education is mirrored in the labour force experience of young people. Young women and men continue to be streamed to different areas of work, with an associated wage gap. Meanwhile, the educational and work environments alike reflect the male domination in society in general as young women in particular are subjected to sexual harassment. Meanwhile, not enough has been done to assist either female or minority youth in their educational or employment experiences.

Young People's Relationships

Of particular note is the link between worsened youth labour markets and the dependency of young single mothers on welfare. Being a young parent has not always been problematic, but Western countries are creating circumstances in which it is impossible for young women to raise children without state assistance. These women get stigmatized while they are in the difficult situation in which they cannot make enough money from wages, and are forced into dependency on the state. Many fathers of the children of these young women are neither around nor held accountable for their actions.

In addition to illustrating the patriarchal oppression of young women by the individual men they get involved with and by society at large, the example of teenage pregnancy also illustrates that it is economically difficult for young couples to create a family unit. This is also seen in the increasing proportions of young people who choose either to delay marriage or to live common-law. Young people are living in a semi-independent state for a longer time, extending their education and delaying economic sustainability, putting their personal lives on hold. Thus, supporting a family is difficult for all youth, and may partly explain, although not excuse, the rate at which young males neglect their responsibilities toward their dependants. Young people's couple relationships generally mirror the stresses they are subjected to in a capitalist and patriarchal society. These overlapping power relationships are manifested in the lives of young couples in the continuation of an unequal division of household labour, traditional expectations that stress women's role in adjusting their wage work patterns to fit family and child care needs, and in an extreme form in the prevalence of females' abuse by their male partners.

Thus, forming relationships that focus on sexuality and romance is more complicated than even a couple of decades ago. Further, although there is increased acceptance of homosexuality and bisexuality, gay and lesbian youth who come out still face serious problems, including abuse, from their families and friends alike. The sexual activities and involvements of young people are much more accepted today, but pose their own problems. In addition to the fear of teenage pregnancy, there is fear of sexually transmitted diseases, and specifically HIV/AIDS. Both issues raise concerns over the heightened risk of specific youth populations. As discussed in Chapter 6, information and services are more readily available in more affluent areas, while youth in less well-to-do areas fare a lot worse, with the noted overlap with social class and minority group status.

Criminalizing Youth

Gender and social class distinctions are manifested in separate youth cultures among males and females of different social echelons. Additionally, there are distinct youth cultures based on race or ethnicity. What unites all youth is the extensive invasion of media and advertising into areas where youth create their own identity and culture. Mass media perpetuate divisions among youth that follow different trends, while creating an atmosphere of relentless consumerism. This is seen in the countless youth fads of the 20th century, and also in one of the new 21st-century youth trend: raves. Raves began as an authentic youth phenomenon, but they have been gradually targeted for consumerism, including clothes and CDs and other goods. In their ugliest manifestation, business interests invade young people's lives in the form of a range of drugs, including tobacco, alcohol, and other state-altering substances. Ironically, drug use among youth is turned against them. The state targets youth with state-control mechanisms and policing instead of focusing effort on catching the criminals who make the destruction of youthful bodies and minds their business.

Similar patterns of criminalizing youth are seen in other areas. Some youth, for no fault of their own, are pushed to the fringes of society, and can be found in the informal work sector, such as "squeegeeing." This legitimate attempt to make a living without engaging in crime has been made difficult by legislation banning this type of activity, with the anticipated result that more youth will become involved in other illegal and criminal activities, including selling drugs and stealing. That this law-and-order approach is not working is also seen in the juvenile justice system where harsher measures push young people further and further from any chance of establishing a normal life, and instead push them into the fringes of society.

The tendency to blame the youthful victims and create moral panics over their behaviour can also be seen in the area of youth crime and violence. Although youth are more likely to be victims than perpetrators of violence, media images of "youth run amok" persist, and politicians are jumping on the bandwagon of boot camps and other increasingly harsh measures to deal with a crisis that has little bearing on reality. Here, too, social class, gender, ethnic, and racial inequalities persist, with images such as increased violence and gang behaviour among young women and Black youth.

What the proponents of the tough law-and-order measures ignore are the true causes of youth criminal and violent behaviour: poverty and marginalization, with their associated ill effects on family life. Thus, these tougher measures would further alienate young people who are already dissociated from social bonds that would help them get engaged in more constructive ways. The warning signs of the total detachment of youth in the face of their marginalized position are to be seen in one of the most dangerous manifestations of youth alienation: the prevalence of hate groups. The misdirected hate of young people against other even more powerless groups in society is understandable in the light of a general ambience of competition created in the capitalist economy. Youth are more likely to adopt a zero-sum concept of distribution of social goods, in which anything that "they" get is something that is taken away from "me" or "us." Media add fuel to this fire with their misrepresentations of minority groups and equity programs. No wonder then that some youth are lashing out.

Health

One of the best ways to measure inequality is to examine people's health status. It is evident from many of the chapters in this book that large segments of youth suffer from a wide range of health problems that are not adequately addressed by health care systems, whether publicly funded or not. There is a real crisis in young people's mental health, manifested in an unacceptably high incidence of depression and suicides. Young women particularly are being bombarded by widely prevalent and publicly endorsed messages that drive them toward poor self-esteem and body image. The resultant increasing cohorts of dieters, anorexics, and bulimics are a testimonial to governments' endorsement of rampant business interests instead of curbing the advertising and music industries' worst practices, which are destructive to the bodies and minds of youth.

A similar crisis prevails around substance use, particularly alcohol, which is used by more youth at increasingly early ages. The use of tobacco, alcohol, and illegal drugs clearly reflects social class, race, and gender divides. Tobacco and associated ill health effects are more common among youth in lower-income groups who are both more likely to smoke and be exposed to second-hand smoke, compared to higher-income groups. Alcohol and drug use is more prevalent among boys than girls, and particularly problematic among marginalized racialized groups, and becomes even more so among immigrant youth through longer-term settlement. The fact that immigrants are likely to experience lower incomes as their settlement progresses is evidence of a link between substance use and marginalization.

In a world that is based on the superior economic and social standing of men, it is to be expected that it is a part of young people's relationships. Indeed, dating violence by young men is a serious issue. The violence in youth's intimate relationships mirrors the violence they experience at the hands of acquaintances and family members. No social category is devoid of violence. Though fingers are often pointed at immigrants in this regard, the main difference is that the types of and reasons for violence differ, not that immigrants are more likely to be abusive than longer-term residents in any country. Many boys and girls are subjected to physical, sexual, and emotional violence, which leaves scars and establishes patterns that may be repeated in their own relationships. Some youth also retaliate by lashing out at their siblings or parents.

The link between social and economic marginalization and poor health status is exemplified in the catastrophically poor health of homeless youth on the streets. Their multiple problems started gradually, from abusive and neglectful families, to uncaring social institutions including schools and communities, and ended up at our doorsteps in downtown core areas. The violence, substance abuse, and horrible urban street conditions, including sexual exploitation, drive a cycle of poor physical and mental health, substance abuse and self-destructive behaviours. For every youth on the streets, there had to be a series of abusive, neglectful, and even wilfully cruel acts that express the contempt societies hold for their young.

Political Engagement

What is encouraging among the depressing news about the state of youth is that young people are finding different ways of resisting the forces that pull them down. Young people's interest in politics is taking a different form from their parents or other adults. Given the rough ride they are given, it is understandable that many youth have inherent suspicion about adult-led organizations and institutions. Instead, they opt for informal and formal types of resistance that involve their peers. As indicated in many of the chapters of this book, examples of these can be found in schools, workplaces, communities, and society at large. This does not mean that all types of youth group activity can be seen as a form of protest, but that more attention needs to be paid to those groups and organizations and events that are organized and led by young people themselves. Ultimately, it is their voices that need to be heard in building effective policies that actually make a difference in the way societies treat them.

What Is the Real Problem and What Can Be Done about It?

The main trends in policy making in the three countries since the 1990s have been labelled liberal, and most recently, neo-liberal, approaches to the welfare state (Marquardt, 1998, pp. 110–111; Pulkingham & Ternowetsky, 1996; Bell & Jones, 2000; American Youth Policy Forum, 1995; Yankelovich, 1998). What holds up this type of system is a prevailing acceptance of the view that individuals and their families, instead of the state, are ultimately responsible for their well-being. The welfare state is seen only as a final resort, in cases where there are individual failures or a lack of familial supports (Pupo, 1994, p. 128; Chappell, 1997, pp. 10–13).

Let's flesh out the two main premises of neo-liberalism as it pertains to young people's lives. First, it is assumed that families will look after their adolescents and youth. There is a prevalent rhetoric that the family is a private institution, and that state policies should not apply to it. In reality, the state has a great deal to do with families, most of all because families are not always in a position to look after their members, and it is left up to the state to deal with the costs. Because of the widening gap between haves and have-nots, there are more young people in need of assistance, and it is all the more convenient for the state to make families or the private sector rather than itself responsible for costs (Mitchell & Gee, 1996, pp. 68–69; Brodie, 1996, pp. 22–23; American Youth Policy Forum, 1995; Yankelovich, 1998; Côté, 2005).

There is a second major assumption in the idea that state responses are required only whenever there is a specific problem. This problem-centred approach means that policies related to youth have been developed in a piecemeal fashion. There are separate policies that relate to, for example, youth in education, employment, the justice system, and general family policies that apply to young people in general (see, e.g., Chappell, 1997, pp. 233–258; American Youth Policy Forum, 1995; Yankelovich, 1998; Bell & Jones, 2000, 2002).

Out of this general philosophy arises one of the major dilemmas in social policy related to youth, i.e., the targeting of specific groups as recipients of specialized services. For example, youth policies and programs typically target teen mothers, Aboriginal youth, Black youth, or young criminals. These group-specific measures are seen to respond to a specific need, and are arguably necessary to bring much required help to segments that are seen to be in a crisis. However, the end result of these programs, as seen throughout this book, is the extensive stigmatization of the populations in question. These "warning signs" of neoliberalism in youth programs are further explored in Box 10.2.

Through ideologically laden media coverage, the general public gets the impression that problems among youth are not due to a lack of help, but with the specific populations themselves. Negative stereotypes prevail: Teenage mothers are amoral girls from poverty-stricken and ignorant families; Black youth are naturally prone to crime; Aboriginal youth are lazy kids who cannot handle their alcohol; and street youth are thugs who need to be sent to boot camps. However, targeting these groups is most likely to fail because they are isolated from the rest of the community while being ghettoized into specialized programs that offer little help in getting away from a bad situation. Thus, we have high rates of recidivism among incarcerated juvenile offenders; poverty-stricken teenage mothers and street youth; and Aboriginal youth who are unable to break away from the cycle of poverty.

Meanwhile, the ineffectiveness of the existing policy measures alone should be a warning sign to decision makers that things are just not working. Ironically, in these times when politicians and the public are concerned with fiscal accountability, the failure of the numerous targeted programs has produced a waste countable in billions of dollars. The problems continue to exist, and the targeted groups continue to be vilified for their lack of progress.

Ultimately, targeting means that the real source of the problems is not acknowledged. When a society is fundamentally based on inequalities, we need to systematically attack those inequalities in order for any policies to be effective.

An Integrated Life-Course Approach to Policies Related to Youth

As indicated above, there are a growing number of voices that call for a much more integrated approach to social policy. One such proposal is that programs related to youth need to take a life-course perspective, including both youth and adult service delivery systems. These need to be coordinated so that a consensus is reached across programs and their goals. This is important because, first, what happens earlier in people's lives

Box 10.2: Signs of Neoliberalism in Youth Programs

This list of characteristics of neoliberal youth programs comes from *CommonAction* (2013), an organization committed to social activism on behalf of children and youth in United States and Canada.

Bean counting. Counting youth-adult "encounters" as a measurement of change. This makes youth-adult interactions *transactions* similar to the way a salesman encounters a customer.

Pay to play. Charging youth to participate in historically free programs, including educational, recreational, cultural, and similar activities. Reducing youth work to a fiscal transaction incapacitates youth workers and denies the human right all young people have to access the resources of their communities.

Pre-packaged programs. Increasing "impact" in the lives of youth through by increasing the number of adult-facilitated, corporate-produced, curriculum-driven programs. This makes youth attendance in pre-packaged programs consumption, like a candy bar that is filled with empty carbs and nothing healthy.

Racist implications. When the same organization offers wildly different programs in different neighborhoods to meet different youth needs, they're being responsive. When they track poor youth and youth or color into different programs than white youth and middle class youth, they're being racist.

Tracking to fast food. Teaching youth that the only jobs they're eligible to get and the only impact they can make on their families and communities is through fast food and other service sector jobs denies their democratic roles and responsibilities.

Signed in blood. Using contracts between youth and adults as a basis for interactions. This makes behavior and attendance a consumer interaction, and equates it to a consumer contract enforceable by law.

Poverty pimps. Selling donors on the horrors faced by youth in their neighborhoods without exposing the reality they're faced to, including deep neighborhood roots, strong family backgrounds, and positive adult role models, is neoliberal to the core. It relies on feelings of *noblese oblige* for donations, and sells the worst side of youth today.

Youth as consumers. Referring to and understanding youth or parents as consumers of programs. This reduces nonprofit programs into supermarkets, and sells youth on the idea that "The customer is always right."

Dramatizing reality. Writing grant applications or recruiting youth by over-emphasizing neighborhood challenges or youth inabilities is responsible and belittling. It sells programs on perceived need and hysteria rather than practical applications and meaningful community building.

Zero tolerance. Enforcing zero-tolerance rules, particularly in low-income communities and with youth of color, who attend youth programs. This makes youth who comply eligible to participate, and pushes those who don't further to the fringes, promoting a youth program-to-prison pipeline.

Being buddy-buddy. Partnering nonprofits and for-profits in relationships that emphasize company values, corporate ideas, or consumerist perspectives.

Not all that counts... Using rigid evaluations and assessments of youth, youth performance, and program impacts in order to justify funding, employment, and youth activities. This makes all the impacts that aren't measureable largely irrelevant, and promotes a "what you see is what you get" mentality, undermining the fabric of community in order to maximize the look of programs.

Sleeping with the enemy. Using corporate volunteers from local businesses to teach youth about financial responsibility and equity is an easy way to infuse youth with anti-democratic ideology and community apathy.

Over counting. Measuring every single component of a program. This makes all program activities artificially responsible for impacting youth, when there are many activities that indirectly affect them or don't effect them at all that need to be done.

influences what their later lives will be like. Second, the same structural limitations based on social class, gender, race, ethnicity, sexual orientation, ability, and rural/urban differences exert their influence across an individual's life span (Hiebert & Thomlison, 1996, pp. 56–57; Copeland et al., 1996, pp. 272–273; McAlpine et al., 1996, p. 311).

A more integrated approach to youth proposes important links among generations and different segments of society. Whereas most approaches to youth emphasize the notion of "independence," particularly self-support based on salaried employment, Galaway and Hudson (1996, p. xix) ask a crucially important question:

> Isn't adulthood more than [independence]? Are we really seeking independence or is interdependence a more appropriate concept? Interdependence would imply the ability to function in a community—both to receive benefits and to contribute to the well-being of others.

Attention to interdependence rather than dependence as a guiding principle of policy formation would pay attention to the ways in which youth simultaneously perform the "roles of income earner, parent, and home manager," as well as take responsibility over the general well-being of the members of their communities and neighbourhoods (Galaway & Hudson, 1996, p. xix; see also McDaniel, 1997). In other words, in order to succeed in life, youth need to be better integrated in all aspects of society rather than isolated from adult lives and institutions. In this way, their skills and capabilities are emphasized, and they are given a voice in their own lives.

This more cohesive life-course approach is evident in some specific policies discussed in this book. One example is measures that would integrate juvenile offenders into their communities and make them accountable and responsible to their neighbours for their actions. This type of approach is more integrative than those that emphasize long-term isolation of youth in juvenile detention centres where they have little chance of future adjustment into a normal life. This more comprehensive approach would also support and strengthen those policies that help youth in making the transition from school to work. A major part of creating programs that work better in this area is to put in place checks and balances to make sure that youth are not exploited while they are combining schooling with employment.

The most difficult aspect of making more cohesive life-course-based programs work is the issue of youth populations that are marginalized. It is likely that special school-based, work-based, or community-based programs will continue to fail unless there is more of an effort to integrate marginalized youth into the mainstream. This is a larger project, requiring coordination among the generations, among families, communities, and different levels of government. Because, ultimately, what we are talking about are general and universal programs that make it possible for all members of society to have equitable access to and success in different areas of social life.

In general, successful policies would account for the wide range of transitions that youth are making on their way to adulthood as they relate to their education, employment, families, and relationships with their peers. Looker and Lowe (1996, p. 139) argue that

> the definition of success must be broadened to help young people understand that fulfilment is not solely linked to economic status and participation in the full-time labour force. There are linkages between the different transitions to adulthood,

transitions between school and work, out of the parental home, to post-secondary institutions, and those involving marriage and parenting. A program designed to deal with one transition is unlikely to be effective if it ignores the relevance of other transitions. Family and community ties are important to the transitions of young people. Government programs should help to nurture support and resources available from families and community, and provide active backup in communities where naturally occurring supports are inadequate. Efforts should be made to ensure that programs are not concentrated solely in urban centres, ignoring the needs of youth in rural and remote areas. It is important for youth to feel that they belong and are in control of their lives; intervention programs should build on the skills that young people have, rather than focusing on their academic, social, physical, or psychological inadequacies.

Critical Thinking Questions

1. What do you think is the biggest area of priority for policy related to youth in the 21st century?
2. How would you go about effecting change in youth policy?
3. How do you think youth should be involved in policy planning related to their own lives?

References

Aapola, S., Gonick, M., & Harris, A. (2005). *Young femininity: Girlhood, power, and social change.* London: Palgrave McMillan.

Abu-Ras, W., Ahmed, S., & Arken, C.L. (2010). *Alcohol use among Muslim youth: Protective and risk factors.* Society for Social Work and Research 14th Annual Conference: A World of Possibilities, Fairfax, VA, January 16. Retrieved June 9, 2013, from http://sswr.confex.com/sswr/2010/webprogram/Paper13231.html

Adams, M.L. (1997). *The trouble with normal: Postwar youth and the making of heterosexuality.* Toronto: University of Toronto Press.

Adamczyk, A., & Hayes, B.E. (2012). Religion and sexual behaviors: Understanding the influence of Islamic cultures and religious affiliation for explaining sex outside of marriage. *American Sociological Review, 77*(5), 723–746.

Addelson, K.P. (1999). How should we live? Some reflections on procreation. In J. Wong & D. Checkland (Eds.), *Teen pregnancy and parenting: Social and ethical issues* (pp. 81–98). Toronto: University of Toronto Press.

Adjacic-Gross, V., Killias, M., Hepp, U., Gadola, E., Bopp, M., Lauber, C., Schnyder, U., Gutzwiller, F., & Rössier, W. (2006). Changing times: A longitudinal analysis of international firearm suicide data. *American Journal of Public Health, 96*(10), 1752–1757. Retrieved February 10, 2008, from the Academic Search Premier database.

Administration for Children and Families. (2007). *Trends in foster care and adoption—FY 2002–FY 2006.* Washington, DC: Administration for Children and Families. Retrieved January 12, 2008, from http://www.acf.hhs.gov/programs/cb/stats_research/afcars/trends.htm

AdWeekMedia. (2007, September 10). Digital hot list: The best of the Web 2007. *Adweek Media.* Retrieved January 20, 2008, from http://zsnewsbits.blogspot.com/2007/09/ad-week-publishes-digital-hotlist-best.html

Africa Reparations Movement. (2007). *A brief chronology of slavery, colonialism, and neo-colonialism.* Retrieved April 30, 2007, from http://www.arm.arc.co.uk/CronOfColonialism.html

African Heritage Educators' Network and the Ontario Women's Directorate. (1996). *Succeeding young sisters: A guide to the development of after-school encouragement and mentoring programs for young Black women.* Toronto: Ontario Women's Directorate.

Akers, J., Jones, R., & Coyl, D. (1998). Adolescent friendships pairs: Similarities in identity development, behaviors, attitudes, and intentions. *Journal of Adolescent Research, 13*(2), 178–195.

Akom, A.A. (2006). The racial dimensions of social capital: Toward a new understanding of youth empowerment and community organizing in America's urban core. In S. Gingwright, P. Noguera,

& J. Cammarota (Eds.), *Beyond resistance! Youth activism and community change: New democratic possibilities for practice and policy for America's youth* (pp. 81–92). New York: Routledge.

Albanese, P. (2005). Ethnic families. In M. Baker (Ed.), *Families: Changing trends in Canada* (pp. 121–142). Toronto: McGraw-Hill.

Albas, C., Albas, D., & Rennie, D. (1994). Dating, seeing, and going out with: An ethnography of contemporary courtship. *International Journal of Contemporary Family and Marriage, 1*(1), 61–81.

Alexander, C.E. (1996). *The art of being Black: The creation of Black British youth* identities. Oxford: Clarendon Press.

Ali, M., & Kilbride, K. (2004). *Forging new ties: Improving parenting and family support services for new Canadians with young children.* Ottawa: Human Resources and Skill Development Canada.

Allahar, A.L., & Côté, J.E. (1998). *Richer & poorer: The structure of inequality in Canada.* Toronto: Lorimer.

Allatt, P. (2001). Critical discussion: Globalization and empowerment. In H. Helve & C. Wallace (Eds.), *Youth, citizenship, and empowerment* (pp. 250–259). Aldershot: Ashgate Publishing Limited.

Allen, M., Harris, S., & Butlin, G. (2003). *Finding their way: A profile of young Canadian graduates.* Ottawa: Statistics Canada. Retrieved June 1, 2013, from http://publications.gc.ca/Collection/Statcan/81-595-MIE/81-595-MIE2003003.pdf

Alphonso, C. (2007, February 3). Schools want to ban my cell phone!! *The Globe and Mail,* A13.

Ambert, A.M. (1992). *The effect of children on parents.* Binghamton: Haworth Press.

Ambert, A.M. (1997). *Parents, children, and adolescents: Interactive relationships and development in context.* Binghamton: Haworth Press.

Ambert, A.M. (2007). *The rise in the number of children and adolescents who exhibit problematic behaviors: Multiple causes.* Ottawa: The Vanier Institute of the Family, Contemporary Family Trends. Retrieved March 20, 2007, from http://www.vifamily.ca/library/cft/behavior.html

Ambert, A.M. & Krull, C. (2006). *Changing families: Relationships in context* (Canadian ed.). Toronto: Pearson.

Ambrose, L.M. (1991). Collecting youth opinion: The research of the Canadian Youth Commission, 1943–1945. In R. Smandych, G. Dodds, & A. Esau (Eds.), *Dimensions of childhood: Essays on the history of children and youth in Canada.* Winnipeg: Legal Research Institute of the University of Manitoba.

American Association of University Women. (2011). *Crossing the line.* Retrieved May 23, 2013, from http://www.care2.com/causes/national-study-reveals-striking-findings-on-school-sexual-harassment.html#ixzz2U8SfbNfg

American Youth Policy Forum. (1995). *Contract with America's youth: Toward a national youth development agenda.* Washington: American Youth Policy Forum. Retrieved February 22, 2007, from http://eric.ed.gov/ERICWebPorta.custom/portlets/recordDetails…

Amnesty International, UK. (2005). *USA: New report shows USA only country in world sentencing thousands of children to live without parole.* London: Amnesty International, UK. Retrieved March 12, 2007, from: http://amnesty.org.uk/news_details.asp?NewsID=16476

Amnesty International, US. (2004). *Threat and humiliation: Racial profiling, domestic security, and human rights in the United States.* New York: Amnesty International, US. Retrieved May 15,

2007, from ttp://www.amnestyusa.org/Other/RP_Report__Threat_and_Humiliation/page. do?id=1106664&n1=3&n2=850&n3=1532

Anderson, S.A., & Sabatelli, R.M. (1999). *Family interaction: A multigenerational developmental perspective* (2nd ed). Toronto: Allyn & Bacon.

Anderssen, E. (2007, March 31). Hooking up in a hooked-up world. *Globe and Mail*, p. A8.

Andreß, H.-J., Borgloh, B. Bröckel, M., Giesselmann, M., & Hummelsheim, D. (2006). The economic consequences of partnership dissolution—A comparative analysis of panel studies from Belgium, Germany, Great Britain, Italy, and Sweden. *European Sociological Review, 22*(5), 533–560.

Anisef, P. (1994). *Learning and sociological profiles of Canadian high school students.* Lewiston/ Queenston/Lampeter: The Edwin Mellen Press.

Anisef, P., & Kilbride, K.M. (2000). *The needs of newcomer youth and the emerging "best practices" to meet those needs.* Toronto: Joint Centre of Excellence for Research on Immigration and Settlement.

Anisef, P., Kilbride, K.M., Ochocka, J., & Janzen, R. (2001). *Parenting issues of newcomer families in Ontario.* Kitchener: Centre for Research & Education in Human Services & Centre of Excellence for Research on Immigration & Settlement.

Anisef, P., Paasche, J.G., & Turrittin, A.H. (1980). *Is the die cast? Educational achievements and work destinations of Ontario youth: A six-year follow-up of the critical juncture for high school students.* Toronto: Ministry of Colleges and Universities, Ontario.

Arat-Koc, S. (1993). Neo-liberalism, state restructuring, and immigration: Changes in Canadian policies in the 1990s. *Journal of Canadian Studies, 34*(2), 31–56.

Arat-Koc, S. (1997). From "mothers of the nation" to migrant workers. In A.B. Bakan & D. Stasiulis (Eds.), *Not one of the family: Foreign domestic workers in Canada* (pp. 53–79). Toronto: University of Toronto Press.

Archambault, R., & Grignon, R. (1999). Decline in youth participation in Canada in the 1990s: Structural or cyclical? *Canadian Business Economics, 7*(2), 71–87.

Archer, J., & Ray, N. (1989). Dating violence in the United Kingdom. *Aggressive Behaviour, 15*, 337–343.

Argenti, N. (2002). Youth in Africa: A major resource for change. In A. De Waal & N. Argenti (Eds.), *Young Africa: Realising the rights of children and youth* (pp. 123–154). Trenton: Africa World Press, Inc.

Arnett, J.J. (2001). *Adolescence and emerging adulthood.* Upper Saddle River: Prentice Hall.

Arnup, K. (2005). Lesbian and gay parents. In N. Mandell & A. Duffy (Eds.), *Canadian families: Diversity, conflict, and change* (3rd ed.) (pp. 176–209). Toronto: Thomson Nelson.

Arruda, A.F. (1993). Expanding the view: Growing up in Portuguese-Canadian families, 1962–1980. *Canadian Ethnic Studies, 25*(3), 8–25.

Arulampalam, W. (2001). Is unemployment really scarring? Effects of unemployment experiences on wages. *The Economic Journal, 111*(475), 585–606.

Association of Public Health Observatories. (2006). *Indications of public health in the English regions.* London: Association of Public Health Observatories. Retrieved February 22, 2008, from the Academic Search Premier database.

Back, L. (1996). *New ethnicities and urban culture: Racism and multiculture in young lives.* New York: St. Martin's Press.

Báez, A.C. (2003). Scholar-activism and the global movement for socioeconomic justice. In S. John & S. Thomson (Eds.), *New activism and the corporate response* (pp. 241–260). New York: Palgrave Macmillan.

Bahdi, R. (2003). No exit: Racial profiling and Canada's war against terrorism. *Osgoode Hall Law Journal, 41*(2 & 3), 293–316. Retrieved May 15, 2007, from Academic Search Premier database.

Bailey, M.J. (1991). Servant girls and masters: The tort of seduction and the support of bastards. *Canadian Journal of Family Law, 10*(1), pp. 3–23.

Bailey, S. (1999, November 8). Graduates under increasing pressure to pay back soaring student loans. *Globe and Mail*, p. A7.

Bakan, A.D., & Stasiulis, D. (1996). Structural adjustment, citizenship, and foreign domestic labour: The Canadian case. In I. Bakker (Ed.), *Rethinking restructuring: Gender and change in Canada* (pp. 217–242). Toronto: University of Toronto Press.

Baker, M. (1989). *Families in Canadian society: An introduction.* Toronto: McGraw-Hill Ryerson Limited.

Baker, M. (1996a). Introduction to family studies: Cultural variations and family trends. In M. Baker (Ed.), *Families: Changing trends in Canada* (3rd ed.). Toronto: McGraw-Hill Ryerson Limited.

Baker, M. (1996b). The future of family life. In M. Baker (Ed.), *Families: Changing trends in Canada* (3rd ed.). Toronto: McGraw-Hill Ryerson Limited.

Baker, M., & Dryden, J. (1993). *Families in Canadian society* (2nd ed.). Toronto: McGraw-Hill Ryerson Limited.

Banerji, S. (2004). Report: Higher education fiscal crisis hardest on Hispanic, low-income students. *Black Issues in Higher Education, 21*(6), 10.

Barber, J. (1999, November 11). Innu people devastated by latest teen suicide. *Globe and Mail*, p. A9.

Barnhorst, R. (2004). The Youth Criminal Justice Act: New directions and implementation issues. *Canadian Journal of Criminology and Criminal Justice, 46*(3), 231–250.

Baron, S.W. (1997). Canadian male street skinheads: Street gang or street terrorist? *The Canadian Review of Sociology and Anthropology, 34*(1), 125–154.

Baron, S.W. (1999). Street youths and substance abuse: The role of background, street lifestyle, and economic factors, *Youth & Society, 31*(1), 3–26.

Barrett, D. (2003, February 6). Girls form addictions faster, study suggests. *The Arizona Republic.* Retrieved from http://www.arizonarepublic.com/news/articles/0206girldrugs06.html

Barron, C.L. (2000). *Giving youth a voice: A basis for rethinking adolescent violence.* Halifax: Fernwood Publishing.

Barron, C., & Lacombe, D. (2005). Moral panic and the nasty girl. *The Canadian Review of Sociology and Anthropology, 42*(1), 51–69.

Bartollas, C., & Miller, S.J. (2001). *Juvenile justice in America* (3rd ed.), Upper Saddle River: Prentice Hall.

Battiste, M., & Barman, J. (2003). *First Nations education in Canada: The circle unfolds.* Toronto: Oxford University Press.

BBC Commissioning. (2006). 16–24-year-olds, youths—What is the role of TV? *BBC News.* Retrieved May 10, 2007, from http://www.bbc.co.uk/commissioning/marketresearch/audiencegroup2.shtml.

BBC News. (2001). Bradford counts the cost of riots. *BBC News*. Retrieved May 2, 2013, from http://news.bbc.co.uk/2/hi/uk_news/1428673.stm

BBC News. (2002). Communities troubled by youth crime. *BBC News*. Retrieved March 12, 2007, from http://news.bbc.co.uk/1/hi/uk/1932803.stm

BBC News. (2003). University fees to rise. *BBC News*. Retrieved May 9, 2007, from http://news.bbc.co.uk/2/hi/uk_news/education/2683573.stm

BBC News. (2007a). Q & A: Student fees. *BBC News*. Retrieved May 9, 2007, from http://news.bbc.co.uk/2/hi/uk_news/education/3013272.stm

BBC News. (2007b). McDonald seeks "McJob" rewrite. *BBC News*. Retrieved January 16, 2008, from http://news.bbc.co.uk/1/hi/business/6469707.stm

BBC World Service. (2007). The story of Africa: Slavery. *BBC World Service*. Retrieved April 20, 2007, from http://www.bbc.co.uk/worldservice/africa/features/storyofafrica/9chapt

Beaujot, R. (2000). *Earning and caring in Canadian families*. Peterborough: Broadview.

Beaumont, S.L. (1996). Adolescent girls' perceptions of conversations with mothers and friends. *Journal of Adolescent Research, 11*(3), 325–346.

Beauvais, C., McKay, L., & Seddon, M. (2001). *A literature review of youth and citizenship*. CPRN discussion paper no. CPRN/02. Ottawa: Canadian Policy Research Networks. Retrieved June 20, 2006, from http://cprn.org/documents/4031_en.pdf

Beiser, M., Hou, F., Hyrnan, I., & Tousignant, M. (2002). Poverty, family process, and the mental health of immigrant children in Canada. *American Journal of Public Health, 92*(2), 220–228.

Beiser, M., Hou, F., Kasper, V., & Who, S. (2000). *Changes in poverty status and developmental behaviour: A comparison of immigrant and non-immigrant children in Canada*. Hull: Applied Research Branch, Strategic Policy Division, Human Resources Development Canada.

Beishon, S., Modood, T., & Virdee, S. (1998). *Ethnic minority families*. London: Joseph Rowntree Foundation. Retrieved May 18, 2007, from http://www.jrf.org.uk/knowledge/findings/social-policy/spr938.asp

Bell, B.T., Lawton, R., & Dittmar, H. (2007). The impact of thin models in music videos on adolescent girls' body dissatisfaction. *Body Image, 4*, 137–145. Retrieved January 15, 2008, from the Academic Search Premier database.

Bell, D.N.F., & Blanchflower, D.G. (2009). *Youth unemployment: Déjà vu?* Retrieved July 17, 2103, from http://www.dartmouth.edu/~blnchflr/papers/speech379paper.pdf

Bell, L., Burtless, G., Gornick, J., & Smeeding, T.M. (2006). *A cross-national survey of trends in the transition to economic independence*. Washington: The Network on Transitions to Adulthood. Retrieved June 20, 2007, from http://www.transad.pop.upenn.edu/downloads/Bell-Burt-Gornick-Smeed_May-8-2006_FINAL.pdf

Bell, R., & Jones, G. (2000). *Youth, parenting, and public policy*. York: Joseph Rowntree Foundation. Retrieved February 22, 2008, from http://www.jrf.org.uk/knowledge/findings/socialpolicy/590.asp

Bell, R., & Jones, G. (2002). *Youth policies in the UK: A chronological map*. Keele: Keele University, School of Social Relations. Retrieved February 22, 2007, from http://www.keele.ac.uk/depts/so/youthchron/index.htm

Bell, S.J. (1999). *Young offenders and juvenile justice a century after the fact*. Toronto: International Thompson Publishing Company.

Belle, M., & McQuillan, K. (2000). Births outside marriage: A growing alternative. *Canadian Social Trends* (Vol. 3) (pp. 112–116). Toronto: Thompson Educational Publishing.

Belyea, S., & Dubinsky, K. (1994). "Don't judge us too quickly": Writing about teenage girls and sex. In S. Prentice (Ed.), *Sex in schools: Canadian education & sexual regulation* (pp. 19–43). Toronto: Our Schools/Ourselves.

Berkner, L., Wei, C.C., & Griffith, J. (2006). *Student financing of undergraduate education: 2003–2004. With a special analysis of the net price of attendance and federal education tax benefits.* Washington: National Centre for Education Statistics, Institute of Education Science. Retrieved May 21, 2007, from http://nces.ed.gov/pubs2006/2006186.pdf

Bernhard, J.K., Landolt, P., & Goldring, L. (2005). *Transnational, multi-local motherhood: Experiences of separation and reunification among Latin American families in Canada.* Working paper no. 40. Toronto: CERIS.

Bernhard, J.K., Lefebvre, M.L., Chud, G., & Lange, R. (1996). Linguistic match between children and caregivers in Canadian early childhood education. *Canadian Journal of Research in Early Childhood Education, 5*(2), 5–18.

Berry, J.W. (2007). Acculturation strategies and adaptation. In J.E. Lansford, K. Dieter-Deckard, & M.H. Bornstein (Eds.), *Immigrant families in contemporary society* (pp. 69–82). New York: Guilford Press.

Bethune, B. (2000, April 24). Inquiry into the agony of ecstasy. *Maclean's, 113*(17), 41.

Bibby, R.W. (2001). *Canada's teens: Today, yesterday, and tomorrow.* Toronto: Stoddart.

Birbalsingh, K. (2013, June 8). These riots were about race. Why ignore the fact? *The Telegraph.* Retrieved June 8, 2013, from http://blogs.telegraph.co.uk/news/katharinebirbalsingh/100099830/these-riots-were-about-race-why-ignore-the-fact/

Bishop, H.N., & Casida, H. (2011). Preventing bullying and harassment of sexual minority students in schools. *The Clearing House: A Journal of Educational Strategies, Issues and Ideas, 84*(4), 134–138.

Blackman, S.J. (1995). *Youth: Positions and oppositions.* Aldershot: Avebury.

Blanchflower, D., & Freeman, R. (1998). Why youth unemployment will be hard to reduce. *Policy Options Politiques, 3,* 3–7.

Blatchford, A. (2007, March 3). FIFA should have overruled hijab ban: Ejected girl's mother. *Globe and Mail.* Retrieved January 29, 2008, from http://www.theglobeandmail.com/servlet/story/RTGAM.20070303.whijab04/BNStory/Front/home

Bloomfield, E., & Bloomfield, G.T. (1991). *Canadian women in workshops, mills, and factories: The evidence of the 1871 census manuscripts.* Guelph: University of Guelph, Department of Geography.

Blum, R., & Harmon, B. (1992). American Indian and Alaska Native youth health. *Journal of American Medical Association, 267*(12), 1637–1644.

Bolter, A. (1999, December 2). Squeegee law overlooks real problem. *London Free Press,* A13.

Bolton, P. (2012). *Student lLoan sStatistics.* London: House of Commence Statistics. Retrieved May 13, 2013, from http://www.parliament.uk/briefing-papers/sn01079.pdf

Borgen, L., & Rumbaut, R.G. (2005). *Coming of age in "America's finest city": Transitions to adulthood among children of immigrants in San Diego.* Philadelphia: Research Network on Transitions to Adulthood, University of Pennsylvania, Department of Sociology. Retrieved May 20, 2007, from http://www.transad.pop.upenn.edu/downloads/Excerpt%20from%20SDiego.pdf

Bourette, S. (1999, January 25). Lowering the boom on genX—again. *Globe and Mail*, pp. A1, A19.

Bowlby, J.W., & McMullen, K.. (2002). *At a crossroads: First results for the 18- to 20-year-old cohort of the youth in transition survey*. Ottawa: Statistics Canada. Retrieved May 12, 2013, from http://www.statcan.gc.ca/pub/81-591-x/81-591-x2000001-eng.pdf

Boyd, M. (2000). Ethnicity and immigrant offspring. In M. Kalbach & W. Kalbach (Eds.), *Race and ethnicity* (pp. 137–154). Toronto: Harcourt Brace.

Boyd, M., & Norris, D. (2000). The crowded nest: Young adults at home. *Canadian Social Trends* (Vol. 3) (pp. 168–170). Toronto: Thomspon Educational Publishing.

Bradbury, B. (1993). Women and the history of their work in Canada: Some recent books. *Journal of Canadian Studies/Revue d'Études Canadiennes, 28*(3), 159–178.

Bradbury, B. (1996). The social and economic origins of contemporary families. In M. Baker (Ed.), *Families: Changing trends in Canada* (3rd ed). Toronto: McGraw-Hill Ryerson Limited.

Brady, E. (2002, April 26). Cheerleading in the USA: A sport and an industry. *USA Today*. Retrieved January 29, 2008, from http://www.usatoday.com/sports/_stories/2002-04-26-cheerleading-cover.htm

Brake, M. (1985). *Comparative youth culture: The sociology of youth culture and youth subgroups in America, Britain, and Canada*. London & New York: Routledge and Kegan Paul.

Brand, D., & Bhaggiyadatta, K.S. (1986). Rivers have sources, trees have roots. In J. Parr & N. Janovicek (Eds.), *Histories of Canadian children and youth* (pp. 277–284). Toronto: Cross Cultural Communication Centre.

Brands, B., Leslie, K., Catz-Biro, L., & Li, S. (2005). Heroin use and barriers to treatment in street-involved youth. *Addiction Research and Theory, 13*(5), 477–487.

Braungart, R.G., & Braungart, M.M. (1990). Youth movements in the 1980s: A global perspective. *International Sociology, 5*(2), 157–181. Retrieved October 15, 2007, from Academic Search Premier database.

Brayton, J. (2007). *Leet speak*. Unpublished paper.

Brearton, S. (1999). "Youth hostile," reality check. *Toronto Life, 33*(1), 2–3.

Brennan, S. (2013). Youth court statistics in Canada, 2010/2011. *Juristat*, Catalogue No. 85-002-X. Retrieved June 5, 2013, from http://www.statcan.gc.ca/pub/85-002-x/2012001/article/11645-eng.htm

Bridge, J.A., Goldstein, T.R., & Brent, D.A. (2006). Adolescent suicide and suicidal behavior. *Journal of Child Psychology and Psychiatry, 47*(3), 372–394. Retrieved February 3, 2008, from the Academic Search Premier database.

Bright, M. (2003). Top-up fees "will widen class divide." *Observer*. Retrieved May 9, 2007, from http://www.guardian.co.uk/politics/2003/feb/23/uk.education

Broadcasters Audience Research Board (2012). *Children's TV viewing: BARB analysis*. Retrieved June 10, 2013, from http://stakeholders.ofcom.org.uk/binaries/research/media-literacy/oct2012/Annex_2.pdf

Brodie, J. (1996). Canadian women, changing state forms, and public policy. In J. Brodie (Ed.), *Women and Canadian public policy* (pp. 1–28). Toronto: Harcourt Brace & Company, Canada.

Brotherton, D. (1999). Old heads tell their stories. *Free Inquiry in Creative Sociology, 27*(1), 77–89.

Brown, C.J. (1990). Generation X: Youth in the 1980s were unemployed, under-employed, marginalized, and poor. *Perception, 14*(2), 62–65.

Brownfield, D., Sorenson, A.M., & Thompson, K. (2001). Gang membership, race, and social class: A test of the group hazard and master status hypotheses. *Deviant Behaviour: An Interdisciplinary Journal, 22,* 73–89.

Brownfield, D., & Thompson, K. (1991). Attachment to peers and delinquent behaviour. *Canadian Journal of Criminology, 33*(1), 45–60.

Brunner, B., & Haney, E. (2000–2007). *Civil rights timeline: Milestones in the modern civil rights movement.* Online resource, Pearson Education. Retrieved May 3, 2007, from http://www.infoplease.com/spot/civilrightstimeline1.html

Bryson, A., Gomez, R., Gunderson, M., & Meltz, N. (2001). *Youth-adult differences in the demand for unionization: Are American, British, and Canadian workers all that different?* London: Centre for Economic Performance, London School of Economics and Political Science. Retrieved January 15, 2008, from http://cep.lse.ac.uk/pubs/download/DP0515.pdf

Brzozowski, J. (2004). *Family violence in Canada: A statistical profile 2004.* Ottawa: Ministry of Industry. Retrieved February 20, 2008, from http://www.phac-aspc.gc.ca/ncfv-cnivf/familyviolence/pdfs/fv-85-224-XIE2004000_e.pdf

Buckingham, D. (2000). *The making of citizens.* London & New York: Routledge.

Bui, H., & Morash, M. (1999). Domestic violence in the Vietnamese immigrant community: An exploratory study. *Violence against Women, 5*(6), 769–795.

Bureau of Labor Statistics (2013). *New Release: Employment Situation—April 2013.* Washington: US Department of Labor. Retrieved May 20, 2013, from http://www.bls.gov/news.release/pdf/empsit.pdf

Burfoot, D. (2003). Children and young people's participation: Arguing for a better future. *Youth Studies Australia, 22*(3), 44–51.

Burrows, M., & Olsen, L. (1998). A holistic peer education program to reduce STD infection among transient young adults in a resort community. *The Canadian Journal of Human Sexuality, 7*(4), 365–370.

Button, J.W., & Rienzo, B.A. (2002). *The politics of youth, sex, and health care in American schools.* New York, London & Oxford: Haworth Press.

Bynner, J., & Parsons, S. (2002). Social exclusion and the transition from school to work: The case of young people not in education, employment, or training (NEET). *Journal of Vocational Behavior, 60,* 289–309.

Calliste, A. (1996). Black families in Canada: Exploring the interconnections of race, class, and gender. In M. Lynn (Ed.), *Voices: Essays on Canadian families* (pp. 199–220). Toronto: Nelson Canada.

Calvin, E. (2004). *Legal strategies to reduce the unnecessary detention of children.* Washington: National Juvenile Defender Center. Retrieved June 5, 2013, from http://www.njdc.info/pdf/detention_guide.pdf

Cambridge Reporter. (2000, February 2). Lawyers set to challenge Ontario's squeegee ban. *Cambridge Reporter,* p. 5A.

Cameron, S. (2000). *Poverty: A student learning resource.* Vancouver: End Legislated Poverty. Retrieved May 11, 2000, from www.bctf.bc.ca/lessonsaid/online/la2030.htm

Campaign 2000. (2012). *Needed: A federal action plan to eradicate child and family poverty in Canada.* Toronto: Family Services Toronto, United Way Member Agency. Retrieved May 11, 2013, from http://www.campaign2000.ca/reportCards/national/C2000ReportCardNov2012.pdf

Canadian Centre for Justice Statistics. (1997–1998). *Alternative measures for youth in Canada 1997/98.* Retrieved April 11, 1999, from qsilver.queensu.ca./rcjnet/research/youth.html

Canadian Centre for Occupational Health and Safety. (2013). *Young workers zone: The truth hurts.* Retrieved May 31, 2013, from http://www.ccohs.ca/youngworkers/resources/truth-Hurts.html

Canadian Centre for Policy Alternatives. (2004). *Highlights—Missing pieces V: An alternative to Canadian post-secondary education.* Retrieved January 12, 2005, from www.policyalterna-tives.ca

Canadian Centre on Substance Abuse. (1999). *Canadian profile 1999—special populations: Highlights.* Ottawa: Canadian Centre on Substance Abuse and the Centre for Addiction and Mental Health. Retrieved March 20, 2006, from http://www.ccsa.ca/CCSA/EN/Statistics/CanadianProfile1999.htm

Canadian Coalition for the Rights of Children. (n.d.). *Young People and Bill C-10.* Retrieved June 8, 2013, from http://rightsofchildren.ca/wp-content/uploads/Young-People-and-Bill-C-10-CCRC-Statement.pdf

Canadian Council on Social Development. (1998). *The progress of Canada's children: Focus on youth.* Ottawa: CCSD.

Canadian Council on Social Development. (1999–2000). *The progress of Canada's children.* Ottawa: CCSD. Retrieved September 11, 2001, from http://www.ccsd.ca/pubs/pcc00/hl.htm

Canadian Council on Social Development. (2000). *Immigrant youth in Canada.* Ottawa: CCSD. Retrieved September 11, 2001, from http://www.ccsd.ca/subsites/cd/docs/iy/

Canadian Council on Social Development. (2005). *Employment and persons with disabilities in Canada. Information Sheet #18.* Ottawa: Canadian Council on Social Development. Retrieved May 20, 2007, from http://www.ccsd.ca/drip/research/drip18/drip18.pdf

Canadian Council on Social Development. (2006). *The progress of Canada's youth and children.* Retrieved April 2, 2007 from http://www.ccsd.ca/pccy/2006/pdf/pccy_civicvitality.pdf.

Canadian Council on Social Development. (2007). *A profile on the labour market in Canada.* Fact sheet #1: Labour force rates. Retrieved May 31, 2012, from http://www.ccsd.ca/factsheets/labour_market/rates/index.htm

Canadian Institute for Health Information. (2005). *Improving the health of young Canadians.* Ottawa: Canadian Institute for Health Information. Retrieved February 20, 2008, from http://www.cihi.ca/cihiweb/dispPage.jsp?cw_page=PG_380_E&cw_topic=380&cw_rel=AR_1217_E

Caputo, T., & Vallée, M. (2010). *A comparative analysis of youth justice approaches.* Review of the roots of youth violence: Research papers, Vol. 4. Ontario Ministry of Children and Youth Services. Retrieved June 5, 2013, from http://www.children.gov.on.ca/htdocs/English/top-ics/youthandthelaw/roots/volume4/comparative_analysis.aspx

Caragata, L. (1999). The construction of teen parenting and the decline of adoption. In J. Wong & D. Checkland (Eds.), *Teen pregnancy and parenting: Social and ethical issues* (pp. 99–120). Toronto: University of Toronto Press.

Career World. (2004). Nightmare jobs! *Career World, 33*(3), 5. Retrieved January 13, 2008, from Academic Search Premier database.

Carrigan, D.O. (1998). *Juvenile delinquency in Canada: A history.* Concord: Irwin Publishing.

Carrington, P.J. (1999). Trends in youth crime in Canada, 1977–1996. *Canadian Journal of Criminology,* 41(1), 1–32.

Carrington, B., & Wilson, B. (2002). Global clubcultures: Cultural flows and late modern dance music cultures. In M. Cieslik & G. Pollock (Eds.), *Young people in risk society: The restructuring of youth identities in late modernity* (pp. 140–157). Aldershot: Ashgate.

Carter, T., Vachon, M., Biles, J., Zamprelli, J., & Tolley, E. (Eds.). (2006). *Canadian Journal of Urban Research, 15*(2) (Special Issue: *Our Diverse Cities: Challenges and Opportunities*).

Cashmore E., & Troyna, B. (Eds.). (1982). *Black youth in crisis.* London & Boston: Allen & Unwin.

CBC News. (2001). "Squeegee kids" law upheld in Ontario. *CBC News.* Retrieved February 20, 2008, from http://www.cbc.ca/story/canada/national/2001/08/03/squeegee_010803.html

CBC News. (2005). Child poverty levels in Canada constant. *CBC News.* Retrieved May 18, 2013, from http://www.cbc.ca/news/canada/story/2005/11/23/poverty051123.html

CBC News. (2010). Bullying and sexual orientation by the numbers. *CBC News.* Retrieved May 23, 2013, from http://www.cbc.ca/news/canada/story/2010/10/29/gay-bullying-statistics.html

Center for Human Rights and Global Justice. (2006). *Irreversible consequences: Racial profiling and lethal force in the "war on terror."* New York: NYU School of Law. Retrieved May 17, 2007, from http://www.chrgj.org/docs/CHRGJ%20Irreversible%20Consequences.pdf

Centers for Disease Control and Prevention. (2013). *Youth violence: National statistics.* Retrieved June 5, 2013, from http://www.cdc.gov/violenceprevention/youthviolence/stats_at-a_glance/vca_temp-trends.html

Centre for Social Justice. (2007–2013). Key issues: Aboriginal issues. Retrieved May 31, 2013, from http://www.socialjustice.org/index.php?page=aboriginal-issues

Cervantes, R., Vazquez, E., & Mata, A.G. (2000). Sociocultural issues and youth violence. *Free Inquiry in Creative Sociology, 28*(2), 43–51.

Chandler, K. (1995). *Passages of pride: Lesbian and gay youth come of age.* New York: Times Books.

Chandler, M.J. & Lalonde, C.E. (2008). Cultural continuity as a protective factor against suicide in First Nations youth. *Horizons, 10*(1), 68–72. Retrieved June 9, 2013, from http://www.ccyp.wa.gov.au/files/Chandler

Chappell, R. (1997). *Social welfare in Canadian society.* Toronto: ITP Nelson.

Charles, N. (2002). *Gender in modern Britain.* New York: Oxford University Press.

Cheney, P. (1999, September 22). Judge lays blame for reserve suicides. *Globe and Mail,* p. A3.

Child Health USA. (2003). *Population of children.* Washington: Child Health USA. Retrieved May 22, 2007, from http://mchb.hrsa.gov/chusa03/

Child Trends Data Bank. (2006). *High school dropout rates.* Retrieved October 15, 2007, from http://www.childtrendsdatabank.org/indicators/1highschooldropout.cfm

Child Trends Data Bank. (2012) *High school dropout rates: Indicators on children and youth.* Bethesda, MD: Child Trends. Retrieved May 15, 2013, from http://www.childtrendsdatabank.org/sites/default/files/01_Dropout_Rates.pdf

Chisholm, L., & Hurrelmann, K. (1995). Adolescence in modern Europe: Pluralized transition patterns and their implications for personal and social risks. *Journal of Adolescence, 18,* 129–158.

Christensen, C.P., & Weinfeld, M. (1993). The Black family in Canada: A preliminary exploration of family patterns and inequality. *Canadian Ethnic Studies, 25*(3), 26–44.

Chui, T., & Maheux, H. (2011). *Census 2006: Visible minority women.* Statistics Canada catalogue no. 89-503-X. Ottawa: Statistics Canada. Retrieved May 13, 2013, from http://www.statcan.gc.ca/pub/89-503-x/2010001/article/11527-eng.pdf

Claes, M., Lacourse, E., Ercolani, A.P., Pierro, A., Leone, L., & Presaghi, F. (2005). Parenting, peer orientation, drug use, and anti-social behavior in late adolescence: A cross-national study. *Journal of Youth and Adolescence, 34*(5), 401–411.

Clark, A. (1999, March 22). How teens got the power: Gen Y has the cash, the cool—and a burgeoning consumer culture. *Maclean's,* p. 42.

Clark, S. (1999). What do we know about unmarried mothers? In J. Wong & D. Checkland (Eds.), *Teen pregnancy and parenting: Social and ethical issues* (pp. 10–24). Toronto: University of Toronto Press.

Cochrane, M. (1988). Addressing youth and family vulnerability: Empowerment in an ecological context. *Canadian Journal of Public Health Supplement, 79,* S10–S16.

Codjoe, H. (2006). The role of an affirmed Black cultural identity and heritage in the academic achievement of African-Canadian students. *Intercultural Education, 17*(1), 33–54.

Cohen, C.J., Celestine-Michener, J., Holmes, C., Merseth, J.L., & Ralph, L. (2007). *The attitudes and behaviours of young Black Americans: Research summary.* Chicago: University of Chicago, Centre for the Study of Race, Politics, and Culture. Retrieved December 5, 2007, from www.blackyouthproject.com

Cohen, R. (2000). "Mom is a stranger": The negative impact of immigration policies on the family life of Philipina domestic workers. *Canadian Ethnic Studies, 32*(3), 76–88.

Coker, A.L., McKeown, R.E., Sanderson, M., Davis, K.E., Valois, R.F., & Huebner, E.S. (2000). Severe dating violence and quality of life among South Carolina high school students. *American Journal of Preventative Medicine, 19*(4), 220–227.

Coleman, L., & Cater, S. (2005). Underage "binge" drinking: A qualitative study into motivations and outcomes. *Drugs: Education, Prevention & Policy, 12*(2), 125–136. Retrieved February 17, 2008, from Academic Search Premier database.

Commission des droits de la personne et des droits de la jeunesse. (2011). *Racial profiling and systemic discrimination of racialized youth: Report on the consultation on racial profiling and its consequences.* Montreal: Commission des droits de la personne et des droits de la jeunesse. Retrieved June 8, 2013, from http://www.cdpdj.qc.ca/publications/Profiling_final_EN.pdf

CommonAction. (2013). Neoliberalism in youth programs. *CommonAction,* March 5. Retrieved June 10, 2013, from http://commonaction.blogspot.ca/2013/03/signs-of-neoliberalism-in-youth-programs.html

Conference Board of Canada. (2013). *Gender income gap.* Retrieved May 24, 2013, from http://www.conferenceboard.ca/hcp/details/society/gender-income-gap.aspx

Connolly, J., Craig, W., Goldberg, W., & Pepler, D. (1999). Conceptions of cross-sex friendships and romantic relationships in early adolescence. *Journal of Youth and Adolescence, 28*(4), 481–494.

Cook, E.-D., & Howe, D. (2004). Aboriginal languages of Canada. In W. O'Grady & J. Archibald (Eds.), *Contemporary linguistic analysis* (pp. 294–309). Toronto: Addison Wesley Longman.

Cook, P.J., & Ludwig, J. (2002). The costs of gun violence against children. *Children, Youth, and Gun Violence, 12*(2), 25–37. Retrieved January 27, 2007, from www.futureofchildren.org

Cooper, A. (2007, March 25). The invisible history of the slave trade. *Toronto Star*, p. A15.

Cooper, C., & Roe, S. (2012). *An estimate of youth crime in England and Wales: Police recorded crime committed by young people in 2009/10*. UK Home Office, Research Report 64. Retrieved June 5, 2013, from https://www.gov.uk/government/uploads/system/uploads/attachment_data/file/167982/horr64.pdf

Copeland, B., Armitage, A., & Rutman, D. (1996). Preparation for responsible community living. In B. Galaway & J. Hudson (Eds.), *Youth in transition: Perspectives on research and policy.* Toronto: Thompson Educational Publishing, Inc.

Corak, M. (1999, January). Long-term prospects of the young. *Canadian Economic Observer, 12*(1). Ottawa: Minister of Industry.

Corbeil, J.P. (2000). Sport participation in Canada. *Canadian Social Trends* (Vol. 3) (pp. 214–215). Toronto: Thompson Educational Publishing.

Corrado, R.R., Odgers, C., & Cohen, I.M. (2000). The incarceration of female young offenders: Protection for whom? *Canadian Journal of Criminology, 42*(2), 189–207.

Correctional Service Canada. (1999b). *Substance use by adolescents and subsequent adult criminal activity.* Ottawa: Correctional Service Canada. Retrieved January 11, 2000, from scc.ca/text/pblct/forum/e033/e033f.shtm.

Côté, J. (2005). Trends in youth studies in (English-speaking) North America. In H. Helve & G. Holm (Eds.), *Contemporary youth research: Local expressions and global connections* (pp. 35–38). Aldershot: Ashgate.

Côté, J.A., & Allahar, L.A. (1994). Generation on hold. *Coming of age in the late twentieth century.* Toronto: Stoddart.

Coulter, R.P. (2005). "Girls just want to have fun": Women teachers and the pleasures of the profession. In R.P. Coulter & H. Harper (Eds.), *History is hers: Women educators in twentieth century Ontario* (pp. 211–229). Calgary: Detselig.

Council of Ministers of Education Canada. (1999). *Education indicators in Canada. Report of the pan-Canadian education indicators program 1999*. Ottawa: Council of Ministers of Education Canada. Retrieved November 17, 2007, from http://www.statcan.ca/english/freepub/81-582-XIE/1999001/1999001.htm.

Council of Ontario Universities. (2013). *Facts and figures: Applications and enrollment.* Toronto: Council of Ontario Universities. Retrieved May 9, 2013, from http://www.cou.on.ca/applications-enrolment/

Cox, K. (2000, November 25). Innu to show video of gas-sniffers in agony. *Globe and Mail*, p. A7.

Cozzens, L. (1998). *School integration in Little Rock, Arkansas.* Online resource. Retrieved May 3, 2007, from http://www.watson.org/~lisa/blackhistory/school-integration/lilrock/

Crago, A.L. (1996). Queer and young and so much else. *Canadian Woman Studies, 16*(2), 15–17.

Craig, R.K.J., & Hodson, S. (2000). Homeless youth in London: Accommodation, employment, and health outcomes at 1 year. *Psychological Medicine, 30*, 187–194. Retrieved February 19, 2008, from the Academic Search Premier database.

Crawford, J. (1995, Winter). Endangered Native American languages: What is to be done, and why? *The Bilingual Research Journal, 19*(1), 17–38. Retrieved May 4, 2007, from http://www.ncela.gwu.edu/pubs/nabe/brj/v19/19_1_crawford.pdf

Creese, G., Dyck, I., & McLaren, A. (1999). *Reconstituting the family: Negotiating immigration and settlement.* Working paper 99-10. Vancouver: Centre for Excellence, RIIM.

Crime in America (2010). *Female involvement in crime growing: Crime news.* March 15. Retrieved June 8, 2013, from http://www.crimeinamerica.net/2010/03/15/female-involvement-in-crime-growing-crime-news/

Crisis. (2012). *Research briefing: Young, hidden and homeless.* London: Crisis. Retrieved May 19, 2013, from http://www.crisis.org.uk/data/files/publications/Crisis%20briefing%20-%20 youth%20homelessness.pdf

Cross, M. (1982). Unemployment of black youth. In E. Cashmore & B. Troyna (Eds.), *Black youth in crisis* (pp. 50–75). London: Allen & Unwin.

Cross, W.E. (2003). Tracing the historical origins of youth delinquency & violence: Myths & realities about Black culture. *Journal of Social Issues, 59*(1), 67–82. Retrieved March 14, 2007, from Academic Search Premier database.

Crysdale, S. (1991). *Family under stress.* Toronto: Thompson.

Cuddington, L. (1995, January). Young offenders: A correctional policy perspective. *Forum on Corrections Research, 7*(1), 43–45.

Currie, D. (1999). *Girl talk: Adolescent magazines and their readers.* Toronto: University of Toronto Press.

Currie, F., & Covell, K. (1998). Juvenile justice and juvenile decision making: A comparison of young offenders with their non-offending peers. *International Journal of Children's Rights, 6,* 125–136.

Cusick, L. (2002). Youth prostitution: A literature review. *Child Abuse Review, 11,* 230–251.

Dachner, N., & Tarasuk, V. (2002). Homeless "squeegee kids": Food insecurity and daily survival. *Social Science & Medicine, 54,* 1039–1049.

Dado, N. (2103, April 11). Hate crimes against Muslims only escalating 10 years after 9/11. *The Arab American News.* Retrieved June 8, 2103, from http://www.arabamericannews.com/ news/index.php?mod=article&cat=Community&article=6246

Dahinten, V.S. & Willms, J.D. (2002). The effects of adolescent childbearing on children's outcomes. In J.D. Willms (Ed.), *Vulnerable children: Findings from Canada's National Longitudinal Survey of Children and Youths* (pp. 243–258). Edmonton: University of Alberta Press.

Dallaire, C., & Denis, C. (2005). Assymetrical hybridities: Youths at francophone games in Canada. *Canadian Journal of Sociology, 30*(2), 143–168.

Danesi, M. (1994). *Cool: The signs and meanings of adolescence.* Toronto: University of Toronto Press.

Darling, N., Dowdy, B.B., Lee Van Horn, M., & Caldwell, L. (1999). Mixed-sex settings and the perception of competence. *Journal of Youth and Adolescence, 28*(4), 461–480.

Das, S., Eargle, L.A., & Butts, F.M. (2011). The effects of religiosity on perceptions about premarital sex. *Sociation Today, 9*(1). Retrieved June 2, 2013, from http://www.ncsociology.org/ sociationtoday/v91/das.htm

Davies, G. (1995). Private education for women in early Nova Scotia: 1784–1894. *Atlantis, 20*(1), 9–19.

Davies, L., McKinnon, M., & Rains, P. (1999). "On my own": A new discourse of dependence and independence from teen mothers. In J. Wong & D. Checkland (Eds.), *Teen pregnancy and parenting: Social and ethical issues* (pp. 38–51). Toronto: University of Toronto Press.

Davies, S. (1994). In search of resistance and rebellion among high school dropouts. *The Canadian Journal of Sociology, 19*(1), 331–350.

Davies, S., & Guppy, N. (1998). Race and Canadian education. In V. Satzewitch (Ed.), *Racism and social inequality in Canada: Concepts, controversies, and strategies of resistance.* Toronto: Thompson Educational Publishing, Inc.

Davis, E.C., & Friel, L.V. (2001). Adolescent sexuality: Disentangling the effects of family structure and family context. *Journal of Marriage and Family, 63*, 669–681.

Dearden, L., Emmerson, C., Frayne, C., & Meghir, C. (2006). *Education subsidies and school dropout rates.* London: London School of Economics, Centre for the Economics in Education. Retrieved May 11, 2007, from http://www.ifs.org.uk/wps/wp0511.pdf

DeKeseredy, W.S. (1996). Patterns of family violence. In M. Baker (Ed.), *Families: Changing trends in Canada* (3rd ed.) (pp. 238–266). Toronto: McGraw-Hill Ryerson Limited.

Delgado, M. (2002). *New frontiers for youth development in the twenty-first century: Revitalizing and broadening youth development.* New York: Columbia University Press.

DeNavas-Walt, D., Proctor, B.D., & Smith, J.C. 2012. *Income, poverty and health insurance coverage in the United States: 2011: Current population reports.* Washington: U.S. Department of Commerce. Retrieved May 13, 2013, from http://www.census.gov/prod/2012pubs/p60-243.pdf

Department for Education and Employment, UK. (1999). *More young Asians go to university.* Retrieved December 12, 2003, from http://www.gnn.gov.uk/80256CAC005CC584/Searc h/3F96E495FA72E74480256746003

Department for Education and Employment, UK. (2000). *Boys need school culture where it's cool to succeed—Morris.* London: Department for Education and Employment. Retrieved December 12, 2003, from http://www.gnn.gov.uk/80256CACC584/Search/ D3720DD8E933023E8025687F00

Department of Finance Canada. (2006). *Advantage Canada: Building a strong economy for Canadians.* Ottawa: Department of Finance Canada. Retrieved July 17, 2013, from http:// www.fin.gc.ca/ec2006/pdf/plane.pdf

Department of Health, UK. (1999). *Position paper on prevention of teenage pregnancy.* London: Department of Health. Retrieved February 20, 2007, from http://www.riph.org.uk/prevention_teenage_pregnancies.html.

Department of Health, UK. (2006). *Abortion Statistics, England, and Wales: 2005—Statistical Bulletin.* London: Department of Health. Retrieved April 30, 2007, from http://www. dh.gov.uk/en/Publicationsandstatistics/Publications/PublicationsStatistics/D_4136852

Desai, S., & Subramanian, S. (2000). *Colour, culture, and dual consciousness: Issues identified by South Asian immigrant youth in the Greater Toronto Area.* Toronto: Council of Agencies Serving South Asians and South Asian Women's Centre.

Desjardins, L. & King, D. (2011). *Expectations and labour market outcomes of doctoral graduates from Canadian universities.* Ottawa: Statistics Canada. Retrieved May 21, 2013, from http:// www.statcan.gc.ca/pub/81-595-m/81-595-m2011089-eng.pdf

De Waal, A. (2002). Realising child rights in Africa: Children, young people, and leadership. In A. De Waal & N. Argenti (Eds.), *Young Africa: Realising the rights of children and youth* (pp. 1–28). Trenton: Africa World Press, Inc.

De Waal, A., & Argenti, N. (Eds.). (2002). *Young Africa: Realising the rights of children and youth*. Trenton: Africa World Press, Inc.

Dhruvarajan, V. (2003). Hindu Indo-Canadian families. In M. Lynn (Ed.), *Voices: Essays on Canadian families* (2nd ed.) (pp. 301–328). Toronto: Nelson Canada.

Di Done, R. (2002). *Child poverty: Scope and solutions. Material, emotional, social, and spiritual poverty in the G7 countries*. Paper presented for the World Summit on Sustainable Development's Global NGO Forum, Strategies for Sustainable Development Event, August 29, 2002, Johannesburg Expo Centre, South Africa. Retrieved May 17, 2007, from http://www.osde.ca/pdf/OPCR_Child_Poverty_in_G7_Countries_%20Johannesburg_2002.pdf

Dittus, P.J., & Jaccard, J. (2000). Adolescents' perceptions of maternal disapproval of sex: Relationship to sexual outcomes. *Journal of Adolescent Health, 26*, 268–278.

Donnelly, J. (2007). Sobering statistics. *Listen, 61*, 18–19. Retrieved February 18, 2008, from ProQuest database.

Doob, A., & Cesaroni, C. (2004). *Responding to youth crime in Canada*. Toronto: University of Toronto Press.

Dortch-Tiger, G. (1957, September 19). *Central High thrown into national spotlight as it faces integration: Settlements pending in federal courts*. Little Rock Central 40th Anniversary Web site. Retrieved May 3, 2007, from http://www.centralhigh57.org/the_tiger.htm

Dowd, J.J. (1981). Age and inequality: A critique of the age stratification model. *Human Development, 24*, 157–171.

Dowden, C., & Brennan, S. (2010). Police-reported hate crime in Canada, 2010. *Juristat*. Statistics Canada catalogue no. 85-002-X. Ottawa: Statistics Canada. Retrieved June 8, 2013, from http://www.statcan.gc.ca/pub/85-002-x/2012001/article/11635-eng.htm

Downe, P., & "Ashley-Mika." (2003). "The people we think we are": Social identities of girls involved in prostitution. In K. Gerkoff & J. Runner (Eds.), *Being heard: The experiences of young women in prostitution* (pp. 46–67). Halifax: Fernwood Publishing and Research and Education for Solutions to Violence and Abuse.

Driedger, L. (2001). Changing visions in ethnic relations. *Canadian Journal of Sociology, 26*(3), 421–442.

Drolet, M. (2005). *Participation in post-secondary education in Canada: Has the role of parental income and education changed over the 1990s?* Ottawa: Statistics Canada. Retrieved May 7, 2013, from http://www.statcan.gc.ca/pub/11f0019m/11f0019m2005243-eng.pdf

Dryburgh, H. (2001). *Changing our ways: Why and how Canadians use the Internet*. Statistics Canada Catalogue No. 56F0006XIE2000001. Retrieved May 10, 2007, from http://www.statcan.ca/english/research/56F0006XIE/56F0006XIE2000001.pdf.

Duffy, A., & Momirov, J. (1997). *Family violence: A Canadian introduction*. Toronto: James Lorimer & Company, Publishers.

Duncan, S. (2000). *Is there a generation gap?* Billings: Montana State University, Communication Services. Retrieved January 7, 2008, from http://www.montana.edu/wwwpb/home/gap.html

Dunn, K.A., Runyah, C.W., Cohen, L.R., & Schulman, M.D. (1998). Teens at work: A statewide study of jobs, hazards, and injuries. *Journal of Adolescent Health, 22*(1), 19–25. Retrieved January 13, 2008, from Academic Search Elite homepage.

Dupont, C. (2000). Unrebellious youth: Old assumptions about marketing to the young don't work with the screenagers. *Marketing, 105*(1), 20.

Durham, M. (1999). Girls, media, and the negotiation of sexuality: A study of race, class, and gender in adolescent peer groups. *Journalism and Mass Communication Quarterly, 76*(2), 193–216.

Earls, F., & Carlson, M. (2002). Adolescents as collaborators: In search of well-being. In M. Tienda & W.J. Wilson (Eds.), *Youth in cities: A cross-national perspective* (pp. 58–86). Cambridge: Cambridge University Press.

East Midlands Public Health Observatory. (2005). *Teenage pregnancy.* London: Office for National Statistics. Retrieved April 30, 2007, from http://www.empho.org.uk/pages/viewResource. aspx?id=9807 *Data for 2005 are provisional.*

Eaton, J. (1997, September 1). Labor's love lost? *Toronto Star*, p. E1.

Eddington, R., & Parker, H. (2002). From one-off triers to regular users: Measuring the regularity of drug taking in a cohort of English adolescents (1996–1999). *Addiction Research and Theory, 10*(1), 97–114. Retrieved February 18, 2008, from the Academic Search Premier database.

Education Today. (1996). Post-schooling employment. *Education Today, 8*(1), 5.

Edwards, R., Gonsalves, L.M., & Willie, C.V. (2000). The school reform movement and the education of African-American youth. *Journal of Negro Education, 69*(4), 252–254.

Egley, A., & Howell, J.C. (2012, April). *Highlights of the 2010 National Youth Gang Survey.* Office of Juvenile Justice and Delinquency Prevention Fact Sheet. Retrieved June 8, 2103, from http://www.ojjdp.gov/pubs/237542.pdf

Eichler, M., & Pedersen, A-M. (2012). *Marriage and divorce.* The Canadian Encyclopedia. Retrieved June 2, 2013, from http://www.thecanadianencyclopedia.com/articles/marriage-and-divorce

Elton, S., & Brearton, S. (1997). Youth and work. *This Magazine, 31*(1), 4–5.

Engen, R.L., Steen, S., & Bridges, G.S. (2002). Racial disparities in the punishment of youth: A theoretical and empirical assessment of the literature. *Social Problems, 49*(2), 194–220.

Etherington, B. (1997). *Review of multiculturalism and justice issues: A framework for addressing reform.* Ottawa: Research and Statistics Directorate, Department of Justice, Canada.

European Commission. (1998). *Sexual harassment in the workplace in the European Union.* Retrieved May 31, 2013, from http://www.un.org/womenwatch/osagi/pdf/shworkpl.pdf

European Travel Commission (2012). *New media trend watch: Usage patterns and demographics.* Retrieved June 10, 2013, from http://www.newmediatrendwatch.com/markets-by-country/18-uk/148-usage-patterns-and-demographics

Eurostats. (2009). *Youth in Europe: A statistical portrait.* Luxembourg: Publications Office of the European Union. Retrieved May 17, 2013, from http://epp.eurostat.ec.europa.eu/cache/ITY_OFFPUB/KS-78-09-920/EN/KS-78-09-920-EN.PDF

Everatt, D. (2001). From urban warrior to market segment? Youth in South Africa 1990–2000. In H. Helve & C. Wallace (Eds.), *Youth, citizenship, and empowerment* (pp. 290–299). Aldershot: Ashgate Publishing Limited.

Facer, K., & Furlong, R. (2001). Beyond the myth of the "cyberkid": Young people and the margins of the information revolution. *Journal of Youth Studies, 4*(4), 451–469.

Farber, P., Provenzo, E.F., & Holm, G. (1994). *Schooling in the light of popular culture.* New York: State University of New York Press.

FBI (Federal Bureau of Investigation). (2012). *Hate crime statistics 2011*. Retrieved June 8, 2013, from http://www.fbi.gov/news/stories/2012/december/annual-hate-crimes-report-released/ annual-hate-crimes-report-released

Federal Interagency Forum on Child and Family Statistics. (2012). *American's children in brief: Key national indicators of well being, 2012*. Retrieved May 9, 2013, from http://www.child-stats.gov/americaschildren/famsoc.asp

Feiring, C., Deblinger, E., Hoch-Espada, A., & Haworth, T. (2002). Romantic relationship aggression and attitudes in high school students: The role of gender, grade, and attachment and emotional styles. *Journal of Youth and Adolescence, 31*(5), 373–385.

Fekete, L. (2006). Racial profiling and shoot to kill. *IRR News. Independent Race and Refugee News Network*. Retrieved May 11, 2007, from http://www.irr.org.uk/2006/may/ha000019.html

Feng, Y., Dubey, S., & Brooks, B. (2007). *Persistence on low income among non-elderly unattached individuals*. Income Research Paper Series. Statistics Canada catalogue no. 75F0002MIE - No. 5. Retrieved May 24, 2013, from http://www.statcan.gc.ca/pub/75f0002m/75f0002 m2007005-eng.pdf

Ferguson, S. (2000, May 29). Wired teens: A new study documents the embraces of the Internet by Canadian kids—and lifts the veil on how they use it. *Maclean's, 113*(22), 38.

Ferman, B. (2005). Youth civic engagement in practice: The youth VOICES program. *The Good Society, 14*(3), 45–50. Retrieved February 20, 2008, from ProQuest database.

Fieldhouse, E.A., Kalra, V.S., & Alam, S. (2002). A new deal for young people from minority ethnic communities in the UK. *Journal of Ethnic and Migration Studies, 28*(3), 499–513.

Finch, N. (2003). *Demographic trends in the UK. First report for the project: Welfare policy and employment in the context of family change*. Heslington: Social Policy Research Unit, University of York. Retrieved May 20, 2007, from http://www.york.ac.uk/inst/spru/research/nordic/ ukdemo.PDF

Fine, S. (1999, October 11). Teenage daughters still find dad distant. *Globe and Mail*, pp. A1, A6.

Fine, S. (2000, August 29). University fee hikes slowing: Statscan. *Globe and Mail*, p. A8.

Finer, L.B. (2007). Trends in premarital sex in the United States, 1954–2003. *Public Health Report, 122*(1), 73–8.

Fingerhut, L.A., & Christoffel, K.K. (2002). Firearm-related death and injury among children and adolescents. *Children, Youth, and Gun Violence, 12*(2), 25–37. Retrieved January 12, 2008, from www.futureofchildren.org

Fisher, W.A., & Boroditsky, R. (2000). Sexual activity, contraceptive choice, and sexual and reproductive health indicators among single Canadian women aged 15-29: Additional findings from the Canadian contraception study. *Canadian Journal of Human Sexuality, 9*(2), 79–93.

Fiske, J.A., & Johnny, R. (1996). The Nedut'en family: Yesterday and today. In M. Lynn (Ed.), *Voices: Essays on Canadian families*. Toronto: Nelson Canada.

Fitzgerald, M.D. (1995). Homeless youths and the child welfare system: Implications for policy and service. *Child Welfare, 74*(3), 717–731.

Flanagan, C. (2006). *Developmental roots of political engagement*. University Park: Pennsylvania State University, the Network on Transitions to Adulthood. Reprint of: Flanagan, C.A. (2003). Developmental roots of political engagement. *PS: Political Science and Politics,*

36(2), 257–261. Retrieved January 20, 2008, from http://www.transad.pop.upenn.edu/downloads/flanagan-politengagment-to%20USA.pdf

Florian-Lacy, D.J., Jefferson, J.L., & Fleming, J. (2002). The relationship of gang membership to self-esteem, family relations, and learning disabilities. *TCA Journal, 30*(1), 4–16.

Floyd, F.J., Stein, T.S., Harter, K.S.M., Allison, A., & Nye, C.L. (1999). Gay, lesbian, and bisexual youths: Separation-individuation, parental attitudes, identity consolidation, and well-being. *Journal of Youth and Adolescence, 28*(6), 719–739.

Foner, N. (1997). The immigrant family: Cultural legacies and cultural changes. *International Migration Review, 31*(4), 961–974.

Fontes, M., & Margolies, K. (2010). *Youth and unions*. Cornell University, ILR School. Retrieved June 1, 2013, from http://digitalcommons.ilr.cornell.edu/cgi/viewcontent.cgi?article=1103&context=workingpapers

Fontes, M., & Roach, P. (2007). Predictors and confounders of unprotected sex: A UK Web-based study. *The European Journal of Contraception and Reproductive Health, 12*(1), 36–45. Retrieved January 10, 2007, from the Academic Search Premier database.

Foshee, V.A., Lindner, F., MacDougall, J.E., & Bangdiwala, S. (2001). Gender differences in the longitudinal predictors of adolescent dating violence. *Preventative Medicine, 32*, 128–141.

Foster, K. (2012, October). Youth employment and un(der)employment in Canada: More than a temporary problem? *Behind the numbers*. Canadian Centre for Policy Alternatives. Retrieved June 1, 2013, from http://www.policyalternatives.ca/sites/default/files/uploads/publications/National%20Office/2012/10/Youth%20Unemployment.pdf

Fowler, B. (2011). Justin Bieber sets YouTube record, hits 2 billion views. *ENews*. Retrieved June 4, 2013, from http://ca.eonline.com/news/272657/justin-bieber-sets-youtube-record-hits-2-billion-views

Frank, B. (1994). Queer selves/queer in schools: Young men and sexualities. In S. Prentice (Ed.), *Sex in schools: Canadian education & sexual regulation* (pp. 44–59). Toronto: Our Schools/Ourselves.

Frank, J. (2000). 15 years of AIDS in Canada. *Canadian Social Trends* (Vol. 3) (pp. 60–64). Toronto: Thompson Educational Publishing.

Frankel, G., & Jones, T. (2005, July 27). In Britain, a divide over racial profiling. Mistaken killing by police sets off debate. *Washington Post*. Retrieved May 11, 2007, from http://www.washingtonpost.com/wp-dyn/content/article/2005/07/26/AR2005072601789.html

Franz, B. (2007). Europe's Muslim youth: An inquiry into the politics of discrimination, relative deprivation, and identity formation. *Mediterranean Quarterly, 18*(1), 89–112. Retrieved January 15, 2008, from Academic Search Premier database.

Frederick, J.A., & Boyd, M. (1998). The impact of family structure on high school completion. *Canadian Social Trends, 48*, 12–14.

Freeze, C. (1999, September 27). Teen dies in a dough-making machine. *Globe and Mail*, p. A8.

Frenette, M. (2005). *The impact of tuition fees on university access: Evidence from a large-scale price deregulation in professional programs*. Ottawa: Statistics Canada.

Frenette, M., & Morissette, R. (2005). Will they ever converge? Earnings of immigrant and Canadian-born workers over the last two decades. *International Migration Review, 39*(1), 228–258.

Friesen. J. (2007, January 21). Hundreds of girls work Winnipeg's sex trade. *The Globe and Mail*, A1, A7.

Fuligni, A.J. (1997). The academic achievement of adolescents from immigrant families: The roles of family background, attitudes, and behavior. *Child Development, 68*(2), 351–363.

Fuligni, A.J., & Yoshikawa, K. (2003). Socioeconomic resources, parenting, and the child development among immigrant families. In M. Bornstein & R. Bradley (Eds.), *Socioeconomic status, parenting, and child development* (pp. 107–124). Mahwah: Lawrence Erlbaum Associates, Inc.

Fuller, M. (1982). Young, female and black. In B. Troyna & R. Hatcher (Eds.), *Black youth in crisis* (pp. 87–99). London: Allen & Unwin.

The Future of Children. (2002). Children, youth, and gun violence: Analysis. *The Future of Children, 12*(2), 1–4. Retrieved June 8, 2013, from http://www.princeton.edu/futureofchildren/publications/docs/12_02_ExecSummary.pdf

Gabor, P., Thibodeau, S., & Manychief, S. (1996). Taking flight? The transition experiences of Native youth. In B. Galaway & J. Hudson (Eds.), *Youth in transition: Perspectives on research and policy* (pp. 79–89). Toronto: Thompson Educational Publishing, Inc.

Gadalla, T.M. (2008). Gender differences in poverty rates after marital dissolution: A longitudinal study. *Journal of Divorce & Remarriage* 49(3/4), 225–238.

Gaetz, S., O'Grady, B., & Vaillaincourt, B. (1999). *Making money: The Shout Clinic report on homeless youth and employment.* Toronto: Central Toronto Community Health Centres.

Galabuzi, G. E. (2005). *The racialization of poverty in Canada: Implications for Section 15 Charter protection.* The National Anti-Racism Council of Canada National Conference Ottawa, Nov. 10-13. Retrieved May 31, 2013, from http://action.web.ca/home/narcc/attach/GEGSection%2015%20Implications%20of%20Racialization%20of%20Poverty.pdf

Galambos, N.L., & Kolaric, G.C. (1994). *Canada.* In K. Hurrelman (Ed.), *International handbook of adolescence* (pp. 92–107). Westport: Greenwood Press.

Galarneau, D., & Morissette, R. (2008). *Immigrants' education and required job skills.* Ottawa: Statistics Canada. Retrieved May 4, 2013, from http://www.statcan.gc.ca/pub/75-001-x/2008112/pdf/10766-eng.pdf

Galarneau D., & Radulescu, M. (2009). *Employment among the disabled.* Ottawa: Statistics Canada. Retrieved May 21, 2013, from http://www.statcan.gc.ca/pub/75-001-x/75-001-x2009105-eng.pdf

Galaway, B., & Hudson, J. (Eds.). (1996). *Youth in transition: Perspectives on research and policy.* Toronto: Thompson Educational Publishing.

Galt, V. (1999a, November 15). Fighting "poor" label earns Parkdale kids special recognition. *Globe and Mail*, p. A7.

Galt, V. (1999b, December 13). I can't afford it any more. I'm 20 grand in debt. *Globe and Mail*, p. A16.

Gandhi, U. (2007, January 21). Alberta—Contentious child legislation. *The Globe and Mail*, A7.

Gatti, U., Tremblay, R.E., Vitaro, F., & MacDuff, P. (2005). Youth gangs, delinquency, and drug use: A test of the selection, facilitation, and enhancement hypotheses. *Journal of Child Psychology and Psychiatry, 46*(11), 1178–1190.

Gauthier, M. (2003). The inadequacy of concepts: The rise of youth interest in civic participation in Quebec. *Journal of Youth Studies, 6*(3), 265–277. Retrieved January 19, 2008, from Academic Search Premier database.

Gennaro, S. (2005). Purchasing the Canadian teenage identity: American media and brand-name consumption. *International Social Science Review, 80*(3/4), 119–136.

Gerbner, G. (1995). Casting and fate: Women and minorities on television drama, game shows, and news. In E. Hollander, C. van der Linden, & P. Rutten (Eds.), *Communication, cultures, and community* (pp. 3–33). Houten: Bohn Stafleu van Logham.

Gerbner, G. (1998). Who is shooting whom? The content and the context of media violence. In M. Pomerance & J. Sakeris (Eds.), *Bang bang shoot shoot: Essays on guns and popular culture* (pp. 69–78). Toronto: Media Studies Working Group.

Gfellner, B.M., & Hundleby, J.D. (1990). The status of Canadian research on adolescence: 1980–1987. *Canadian Psychology, 31*(2), 132–137.

Ghuman, P.A.S. (1999). *Asian adolescents in the West.* Leicester: British Psychological Society Books.

Giguère, B., Lalonde, R., & Lou, E. (2010). Living at the crossroads of cultural worlds: The experience of normative conflicts by second generation immigrant youth. *Social and Personality Psychology Compass, 4*(1), 14–29.

Gillis, J.R. (1981). *Youth and history: Tradition and change in European age relations, 1770–present* (Expanded student ed.). Orlando: Academic Press, Inc.

Gilroy, P. (1987). *"There ain't no black in the Union Jack": The cultural politics of race and nation.* Chicago: The University of Chicago Press.

Gingwright, S., & Cammarota, J. (2006). Introduction. In S. Gingwright, P. Noguera, & J. Cammarota (Eds.), *Beyond resistance! Youth activism and community change: New democratic possibilities for practice and policy for America's youth* (pp. xiii–xxi). New York: Routledge.

Girls Action Foundation. (2011). *Girls in Canada today: National opinion poll and report on the status of girls.* Montreal: Girls Action Foundation. Retrieved July 17, 2013, from http://girlsactionfoundation.ca/files/girls_in_canada_today_report_by_girls_action_foundation.pdf

Giroux, H.A. (2003). *The abandoned generation: Democracy beyond the culture of fear.* New York: Palgrave Macmillan.

Globe and Mail. (1999, July 31). More students burdened by loans, study finds. *Globe and Mail,* p. A2.

Globe and Mail. (2007, February 22). So, how are the kids? *Globe and Mail,* p. A16.

GLSEN (Gay, Lesbian and Straight Education Network). (2009). *The 2009 national school climate survey.* Retrieved May 23, 2013, from http://www.glsen.org/cgi-bin/iowa/all/news/record/2624.html

Gordon, D. (2000, June 17). Glow sticks all the rave. *Toronto Star,* p. R14.

Gordon, E. (1999). *Separation, reunification, and the hybridization of culture: A study of Caribbean immigrant families in Toronto.* MA thesis. Toronto: York University.

Gordon, R. (2000). Criminal business organizations, street gangs and 'wanna-be' groups: A Vancouver perspective. *Canadian Journal of Criminology, 42*(1), 39–60.

Gorkoff, K., & Runner, J. (2003). Children and youth exploited through prostitution. In K. Gorkoff & J. Runner (Eds.), *Being heard: The experiences of young women in prostitution* (pp. 12–27). Halifax: Fernwood Publishing and Research and Education for Solutions to Violence and Abuse.

Gourevitch, P. (1993). The Crown Heights riot and its aftermath. *Commentary,* 29(1), 29.

Government of Canada. (1998). *Tobacco and health: Government responses.* Ottawa: Government of Canada. Retrieved January 12, 1999, from http://dsp-psd.pwgsc.gc.ca/Collection-R/LoPBdP/modules/prb98-8-tobacco/index-e.htm

Government of Canada. (2013). *Workplace safety.* Services for Youth. Retrieved May 31, 2013, from http://www.youth.gc.ca/eng/topics/jobs/safety.shtml

Government of Ontario. (2008). *The review of the roots of youth violence.* Toronto: Government of Ontario. Retrieved June 8, 2013, from http://www.children.gov.on.ca/htdocs/english/documents/topics/youthandthelaw/rootsofyouthviolence-summary.pdf

gov.uk. (2013). *National minimum wage rates.* Retrieved May 24, 2013 from https://www.gov.uk/national-minimum-wage-rates

Goyette, K., & Xie, Y. (1999). Educational expectations of Asian-American youths: Determinants and ethnic differences. *Sociology of Education, 72,* 22–36.

Grainger, H. (2006). *Trade union membership 2005.* London: Employment Market Analysis and Research, Department of Trade and Industry. Retrieved December 3, 2007, from http://www.berr.gov.uk/files/file25737.pdf

Graydon, S. (1997). *Round table report on the portrayal of young women in the media.* Ottawa: Status of Women Canada. Retrieved May 15, 2000, from http://www.swc-cfc.gc.ca/pubs/roundtablemedia/roundtablemedia_e.pdf

Green, H. (2007, April 8). The greening of America's campuses: College students across the country are fired up about global warming, and they're gathering online to agitate for change. Is this the next big youth movement? *Business Week, 4029,* 62. Retrieved February 5, 2008, from ABI/INFORM Global database.

Greenwood, J., Fernández-Villaverde, J. & Guner, N. (2010). *From shame to game in one hundred years: An economic model of the rise in premarital sex and its de-stigmatization.* Discussion Paper No. 4708. Bonn: Institute for the Study of Labour (IZA). Retrieved June 2, 2013, from http://www.econstor.eu/dspace/bitstream/10419/36030/1/619869844.pdf

Gregg, P., & Tominey, E. (2004). *The wage scar from youth unemployment.* The Centre for Market and Public Organisation, Department of Economics, University of Bristol, UK. Retrieved July 17, 2013, from http://ideas.repec.org/p/bri/cmpowp/04-097.html

Grewal, S., Bottorff, J.L., & Hilton, B. (2005). The influence of family on immigrant South Asian women's health. *Journal of Family Nursing, 11*(3), 242–263.

Griffiths, M.J. (2013, February 26). The unhappy hookah. *The Wall Street Journal.* Retrieved June 10, 2103, from http://online.wsj.com/article/SB1000142412788732419620457829636003470836 2.html

Grinder, R.E. (1973). *Adolescence.* Toronto: John Wiley & Sons.

Grittani-Livingston, M. (2007, May 29). McJob: Fun, well-regarded, much-desired employ? *Quill & Quire.* Retrieved January 16, 2008, from http://www.quillandquire.com/blog/index.php/2007/05/29/mcjob-fun-well-regarded-much-desired-employ/

Grover, S. (2005). Pushing under-18s onto the street: A Canadian charter analysis of Ontario's welfare-to-work scheme. *International Journal of Human Rights, 9*(1), 37–48. Retrieved October 22, 2007, from Academic Search Premier database.

Guttman, J., & Alice, M. (1991). Issues in the career development of adolescent females: Implications for educational and guidance practices. *Guidance & Counselling, 6*(3), 59–75.

Haddad, T., & Lam, L. (1988). Canadian families—men's involvement in family work: A case study of immigrant men in Toronto. *International Journal of Comparative Sociology, 29*(3–4), 269–281.

Hamilton, B.E., Martin, J.A., & Ventura, S.J. (2006). *National vital statistics report. Births: Preliminary data for 2005.* Washington: National Center for Health Statistics. Retrieved April 30, 2007, from http://www.cdc.gov/nchs/products/pubs/pubd/hestats/prelimbirths05/prelimbirths05.htm

Hammer, K. (2012, August 24). TDSB allows cellphones back in the classroom. *The Globe and Mail.* Retrieved July 17, 2013, from http://www.theglobeandmail.com/news/toronto/tdsb-allows-cellphones-back-in-the-classroom/article598155/

Hampson, K. (1996). Authenticity, music, television. In M. Pomerance & J. Sakeris (Eds.), *Pictures of a generation on hold: Selected papers* (pp. 74–87). Toronto: Media Studies Working Group.

Handa, A. (1997). *Caught between omissions: Exploring "culture conflict" among second-generation South Asian women in Canada.* PhD thesis. Toronto: University of Toronto.

Harcourt, B.E. (2006). *Muslim profiles post 9/11: Is racial profiling an effective counterterrorist measure and does it violate the right to be free from discrimination? Public law and legal theory.* Working paper no. 123. Chicago: The University of Chicago, The Law School. Retrieved May 11, 2007, from http://papers.ssrn.com/sol3/papers.cfm?abstract_id=893905

Hargrove, B. (2000, July 19). Dying to work: We should protect our young. *Globe and Mail,* p. A11.

Harper, T. (2007, March 25). Youth crime ... and punishment. *Toronto Star,* p. A11.

Hartnagel, T.F. (1998). Labour-market problems and crime in the transition from school to work. *The Canadian Review of Sociology and Anthropology, 35*(3), 435–460.

Hatcher, M. (2003). Public affairs challenges for multinational corporations. In S. John & S. Thomson (Eds.), *New activism and the corporate response* (pp. 97–14). New York: Palgrave Macmillan.

Haw, C., & Hawton, K. (2007). Deliberate self-harm in young people: Characteristics and subsequent mortality in a 20-year cohort of patients presenting to hospital. *Journal of Clinical Psychiatry, 68*(10), 1574–1583.

Hazards. (2006). Too young to die. *Hazards Magazine, 95* (July/September). Retrieved January 30, 2008, from http://www.hazards.org/2young2die/index.htm#introduction

Health and Welfare Canada. (1992). Research update. *Health Promotion, 31*(2), 16–17.

Health Canada. (1995). *1994 Youth Smoking Survey.* Ottawa: Health Canada. Retrieved November 12, 2007, from http://www.hc-sc.gc.ca/hl-vs/pubs/tobac-tabac/yss-etj-1994/ch2_e.html.

Health Canada. (2000). *Examining youth smoking and relapse prevention: A review of the literature.* Ottawa: Health Canada. Retrieved May 20, 2000, from http://www.hc-sc.gc.ca/hecs-sesc/tobacco/prog_arc/youth_smoking/index.html

Health Canada. (2011). *Major findings from the Canadian Alcohol and Drug Use Monitoring Survey (CSUMS).* Retrieved June 9, 2013, from http://www.hc-sc.gc.ca/hc-ps/drugs-drogues/stat/index-eng.php

Health Canada. (2012). *Summary of the results from the 2010–2011 Youth Smoking Survey.* Retrieved June 9, 2013, from http://www.hc-sc.gc.ca/hc-ps/tobac-tabac/research-recherche/stat/_survey-sondage_2010-2011/result-eng.php

Health Protection Agency, UK. (2006a). *Health Protection Agency points to "increasing pool" of UK HIV cases.* London: Health Protection Agency. Retrieved January 12, 2008, from http://www.privatehealth.co.uk/news/november-2006/uk-hiv-statistics-294/

Health Protection Agency, UK. (2006b). *63,500 adults now living with HIV in the UK.* London: Health Protection Agency. Retrieved January 12, 2008, from http://www.hpa.org.uk/webw/HPAweb&HPAwebStandard/HPAweb_C/1195733729992?p=1158945066097

Hébert, Y. (2001). Identity, diversity, and education: A critical review of the literature. *Canadian Ethnic Studies, 32,* 111–125

Heckman, J.J. (1994). Is job training oversold? *Public Interest, 115,* 91–115. Retrieved December 15, 2007, from Academic Search Premier database.

Heitmeyer, W. (2002). Have cities ceased to function as "integration machines" for young people? In M. Tienda & W.J. Wilson (Eds.), *Youth in cities: A cross-national perspective* (pp. 87–112). Cambridge: Cambridge University Press.

Helve, H., & Wallace, C. (Eds.). (2001). *Youth, citizenship, and empowerment.* Aldershot: Ashgate Publishing Limited.

Henry, F., & Tator, C. (1994). Racism and the university. *Canadian Ethnic Studies, 26*(3), 74–91.

Henry, F., Tator, C., Mattis, W., & Rees, T. (2000). Racism in Canadian education. In F. Henry, C. Tator, W. Mattis & T. Rees (Eds.), *The colour of democracy: Racism in Canadian society* (2nd ed.) (pp. 231–261). Toronto: Harcourt Brace & Company.

Henry J. Kaiser Family Foundation. (2005). *Generation M: Media in the lives of 8–18-year-olds.* Washington: Henry J. Kaiser Family Foundation. Retrieved May 10, 2007, from http://www.kff.org/entmedia/upload/Generation-M-Media-in-the-Lives-of-8-18-Year-olds-Report.pdf

Hernandez, F.J., Denton, N.A., & Macartney, S.E. (2007). Family circumstances of children in immigrant families: Looking to the future of America. In J.E. Lansford, K. Dieter-Deckard, & M.H. Bornstein (Eds.), *Immigrant families in contemporary society* (pp. 9–29). New York: Guilford Press.

Herrera, V.M., & McCloskey, L.A. (2001). Gender differences in the risk for delinquency among youth exposed to family violence. *Child Abuse and Neglect, 25,* 1037–1051.

Hewitt, D., Vinje, G., & MacNeil, P. (1995). *Young Canadians' alcohol and other drug use: Increasing our understanding.* Ottawa: Horizons Three.

Hiebert, B., & Thomlison, B. (1996). Facilitating transitions to adulthood: Research and policy implications. In B.Galaway & J. Hudson (Eds.), *Youth in transition: Perspectives on research and policy.* Toronto: Thompson Educational Publishing, Inc.

Hier, S.P. (2002). Raves, risks, and ecstacy panic: A case study in the subversive nature of moral regulation. *Canadian Journal of Sociology, 27*(1), 33–57.

Hill, A.J. (2006). Motivation for eating behaviour in adolescent girls: The body beautiful. *Proceedings of the Nutrition Society, 63,* 376–384. Retrieved January 10, 2008, from the Academic Search Premier database.

Hill, D. (Ed.). (1981). *A Black man's Toronto 1914–1980: The reminiscences of Harry Cairey.* Toronto: The Multicultural History Society of Ontario.

Hill, R.F., & Fortenberry, D. (1992). Adolescence as a culture-bound syndrome. *Social Science & Medicine, 35*(1), 73–80.

Hill-Smith, A.J., Hugo, P., Fonagy, P., & Hartman, D. (2002). Adolescent murderers: Abuse and adversity in childhood. *Journal of Adolescence, 25,* 221–230.

Hird, M.J. (2000). An empirical study of adolescent dating aggression in the UK. *Journal of Adolescence, 23*, 69–78.

Hobart, C. (1996). Intimacy and family life: Sexuality, cohabitation, and marriage. In M. Baker (Ed.), *Families: Changing trends in Canada* (3rd ed.) (pp. 143–173). Toronto: McGraw-Hill Ryerson Limited.

Hodge, S.R, Burden, J.W., Robinson, L.E., & Bennet, R.A. (2008). Theorizing on the stereotyping of black male student-athletes: Issues and implications. *Journal for the Study of Sports and Athletes in Education, 2*(2), 203–226.

Holmes, J., & Silverman, E.L. (1992). *We're here, listen to us! A survey of young women in Canada.* Ottawa: Canadian Advisory Council on the Status of Women.

Holt, M.K., & Espelage, D.L. (2007). Perceived social support among bullies, victims, and bully-victims. *Journal of Youth and Adolescence, 36*(8), 989–994.

Home Office, UK. (2000). *Radical new measures to tackle youth crime get underway.* London: Home Office. Retrieved December 12, 2003, from http://213.38.88.204/80256CAC005 CC584/Search/D29BF0CC705802568F1002

Horowitz, J.L., & Newcomb, M.D. (2001). A multidimensional approach to homosexual identity. *Journal of Homosexuality, 42*(2), 34–53.

Horowitz, M., & Kaufman, M. (1987). Male sexuality: towards a theory of liberation. In M. Kaufman (Ed.) *Beyond patriarchy: Essays by men on pleasure, power, and change (pp. 81–102).* Toronto: Oxford University Press.

House of Commons Library. (2004). *Ethnic minorities in politics and government.* London: House of Commons Library. Retrieved November 12, 2007, from http://www.parliament.uk/commons/lib/research/notes/snsg-01156.pdf

Howard, T.C. (2002). Hearing footsteps in the dark: African American students' descriptions of effective teachers. *Journal of Education for Students Placed at Risk, 7*(4), 425–444. Retrieved June 9, 2013, from http://www.appstate.edu/~koppenhaverd/rcoe/5710/read/africanam/howard02.pdf

Howe, N., & Bukowski, N.W. (1996). What are children and how do they become adults? Childrearing and socialization. In M. Baker (Ed.), *Families: Changing trends in Canada* (3rd ed.) (pp. 180–190). Toronto: McGraw-Hill Ryerson Limited.

Hudon, R., Fournier, B., & Métivier, L., with the assistance of Hébert, B.P. (1991). To what extent are today's young people interested in politics? Inquiries among 16- to 24-year-olds. In K. Megyery (Ed.), *Youth in Canadian politics: Participation and involvement,* vol. 8 of the Research Studies (pp. 3–59). Royal Commission on Electoral Reform and Party Financing and Canada Communication Group—Publishing, Supply and Services Canada. Toronto & Oxford: Dundurn Press.

Huerta, M. (2007). *Intersections of race and gender in women's experiences of harassment.* University of Michigan. ProQuest Dissertations Publishing.

Human Resources Development Canada. (1999a). National Longitudinal Survey of Children and Youth. *Developments, 4*(1), 5–6.

Human Resources Development Canada. (1999b). Post-secondary education in Canada: Still a good investment. *Applied Research Bulletin, 5*(1), 12–13.

Human Resources Development Canada. (1999c). Dropping out and working while studying. *Applied Research Bulletin, 5*(1), 17–19.

Human Resources Development Canada. (2001). The school-to-work transition of post-secondary graduates in Canada. *Applied Research Bulletin, 7*(1), 5–15.

Human Resources Development Canada. (2002). Quarterly labour market and income review. *Applied Research—Socio-Economic Studies, 3*(1), 16–22.

Human Resources and Skills Development Canada. (2011). *Indicators of well-being in Canada: Work - unemployment rate.* Retrieved May 31, 2013, from http://www4.hrsdc.gc.ca/.3ndic.1t.4r@-eng.jsp?iid=16

Human Resources and Skills Development Canada. (2013). *Canadians in context - household and families.* Retrieved May 5, 2013, from http://www4.hrsdc.gc.ca/.3ndic.1t.4r@-eng.jsp?iid=37

Hung, K., & Lipinski, S. (1995). Questions and answers on youth and justice. *Forum on Corrections Research, 7*(1). Ottawa: Correctional Service Canada. Retrieved from http://www.csc-scc.ca/text/pblct/forum/e07/e071b.shtm

Hurley, M.C. (2005). *Legislative summary. Bill C-38: The Civil Marriage Act.* Ottawa: Library of Parliament. Retrieved May 18, 2007, from http://www.parl.gc.ca/common/bills_ls.asp?Parl=38&Ses=1&ls=c38

Hussain, Y., Atkin, K., & Ahmad, W. (2002). *South Asian young disabled people and their families.* London: Foundation by the Polity Press. Retrieved May 18, 2007, from http://www.jrf.org.uk/knowledge/findings/socialcare/742.asp

Iacovou, M. (2002). Regional differences in the transition to adulthood. *ANNALS, AAPSS (Annals of the American Academy), 580,* 40–69.

Ighodaro, M. (1997). *Experiences of Somali students in the Metro-Toronto school system.* Unpublished MEd Thesis, York University, Toronto.

ILO (International Labour Organization). (2005). *Youth: Pathways to decent work. Report VI Promoting youth employment—Tackling the challenge.* Geneva: International Labour Conference, 93rd Session. Retrieved June 19, 2007, from http://www.ilo.org/public/libdoc/ilo/2005/105B09_97_engl.pdf

ILO (International Labour Organization). (2013). *Global employment trends for youth 2013: A generation at risk.* Geneva: International Labour Office. Retrieved May 20, 2013, from http://www.ilo.org/wcmsp5/groups/public/---dgreports/---dcomm/documents/publication/wcms_212423.pdf

Infoplease. (2000–2007). *Timeline of slavery in America.* Pearson Education online. Retrieved January 12, 2008, from http://www.infoplease.com/timelines/slavery.html

Infoplease. (2010). *Median age at first marriage, 1890–2010.* Pearson Education online. Retrieved June 10, 2013, from http://www.infoplease.com/ipa/A0005061.html#ixzz2UzHj5JgU

Ipsos MORI. (2010). How Britain voted in 2010. Retrieved June 10, 2013, from http://www.ipsos-mori.com/researchpublications/researcharchive/poll.aspx?oItemId=2613

Irvine, M. (1997, August 18). Young and unionizing. *Toronto Star,* p. E3.

Jackson, D.J., & Darrow, T.I.A. (2005). The influence of celebrity endorsements on young adults' political opinions. *Press, Politics, 10*(3), 80–98.

Jaffe, P.G., & Baker, L.L. (1999). Why changing the YOA does not impact youth crime: Developing effective prevention programs for children and adolescents. *Canadian Psychology, 40*(1), 22–29.

Jain, A., & Belsky, J. (1997). Fathering and acculturation: Immigrant Indian families with young children. *Journal of Marriage and Family, 59,* 873–883.

James, C.E. (1990). *Making it: Black youth, racism, and career aspirations in a big city.* Toronto: Mosaic Press.

James, C.E. (1998). "Up to no good": Black on the streets and encountering police. In V. Satzewitch (Ed.), *Racism & social inequality in Canada: Concepts, controversies & strategies of resistance.* Toronto: Thompson Educational Publishing, Inc.

James, C.E. (1999). *Seeing ourselves: Exploring race, ethnicity, and culture* (2nd ed.). Toronto: Thompson Educational Publishing, Inc.

James, C.E. (2003). *Seeing ourselves: Exploring race, ethnicity, and culture* (3rd ed.). Toronto: Thompson Educational Publishing, Inc.

James, C.E. (2005). *Race in play: Understanding the socio-cultural world of student athletes.* Toronto: Canadian Scholars' Press Inc.

Jang, S.J. (2002). Race, ethnicity, and deviance: A study of Asian and non-Asian adolescents in America. *Sociological Forum, 17*(4), 647–680.

Janovicek, N. (2003). Colonial childhood, 1700–1880. In N. Janovicek & J. Parr (Eds.), *Histories of Canadian children and youth* (pp. 25–41). Toronto: Oxford University Press.

Jayakody, A.A., Viner, R.M., Haines, M.M., Bhui, K.S., Head, J.A., Taylor, S.J.C., Booy, R., Klineberg, E., Clark, C., & Stansfeld, S.A. (2006). Illicit and traditional drug use among ethnic minority adolescents in East London. *Public Health, 120,* 329–338. Retrieved February 20, 2008, from the Academic Search Premier database.

Jennings, D. (2002). One year juvenile reconviction rates: July 2000 cohort. London: Home Office Research Development and Statistics Directorate.

Jennings, P. (1998, April). School enrolment and the declining youth participation rate. *Policy Options Politiques,* 10–14.

Jimenez, M. (2006, September 8). For Muslims, guilt by association. *Globe and Mail.* Retrieved May 11, 2007, from http://www.stopracialprofiling.ca/2006/09/10/for-muslims-guilt-by-association/

Jiwani, Y. (2001). *Intersecting inequalities: Immigrant women of colour, violence, and health care.* Vancouver: The BC Centre of Excellence for Women's Health, The Vancouver Foundation. Retrieved June 20, 2006, from http//:www.harbour.sfu.ca/Freda/articles.hlth.htm

Joe, D., & Robinson, N. (1980). Chinatown's immigrant gangs: The new young warrior class. *Criminology, 18*(3), 337–345.

John Jay College of Criminal Justice. (2012). *Violent crime rates continue to fall among juveniles and young adults: research and evaluation databits.* New York: John Jay College of Criminal Justice. Retrieved June 5, 2013, from http://johnjayresearch.org/wp-content/uploads/2012/04/databit2012_06.pdf

Johnson, H. (1996). *Dangerous domains: Violence against women in Canada.* Toronto: Nelson Canada.

Johnston, L.D., O'Malley, P.M., Bachman, J.G., & Schulenberg, J.E. (2006). *Monitoring the future: National results of adolescent drug use. Overview of key findings, 2006.* Bethesda: National Institute of Drug Abuse. Retrieved February 18, 2008, from http://www.monitoringthefuture.org/pubs/monographs/overview2005.pdf

Jones, G. (2000). Experimenting with households and inventing "home." *International Social Science, 52*(2), 183–194.

Jones, G., & Wallace, C. (1992). *Youth, family, and citizenship*. Buckingham: Open University Press.

Jones, S. (1988). *Black culture, white youth: The reggae tradition from JA to UK*. Houndsmills & London: Macmillan Education Ltd.

Justice for Children and Youth. (2011). *Justice for Children and Youth's submissions on Bill C-10: Youth Criminal Justice Act amendments*. Retrieved June 8, 2013, from http://www.jfcy.org/PDFs/BillC10_Nov2011.pdf

Kalbach, M.A., & Kalbach, W.E. (1999). Becoming Canadian: Problems of an emerging identity. *Canadian Ethnic Studies, 31*(2), 1–16.

Kamerman, S., Neuman, M., Waldfogel, J., & Brooks-Gunn, J. (2003). *Social policies, family types, and child outcomes in selected OECD countries*. Paris: Organisation for Economic Co-operation and Development. Social, employment, and migration working paper no. 6. Retrieved May 17, 2007, from http://www.oecd.org/dataoecd/26/46/2955844.pdf

Kao, G. (2002). Ethnic differences in parents' educational aspirations. *Schooling and Social Capital in Diverse Cultures, 13*, 85–103.

Karakayali, N. (2005). Duality and diversity in the lives of immigrant children: Rethinking the "problem of the second generation" in light of immigrant autobiographies. *The Canadian Review of Sociology and Anthropology, 42*(2), 325–343.

Kaufman, C., Beals, J., Mitchell, C., Lemaster, P., & Fickhenscher, A. (2004). Stress, trauma, and risky sexual behaviour among American Indians in young adulthood. *Culture, Health & Sexuality, 16*(4), 301–318. Retrieved February 17, 2008, from Academic Search Premier database.

Kaufman, M. (1999). Day-to-day ethical issues in the care of young parents and their children. In J. Wong & D. Checkland (Eds.), *Teen pregnancy and parenting: Social and ethical issues* (pp. 25–37). Toronto: University of Toronto Press.

Kaushal, N., & Reimers, C. (2007). How economists have studied the immigrant family. In J.E. Lansford, K. Deater-Deckar, & M.H. Bornstein (Eds.), *Immigrant families in contemporary society* (pp. 100–120). New York: Guilford Press.

Kelly, D.M. (1999). A critical feminist perspective on teen pregnancy and parenthood. In J. Wong & D. Checkland (Eds.), *Teen pregnancy and parenting: Social and ethical issues* (pp. 52–70). Toronto: University of Toronto Press.

Kelly, J. (1998). *Under the gaze: Learning to be Black in a White society*. Halifax: Fernwood.

Kelly, K., & Howatson-Leo, L., & Clark, W. (2000). I feel overqualified for my job. *Canadian Social Trends* (Vol. 3) (pp. 180–184). Toronto: Thompson Educational Publishing.

Kelly, M.B. (2013). *Payment patterns of child and spousal support*. Statistics Canada catalogue no. 85-002-X. Ottawa: Statistics Canada. Retrieved May 6, 2013, from http://www.statcan.gc.ca/pub/85-002-x/2013001/article/11780-eng.pdf

Kendal, D., Murray, J., & Linden, R. (1997). *Sociology in our times*(1st Canadian ed.). Scarborough: International Thomson Publishing.

Kerckhoff, A.C. (1990). *Getting started: Transition to adulthood in Great Britain*. Boulder, San Francisco & Oxford: Westview Press.

Kerr, K.B. (1997). *Youth unemployment trends*. Ottawa: Government of Canada, Depository Services Program, p. BP-448E

Kerr, K.B. (1999). *Youth unemployment in Canada.* Ottawa: Government of Canada, Depository Services Program, p. 82-4E.

Khanlou, N., & Crawford, C. (2006). Post-migratory experiences of newcomer female youth: Self-esteem and identity development. *Journal of Immigrant and Minority Health, 8*(1), 45–56.

Khanna, M. (1999). *Hate/bias motivated acts perpetrated by and against youth: A research overview.* Ottawa: Canadian Heritage.

Kidder, K., & Rogers, D. (2004). *Why Canada needs a national youth policy agenda.* Ottawa: National Children's Alliance. Retrieved February 22, 2007, from http://www.nationalchild-rensalliance.com/nca/pubs/2004/youthpolicypaper.htm

Kiernan, K. (2003). *Cohabitation and divorce across nations and generations. CASE paper 65.* London: Centre for Analysis of Social Exclusion, London School of Economics. Retrieved May 17, 2007, from http://sticerd.lse.ac.uk/dps/case/cp/CASEpaper65.pdf

Kilbride, K.M., Anisef, P., Baichman-Anisef, E., & Khattar, R. (2001). *Between two worlds: The experiences and concerns of immigrant youth in Ontario.* Toronto: Joint Centre of Excellence for Research on Immigration and Settlement (CERIS).

Kim, E. (2002). The relationship between parental involvement and children's emotional achievement. *Journal of Comparative Family Studies, 33*(4), 529–540.

Kim, K., & Rohner, R.P. (2002). Parental warmth, control, and involvement in schooling: Predicting academic achievement among Korean-American adolescents. *Journal of Cross Cultural Psychology, 33*(2), 127–140.

King, A., Perreault, R., & Roeter, K. (1988). Results of an Ontario secondary school study. *Canadian Journal of Public Health, Supplement, 79,* S46–47.

King, D., Eisl-Culkin, J. & Desjardins, L. (2008). *Doctorate education in Canada: Findings from the Survey of Earned Doctorates, 2005/2006.* Ottawa: Statistics Canada. Retrieved May 8, 2013, from http://www.statcan.gc.ca/pub/81-595-m/81-595-m2008069-eng.pdf

Kingsmill, S., & Schlesinger, B. (1998). *The family squeeze: Surviving the sandwich generation.* Toronto: University of Toronto Press.

Kingsnorth, P. (2001, March). If it's Tuesday, it must be Seattle. *The Ecologist, 31,* 2. Retrieved February 2, 2008, from ProQuest database.

Kingstone, J. (2000, June 28). Ecstasy kills mom, 21 was at rave club. *Toronto Sun,* p. 10.

Kingston, P.W., Hubbard, R., Lapp, B., Schroeder, P., & Wilson, J. (2003). Why education matters. *Sociology of Education, 76,* 53–70.

Kirby, D. (2009). Teaching schools a lesson: Undaunted by the opposition, gay students are giving their schools a lesson in tolerance. *The Advocate,* 809. Retrieved May 23, 2013, from ProQuest.

Kirby, E.H., & Marcelo, K.B. (2006). *Young voters in the 2006 elections.* College Park: School of Public Policy, University of Maryland. Retrieved January 29, 2008, from http://www.civicyouth.org/quick/youth_voting.htm

Kirchheimer, S. (2003). Does rap put teens at risk? Study: Association found between video viewing time and risky behaviours. *WebMD Medical News.* Retrieved March 12, 2007, from http://www.webmd.com/baby/news/20030303/does-rap-put-teens-at-risk

Kitchener-Waterloo Record. (1998, September 4). Women signing up for unions faster than men, report says. *Kitchener-Waterloo Record,* p. F5.

Koller, M.R. (1974). *Families: A multigenerational approach.* Toronto: McGraw-Hill.

Kreider, R.M. (2007, August 12). *Young adults living in their parents' home.* Paper presented at the ASA Annual Meetings, New York. Retrieved June 1, 2013, from https://www.census.gov/hhes/families/files/young-adults-in-parents-home.pdf

Kuryllowicz, K. (1996). Youth crime: Behind the stats. *What! A Magazine, 10*(1), 20–23.

Lafrance, M.N., Zivian, M.T., & Myers, A.M. (2000). Women, weight, and appearance dissatisfaction: An ageless pursuit of thinness. In B. Miedema, J.M. Stoppard, & V. Anderson (Eds.), *Women's bodies, women's lives: Health, well-being, and body-image* (pp. 227–240). Toronto: Sumach Press.

Lagille, A. (2013). *Unpaid internships bad for economy, young workers.* Youth and Work. Retrieved June 9, 2013, from http://www.youthandwork.ca/2013/03/unpaid-internships-bad-for-economy.html

Laidler, K.J., & Hunt, G. (2001). Accomplishing femininity among the girls in the gang. *Centre for Crime and Justice Studies, 41*, 656–678.

Larkin, J. (1994). *Sexual harassment: High school girls speak out.* Toronto: Second Story Press.

Latimer, J. (2001). A meta-analytic examination of youth delinquency, family treatment, and recidivism. *Canadian Journal of Criminology, 43*(2), 237–253.

Latimer, J., & Foss, J.C. (2005). The sentencing of Aboriginal and non-Aboriginal youth under the Young Offenders Act: A multivariate analysis. *Canadian Journal of Criminology and Criminal Justice, 47*(3), 481–500.

Law Now. (1996). Youth crime—what do we know? *Law Now, 21*(1), 12.

Leapman, B. (2008, January 20). Violent youth crime up a third. *The Telegraph.* Retrieved June 5, 2013, from http://www.telegraph.co.uk/news/uknews/1576076/Violent-youth-crime-up-a-third.html

LeBlanc, M., Vallieres, E., & McDuff, P. (1993). The prediction of males' adolescent and adult offending from school experience. *Canadian Journal of Criminology, 35*(1), 459–478.

Leeder, J., Reinhart, A., & Koring, P. (2007, April 18). Cho Seung-Hui was a dark and demented student. Liviu Librescu survived the Holocaust and tyranny. They will be remembered for their final moments. *Globe and Mail,* p. A1.

Lenhart, A. (2012). *Teens, smartphones & texting.* Pew Research Centre. Retrieved June 10, 2013, from http://www.pewinternet.org/Reports/2012/Teens-and-smartphones.aspx

Lenhart, A., Purcell, K., Smith, A., & Zickuhr, K. (2010, February 3). *Social media and young adults.* Pew Internet. Retrieved June 10, 2013, from http://www.pewinternet.org/Reports/2010/Social-Media-and-Young-Adults/Summary-of-Findings.aspx

Lenskyj, H. (1990). Beyond plumbing and prevention: Feminist approaches to sex education. *Gender & Education, 2*(2), 217–221.

Li, P.S. (1988). *Ethnic inequality in class society.* Toronto: Thompson Educational Publishing.

Li, Q. (2006). Cyberbullying in schools: A research on gender differences. *School Psychology International, 27*, 1–14.

Links, P.S. (1998). Suicide and life: The ultimate juxtaposition. *Canadian Medical Association Journal, 158*(4), 514–515.

Library of Parliament Research Publications. (2010). *Youth voter turnout in Canada: 1. Trends and issues.* Ottawa: Parliament of Canada. Retrieved June 10, 2013, from http://www.parl.gc.ca/Content/LOP/ResearchPublications/2010-19-e.htm

Liu, J., & Kerr, D. (2003). Family change and economic well-being in Canada: The case of recent immigrant families with children. *International Migration, 41*(4), 113–140.

Livingstone, D.W. (1999). *The education-jobs gap.* Toronto: Garamond Press.

Lojowsky, M. (2001). The new dawn of the student revolution. *The Humanist, 61,* 9–11. Retrieved February 2, 2008, from ProQuest database.

Looker, E.D. (1996). The transitions to adult roles: Youth views and policy implications. In B. Galaway & J. Hudson (Eds.), *Youth in transition: Perspectives on research and policy* (pp. 152–161). Toronto: Thompson Educational Publishing, Inc.

Looker, E.D., & Lowe, G.S. (1996). Preparation for the world of work: Research and policy implications. In B. Galaway & J. Hudson (Eds.), *Youth in transition: Perspectives on research and policy (pp. 125–141).* Toronto: Thompson Educational Publishing.

Looker, E.D. & Thiessen, V. (2008). *The second chance system: Results from the three cycles of the Youth in Transition Survey.* Ottawa: Human Resource and Skill Development, Learning Policy Directorate. Retrieved May 16, 2013, from http://publications.gc.ca/collections/collection_2008/hrsdc-rhdsc/HS28-142-2008E.pdf

Lopez, N. (2002). Race-gender experiences and schooling: Second-generation Dominican, West Indian, and Haitian youth in New York City. *Race, Ethnicity, and Education, 5*(1), 67–89.

Lorriggio, P. (2011, December 11). Protests, Occupy could lead to full-blown Canadian youth movement: experts. *Global TV News.* Retrieved June 4, 2013, from http://globalnews.ca/news/191844/protests-occupy-could-lead-to-full-blown-canadian-youth-movement-experts-4/

Lowe, G.S., & Krahn, H. (1994–1995). *Job-related education and training among young workers. Queen's Papers in Industrial Relations.* Working paper series. Kingston: Queen's University, School of Industrial Relations/Industrial Relations Centre.

Lowe, J. (1990). Youth environmental movement flourishing. *Earth Island Journal, 5*(4), 17–18.

Lynn, M., & O'Neill, E. (1995). Families, power, and violence. In N. Mandell & A. Duffy (Eds.), *Canadian families: Diversity, conflict, and change.* Toronto: Harcourt Brace & Company, Canada.

Macartney, S. (2011). *Child poverty in the United States 2009 and 2010: Selected race groups and Hispanic origin: American community survey briefs.* Washington: U.S. Department of Commerce. Retrieved May 13, 2013, from http://www.census.gov/prod/2011pubs/acsbr10-05.pdf

Mackie, M. (1987). *Constructing women and men: Gender socialization.* Toronto: Holt, Rinehart and Winston.

MacKinnon, M. (2000a, November 6). Young voters feel disaffected. *Globe and Mail,* pp. A1, A9.

MacKinnon, M. (2000b, May 31). Canadian tobacco firms after young, Wigand says. *Globe and Mail,* p. A7.

MacKinnon, M. (2000c, May 29). Tobacco sales target was youth. *Globe and Mail,* pp. A1, A7.

Maclean's (2000, April 24). Wild ones through the ages: Some of the youth movements that have captivated kids—and, in most cases, scandalized parents—over the past 80 years. *Maclean's,* 43.

MacLeod, L., & Shin, M. (1993). *"Like a wingless bird…" A tribute to the survival and courage of women who are abused and who speak neither English nor French.* Ottawa: National Clearinghouse on Family Violence.

Madge, N., & Harvey, J.G. (1999). Suicide among the young—the size of the problem. *Journal of Adolescence, 22*, 145–155.

Madsen, J. (2000). *Linguistic classification of American Indians.* John Madsen Web site. Retrieved May 11, 2007, from http://hjem.tele2adsl.dk/johnmadsen/Indian/indian0.html

magnifydigital.com. (2013). *Using a flash mob to create brand awareness.* Retrieved June 4, 2013, from http://www.magnifydigital.com/business/using-a-flash-mob-to-create-brand-awareness/

Mahl, D. (2001). The influence of parental divorce on the romantic relationship beliefs of young adults. *Journal of Divorce and Remarriage, 34*(3/4), 89–118.

Mahony, T.H. (2011). *Women and the criminal justice system.* Statistics Canada catalogue no. 89-503-X. Retrieved June 8, 2013, from http://www.statcan.gc.ca/pub/89-503-x/2010001/article/11416-eng.htm

Maira, S. (2004). Youth culture, citizenship, and globalization: South Asian Muslim youth in the United States after September 11th. *Comparative Studies of South Asia, Africa, and the Middle East, 24*(1), 219–231. Retrieved September 25, 2007, from Academic Search Premier database.

Maiter, S., Trocme, N., & George, U. (2003). Building bridges: The collaborative development of culturally appropriate definitions of child abuse and neglect for the South Asian community. *Affilia: Journal of Women and Social Work, 18*(4), 411–420.

Males, M.A. (1996). *The scapegoat generation: America's war on adolescents.* Monroe: Common Courage Press.

Man, G. (2003). The experience of middle-class women in recent Hong Kong Chinese immigrant families in Canada. In M. Lynn (Ed.), *Voices: Essays on Canadian families* (2nd ed.) (pp. 271–300). Toronto: Thomson Nelson.

Mandell, N. (1988). The child question: Links between women and children in the family. In N. Mandell & A. Duffy (Eds.), *Reconstructing the Canadian family: Feminist perspectives* (pp. 285–312). Toronto: Butterworths.

Mandell, N., & Crysdale, S. (1993). Gender tracks: Male-female perceptions of home-school-work transitions. In P. Anisef & P. Axelrod (Eds.), *Transitions: Schooling and employment in Canada* (pp. 21–44). Toronto: Thompson Educational Publishing.

Mandell, N., & Duffy, A. (Eds.). (1995). *Canadian families: Diversity, conflict, and change.* Toronto: Harcourt Brace & Company, Canada.

Manderson, L., & Liamputtong, P. (2002). Introduction: Youth and sexuality in contemporary Asian societies. In L. Manderson & P. Liamputtong (Eds.), *Coming of age in South and Southeast Asia: Youth, courtship, and sexuality* (pp. 1–12). Richmond: Curzon.

Manning, W. D., Longmore, M.A., & Giordano, P.C. (2005). Adolescents' involvement in non-romantic sexual activity. *Social Science Research, 34*, 384–407.

Manzo, J.F., & Bailey, M.M. (2005). On the assimilation of racial stereotypes among Black Canadian young offenders. *The Canadian Review of Sociology, 42*(3), 283–300.

Marchessault, G. (2000). One mother and daughter approach to resisting weight preoccupation. In B. Miedema, J.M. Stoppard, & V. Anderson (Eds.), *Women's bodies, women's lives: Health, well-being, and body-image* (pp. 203–226). Toronto: Sumach Press.

Mark, G.Y. (2000). Oakland Chinatown's first youth gang: The Suey Sing Boys. *International Review of Modern Sociology & International Journal of Sociology of the Family (Special Issue: Gangs, Drugs and Violence), 28*(1), 31–39.

Marshall, K. (2010). *Employment patterns of postsecondary students.* Statistics Canada catalogue no. 75-001-X. Ottawa: Statistics Canada. Retrieved May 13, 2013, from http://www.stat-can.gc.ca/pub/75-001-x/2010109/article/11341-eng.htm

Marquardt, R. (1998). *Enter at your own risk: Canadian youth and the labour market.* Toronto: Between the Lines.

Martin, D., & Mosher, J. (1995). Unkept promises: Experiences of immigrant women with the neo-criminalization of wife abuse. *Canadian Journal of Women and the Law, 8,* 3–44.

Martinez, M. (2002). The challenge of a new ideology. *Canadian Dimension, 36*(1), 28–31. Retrieved January 29, 2008, from Academic Search Premier database.

Marwick, A.E. (2008). To catch a predator? The MySpace moral panic. *First Monday: Peer Reviewed Journal on the Internet, 13*(6). Retrieved June 4, 2013, from http://firstmonday.org/ojs/index.php/fm/article/view/2152/1966

Mathews, F. (1996). *The invisible boy: Revisioning the victimization of male children and teens.* Ottawa: Health Canada.

Maticka-Tyndale, E., Herold, E.S., & Mewhinney, D. (1998). Casual sex on spring break: Intentions and behaviors of Canadian students. *Journal of Sex Research, 35*(3), 254–264. [Reprinted in M. Kimmel & R.F. Plante (Eds.), *Sexualities: Identities, Behaviors, and Society,* New York & Oxford: Oxford University Press, 2004).]

Matsudaira, J.D. (2006). *Economic conditions and the living arrangements of young adults.* Philadelphia: Network on Transitions to Adulthood. Retrieved May 22, 2007, from http://www.transad.pop.upenn.edu/downloads/matsudaira-formatted.pdf.

Matsueda, R.L., & Heimer, K. (1997). A symbolic interactionist theory of role transitions, role commitments, and delinquency. In T. Thornberry (Ed.), *Advances in criminological theory: Vol. 7. Developmental theories of crime and delinquency* (pp. 163–213). New Brunswick, NJ: Transaction.

Matthews, H., & Limb, M. (2003). Another white elephant? Youth councils as democratic structures. *Space and Polity, 7*(2), 173–192. Retrieved February 2, 2008, from ProQuest database.

Mattson, K. (2003). *Engaging youth: Combating the apathy of young Americans towards politics.* New York: The Century Foundation Press.

Maxwell, M.P., & Maxwell, J.D. (1994). Three decades of private school females' ambitions: Implications for Canadian elites. *Canadian Review of Sociology and Anthropology, 31*(2), 137–167.

May-Chahal, C. & Cawson, P. (2005). Measuring child maltreatment in the United Kingdom: A study of the prevalence of child abuse and neglect. *Child Abuse & Neglect, 29,* 969–984. Retrieved February 12, 2008, from the Academic Search Premier database.

Maynard, S. (1997). "Horrible temptations": Sex, men, and working-class male youth in urban Ontario, 1890–1935. *The Canadian Historical Review, 78*(2), 191–235.

McAllister, F. (1999). *Effects of changing material circumstances on the incidence of marital breakdown.* In Lord Chancellor's Department. High divorce rates: The state of the evidence on reasons and remedies, vol. 1 (Papers 1–3)—Research series no. 2/99. London: Lord Chancellor's Department. Retrieved May 14, 2007, from http://www.oneplusone.org.uk/Publications/ReviewPapers/2%20-%20effects%20of%20changing%20material%20circumstances.pdf

McAlpine, D.D., Grindstaff, C.F., & Sorenson, A.M. (1996). Competence and control in the transition from adolescence to adulthood: A longitudinal study of teenage mothers. In B. Galaway & J. Hudson (Eds.), *Youth in transition: Perspectives on research and policy* (pp. 302–312). Toronto: Thompson Educational Publishing, Inc.

McCormick, N., & Jesser, C.J. (1991). The courtship game: Power in the sexual encounter. In J.E. Veevers (Ed.), *Continuity and change in marriage & family* (pp. 64–86). Toronto: Holt, Reinhart & Winston Canada.

McCreary Centre Society. (1998). *Results from the Adolescent Health Survey.* Vancouver: McCreary Centre Society.

McDaniel, S. (1997). Intergenerational transfers, social solidarity, and social policy: Unanswered questions and policy challenges. *Canadian Public Policy/Canadian Journal on Aging* [Special Joint Issue], 1–21.

McDiarmid, J. (2013, June 4). Teens use, divulge on social media at unprecedented levels. *The Toronto Star.* Retrieved June 4, 2013, from http://www.thestar.com/business/tech_news/2013/05/22/teens_use_divulge_on_social_media_at_unprecedented_levels.html

McElrath, J. (2007a). *Timeline of the reconstruction era.* About: African-American history (Online). Retrieved May 3, 2007, from http://afroamhistory.about.com/od/reconstruction/timeline_recon.htm

McElrath, J. (2007b). *The Black codes of 1865.* About: African-American history (Online). Retrieved May 3, 2007, from http://afroamhistory.about.com/od/blackcodes/a/black-codes1865.htm

McElroy, W. (2004). *West Africa and colonialism.* Fairfax: The Future of Freedom Foundation. Retrieved April 30, 2007, from http://www.lewrockwell.com/mcelroy/mcelroy55.html

McIlroy, A. (1999, June 23). Illegal sales of cigarettes to minors rising, study finds. *Globe and Mail,* p. A7.

McIntosh, R. (2000). *Boys in the pits: Child labour in coal mines.* Montreal: McGill-Queens University Press.

McKay, A., & Holowaty, P. (1997). Sexual health education: A study of adolescents' opinions, self-perceived needs, and current and preferred sources of information. *Canadian Journal of Human Sexuality, 6*(1), 29–38.

McKay, S. (2002). The dynamics of lone parents, employment and poverty in Great Britain. *Sociologia e politica sociale, 2,* 1–26.

McKechnie, J., & Hobbs, S. (2002). Work by the young: The economic activity of school-aged children. In M. Tienda & W.J. Wilson (Eds.), *Youth in cities: A cross-national perspective* (pp. 217–245). Cambridge: Cambridge University Press.

McKenzie, C. (2006). Racial profiling: Our national shame. The race against profiling. *Hour.ca—News.* Retrieved May 11, 2007, from http://www.hour.ca/news/news.aspx?iIDArticle=8621

McKinley, E.G. (1996). In the back of your head: "Beverly Hills 90210," "Friends," and the discursive construction of identity. In M. Pomerance & J. Sakeris (Eds.), *Pictures of a generation on hold: Selected papers* (pp. 110–125). Toronto: Media Studies Working Group.

McQuire, J.K., Anderson, C.R., Toomey, R.B., & Russell, S.T. (2010). School climate for transgender youth: A mixed method investigation of student experiences and school responses. *Journal of Youth and Adolescence, 39,* 1175–1188.

Measor, L. (2006). Condom use: A culture of resistance. *Sex Education, 6*(4), 393–402. Retrieved December 15, 2007, from the Academic Search Premier database.

Media Watch. (2000). *Analyzing the "tween" market: A report by The Health Communication Unit (THCU).* Toronto: Centre for Health Promotion, University of Toronto, and MediaWatch.ca.

Meloff, W., & Silverman, R.A. (1992). Canadian kids who kill. *Canadian Journal of Criminology, 34*(1), 15–34.

Mendes, P., & Moslehuddin, B. (2004). Graduating from the child welfare system: A comparison of the UK and Australian leaving care debates. *International Journal of Social Welfare, 13,* 332–339.

Menjivar, C., & Salcido, O. (2002). Immigrant women and domestic violence: Common experiences in different countries. *Gender and Society, 16*(6), 898–920.

The Mental Health Foundation. (2006). *Making the link between mental health and youth homelessness: A pan-London study.* London: The Mental Health Foundation. Retrieved February 10, 2008, from the Academic Search Premier database.

Mesch, G.S. (2009). The internet and youth culture. *The Hedgehog Review, 11*(1), 50–60. Retrieved June 4, 2013, from http://www.iasc-culture.org/THR/archives/YouthCulture/Mesch.pdf

Meyerson, L.A., Long, P.J., Miranda, R. Jr., & Marx, B.P. (2002). The influence of childhood sexual abuse, physical abuse, family environment, and gender on the psychological adjustment of adolescents. *Child Abuse and Neglect, 26*(4), 387–405.

Mikkonen, J., & Raphael, D. (2010). *Social determinants of health: The Canadian facts.* Toronto: York University School of Health Policy and Management.

Milan, A. (2000, Spring). One hundred years of families. *Canadian Social Trends.* Retrieved June 2, 2013, from http://publications.gc.ca/Collection-R/Statcan/11-008-XIE/0049911-008-XIE.pdf

Milan, A., & Tran, K. (2004). Social trends: Blacks in Canada: A long history. Statistics Canada catalogue no. 11-008. Ottawa: Statistics Canada. Retrieved May 7, 2013, from http://www.ualberta.ca/~jrkelly/blacksinCanada.pdf

Miles, S. (2000). *Youth lifestyles in a changing world.* Buckingham & Philadephia: Open University Press.

Miller, P., Donahue, P., Este, D., & Hofer, M. (2004). Experiences of being homeless or at risk of being homeless among Canadian youths. *Adolescence, 39*(156), 735–755.

Mintz, E. (1993, Winter). Two generations: The political attitudes of high school students and their parents. *International Journal of Canadian Studies/Revue internationale d'études canadiennes* (Special Issue), 59–71.

The Mirror. (1825). Slaves and slavery in the United States. *Mirror of Literature, Amusement and Instruction, 6*(154), 100. Retrieved April 20, 2007, from ProQuest database.

The Mirror. (1844). Slavery forever, in the United States. *Mirror of Literature, Amusement and Instruction, 1*(24), 374. Retrieved April 20, 2007, from ProQuest database.

Mitchell, B. (1998). Too close for comfort? Parental assessments of "boomerang kid" living arrangements. *Canadian Journal of Sociology, 23*(1), 21–46.

Mitchell, B. (2001). Ethnocultural reproduction and attitudes toward cohabiting relationships. *Canadian Review of Sociology and Anthropology, 38*(4), 391–414.

Mitchell, B.A., & Gee, E.M. (1996). Young adults returning home: Implications for social policy. In B. Galaway & J. Hudson (Eds.), *Youth in transition: Perspectives on research and policy* (pp. 61–71). Toronto: Thompson Educational Publishing, Inc.

Momirov, J., & Kilbride, K. (2005). Family lives of Native peoples, immigrants, and visible minorities. In N. Mandel & A. Duffy (Eds.), *Canadian families: Diversity, conflict, and change* (pp. 87–110). Toronto: Thomson Nelson.

Monbiot, G. (2006, July 7). Willy Loman Syndrome. *The Guardian*. Retrieved March 21, 2007, from http://www.monbiot.com/archives/2006/07/07/willy-loman-syndrome/#more-996

Monger, R. & Yankay, J. (2013). *U.S. legal permanent residents: 2012*. Washington: U.S. Department of Homeland Security. Retrieved May 7, 2013, from http://www.dhs.gov/sites/default/files/publications/ois_lpr_fr_2012_2.pdf

Moogk, P.N. (1982). Les petits sauvages: The children of eighteenth-century New France. In J. Parr & N. Janovick (Eds.), *Childhood and family in Canadian history* (pp. 36–56). Toronto: McClelland & Stewart.

Moore, K., Jones, N., & Broadbent, E. (2008). *School violence in OECD countries*. Woking, Surrey, UK: Plan Limited. Retrieved June 5, 2013, from http://plan-international.org/learnwithoutfear/files/school-violence-in-oecd-countries-english

Morgan, J. (2012, September 28). Harassment of gay students falling, says study. *Gaystarnews*. Retrieved May 23, 2013, from http://www.gaystarnews.com/article/harassment-gay-students-falling-says-study080912

Morrison, L., Guruge, S., & Snarr, K.A. (1999). Sri Lankan Tamil immigrants in Toronto: Gender, marriage patterns, and sexuality. In G. Kelson & D. DeLaet (Eds.), *Gender and immigration* (pp. 144–162). New York: New York University Press.

Mroz, T.A., & Savage, T.H., (2006). The long-term effects of youth unemployment. *Journal of Human Resources, 41*(2), 259–293.

MSN Money Partner. (2012). Young, broke and spending on luxury. *MSN Money*. Retrieved June 4, 2013, from http://money.msn.com/saving-money-tips/post.aspx?post=8db66948-b50f-4f01-9fb5-54739766e6c1

Munroe, S. (2013). Minimum wage in Canada: Minimim wage rates in Canada by province. *About.com Guide*. Retrieved May 24, 2013, from http://canadaonline.about.com/od/labourstandards/a/minimum-wage-in-canada.htm

Muzzatti, S.L. (2004). Criminalising marginality and resistance: Marilyn Manson, Columbine, and cultural criminology. In J. Ferrell, K. Hayward, W. Morrison, & M. Presdee (Eds.), *Cultural criminology unleashed* (pp. 143–152). London: Glasshouse Press.

Myerson, L.A., Long, P.J., Miranda, R., & Marx, B.P. (2002). The influence of childhood sexual abuse, physical abuse, family environment, and gender on the psychological adjustment of adolescents. *Child Abuse and Neglect, 26*, 387–405.

Naiman, J. (2000). *How societies work: Class, power and change in a Canadian context* (3rd ed.). Toronto: Irwin.

Nakamura, A., & Wong, G. (1998, April). Rethinking our national stay-in-school rhetoric. *Policy Options*, 7–10.

Natale, L., & Williams, N. (2012). Youth crime in England and Wales. *Civitas Crime Fact Sheets*. Retrieved June 5, 2013, from http://www.civitas.org.uk/crime/factsheet-youthoffending.pdf

National Archives. (2007). *Slavery: How did the Abolition Acts of 1807 and 1866 affect slavery?* London: National Archives, Electronic resource. Retrieved April 30, 2007, from http://learningcurve.gov.uk/snapshots/snapshot 27/snapshot27.htm

National Centre for Education Statistics. (2003). *The condition of education 2003.* Washington: US Department of Education, Institute of Education Sciences. Retrieved November 17, 2007, from http://nces.ed.gov/pubs2003/2003067.pdf.

National Center for Health Statistics. (2007). *Health, United States 2007, with chartbook on trends in the health of Americans.* Hyattsville: National Center for Health Statistics. Retrieved February 21, 2008, from http://www.cdc.gov/nchs/data/hus/hus07.pdf

National Coalition for the Homeless. (2008). *Homeless youth.* Washington: National Coalition for the Homeless. Retrieved May 18, 2013, from http://www.nationalhomeless.org/factsheets/youth.html

National Council of Welfare. (2012). *Poverty profile: Special edition.* Retrieved May 31, 2013, from http://publications.gc.ca/collections/collection_2012/cnb-ncw/HS51-2-2012S-eng.pdf

National Council on Disability. (2000, November 1). *Transition and post-school outcomes for youth with disabilities: Closing the gaps to post-secondary education and employment.* Washington: National Council on Disability. Retrieved February 12, 2008, from http://www.ncd.gov/newsroom/publications/2000/transition_11-01-00.htm

National Crime Prevention Council (1997). *Young people say: Report from the youth consultation initiative.* Ottawa: NCPC.

National Crime Prevention Council. (2000). *Young people say: Report from the youth consultation initiative.* Ottawa: NCPC.

National Crime Prevention Council of Canada. (1996). *Is youth crime a problem?* Ottawa: NCPC. Retrieved November 22, 1999, from crime-prevention.org/ncpc/publications/children/family/introd_e.htm

National Criminal Justice Reference Services (2012). *Women & girls in the criminal justice system.* Retrieved June 8, 2103, from https://www.ncjrs.gov/spotlight/wgcjs/summary.html

National Film Board. (1990). *Playing for keeps: A film about teen mothers.*Documentary. Montreal: National Film Board.

National Film Board. (1992). *Speak it! From the heart of Nova Scotia.* Documentary. Halifax: National Film Board, Atlantic Centre.

National Film Board. (1997). *All the right stuff.* [Documentary.] Montreal: National Film Board.

National Post. (2006). Youth crime down: StatsCan. *National Post.* Retrieved March 12, 2007, from http://www.canriancrc.com/Youth/Justice/Webpage/Youth_Crime.htm

National Statistics (Online). (2002, December 12). *Minority ethnic groups in the UK.* Retrieved January 17, 2008, from http://www.statistics.gov.uk/pdfdir/meg1202.pdf

National Statistics (Online). (2003a). *Age distribution: Ethnic groups have younger age structure.* London: National Statistics. Retrieved December 12, 2003, from http://www.statistics.gov.uk/cci/nugget.asp?id=272

National Statistics (Online). (2005a). *Age at marriage by sex and previous marital status, 1991, 2001–2005.* London: National Statistics. Retrieved April 18, 2007, from http://www.statistics.gov.uk/STATBASE/ssdataset.asp?vlnk=9599

National Statistics (Online). (2005b). *Social Trends 37: Voting turnout in the 2005 general election, Great Britain*. Retrieved April 2, 2007, from http://www.statistics.gov.uk/statbase/Product.asp?vlnk=13675.

National Statistics. (Online). (2005c). *Focus on families*. London: Office for National Statistics. Retrieved May 6, 2013, from http://www.ons.gov.uk/ons/rel/family-demography/focus-on-families/2005/index.html

National Statistics. (Online). (2010). *Marriage in England and Wales, 2010*. London Office for National Statistics. Retrieved May 7, 2013, from http://www.ons.gov.uk/ons/dcp171778_258307.pdf

National Statistics. (Online) (2011a). *Population estimates by ethnic group: Current estimates, population estimates by ethnic group mid-2009*. London: Office for National Statistics. Retrieved May 5, 2013, from http://www.ons.gov.uk/ons/taxonomy/index.html?nscl=Population+Estimates+by+Ethnic+Group#tab-data-tables

National Statistics. (Online). (2011b). *Divorces in England and Wales, 2010*. London: Office for National Statistics. Retrieved May 5, 2013, from http://www.ons.gov.uk/ons/rel/vsob1/divorces-in-england-and-wales/2010/stb-divorces-2010.html#tab-Key-findings

National Statistics (Online). (2011c). *People with disabilities in the labour market, 2011*. London, UK: Office of National Statistics. Retrieved May 21, 2013, from http://www.ons.gov.uk/ons/dcp171776_242963.pdf

National Statistics. (Online). (2012a). *Divorces in England and Wales, 2011*. London: Office for National Statistics. Retrieved May 5, 2013, from http://www.ons.gov.uk/ons/rel/vsob1/divorces-in-england-and-wales/2011/stb-divorces-2011.html

National Statistics. (Online) (2012b). *Families and households 2012: Statistics bulletin*. London: Office for National Statistics. Retrieved May 5, 2013, from http://www.ons.gov.uk/ons/dcp171778_284823.pdf

National Statistics. (Online) (2012c). *Birth summary tables, England and Wales, 2011*. London: Office for National Statistics. Retrieved May 16, 2013, from http://www.ons.gov.uk/ons/rel/vsob1/birth-summary-tables--england-and-wales/2011--provisional-/index.html

National Statistics. (Online). (2012d). *Child Support Agency quarterly summary of statistics for Great Britain*. London: Department of Work and Pensions. Retrieved May 5, 2013, from http://statistics.dwp.gov.uk/asd/asd1/child_support/2012/csa_qtr_summ_stats_dec12.pdf

National Statistics (Online). (2012e). *Unemployment levels and rates for people in London, aged 16 to 24*. London: Office of National Statistics. Retrieved May 20, 2013, from http://www.ons.gov.uk/ons/search/index.html?pageSize=50&sortBy=none&sortDirection=none&newquery=youth+unemployment+ethnic

National Statistics. (Online) (2013a). *Labour market statistics, May 2013*. London: Office of National Statistics. Retrieved May 20, 2013, from http://www.ons.gov.uk/ons/rel/lms/labour-market-statistics/may-2013/index.html

National Statistics. (Online) (2013b). *Table A06: Educational status, economic activity and inactivity of young people*. London: Office of National Statistics. Retrieved May 20, 2013, from http://www.ons.gov.uk/ons/search/index.html?newquery=youth+unemployment

Nelson, E.D., & Robinson, B.W. (1999). *Gender in Canada*. Scarborough: Prentice Hall Allyn and Bacon Canada.

Nett, E.M., (1993). *Canadian families: Past and present* (2nd ed.). Toronto: Butterworths.

Netting, N.S. (1992). Sexuality in youth culture: Identity and change. *Adolescence, 27*(108), 961–976.

Netting, N.S. (2001, May). *Indo-Canadian youth: Love and identity*. Paper presented at the Annual meeting of the Canadian Sociology and Anthropology Association, Laval University, Quebec City, Canada.

Netting, N.S. (2006). Two lives, one partner: Indo-Canadian youth between love and arranged marriage. *Journal of Comparative Family Studies, 37*(1), 129–146.

Netting, N.S., & Burnett, M. (2001, May). *Still a kiss? Still a sigh? Love and sexuality among students, as time goes by.* Presentation at the annual meeting of the Canadian Sociology and Anthropology Association, Laval University, Quebec City, Canada.

Netting, N.S., & Burnett, M. (2004). Twenty years of student sexual behaviour. *Adolescence, 39*(153), 19–38.

Newman, M. (1992, May 11). After the riots: Riots put focus on Hispanic growth and problems in South Central area. *The New York Times*. Retrieved May 5, 2013, from http://www.nytimes.com/1992/05/11/us/after-riots-riots-put-focus-hispanic-growth-problems-south-central-area.html?pagewanted=all&src=pm

Nguyen, A.N., Taylor, J., & Bradley, S. (2001). *High school dropouts: A longitudinal analysis*. Lancaster University Management School Working paper 2001/004. Lancaster: The Department of Economics. Retrieved May 20, 2007, from http://www.lums.lancs.ac.uk/publications/viewpdf/000037/

Nguyen, L. (1999, August 8). Protest in the park. *The Toronto Star*, A18.

Niemiere, V. (2008). Cheers, chants, and yells for cheerleaders. *About.com: Cheerleading*. Retrieved January 29, 2008, from http://cheerleading.about.com/od/cheerschantsyells/a/cheers7.htm

Noguera, P., & Cannella, C.M. (2006). Conclusion. Youth agency, resistance, and civic activism: The public commitment to social justice. In S. Gingwright, P. Noguera, & J. Cammarota (Eds.), *Beyond resistance! Youth activism and community change: New democratic possibilities for practice and policy for America's youth* (pp. 333–348). New York: Routledge.

Noivo, E. (1993). Ethnic families and the social injuries of class, migration, gender, generation, and minority status. *Canadian Ethnic Studies, 23*(3), 66–76.

Noller, P., & Fitzpatrick, M.A. (1993). *Communication in family relationships*. Englewood Cliffs: Prentice Hall.

Normand, J. (2000). Education of women in Canada. *Canadian Social Trends* (Vol. 3) (pp. 73–77). Toronto: Thompson Educational Publishing.

Oaksford, K., & Frude, N. (2001). The prevalence and nature of child sexual abuse: Evidence from a female university sample in the UK. *Child Abuse Review, 10*, 49–59. Retrieved February 11, 2008, from the Academic Search Premier database.

Obama, B. (2013). *Education*. Washington: The White House. Retrieved July 17, 2013, from http://www.whitehouse.gov/issues/education

O'Brien, C.A., & Weir, A. (1995). Lesbians and gay men inside and outside families. In N. Mandell & A. Duffy (Eds.), *Canadian families: Diversity, conflict, and change*. Toronto: Harcourt Brace & Company, Canada.

O'Connor, C. (1999). Race, class, and gender in America: Narratives of opportunity among low-income African-American youths. *Sociology of Education, 72*, 137–157.

O'Donnell, M. (1985). *Age and generation*. New York: Society Now.

Oderkirk, J. (2000). Marriage in Canada: Changing beliefs and behaviours 1600–1900. *Canadian Social Trends* (Vol. 3) (pp. 50–54). Toronto: Thompson Educational Publishing.

OECD (Organisation for Economic Co-operation and Development). (1986). *Girls and women in education: A cross-national study of sex inequalities in upbringing and in schools and colleges.* Paris: OECD.

OECD (Organisation for Economic Co-operation and Development). (2003). *Introduction: Towards more and better jobs (employment outlook).* Paris: OECD.

OECD (Organisation for Economic Co-operation and Development). (2004). *Education at a glance 2004.* Paris: OECD, Directorate for Education. Retrieved September 22, 2007, from http://www.cmec.ca/stats/Profile2004.en.pdf

OECD (Organisation for Economic Co-operation and Development). (2008a). *Jobs for youth/ Des emplois pour les jeunes: Canada.* Paris: OECD. Retrieved June 1, 2013, from http://www.oecd.org/els/40808376.pdf

OECD (Organisation for Economic Co-operation and Development). (2008b). *Jobs for youth/ Des emplois pour les jeunes: United Kingdom.* Paris: OECD. Retrieved June 1, 2013, from http://www.oecd.org/els/emp/40912683.pdf

OECD (Organisation for Economic Co-operation and Development). (2009a). Poverty among children. In *Society at a Glance 2009: OECD Social Indicators.* Paris: OECD. Retrieved May 8, 2013, from http://dx.doi.org/10.1787/soc_glance-2008-18-en

OECD (Organisation for Economic Co-operation and Development). (2009b). *Tertiary level education attainment for age group 25 to 64.* Paris: OECD. Retrieved May 8, 2013, from http://www.oecd-ilibrary.org/education/tertiary-level-educational-attainment-for-age-group-25-64_20755120-table3

OECD (Organisation for Economic Co-operation and Development). (2010a). *Off to a good start? Jobs for youth.* OECD Multilingual Summaries. Summary in English. Paris: OECD. Retrieved June 1, 2013, from http://www.oecd.org/els/emp/46748099.pdf

OECD (Organisation for Economic Co-operation and Development). (2010b). *Cohabitation rate and prevalence of other forms of partnership.* OECD Family Database. Paris: Directorate of Employment, Labour and Social Affairs. Retrieved June 1, 2013, from http://www.oecd.org/els/soc/41920080.pdf

OECD (Organisation for Economic Co-operation and Development). (2011). *Doing better for families.* Retrieved July 17, 2013, from http://www.oecd.org/els/soc/doingbetterforfamilies.htm

OECD (Organisation for Economic Co-operation and Development). (2013a). *Youth unemployment rates in OECD countries, December 2007 to March 2012.* Paris: OECD. Retrieved May 20, 2013, from www.oecd.org/els/emp/50305438.xlsx

OECD (Organisation for Economic Co-operation and Development). (2013b). *Crisis squeezes incomes and puts pressure on inequality and poverty: New results from the OECD income distribution database.* Retrieved May 31, 2013, from http://www.oecd.org/edu/skills-beyond-school/EDIF%202013--N°13%20(eng)--FINAL.pdf

OECD (Organisation for Economic Co-operation and Development). (2013c). How difficult is it to move from school to work? *Education Indicators in Focus,* 2013/04 (April). Retrieved May 20, 2013, from http://www.oecd.org/edu/skills-beyond-school/EDIF%20 2013--N0130/020(end)--FINAL.pdf

Ofcom. (2012). UK is now texting more than talking. *Ofcom*. Retrieved June 10, 2013, from http://consumers.ofcom.org.uk/2012/07/uk-is-now-texting-more-than-talking/

Offer, D., & Offer, J. (1972). Developmental psychology of youth. In S.J. Samsie (Ed.), *Youth: Problems and approaches* (pp. 55–78). Philadelphia: Lea & Febiger.

Office for National Statistics, UK. (2005). *Age at marriage by sex and previous marital status, 1991, 2001–2005*. London: Office for National Statistics, UK. Retrieved April 18, 2007, from http://www.statistics.gov.uk

Office for National Statistics, UK. (2010). *Statistical bulletin: Marriages in England and Wales, 2010*. London: Office for National Statistics, UK. Retrieved August 1, 2013, from http://www.ons.gov.uk/ons/rel/vsob1/marriages-in-england-and-wales--provisional-/2010/marriages-in-england-and-wales--2010.html#tab-Age-at-Marriage

Office of Disability Issues. (2013). *Disability facts and figures: An overview of official UK disability statistics from the Office for Disability Issues*. London: Department for Work and Pensions. Retrieved May 21, 2013, from http://odi.dwp.gov.uk/disability-statistics-and-research/disability-facts-and-figures.php

Office of Justice Programs. (2013). *Juveniles*. Retrieved June 5, 2013, from http://www.crimesolutions.gov/topicdetails.aspx?id=5

Office of Juvenile Justice and Delinquency Prevention. (2004). *Victims of violent juvenile crime*. U.S. Department of Justice, Office of Justice Programs. Retrieved June 5, 2013, from https://www.ncjrs.gov/pdffiles1/ojjdp/201628.pdf

O'Grady, B., Bright, R., & Cohen, E. (1998). Sub-employment and street youths: An analysis of the impact of squeegee cleaning on homeless youths. *Security Journal, 11*, 315–323.

Oh, S. (2000, April 24). Rave fever: Raves are all the rage, but drugs are casting a pall over their sunny peace-and-love ethos. *Maclean's, 113*(17), 38.

O'Higgins, N. (1997). *The challenge of youth unemployment*. Geneva: Employment and Training Department, International Labour Office. Retrieved June 20, 2006, from http://www.ilo.org/public/english/employment/strat/publ/etp7.htm

O'Keeffe, S., McGrath, D., & Smith, M. (2006). *Crisis pregnancy agency statistical report 2006: Teenage pregnancy data*. Dublin: Crisis Pregnancy Agency. Retrieved April 30, 2007, from http://www.crisispregnancy.ie/pub/statistical_report2006.pdf

Olubusola, A., & Appiah, K. (2006). Teenage pregnancy in the United Kingdom: Are we doing enough? *European Journal of Contraception and Reproductive Health Care, 11*(4), 314–318. Retrieved February 13, 2008, from ProQuest database.

Oman, R.F., Vesely, S.K., Aspy, C.B., & Tolma, E. (2006). Youth assets and sexual abstinence in Native American youth. *Journal of Health Care for the Poor and Undeserved, 17*(4), 775–788. Retrieved February 19, 2008, from ProQuest database.

O'Rand, A.M. (1990). *Stratification and the life course*. In R. Binstock & L.K. George (Eds.), *The handbook of aging and the social sciences* (3rd ed.) (pp. 130-148). New York: Academic Press.

Oreopoulos, P., von Wachter,T., & Heisz, A. (2006). *The short- and long-term career effects of graduating in a recession: Hysteresis and heterogeneity in the market for college graduates*. NBER Working Paper No. 12159. Retrieved July 17, 2013, from http://www.columbia.edu/~vw2112/papers/cycl_upgr_oreovonwaheisz.pdf

Ornstein, M. (2000). *Ethno-racial inequality in the City of Toronto: An analysis of the 1996 Census*. Toronto: City of Toronto.

Orton, M.J. (1999). Changing high-risk policies to reduce high-risk sexual behaviours. In J. Wong & D. Checkland (Eds.), *Teen pregnancy and parenting: Social and ethical issues* (pp. 121–150). Toronto: University of Toronto Press.

Otis, J., Levy, J., Samson, J.M., Pilote, F., & Fugere, A. (1997). Gender differences in sexuality and interpersonal power relations among French-speaking young adults from Quebec: A province-wide study. *Canadian Journal of Human Sexuality, 6*(1), 17–28.

Paetch, J.J., & Bertrand, L.D. (1999). Victimization and delinquency among Canadian youth. *Adolescence, 34*(134), 351–367.

Pagani, L., Larocque, D., Vitaro, F., & Tremblay, R.E. (2003). Verbal and physical abuse toward mothers: The role of family configuration, environment, and coping strategies. *Journal of Youth and Adolescence, 32*(3), 215–222.

Panagakos, A. (2004). Recycled odyssey: Creating transnational families in the Greek diaspora. *Global Networks, 4*(3), 299–311.

Panitch, L. & D. Swartz. (2006). Neo-liberalism, labour and the Canadian state. In V. Shalla (Ed.), *Working in a global era: Canadian perspectives* (pp. 347–378). Toronto: Canadian Scholars' Press Inc.

Paperny, A.M. (2012, September 6). Canada's youth crime plans bewilder international observers. *The Globe and Mail*. Retrieved June 8, 2013, from http://www.theglobeandmail.com/news/national/time-to-lead/canadas-youth-crime-plans-bewilder-international-observers/article592992/

Pappano, L. (2011, July 22). The Master's and the new Bachelor's. *The New York Times*. Retrieved June 1, 2103, from http://www.nytimes.com/2011/07/24/education/edlife/edl-24masters-t.html?pagewanted=all&_r=0

Parker, H. (2005). Normalization as a barometer: Recreational drug use and the consumption of leisure by younger Britons. *Addiction Research and Theory, 13*(3), 205–215. Retrieved February 19, 2008, from the Academic Search Premier database.

Pate, K. (1999). Young women and violent offences: Myths and realities. *Canadian Woman Studies, 19*(1&2), 39–43.

Patterson, S. (1965). *Dark strangers: A study of West Indians in London*. London: Penguin Books.

Paul, P. (2003, September 3). The permaparent trap. *Psychology Today*. Retrieved May 18, 2007, from http://psychologytoday.com/articles/pto-2993.html

Paulson, S.E., & Sputa, C.L. (1996). Patterns of parenting during adolescence: Perceptions of adolescents and parents. *Adolescence, 31*(122), 369–382.

Pearson, P. (1993, May 1). Teenage mutant Ninja Canadians? *Chatelaine, 66*(3), 72–75, 116.

Pepler, D., Connolly, J., & Craig, W. (1999). *School experiences of immigrants and ethnic minority youth: Risk and protective factors in coping with bullying and harassment*. Research report 1997–1998. Toronto: CERIS—The Ontario Metropolis Centre. Retrieved March 11, 2007, from http://ceris.metropolis.net/frameset_e.html

Perkins, U.E. (2005). *Harvesting new generations: The positive development of Black youth* (2nd ed.). Chicago: Third World Press.

Perreault, S. (2011). Self-reported internet victimization in Canada, 2009. *Juristat*. Statistics Canada catalogue no. 85-002-X. Ottawa: Minister of Industry.

Philp, M. (2000, July 10). Young workers face high risks. *Globe and Mail*, p. A2.

Picard, A. (2005, October 20). It takes more than their peer group to make teens happy, study finds. *Globe and Mail*, p. A3.

Picot, G., & Myles, J. (2000). Children in low-income families. *Canadian Social Trends* (Vol. 3) (pp. 129–132). Toronto: Thompson Educational Publishing.

Pipher, M. (1994). *Reviving Ophelia: Saving the selves of adolescent girls*. New York: Penguin.

Platt, L. (2009). *Ethnicity and family relationships within and between ethnic groups: An analysis using the Labour Force Survey*. London: Equity and Human Rights Commission. Retrieved May 9, 2013, from http://www.equalityhumanrights.com/uploaded_files/raceinbritain/ethnicity_and_family_report.pdf

Policy Studies Institute. (2003). *University top up fees—threat to widening participation?* London: Policy Studies Institute. Press release. Retrieved May 9, 2007, from http://www.psi.org.uk/news/pressrelease.asp?news_item_id=121

Politics.co.uk. (2013). Tuition fee: What are tuition fees? *Politics.co.uk*. Retrieved May 10, 2013, from http://www.politics.co.uk/reference/tuition-fees

Potter, R.H., & Potter, L.A. (2001). The internet, cyberporn, and sexual exploitation of children: Media moral panics and urban myths for middle-class parents? *Sexuality and Culture, 5*(3), 31–48. Retrieved June 4, 2013, from http://link.springer.com/article/10.1007%2Fs12119-001-1029-9

Pratt, A. (1995). New immigrant and refugee battered women: The intersection of immigration and criminal justice policy. In Centre for Criminology (Ed.), *Wife assault and the Canadian criminal justice system* (pp. 27–47). Toronto: Centre for Criminology, University of Toronto.

Presdee, M. (1999). The diversity of youth reviewed [Review Essay]. *Sociology, 33*(3), 639–643.

Press TV. (2013, June 8). Islamophobic hate crimes surge in UK following Woolwich incident. *Press TV.* Retrieved June 8, 2013, from http://www.presstv.ir/detail/2013/05/25/305315/islamophobic-hate-crimes-surge-in-uk/

Preston, B. (2001). *A booklet for service providers who work with immigrant families on issues relating to child discipline, child abuse and child neglect*. Ottawa: National Clearinghouse on Family Violence.

Price, L.S. (1989). *Patterns of violence in the lives of girls and women: A reading guide*. Vancouver: Women's Research Centre.

Progressive Conservative Party of Ontario. (1999). *PC Blueprint.* Toronto: PC Party of Ontario.

Pryce, K. (1986). *Endless pressure*. Bristol: Bristol Classical Press.

Public Safety Canada. (2002). The effects of punishment on recidivism. *Research Summary, 7*(3). Retrieved June 5, 2013, from http://www.publicsafety.gc.ca/res/cor/sum/cprs200205_1-eng.aspx

Public Safety Canada. (2012). *A statistical snapshot of youth at risk and youth offending in Canada*. Statistics Canada catalogue no. PS4-126/2012E-PDF. Retrieved June 5, 2013, from http://www.publicsafety.gc.ca/res/cp/res/ssyr-eng.aspx#sec02.1

Pulkingham, J., & Ternowetsky, G. (Eds.). (1996). *Remaking Canadian social policy: Social security in the late 1990s*. Halifax: Fernwood Publishing.

Pupo, N. (1994). Dissecting the role of the state. In D. Glenday & A. Duffy (Eds.), *Canadian society: Understanding and surviving in the 1990s*. Toronto: McClelland & Stewart.

Purkayastha, B. (2000). Liminal lives: South Asian youth and domestic violence. *Journal of Social Distress and Homelessness, 9*, 201–219.

Push Projects. (2013). *Transgender coming out stories*. Retrieved June 2, 2013, from http://www.pushprojects.moonfruit.com/#/transgender-coming-out-stories/4558314999

Raby, R. (2005a). Polite, well-dressed, and on time: High school conduct codes and the production of docile citizens. *Canadian Review of Sociology and Anthropology, 42*(1), 71–91.

Raby, R. (2005b). What is resistance? *Journal of Youth Studies, 8*(2), 151–171.

Rahman, M. (2001). The globalization of childhood and youth: New actors and networks in protecting street children and working children in the south. In H. Helve & C. Wallace (Eds.), *Youth, citizenship, and empowerment* (pp. 262–275). Aldershot: Ashgate Publishing Limited.

Rahwoni, O. (2002). Reflections on youth and militarism in contemporary Africa. In A. De Waal & N. Argenti (Eds.), *Young Africa: Realising the rights of children and youth* (pp. 155–170). Trenton: Africa World Press, Inc.

Rains, C. (2000). *Little Rock Central High 40th anniversary.* Little Rock: Craig Rains/Public Relations, Inc. Retrieved January 23, 2008, from http://www.centralhigh57.org/.

Raising the Roof. (2009). *Youth homelessness in Canada: The road to solutions.* Toronto: Raising the Roof. Retrieved May 11, 2013, from http://www.raisingtheroof.org/RaisingTheRoof/media/RaisingTheRoofMedia/Documents/RoadtoSolutions_fullrept_english.pdf

Ram, B., & Hou, F. (2003). Changes in family structure and child outcomes: Roles of economic and familial resources. *Policy Studies Journal 31*(3), 309–331.

Ramirez-Valles, J., Zimmerman, M.A., & Juarez, L. (2002). Gender differences of neighborhood and social control processes: A study of the timing of first intercourse among low-achieving, urban, African-American youth. *Youth & Society, 33*(3), 418–441.

Ramsden, B., & Brown, N. (2005). *Variable tuition fees in England: Assessing their impact on students and higher education institutions. A first report.* London: Nigel Brown Associates. Retrieved May 5, 2007, from http://bookshop.universitiesuk.ac.uk/downloads/VariableFees2.pdf

Raphael, D. (2009). *Social determinants of health: Canadian perspectives.* (2nd ed.) Toronto: Canadian Scholars' Press Inc.

Rattansi, A., & Phoenix, A. (2005). Rethinking youth identities: Modernist and postmodernist frameworks. *Identity: An International Journal of Theory & Research, 5*(2), 97–123. Retrieved June 20, 2006, from Academic Search Premier database.

Raychaba, B. (1993). *"Pain … lots of pain": Family violence and abuse in the lives of young people in care.* Ottawa: National Youth Care Network.

Redmond, M.A. (1985). Attitudes of adolescent males toward adolescent pregnancy and fatherhood. *Family Relations, 34*, 337–342.

Redmount, E. (2002). Cyclical patterns in school attrition and attendance: A study in the labor-market behavior of children. *Economic Development and Cultural Change, 51*(1), 135–160.

Rees, G., & Stein, M. (1999). *The abuse of adolescents within the family: Summary of research and findings.* London: National Society for Prevention of Cruelty against Children. Retrieved February 15, 2008, from www.nspcc.org.uk/inform

Reich, K., Culcross, P.L., & Behrman, R.E. (2002). Children, youth, and gun violence: Analysis and recommendations. *The Future of Children, 12*(2), 4–23. Retrieved May 30, 2006, from http://www.futureofchildren.org/pubs-info2825/pubs-info_show.htm?doc_id=154414

Reid, J.L., Hammond, D., Burkhalter, R., & Ahmed, R. (2012). *Tobacco use in Canada: Patterns and trends*, 2012 edition. Waterloo, ON: Propel Centre for Population Health Impact, University of Waterloo. Retrieved June 9, 2013, from http://www.tobaccoreport.ca/2012/TobaccoUseinCanada_2012.pdf

Reuters. (2013, March 28). Newtown school gunman fired 154 rounds in less than 5 minutes. *Reuters*. Retrieved June 8, 2013, from http://www.reuters.com/article/2013/03/28/us-usa-shooting-connecticut-idUSBRE92R0EM20130328

Rex, J. (1982). West Indian and Asian youth. In E. Cashmore & B. Troyna (Eds.), *Black youth in crisis* (pp. 50–75). London: Allen & Unwin.

Reynolds, C. (1998). The educational system. In N. Mandell (Ed.), *Feminist issues: Race, class, and sexuality* (2nd ed.) (pp. 272–293). Scarborough: Prentice Hall Allyn and Bacon Canada.

Rhodes, C.N., Mihyar, H.A., & El-Rous, G.A. (2002). Social learning and community participation with children at risk in two marginalized urban neighborhoods in Amman, Jordan. In M. Tienda & W.J. Wilson (Eds.), *Youth in cities: A cross-national perspective* (pp. 191–216). Cambridge: Cambridge University Press.

Rhynard, J., & Krebs, M. (1997). Sexual assault in dating relationships. *Journal of School Health, 67*(3), 89–97.

Richardson, C.J. (1996). Divorce and remarriage. In M. Baker (Ed.), *Families: Changing trends in Canada* (3rd ed.) (pp. 215–246). Toronto: McGraw-Hill Ryerson Limited.

Ritzer, G. (1993). *The McDonalidization of society*. Thousand Oaks, CA: Pine Forge Press.

Robson, K., & Anderson, G. (2006). Male adolescents' contributions to household labor as predictors of later-life participation in housework. *Journal of Men's Studies, 14*(1), 1–12.

Roe, K. (1999). Music and identity among European youth: Music as communication (Online). In P. Rutten (Ed.), *Music, culture, and society in Europe* (pp. 85–97). Part II of European Music Office, Music in Europe. Brussels: European Music Office. Retrieved March 12, 2007, from http://www.icce.rug.nl/~soundscapes/DATABASES/MIE/Part2_chapter03.shtml

Rogers, R.S. (1997). The making and moulding of modern youth: A short history. In J. Roche & S. Tucker (Eds.), *Youth in society: Contemporary theory, policy and practice* (pp. 8–16). London: Sage Publications.

Roggero, P., Tarricone, R., Nicoli, M., & Mangiaterra, V. (2006). What do people think about disabled youth and employment in developed and developing countries? Results from an e-discussion hosted by the World Bank. *Disability & Society, 21*(6), 645–650. Retrieved January 18, 2008, from Academic Search Elite database.

Rokach, A. (2005). The causes of loneliness in homeless youth. *The Journal of Psychology, 139*(5), 469–480.

Rollins, A., & Hunter, A.G. (2013). Racial socialization of biracial youth: Maternal messages and approaches to address discrimination. *Family Relations, 62*(February), 140–153. Retrieved June 9, 2013, from http://www.academia.edu/2562644/Racial_Socialization_of_Biracial_Youth_Maternal_Messages_and_Approaches_to_Address_Discrimination

Rosario, M., Schrimshaw, E., Hunter, J., & Braun, J. (2006). Sexual identity development among lesbian, gay, and bisexual youths: Consistency and change over time. *The Journal of Sex Research, 43*(1), 46–58.

Rossiter, K. (2000). Shattering the mirror: A young woman's story of weight preoccupation. In B. Miedema, J.M. Stoppard, & V. Anderson (Eds.), *Women's bodies/women's lives: Health, well-being, and body image* (pp. 194–202). Toronto: Sumach Press.

Rotermann, M. (2005). Sex, condoms and STDs among young people. *Health Reports, 16*(3), 39–45. Retrieved October 27, 2007, from http://www.sexualityandu.ca/teachers/data-1.aspx

Rotermann, M. (2008). *Trends in teen sexual behaviour and condom use.* Statistics Canada catalogue no. 82-003-X. Retrieved June 2, 2013, from http://www.statcan.gc.ca/pub/82-003-x/2008003/article/10664-eng.pdf

Royal Commission on Aboriginal Peoples. (1991). *Report of the Royal Commission on Aboriginal Peoples.* Ottawa: Indian and Northern Affairs Canada.

Rozie-Battle, Judith L. (Ed.). (2002). *African-American adolescents in the urban community: Social services policy and practice interventions.* New York: Haworth.

Runyan, C.W., & Zakocz, R.C. (2000). Epidemiology and prevention of injuries among adolescent workers in the United States. *Annual Review of Public Health, 21,* 247–269. Retrieved January 13, 2008, from Academic Search Premier database.

Russell, C. (1996–1997). *Education, employment, and training policies and programmes for youth with disabilities in four European countries.* Geneva: International Labour Office. Retrieved January 16, 2008, from http://www.ilo.org/public/english/employment/strat/publ/etp21.htm

Saffron, L. (1998). Raising children in an age of diversity—Advantages of having a lesbian mother. In G.A. Dunne (Ed.), *Living "difference": Lesbian perspectives on work and family life* (pp. 35–47). Bristol: Haworth.

Sangster, J. (2002). *Girl trouble: Female delinquency in English Canada.* Toronto: Between the Lines.

Savin-Williams, R.C. (2001). A critique of research on sexual-minority youths. *Journal of Adolescence, 24,* 5–13.

Savoie, J. (1999). *Youth violent crime. Juristat, 19*(13). Catalogue no. 85-002-XPE. Ottawa: Canadian Centre for Justice Statistics, Statistics Canada.

Scarpetta, S., Sonnet, A., & Manfredi, T. (2010). *Rising youth unemployment during the crisis: How to prevent negative long-term consequences on a generation?* OECD Social, Employment and Migration Papers, No. 6. Paris: OECD. Retrieved June 1, 2013, from http://www.oecd.org/employment/youthforum/44986030.pdf

Schellenberg, E.G., Hirt, J., & Sears, A. (1999). Attitudes toward homosexuals among students at a Canadian university. *Sex Roles, 40*(1/2), 139–152.

Schiff, K.G. (2000). Give it to us straight. *Newsweek, 136*(3), 28. Retrieved February 2, 2008, from ProQuest database.

Schiff, M., & McKay, M.M. (2003). Urban youth disruptive behavioral difficulties: Exploring association with parenting and gender. *Family Process, 42*(4), 517–529.

Schilt, K. (2003). "I'll resist with every inch and every breath": Girls and zine making as a form of resistance. *Youth & Society, 35*(1), 71–97. Retrieved November 15, 2007, from Academic Search Premier database.

Schissel, B. (1997). *Blaming children: Youth crime, moral panics, and the politics of hate.* Halifax: Fernwood Publishing.

Schissel, B. (2000). Boys against girls: The structural and interpersonal dimensions of violent patriarchial culture in the lives of young men. *Violence against Women, 6*(9), 960–986.

Schissel, B. (2006). *Still blaming children: Youth conduct and the politics of child hurting.* Halifax: Fernwood Publishing.

Scott, J.L. (2003). English language and communication: Issues for African and Caribbean immigrant youth in Toronto. In P. Anisef & K.M. Kilbride (Eds.), *Managing two worlds: Immigrant youth in Ontario* (pp. 96–117). Toronto: Canadian Scholars' Press Inc.

Sears, H.A., & Armstrong, V.H. (1998). A prospective study of adolescents' self-reported depressive symptoms: Are risk behaviours a stronger predictor than anxiety symptoms? *Journal of Behavioural Science, 30*(4), 225–233.

Sefa Dei, G.J. (1993). Narrative discourses of Black/African-Canadian parents and the Canadian public school system. *Canadian Ethnic Studies, 25*(3), 45–66.

Sellick, C. (2006). From famine to feast: A review of the foster care research literature. *Children and Society, 20,* 67–74. Retrieved February 10, 2008, from the Academic Search Premier database.

Seltzer, V.C. (1989). *The psychosocial worlds of the adolescent: Public and private.* Toronto: John Wiley & Sons.

Sermons, M.W. & Henry, M. (2009). *Homelessness counts: Changes in homelessness from 2005 to 2007.* Washington: The Homelessness Research Institute of the National Alliance to End Homelessness.

Service Canada. (2005). *Canadian youth: Who are they and what do they want?* Ottawa: Service Canada. Retrieved May 14, 2007, from http://www.youth.gc.ca/yoaux.jsp?lang=en&auxpa geid=846&ta=1&flash=1

Sev'er, A. (2002). *Fleeing the house of horrors: Women who have left abusive partners.* Toronto: University of Toronto Press.

Settersten, R.A. (2006). *Becoming adult: Meanings and markers for young Americans.* Philadelphia: Network on Transitions to Adulthood Research Network Working Paper. Retrieved July 17, 2013, from http://www.youthnys.org/InfoDocs/BecomingAnAdult-3-06.pdf

Sex Information and Education Council of Canada. (2012). Statistics related to trends in sexual behaviours of Canadian teenagers. *Check the Research,* July/August 2012. Retrieved June 2, 2013, from http://sexualityandu.ca/uploads/files/CTR_TeenageStatistics_JULYAUG2012-EN.pdf

Seyfried, S.F., & Chung, I.-J. (2002). Parent involvement as parental monitoring of student motivation and parent expectations: Predicting later achievement among African-American and European-American middle school-age students. *Journal of Ethnic & Cultural Diversity in Social Work, 11*(1/2), 109–131.

Shahidian, H. (1999). Gender and sexuality among immigrant Iranians in Canada. *Sexualities 2*(2), 189–222.

Sharp, L.A. (2002). *The sacrificed generation: Youth, history, and the colonized mind in Madagascar.* Berkeley: University of California Press.

Sharpe, D., & Taylor, J.K. (1999). An examination of variables from a social-developmental model to explain physical and psychological dating violence. *Canadian Journal of Behavioural Science, 31*(3), 165–175.

Sherrod, L.R. (2006). Promoting citizenship and activism in today's youth. In S. Gingwright, P. Noguera, & J. Cammarota (Eds.), *Beyond resistance! Youth activism and community change: New democratic possibilities for practice and policy for America's youth* (pp. 287–300). New York: Routledge.

Sherwood, J. (1993). Teaching tolerance. *Canada & the World, 59*(2), 22–24.

Shields, I.W. (1995). Young sex offenders: A comparison with a control group of non-sex offenders. *Correctional Service Canada, Safety, Dignity, and Respect for All, 7*(1), 17–19. Retrieved from www.cscscc.ca/text/pblct/forum/e07/e071e.shtm

Shields, J. (2004). *No safe haven: Markets, welfare, and migrants.* CERIS Working paper no. 22. Toronto: Joint Centre of Excellence for Research on Immigration and Settlement (CERIS).

Shimoni, E., Este, D., & Clark, D. (2003). Paternal engagement in immigrant and refugee families. *Journal of Comparative Family Studies, 34*(4), 555–571.

Shore, H. (1999). *Artful dodgers: Youth and crime in early nineteenth-century London.* London: Boydell Press.

Sifferlin, A. (2012, August 9). Teens and tobacco use: Why declines in youth have stalled. *Time.* Retrieved June 9, 2013, from http://healthland.time.com/2012/08/09/teens-and-tobacco-use-why-declines-in-middle-and-high-school-students-stalled/

Silcott, M. (2000a). Built for speed: In the rave scene, ecstasy is no longer the drug of choice. Which is not good news. *Saturday Night, 115*(6), 68.

Silcott, M. (2000b, February 19). Raves roots. *Toronto Star,* p. M1.

Simiyu, N.W.W. (2009). Triple tragedy of the black student athlete. *The Sports Digest, 17*(3). Retrieved June 4, 2013, from http://thesportdigest.com/archive/article/triple-tragedy-black-student-athlete

Single, E., Maclennan, A., & MacNeil, P. (1994). *Horizons: Alcohol and other drug use in Canada.* Ottawa: Health Canada, and the Canadian Centre on Substance Abuse.

Sippola, L.K. (1999). Getting to know the "other": The characteristics and developmental significance of other-sex relationships in adolescence. *Journal of Youth and Adolescence, 28*(4), 407–418.

Small, S. (1994). *Racialised barriers: The Black experience in the United States and England in the 1980s.* London & New York: Routledge.

Smandych, R.C. (2001). *Youth crime: Varieties, theories, and prevention.* Toronto: Harcourt Canada.

Smith, E. (2004). *Nowhere to turn? Responding to partner violence against immigrant and visible minority women.* Ottawa: Department of Justice Canada, Sectoral Involvement in Departmental Policy Development (SIDPD).

Smith, A., Schneider, B.H., & Ruck, M.D. (2005). "Thinking about makin' it": Black Canadian students' beliefs regarding education and academic achievement. *Journal of Youth and Adolescence, 34*(4), 347–359.

Smith, A., & Twomey, B. (2002). Labour market experiences of people with disabilities. *Labour Market Trends, 110*(8). Published in Web format August 8, 2002. Retrieved January 16, 2008, from http://findarticles.com/p/articles/mi_qa3999/is_200208/ai_n9121000

Smith, N., Lister, R., Middleton, S., & Cox, L. (2005). Young people as real citizens: Towards an inclusionary understanding of citizenship. *Journal of Youth Studies, 8*(4), 425–443.

Solomon, Y., Warin, J., Lewis, C., & Langford, W. (2002). Intimate talk between parents and their teenage children: Democratic openness or covert control? *Sociology, 36*(4), 965–983.

Solomos, J. (2003). *Race and racism in Britain* (3rd ed.). London: Palgrave McMillan.

Somerville, K. (2008). Transnational belonging among second generation youth: Identity in a globalized world. *Journal of Social Sciences, 10*, 23–33.

Span, C.M. (2002). Educational and social reforms for African-American juvenile delinquents in 19th-century New York City and Philadephia. *Journal of Negro Education, 71*(3), 108–117.

Spears, J. (1999, August 4). Mayor's program called attack on poor. *Toronto Star.*

Special Senate Committee on Youth. (1986). *Youth: A plan of action.* Ottawa: Special Senate Committee on Youth.

Springhall, J. (1986). *Coming of age: Adolescence in Britain 1860–1960*. Dublin: Gill and Macmillan.

Sprott, J.B. (1996). Understanding public views of youth crime and the youth justice system. *Canadian Journal of Criminology, 38*(3), 271–290.

Stahura, K., & Parks, K. (2005). Race issues within intercollegiate athletics: African-American versus Caucasian-American athletes' perceptions of athletic, academic, and community social climate. *Research Quarterly for Exercise and Sport, 76*(1), A111. Retrieved February 20, 2008, from ProQuest database.

Stald, G. (2008). Mobile identity: Youth, identity, and mobile communication media. In D. Buckingham (Ed.), *Youth, identity, and digital media* (pp. 143–164). Cambridge, MA: The MIT Press.

Stanleigh, S. (2000, August 4). Peaceful rave rally was a seminal event: Youth accented positive vibe to city politicians. *Toronto Star*, p. B4.

Statistic Brain. (2012). *Teenage consumer spending statistics*. Statistic Brain. Retrieved June 4, 2013, from http://www.statisticbrain.com/teenage-consumer-spending-statistics/

Statistics Canada. (1993–1997). *Community college postsecondary enrolment, 1993–1997*. Publication no. 81-229-XIB. Ottawa: Statistics Canada.

Statistics Canada. (1996–1997). *Smoking behaviour of Canadians*. Ottawa: Statistics Canada. Retrieved November 11, 2007, from http://www.hc-sc.gc.ca/ahc-asc/media/nr-cp/1999/1999_12bk1_e. html.

Statistics Canada. (1998a). 1996 Census: Education, mobility and migration. *The Daily*. Retrieved from http://www.statcan.ca/English/dai-quo/.

Statistics Canada. (1998b). Multiple risk behaviour in teenagers and young adults, 1994/95. *The Daily*. Retrieved from http://www.statcan.ca/English/dai-quo/.

Statistics Canada. (1999a). *Labour force characteristics by age and sex*. Retrieved June 23, 2000, from http://www.statcam.ca/english/Pgdb/People/Labour05.htm

Statistics Canada. (1999b). *Labour force participation rates*. Retrieved June 23, 2000, from http://www.statcam.ca/english/Pgdb/People/Labour05.htm

Statistics Canada. (1999c). *Population 15 years and over by sex, age groups, and labour force activity, for Canada, provinces and territories, 1981–1996 Censuses (20% sample data)*. Nation Series. Publication no. 93F0027XDB96001. Ottawa: Statistics Canada.

Statistics Canada. (1999d). *Selected notifiable diseases*. Publication no. 82F0075XCB. Ottawa: Statistics Canada.

Statistics Canada (1999e). *Youths and adults charged in criminal incidents, Criminal Code, and federal statutes, by sex*. CANSIM, Matrices 2198 and 2199. Ottawa: Statistics Canada.

Statistics Canada. (1999f). Youths and the labour market, 1998–99. *Labour Force Update, 3*(4).

Statistics Canada. (2000a). *Average hours per week of television watching*. Catalogue no. 87F0006XIB. Ottawa: Statistics Canada.

Statistics Canada. (2000b). *Family violence in Canada: A statistical profile 2000*. Catalogue no. 85-224-XIE. Ottawa: Canadian Centre for Justice Statistics.

Statistics Canada. (2000c). *Labour force survey*. Retrieved May, 2000, from http://www.statcan. ca/Daily/English/000505/d000505a.htm

Statistics Canada. (2002a). *Profile of Canadian families and households: Diversification continues.* Ottawa: Statistics Canada. Retrieved May 18, 2007, from http://www12.statcan.ca/english/census01/Products/Analytic/companion/fam/pdf/96F0030XIE2001003.pdf

Statistics Canada. (2002b). 2001 Census: Marital status, common-law status, families, dwellings, and households. *The Daily.* Retrieved May 16, 2007, from http://www.statcan.gc.ca/Daily/English/021022/d021022a.htm

Statistics Canada. (2003a). Family income and participation in postsecondary education. *The Daily.* Retrieved November 22, 2007, from http://www.statcan.ca/Daily/English/031003/d031003b.htm

Statistics Canada. (2003b). *2001 Census: Analysis series. Aboriginal peoples in Canada: A demographic profile.* Ottawa: Ministry of Industry. Retrieved April 20, 2007, from http://www12.statcan.ca/english/census01/products/analytic/companion/abor/contents.cfm

Statistics Canada. (2003c). *Pregnancy outcomes.* Catalogue no. 82-224-XIE. Statistics Canada, Canadian Vital Statistics, Birth Database and Stillbirth Database; Canadian Institute for Health Information, Hospital Morbidity Database and Therapeutic Abortion Database (CANSIM table 106-9002). Retrieved April 30, 2007, from http://www.statcan.ca/english/freepub/82-224XIE/82-224-XIE2003000.pdf

Statistics Canada. (2004a). University tuition fees. *The Daily.* Retrieved September 20, 2006, from http://www.statcan.ca/Daily/English/040902/d040902a.htm

Statistics Canada. (2004b). Study: Saving for post-secondary education. *The Daily.* Retrieved September 20, 2006, from http://www.statcan.ca/Daily/English/040723/d040723b.htm

Statistics Canada. (2004c). Divorces 2001 and 2002. *The Daily.* Ottawa: Statistics Canada. Retrieved May 16, 2007, from http://www.statcan.ca/Daily/English/040504/d040504a.htm

Statistics Canada. (2004d). Youth in transition survey. *The Daily.* Catalogue no. 11-001-XIE ISSN 0827-0465. Ottawa: Statistics Canada.

Statistics Canada. (2005a). The impact of family background on access to postsecondary education. *The Daily.* Retrieved November 22, 2007, from http://www.statcan.ca/Daily/English/050118/d050118c.htm

Statistics Canada. (2005b). Study: How Canada compares in the G8. *The Daily.* Retrieved May 16, 2007, from http://www.statcan.ca/Daily/English/050621/d050621c.htm

Statistics Canada. (2005c, June 28). Canada's aboriginal population in 2017. *The Daily.* Ottawa: Statistics Canada. Retrieved October 14, 2007, from http://www.statcan.ca/Daily/English/050628/d050628d.htm

Statistics Canada. (2005d, May 11). Adult literacy and life skills survey. *The Daily.* Retrieved May 11, 2013, from http://www.statcan.gc.ca/daily-quotidien/050511/dq050511b-eng.htm

Statistics Canada. (2006a). Study: Self-reported delinquency among young people in Toronto. *The Daily.* Retrieved December 31, 2007, from http://www.statcan.ca/Daily/English/070925/d070925a.htm

Statistics Canada. (2006b). Television viewing. *The Daily.* Retrieved May 10, 2007, from http://www.statcan.ca/Daily/English/060331/d060331b.htm

Statistics Canada. (2006c, September 1). University tuition fees. *The Daily.* Ottawa: Statistics Canada. Retrieved November 22, 2007, from http://www.statcan.ca/Daily/English/060901/d060901a.htm

Statistics Canada. (2006d). *Women and men aged 15 years and over, by living arrangement and visible minority status, Canada, 2006.* Statistics Canada catalogue no. 89-503-X. Ottawa: Statistics Canada. Retrieved May 13, 2013, from http://www.statcan.gc.ca/pub/89-503-x/2010001/article/11546/tbl/tbl004-eng.htm

Statistics Canada. (2006e). *2006 Census: Educational portrait of Canada, 2006 Census: National picture.* Ottawa: Statistics Canada. Retrieved May 12, 2013, from http://www12.statcan.ca/census-recensement/2006/as-sa/97-560/p6-eng.cfm

Statistics Canada. (2007a). *General Social Survey (GSS), 2005, Cycle 19: Time use diary.* (Subset compiled from public-use microdata file.) Ottawa: Statistics Canada (producer). Using IDLS (distributor). Retrieved September 30, 2007, from http://www.chass.utoronto.ca

Statistics Canada. (2007b). Marriages. *The Daily.* Retrieved April 18, 2007, from http://www.statcan.ca/Daily/English/070117/d070117a.htm

Statistics Canada. (2007c). *The Canadian labour market at a glance.* Labour Statistics Division. Ottawa: Statistics Canada. Retrieved May 5, 2013, from http://www.statcan.gc.ca/pub/71-222-x/71-222-x2008001-eng.pdf

Statistics Canada. (2008a). *Education matters: Insights on education, learning and training in Canada: Children of Immigrants: How well do they do in school?* (CANSIM table 81-004-XIE). Ottawa: Statistics Canada. Retrieved May 6, 2013, from http://www5.statcan.gc.ca/bsolc/olc-cel?catno=81-004-XRCHROPG=1&lang=eng

Statistics Canada, (2008b). *Immigrant status and place of birth (38), immigrant status and period of immigration (8A), age groups (8), sex (3) and selected demographic, cultural, labour force, educational and income characteristics (277), for the total population of Canada, provinces, territories, census metropolitan areas and census agglomerations, 2006 Census—20% Sample Data.* Statistics Canada catalogue no. 97-564-XCB2006008. Ottawa: Statistics Canada.

Statistics Canada (2008c, June 12). Canadian internet use survey. *The Daily.* Retrieved June 14, 2013, from http://www.statcan.gc.ca/daily-quotidien/080612/dq080612b-eng.htm

Statistics Canada. (2008d). Health care use among gay, lesbian and bisexual Canadians. Statistics Canada catalogue no. 82-003-XWE. *Health Reports, 19*(1). Retrieved June 2, 2013, from http://www.statcan.gc.ca/pub/82-003-x/2008001/article/10532/5002598-eng.htm

Statistics Canada. (2009a). *Income in Canada.* Statistics Canada catalogue no. 75—202-X. Ottawa: Statistics Canada. Retrieved May 6, 2013, from http://www.statcan.gc.ca/pub/75-202-x/75-202x2007000-eng.pdf

Statistics Canada. (2009b). *Graduating in Canada: Profile, labour market outcomes and student debt of the class of 2005.* Retrieved May 17, 2013, from http://www.statcan.gc.ca/pub/81-595-m/81-595-m2009074-eng.pdf

Statistics Canada. (2010). Measuring up: Canadian results of the OECD PISA study: The performance of Canada's youth in reading, mathematics and science. Ottawa: Statistics Canada. Retrieved May 16, 2013, from http://www.statcan.gc.ca/pub/81-590-x/81-590-x2010001-eng.pdf

Statistics Canada. (2011a). *Divorces and crude divorce rates, Canada, provinces and territories, annual* (CANSIM table 101-6501). Ottawa: Statistics Canada.

Statistics Canada. (2011b). *Census families by number of children at home, by province and terirtory (2011 Census).* Statistics Canada catalogue no. 98312XCB. Ottawa: Statistics Canada. Retrieved May 16, 2013, from http://www.statcan.gc.ca/tables-tableaux/sum-som/l01/cst01/famil50a-eng.htm

Statistics Canada. (2011c). *Census 2011: Portrait of families and living arrangements in Canada.* Ottawa: Statistics Canada. Retrieved May 18, 2013, from http://www12.statcan.ca/census-recensement/2011/as-sa/98-312-x/98-312-x2011001-eng.cfm#a2

Statistics Canada. (2011d). *Education indicators in Canada: Spending on post secondary education.* Statistics Canada catalogue no. 81-599-X—Issue no. 007. Ottawa: Statistics Canada. Retrieved May 18, 2013, from http://www.statcan.gc.ca/pub/81-582-x/81-582-x2013001-eng.htm

Statistics Canada. (2011e). *Canadian vital statistics, marriage database and demography division (population estimates),* Ottawa: Statistics Canada.

Statistics Canada. (2011f). *Aboriginal peoples.* Statistics Canada catalogue no. 11-402X. Retrieved May 31, 2014, from http://www.statcan.gc.ca/pub/11-402-x/2011000/chap/ap-pa/ap-pa-eng.htm

Statistics Canada (2012a, September 19). 2011 Census of population: Families, households, marital status, structural type of dwelling, collectives. *The Daily.* Ottawa: Statistics Canada. Retrieved May 18, 2013, from http://www.statcan.gc.ca/daily-quotidien/120919/dq120919a-eng.pdf

Statistics Canada. (2012b). *2011 census in brief: Living arrangements of young adults aged 20 to 29 years.* Ottawa: Statistics Canada. Retrieved May 18, 2013, from http://www12.statcan.gc.ca/census-recensement/2011/as-sa/98-312-x/98-312-x2011003_3-eng.pdf

Statistics Canada. (2012c). *Educational attainment and employment: Canada in an international context.* Statistics Canada catalogue no. 81-599-X—Issue no. 008. Ottawa: Statistics Canada. Retrieved May 18, 2013, from http://www.statcan.gc.ca/pub/81-599-x/81-599-x2012008-eng.pdf

Statistics Canada. (2012d). *Labour force survey 2012.* Ottawa: Statistics Canada.

Statistics Canada. (2012e). *Education attainment: Public postsecondary enrolments by institution type, sex and field of study.* Ottawa: Statistics Canada.

Statistics Canada. (2012f). *Labour force survey estimates (LFS), by sex and detailed age group, annual* (CANSIM Table 282-0002). Ottawa: Statistics Canada.

Statistics Canada. (2013a). Undergraduate tuition fees for full time Canadian students, by discipline, by province. Retrieved May 18, 2013, from http://www.statcan.gc.ca/tables-tableaux/sum-som/l01/cst01/educ50a-eng.htm

Statistics Canada. (2013b, May 10). Labour force survey, April 2013. *The Daily.* Ottawa: Statistics Canada. Retrieved May 20, 2013, from http://www.statcan.gc.ca/daily-quotidien/130510/dq130510a-eng.pdf

Sternheimer, K. (2007). Do video games kill? *Contexts, 6*(1), 13–17. Retrieved March 26, 2007, from http://www/ucpressjournals.com/

Stevenson, K., & Besserer, S. (1997). *A profile of youth justice in Canada.* Ottawa: Canadian Centre for Justice Statistics.

Stevenson, K., Tufts, J., Hendrick, D., & Kowalski, M. (2000). Youth and crime. *Canadian Social Trends, 3,* 222–228.

Stewart, C. (2002). Family factors of low-income African-American youth associated with substance use: An exploratory analysis. *Journal of Ethnicity in Substance Abuse, 1*(1), 97–111.

Stewart, D. (1998, November 2). High school rules: Recognizing high school as cultural centres leads to a better understanding of teens. *Marketing Magazine,* 26.

Stone, N., Hatherall, B., Ingham, R., & McEachran, J. (2006). Oral sex and condom use among young people in the United Kingdom. *Perspectives on Sexual and Reproductive Health, 38*(1), 6–12. Retrieved February 13, 2008, from ProQuest database.

Strange, C. (1995). *Toronto's girls problem: The perils and pleasures of the city, 1880–1930.* Toronto: University of Toronto Press.

Strange, C. (1997). Sin or salvation? Protecting Toronto's working girls. *Beaver, 77*(3), 8–13.

Strauss, L.T., Herndon, J., Chang, J., Parker, W.Y., Bowens, S.V., & Berg, C.J. (2005). *Abortion surveillance—United States, 2002.* Washington: Centers for Disease Control and Prevention: Morbidity and Mortality Weekly Report. Retrieved April 30, 2007, from http://www.cdc.gov/mmwr/preview/mmwrhtml/ss5407a1.htm

Strickland, R. (Ed.). (2002). *Growing up postmodern: Neoliberalism and the war on the young.* Oxford: Rowman & Littlefield Publishers, Inc.

Student Voices Pennsylvania. (2006). *How can Pennsylvania solve the dropout problem?* The Annenberg Public Policy Center. Retrieved May 9, 2007, from http://student-voices.org/discussions/discussion.php?DiscussionID=480

Substance Abuse and Mental Health Services Administration. (2006). *Results from the 2005 National Survey on Drug Use and Health: National findings.* Office of Applied Studies, NSDUH Series H-30, DHSS Publication no. SMA 06-4194. Rockville: Substance Abuse and Mental Health Services Administration. Retrieved January 20, 2008, from http://www.oas.samhsa.gov/NSDUH/2k5NSDUH/2k5results.htm

Tait, G. (2000). *Youth, sex, and government.* New York: Peter Lang Publishing, Inc.

Tait, H. (2000). Educational achievement of young Aboriginal adults. *Canadian Social Trends* (Vol. 3) (pp. 257–259). Toronto: Thompson Educational Publishing.

Tam, S. (2005). Engendering youth: Shortcomings of Canadian youth employment programs. *Women and Environments International Magazine 66/67,* 34–36. Retrieved from Academic Search Premier database.

Tanner, J. (1990). Reluctant rebels: A case study of Edmonton high school drop-outs. *Canadian Review of Sociology and Anthropology, 27*(1), 74–94.

Tanner, J. (1996). *Teenage troubles: Youth and deviance in Canada.* Toronto: Nelson Canada.

Tanner, J. (2001). *Teenage troubles: Youth and deviance in Canada* (2nd ed.). Toronto: Nelson.

Tannock, S. (2001). *Youth at work: The unionized fast-food and grocery workplace.* Philadelphia: Temple University Press.

Taylor, P.S. (1997). Getting the drop on dropouts. *Canadian Business, 70*(13), 22–24.

Thiessen, V., & Blasius, J. (2002). The social distribution of youth's images of work. *The Canadian Review of Sociology and Anthropology, 39*(1), 49–78.

Television Bureau of Canada. (2013). *TVBasics 2012–2013.* Retrieved June 10, 2013, from http://www.tvb.ca/page_files/pdf/InfoCentre/TVBasics.pdf

Thiessen, V.E., & Looker, D. (1993, Winter). Generation, gender, and class perspectives on work. *International Journal of Canadian Studies/Revue Internationale d'etudes canadiennes* (Special Issue), 39–57.

Thompson, S. (2004). Fashion flirts with political messages. *Advertising Age [Midwest region edition], 75*(33), 10–11. Retrieved February 2, 2008, from ProQuest database.

Thomson, C.A. (1979). *Blacks in deep snow: Black pioneers in Canada.* Don Mills: James Dent & Sons (Canada) Limited.

Thomson, R., Holland, J., McGrellis, S., Bell, R., Henderson, S., & Sharpe, S. (2004). Inventing adulthoods: A biographical approach to understanding youth citizenship. *Sociological Review, 52*(2), 218–239.

Tienda, M., & Wilson, W.J. (Eds.). (2002a). *Youth in cities: A cross-national perspective.* Cambridge: Cambridge University Press.

Tienda, M., & Wilson, W.J. (2002b). Comparative perspectives of urban youth: Challenges for normative development. In M. Tienda & W.J. Wilson (Eds.), *Youth in cities: A cross-national perspective* (pp. 3–20). Cambridge: Cambridge University Press.

Tirone, S., & Pedlar, A. (2005). Leisure, place, and diversity: The experience of ethnic minority youth. *Canadian Ethnic Studies, 37*(2), 32–48.

Tolman, D.L., Spencer, R., Rosen-Reynoso, M., & Porche, M.V. (2003). Sowing the seeds of violence in heterosexual relationships: Early adolescents narrate compulsory heterosexuality. *Journal of Social Issues, 59*(1), 159–178.

Tonnesen, S.C. (2013). "Hit it and quit it": Responses to Black girls' victimization in school. *Berkeley Journal of Gender, Law & Justice, 28*(1), 1–30.

Toomey, E.T., & Nelson, E.S. (2001). Family conflict and young adults' attitudes toward intimacy. *Journal of Divorce and Remarriage, 34*(3/4), 49–69.

Toronto Star. (2000a, June 14). Challenge to the Safe Streets Act. *Toronto Star*, p. B4.

Toronto Star. (2000b, August 6). Right decision on raves. *Toronto Star*, p. A12.

Totten, M.D. (2009). Aboriginal youth and violent gang involvement in Canada: Quality prevention strategies. *IPC Review, 3*, 135–156. Retrieved June 10, 2013, from http://www.sciencessociales.uottawa.ca/ipc/eng/documents/IPCR3Totten.pdf

The Truth and Reconciliation Commission of Canada. (2012). *They came for the children.* Winnipeg, MB: The Truth and Reconciliation Commission of Canada.

Trypuc, B., & Robinson, J. (2009). *Homelessness in Canada: A funder's primer in understanding the tragedy on Canada's streets.* King City, ON: Charity Intelligence Canada. Retrieved May 15, 2013, from http://www.charityintelligence.ca/images/Ci-Homeless-in-Canada.pdf

Turcotte, P., & Belanger, A. (2000). Moving in together: The formation of first common-law unions. *Canadian Social Trends* (Vol. 3) (pp. 105–108). Toronto: Thompson Educational Publishing.

Tyyskä, V. (1998). Changing family structure and children's welfare: Global Perspectives. In A. Sev'er (Ed.), *Frontiers in women's studies: Canadian and German perspectives* (pp. 45–58). Toronto: Canadian Scholars' Press Inc.

Tyyskä, V. (2002). *Report of individual interviews with parents—Toronto. Improving parenting and family supports for new Canadians with young children: Focus on resources for service providers.* Kitchener-Waterloo and Toronto: Centre for Research and Education in Human Services and Joint Centre of Excellence for Research in Immigration and Settlement.

Tyyskä, V. (2003a). *Report of focus groups with newcomer parents—Toronto. Toronto: Improving parenting and family supports for new Canadians with young children: Focus on resources for service providers.* Kitchener-Waterloo and Toronto: Centre for Research and Education in Human Services and Joint Centre of Excellence for Research in Immigration and Settlement.

Tyyskä, V. (2003b). Solidarity and conflict: Teen-parent relationships in Iranian immigrant families in Toronto. In M. Lynn (Ed.), *Voices: Essays on Canadian families* (2nd ed.) (pp. 312–331). Toronto: Nelson Canada.

Tyyskä, V. (2005). Immigrant adjustment and parenting of teens: A study of newcomer groups in Toronto, Canada. In V. Puuronen, J. Soilevuo-Grønnerød, & J. Herranen (Eds.), *Youth— similarities, differences, inequalities* (pp. 118–132). Reports of the Karelian Institute, no. 1/2005. Joensuu: Joensuu University.

Tyyskä, V. (2006). *Teen perspectives on family relations in the Toronto Tamil community.* CERIS Working paper no. 45. Toronto: CERIS.

Tyyskä, V. (2011). Immigrant and racialized families. In N. Mandell & A. Duffy (Eds.), *Canadian families: Diversity, conflict, and change* (pp. 86–122). (4th ed.) Toronto: Nelson Education.

Tyyskä, V., & Colavecchia, S. (2001). *Report on individual interviews in Toronto: Study of parenting issues of newcomer families in Ontario.* Report for the Centre for Research & Education in Human Services (CREHS), Joint Centre of Excellence for Research on Immigration and Settlement (CERIS). Kitchener-Waterloo: CREHS.

UFCW (United Food and Commercial Workers). (2010). *Workplace sexual harassment: References and rights guide.* Retrieved May 31, 2013, from http://www.ufcw.ca/templates/ufcwcanada/ images/women/publicatios/harassment_brosh_jan2011_en.pdf

Ulman, A., & Straus, M.A. (2003). Violence by children against mothers in relation to violence between parents and corporal punishment by parents. *Journal of Comparative Family Studies, 34*(1), 41–60.

Unesco. (1981). *Youth in the 1980s.* Paris: United Nations Educational, Scientific, and Cultural Organization.

Unicef. (2005). *The state of the world's children in 2006: Excluded and invisible.* New York: Unicef. Retrieved May 11, 2013, from http://www.unicef.org/sowc06/pdfs/sowc06_fullreport.pdf

Universities and Colleges Admission Systems. (2013). *Data summary: Total UCAS applications, applicants and accepted applicants.* Cheltenham, UK: Universities and Colleges Admission Systems. Retrieved May 18, 2013, from http://www.ucas.com/about_us/stat_services/stats_ online/data_tables/datasummary

United States Conference of Mayors. (2008). Hunger and homelessness survey: A status report on hunger and homelessness in America's cities. Retrieved May 18, 2013, from http://us-mayors.org/pressreleases/documents/hungerhomelessnessreport_121208.pdf

USA Today. (2001, April 10). Study: Media coverage of youth crime unbalanced. *USA Today.* Retrieved March 12, 2007, from http://www.usatoday.com/news/nation/2001-04-10-media.htm.

US Census Bureau. (2002–2003). *American Community Survey 2002–2003, Census Supplementary Survey 2000–2001.* Retrieved April 18, 2007, from http://www.census.gov

US Census Bureau. (2003a). *Marital status: 2000. Census 2000 brief.* Washington: US Department of Commerce, Economics, and Statistics Administration, US Census Bureau. Retrieved May 17, 2007, from http://www.census.gov/prod/2003pubs/c2kbr-30.pdf.

US Census Bureau. (2003b). *Households and families: 2000. Census 2000 brief.* Washington: US Department of Commerce, Economics, and Statistics Administration, US Census Bureau. Retrieved May 17, 2007, from http://www.census.gov/prod/2001pubs/c2kbr01-8.pdf

US Census Bureau. (2003c). *Computer and Internet use in the United States: October 2003.* Washington: US Census Bureau. Retrieved May 10, 2007, from http://www.census.gov/population/www/socdemo/computer/2003.html

US Census Bureau. (2006). *We the people: American Indians and Alaska Natives in the United States: Census 2000 special reports.* Washington: US Census Bureau. Retrieved January 22, 2008, from http://www.census.gov/prod/2006pubs/censr-28.pdf

US Census Bureau. (2007). *Statistical abstracts of the United States: 2007* (126th ed.). Washington: US Census Bureau.

US Census Bureau (2008). *2008 National population projections.* Washington: Department of Commerce. Retrieved May 11, 2013, from http://www.census.gov/population/www/projections/2008projections.html

US Census Bureau. (2009). *Voter turnout increases by 5 million in 2008 presidential election, U.S. Census Bureau reports.* Retrieved June 10, 2013, from http://www.census.gov/newsroom/releases/archives/voting/cb09-110.html

US Census Bureau. (2010). *Educational attainment: Table 1: Enrollment status of the population 3 years old and over, by sex, age, race, Hispanic origin, foreign born, and foreign-born parentage: October 2010.* Washington: Department of Commerce.

US Census Bureau. (2011a). *The Hispanic population in the United States: Table 1: Population by sex, age, Hispanic origin, and race: 2011.* Washington: U.S. Department of Commerce. Retrieved May 18, 2013, from http://www.census.gov/population/hispanic/data/2011.html

US Census Bureau. (2011b). *The Asian alone population in the United States: Table 1: Population by sex, age, Asian origin, and race: 2011.* Washington: U.S. Department of Commerce. Retrieved May 18, 2013, from http://www.census.gov/population/race/data/ppl-aa11.html

US Census Bureau. (2011c). *The Black alone population in the United States: 2011: Table 1. Population by sex, age, Black alone and White alone, not Hispanic: 2011.* Washington: U.S. Department of Commerce. Retrieved May 18, 2013, from http://www.census.gov/population/race/data/ppl-ba11.html

US Census Bureau. (2011d). *Custodial mothers and fathers and their child support: 2009.* Washington: U.S. Department of Commerce. Retrieved May 11, 2013, from http://www.census.gov/prod/2011pubs/p60-240.pdf

US Census Bureau. (2012a). Births, deaths, marriages and divorces: marriages and divorce 2009. Washington: U.S. Department of Commerce. Retrieved May 8, 2013, from http://www.census.gov/compendia/statab/cats/births_deaths_marriages_divorces/marriages_and_divorces.html

US Census Bureau. (2012b). *America's family living arrangements: Marital status of people 15 years and over, by age, sex, personal earnings, race, and Hispanic origin.* Washington: U.S. Department of Commerce. Retrieved May 18, 2013, from http://www.census.gov/hhes/families/data/cps2012.html

US Census Bureau. (2012c). *America's family living arrangements: Living arrangements of children under 18 years and marital status of parents, by age, sex, race, and Hispanic origin and selected characteristics of the child for all children.* Washington: U.S. Department of Commerce. Retrieved May 9, 2013, from http://www.census.gov/hhes/families/data/cps2012.html

US Census Bureau. (2012d). *Households and families: 2010 census brief.* Washington: U.S. Department of Commerce. Retrieved May 16, 2013, from http://www.census.gov/prod/cen2010/briefs/c2010br-14.pdf

US Census Bureau. (2012e). *CPS historical time series tables: Table A-2: Percent of people 25 years and over who have completed high school or college, by race, Hispanic origin and sex: Selected years 1940 to 2012.* Washington: Department of Commerce.

US Census Bureau. (2012f). *School enrollment.* Washington: Department of Commerce. Retrieved May 18, 2013, from http://www.census.gov/population/www/socdemo/school.html

US Census Bureau. (2012g). *The 2012 statistical abstract: The national data book: Education.* Washington: Department of Commerce.

US Department of Health and Human Services. (2003). *Child health USA 2003.* Rockville, Maryland: US Department of Health and Human Services, Health Resources and Services Administration, Maternal and Child Health Bureau. Retrieved May 20, 2007, from http://mchb.hrsa.gov/chusa03/pages/population.htm

US Department of Health and Human Services. (2007). *The surgeon general's call to action to prevent and reduce underage drinking.* Washington: US Department of Health and Human Services, Office of the Surgeon General. Retrieved February 20, 2008, from http://www.surgeongeneral.gov/topics/obesity/calltoaction/toc.htm

US Department of Health and Human Services. (2012, July). HIV-related risk among U.S. high school students: Trends from the National Youth Risk Behaviour Survey since 1991. *CDC Fact Sheet.* Retrieved July 17, 2013, from http://www.cdc.gov/nchhstp/newsroom/docs/2013/YRBS-Fact-Sheet-FINAL-508.pdf

US Department of Labor. (2008). *Training: Youth programs.* Washington: US Department of Labor. Retrieved January 13, 2008, from http://www.dol.gov/dol/topic/training/youth.htm

US Department of Labor. (2013a). *Youth employment rate.* Washington: Office of Disability Employment Policy. Retrieved May 21, 2013, from http://www.dol.gov/odep/categories/youth/youthemployment.htm

US Department of Labor. (2013b). *Minimum wage laws in the states - January 1, 2013.* Retrieved May 24, 2013, from http://www.dol.gov/whd/minwage/america.htm

USInfo. (2007). *Native Americans of North America.* Washington: US Department of State, International Information Programs. Retrieved January 20, 2008, from http://usinfo.state.gov/scv/history_geography_and_population/population_and_diversity/native_americans.html

US Justice Fund (2007, Fall). Dream and reality: Searching for racial justice in the United States. *Open Society News.* Washington, DC: US Justice Fund. Retrieved January 27, 2008, from http://www.soros.org/resources/articles_publications/publications/osinews_20071105

Van der Veen, W. (1994). Young people and the environment: A comparative analysis of young environmentalists and decision-makers in Australia and Canada. *Youth Studies, 13*(4), 24–30.

Van der Ploeg, J., & Scholte, E. (1997). *Homeless youth.* London, Thousand Oaks, & New Delhi: Sage.

Van Gelder, S. (2011). Introduction: How Occupy Wall Street changes everything. In S. Van Gelder & The Staff of *YES! Magazine* (Eds.), *This changes everything: Occupy Wall Street and the 99% movement* (pp. 1–12). San Francisco: Berrett-Koehler Publishers.

Van Roosmalen, E., & Krahn, H. (1996). Boundaries of youth. *Youth & Society, 28*(1), 3–39.

Van Wert, B. (1997). Change your future: Transition programs for minority youth. *Guidance and Counselling, 13*(1), 16–18.

Vanier Institute of the Family. (2000). *Profiling Canada's families II.* Nepean: The Vanier Institute of the Family.

Vanier Institute of the Family. (2010). *Family count: Profiling Canada's families IV.* Ottawa, ON: Vanier Institute of the Family.

Varpalotai, A. (1996). Canadian girls in transition to womanhood. In B. Galaway & J. Hudson (Eds.), *Youth in transition: Perspectives on research and policy* (pp. 90–98). Toronto: Thompson Educational Publishing.

Vedder, R. (2010, December 9). The great college-degree scam. *The Chronicle of Higher Education.* Retrieved June 1, 2013, from http://chronicle.com/blogs/innovations/the-great-college-degree-scam/28067

Verhulst, J., & Walgrave, S. (2007). Protest and protesters in advanced industrial democracies: The case of the 15 February global anti-war demonstrations. In D. Purdue (Ed.), *Civil societies and social movements: Potentials and problems* (pp. 125–144). London & New York: Routledge.

Vertinsky, P. (1989). Substance abuse prevention programs: The state of the art in school health. *Health Promotion, 27*(4), 8–14.

Vinken, H. (2005). Young people's civic engagement: The need for new perspectives. In H. Helve & G. Holm (Eds.), *Contemporary youth research: Local expressions and global connections* (pp. 147–158). Aldershot: Ashgate.

Vobejda, B., & Perlstein, L. (1998, June 18). Girls will be … boys—and it's not a pretty sight. *Toronto Star,* p. A1.

Wackett, J. (1998). A theory-based initiative to reduce the rates of chlamydia trachomitis infection among young adults in the Yukon. *The Canadian Journal of Human Sexuality, 7*(4), 347–370.

Wade, T.J., & Brannigan, A. (1998). The genesis of adolescent risk-taking: Pathways through family, school, and peers. *Canadian Journal of Sociology, 23*(1), 1–20.

Wadhera, S., & Millar, W.J. (1997). Teenage pregnancies, 1974 to 1994. *Statistics Canada, Health Reports, 9*(3), 9–17.

Waisman, R. (2002). Robbie Waisman. Romek Wajsman, b. 1931, Skarszysko, Poland. In Vancouver Holocaust Education Centre, *Open hearts—Closed doors: The war orphans project.* Retrieved November 15, 2007, from http://www.virtualmuseum.ca/Exhibitions/orphans/english/biographies/waisman/

Waldie, P. (1993, June 19). Kids at work: Recession is forcing more Canadian children to become partial family breadwinners. *Financial Post,* p. S18.

Walker, J.W.S. (1985). *Racial discrimination in Canada: The Black experience.* Historical booklet no. 41. Ottawa: Canadian Historical Association.

Wall, J., Covell, K., & MacIntyre, P.D. (1999). Implications of social supports for adolescents' education and career aspirations. *Canadian Journal of Behavioural Science, 31*(2), 63–71.

Walton, D. (2007, January 21). Vancouver: Lack of options drives problem. *The Globe and Mail,* p. A7.

Wang, J., Waildman, L., & Calhoun, G. (1996). The relationship between parental influences and student achievement in seventh grade mathematics. *School Science and Mathematics, 96*(8), 395–399.

Washington Post. (1991). Mount Pleasant riot [Final Edition]. *The Washington Post*, p. A18.

Wasik, B. (2006, March). My crowd, or, phase 5: A report from the inventor of the flash mob. *Harper's Magazine.* Retrieved July 17, 2013, from http://harpers.org/archive/2006/03/my-crowd/

Waters, J.L. (2002). Flexible families? "Astronaut" households and the experiences of lone mothers in Vancouver, British Columbia. *Social and Cultural Geography, 3*(2), 117–134.

Waters, T. (1999). *Crime and immigrant youth.* Thousand Oaks: Sage.

Watt, T.T., & Sharp, S.F. (2002). Race differences in strains associated with suicidal behavior among adolescents. *Youth & Society, 34*(2), 232–256.

Wawatay News. (2013, March 27). Human traffickers target Aboriginal girls, women. *Wawatay News.* Retrieved June 9, 2013, from http://www.wawataynews.ca/archive/all/2013/3/27/human-traffickers-target-aboriginal-girls-women_24317

Webber, M. (1991). *Street kids: The tragedy of Canada's runaways.* Toronto: University of Toronto Press.

Welch, M., Price, E.A., & Yankey, N. (2002). Moral panic over youth violence: Wilding and the manufacture of menace in the media. *Youth & Society, 34*(1), 3–30.

White, M. (2010, June 19). Gay proms held across Canada. *Leader Post*, p. B8.

White, R. (2002). Youth crime, community development, and social justice. In M. Tienda & W.J. Wilson (Eds.), *Youth in cities: A cross-national perspective* (pp. 138–164). Cambridge: Cambridge University Press.

Whitesell, N.R., Beals, J., Mitchell, C.M., & Novins, D.K. (2007). Marijuana initiation in 2 American Indian reservation communities: Comparison with a national sample. *American Journal of Public Health, 97*(7), 1311–1318. Retrieved February 19, 2008, from ProQuest database.

Whittington-Walsh, F. (2006). The broken mirror: Young women, beauty and facial difference. *Women's Health and Urban Life: An International & Interdisciplinary Journal, 5*(2), 7–24.

Whyte, M. (2007, March 18). The 12-year-old arbiter of cool. *Toronto Star*, p. A6.

Wiebe, K. (1991). *Violence against immigrant women and children: An overview of community workers* (2nd ed.). Vancouver: Women against Violence against Women/Rape Crisis Centre.

Wilde, R. (2007). The European overseas empires. Electronic resource. *About: European History.* Retrieved April 30, 2007, from http://europeanhistory.about.com/od/colonimperialism/a/ovoverempires.htm

Willms, J.D. (1997). *Literacy skills of Canadian youth.* Publication no. 89-552-MPE, no. 1. Ottawa: Statistics Canada.

Willms, J.D. (1999). *Inequalities in literacy skills among youth in Canada and the United States.* Ottawa: Statistics Canada, Human Resources Development Canada.

Willms, J.D. (Ed.). (2002). *Vulnerable children: Findings from Canada's national longitudinal survey on children and youth.* Edmonton: The University of Alberta Press.

Wills, W., Backett-Milburn, K., Gregory, S. & Lawton, J. (2006). Young teenagers' perceptions of their own and others' bodies: A qualitative study of obese, overweight, and "normal" weight young people in Scotland. *Social Science & Medicine, 62*, 396–406. Retrieved February 2, 2008 from the Academic Search Premier database.

Wilson, B. (2002). The Canadian rave scene and five theses on youth resistance. *Canadian Journal of Sociology, 27*(3), 373–412.

Wilson, B., & Jette, S. (2005). Making sense of the cultural activities of Canadian youth. In N. Mandell & A. Duffy (Eds.), *Canadian families: Diversity, conflict, and change* (3rd ed.) (pp. 64–86). Toronto: Thomson Nelson.

Wilson, J. (1998). Generation X: Who are they? What do they want? *The NEA Higher Education Journal*, 14, 9–18.

Wincup, E., Buckland, G., & Bayliss, R. (2003). *Youth homelessness and substance use: Report to the drugs and alcohol research unit. Home Office Research Study 258*. London: Home Office Research, Development, and Statistics Directorate.

Winks, R.W. (1997). *The Blacks in Canada: A history* (2nd ed.). Montreal & Kingston: McGill-Queen's University Press.

Winterman, D. (2006). *The flip side of a McJob*. London: BBC News. Retrieved January 16, 2008, from http://news.bbc.co.uk/1/hi/magazine/5052020.stm

womenshealth.gov. (2013). *Body image*. A Project of the U.S. Department of Health and Human Services Office on Women's Health. Retrieved June 2, 2013, from http://www.women-shealth.gov/body-image/eating-disorders/

Wong, B.P. (2007). Immigration, globalization, and the Chinese-American family. In J.E. Lansford, K. Dieter-Deckard, & M.H. Bornstein (Eds.), *Immigrant families in contemporary society* (pp. 212–230). New York: Guilford Press.

Wong, J., & Checkland, D. (Eds.). (1999). *Teen pregnancy and parenting: Social and ethical issues*. Toronto: University of Toronto Press.

Wong, S.K. (1999). Acculturation, peer relations, and delinquent behaviour of Chinese-Canadian youth. *Adolescence, 34*(133), 107–119.

Wood, D., & Griffiths, C.T. (1996). The lost generation: Inuit youth in transition to adulthood. In B. Galaway & J. Hudson (Eds.), *Youth in transition: Perspectives on research and policy*. Toronto: Thompson Educational Publishing, Inc.

Woodgate, R.L., & Leach, J. (2010). Youth's perspectives on the determinants of health. *Qualitative Health Research, 20*(9), 1173–1182. Retrieved June 9, 2013, from http://www.hpclearinghouse.ca/pdf/youthperspective.pdf

World Health Organization. (2001). *The world health report 2001: Mental health: New understanding, new hope*. Geneva: WHO.

World Health Organization. (2012). *Mental health: Suicide prevention and special programmes*. Retrieved June 10, 2013, from http://www.who.int/mental_health/prevention/suicide/country_reports/en/index.html

Wortley, S., & Tanner, J. (2005). Inflammatory rhetoric? Baseless accusations? A response to Gabor's critique of racial profiling research in Canada. *Canadian Journal of Criminology and Criminal Justice, 47*(3), 581–609.

Wortley, S., & Tanner, J. (2006). Immigration, social disadvantage, and urban youth gangs: Results of a Toronto-area survey. *Canadian Journal of Urban Research, Supplement, 15*(2), 18–37.

Wotherspoon, T. (1998). *The sociology of education in Canada: Critical perspectives.* Toronto: Oxford University Press.

Wu, L.L., & Thomson, E. (2001). Race differences in family experience and early sexual initiation: Dynamic models of family structure and family change. *Journal of Marriage and Family, 63,* 682–696.

Wyn, J., & White, R. (1997). *Rethinking youth.* London: Sage.

Wynn, N.A. (1993). *The Afro-American and the Second World War.* New York: Holmes & Meier.

Yankelovich, D. (1998). America's youth problem: The forgotten half revisited. In S. Halperin (Ed.), *America's youth problem: The forgotten half revisited.* Washington: The American Youth Policy Forum 1998. Retrieved February 22, 2007, from www.danyankelovich.com/americasyouth.html

Youth Justice Board. (2009). *Girls and offending—patterns, perceptions and interventions.* Retrieved June 8, 2013, from http://www.yjb.gov.uk/publications/resources/downloads/girls_offending_fullreport.pdf

Youth Justice Board. (2013). *Youth justice statistics 2011/12—England and Wales.* Home Office Ministry of Justice. Retrieved June 5, 2013, from https://www.gov.uk/government/uploads/system/uploads/attachment_data/file/163526/yjb-stats-2011-12.pdf.pdf

Zaidi, A., & and Shuraydi, M. (2002). Perceptions of arranged marriages by young Pakistani Muslim women living in Western society. *Journal of Comparative Family Studies, 33*(4), 37–57.

Zhao, J.Z., Rajulton, F., & Ranavera, Z.R. (1995). Leaving parental homes in Canada: Effects of family structure, gender, and culture. *Canadian Journal of Sociology, 20*(1), 31–50.

Zurbriggen, E.L., Collins, R.L., Lamb, S., Roberts, T., Tolman, D.L., Ward, L.M., & Blake, J. (2007). *Report of the APA task force on the sexualization of girls.* Washington: American Psychological Association. Retrieved November 22, 2007, from http://www.apa.org/pi/wpo/sexualization.html

Copyright Acknowledgements

Index

abolition, 28

Aboriginal youth, Canadian, 36–40

    alcohol use, 285, 295, 297, 300; colonial legacy, 36–40; crime, 252; dating violence, 309; depression, 285; dropping out, 93; drug use, 289, 295; education, 110–111; family violence, 320–321; gangs, 201, 254, 263; health, 284, 285; prostitution, 328; solvent abuse, 289; suicide, 285, 289; tobacco use, 301; unemployment, 143–144

abortion, 182–184, 187

abuse

    adolescent, 315–317; alcohol, 298–300, 322; child, 259, 315–317; crime and, 252, 258–260; effects of, 259, 317; employment and, 136–137, 140–141; parent, 319–320; physical, 124, 310, 314, 316, 320; prescription drug, 295, 296; psychological, 124, 178, 310; sexual, 50, 84, 186, 259–260, 308, 310, 315–319; sibling, 317–319; substance, 40, 84–85, 181, 186, 252, 259, 285–286, 289–290, 295–298, 301, 308, 317, 320, 322; verbal, 122, 310

academic success, 50

    boys and, 104–105; Black students and, 112, 118–119; combining work and school and, 147–148; dropping out and, 92–93; girls and, 105–108; parenting and, 65–66

acculturation thesis, 212

acquaintance rape, 300, 309, 311, 314

activism, 45, 203–207

    anti-globalization, 204; environmental, 203; Occupy movement, 204–206

adolescence

    as "inherently pathological," 7–9; as life stage, 8–11, 51; creation of concept of, 6; definition of, 3–6; emergence of, 42–46; obsolescence of, 46; perpetual, 4, 235; physiological changes in, 9; prolongation of, 51–52

adolescents

    communication with parents, 72; perceptions of parenting styles, 66–67; perceptions of friendship, 124, 162, 210–213; perceptions of romance, 162, 163, 171, 218; relationship with parents, 56, 61–84; role of in socialization of parents, 67–69; stereotype of, 45, 55; stigmatization of, 340; vagrancy and, 46–47

adopted children, 81

adulthood

    as distinct from childhood, 8–12; emerging, 5; perceptions of, 6–7; preparation for, 7–8, 11, 17–19, 51; transition to, 6–12; 14, 27, 47, 78, 162, 343–344

advertising, 98, 218, 234–237, 242, 291, 302, 337

    identity and, 218–219

Afrocentric schools, 119

age

    divorce and, 57; drug use and, 295–297; friendship and, 162, 210; identity and, 9, 179; of becoming a parent, 5, 42,181–184; of entering labour force, 49; of leaving home, 79–80; of living with partner, 189–191; of marriage, 189–191; of sexual experience, 166–168